Texas Learning Outcomes and Core Objectives:

The State of Texas not only covers the new Learning Outcomes and Core Objectives for GOVT 2306, but also does so in a way that makes the program SACS-compliant. The State of Texas deeply incorporates the state Core Objectives (COs) and Texas Learning Outcomes (TLOs) in both the print and digital products.

S0-BHZ-345

87% *

of college students report that access to learning analytics can positively impact their learning experience.

75% *

of students using adaptive technology report that it is "very helpful" or "extremely helpful" in aiding their ability to retain new concepts.

> "I can honestly say that the first time I used SmartBook after reading a chapter I understood what I had just read better than I ever had in the past."
> – Nathan Herrmann, Oklahoma State University

> "I really enjoy how it has gotten me engaged in the course and it is a great study tool without having to carry around a heavy textbook."
> – Madeline Uretsky, Simmons College

Professors spend:

Less time on administrative tasks

72% **

90% **

More time on active learning

> "Connect keeps my students engaged and motivated. Requiring Connect assignments has improved student exam grades."
> – Sophia Garcia, Tarrant County College

Mc Graw Hill Education

Because learning changes everything.™

To learn more about Texas Government visit the McGraw-Hill Education American Government page: bit.ly/MHEAmGov

* *The Impact of Technology on College Student Study Habits 2015*
** *The Impact of Connect on Student Success, McGraw-Hill Connect Effectiveness Study 2016*

THE STATE OF TEXAS:
Government, Politics, and Policy

THIRD EDITION

THE STATE OF TEXAS:
Government, Politics, and Policy

THIRD EDITION

Sherri Mora

William Ruger

THE STATE OF TEXAS: GOVERNMENT, POLITICS, AND POLICY, THIRD EDITION

Published by McGraw-Hill Education, 2 Penn Plaza, New York, NY 10121. Copyright © 2017 by McGraw-Hill Education. All rights reserved. Printed in the United States of America. Previous editions © 2015, and 2014. No part of this publication may be reproduced or distributed in any form or by any means, or stored in a database or retrieval system, without the prior written consent of McGraw-Hill Education, including, but not limited to, in any network or other electronic storage or transmission, or broadcast for distance learning.

Some ancillaries, including electronic and print components, may not be available to customers outside the United States.

This book is printed on acid-free paper.

1 2 3 4 5 6 7 8 9 0 LWI 21 20 19 18 17

ISBN 978-1-259-54821-5
MHID 1-259-54821-X

Chief Product Officer, SVP Products & Markets: *G. Scott Virkler*
Vice President, General Manager, Products & Markets: *Mike Ryan*
Vice President, Content Design & Delivery: *Betsy Whalen*
Managing Director: *Katie Stevens*
Brand Manager: *Jason Seitz*
Lead Product Developer: *Dawn Groundwater*
Digital Product Analyst: *Susan Pierre-Louis*
Product Developer: *Denise Wright*
Marketing Manager: *Alexandra Hodges*
Marketing Development Manager: *Stacy Ruel*
Director, Content Design & Delivery: *Terri Schiesl*
Program Manager: *Marianne Musni*
Content Project Managers: *Rick Hecker/George Theofanopoulos*
Senior Buyer: *Laura Fuller*
Designer: *Matt Diamond*
Content Licensing Specialists: *Text: Lori Slattery; Photos: Ann Marie Jannette*
Typeface: *10.5/12.5 STIX Mathjax Main*
Compositor: *SPi Global*
Printer: *LSC Communications*

All credits appearing on page or at the end of the book are considered to be an extension of the copyright page.

Library of Congress Cataloging-in-Publication Data

Names: Mora, Sherri, author. | Ruger, William, author.
Title: The state of texas: government, politics, and policy / Sherri Mora,
    William Ruger.
Description: Third edition. | New York, NY : McGraw-Hill Education, 2017.
Identifiers: LCCN 2016040526 | ISBN 9781259548215 (paperback)
Subjects: LCSH: Texas—Politics and government. | BISAC: POLITICAL SCIENCE /
    Government / State & Provincial.
Classification: LCC JK4816 .M67 2017 | DDC 320.4764—dc23 LC record available
at https://lccn.loc.gov/2016040526

The Internet addresses listed in the text were accurate at the time of publication. The inclusion of a website does not indicate an endorsement by the authors or McGraw-Hill Education, and McGraw-Hill Education does not guarantee the accuracy of the information presented at these sites.

mheducation.com/highered

GROUNDED IN YOUR CORE OBJECTIVES, DEVELOPED FOR YOUR STUDENTS

The State of Texas: Government, Politics, and Policy, 3e, combines concise content with effective digital tools that provide a personalized learning path for every student. Built to align directly with state learning outcomes and core objectives, this highly readable program provides students with the content and tools to make Texas government relevant in their lives.

The State of Texas is designed around the Learning Outcomes and Core Objectives for GOVT 2306 as defined by the Texas Higher Education Coordinating Board. With a comprehensive content program, a revision that was informed by student data, and numerous assignable activities in Connect Texas Government®, *The State of Texas* includes ample material for a full semester course on Texas government. Connect Texas Government with LearnSmart and Smartbook is organized around the Texas Learning Outcomes and provides the ability to assess directly on those outcomes.

Informing and Engaging Students on Government Concepts

Using Connect Texas Government, students can learn the course material more deeply and study more effectively than ever before.

At the *remember* and *understand* levels of Bloom's taxonomy, **Concept Clips** help students break down key concepts in government. Using easy-to-understand audio narration, visual cues, and colorful animations, Concept Clips provide a step-by-step presentation that aids in student retention. Concept Clips for the Third Edition address the following:

- What is Federalism?
- What is Selective Incorporation?
- How are State Judges Selected?
- What are the Voting Decision Rules?
- How are Public Opinion Polls Evaluated?
- What are the Merit and Spoils Systems?
- What Does Separation of Powers Mean?
- What is Judicial Review?
- What is the Difference Between De Jure and De Facto Segregation?

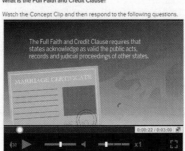

CONCEPT CLIP

What is the Full Faith and Credit Clause?

Watch the Concept Clip and then respond to the following questions.

The Full Faith and Credit Clause requires that states acknowledge as valid the public acts, records and judicial proceedings of other states.

MARRIAGE CERTIFICATE

0:00:22 / 0:03:00

x1

- What is Social Contract Theory?
- What is the Full Faith and Credit Clause?
- What is Electioneering?
- What are the Powers of Congress?
- How Does the Electoral College Work
- What is the Public Policy Cycle?
- How Does Media Shape the Public Agenda?
- Why Two Parties?

Also at the remember and understand levels of Bloom's, **Newsflash** exercises tie current news stories to key Texas government concepts and learning objectives. After interacting with a contemporary news story, students are assessed on their ability to make the connection between real life events and course content.

At the *apply, analyze,* and *evaluate* levels of Bloom's taxonomy, **critical thinking activities** allow students to engage with the political process and learn by doing. For example, students will understand how Texas is a majority-minority state.

Better Data, Smarter Revision, Improved Results

Students study more effectively with LearnSmart® and SmartBook®. LearnSmart is an adaptive learning program designed to help students learn faster, study smarter, and retain more knowledge for greater success. Distinguishing what students know from what they don't, and focusing on concepts they are most likely to forget, LearnSmart continuously adapts to each student's needs by building an individual learning path. Millions of students have answered more than a billion questions in LearnSmart since 2009, making it the most widely used and intelligent adaptive study tool that's proven to strengthen memory recall, keep students in class, and boost grades.

Fueled by LearnSmart, SmartBook is the first and only adaptive reading experience currently available.

- **Make It Effective.** SmartBook creates a personalized reading experience by highlighting the most impactful concepts a student needs to learn at that moment in time. This ensures that every minute spent with SmartBook is returned to the student as the most value-added minute possible.

- **Make It Informed.** The reading experience continuously adapts by highlighting content based on what the student knows and doesn't know. Real-time reports quickly identify the concepts that require more attention from individual students—or the entire class. SmartBook detects the content a student is most likely to forget and brings it back to improve long-term knowledge retention.

Students helped inform the revision strategy:

STEP 1. Over the course of two years, data points showing concepts that caused students the most difficulty were anonymously collected from the Connect Texas Government LearnSmart product.

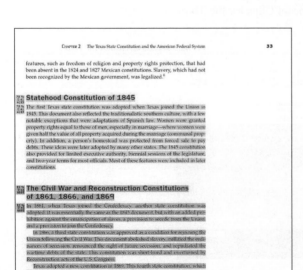

STEP 2. The data from LearnSmart was provided to the authors in the form of a **Heat Map,** which graphically illustrated "hot spots" in the text that impacted student learning (see image to the right).

STEP 3. The authors used the **Heat Map** data to refine the content and reinforce student comprehension in the new edition. Additional quiz questions and assignable activities were created for use in Connect Texas Government to further support student success.

RESULT: Because the **Heat Map** gave the authors empirically based feedback at the paragraph and even sentence level, they were able to develop the new edition using precise student data that pinpointed concepts that caused students the most difficulty.

Real-Time Reports, On the Go, Made Easier

Student performance reports show you their progress.

Connect Insight is a one-of-a-kind visual analytics dashboard—now available for both instructors and students—that provides at-a-glance information regarding student performance.

- **Make It Intuitive.** You receive instant, at-a-glance views of student performance matched with student activity.
- **Make It Dynamic.** Connect Insight puts real-time analytics in your hands so you can take action early and keep struggling students from falling behind.
- **Make It Mobile.** Connect Insight travels from office to classroom, available on demand wherever and whenever it's needed.

Increased Coverage of Criminal Justice, Media, and the Hispanic Experience

The Third Edition features increased coverage of core content areas.

- **New! Chapter 12, "The Criminal Justice System in Texas,"** covers criminal and civil courts, prisons, the death penalty, and reforms.
- **New! Chapter 14, "Public Opinion and the Media in Texas,"** available in Connect Texas Government only, covers the historical and current media landscape as it relates to Texas government.
- **New! Focus On** features present students with engaging examples of how Hispanic and Latino individuals, groups, and culture play an important role in Texas political life. Chapter 8, for example, focuses on "The Hispanic Population and Bilingual Ballots."

Content Changes

As mentioned, the Third Edition was revised in response to student heat map data that pinpointed the topics and concepts where students struggled the most. This was reflected primarily in the chapters on the Texas State Constitution and the American Federal System, the Court System in Texas, Local Governments in Texas, Public Policy in Texas, and Financing State Government.

Chapter 1

- Updated section on post-Reconstruction Texas, including the most recent data available on the state's economy, politics, and demographics
- Updated section on Texas today, including the most recent data available on poverty, education, and immigration in Texas
- Revised section on political culture to clarify Texas's political culture and the philosophical traditions contributing to it
- Expanded Conclusion section
- New Focus On feature on how the government defines the term "Hispanic"

Chapter 2

- Updated section on characteristics common to state institutions with a recent example on conflicts between local law and state law
- Updated section comparing state constitutions to reflect their most current version, as of 2015
- Updated section on amending state constitutions, including the most recent voter turnout numbers from 2015
- Significantly revised section, "Relations between States in the Federal System," focusing on the 2015 Supreme Court case *Obergefell v. Hodges,* which legalized gay marriage in the United States
- New Focus On feature on Tejano contributions to the Texas founding, specifically through the deeds of José Antonio Navarro

Chapter 3

- Updated section on legislator qualifications and demographics, including the most recent data available on the members of the Texas state legislature

- Updated district maps for the state legislature
- Updated coverage of redistricting issues in Texas
- Updated list of legislative committees and process for legislative oversight of state agencies
- Revised section on procedures to include discussion of the change in the "two-thirds" rule, as well as updated coverage of the legislature's use of calendars
- New Focus On feature on the first Hispanic woman in the Texas legislature

Chapter 4

- Updated section, "Informal Qualifications for Governor," including a recent study on the jobs that most often lead into the governorship and updated national statistics on the gender and ethnicity of those holding state governorships in 2016
- Updated map on states with female governors, past and present
- Updated map, "Total Number of Major Statewide Elected Officials for Each State, Executive Branch"
- Updated map, "Term Limits for Governors as of 2015"
- Updated figure, "Employment in the Top Four State Agency Categories by General Appropriation"
- New Focus On feature on the issue of when Texas may have its first Hispanic governor

Chapter 5

- Revised and reorganized section on the structure of state courts
- Updated section "Judicial Selection" reflecting 2015 data, specifically how states currently select their judges
- Significantly revised section "Is There a Best System for Judicial Selection?"
- Revised section "Judicial Selection in Texas," specifically addressing minority representation and campaign contributions
- Updated graph on crime rates in Texas as compared to the United States as a whole
- New Focus On feature on the first Hispanic justice on the Texas Supreme Court, Raul A. Gonzalez, Jr.

Chapter 6

- Revised section on "General Law Cities and Home Rule"
- Updated section on county governments with the most recent data available (number of counties within states and the populations of the largest counties in Texas)
- New Focus On feature on Hispanic representation in local governments, including a brief discussion of the differences between descriptive and substantive representation

Chapter 7

- Revised section on political participation, including a discussion of online political engagement
- Reorganized voting section to present more clearly the current requirements for voting in Texas

- New material on the 2016 presidential primary and general elections
- Updated section on voter turnout with the most recent data available on voter turnout in Texas
- New Focus On feature on Hispanic voter turnout

Chapter 8

- Reorganized subsection "Party Caucus" introducing concepts of primary elections and open vs. closed primary systems
- Updated chart on the primary systems used in state elections as of 2015
- Revised section on the Federal Voting Rights Act to more clearly explain the Supreme Court case *Shelby County v. Holder* (2013) and its effect on voting rights
- Updated material on PAC money in state campaigns with the most recent data available
- New Focus On feature on the use of bilingual ballots as required by the Federal Voting Rights Act

Chapter 9

- Reorganized to present the history and evolution of political parties in the United States as background for subsequent material
- Revised section on the evolution of political parties in Texas to include the concept of candidate-centered politics
- Expanded coverage of realignment and dealignment to clarify these concepts and how they apply to Texas politics
- Updated material on Texas parties and election results with the most recent data available
- Expanded coverage of caucus and primary delegate selection systems
- New Focus On feature on Hispanic party affiliation

Chapter 10

- Updated section on interest group typology, including the most recent data available on Texas interest groups
- Expanded discussion of grassroots lobbying
- New material on litigation as a technique interest groups use to achieve their goals
- New Focus On feature on litigation by Hispanic interest groups

Chapter 11

- Updated section on policy liberalism, including the most recent version of the State Policy Index (SPI)
- Updated section on public policy areas, including the most recent data on state policy regarding business regulation, welfare, health care, education, firearms, gay rights, abortion, immigration, water, and veterans
- Expanded discussion of the Affordable Care Act (ACA), including its provisions
- Expanded discussion of the intersection between federal and state policy
- New Focus On feature on bilingual education

Chapter 12

- New to this edition, this chapter covers criminal and civil courts, prisons, the death penalty, and reforms in the Texas criminal justice system.

Chapter 13

- Significantly revised section "Why Do Governments Provide Services to Citizens?" including a more explicit discussion of public goods and how they are nonexclusive and nonexhaustive
- Revised table comparing revenue for the 15 most populous states
- Updated table on the 10 most regressive state tax systems to 2015
- Updated figures on state and local taxes in Texas and all states to 2015
- Expanded Budget Fix subsection to include discussion of dedicated and non-dedicated revenue
- Updated section on state finance to include discussion of fluctuating oil prices
- New Focus On feature on the tax contributions of Hispanic households

Chapter 14

- New to this edition and available in Connect Texas Government only, this chapter covers the historical and current media and public opinion landscape as it relates to Texas government.

Learning Outcomes and Core Objectives

GOVT 2306 is one of the foundational component areas within the Core Curriculum identified by the Undergraduate Education Advisory Committee (UEAC) of the Texas Higher Education Coordinating Board (THECB). The UEAC has identified six core objectives, of which four—critical thinking skills, communication skills, social responsibility, and personal responsibility—must be mapped to content in GOVT 2306. Those four core objectives are mapped to specific *The State of Texas* content here and throughout each chapter.

Institutions must assess learning outcomes (provided in the *UEAC's Academic Course Guide Manual*); for example, the student's demonstrated ability to explain the origin and development of the Texas constitution, consistent with assessment practices required by the Commission on Colleges of the Southern Association of Colleges and Schools (SACS-COC).

These requirements include an explanation of measures, methodology, frequency, and timeline of assessment; an explanation of targets and benchmarks of "Core Objective" attainment; evidence of attainment of the required core objectives; interpretation of assessment information; and the use of results for improving student learning. SACS principles of accreditation 3.3.1.1 requires institutions to identify expected learning outcomes, assess the extent to which it achieves these outcomes, and provide evidence of improvement based on analysis of the results.

Adopting *The State of Texas* and using the provided assessment tools makes SACS compliance easy while meeting the purpose of the Core Curriculum.

Learning Outcomes and Core Objectives Correlation Table

CHAPTER 1	**Learning Outcome:** Explain the history, demographics, and political culture of Texas.	**Thinking Critically**	How have settlement patterns impacted Texas? Give current examples.
	Learning Outcome: Explain the history, demographics, and political culture of Texas.	**Communicating Effectively**	Write a short synopsis of Texas's changing economy and its role in international trade.
	Learning Outcome: Explain the history, demographics, and political culture of Texas.	**Taking Personal Responsibility**	What can you do to become well informed about political issues so that you can make good decisions at election time?
	Learning Outcome: .Explain the history, demographics, and political culture of Texas.	**Being Socially Responsible**	Understanding the relationship between religious affiliations and politics can improve civic knowledge. How would you use this knowledge to engage effectively in your community?
CHAPTER 2	**Learning Outcome:** Describe separation of powers and checks and balances in both theory and practice in Texas.	**Communicating Effectively**	Analyze the diagram in Figure 2.1 and the division of powers in Table 2.1 to describe the separation of powers and checks and balances in both theory and practice in Texas.
	Learning Outcome: Explain the origin and development of the Texas Constitution.	**Thinking Critically**	What is the impact of a constitutional convention dominated by one party? What were the consequences of the 1875 constitutional convention in the development of the Texas Constitution?
	Learning Outcome: Describe state and local political systems and their relationship with the federal government.	**Being Socially Responsible**	Considering the argument that the national government has eroded state power, to what extent should the government "promote general welfare?" What does promoting general welfare mean to you? In developing an understanding of state and local political systems and their relationship with the federal government, who do you think should play a greater role—the states or the federal government?
	Learning Outcome: Describe state and local political systems and their relationship with the federal government.	**Taking Personal Responsibility**	As a resident of Texas and a citizen of the United States, can you identify and discuss examples that reinforce the Full Faith and Credit Clause and the Privileges and Immunities Clause of the U.S. Constitution? Can you identify examples that, in your opinion, violate these principles?
CHAPTER 3	**Learning Outcome:** Describe the legislative branch of Texas government.	**Communicating Effectively**	It has been argued that smaller constituencies might allow a wider array of people to participate in state politics, rather than just the "rich" or "well born." How would you argue in favor of or against this statement?
	Learning Outcome: Describe the legislative branch of Texas government.	**Being Socially Responsible**	To what extent should legislators use race when redistricting? Do you think redistricting is an appropriate tool to increase intercultural competency? Why or why not?
	Learning Outcome: Describe the legislative branch of Texas government.	**Thinking Critically**	Both demographics and voting patterns have changed in Texas, and some districts have become more competitive, especially for Democrats in South Texas and in inner-city districts. Discuss what these shifts mean for future elections and the composition of the Texas House and Senate. Reference Table 3.6 in your answer.
	Learning Outcome: Describe the legislative branch of Texas government.	**Taking Personal Responsibility**	It has been stated that the success of legislation depends largely on a relative few individuals who make up the leadership in the Texas House and Senate. Do you think the speaker of the house and the lieutenant governor have too much control over the passage of bills? How can you influence legislation? What can individuals do to affect legislation?

CHAPTER 4	**Learning Outcome:** Explain the structure and function of the executive branch of Texas government.	Communicating Effectively	Analyze Map 4.1. What inferences can be drawn from the data?
	Learning Outcome: Explain the structure and function of the executive branch of Texas government.	Being Socially Responsible	How does the comptroller promote effective involvement in regional, national, and global communities?
	Learning Outcome: Explain the structure and function of the executive branch of Texas government.	Taking Personal Responsibility	What can you do to become more actively engaged in the civic discourse about the role of the State Board of Education?
	Learning Outcome: Explain the structure and function of the executive branch of Texas government.	Thinking Critically	The six factors that influence the strength of the power of the governor are the number of elected statewide executives, tenure of office, the governor's appointive powers, the governor's budgetary powers, the governor's veto powers, and the extent to which the governor controls his or her political party. What can you conclude about the powers of the governor?
CHAPTER 5	**Learning Outcome:** Describe the structure and function of the judicial branch of Texas government.	Communicating Effectively	Analyze Figure 5.1. Describe the appeals process for a civil case filed in county court.
	Learning Outcome: Describe the structure and function of the judicial branch of Texas government.	Being Socially Responsible	What impact, if any, do you think partisan election of judges has on judicial outcomes?
	Learning Outcome: Describe the structure and function of the judicial branch of Texas government.	Thinking Critically	Reflecting on the discussion about representation of minorities and women in the Texas judicial system, do you think it is important to have a judiciary that is representative of the general population? Why or why not?
	Learning Outcome: Describe the structure and function of the judicial branch of Texas government.	Taking Personal Responsibility	Given what you read in this section, it would seem that citizens have little impact in disciplining and/or removing judges. What do you think is a citizen's responsibility in this matter? How can individuals take greater personal responsibility to ensure that judges perform properly?
CHAPTER 6	**Learning Outcome:** Describe local political systems in Texas.	Communicating Effectively	Compare Figures 6.1, 6.3, and 6.4 with Table 6.2. Discuss the fundamental differences between weak mayor, strong mayor, and council-manager forms of government. Which do you prefer and why?
	Learning Outcome: Describe local political systems in Texas.	Being Socially Responsible	Compare at-large election systems and single-member district systems. An argument in favor of single-member district systems is that they increase minority representation in local government. In your opinion, does increased minority representation increase intercultural competency? Why?
	Learning Outcome: Describe local political systems in Texas.	Taking Personal Responsibility	Local government directly impacts people in their daily lives. What can you do to improve local governance?
	Learning Outcome: Describe local political systems in Texas.	Thinking Critically	Identify some of the problems facing county governments. What solutions would you propose?

Learning Outcomes and Core Objectives Correlation Table continued

CHAPTER 7	**Learning Outcome:** Identify the rights and responsibilities of citizens.	**Taking Personal Responsibility**	What activities do you engage in that are related to governance? Which forms of political participation do you think are the most effective?
	Learning Outcome: Identify the rights and responsibilities of citizens.	**Thinking Critically**	How do you think the Texas voter ID law impacts voter turnout in Texas? Where do you stand on the issue? Explain why you favor or oppose voter ID laws.
	Learning Outcome: Identify the rights and responsibilities of citizens.	**Being Socially Responsible**	Considering the discussion of the socioeconomic factors that affect voter turnout, identify effective ways to increase civic knowledge in culturally diverse communities.
	Learning Outcome: Identify the rights and responsibilities of citizens.	**Communicating Effectively**	Write a one-page summary of the rationalist explanations for low voter turnout.
CHAPTER 8	**Learning Outcome:** Analyze the state and local election process in Texas.	**Thinking Critically**	Explain the challenges that hinder minor party candidates from succeeding in statewide elections.
	Learning Outcome: Analyze the state and local election process in Texas.	**Communicating Effectively**	Do you think the Voting Rights Act requirement that Texas provide a bilingual ballot increases voter turnout? Construct an argument in favor or against this provision of the Voting Rights Act.
	Learning Outcome: Analyze the state and local election process in Texas.	**Being Socially Responsible**	What responsibility do you think the media have in covering campaigns and elections? Are the media living up to your expectations?
	Learning Outcome: Analyze the state and local election process in Texas.	**Taking Personal Responsibility**	If you choose to contribute to a candidate's campaign, to what extent is the candidate obligated to you as a contributor? Should your contribution influence public policy? What about corporate contributions?
CHAPTER 9	**Learning Outcome:** Evaluate the role of political parties in Texas.	**Communicating Effectively**	Explain how political reforms have weakened political parties.
	Learning Outcome: Evaluate the role of political parties in Texas.	**Taking Personal Responsibility**	Examine your political values and compare them to the expressed values of both parties. Do your ideas about the role of government, politics, and policy align with one particular party?
	Learning Outcome: Evaluate the role of political parties in Texas.	**Being Socially Responsible**	What impact, if any, do factions have on enhancing or diminishing civic engagement? In your opinion, do factions promote acceptance of diverse opinions?
	Learning Outcome: Evaluate the role of political parties in Texas.	**Thinking Critically**	For a variety of reasons, third parties do not currently have much impact on Texas politics. What measures might be taken to level the playing field for third parties and improve their competitiveness in elections?
CHAPTER 10	**Learning Outcome:** Evaluate the role of interest groups in Texas.	**Thinking Critically**	Review Table 10.1. Are you a participant in a membership organization? If so, how does the organization represent your interests? If not, how are your interests represented at the state and federal levels of government?
	Learning Outcome: Evaluate the role of interest groups in Texas.	**Taking Personal Responsibility**	Socrates suggested, "know thyself," and Shakespeare's Hamlet admonished "to thine own self be true." It is important to know what your interests are and how they are represented in government. Consider what you have read in this chapter and determine how interest group efforts align with your personal interests. If they do not, what can you do to ensure that government addresses your interests or the interests of those who share similar values?
	Learning Outcome: Evaluate the role of interest groups in Texas.	**Communicating Effectively**	Review the data presented in Table 10.4. Identify the interest group category that spent the most money in 2014. Discuss the impact that PAC spending has on government.
	Learning Outcome: Evaluate the role of interest groups in Texas.	**Being Socially Responsible**	How can geographic distribution of interest groups improve political awareness between culturally diverse populations?

CHAPTER 11	**Learning Outcome:** Analyze important public policy issues in Texas.	Taking Personal Responsibility	How can you impact public policy decisions? At what point in the policy cycle could you voice your preferences?
	Learning Outcome: Analyze important public policy issues in Texas.	Being Socially Responsible	To what extent should Texas be responsible for ensuring equal funding for wealthy school districts and poor school districts?
	Learning Outcome: Analyze important public policy issues in Texas.	Communicating Effectively	Summarize the legislation that Texas has passed on abortion. Discuss the advantages and disadvantages of state involvement in this policy issue.
	Learning Outcome: Analyze important public policy issues in Texas.	Thinking Critically	Given the water-related challenges facing Texas, what measures would you recommend to ensure all Texans have access to water? What might be some negative or unintended consequences of your recommendations?
CHAPTER 12	**Learning Outcome:** Analyze issues and policies in Texas.	Communicating Effectively	Explain the difference between criminal and civil law, including how the standard of proof differs for each. Provide an example of each type of case.
	Learning Outcome: Analyze issues and policies in Texas.	Taking Personal Responsibility	Currently, at what age does the state of Texas consider a person an adult in criminal and civil proceedings? At what age do you think the state should require individuals to take personal responsibility? Why?
	Learning Outcome: Analyze issues and policies in Texas.	Being Socially Responsible	Why might the use of special courts to punish crimes like prostitution provide a cost savings for the criminal justice system?
	Learning Outcome: Analyze issues and policies in Texas.	Thinking Critically	Given the current challenges faced by the criminal justice system, what types of reforms would you recommend? What might be some of the negative or unintended consequences of your recommendations?
CHAPTER 13	**Learning Outcome:** Analyze state financing issues and policies in Texas.	Thinking Critically	What goods and services do you think state government should provide? Consider the consequences of your answer. What would the possible impact to society be, given your position?
	Learning Outcome: Analyze state financing issues and policies in Texas.	Being Socially Responsible	Texas taxes prepared food items, but does not tax unprepared food items (e.g., raw meats and fresh produce). If, as noted earlier in this chapter, individuals can be excluded from receiving services, such as electricity, because of the inability to pay, how does taxing prepared food impact our state's poorest citizens?
	Learning Outcome: Analyze state financing issues and policies in Texas.	Communicating Effectively	Consider Table 13.7, which illustrates how specific appropriations are restricted. What percentage of funds is not restricted? How does restricting funds impact budget flexibility?
	Learning Outcome: Analyze state financing issues and policies in Texas.	Taking Personal Responsibility	Although few individuals would express a preference for higher taxes, given the information in this chapter about the goods and services the state provides and the revenue data presented in Figure 13.9 and Table 13.9, should Texans advocate for a personal income tax? Why or why not?
CHAPTER 14	**Learning Outcome:** Evaluate public opinion and the role of the media in Texas politics.	Thinking Critically	Compare and contrast the factors of socialization and explain how they have informed your political opinions.
	Learning Outcome: Evaluate public opinion and the role of the media in Texas politics.	Taking Personal Responsibility	What can you do to improve the content on social media networks?
	Learning Outcome: Evaluate public opinion and the role of the media in Texas politics.	Being Socially Responsible	Explain what social obligation the media has in the political campaign process.
	Learning Outcome: Evaluate public opinion and the role of the media in Texas politics.	Communicating Effectively	Write an essay summarizing government's efforts to regulate the Internet.

BRIEF CONTENTS

McGraw Hill Education **connect**

CONTENTS

About the Authors

Sherri Mora is the Associate Chair and Undergraduate Program Coordinator for Political Science and Public Administration at Texas State University. She earned advanced degrees in political science, public administration, and education from Texas State University. She has published on teaching and learning in political science and has served as a vertical team member on College and Career Readiness Standards since 2004. As an active member of the assessment group, Mora is responsible for core curriculum assessment and programmatic review in the Department of Political Science at Texas State. She has received numerous awards from the university for distinction as a professor, coordinator, and scholar, including the College of Liberal Arts Achievement Award for Excellence in Service and the Foundation of Excellence Award.

William Ruger is a political scientist who specializes in state politics, international relations, and political economy. He has worked for two decades in the university and educational nonprofit worlds, including teaching stints at two Texas universities: Texas State University (where he was a tenured professor) and the LBJ School of Public Affairs at the University of Texas-Austin. Ruger authored *Milton Friedman* and co-authored four editions of *Freedom in the 50 States: An Index of Personal and Economic Freedom*. His most notable scholarship appeared in *State Politics and Policy Quarterly*, *International Studies Quarterly*, *Civil Wars*, and *Review of Political Economy*. He is a frequent guest on television and radio, and his op-eds have appeared in several national publications, including *Time*, *USA Today*, *Investor's Business Daily*, and the *New York Daily News*. Ruger earned an A.B. from the College of William and Mary and his Ph.D. in Politics from Brandeis University. He is also a veteran of the Afghanistan War.

ACKNOWLEDGMENTS

We would like to thank Jennifer Ruger and Jamie Falconnier for their exceptional research assistance for the third edition. We also want to thank the anonymous reviewers of the first and second editions, whose questions and comments made this a better edition. At McGraw-Hill Education and Southern Editorial, we are indebted to Denise Wright, Jason Seitz, Dawn Groundwater, Marianne Musni, Laura Wilk, Eliana White, April Cole, Michelle Greco, Dolly Womack, Tamara Newlin, Will Walter, and Rick Hecker. For their help with the manuscript, our gratitude goes out to the following individuals: Tracy Cook at Central Texas College for her thoughtful comments; Christopher Brown and Brendan Scott at Texas State University, Sandra Geiseler at Alamo Colleges, David McClendon at Tyler Junior College, Jerod Patterson at the University of Texas-Austin, Cindy Pressley at Austin State University, Jason Sorens at Dartmouth College, and Christy Woodward-Kaupert at San Antonio College for their helpful contributions; and Meredith Grant for helping make this all happen in the first place.

Additional thanks goes to the following reviewers:
Millie Black, Collin College, Plano
Darrell Castillo, Weatherford College
Henry Esparza, University of Texas, San Antonio
Brandon Franke, Blinn College
Rodolfo (Rudy) Hernandez, Texas State University, San Marcos
Alan Lehmann, Blinn College
Sharon Manna, North Lake College
David McClendon, Tyler Junior College
Lindsey B. McLennan, Kilgore College
Eric Miller, Blinn College, Bryan
Chad Mueller, Weatherford College
Martha Musgrove, Tarrant County College, South
Sharon Navarro, University of Texas, San Antonio
John M. Osterman Jr., San Jacinto College, Pasadena
William Parent, Houston Community College, San Jacinto
Paul Philips, Navarro College
Blayne J. Primozich, El Paso Community College, Verde
Prudencio Ramirez, San Jacinto College, Pasadena
Wesley Riddle, Central Texas College, Killeen
Jeff Stanglin, Kilgore College
Steven Tran, Houston Community College
Ronald Vardy, Wharton County Junior College

CHAPTER 1

Introduction to Texas History and Politics

Texas Learning Outcomes

- Explain the history, demographics, and political culture of Texas.

History and politics are inevitably intertwined, and this is also the case in Texas. Today's Texas is the product of a variety of factors: cultural influences, a unique geography including a vast amount of land that borders a foreign nation and has thriving ports, complicated historical relations with European powers, a distinctive experience with the U.S. Civil War and Reconstruction, economic shifts from agriculture to industry, shifts in political dominance from one party to the other, and changing demographics due to waves of opportunity. The current challenges Texas faces are also tied to national events. To gain a full appreciation for Texas government, we must examine the Texas of the past as well as today's Texas and put them in a framework within which we can understand them—the framework of political culture. By doing this, we can begin to appreciate the special position Texas occupies within the United States, the ways in which it is very much "American," and the ways in which it is uniquely Texan.

Chapter Learning Objectives

- Explain the significance of Texas's six flags.
- Describe the Civil War and Reconstruction in Texas.
- Describe post-Reconstruction Texas.
- Explain the challenges facing Texas today.
- Explain U.S. and Texas political cultures.

The Six Flags of Texas: From Spain to Statehood

Learning Objective: Explain the significance of Texas's six flags.

Settlement of the territory known as Texas began with north Asian tribal groups migrating down from the Bering land bridge into the Americas. These groups spread out throughout the Americas, and several eventually occupied the plains, grasslands, and coastal woodlands that are now called Texas. The Caddo Indians settled primarily in the eastern parts of Texas. The Wichita Indians claimed much of the Red River Valley and the lowland grass plains. The Karankawas made their home along the coastal plains, and the western parts of the state were settled by those tribes that eventually became part of the great horse cultures in North America: the Comanches, Apaches, Kiowas, and Tonkawas. Each of these groups would have an impact on later European settlers.

Spain

Spain was the first of the modern European nations to lay claim to the territory of Texas, although Spanish Texas included only a small part of today's state. Alonso Alvarez de Pineda explored and mapped the Texas coastline as early as 1519, more than 100 years before the Pilgrims landed at Plymouth Rock. However, it was not until 1540 that Francisco Vasquez de Coronado intentionally surveyed the interior of Texas. After Coronado dispelled rumors that the land was brimming with treasures, Spain all but abandoned Texas for almost a century and a half. Still, Spain had raised the first of the six flags that would eventually fly over Texas.

France, Briefly

France was the second nation to lay claim and bring its flag, briefly, to the territory of Texas. After the European discovery of North America, France laid claim to all the territory encompassing the Mississippi River system (bordering much of the territory of Texas in the east and north along the Red River) as well as parts of the Spanish claims in the northwestern territories of Mexico. One settlement attempt, led by René-Robert Cavelier, Sieur de La Salle, began in 1685 (mostly by accident) when his expedition overshot New Orleans and landed on the Texas coast near Matagorda Bay. Fort Saint Louis, however, was a dismal failure because the expedition was inadequately supplied and La Salle was a poor leader. When La Salle left in 1687, taking an overland route to seek assistance from New Orleans, he was killed by his own men. The next year, Karankawa Indians destroyed the fort and either killed or captured the remaining settlers.

Spain Returns

After the remains of Fort Saint Louis were discovered in 1689, the Spanish crown decided to increase settlement efforts by establishing missions and presidios (fortified settlements) in the eastern part of its territory. The goal was to fend off future French claims by bringing Spanish settlers from Mexico into Texas territory. These Spanish settlers were known as Tejanos, and the first area they settled was the Rio Grande Valley. They established settlements along the Rio Grande and as far north and east as San Antonio. (Spanish settlements in other parts of the state lasted for only a few years, with the exception of Nacogdoches.) Although permanent Spanish settlement did not penetrate much beyond San Antonio, Spanish influence permeated the entire state. For example, most of the major rivers in Texas have Spanish names, as do other geographic features and a number of cities and counties. Notably, the Spanish introduced horses, sheep, and cattle into Texas. Spanish legal systems also left their legacy on state laws, especially those regarding land ownership and rights. For example, current laws regarding community property and protections against the forced sale of property (to pay off a debt or court-ordered judgment) have their origins in Spanish law.[1] The homestead exemption is another such legacy.[2]

When the United States purchased the Louisiana Territory from France in 1803, new settlement and immigration patterns emerged in East Texas. As **Anglos** encroached through Louisiana, Spain continued to promote settlement. But Spanish-Mexican relations were deteriorating, and Mexico declared its independence from Spain in 1821.

Anglo
Here, refers to non-Hispanic white North Americans of European descent, typically (but not exclusively) English speaking

The Republic of Mexico

The third flag to fly over Texas was that of the Republic of Mexico, which included what had been Spanish Texas. By 1824 Texas, the northeastern-most territory of the new nation, had been combined with another province to form the new, Mexican state of Coahuila and Texas.[3] The **empresario** land-grant system that had begun under the Spanish continued. (Stephen Austin renegotiated his father's Spanish grant with the new Mexican government.) Mexico continued to attract settlers into East Texas. Southern U.S. Anglos and the African American slaves they brought with them began settling there in the 1820s. These southern white Protestants were decidedly different from the Spanish Catholic settlers who already occupied Texas. Because of Mexico's own history of ethnic diversification, a strong antislavery movement was brewing. When President Santa Anna effectively declared himself dictator of Mexico and issued decrees limiting property rights and economic freedom for Anglos, the simmering conflict led to increased Anglo-Texan calls for rebellion.

empresario
A person who contracted with the Spanish or Mexican government to recruit new settlers to Texas in exchange for the ability to claim land

Open revolt began in late 1835 when Texan and Mexican forces fought over a small six-pound cannon in Gonzales, Texas. Famously, the defenders of the cannon at Gonzales raised a flag with the words "Come and Take It" underneath a lone star and cannon. A Texan victory fed the fever of revolt, and political leaders began planning for rebellion against Mexico. Internal conflicts in Texas complicated matters. Many of the Catholic Spanish remained loyal to Mexico, while the more recently arrived Protestant Anglos generally favored independence.

Gonzales Flag
© *Gallery of the Republic*

The Battle of the Alamo, Percy Moran, 1912
Source: Library of Congress Prints and Photographs Division LC-USZC4-2133

Santa Anna himself took command of the Mexican forces and marched north into Texas for the stated purpose of suppressing the rebellion and expelling the Anglos. His first battle was the siege of the Alamo (an old mission turned fortress) in San Antonio in February 1836. Texan forces under the command of William B. Travis were hopelessly outnumbered and had no real chance to be reinforced. The siege lasted two weeks, ending with the death of all 187 Alamo defenders on March 6, 1836. The brave resistance by the Alamo's defenders provided additional motivation for the independence movement and is today seen as the Texan equivalent of the famous Battle of Thermopylae between the Greek forces led by the Spartan 300 and the Persians. On March 2, 1836, just before the Alamo's fall, the provisional government of Texas declared its independence from Mexico.

The Republic of Texas

The Republic of Texas flew the fourth national flag. The immediate problem for the new republic was surviving the war with Mexico. The republic did not have an organized army, and the one being assembled had little to no experience. Sam Houston, the general of the Texan army, knew that he needed time to organize and train if Texas was to have a chance at victory. Meanwhile, Santa Anna continued his march north and captured and killed all 350 of James Fannin's troops at what is now called the Goliad Massacre. It was becoming increasingly clear that Santa Anna intended to wipe out the Anglo-American presence in Texas permanently. In what came to be known as the "Runaway Scrape," Texans and Texas forces retreated for several weeks, fleeing ahead of Santa Anna's army toward Louisiana. Finally, on the banks of the San Jacinto River on April 21, 1836, Houston found himself with a tactical advantage; he attacked and defeated Santa Anna's army. Santa Anna was captured and forced to sign the Treaty of Velasco, recognizing Texas's independence from Mexico.

In the aftermath of the revolution, Texas found itself a new nation with no real desire to *be* a nation. With limited resources and infrastructure, the new government was quickly bound by debt and struggled to meet its minimum obligations to its citizens. Houston had been elected the first president of Texas, and as one of the first acts of the new republic, he petitioned the government of the United States for statehood. Because the vast majority of Anglo settlers considered themselves Americans, it seemed fitting for Texas to become part of the United States. However, the petition for statehood was denied because of the intensely political and divisive issue of slavery. At that time, if Texas was admitted into the Union as a slave state, a corresponding free state would need to be created. This balancing act was not possible then, and Texas was forced to stand on its own. The United States recognized Texas's independence and set up diplomatic relations.

From 1836 to 1845, the Republic of Texas struggled to survive. Poor relations and border disputes with Mexico to the south and open hostilities with Indians in the west made governing Texas difficult. Lack of revenue and poor infrastructure continued to plague the nascent republic and made economic development challenging. Nonetheless, Texas promoted settlement of its frontier to Americans and Anglo-Europeans by offering the one thing it did have: land. In the 1840s, an organization called the **Adelsverein Society** aided this appeal for settlers by actively promoting German immigration to Texas. By 1847 this society had brought more than 7,000 Germans to Texas, most of whom settled in the vicinity of Fredericksburg in what is now known as "Hill Country."[4] By 1850, German settlers composed 5.4 percent of the population.[5]

Adelsverein Society
An organization that promoted German immigration to Texas in the 1840s

CORE OBJECTIVE

Thinking Critically . . .
How have settlement patterns impacted Texas? Give current examples.

© National Park Service

The Twenty-Eighth State of the Union

Meanwhile, the idea of Manifest Destiny was gaining popularity in the United States. Many in Washington wanted to ensure that Texas and all its lands would be part of this nation, one that would stretch from the Atlantic to the Pacific. Although the diplomatic efforts to bring Texas into the Union were complex, on December 29, 1845, President Polk signed the act making Texas the twenty-eighth state of the Union. When Texas entered the Union, it retained its public debt and its public lands, forcing the U.S. government to purchase all land

MAP 1.1   Compromise of 1850 Present state boundaries are shown along with territory transferred to the federal government as part of this agreement.

that was to be designated as federal. During the Compromise of 1850 (see Map 1.1), when Texas's boundary lines were finally settled, the U.S. government purchased lands that were formerly the west and northwest parts of Texas (now much of present-day New Mexico and parts of Colorado, Wyoming, Kansas, and Oklahoma).[6]

Thus the U.S. flag became the fifth to fly over Texas. But Mexico did not give up easily. Still claiming all of Texas as its own, Mexico had voiced objections to U.S. annexation of Texas and broke diplomatic relations with the United States in early 1845. Moreover, Mexican territory at that time extended as far north as the Great Salt Lake and west to the Pacific, in direct opposition to the U.S. goal of spreading across the whole continent. Crossing the Rio Grande on April 25,1846, Mexican troops attacked U.S. troops provocatively stationed in a disputed area, leading the U.S. Congress to declare war. The resulting Mexican-American War lasted from 1846 to 1848, ending with a decisive victory for the United States. In the Treaty of Guadalupe Hidalgo (in conjunction with the Gadsden Purchase in 1853), the United States officially gained Texas, California, and all the land between them. However, Texas had entered the Union at a time when the very structure of that Union was becoming tenuous.

The Confederate State of Texas

From 1848 to 1860, settlement increased dramatically, with more and more immigrants coming from the southern United States and Europe. Increasingly, Texas's economy became tied to that of the southern states and the slave system. These ties were the primary reason Texas seceded from the Union in 1861 and joined the Confederacy. Texas was not among the first states to do so, because its constitutional requirements were more stringent than other southern states, but in the end, the Confederate flag was the sixth national flag to fly over Texas.

Civil War and Reconstruction: A Time of Transition

Learning Objective: Describe the Civil War and Reconstruction in Texas.

The Civil War was a costly and brutal conflict, but Texas was lucky compared to many Confederate states. Politics and geography combined to create that "luck." Oddly enough, the machinations of Napoleon III of France played a role in the war in Texas. France had invaded Mexico in 1861. Napoleon's goal was to set up a new government in Mexico, with Archduke Ferdinand Maximilian of Austria as emperor, under French protection. Napoleon was openly pro-Confederate but did not want to risk warfare with the United States. Despite the Confederacy's desperate need for French funds and official recognition, events in Europe combined with U.S. threats to keep the French from fully committing to Confederate support. Union General Nathaniel P. Banks, commanding the Army of the Gulf, was ordered to invade Texas, partly as a show of force to discourage French support of the Confederacy and partly to occupy the state. Both of Banks's attempts to do so ultimately failed. Thanks to a complex series of events worthy of the most intrigue-laden novels, Maximilian did eventually become emperor of Mexico (though only for a brief time, and he ended up being executed in 1867 by Mexicans fighting for independence); Banks was relieved of field command; France did not throw her support behind the Confederacy; and Texas for the most part avoided the battles and physical devastation, stemming from invasion and occupation, that affected much of the rest of the Confederacy.[7] After the war ended in 1865, 50,000 U.S. troops were stationed in Texas, primarily along the border with Mexico to oppose the "French Intervention." However, conflict did not break out between the U.S. and Mexico at that time.

Geography also played a role in limiting Texas's exposure to the ravages of war. A line runs from the Red River to present-day Fort Worth and south through Waco and Austin to San Antonio, and the settlements of Anglo southerners did not extend west much beyond this line. (This line is a natural geological feature, known as the Balcones Escarpment, which separates the Coastal Plains and pine forest regions of Texas from the middle and High Plains regions of the state.) In fact, most areas west of this line were not settled by whites until after the Civil War, for two reasons. First, Native American tribes—Comanche, Lipan Apache, Kiowa, and Tonkawa Indians—already inhabited the region. In the 1850s, the U.S. Army tried to control this region by constructing a series of forts on the edge of the Cross Timbers area. Forts Belknap, Cooper, Phantom Hill, Chadborne, McKavett, and Terrett were part of this plan. During the Civil War, however, the U.S. government abandoned these forts, and the Indian presence in the region reemerged. (Indeed, both Union and Confederate forces engaged in skirmishes with Native Americans in Texas during the Civil War.) Indian domination of the area continued until 1875, when Comanche Chief Quanah Parker was captured in Palo Duro Canyon, near present-day Amarillo. The second geography-related reason settlement was limited was that the dry, arid, treeless plains west of the Balcones Escarpment (Grande Prairie, Cross Timbers, lower plains, and High Plains) were not conducive to the wood, water, and plantation culture that southern Anglos brought with them. (This terrain likewise did not offer bountiful provisions for an invading army trying to live off the land.)

Despite Texas's relative "luck" during the war years from 1861 to 1865, it was the home of some important Civil War events. Foremost among them were the Battle of Sabine Pass and the Battle of Galveston, both fought in 1863. In the former, a small Confederate force prevented a larger Union force, led by General Banks, from moving into Texas. In the latter, Confederate forces on land recaptured Galveston while its naval forces captured the USRC *Harriet Lane,* despite being heavily outnumbered and losing CS *Neptune.* Other noteworthy actions included the Union blockade of the Texas coast, General Henry Sibley's march to El Paso in an attempt to take New Mexico and other federal territories beyond for the Confederacy, and

Battle of Galveston, Harper's Weekly, January 31, 1863
© *Courtesy of Texas State Library & Archives Commission*

the final land conflict of the war, the Battle of Palmito Ranch (which took place more than a month after Lee's surrender in Virginia). It is also worth noting that roughly 90,000 Texans served in the war.[8] Overall, the lives lost in battle and the time and money lost to the conflict were devastating to both Texas and the nation.

In the immediate aftermath of the Civil War, Texas, like many other states of the former Confederacy, found itself deeply in debt and under the military control of the Union army. The era that began in 1865 and was known as Reconstruction had two primary political goals. First, the Union wanted to restore law and order to a society recovering from war and allow Southern states to be readmitted to the Union. Second, the Union sought to finally dismantle the institution of slavery. As historians James M. McPherson and James K. Hogue stated, "No single generalization can encompass the variety of ways in which freedom came to the slaves."[9] In Texas, Union General Gordon Granger started the process of emancipation on his arrival at Galveston by issuing General Order Number 3 on June 19, 1865. This order informed Texans that "in accordance with a proclamation from the Executive of the United States, all slaves are free." Importantly, it went on to note that "This involves an absolute equality of personal rights and rights of property between former masters and slaves, and the connection heretofore existing between them becomes that between employer and hired labor." This is the origin of the "Juneteenth" holiday in Texas and other states.[10] By the time the Thirteenth Amendment became the law of the land in December 1865, U.S. slavery was outlawed. It would prove more difficult to reunite the country and truly protect the rights of African Americans in the former states of the Confederacy.

Reconstruction's goals created a culture clash between the two major ideological groups in Texas. One group was the dominant Confederate sympathizers (typically southern Democrats) who wanted to maintain the status quo of society as much as possible. The second group was composed of Union supporters, including Republican "carpetbaggers," a pejorative term used to describe Republicans who moved to the South to be appointed to political office during Reconstruction, and "scalawags," an equally derisive descriptor of Southerners who supported Reconstruction policies. During this time, being a Republican in the South essentially came to mean that you were an outsider and could not be trusted by "true" (meaning white) Southerners.

In 1866, Texas adopted a new constitution that abolished slavery, nullified the ordinances of secession, renounced the right of future secession, and repudiated the state's wartime debt. This constitution was short-lived; it was replaced with another in 1869 as a result of the Reconstruction acts of the U.S. Congress and subsequent military rule imposed on Texas. This alleged "carpetbagger's constitution" was a drastic departure from other Texas constitutions, past and future (see Chapter 2), and granted African Americans the right to vote while also disenfranchising whites who had participated in the Civil War. Texas formally rejoined the Union in 1870.

Southern Democrats were able to regain control of state government with the election of 1874. The new governor, Richard Coke, called for a convention to write yet another constitution. When Texas adopted its new constitution in 1876, the document demonstrated a strong distrust in the institutions of government and a heavy emphasis on the freedoms and liberties of its citizens. Although it has changed dramatically due to hundreds of amendments over the years, the 1876 constitution remains the outline of our fundamental law for the state of Texas. The Coke administration also marked the beginning of one-party Democratic politics in Texas that lasted about 100 years. Without the legal tools created by the policies of Reconstruction, or the broad political support necessary to win any public office, Republicans began to vanish from the political scene. Democrats were triumphant in Texas.

Post-Reconstruction Texas

Learning Objective: Describe post-Reconstruction Texas.

A state's economy plays a role in its politics (and vice versa). For most of its history, the Lone Star State has had a **land-based economy**. However, that economy has evolved in the many decades following Reconstruction. Texas is no longer simply a rural state with an economy dominated by cattle, cotton, and oil (although these are still important elements).

land-based economy
An economic system in which most wealth is derived from the use of the land

Land

Early in Texas's history, many settlers were lured to the region by offers of free land. The Spanish and, later, Mexican governments provided generous land grants to any family willing to settle in the state. Each family could receive one *sitio* or *legua* (Spanish for "league"), the equivalent of about 4,428 acres of land, and a single person could receive 1,500 acres. By the 1820s it took generous incentives to convince people to settle in Texas, given the hardships of travel and simple survival there. "GTT" ("Gone to Texas") was a common sign left behind

Queen of Waco gusher. Spindletop, Beaumont, Port Arthur, and vicinity. Texas oil industry ca. 1901.

Source: Library of Congress Prints and Photographs Division LC-USZ62-26332

by those escaping debt or the long arm of the law. In a letter dated 1855 from Fort Clark, Texas, General P. H. Sheridan said, "If I owned Hell and Texas, I'd rent out Texas and live in Hell."[11]

Land issues also played a role in the Texas revolution in 1836 and subsequent annexation of Texas by the United States in 1845. The sheer vastness of Texas—all those acres of land—has played a role in Texas history for generations.

The Texas Economy: From Agriculture to Oil to the Service Sector

From the 1820s to 1860s, the primary use of that land was for cotton farming, which dominated the Texas economy. King Cotton was the state's major cash crop, helping Texas pay its bills from Independence through Reconstruction. The giant cattle ranches in south and west Texas also helped develop the cowboy culture and mystique of the frontier Texan. In the years following the Civil War, cattle became Texas's economic mainstay. In 1901, however, the Spindletop oil field was tapped near Beaumont, and the economy and politics of the state began to change dramatically.

The discovery of oil transformed Texas in three major ways over the next century:

- Oil sparked the transition from an agricultural economy to an industrial economy. In addition to jobs directly related to the oil industry, high-tech peripheral jobs and industries developed to support or benefit from the oil industry.[12]
- Oil accelerated the growth of Texas's population and brought in new citizens from all over the United States and abroad, looking for work. These new citizens brought with them ideas about government and economics that challenged and diversified the ideas of Texas Democrats and Republicans.
- Oil accelerated the demographic shift from a rural society to an urban society. In 1900, less than 20 percent of Texans lived in urban areas. In 1950, about 63 percent lived in urban areas. By 1990, that number had increased to more than 80 percent.[13]

During the 1970s and early 1980s, the state economy experienced tremendous growth because of an increase in oil prices. But oil was not always reliable. In the mid-1980s, the price of oil declined, and with it the economy of the entire state. To many, the economic recession of the 1980s pointed to a need for more economic diversity. Perhaps the old land-based economy, which had been so important in Texas's history, could not carry the state into the twenty-first century. Passage of the North American Free Trade Agreement (NAFTA), which went into effect in 1994, offered the promise of significant economic growth because of increased trade with Mexico. Furthermore, new high-tech industries, especially in Austin, Dallas, and Houston, significantly bolstered the Texas economy. Texas Instruments helped turn the calculator into a common household item in the 1970s, and today's Texas boasts a thriving software, equipment, telecommunications, and semiconductor industry. To support this industry,

Texas has become a leader in scientific and technological research and development. A good indicator of technological innovation is the number of international patent applications filed under the Patent Cooperation Treaty. In 2008, Texas ranked fourth among the 50 states in the number of patents filed, trailing only California, New York, and Massachusetts. According to the U.S. Patent and Trademark Office, Texas was second among the 50 states in total patents granted in 2014 (although this ranking is not nearly as high when considered on a per capita basis).[14] When Texas entered the twenty-first century, the economy of the state was far more diverse than it was even 20 years earlier. Although energy and agriculture are still important elements in the state's economy, they are balanced today by many new elements.

Today, the service industry dominates the Texas economy. According to the U.S. Bureau of Labor Statistics, service-providing industries include trade, transportation, utilities, information and financial activities, real estate, professional and business services, education, health care, and leisure and hospitality, among others. In November 2015, service industries employed 77 percent of the private sector workforce in Texas. Moreover, that number increases to 82 percent if farm labor is excluded.[15] The state's location, its proximity to Mexico, and its centrality within the continental United States has pushed this sector's growth. Trade has expanded rapidly owing to both NAFTA and globalization, and Texas has become a transportation hub. Increased trade has also fueled the growth of professional and business services in areas such as accounting and legal and computer services, as well as construction, engineering, and management. Meanwhile, population expansion has led to a marked increase in the need for health care and education services. Simultaneously, the rise in both trade and population has sparked the growth of the leisure and hospitality industry.

Texas has become a major trading power in its own right, leading the 50 U.S. states in exports. When Congress passed NAFTA in 1993, Texas anticipated significant economic growth because of increased trade, primarily with Mexico. But in reality, Texas has become a major center of international trade. From 2003 to 2014, it led all states in U.S. exports. In 2014, Texas exported $288 billion in goods, whereas California, in second place, exported only $174 billion. Texas by itself accounted for 17.8 percent of all U.S. exports. The state's major trading partners are Mexico and Canada, followed by countries in South America, Asia, and Europe. Mexico's importance is not to be underestimated, however; that nation alone received more than 35 percent of Texas's exports in 2014 (see Figure 1.1 for major categories of exports).[16]

CORE OBJECTIVE

Communicating Effectively . . .

Write a short synopsis of Texas's changing economy and its role in international trade.

© George Lavendowski/USFWS

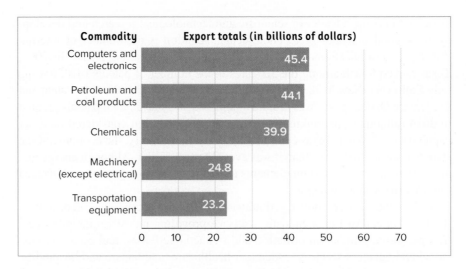

FIGURE 1.1 **Top Five Exports from Texas (in billions)**

SOURCE: Adapted from U.S. Department of Commerce, International Trade Administration, "Texas Exports, Jobs, and Foreign Investment," http://www.trade.gov/mas/ian/statereports/states/tx.pdf.

Texas's Economic Regions

economic regions

Divisions of the state based on dominant economic activity

The state comptroller's office has divided Texas into 12 **economic regions** as a convenient way to talk about areas of the state.[17] To simplify discussion, this book merges these 12 regions into six, as shown in Figure 1.2. A basic knowledge of these regions will be useful in considering how Texas's economic diversity impacts its government.

The East Texas or Piney Woods region was traditionally dominated by agriculture, timber, and oil. Today, agriculture is less important, and oil is declining, but timber is still important. Some diversification has occurred, with manufacturing becoming a more important element in the economy of this area.

The Plains region of the state, with Lubbock and Amarillo as its major cities, has historically been dominated by agriculture (especially cotton, wheat, and maize) and by ranching and cattle feedlots. In recent years, the economy of this region has become more diversified and less dominated by agriculture.

The Gulf Coast region, extending from Corpus Christi to Beaumont/Port Arthur/Orange and including Houston, is dominated by petrochemical industries, manufacturing, shipping, and fishing. In recent years, this area has further diversified with the addition of high-tech industries. It is also the area with the highest concentration of organized labor unions in the state.

The border area of South Texas and the Rio Grande Valley, stretching from Brownsville to El Paso, is noted primarily for its agricultural production of citrus fruits and vegetables. In recent years, trade with Mexican border cities has diversified the economy of this region, a process increased by the passage of NAFTA.

The Metroplex, or Dallas/Fort Worth area, is considered the financial center of the state. This region is the most economically diversified, with a combination of banking, manufacturing, high-tech, and aerospace industries.

The Central Corridor, or midstate region, is an area stretching roughly from College Station in the east to Waco in the north and Austin and San Antonio in the southwest. This area is dominated by two large state universities—Texas

FIGURE 1.2 **Economic Regions of Texas**

Industrial landscape: © Hal Bergman/Getty Images; *cityscape:* © Molly Dean/Getty Images; *crane:* © Greg Cooksey/Getty Images; *riverscape:* © ericfoltz/Getty Images

A&M University and the University of Texas at Austin—along with high-tech industries in Austin and San Antonio and major military bases in the Waco/Temple/Killeen and San Antonio areas.

Texas Politics: From Democrat to Republican

The Democratic Party dominated Texas politics from the end of Reconstruction until the mid-1970s. In the absence of a strong and viable Republican Party, third parties became the primary challengers to the Democratic Party during the "Progressive Era" of American politics. Groups such as the Greenback Party, the Farmers Alliance, and the Populists became known as progressives because they believed in the "doctrine of progress"—the concept that governing institutions can be improved by bringing science to bear on public problems.[18] Each of these groups had as their goal the use of government to try to positively impact the economy, by either increasing the value of agriculture or reining in the power of business and banking.[19] The Democratic Party successfully responded to these challenges by adopting many progressive reform proposals into its own platform. By the start of the twentieth century, Texas was effectively a one-party state with Progressive Democrats and Conservative Democrats contesting offices. In fact, a lack of meaningful competition from Republicans often led to straight-ticket party voting in elections. The term "Yellow Dog Democrat," coined to describe an individual who would vote only for Democratic candidates, aptly described the voting habits of many Texans (that is, "He would vote for a yellow dog if it ran as a Democrat").

From the 1920s through World War II, the oil industry helped shape state and local politics. The majority of Texas Democrats were conservative in their political ideology. Conservative business interests actually aligned more with the national Republican Party at times, and the state supported Herbert Hoover in 1928—one of only four instances from the end of Reconstruction to the mid-1970s in which a majority of Texas voters favored the Republican candidate in a presidential election.[20] The Great Depression, however, soured Texans on the Republican Party again, and the Democratic New Deal brought Texans back into the party fold. Progressive Democrats supporting jobs programs and military development helped attract more liberal-minded citizens to the party.

The next time a majority of Texas voters supported the Republican candidate was in 1952, when Dwight Eisenhower was elected president. He was backed by the "Shivercrats," a faction of Texas Democrats who followed conservative Democratic Governor Allan Shivers. Texans supported Eisenhower again in 1956.

As the national Democratic Party increased the federal government's role in the lives of individuals and businesses through the New Deal, the Fair Deal, and Great Society programs, conservative Texas Democrats became disenchanted with the national party and chose not to support it in national races. This coincided with an increase in the number of liberal Democrats joining the party and achieving leadership positions. The Civil Rights movement of the late 1950s and 1960s also pushed socially conservative Democrats away from the Democratic Party and started pulling them toward the Republican Party. John Tower's 1961 election, the first time Texas had sent a Republican to the U.S. Senate since 1870, reflected the beginning of this shift.[21] A majority of Texas voters supported Richard Nixon, a Republican, for president in 1972.

This pattern of supporting Republicans for national political offices eventually evolved into supporting Republican candidates for state offices (for example, Bill Clements for Governor in 1978) and, eventually, supporting Republican candidates for local office. For example, beginning with the election of Ronald Reagan in 1980, a majority of Texans have voted Republican in every presidential election to date.[22] Texas fully transitioned from a predominantly Democratic (conservative) majority to a fully Republican statewide majority by 2002. After the 1994 political party realignment, which swept away Democratic majorities in the U.S. House and Senate, Texans voted a large sector of experienced, powerful Democratic officeholders out of public office. Anglo male voters, as well as businesses and conservatives seeking big changes in the state's legal and regulatory system, found and supported Republican candidates at all levels. By 1998, all statewide elective officeholders were Republicans, and by 2002, the Texas House of Representatives had a Republican majority for the first time in its history, also a testament to the significance of redistricting. (See the Chapter 3 section titled "Reapportionment and Redistricting Issues" for an in-depth discussion of redistricting.) During the past two decades, the Republican Party has grown so much in Texas that the state is again virtually a one-party dominant state, but now the advantage goes to the Republicans.

There are other, non-ideological reasons for the shift toward a one-party, Republican state. Culturally, there are likely many more individuals who would self-identify as Democrats or who would vote for Democratic candidates than are currently registered or voting. Structurally, however, there are problems with making today's Democratic Party a competitive entity. Many likely Democratic voters either do not register or do not vote (see Chapter 7 for more on why people vote), some independents might vote Democratic if that party had a better chance of winning statewide seats or legislative control, and redistricting has virtually guaranteed Republican majorities in the state and federal representative races. Additionally, the Texas Democratic Party has not offered much in the way of dynamic candidates or organization.

Evidence from the 2008 election suggests that if these conditions changed, very different political outcomes could occur in Texas. In the March 2008 presidential primary election, nearly 3 million Texans voted in the Democratic primary, compared to only 1.3 million in the Republican primary (though the poor turnout on the Republican side was because eventual party nominee John McCain had all but sewn up the nomination).[23] In the general election, 8 million Texans cast ballots, and although Republican John McCain won the state, Democrats (with a strong presidential candidate with coattails in Barack Obama) made significant gains in the Texas House, closely missing a tie with 74 seats.

The situation, though, changed quickly and dramatically. Aggressive reaction to the Obama presidency in 2010 and 2012 prompted a tidal wave of small-government or social conservatives to run for office, and many succeeded in winning primaries, unseating a number of long-standing Democrats in both the state and U.S. House of Representatives. However, in 2013, Democratic operatives launched "Battleground Texas," a **political action committee** (**PAC**) whose goal was to revitalize the Democratic Party in the state and ultimately "turn Texas blue."[24] Unfortunately for Democrats, the 2014 election was not kind to these efforts. As discussed in Chapter 9, the Democratic Party's gubernatorial candidate Wendy Davis failed to defeat Republican Greg Abbott and actually performed worse than its candidate Bill White did against incumbent governor Rick Perry in 2010. Davis received fewer total votes than White (1,835,596 to 2,106,395) and only 39% of the total statewide vote compared to the 42% he had received. Likewise, Democrats had 55 seats in the House and 12 in the Senate for the 83rd legislative session. The party's numbers slipped to 52 seats in the House and 11 in the Senate for the 84th Legislature that convened in 2015. In the 2016 primary, 2.84 million voters chose from among a crowded Republican field that included Texas Senator Ted Cruz, while only about half that number (1.44 million) voted in a two-person match-up between Hillary Clinton and Bernie Sanders on the Democratic Party's side.

It should be noted that although political party realignment has occurred in the past 50 years, the ideological landscape of Texas has not really changed.

political action committee (PAC)
Spin-offs of interest groups that collect money for campaign contributions and other activity

When public opinion polls ask about political ideology, a solid plurality of Texans continue to identify themselves as conservative (rather than moderate, independent, or liberal). One of the characteristics of Texas political culture has been its strong tendency toward conservative ideological principles in all areas of public policy. In fact, "ideology" has meant more to many Texas voters than political party labels. This strong ideological association helps explain why Texas voters realigned between the two major parties during the latter part of the twentieth century. For most Texas voters, whether a candidate was a Democrat or a Republican was not relevant; the most "conservative" candidate would likely win most elections.

CORE OBJECTIVE

Taking Personal Responsibility . . .

What can you do to become well informed about political issues so that you can make good decisions at election time?

Source: United States Department of Agriculture Agricultural Research Service

Demographics: The Road to Majority-Minority

Demography refers to the statistical characteristics of a population. Typically, data used to develop and describe population statistics come from the United States Census, which is conducted every 10 years. Regardless of the best efforts, the census is subject to error, particularly in the form of an undercount. Nonetheless, census questions and the information derived from them provide a means of measuring meaningful features of a population. Population trends reflect much about the political, social, and cultural features of a given region and are very important indicators for government at all levels. Population data allow governments to plan well, and well in advance, in providing the vital needs for which they are responsible.

Of the 50 states, Texas ranks second not only in total land size but also in terms of population. Moreover, that population has been growing at an explosive rate. In 1970, Texas's population was 11.2 million; by 1990 it had increased to almost 17 million. In 2010, the U.S. Census Bureau calculated the state's official population at 25,145,561. The 2015 estimate jumped to 27,469,114, reflecting a rapid increase of 9.2 percent, or more than 2.3 million residents in five years. This compares to national growth of only 4.1 percent over the same five-year period.[25] (See Figure 1.3 for a comparison of the Lone Star State's population growth with that of other states.) Although birthrates account for part of this growth, it is also attributable to the arrival of newcomers from other states and countries.

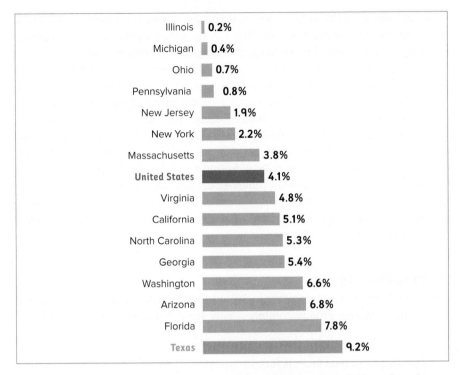

FIGURE 1.3 Percentage Change in Population for the 15 Most Populous States, 2010–2015

SOURCE: Adapted from U.S. Census Bureau, Population Estimates, Table 2. Cumulative Estimates of Resident Population Change for the United States, Regions, States, and Puerto Rico and Region and State Rankings: April 1, 2010 to July 1, 2015; http://www.census.gov/popest/data/State/totals/2015/index.html.

This incredible growth has had an impact on Texas's standing in national politics. As a result of the 2010 Census, Texas was awarded four additional seats—the biggest gain of any state—in the U.S. House of Representatives.[26] The location of the four new districts highlights two very salient shifts in political power in the state: from rural to urban and suburban areas and increasing majority/minority demographics.

Urban and Rural

As *The Economist* noted, "The imagery of Texas is rural—cattle, cotton, cowboys and, these days, wind turbines whirring against the endless sky. But the reality is increasingly urban."[27] Although definitions of rural and urban can vary, the U.S. Census Bureau uses the following distinction for densely populated areas: "Urbanized Areas (UAs) consist of 50,000 or more people; Urban Clusters (UCs) comprise at least 2,500 but less than 50,000 people, and 'rural' encompasses all population, housing, and territory not included within an urban area."[28] Applying this definition to 2010 census data, 21,298,039 Texans lived in urban areas that year. This constituted 84.7 percent of the state's population, leaving 15.3 percent of the population (or 3.8 million people) in rural areas.[29] By comparison, in 2000, 17.5 percent of Texans (or 3.6 million people) were considered "rural."[30] In other words, while the overall population of Texas has increased, the proportion of Texans living in rural areas is declining. The state comptroller's office has projected that over the next 40 years, urban areas will continue to grow much more rapidly than rural areas.[31] In Map 1.2, the urban nature of today's Texas is apparent, with so many Texans living in a handful of populous counties.

As stated previously, Texas has added four new congressional districts: numbers 33, 34, 35, and 36. These new districts were primarily established in or near urban centers and are capable of capturing significant numbers of minority voters. District 33 includes Dallas and Tarrant counties and covers parts of the Dallas-Fort Worth metropolitan area. District 34 covers the Gulf Coast between Brownsville and Corpus Christi. District 35 covers multiple counties including parts of San Antonio and Austin. District 36 likewise includes multiple counties in southeast Texas near Houston.[32] Minority groups are particularly concentrated in major cities because of minority migration to urban centers and higher birth rates for minorities, along with white migration to suburban areas. The role of minority groups is particularly important in Texas.

majority-minority
Minority groups make up a majority of the population of the state

Majority-Minority

Since 2004, Texas has been a "**majority-minority**" state, meaning that all racial and ethnic minority groups combined now form a majority of the population

Percentage of All Texas Voters in 2012, By County

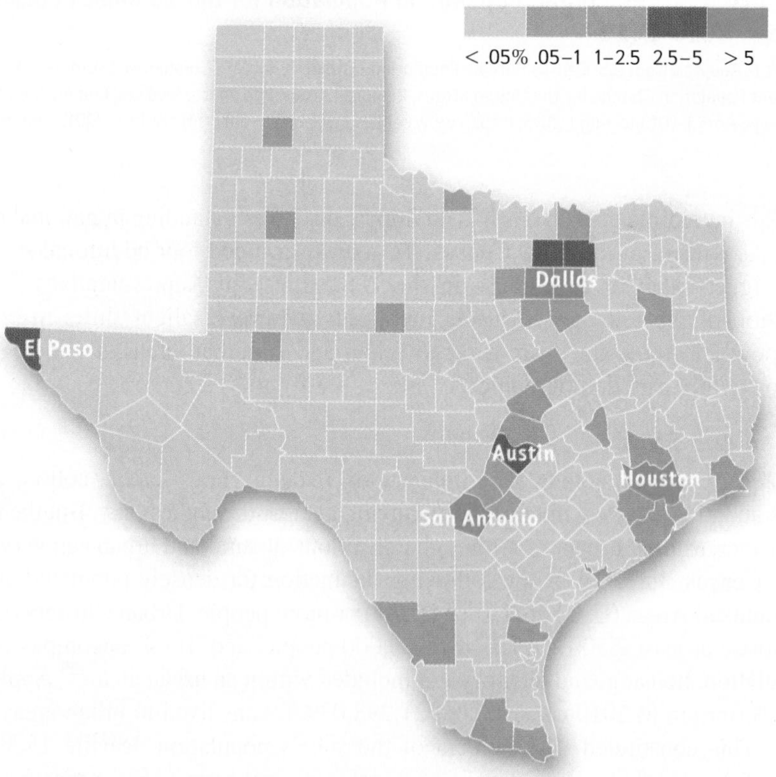

< .05%   .05–1   1–2.5   2.5–5   > 5

MAP 1.2   Population Density as Indicated by Percentage of Voters in Each County

and outnumber the non-Hispanic white population.[33] As of 2014, white non-Hispanics made up 43.5 percent of the total state population, making them a numerical, statistical minority.[34] Public school enrollments have been majority-minority for some time. According to the Texas Education Agency, 2001–2002 was the first school year in which Hispanic students outnumbered whites. By 2013-2014, Hispanic enrollment was over half of all students (51.8 percent), and white enrollment had declined to 29.5 percent of the total school population.[35] These changes in majority and minority status have significant implications for state politics as well as public policy decisions.

FOCUS ON

How the Government Defines "Hispanic"

Many forms ask respondents to indicate whether or not they are "Hispanic" or "Latino," but what do these terms mean? How do people and the government define "Hispanic" and "Latino"? As with many questions, the answer depends upon whom you ask!

First championed by a Hispanic bureaucrat in the 1970s,[36] U.S. government use of the term "Hispanic" has grown steadily. One of the earliest references was a 1976 law directing various federal departments to collect data regarding "Americans of Spanish origin or descent."[37] This group was originally defined as people who are "of Spanish-speaking background and trace their origin or descent from Mexico, Puerto Rico, Cuba, Central and South America, and other Spanish-speaking countries."[38] The actual term "Hispanic" first appeared on U.S. Census forms in 1980.[39] In 1997, the federal Office of Management and Budget (OMB) revised the definition of "Hispanic" to refer to "persons who trace their origin or descent to Mexico, Puerto Rico, Cuba, Central and South America, and other Spanish cultures." The OMB also began to use "Latino" in conjunction with "Hispanic" at that time. As justification, the OMB cited regional conventions, suggesting that "Hispanic" was often used in the eastern U.S. and "Latino" preferred in the western U.S.[40] (In some contexts, "Latino" may be a more inclusive term reflecting origins anywhere in Latin America—such as Brazil where

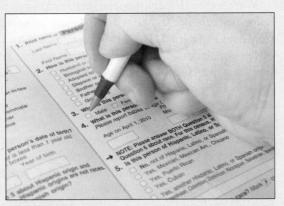

© Darren Brode/Shutterstock.com

Portuguese is the primary language—not just Spanish-speaking countries. Others have suggested the use of "Latino"/"Latina" may be associated with certain age groups or political affiliations.)[41] Despite the existence of these official governmental definitions, no proof or documentation is required to establish membership in this group. For census purposes, determining whether someone is Hispanic is based solely on self-identification. In other words, if one says one is Hispanic or Latino, then one is considered Hispanic or Latino.[42] According to the federal government's approach, race is a separate classification. The Census Bureau states people "who report themselves as Hispanic can be of any race."[43] This may differ from the perception of many Hispanics. According to a recent study by Pew Research Center, more than half of Hispanic adults surveyed considered their Hispanic background to be part of both their origin and their race.[44] Much of the demographic information in this book is based on census data.

Critical Thinking Questions

1. Why might the federal government collect data regarding particular ethnic groups?

2. In what way is the federal government's definition of the term "Hispanic" appropriate or inappropriate? What might be a better definition?

Raul A. Gonzales, Jr.

Courtesy of Raul A. Gonzalez

Hispanic immigration from Mexico to Texas has steadily increased over the course of the past half-century and has become a major factor in state politics. In 1960, Hispanics represented 15 percent of the total population of Texas. That increased to 18 percent by 1970, 21 percent in 1980, and 25 percent in 1990. According to the U.S. Census Bureau, Hispanics or Latinos made up 38.6 percent of the state's total population in 2014.[45]

With the aid of liberalized voter registration procedures, Hispanics have begun to dominate politics in the border areas, in some sections of South Texas and the Gulf Coast, and in the San Antonio area. They have successfully elected local officials to city and county government and school boards, to the state legislature, and to Congress. The first Hispanic either appointed or elected to statewide office was Raul Gonzales, in 1984, to the Texas Supreme Court.[46] Dan Morales was subsequently elected state attorney general in 1990 and served until 1999. In 2002, Tony Sanchez was the first Hispanic to become a major-party candidate for governor. The 2012 election of Ted Cruz to the U.S. Senate marked the first time the state sent a Hispanic to the upper chamber of Congress.[47] In 2015, George P. Bush (whose mother, Columba, is a native of Mexico who became a U.S. citizen in 1979) took office as Commissioner of the General Land Office (the state's fifth-highest elected position), and Carlos Cascos was appointed Texas Secretary of State.[48] It is clear that Hispanic voters and leaders will continue to be a major force in Texas state politics in the future.

Whereas the Hispanic population has grown as a percentage of total state population since the 1960s, the African American population has remained fairly constant over that period. The 2014 estimate for African Americans was 12.5 percent of the population.[49] African Americans tend to be concentrated in three metropolitan areas: Houston, Dallas/Fort Worth, and Austin. African Americans have had some political success winning election to local offices (school boards, city councils, and county offices) and the state legislature, in addition to winning a few seats in the U.S. Congress. Only one African American, Morris Overstreet, has been elected to statewide office. From 1990 to 1999, Judge Overstreet served on the Texas Court of Criminal Appeals, the highest court for criminal matters in the state. In 2002, Ron Kirk, the popular African American mayor of Dallas, ran for a U.S. Senate seat. Although polls showed Kirk to be in a dead heat with Republican John Cornyn, Kirk lost the race by a margin of almost 12 percent (43 percent for Kirk compared to 55 percent for Cornyn).[50]

Asian Americans constituted less than 1 percent of the population of Texas in 1980 but composed 4.5 percent of the state population by 2014.[51] The state's Asian American population is projected to continue increasing in the years ahead. In fact, the state demographer's office argues that "the non-Hispanic Other group, consisting of mostly Asian Americans, will grow at the fastest rate, when compared to other racial/ethnic categories."[52] Most of Texas's Asian American population is concentrated in the Houston area. In fact, one section of Houston has such a large proportion of Chinese Americans that some of the street signs are in Chinese. However, there are also significant concentrations of Korean Americans in the Dallas/Fort Worth Metroplex and in Killeen. Asian Americans in the Houston area have had some success in electing local officials, including one city council member and a county court of law judge. In 2002, Martha Wong was elected to represent the Houston area in the Texas statehouse. Wong was only the second Asian American to serve in the Texas House and the first Republican of Asian descent. In 2004, Hubert Vo was the first Vietnamese American elected to serve as a state representative, and he continues to represent his Houston area district. The first Asian American elected to the Texas House was Tom Lee from San Antonio. As of 2016, there have been five Asian Americans in the Texas House, including three in the current legislature.[53]

Religion in Texas

Religion in Texas bears the Roman Catholic imprint of its Spanish and Mexican roots as well as the conservative Protestantism of its later Anglo settlers. According to a 2014 survey by the Pew Research Center, (see Table 1.1) approximately 82 percent of Texans affiliate with a religious tradition. About 3 in 4 Texans identify as Christians, with Protestants accounting for 50 percent of the population and Catholics accounting for another 23 percent.[54]

Due in part to the state's large population of evangelical Protestants and also its large metropolitan areas, Texas is home to some of America's largest churches. The Houston area, for example, boasts the largest congregation in the United States: Joel Osteen's Lakewood Church has a weekly attendance in excess of 40,000. According to the Hartford Institute for Religion Research, 207 Protestant churches in Texas have an average weekly attendance of at least 2,000 persons, making them "megachurches."[55]

Religion is also an important feature of Texas politics, and Republican politics in particular. For example, shortly before former Governor Rick Perry launched his 2012 presidential primary campaign, he organized a national televised prayer meeting in Houston. A 2012 report by the Irma Rangel Public Policy Institute at the University of Texas at Austin on religion and the Texas electorate helped to underscore the relationship between religion and politics in Texas. The

Lakewood Church, the largest congregation in the country, meets in a former sports arena in Houston.

© Eric Kayne/Houston Chronicle/AP Images

TABLE 1.1

Religious Affiliation in Texas

Evangelical Protestant	31%	Jewish	1%
Mainline Protestant	13%	Muslim	1%
Historically Black Protestant	6%	Buddhist	1%
Catholic	23%	Hindu	1%
Mormon	1%	Other World Religions	< 1%
Jehovah's Witness	1%	Other Faiths	1%
Orthodox Christian	< 1%	Unaffiliated	18%
Other Christian	1%		

Source: U.S. Religious Landscape Survey, Pew Research Center, 2014

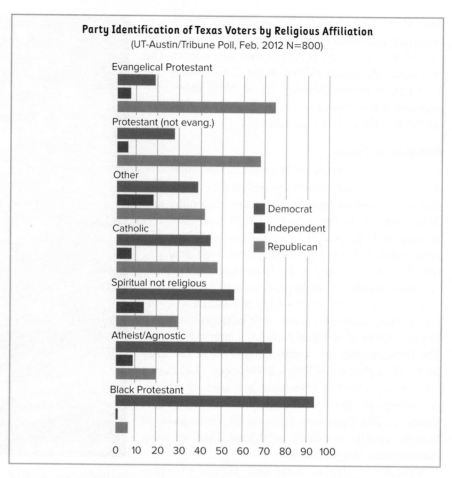

FIGURE 1.4   **Party Identification of Texas Voters by Religious Affiliation**

approximately one-third of Texans who are evangelical Protestants are over-whelmingly Republican, whereas Roman Catholics are fairly evenly split in party affiliation. Protestants of the black church tradition, those who identify as atheist or agnostic, and those who do not identify with an organized religion are overwhelmingly Democratic (see Figure 1.4).

CORE OBJECTIVE

Being Socially Responsible . . .

Understanding the relationship between religious affiliations and politics can improve civic knowledge. How would you use this knowledge to engage effectively in your community?

Current Challenges: Texas Today

Learning Objective: Explain the challenges facing Texas today.

Today, Texas is confronted with national issues that affect all states to some degree, as well as issues specific to the state. The impact of these issues on the state, and the state's role in the nation, are crucial to understanding today's Texas government.

The Recent Recession

Texas's diverse and growth-oriented economy weathered the 2008 financial meltdown-turned-recession better than other large states. Texas had diversified and transitioned its economy to a combination of energy, agriculture, trade, and an array of professional and business services, utilities, and general services. Due in part to this diversification and its relatively business-friendly fiscal and regulatory policies, Texas both entered the recession later and emerged from it more quickly than other states.[56] The state's gross domestic product (GDP), a measure of economic growth and production and therefore an indicator of the state's economic health,[57] actually fell during 2009.[58] (This had not happened in Texas since the mid-1980s, the last phase of the state's boom-and-bust oil economy.) According to the U.S. Bureau of Economic Analysis, automotive manufacturing and mining sectors suffered the biggest percentage declines in Texas in 2009.[59] The state unemployment rate peaked at 8.2 percent in December 2009 and remained at that level for most of 2010.[60] The economic sector for state and local government services and layoffs for government employees added to the state's unemployment spike in 2010. Nonetheless, Texas unemployment was consistently lower than the national average for the period 2008 to 2012.[61] Despite a large number of mortgage foreclosures, home prices remained fairly stable in Texas throughout the recession, with housing demand propped up by the state's dramatic increase in population. Housing costs in the state were lower than the national average to begin with (and remain so), suggesting that not much of a bubble existed in Texas housing prices prior to the recession.[62] The state comptroller reported that for September 2012, the Texas foreclosure rate was "one in every 1,336 mortgages," lower than figures released for Florida, California, and Illinois.[63]

National Issues

The issues of education and income garner perennial attention on the national stage. That there is a relationship between the two is not contested: ample research has demonstrated that individuals with higher educational attainment tend to have higher earnings.[64] On the other hand, low incomes may adversely impact educational attainment, or both income and education attainment may reflect other causes.

Income and Poverty

Available figures suggest that, on average, incomes in Texas run slightly lower than the national mean, and poverty rates track slightly higher than the national average. According to data from the U.S. Bureau of Economic Analysis, Texas's 2014 per capita personal income of $45,669 fell slightly below the national average of $46,049.[65] Likewise, Texas's median household income of $52,576 was lower than the national average of $53,482. Poverty rates for that period are higher than the national figures, with 17.2 percent of Texas residents estimated to be below the poverty level in 2014, compared to 15.5 percent for the U.S. overall.[66]

Education

States are constantly collecting data about and making changes to their educational systems in an effort to improve educational outcomes. Texas is no exception. (See the Chapter 11 section titled "Primary and Secondary Education in Texas" for a detailed discussion of education policy.) For seven consecutive years, the state has reported rising high school graduation rates. The Class of 2014 (the most recent class for which data is available), had an on-time graduation rate of 88.3 percent, meaning that 88.3 percent of students who began ninth grade in Texas public schools obtained a high school diploma in four years. This rate was second only to one other state, Iowa. The Texas Education Agency (TEA), which oversees public K-12 education in Texas, has credited the efforts of teachers and students across the state for this improvement; skeptics have alleged that data manipulation accounts for the impressive statistics.[67] Census bureau data suggest that Texas continues to lag behind the national average in terms of its proportion of adults age 25 or older who have graduated from high school or completed a bachelor's degree.[68]

According to Steve Murdock, former census bureau chief during the Bush administration and former state demographer of Texas, "Poverty is typically a strong indicator of educational attainment."[69] This relationship is evident upon closer examination of the state's public school dropout numbers. According to the TEA, 60.4 percent of twelfth-grade students who dropped out of Texas high schools in 2014 were considered "economically disadvantaged." Viewed from another perspective, economically disadvantaged students had a graduation rate of 85.2 percent in 2014, compared to the statewide graduation rate of 88.3 percent. The dropout rate was higher among Hispanic and African American students than for Asian and white students.[70]

Immigration and In-Migration Today

Texas has been affected by two types of migration: movement of people into Texas from other U.S. states (often called in-migration) and from other countries (immigration).

In-Migration

A look at population trends in the twenty-first century indicates that in-migration to Texas from other states is a reflection of both push and pull forces. In particular, economic, social, and political trends outside the state are pushing people to leave their home states and, in many cases, come to Texas. From 2000 to 2011, Texas had a net in-migration rate of 4.2 percent (meaning that Texas gained almost 900,000 more people who moved in from other states than it lost) and the second highest (to Florida) absolute gain of any state in the country.[71] One special push during this period was the upheaval caused by Hurricane Katrina in Louisiana in 2005, which led to a significant flow of people to Texas. However, other Texas-specific factors have been pulling people here and continue to attract

TABLE 1.2

Migration to Texas from Other States, 2014

California	63,591
Florida	40,930
Oklahoma	25,096
Louisiana	23,805
Illinois	23,258
New York	21,347
Georgia	19,023

Source: Adapted from U.S. Census Bureau.

newcomers, such as the relatively inexpensive housing market and the appealing natural and business climate in the state. From April 2010 to July 2015, Texas had net in-migration of more than 700,000 people.[72] This was the largest absolute jump of any state in the country during that period.

Migration to Texas from other states over past decades has generally reflected well-established patterns of movement, primarily from the rust-belt states of Ohio, Michigan, and New York, and secondarily from California and Florida. More recently, California and Florida, the nation's most populous and third most populous states, respectively, have tended to outpace the other states. Some in-migration clearly reflects economic upheaval from the 2008 home mortgage and banking implosion, coupled with the appeal of Texas's fairly resilient and diverse economy and low cost of living. High-tech workers, in particular, have been drawn to the Texas job market, and the devastation in Florida's housing market led to an exodus from that state.[73] In 2014, the most recent year for which the U.S. Census Bureau has specific information on state-to-state migration flows, California and Florida continued to be the most likely states of origin for in-migrants to Texas (see Table 1.2). More than 100,000 people came from those two states combined. Other large contributors to the Texas population included Oklahoma, Louisiana, Illinois, New York, and Georgia.[74]

Immigration

Push and pull factors also impact international migration to Texas. Texas continues to be an attractive location for immigrants both legal and illegal, but such migration will depend in part on political and economic conditions in the United States and other countries. Because of its long contiguous border with Mexico, Texas is a natural draw for Mexicans. Mexico has traditionally been the leading country of origin for both legal and illegal immigrants to the United States. In 2012, the United States admitted 145,326 legal immigrants from Mexico, more than from any other single nation.[75] Also in 2012, some 6.7 million Mexican immigrants were thought to be living in the United States illegally, according Department of Homeland Security estimates. Out of a nationwide total of 11.4 million unauthorized immigrants, an estimated 1.8 million lived in Texas.[76] However, recent studies have shown that, during the period from 2009 to 2014, the number of Mexican immigrants returning to Mexico exceeded the number coming to the United States. Suggested reasons for this outflow include a desire to reunite with family in Mexico, a less attractive job market in the United States, and enforcement of immigration laws resulting in deportation or discouragement from migrating in the first place.[77] A 2015 report from the state demographer's office indicated that Texas had received "roughly equal numbers of Latin American and Asian immigrants" in 2013;[78] state demographer Lloyd Potter called this a "significant" development.[79] Thus, while immigration from Mexico has declined in recent years, immigration to Texas from India and China is on the rise.

Texas Political Culture

Learning Objective: Explain U.S. and Texas political cultures.

Sections of this chapter have covered historic settlement patterns, the changing makeup of the current population, and demographic characteristics of the state. The reason these factors are important in a study of Texas government is that they contribute to what is called **political culture**. Political culture consists of the attitudes, values, and beliefs that most people in a political community have about the proper role of government. This system of beliefs essentially defines the role of government and the role of citizens within that government. Although the average person might not possess much technical knowledge about government or how it works, most people do have views or opinions, even if poorly defined, about what government should and should not do and what their own personal responsibility should be.

political culture
A system of beliefs and values that defines the role of government and the role of citizens in that government

Types of Political Culture

In the mid-1960s, Daniel J. Elazar, in his book *American Federalism: A View from the States,* developed a system for classifying different types of political culture in the 50 states. That system is still relevant today. Elazar described three distinctive political subcultures in the United States: moralistic, individualistic, and traditionalistic.[80]

In the **moralistic subculture**, politics "is considered one of the great activities of [people in their] search for the good society . . . an effort to exercise power for the betterment of the commonwealth."[81] In other words, government is viewed as a positive instrument for change and a means of promoting all citizens' general welfare. In the moralistic subculture, politics is regarded as the responsibility of all citizens, who have an obligation to participate in government. Individuals seek leadership roles in government not for personal gain, but from a desire to serve the public. In addition, the government has a right and an obligation to intervene in the private affairs of citizens when deemed necessary for the "public good or the well-being of the community."[82]

moralistic subculture
Government viewed as a positive force to achieve a common good for all citizens

An **individualistic subculture** "emphasizes the conception of the democratic order as a marketplace. In its view, a government is created for strictly utilitarian reasons, to handle those functions demanded by the people it is created to serve."[83] That is, government is not concerned with the creation of a "good society," and government intervention in the private sector should be kept to a minimum. From this perspective, politics is not a profession of high calling, but rather something that should be left to those willing to dirty their hands. Participation is considered a necessary evil but not an obligation of every citizen.

individualistic subculture
Government that benefits the individual rather than society in general

The primary function of the **traditionalistic subculture** is maintenance of the existing political order, and participation is confined to a small, self-perpetuating elite. The public has only limited power and influence. Policies that benefit the public are enacted only when the elite allows them to be. In practice, most policies enacted by government benefit the ruling elite and not the public. Political participation by the public is discouraged. A class-based social structure helps to maintain the existing order.

Map 1.3 shows Elazar's proposed distribution of political cultures across the nation. As the map indicates, all the old Confederate states have traditionalistic political cultures, and many of the Midwestern states have individualistic political cultures. Northern and some far western states have a moralistic political culture.

A look at the attitudes and beliefs of Texas's early settlers provides some insight into the state's political culture. Mexican immigrants contributed a strongly traditionalistic culture. This culture had its origins in seventeenth- and eighteenth-century Spanish culture, which was characterized by a dominant, landed aristocracy and elite-controlled government. Southern Anglo settlers of East Texas also brought a strong traditionalistic culture with them. This culture was a natural extension of the practice of slavery and persisted even after the Civil War. African American slaves were forced to adopt the traditionalistic culture of their Anglo slave owners. Conversely, German and Midwestern Anglo settlers in West Texas brought a strong individualistic culture with them. Few, if any, of these settlers were slave owners, and they came to Texas in search of individual opportunities. Based on this heritage, one might expect to find a blend of traditionalistic and individualistic political cultures in Texas.

In fact, the basic structure of state government in Texas fits the traditionalistic/individualistic model quite well. Government is relatively limited. Power is

traditionalistic subculture

Government that maintains the existing political order for the benefit of a small elite

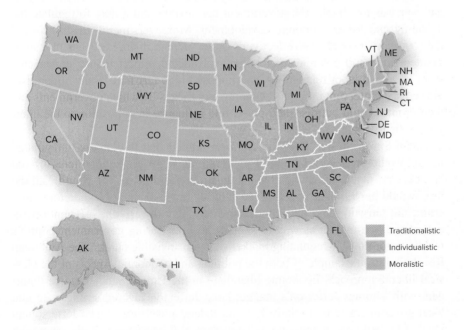

MAP 1.3   Political Culture in the States

divided among many elected officials. Executive authority—namely, the office of the governor—is weak, and most power rests with the state legislature. Few state regulations are placed on business, and many of those that do exist benefit specific businesses. Regulation of the environment is modest.

Examining political culture helps us understand the basic structure of state government, the nature of government policy, and the degree to which citizens are involved in government. Although the name of the party controlling the Texas governor's mansion, all statewide offices, and the state legislature has changed, the state's political culture has not. Texas has transitioned from a state dominated by the Democratic Party to a state dominated by the Republican Party but, crucially, there have been no significant changes in philosophy, ideology, or policy.

Social Conservatism, Classical Liberalism, Populism, and Progressivism

Yet the political culture of Texas reflects a deeper ideological position for most Texans, whose ideology is a mix of elements from classical liberalism and social conservatism, with some strains of populism woven through their political opinions as well. Classical liberalism, in general, has both political and economic components and is associated in the United States with the writings of John Locke, Adam Smith, Thomas Jefferson, and James Madison. Politically, classical liberalism focuses on the protection of individual rights, limited government, the rule of law, and a generally free market economy. Politically, classical liberals have often supported representative government and civil liberties (such as freedom of speech, press, assembly, and petition) as means by which citizens could control their government and secure their (natural) rights.

Just as classical liberalism rejects obtrusive government—whether monarchic or even democratic—it also rejected mercantilism in the economic realm. Mercantilism held that because a country's wealth and power were synonymous and war was inevitable, the government had a right and a duty to regulate the economy and foster economic development. Moreover, mercantilists believed the government could do so effectively. Under mercantilism, European monarchs granted trade and colonial monopolies, subsidized import industries, enacted strict trade and labor regulations, and imposed high tariffs. Classical liberalism viewed such intervention in the economy as a means by which governments and their cronies could buttress their power and influence in opposition to the interests of their people.

Adam Smith, in his *Wealth of Nations,* argued that the largely unregulated market would produce wealth on its own as long as government policies offered "peace, easy taxes, and a tolerable administration of justice." To Smith, "all the rest" would be "brought about by the natural course of things." Therefore, governmental intrusion into the economy would only "thwart" the efficient operation of the free market as well as support an overbearing government. Smith's metaphor for the self-regulating market was the "invisible hand." The American Revolution is an example of both the political and economic aspects of the classical liberal approach. Economic liberalism in the United States became dominant with Thomas Jefferson's inauguration. Jefferson favored strong state and local governments and a relatively weak federal government. The Jeffersonian ideal of limited government opposed governmental intervention in the economy; it did not support a role for the federal government in chartering banks—or in spending money on transportation infrastructure, or what would have been termed "internal improvements."

Texan opposition to taxes and government regulation of the economy is reminiscent of the distrust of the federal government that characterized the presidencies of Thomas Jefferson and Andrew Jackson. State government exists, in the view of these people, to provide a healthy business climate and keep taxes and regulations low. To facilitate commerce, the state may accept federal assistance for construction of roads and bridges. In general, classical liberals in the past—and many Texans today—have held, at least rhetorically, that the government is best that governs least. This philosophy forms the basis of the modern Libertarian Party, as well as some of the planks of the Texas Republican Party. Except for a few periods of reform associated with James Hogg, James Ferguson, and the New Deal, Texas has frequently embraced the economic aspects of classical liberalism. However, many adherents have been willing to compromise this faith for political and personal advantage.

At the same time, many Texans also embrace social conservatism. Salient political issues for social conservatives include but are not limited to abortion, traditional family values, and school prayer. In general, they want *Roe v. Wade* overturned, are against same-sex marriage, want school-conducted prayer allowed, and would like to see alternatives to evolution (for example, creationism or intelligent design) taught in public schools. Many are uncompromising in their beliefs on each of these issues because they see their perspective as grounded in their religious faith.

Another facet of Texas political ideology and culture is populism. Populism is a difficult term to define, although most political analysts agree that it is an important part of U.S. and political history. Populism arose in the 1880s in the southern and western parts of the United States. Populists call for the federal and state government to help small businesses, farmers, and ranchers in the face of competition from large U.S. corporations and foreign businesses. Populists, historically, have wanted the federal government to regulate railroad rates and to ensure a money supply equal to the size of the economy. Populists also distrust banks and want the government to provide credit for industrial production and trade unions. They were, historically, also anti-immigrant. Populism, being primarily a rural and small town movement, supports more conservative religious values. It can also have an anti-intellectual strain, which is voiced as suspicion of experts. The rural anti-union, anti-immigrant, anti-intellectual strain of populism has survived and appears to have merged with social conservatism in Texas and other states.

It is also worth noting that a significant segment of Texans embrace a progressive or modern liberal understanding of the relationship between the people and the government. These contemporary liberals or progressives (like populists before them) are not as skeptical of government intervention in the economy and see the government as a potent force for good. Among other things, they favor a larger social welfare system and more regulation of business while opposing the agenda of social conservatives. Though a minority of Texans, they make up a large part of the modern Democratic Party in Texas and could be a growing force in the state. Indeed, as noted earlier, the "Battleground Texas" operation ultimately hopes to "turn Texas blue"—although its first steps, in the words of a *Texas Monthly* article on its efforts—are "to recruit and train volunteers, foster neighbor-to-neighbor contact about the issues, and enlist voter registrars."[84]

Conclusion

The state of Texas has a complex history. In this chapter we have seen how aspects of that history, and in particular the attitudes and beliefs of early settlers to the area, have shaped the state's political culture. Examining government using the framework of political culture helps us to understand the basic structure of the government, the nature of government policy, and the degree to which citizens are involved in government. Texas's traditionalistic/individualistic political culture has remained essentially unchanged throughout its history despite major shifts in political party dominance.

Texas occupies a special position within the larger United States today, and state government must contend with a number of challenges both common to other states and unique to Texas. Once a primarily rural state with a land-based economy, Texas now has a more diversified economy and is an international trade powerhouse. As it attracts more people through domestic and international channels, the state must deal with unprecedented population growth. That population has shifted toward urban centers, and Texas has become a majority-minority state. These issues provide a backdrop for current policy, and we can use the framework of political culture to understand how state government approaches these challenges.

Summary

LO: Explain the significance of Texas's six flags.

Six nations have ruled either part or all of the territory of Texas during its history: Spain, France, Mexico, the Republic of Texas, the United States of America, and the Confederate States of America. After being claimed by Spain and France, Texas was controlled by Mexico until it became an independent republic. Texas joined the United States but then seceded to become a part of the Confederacy. Thus, six different national flags have flown over Texas.

LO: Describe the Civil War and Reconstruction in Texas.

Though it was home to some important Civil War events, Texas for the most part avoided the battles and physical devastation, stemming from invasion and occupation, that affected much of the rest of the Confederacy. During Reconstruction (the period immediately following the Civil War), Republicans controlled state government, slavery ended, and Texas was readmitted to the Union. The backlash against Republican rule during Reconstruction marked the beginning of 100 years of one-party Democratic dominance in Texas.

LO: Describe post-Reconstruction Texas.

Since Reconstruction, Texas has converted from a land-based economy to a more diversified, primarily service economy. Control of state politics has shifted from the Democratic Party to the Republican Party. In addition, Texas now has the second largest population of any state. That population is growing rapidly, is increasingly urban (as opposed to rural), and has become majority-minority (meaning that racial and ethnic minority groups together make up a majority of the state's population).

LO: Explain the challenges facing Texas today.

Like other states, Texas must contend with issues related to poverty, education, and the national economy. One challenge specific to Texas is the large numbers of people moving into the state, both from other U.S. states (a process called in-migration) and from other countries (immigration). Many factors, including the state's fairly resilient and diverse economy, low cost of living, and appealing natural climate make Texas a strong draw for people outside the state.

LO: Explain U.S. and Texas political cultures.

Political culture is the system of beliefs and values that defines the role of government and the role of citizens in that government. In the U.S., many Midwestern states have individualistic political cultures, whereas Northern and some far western states have a moralistic political culture. Southern (former Confederate) states, including Texas, have traditionalistic political cultures. The traditionalistic subculture is one in which the existing political order is maintained, and political participation is generally confined to a small number of elites.

Key Terms

Anglo
empresario
Adelsverein Society
land-based economy

economic regions
political action committee (PAC)
majority-minority
political culture

moralistic subculture
individualistic subculture
traditionalistic subculture

Notes

1 Texas General Land Office, "History of Texas Public Lands," January 2015. http://www.glo.texas.gov/history/archives/forms/files/history-of-texas-public-lands.pdf.

2 Jean Stuntz, "Spanish Laws for Texas Women: The Development of Marital Property Law to 1850," *The Southwestern Historical Quarterly,* vol. 104 (4), April 2001, 542–559.

3 "Coahuila and Texas," *Handbook of Texas Online,* published by the Texas State Historical Association, accessed November 04, 2012. http://www.tshaonline.org/handbook/online/articles/usc01.

4 Terry G. Jordan, *German Seed in Texas Soil: Immigrant Farmers in Nineteenth Century Texas* (Austin: University of Texas Press, 1966).

5 Robert A. Calvert and Arnold DeLeon, *The History of Texas* (Arlington Heights, Ill.: Harland Davidson, 1990), 99–100.

6 T. R. Fehrendbach, *Lone Star: A History of Texas and the Texans* (New York: Collier, 1980), 276–277.

7 James M. McPherson and James K. Hogue, *Ordeal by Fire: The Civil War and Reconstruction,* 4th edition (New York: McGraw-Hill Higher Education, 2009), 371; 446–447.

8 Texas Historical Commission, Texas in the Civil War. http://www.thc.state.tx.us/public/upload/publications/tx-in-civil-war.pdf; Texas State Historical Association, Civil War. https://tshaonline.org/handbook/online/articles/qdc02.

9 McPherson and Hogue, 428.

10 Texas State Library and Archives Commission, Juneteenth. https: www.tsl.texas.gov/ref/abouttx/juneteenth.html.

11 Roy Morris, *Sheridan: The Life and Wars of General Phil Sheridan* (New York: Crown, 1992).

12 Robert A. Calvert et al., 363.

13 U.S. Census Bureau, Table 1. Urban and Rural Population: 1900 to 1990, https://www.census.gov/population/censusdata/urpop0090.txt.

14 U.S. Patent and Trademark Office, Patent Counts by Origin and Type, Calendar Year 2014, http://www.uspto.gov/web/offices/ac/ido/oeip/taf/st_co_14.htm.

15 U.S. Department of Labor, Bureau of Labor Statistics, Industries at a Glance, Service-Providing Industries, http://www.bls.gov/iag/tgs/iag07.htm; U.S. Department of Labor, Bureau of Labor Statistics, Texas Economy at a Glance, http://www.bls.gov/eag/eag.tx.htm#eag_tx.f.1; U.S. Department of Labor, Bureau of Labor Statistics, Southwest Information Office, Texas, http://www.bls.gov/regions/southwest/texas.htm#eag.

16 U.S. Census Bureau, Foreign Trade, State Exports from Texas, http://www.census.gov/foreign-trade/statistics/state/data/tx.html.

17 Glenn Hegar, Texas Comptroller of Public Accounts, "Regional Economic Data," *Texas Ahead,* http://texasahead.org/regionalrpts/.

18 Jay M. Shafritz, ed., *The Harper Collins Dictionary of American Government and Politics,* (New York: Harper Collins Publishers, Inc., 1992), 469.

19 Robert A. Calvert et al., 228–241.

20 Texas Secretary of State, Presidential Election Results. http://www.sos.state.tx.us/elections/historical/presidential.shtml.

21 Susan Eason, "Tower, John Goodwin," *Handbook of Texas Online,* published by the Texas State Historical Association, accessed March 4, 2016. http://www.tshaonline.org/handbook/online/articles/ftoss.

22 Ibid., 14

23 Though it should be noted that the Republican nominee was not in question at that point (and some Republicans may have shifted over to vote in the Democratic Party primary).

24 Texas Ethics Commission, "Active Political Committees (PACS) and Their Treasurers," (September 2015), https://www.ethics.state.tx.us/tedd/paclista.htm.

25 U.S. Census Bureau, QuickFacts, Texas. http://quickfacts.census.gov/qfd/states/48000.html; U.S. Census Bureau, Texas, Population of Counties by Decennial Census: 1900 to 1990, http://www.census.gov/population/cencounts/tx190090.txt.

[26] Jeannie Kever, "Census shows Texas gains 4 seats in the U.S. House," *Houston Chronicle,* December 21, 2010. http://www.chron.com/news/houston-texas/article/Census-shows-Texas-gains-4-seats-in-the-U-S-House-1700473.php.

[27] "The Trans-Texas Corridor: Miles to Go," *The Economist,* January 7, 2010. http://www.economist.com/node/15213418.

[28] U.S. Census Bureau, Geography, 2010 Census Urban and Rural Classification and Urban Area Criteria. https://www.census.gov/geo/reference/ua/urban-rural-2010.html.

[29] U.S. Census Bureau, Geography, Lists of Population, Land Area, and Percent Urban and Rural in 2010 and Changes from 2000 to 2010, Percent urban and rural in 2010 by state. https://www.census.gov/geo/reference/ua/urban-rural-2010.html.

[30] U.S. Department of Agriculture, Rural Population Indicators for Texas, 2000–2012. http://www.ers.usda.gov/datafiles/Rural_Definitions/StateLevel_Maps/TX.pdf.

[31] Susan Combs, *Texas In Focus: A Statewide View of Opportunities*–2008. http://www.window.state.tx.us/specialrpt/tif/96-1286.pdf.

[32] Texas Legislative Council, Statewide map of U.S. Congressional Districts, 114th Congress 2015-2016, Texas Redistricting. http://www.tlc.state.tx.us/redist/pdf/congress/map.pdf.

[33] Susan Combs, *Texas In Focus: A Statewide View of Opportunities*–2008. http://www.window.state.tx.us/specialrpt/tif/population.html.

[34] U.S. Census Bureau, QuickFacts, Texas. http://quickfacts.census.gov/qfd/states/48000.html.

[35] Texas Education Agency, *Enrollment in Texas Public Schools 2013-14,* (November 2014). http://tea.texas.gov/acctres/enroll_index.html.

[36] Rachel Dry, "Grace Flores-Hughes Interview—She Made 'Hispanic' Official," *Washington Post,* July 26, 2009. http://www.washingtonpost.com/wp-dyn/content/article/2009/07/24/AR2009072402091.html?sid=ST2010031902002.

[37] Jeffrey S. Passel and Paul Taylor, "Who's Hispanic?" Pew Research Center, May 28, 2009. http://www.pewhispanic.org/2009/05/28/whos-hispanic/.

[38] *Joint resolution relating to the publication of economic and social statistics for Americans of Spanish origin or descent,* Public Law 94-311, *U.S. Statutes at Large* 90 (1976): 688. Accessible at http://uscode.house.gov/statviewer.htm?volume=90&page=688.

[39] D'Vera Cohn, "Census History: Counting Hispanics," Pew Research Center, March 3, 2010, http://www.pewsocialtrends.org/2010/03/03/census-history-counting-hispanics-2/; U.S. Department of Commerce, Bureau of the Census, "Twenty Censuses: Population and Housing Questions 1790-1980" (October 1979), https://www.census.gov/history/pdf/20censuses.pdf.

[40] Office of Management and Budget, "Revisions to the Standards for the Classification of Federal Data on Race and Ethnicity," *Federal Register,* October 30, 1997. https://www.whitehouse.gov/omb/fedreg_1997standards.

[41] U.S. Census Bureau, Equal Employment Opportunity, Hispanic Heritage Month, https://www.census.gov/eeo/special_emphasis_programs/hispanic_heritage.html; Rachel Dry, "Grace Flores-Hughes Interview—She Made 'Hispanic' Official," *Washington Post,* July 26, 2009, http://www.washingtonpost.com/wp-dyn/content/article/2009/07/24/AR2009072402091.html?sid=ST2010031902002.

[42] U.S. Census, "Hispanic Origin," http://www.census.gov/population/hispanic/; Jeffrey S. Passel and Paul Taylor, "Who's Hispanic?" Pew Research Center, May 28, 2009, http://www.pewhispanic.org/2009/05/28/whos-hispanic/.

[43] U.S. Census Bureau, "Hispanic Origin." http://www.census.gov/topics/population/hispanic-origin/about.html.

[44] Ana Gonzalez-Barrera and Mark Hugo Lopez, "Is being Hispanic a matter of race, ethnicity or both?" Pew Research Center, June 15, 2015, http://www.pewresearch.org/fact-tank/2015/06/15/is-being-hispanic-a-matter-of-race-ethnicity-or-both/.

[45] Ibid., 20

[46] State Bar of Texas, Texas Legal Legends. http://www.texasbar.com/AM/Template.cfm?Section=Texas_Legal_Legends.

[47] Office of the Secretary of State, 2012 General Election, Election Night Returns. https://team1.sos.state.tx.us/enr/results/nov06_164_state.htm; Fox News Latino, "Election 2012: Ted Cruz Wins Senate Seat in Texas, Makes History," November 6, 2012, accessed November 8, 2012. http://latino.foxnews.com/latino/politics/2012/11/06/election-2012-ted-cruz-wins-senate-seat-in-texas/.

[48] Texas Secretary of State, Statewide Elected Officials, http://www.sos.state.tx.us/elections/voter/elected.shtml; Texas Secretary of State, Biography of Secretary of State Carlos H. Cascos. http://www.sos.state.tx.us/about/sosbio.shtml.

[49] U.S. Census Bureau, QuickFacts, Texas. http://quickfacts.census.gov/qfd/states/48000.html.

[50] Office of the Secretary of State, Race Summary Report, 2002 General Election. http://elections.sos.state.tx.us/elchist95_state.htm.

[51] Ibid., 20

[52] Office of the State Demographer, Texas Population Projections, 2010 to 2050. http://osd.texas.gov/Resources/Publications/2014/2014-11_ProjectionBrief.pdf.

[53] Alexa Ura and Jolie McCullough, "The 84th Texas Legislature, by the Numbers," *Texas Tribune,* January 14, 2015, https://www.texastribune.org/2015/01/14/demographics-2015-texas-legislature/; Corrie MacLaggan, "Texas House Race Draws Focus to Vietnamese Voters," *Texas Tribune,* January 10, 2014. https://www.texastribune.org/2014/01/10/texas-house-race-draws-focus-vietnamese-bloc/.

[54] 2014 U.S. Religious Landscape Study, Pew Research Center. http://www.pewforum.org/religious-landscape-study/state/texas/.

[55] Hartford Institute for Religion Research, Database of Megachurches in the U.S., accessed February 29, 2016. http://hirr.hartsem.edu/cgi-bin/mega/db.pl?db=default&uid=default&view_records=1&ID=*&sb=4&State=TX.

[56] Keith R. Phillips and Jesus Cañas, "Recession Arrives in Texas: A Rougher Ride in 2009," *Southwest Economy* (Federal Reserve Bank of Dallas), first quarter 2009, http://www.dallasfed.org/assets/documents/research/swe/2009/swe0901b.pdf; Susan Combs, "Comptroller's Weekly Economic Outlook," *The Texas Economy,* November 2, 2012. http://www.thetexaseconomy.org/economic-outlook/.

[57] Susan Combs, "Comptroller's Weekly Economic Outlook," *The Texas Economy,* November 2, 2012. http://www.thetexaseconomy.org/economic-outlook/.

[58] U.S. Department of Commerce, Bureau of Economic Analysis, Gross Domestic Product by State. http://www.bea.gov/iTable/iTable.cfm?ReqID570&step51&isuri51&acrdn51.

[59] U.S. Department of Commerce, Bureau of Economic Analysis, GDP by state. http://www.bea.gov/iTable/iTable.cfm?ReqID=70&step=1&isuri=1&acrdn=1.

[60] U.S. Department of Labor, Bureau of Labor Statistics, Local Area Unemployment Statistics. http://data.bls.gov/timeseries/LASST48000003; and see http://www.bls.gov/news.release/laus.nr0.htm.

[61] U.S. Department of Labor, Bureau of Labor Statistics, Labor Force Statistics from the Current Population Survey. http://data.bls.gov/timeseries/LNS14000000.

[62] Wenhua Di, "Residential Foreclosures in Texas Depart from National Trends," *e-Perspectives,* vol. 8(2), 2008. http://www.dallasfed.org/microsites/cd/epersp/2008/2_2.cfm.

[63] Ibid., 23

[64] United States Department of Labor, Bureau of Labor Statistics, Earnings and unemployment rates by educational attainment, 2015. http://www.bls.gov/emp/ep_chart_001.htm.

[65] U.S. Dept. of Commerce, Bureau of Economic Analysis, Personal Income Summary: Personal Income, Population, Per Capita Personal Income. http://www.bea.gov/iTable/iTable.cfm?reqid=70&step=1&isuri=1&acrdn=6#reqid=70&step=29&isuri=1&7022=21&7023=0&7024=non-industry&7001=421&7090=70.

[66] U.S. Census Bureau, Poverty Status in the Past 12 Months (2014 American Community Survey 1-Year Estimates); Income in the Past 12 Months (2010-2014 American Community Survey 5-Year Estimates). http://factfinder.census.gov/faces/tableservices/jsf/pages/productview.xhtml?pid=ACS_12_1YR_S1701&prodType=table.

[67] Texas Education Agency, "Class of 2014 graduation rate sets new mark," TEA News Releases Online, August 5, 2015, http://tea.texas.gov/About_TEA/News_and_Multimedia/Press_Releases/2015/Class_of_2014_graduation_rate_sets_new_mark/; Morgan Smith, "Texas High School Graduation Rate Behind Only Iowa," *Texas Tribune,* February 20, 2015, https://www.texastribune.org/2015/02/20/texas-high-school-graduation-rate-behind-only-iowa/; Terrance Stutz and Holly K. Hacker, "Critics scrutinize Texas' unusual high school dropout rates," *Dallas Morning News,* August 29, 2015, http://www.dallasnews.com/news/education/headlines/20150829-critics-scoff-at-texas-high-school-dropout-rates.ece.

[68] U.S. Census Bureau, QuickFacts, Texas. http://www.census.gov/quickfacts/table/PST045215/48.

[69] Jake Berry, "Democrats say Texas graduation rate fell to 50th under Rick Perry," *Tampa Bay Times,* September 8, 2011. http://www.politifact.com/truth-o-meter/statements/2011/sep/08/new-hampshire-democratic-party/democrats-say-texas-graduation-rate-fell-50th-unde/.

[70] Texas Education Agency, Secondary School Completion and Dropouts in Texas Public Schools 2013-14, August 2015. http://tea.texas.gov/acctres/dropcomp_index.html#reports.

[71] William P. Ruger and Jason Sorens, *Freedom in the 50 States: An Index of Personal and Economic Freedom* (Arlington, VA: Mercatus Center at George Mason University, 2013).

[72] U.S. Census Bureau, Estimates of the Components of Resident Population Change: April 1, 2010 to July 1, 2015, 2015 Population Estimates. http://www.census.gov/popest/data/state/totals/2015/index.html.

[73] William H. Frey, "A Rollercoaster Decade for Migration," The Brookings Institution, December 29, 2009. http://www.brookings.edu/research/opinions/2009/12/29-migration-frey.

[74] U.S. Census Bureau, Migration/Geographic Mobility, State-to-State Migration Flows. https://www.census.gov/hhes/migration/data/acs/state-to-state.html.

[75] Department of Homeland Security, Office of Immigration Statistics, 2013 Yearbook of Immigration Statistics, (August 2014). https://www.dhs.gov/sites/default/files/publications/ois_yb_2013_0.pdf.

[76] Bryan Baker and Nancy Rytina, "Estimates of the Unauthorized Immigrant Population Residing in the United States: January 2012," (March 2013), Department of Homeland Security, Office of Immigration Statistics. https://www.dhs.gov/sites/default/files/publications/ois_ill_pe_2012_2.pdf.

[77] Ana Gonzalez-Barrera, "More Mexicans Leaving Than Coming to the U.S.," Pew Research Center, November 19, 2015, http://www.pewhispanic.org/2015/11/19/more-mexicans-leaving-than-coming-to-the-u-s/. Also accessible at http://www.pewhispanic.org/files/2015/11/2015-11-19_mexican-immigration__FINAL.pdf.

[78] Office of the State Demographer, "Origins of Immigrants to Texas," (May 2015). http://osd.texas.gov/Resources/Publications/2015/2015_05_Origins.pdf.

[79] Lomi Kriel, "Latino immigration to Texas drops as Asian migration grows," *Houston Chronicle,* October 8, 2015. http://www.houstonchronicle.com/news/houston-texas/article/Latino-immigration-to-Texas-drops-as-Asian-6559244.php.

[80] Daniel J. Elazar, *American Federalism: A View from the States* (New York: HarperCollins, 1984; originally published 1966).

[81] Ibid., 90.

[82] Ibid.

[83] Ibid., 86.

[84] Robert Draper, "The Life and Death (and Life?) of the Party," *Texas Monthly,* August 2013. http://www.texasmonthly.com/story/life-and-death-and-life-party?fullpage=1.

CHAPTER 2

The Texas State Constitution and the American Federal System

Although we are familiar with the United States Constitution, it is important to remember that all 50 states have written constitutions, as well. A **constitution** establishes the fundamental rules by which states govern. Constitutions instruct, though not always explicitly, what a government can and cannot do. In the previous chapter, we discussed the political culture of Texas, and the Texas Constitution is very much an embodiment of both the traditionalistic and individualistic subcultures. Although Texas has operated under seven different constitutions, the current constitution of Texas, ratified in 1876, reflects the conservative nature of the state, the distrust of government, and the desire to limit the government's ability to act.

constitution
The basic document that provides a framework for government and limits what the government can do

Examining the several constitutions that have governed Texas since Anglo settlement began gives us a greater understanding of how political culture impacts the formal structure of government. In addition, this chapter examines how Texas and other states operate within a federal system of government.

Principles of Constitutional Government

Learning Objective: Describe the principles of constitutional government.

History, culture, traditions, basic principles, and ideas have an impact on constitutions. Later in this chapter, you will see how the individualistic and traditionalistic political culture of Texas influenced the current constitution. Fundamentally, several important principles specifically underpin the general idea of constitutional government. The first is the idea of **popular sovereignty**. This idea holds that, at root, power rests with the people[1] and, theoretically, legitimate constitutions should articulate the will of the people. Constitutions are written by a popularly elected convention of citizens and not by state legislatures. Thus the citizens must also approve any changes in state constitutions—except in Delaware, where the state legislature can amend the state constitution without voter approval. The current Texas Constitution emphasizes the idea of popular sovereignty in the preamble and bill of rights, prominently positioned at the beginning of the document.

Second, constitutions are contracts or compacts between the citizens and the government and cannot be violated. This principle is embodied in **social contract theory**, the notion that all individuals possess inalienable rights and willingly submit to government to protect these rights. In essence, the constitution binds the government and the people, providing the framework within which interaction occurs. The laws passed by legislatures must fit within the framework of the constitution.

Third, constitutions structure government, divide and assign power, and place limitations on government's power. Many assume that government can do anything not prohibited by the constitution, and thus it is necessary to expressly limit the power of government. The current Texas Constitution is very much an example of limitations on the power of state government.

The men who assembled in a constitutional convention of 1875 (women could not vote until 1920) had as their primary aim limiting the power of state government due to the perceived abuses of Radical Republican Governor Edmund J. Davis. The actions of the Radical Republicans in Congress and in Texas during Reconstruction may have intensified the desires of these men to weaken and limit government, but they were predisposed to this philosophy even before the Civil War. Although the Texas Constitution embraces all three principles, the idea of a limited government, in particular, is wholeheartedly embraced.

Characteristics Common to State Constitutions

Learning Objective: Describe the characteristics common to state constitutions.

Separation of Powers

Besides the ideals of popular sovereignty, compact or contract theory, and limited government, state constitutions share other common characteristics. First, all state constitutions embrace the idea of **separation of powers** provided in

---

popular sovereignty
The idea that power granted in state constitutions rests with the people

social contract theory
The idea that all individuals possess inalienable rights and willingly submit to government to protect these rights

separation of powers
Power divided between the legislative, executive, and judicial branches of government

the U.S. Constitution. Power is divided among an elected executive, an elected legislature, and the judiciary. The separation of powers provides a check on the actions of government. Fear of concentration of power in a single person led the framers of the U.S. Constitution to separate powers and provide for a system of **checks and balances**. Similarly, framers of the current Texas Constitution sought to distribute powers broadly among the branches of Texas government. Figure 2.1 is a diagram of the separation of powers between the three branches of the federal government, and Table 2.1 clearly articulates the powers of the legislature, the governor, and the judiciary in Texas.

checks and balances
Power granted by the Constitution to each branch of government giving it authority to restrain other branches

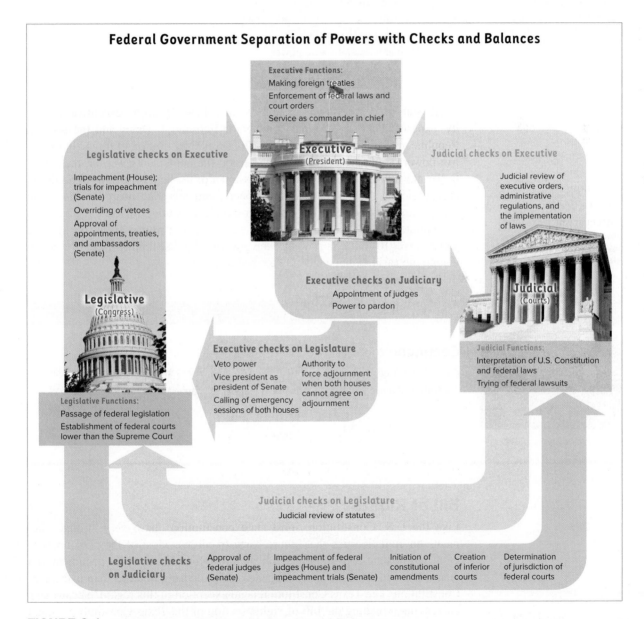

FIGURE 2.1   Separation of Powers with Checks and Balances

Capitol dome: © Photov.com/age fotostock RF; White House: © Photov.com/age fotostock RF; Supreme court: © Hisham Ibrahim/Photographer's Choice RF/Getty Images

TABLE 2.1

Separation of Powers in Texas Government

The Legislature	The Governor	The Judiciary
Propose and pass laws	Limited appointment power of some executive officials and judges in cases of vacancies	Interpret the law
Power to propose constitutional amendments		Settle all disputes in matters of criminal and civil law
Power to tax and set the budget	Submit budget proposal to legislature	Popularly elected
Oversight power of state agencies and departments	Serve on boards; e.g., the Legislative Budget Board	
Impeachment power of judges and executive branch officials	Can call special sessions and dictate special session agenda	
	Veto and line-item veto power	

All state constitutions embrace this idea. Fear of strong executive authority, experienced in Texas under Governor Edmund J. Davis and the Radical Republicans, led the framers of the 1876 Texas Constitution to fragment executive power. Today, voters elect the governor, the lieutenant governor, the comptroller, the attorney general, the commissioner of the land office, the agricultural commissioner, the railroad commissioners, and the state board of education. The secretary of state is the only non-elected executive official; the position is appointed by the governor. This system is called a **plural executive system**, and it serves to limit the power of the governor by distributing executive power among the various independently elected officials.

plural executive system
System in which executive power is divided among several statewide elected officials

CORE OBJECTIVE

© George Lavendowski/USFWS

Communicating Effectively . . .

Analyze the diagram in Figure 2.1 and the division of powers in Table 2.1 to describe the separation of powers and checks and balances in both theory and practice in Texas.

Bill of Rights

Like the U.S. Constitution, most state constitutions have very strong statements on civil liberties that secure basic freedoms. Most of the civil liberties protected in state constitutions duplicate those found in the U.S. document, but many state constitutions are more generous in securing liberties than is the U.S. Constitution. The Texas Constitution is no exception in this regard. The average citizen, upon reading the **bill of rights** section of the Texas Constitution, might well conclude that it is a very permissive document, granting equalities under the law to all citizens regardless of "sex, race, color, creed or national origin."[2]

bill of rights
A list of individual rights and freedoms granted to citizens within a constitution

Supreme Law of the State

Article 6 of the U.S. Constitution contains the **supremacy clause**. This makes the U.S. Constitution the supreme law of the land, and no federal or state **statute** may violate it. Because laws follow a hierarchy (owing to our federal system of government, discussed later in the chapter), federal law preempts state law, and state law preempts local law. Similarly, state law may not violate the state constitution, and state statutes are superior to local government **ordinances**.

A recent example of local ordinances potentially conflicting with a state statute involves the state issuing permits to citizens for carrying concealed handguns. Many local governments (cities, counties, and metropolitan transit authorities) passed regulations prohibiting the carrying of concealed handguns in some public places. Many of these gun laws have been struck down, though not all. Typically, local gun laws have been upheld only when they do not contradict state law, such as when local laws prohibit what the state prohibits, but more strictly. For example, in *Cincinnati v. Baskin* (2006), the defendant argued local law (prohibiting semiautomatic firearms with 10+ round capacity) was in violation of state law (prohibiting semiautomatic firearms with 31+ round capacity). While state law was found to be general law, the local law was determined to not be in conflict and was therefore applicable to the defendant.[3] In 2015, the 84th Texas Legislature passed legislation permitting the "license to carry" firearms, also know as "open carry." This legislation (discussed more fully in Chapter 12) prohibits municipalities from regulating "the transfer, private ownership, keeping, transportation, licensing, or registration of fire arms."[4] In this policy area, local governments are very limited in their ability to act.

supremacy clause
A clause that makes constitutional provisions superior to other laws

statutes
Laws passed by state legislatures

ordinances
Laws passed by local governments

Evolution of the Texas Constitution: 1824–1876

Learning Objective: Describe the development of Texas's constitutions before and after 1876.

We have identified several common features of constitutions. Throughout history, each transitional period for the region that became Texas, whether incorporating under Mexico, gaining independent nation status, becoming part of the United States, or moving through the troubled period before and after the Civil War, necessitated the creation of a new constitution. An examination of the various constitutions that have been drafted throughout Texas's history will show that not only are common features present throughout, but Texas's history and culture have also had a significant influence on the development of each constitution.

Constitutions under the Republic of Mexico

The first constitution to govern Anglos in Texas was the Republic of Mexico's Constitution of 1824. This constitution was federalist in concept, dividing governing authority between the nation and the states, breaking with the Spanish centralist tradition of a strong national government.[5] Under the provisions of the 1824 Constitution, the state of Coahuila y Tejas was formed. The new state was required to enact a state constitution that passed in 1827. It provided for a

Early Texas flag depicting dissatisfaction with the suspension of the Republic of Mexico's 1824 Constitution

© Universal Images Group Limited/Alamy

unicameral legislature, and Texas elected two representatives to the state legislature. This constitution, which lacked a bill of rights, provided a government structure with which the Anglos were mostly comfortable. Anglos simply disregarded sections of the constitution they found disagreeable. The sections with which Anglo settlers were most uncomfortable were those designating Catholicism as the state religion and those that did not recognize slavery.[6]

The suspension of the Mexican national constitution of 1824, and with it the state constitution of 1827, by Mexican president Santa Anna, was a factor that led to the Texas revolution. One of the early Texas flags, supposedly flown at the Alamo, had the number 1824 superimposed on a red, green, and white emblem of the Mexican flag. This was a demand that the Constitution of 1824 be restored.[7]

The Republic of Texas Constitution of 1836

In 1836, when Texas declared itself a republic independent of Mexico (Map 2.1), a new constitution was adopted. This document was a composite of the U.S. Constitution and the constitutions of several southern states. It provided for a unitary, rather than federal, form of government. (See the discussion on systems of government later in this chapter.) Signs of the distrust of government by the traditionalistic southerners who wrote the document are evident. They limited the term of the president to one 3-year term with prohibitions against consecutive reelection. The president was also prohibited from raising an army without the consent of the congress. There were other features, such as freedom of religion and property rights protection, that had been absent in the 1824 and 1827 Mexican

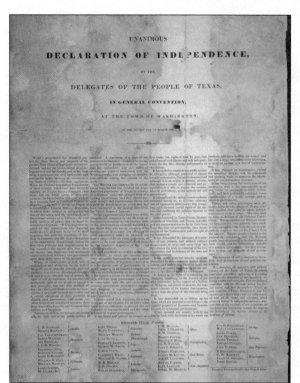

The Declaration of Independence 1836

Courtesy of Texas State Library and Archives Commission

MAP 2.1   Republic of Texas From 1836 until 1845, Texas was an independent nation known as the Republic of Texas. In the treaty forced on Mexico by Texas, Mexico ceded land stretching to the headwaters of the Rio Grande. Although this land was never fully occupied by the government of the Republic, Texas claimed land in what is now part of the states of New Mexico, Oklahoma, Kansas, Colorado, and Wyoming.

Courtesy of Texas State Library and Archives Commission

constitutions. Slavery, which had not been recognized by the Mexican government, was legalized.[8]

Statehood Constitution of 1845

The first Texas state constitution was adopted when Texas joined the Union in 1845. This document also reflected the traditionalistic southern culture, with a few notable exceptions that were adaptations of Spanish law. Women were granted property rights equal to those of men, especially in marriage, where women were given half the value of all property acquired during the marriage (communal property). In addition, a person's homestead was protected from forced sale to pay debts. These ideas were later adopted by many other states. The 1845 constitution also provided for limited executive authority, biennial sessions of the legislature, and two-year terms for most officials. Most of these features were included in later constitutions.

FOCUS ON

The Tejano Contribution to Texas's Founding

One of only three Tejano signatories to the Texas Declaration of Independence and the only Hispanic delegate to the Texas Convention of 1845, José Antonio Navarro played an important part in the evolution of Texas from Mexican province to independent Republic to statehood.

Born on February 27th, 1795, into an elite San Antonio family, Navarro lived a relatively privileged life until his father's death in 1808.[9] Around this same time, there was increasing unrest in Texas as Mexican rebels began clashing with the Spanish army. Navarro, along with his mother's family, actively supported the rebellion.[10] The loss at the Battle of Medina in 1813 forced Navarro, his uncle José Francisco Ruiz, and others to flee to Louisiana. They would return briefly in 1816[11] but not permanently to San Antonio until Mexican independence in 1821.[12]

After Navarro returned to Texas, he became friendly with Stephen F. Austin. Together Navarro and Austin subtly, yet decisively, ensured that slavery would thrive in Mexican Texas[13] and actively pushed for Anglo settlement.[14] Initially, the Mexican government wanted Anglos to help settle Texas, but as Anglos started to sharply outnumber Tejanos, the government's position reversed and a law was passed restricting North American immigration to the province in 1830.[15] In December 1832, the ayuntamiento of San Antonio (a council of elite Tejanos including Navarro) agreed, in defiance of the Mexican government, to encourage North American immigration because of various benefits, such as increased trade, protection against Native American raids, and infrastructure building.[16]

© Pat Eyre/Alamy

As one of only three Tejano delegates to the Independence Convention, Navarro signed the Texas Declaration of Independence, an act that would have been considered treasonous had the Texas revolution failed. After the Texas Revolution, many Anglos became hostile to native Tejanos. Navarro was able to sidestep this prejudice to a degree due to his history of service to Texas and his friendship with a number of Anglo leaders (Not all of his family did, however. His nephew was beaten to death in 1838 for being perceived as "a Mexican sympathizer.").[17] Navarro's unwavering loyalty led many Texans, Anglos included, to see him as a hero.[18]

When the annexation of Texas drew near, Navarro was elected to represent Bexar County at the Constitutional Convention of 1845.[19] Notably, he was the only Hispanic elected in any county and, once there, "was instrumental in having the word 'white' stricken from the requirements for voting in the constitution for the new State of Texas."[20]

Navarro served two terms in the state Senate before retiring in 1849.[21] In recognition of his service to Texas, Navarro County was named in his honor.[22] He died on January 13th, 1871.[23]

The Civil War and Reconstruction Constitutions of 1861, 1866, and 1869

In 1861, when Texas joined the Confederacy, another state constitution was adopted. It was essentially the same as the 1845 document, but with an added prohibition against the emancipation of slaves, a provision to secede from the Union, and a provision to join the Confederacy.

In 1866, a third state constitution was approved as a condition for rejoining the Union following the Civil War. This document abolished slavery, nullified the ordinances of secession, renounced the right of future secession, and repudiated the wartime debts of the state. This constitution was short lived and overturned by Reconstruction acts of the U.S. Congress.

Texas adopted a new constitution in 1869. This fourth state constitution, which was approved under the supervision of the federal government's military rule, is called the Reconstruction constitution, or the "carpetbagger's constitution." It represented a radical departure from past and future documents and reflected the centralization aspirations of the national Republicans. A four-year term was provided for the governor, who was also given the authority to appoint most state and many local officials. County courts were abolished, and much local authority and control was removed from the planter class. Public schools were centralized under state control and funded with a poll tax and the sale of public lands. African Americans were given the right to vote, and whites who had participated in the "rebellion" (Civil War) were disfranchised.[24]

The Constitution of 1876

The current Texas Constitution was written in 1875 at the end of Reconstruction and approved by the voters in 1876. None of the delegates present at the 1875 constitutional convention had participated in writing the 1869 constitution. These men were landowners who had strongly objected to the centralist government under Reconstruction. As T. R. Fehrenbach put it, these men were

Delegates to the 1875 Constitutional Convention

Courtesy of Texas State Library and Archives Commission

> mostly old Texans: John Henry Brown, Sterling C. Robertson, sons of empresarios, Rip Ford (Texas Ranger), John H. Reagan (Ex-Postmaster General of the Confederacy), and a bevy of generals who has [sic] worn the grey. Of the ninety members, more than twenty held high rank in the C.S.A. [Confederate States of America] This was a restoration convention . . . It was a landowners' group, including forty members of the Grange . . . This was an antigovernment instrument: too many Texans had seen what government could do, not for them but to them. It tore up previous frameworks, and its essential aim was to try and bind all state government within tight confines.[25]

The new constitution reflected the antigovernment sentiments of the traditionalistic/individualistic political culture of the state. It reimposed shorter terms of office, reestablished many statewide and local elected offices, and severely restricted the government's authority to act. The powers of both the legislature and the governor were restricted.[26]

CORE OBJECTIVE

Thinking Critically . . .

What is the impact of a constitutional convention dominated by one party? What were the consequences of the 1875 constitutional convention in the development of the Texas Constitution?

Source: National Park Service

Culture Drives Institutions

Learning Objective: Describe how political culture drives institutions.

The various Texas constitutions have all reflected the political climate of the state, demonstrating how political culture drives institutions. Previously in this chapter it was noted that during the annexation period, many Texans distrusted government. Their political culture was influenced by their attitudes about the former Mexican government, as well as their deep-rooted southern traditional beliefs. Consistent with the dominant views of the day, the 1845 constitution provided for limited government with little centralized power. The Civil War and post-Civil War constitutions of 1861 and 1866 continued these principles of limited government. The present 1876 constitution not only reinstated but expanded the ideas of limited government. Only the Reconstruction constitution of 1869, which provided for a strong centralized government, was a departure from these ideas. Its swift repeal at the end of Reconstruction indicates how southern whites utterly rejected these concepts. Many Texans today would not accept these concepts, either. In 1999, voters rejected two amendments that would have expanded the power of the governor to appoint and remove minor state officials. In addition, voters have rejected annual sessions of the legislature on several occasions, and there is a consistent voice for decentralization of decisions down to the local level. In short, the current Texas Constitution is very compatible with the political climate of the state. However, institutions also can independently impact political outcomes as well as shape political culture in the future. The Spanish constitutions (1824 and 1827) contributed several key elements, including community property rights for women, which was a clear departure from English common law.

Important Sections of the Texas Constitution

Learning Objective: Describe the development of Texas's constitutions before and after 1876.

There are 17 articles in the Texas Constitution in addition to a preamble and appendix. Because the Texas Constitution contains nearly 87,000 words, to discuss all sections in depth would be exhaustive. However, quite a few sections stand out as essential. A number of them are reflective of sections found in the U.S. Constitution, but the Texas Constitution is significantly more detailed.

Article 1: Bill of Rights

The first article in the Texas Constitution is the Bill of Rights. Much like the U.S. Constitution, the Texas Constitution provides protection for freedom of speech and religion and protects the rights of the accused. Additional elements can be found in the Texas Constitution. For example, an equal rights amendment was inserted into the Texas Constitution in 1972, guaranteeing equality based on sex, race, color, creed, and national origin. The Texas Constitution ensures that the writ of habeas corpus will not be suspended and gives protection to crime victims. In 2009, the Texas Constitution was amended to give property owners additional rights, stating that private property cannot be taken by government for the purpose of "transfer to a private entity for the primary purpose of economic development or enhancement of tax revenues."[27] These rights add many of the elements of law found in the federal government and in other state constitutions. Some elements and amendments conflict, however. One such conflicting amendment added in late 2005 is Section 32, which defines marriage as a union between one man and one woman.[28] This amendment was struck down as unconstitutional by the United States Supreme Court in February 2015 and is no longer operational.[29]

Article 2: The Powers of Government

Article 2 discusses separation of powers specifically. The Texas Constitution makes it clear that the system contains separate checks, as compared to the more implied structure noted in the U.S. Constitution, by stating "no person, or collection of persons, being of one of these departments, shall exercise any power properly attached to either of the others, except in the instances herein expressly permitted."[30]

Article 3: Legislative Department

Article 3 refers to the legislative branch. The Texas Constitution divides the Texas legislature into two branches: a senate and a house of representatives. The senate is to be composed of 31 members, and the house of representatives is to be 150 members. The constitution provides for the election system, terms of office of members, and required qualifications of both branches. Much like the U.S. Constitution, the qualifications for senators and representatives are minimal. The legislature is to meet every two years for 140 days. Unlike the U.S. Constitution, the Texas Constitution lays out in significant detail the rules of procedure that legislators must follow. Article 3, Section 24, provides the amount of compensation for legislators at $600 per month, with per diem expenses allowed. The Texas Ethics Commission, an agency whose membership is outlined in Article 3, sets the per diem amount and can choose to recommend a higher salary for legislators.

Article 4: Executive Department

Article 4 describes the executive branch, which consists of the governor, lieutenant governor, comptroller of public accounts, commissioner of general land office, and the attorney general, who are all elected. The secretary of state is appointed by the governor. Under Article 4, the Texas legislature sets the annual salary of the governor. The governor's term is set at four years, and the constitution establishes no term limits. The governor is given the right to call a special session (which differs from an extraordinary session), during which members of the "Legislature may not consider any subject other than the appointment of electors at that special session."[31] The Texas Constitution purposefully provides for a fragmented executive branch and limits the powers of the governor. This is in keeping with much of the history and culture of the state, in which a general distrust of centralized power led to a preference for limited government.

Article 5: Judicial Department

Article 5 refers to the judicial branch. This is one of the branches whose structural elements are distinct from the design of the federal branches. The judicial department consists of multiple courts and, rather than having a single high court, the Texas Constitution provides for two high courts: the Supreme Court (eight justices and one chief justice) and the Court of Criminal Appeals (eight judges and one presiding judge). The Texas legislature has the right to create additional courts as it sees fit. Article 5 provides the requirements for judges. For example, a justice on the Texas Supreme Court must be "licensed to practice law in this state and [must be], at the time of election, a citizen of the United States and of this state, and [have] attained the age of thirty-five years, and [have] been a practicing lawyer, or a lawyer or judge of a court of record together at least ten years."[32] It should be noted, however, that not all judges need be lawyers. For example, county judges and justices of the peace are excluded from this requirement. In addition, the Texas Constitution provides for the election, rather than appointment, of judges. This has been a political concern wherein some citizens argue that the partisan election of judges may lead judges to base decisions on political reasons to ensure reelection. However, others argue that the election of judges provides for more direct involvement by the people in the democratic process.

Additional Articles

Article 6 concerns suffrage and provides the list of persons not allowed to vote in the state, including those who are under 18 years of age, individuals deemed mentally incompetent by the court, and persons convicted of felonies. Article 7 focuses on education and provides for a system of free public schools as well as various systems of funding for primary and secondary schools. Article 7 also provides for the establishment of state universities. Articles 9 and 16 define the creation and structure of counties in the state. These portions of the constitution are incredibly detailed, and the structure provided for counties leads to a fairly inflexible system to which counties are required to conform. Article 17 provides the means for amending the Texas Constitution.

Comparing the Structure of State Constitutions

Learning Objective: Describe the characteristics common to state constitutions.

Although they have some common characteristics, vast differences exist among state constitutions. According to legal experts and political theorists, there are some ideal characteristics that constitutions should possess. Ideally, a constitution should be brief and explicit, embody only the general principles of government, and provide the broad outlines of government subject to interpretation, especially through the court's power of judicial review. Constitutions should not be too detailed and specific, but should be broad and flexible. Furthermore, constitutions should provide broad grants of power to specific agencies and hold government officials accountable for their actions. Last, formal amendments to the constitution should be infrequent, deliberate, and significant.

Although it is worth identifying the qualities of an ideal constitution, it is important to understand that an "ideal" constitution does not necessarily equal good governance. The culture in which political institutions operate has a much more significant impact on governance. A good constitution serves to reinforce cultural expectations, but it is not sufficient in and of itself.

The U.S. Constitution meets these "ideal characteristics." There are only 4,543 words in the original document. It broadly outlines the basic principles of government and has been amended only 27 times. All but eight of these amendments involved issues of civil liberty, voting, and electoral questions. Very few of these amendments have altered the basic structure of the federal government. The document is flexible enough to allow for change without altering the basic document.

Few state constitutions can meet the ideal standards of brevity and a small number of amendments. This is especially true of the Texas Constitution. Table 2.2 details information about all 50 state constitutions as of January 1, 2015. Several conclusions are obvious from examining this table. First, most

TABLE 2.2

Comparisons of State Constitutions, January 1, 2015

State or Other Jurisdiction	Number of State Constitutions	Dates of Adoption	Effective Date of Present Constitution	Estimated Length (Number of Words)	Number of Amendments	
					Submitted to Voters	Adopted
Alabama	6	1819, 1861, 1865, 1868, 1875, 1901	Nov. 28, 1901	388,882	1,221	892
Alaska	1	1956	Jan. 3, 1959	13,479	42	29
Arizona	1	1911	Feb. 14, 1912	47,306	275	152
Arkansas	5	1836, 1861, 1864, 1868, 1874	Oct. 30, 1874	59,120	202	102
California	2	1849, 1879	July 4, 1879	67,048	896	529
Colorado	1	1876	Aug. 1, 1876	66,140	342	158
Connecticut	2	1818, 1965	Dec. 30, 1965	16,401	32	30
Delaware	4	1776, 1792, 1831, 1897	June 10, 1897	25,445	0*	145
Florida	6	1839, 1861, 1865, 1868, 1886, 1968	Jan. 7, 1969	56,705	168	122
Georgia	10	1777, 1789, 1798, 1861, 1865, 1868, 1877, 1945, 1976, 1982	July 1, 1983	41,684	98	75
Hawaii	1	1950	Aug. 21, 1959	21,498	138	113
Idaho	1	1889	July 3, 1890	24,626	213	125
Illinois	4	1818, 1848, 1870, 1970	July 1, 1971	16,401	21	14
Indiana	2	1816, 1851	Nov. 1, 1851	11,476	79	47

(Continued)

TABLE 2.2 *(Continued)*

Comparisons of State Constitutions, January 1, 2015

State or Other Jurisdiction	Number of State Constitutions	Dates of Adoption	Effective Date of Present Constitution	Estimated Length (Number of Words)	Number of Amendments	
					Submitted to Voters	Adopted
Iowa	2	1846, 1857	Sept. 3, 1857	11,089	59	54
Kansas	1	1859	Jan. 29, 1861	14,097	127	97
Kentucky	4	1792, 1799, 1850, 1891	Sept. 28, 1891	27,234	76	42
Louisiana	11	1812, 1845, 1852, 1861, 1864, 1868, 1879, 1898, 1913, 1921, 1974	Jan. 1, 1975	69,876	262	182
Maine	1	1819	March 15, 1820	16,313	205	172
Maryland	4	1776, 1851, 1864, 1867	Oct. 5, 1867	43,198	266	230
Massachusetts	1	1780	Oct. 25, 1780	45,283	148	120
Michigan	4	1835, 1850, 1908, 1963	Jan. 1, 1964	31,164	73	30
Minnesota	1	1857	May 11, 1858	11,734	217	120
Mississippi	4	1817, 1832, 1869, 1890	Nov. 1, 1890	26,229	162	126
Missouri	4	1820, 1865, 1875, 1945	March 30, 1945	69,394	186	120
Montana	2	1889, 1972	July 1, 1973	12,790	57	31
Nebraska	2	1866, 1875	Oct. 12, 1875	34,934	354	230
Nevada	1	1864	Oct. 31, 1864	37,418	235	138
New Hampshire	2	1776, 1784	June 2, 1784	13,060	289	145
New Jersey	3	1776, 1844, 1947	Jan. 1, 1948	26,360	85	70
New Mexico	1	1911	Jan. 6, 1912	33,198	303	169
New York	4	1777, 1822, 1846, 1894	Jan. 1, 1895	44,397	303	227
North Carolina	3	1776, 1868, 1970	July 1, 1971	17,177	39	32
North Dakota	1	1889	Nov. 2, 1889	18,746	277	156
Ohio	2	1802, 1851	Sept. 1, 1851	53,239	288	173
Oklahoma	1	1907	Nov. 16, 1907	81,666	363	196
Oregon	1	1857	Feb. 14, 1859	49,016	498	255
Pennsylvania	5	1776, 1790, 1838, 1873, 1968	1968	26,078	36	30
Rhode Island	2	1842, 1986	Dec. 4, 1986	11,407	16	13
South Carolina	7	1776, 1778, 1790, 1861, 1865, 1868, 1895	Jan. 1, 1896	27,421	689	500
South Dakota	1	1889	Nov. 2, 1889	27,774	234	118
Tennessee	3	1796, 1835, 1870	Feb. 23, 1870	13,960	66	43
Texas	5	1845, 1861, 1866, 1869, 1876	Feb. 15, 1876	86,936	662	484
Utah	1	1895	Jan. 4, 1896	17,849	172	118

TABLE 2.2 *(Continued)*

Comparisons of State Constitutions, January 1, 2015

State or Other Jurisdiction	Number of State Constitutions	Dates of Adoption	Effective Date of Present Constitution	Estimated Length (Number of Words)	Number of Amendments	
					Submitted to Voters	Adopted
Vermont	3	1777, 1786, 1793	July 9, 1793	8,565	212	54
Virginia	6	1776, 1830, 1851, 1869, 1902, 1970	July 1, 1971	21,899	56	49
Washington	1	1889	Nov. 11, 1889	32,578	180	106
West Virginia	2	1863, 1872	April 9, 1872	33,324	123	72
Wisconsin	1	1848	May 29, 1848	15,102	195	146
Wyoming	1	1889	July 10, 1890	26,349	129	100

*In Delaware, the state legislature amends the state constitution without voter approval.

Source: Book of the States 2015 (Council of State Governments, http://knowledgecenter.csg.org/kc/content/book-states-2015-chapter-1-state-constitutions).

states have had several constitutions. Only 19 states are still operating under their first constitution, and most of these are newer states in the West. Maine and Massachusetts are the only states of the "original 13" still operating under their first constitutions. Because of the Civil War and its aftermath, former Confederate states have had multiple constitutions.

Second, most state constitutions are very lengthy documents. Alabama's is the longest, with 388,882 words, including the amendments. The average state constitution is about 38,548 words. Some writers have pointed out that state constitutions have to be longer than the U.S. document because of the nature of state responsibility. Although this is true, it can also be argued that most state documents are of excessive length for other reasons, which are discussed later.

Third, most state constitutions have been amended more often than the U.S. Constitution; the average is about 142 times. Alabama is again the leader with 892 amendments. Fourth, state constitutions have a limited life span when compared with the U.S. Constitution. The average life span for a state constitution is ninety-five years.[33]

If we compare the Texas Constitution to the "average" state constitution, we find that it is longer than most, at 86,936 words, and has more amendments. It has been amended 484 times as of January 1, 2015.[34] Only six states have drafted more constitutions. One can easily conclude that most state constitutions, including Texas's, do not meet the criteria for an ideal constitution. Most are lengthy, detailed documents that require frequent alteration and might be more accurately described as statutory or legislative acts rather than constitutional law. This is especially true of the document that governs Texas.

Several other generalizations can be made about state constitutions. First, most create weak executives and strong legislatures. (This is discussed later in the text.) Second, all state constitutions contain articles on taxation and finance that limit how funds can be spent. Often taxes are **earmarked** for specific purposes (a common example is the gasoline tax for state highways). Third, all but

earmarked revenue

Money dedicated to a specific expenditure; for example, the excise tax on gasoline funds highway infrastructure

a few constitutions prohibit deficit expenditures unless approved by voters in the form of a bond election. Finally, most state constitutions contain large amounts of detail. For example, the original Texas Constitution contained a detailed list of items protected by the homestead protection provisions from forced sale for payment of debts. The list included the numbers of chickens, ducks, cows, pigs, dogs, and horses that were exempt.

Amending and Revising State Constitutions

Learning Objective: Explain how state constitutions, including Texas's, are amended and revised.

All state constitutions provide procedures for amending and revising the document. Except in the state of Delaware, two steps are involved in changing constitutions: proposing amendments and citizen approval. In Texas, two-thirds of each house of the legislature must propose amendments, and a majority of the voters who vote on the amendment must approve it.

Some states provide a variety of methods for proposing or recommending changes to the constitution. All state constitutions allow the legislature to propose changes. Most other states require an extraordinary majority vote of both houses to propose an amendment. Seventeen states require only a majority; eighteen states require a two-thirds vote of the state legislature; nine states require a three-fifths vote of the state legislature; and six states use variations thereof.[35]

initiative

A process that allows citizens to propose changes to the state constitution through the use of petitions signed by registered voters; Texas does not allow constitutional revision through initiative

A second method of proposing amendments to constitutions is by voter initiative. **Initiative** requires the collection of a prescribed number of signatures on a petition within a set time. Seventeen states allow initiative. Most states with initiative are western states that entered the Union in the late nineteenth or early twentieth century, when initiative was a popular idea. Only five states that allow for constitutional amendments by initiative are east of the Mississippi River. Texas does not have initiative. The Texas Republican Party pushed the idea of initiative for many years, but in 1996 it was dropped from the party platform.

constitutional convention

An assembly of citizens which may propose changes to state constitutions through voter approval

Most states, including Texas, allow the legislature to submit to the voters the question of calling a **constitutional convention** to propose amendments. This method is normally used for general revision and not for single amendments. Fourteen states have some provision for automatically submitting the question of a general convention to the voters periodically. If the voters approve, a convention is elected, it assembles, and it proposes amendments for voter approval.

Constitutional commissions are most often created by acts of the legislature, although there are other methods. These commissions usually submit a report to the legislature recommending changes. If the legislature approves, the proposed amendments are submitted to the voters. In Florida, the commission can bypass the legislature and go directly to the voters. Texas last used a commission in 1973 when the legislature created a 37-member commission to consider substantive and comprehensive revision to the Texas Constitution. After eight months of meetings and 19 public hearings, the Constitutional Revision Commission submitted recommendations to the 63rd Texas legislature.[36] Many issues, such as "right to work" provisions, were contentious and necessitated compromise. Other provisions, including bringing the multitude of local government clauses together in one article, represented vast improvements. Ultimately the committee's recommendations were rejected by the legislature on July 30, 1974, having failed to garner a two-thirds majority by three votes.

Patterns of Constitutional Change

If we examine state constitutional amendment processes, several patterns emerge. The first involves the frequency of change. State constitutions are amended more frequently than the U.S. Constitution. One reason is that state constitutions deal with a wider range of functions. About 63 percent of state amendments deal with issues not covered in the U.S. Constitution. A good example of this is education. Even if we remove issues not covered in the U.S. Constitution, the rate of amendment is still 3.5 times the national rate.[37] Change is also related to length. Longer state constitutions are more likely to be amended.[38]

The second pattern involves the method used to amend. As indicated, most amendments (90 percent) are proposed by state legislatures. States that require large legislative majorities for initiation have fewer amendments proposed and approved. Most amendments proposed by legislatures also receive voter approval. About 63 percent of all amendments proposed since 1970 have been approved by the voters.[39]

In the 18 states that allow voters to initiate amendments, two patterns emerge: more amendments are proposed, and the voter approval success rate for initiative-generated amendments is about half the rate for those proposed by state legislatures (32 percent versus 64 percent).[40] This tells us that the initiative process does not screen out amendments that lack broad public support. Proposal by legislature does. Amendments that gain support from supermajorities (majorities at a specified level above a simple majority of 50 percent) are more likely to be politically acceptable. The legislature serves as a screening process to rule out unacceptable amendments.

Amending the Texas Constitution

All amendments to the Texas Constitution have been proposed by a two-thirds vote of each house of the state legislature. From 1876 to 2015, the legislature has proposed 670 amendments for voter approval. The voters have approved 491 and have rejected 179 (an 73 percent approval rate).[41]

Voter turnout for amendments tends to be quite low, for a variety of reasons. Most amendments appear on the ballot in November of odd-numbered years, when no statewide offices are up for election. Texas submits more amendments in odd-numbered years than most states. Since 1972, Texas has formally adopted 35 constitutional amendments. Of these, 26 were in odd-numbered years, and 9 were in even-numbered years. Voter turnout for odd-year elections is lower than for even-year elections. In odd-year elections, less than 10 percent of the voting-age population participates (see Table 2.3).[42] This means that as few as 5 percent (plus one voter) could approve an amendment to the constitution. In 2005, there was a slight increase due to the anti-gay marriage amendment that was on the ballot.

Second, statewide voter turnout rates are often skewed by election schedules in counties with large cities. For example, Harris County could have a greater

TABLE 2.3

Voter Turnout in Odd-Year Constitutional Amendment Elections

Year	Percent of Voting-Age Population Voting
2015	8.30
2013	6.14
2011	3.77
2009	5.77
2007	6.31
2005	13.82 (Antigay-marriage amendment)
2003	9.31
2001	5.57
1999	6.69
1997	5.32
1997	8.45 (Special election)
1995	5.55
1993	8.52
1991	16.60 (School tax reform)
1989	9.33
1987	18.60 (School tax reform)
1985	8.24
1983	6.91
1981	8.07

Source: Adapted from Texas Secretary of State (http://www.sos.state.tx.us/elections/historical/70-92.shtml).

impact on statewide elections if many city and school board elections are held in the same election cycle as constitutional amendments. The Harris County vote could be significant if turnout statewide is very low. A strongly contested race for mayor of Houston could inflate the turnout rate in that city and affect statewide election results. The Harris County vote often constitutes about 30 percent of the total statewide votes cast on these amendments, despite the fact that registered voters in Harris County make up approximately 15 percent of the total number of registered voters in the entire state.

Third, **ballot wording** can also contribute to voter confusion and apathy about the political process. The state legislature dictates the ballot wording of all amendments. Sometimes this wording can be misleading or noninstructive unless the voter has studied the issue before the election. This example from the 1978 election is illustrative:

> For or against the constitutional amendment providing for tax relief for residential homesteads, elderly persons, disabled persons, and agricultural land; for personal property exceptions; truth in taxation procedures, including citizen involvement; for a redefinition [sic] of the tax base; for limitations on state spending; and for fair property tax administration.[43]

Most voters probably found this wording irresistible. Could any voter not favor tax exemptions for the elderly, the handicapped, homeowners, and farmers? Does any citizen oppose fair tax administration or citizen involvement? The amendment passed by an overwhelming majority. Another example of ballot-wording bias occurred in an amendment exempting personal property in Texas

ballot wording
Description of a proposed amendment as it appears on the ballot; can be intentionally noninstructive and misleading to voters in order to affect voter outcome

ports—the "freeport" amendment—which failed in 1987. The ballot read: "rendering to the exemption from ad valorem taxation, certain tangible personal property temporarily located within the states." But in 1989 the ballot read: "The constitutional amendment promoting economic growth, job creation and fair tax treatment for Texans who export goods." The amendment passed by a large majority. Ballot wording is apparently an important factor in the passage or rejection of amendments.

Fourth, the number of amendments and the subject matter of most amendments are not of interest to most voters, thus discouraging voter turnout. For example, in 1993, the voters were asked to approve 16 amendments to the constitution. The subjects of most of these amendments were financial: to authorize the issuance of bonds for economic development, pollution control, veterans' land, higher education, prisons, pensions, and agricultural development. In addition, one prohibited the establishment of an income tax without voter approval, and one concerned delinquent taxes. Two separate amendments (Propositions 6 and 8) abolished the office of land surveyor in Jefferson and McLennan counties, and another amendment (number 15) allowed voters in any county to abolish the office of land surveyor. One amendment cleared up Spanish land-grant titles in two counties. Another allowed the legislature to set qualifications for county sheriffs, and yet another allowed corporations additional means of raising capital. Except for one amendment dealing with an income tax prohibition, there was little in these amendments that was of interest to the average voter. This election is typical of most constitutional amendment elections in which the seemingly trivial subject matter contributes to low voter interest and turnout. Only those people most affected by an amendment are likely to understand it and to vote. Most voters stay home because there is little else to bring them out to the polls on Election Day.

Finally, voter ignorance of the issues is also a factor, although numerous sources provide ballot information. Issues are commonly reported in newspapers, on the nightly news, and on public radio broadcasting. Many county websites provide sample ballots beginning about a month in advance of an election. Unfortunately, many people remain uninformed regardless of the numerous avenues through which information can be accessed. This issue is discussed in more detail in Chapter 8.

Thus, odd-year elections, the impact of counties with large cities, confusing or noninstructive ballot wording, issues that interest few voters, and voter ignorance all contribute to low voter turnout (see Table 2.4). A very small number of voters, stimulated by personal interests and supported by an active interest group, can amend the constitution without a majority of the voters becoming involved. Often, many voters are not even aware that an election is being held.

Several other observations can be made regarding the amendment processes in Texas. First, most amendments face little opposition. Texans have approved 491 amendments and rejected 179.[44] Most are supported by an organized interest group willing to spend money, gain support, and work hard for passage. Second, interest groups attempt to have their interests protected in the constitution. A vested interest, protected in the constitution, is more difficult to alter than one protected by state law alone, because state law can be changed easily in the next session of the legislature. The process of constitutional change requires a two-thirds vote of the legislature plus electoral approval.

TABLE 2.4

Reasons for Low Voter Turnout in Constitutional Amendment Elections

Reason	Consequence
Odd-year election	Fewer citizens vote when elections occur in odd years, particularly when there are no other statewide elections on the ballot.
Counties with larger cities skew turnout	If larger cities have issues on the ballot, particularly city offices, more citizens of those cities will turn out than citizens in other areas of a state, thereby giving those particular city citizens greater influence over amendment approval or disapproval.
Poorly worded amendments	Amendment proposals with poor or misleading wording can increase voter apathy due to lack of understanding or can cause voters to vote for an amendment they do not actually want.
Little public interest	Many amendments are not perceived to be of concern to the daily life of a typical voter, such as those on land grants or other government financial matters.
Voter ignorance	Even though there are numerous media outlets for information on upcoming amendment elections, few voters are aware of what any given amendment election is about. This can be attributed to lack of voter interest in learning about these issues and also to the media and political outlets themselves.

A good example of such a protection in the constitution is the Permanent University Fund (PUF). The University of Texas and Texas A&M University are the only state schools that benefit from this fund, which has a value of approximately $11 billion. Other state universities have long felt that they deserved a share of this protected fund. Texas A&M and the University of Texas wanted to protect their funds and formed a coalition with non-PUF schools to support an amendment that created the Higher Education Assistance Fund (HEAF). This fund provides money to non-PUF universities. In the end, higher education funding for all state universities became protected in the state constitution.

Criticisms of the Texas Constitution

Learning Objective: Discuss common criticisms of Texas's constitution.

A number of criticisms can be levied against the Texas Constitution. These include length, wording, unclear organization, excessive detail, inflexibility, and constant change.

The Texas Constitution is the second longest state constitution in the nation, with much of its length in the form of amendments. For example, Article 1, Bill of Rights, contains 33 sections and Article 8, Taxation and Revenue, contains 24 sections. Including the index, the Texas Constitution is 241 pages.[45] Much of it is written in language that is unclear and that some consider outdated. For example, Article 4, Sec. 3, on election returns states:

> The returns of every election for said executive officers, until otherwise
> provided by law, shall be made out, sealed up, and transmitted by the

returning officers prescribed by law, to the seat of Government, directed to the Secretary of State, who shall deliver the same to the Speaker of the House of Representatives, as soon as the Speaker shall be chosen, and the said Speaker shall, during the first week of the session of the legislature, open and publish then in the presence of both Houses of the Legislature . . .

In addition to the difficult language, the Texas Constitution is not organized in a manner that makes it easy to discover where items are located. Thus, there is the necessity of having both a table of contents and an index.

While such detail might not seem problematic at first, the purpose of a constitution is to provide a broad foundation upon which a state government can rest. Although the Texas Constitution contains some broad foundational aspects, many of the components are so specific and detailed that they would be better placed in a legislative enactment. For example, Article 8, Taxation and Revenue, addresses topics such as homestead exemptions, assessment of lands designated for agricultural use, and ad valorem tax relief for items such as mobile drilling equipment and green coffee. Although these items may be important for government to address, their placement in the constitution, in contrast to being part of a statute or agency regulation, illustrates that many parts of the Texas Constitution are focused on specifics rather than on broad foundations.

The criticism that the Texas Constitution is both inflexible and at the same time constantly changing would seem contradictory. However, the inflexibility comes from the excessive detail. Broad statements allow for a wider use of discretion in interpreting and implementing constitutional provisions. The extreme detail found in a number of sections is one reason it is more difficult for government actors to use their discretion in interpretation and implementation. For example, Article 9, Counties, lays out in detail such items as hospital districts, tax rates, and airport authorities. Counties become limited in what they can do under the Texas Constitution. Of course, for some people this is seen as an advantage rather than as a bug in the system. They believe that a constitution that frustrates the use of power by governmental authorities limits government and preserves their freedom.

The constant change comes from the stream of new amendments. These also contribute to excessive length. The changes are constant, but they tend to be incremental in nature, meaning that the Texas Constitution as a whole has not been drastically revised since the 1876 version upon which the current document is based. Although many reformers believe the constitution is therefore in need of a comprehensive revision, it is unlikely that such change can be achieved in the brief biennial legislative session in a state whose citizens tend to have a strong distrust of government.

Conclusion to the Texas Constitution

Learning Objective: Describe the development of Texas's constitutions before and after 1876.

Many legal scholars have pointed out the need for a general revision of the current Texas Constitution. In the 1970s, a serious effort at total revision was unsuccessful. A commission of legal experts, acting as a constitutional commission, made recommendations to the state legislature for major changes. The state legislature, acting as a constitutional convention in 1974, deadlocked and adjourned without making any recommendations for change. The next regular session of the Texas legislature, in 1975, proposed eight separate amendments to the voters. In November 1975, the voters rejected all amendments by a two-to-one margin.

In 1999, two prominent members of the Texas legislature introduced a bill calling for general revision of the Texas Constitution. Then-Senator Bill Ratliff, Republican from East Texas, and Representative Robert Junell, Democrat from San Angelo, were the chairs of budget-writing committees in the senate and house in that session. Their bill called for some substantial changes in the current constitution. This proposal, which would have reduced the size of the current constitution to some 19,000 words in 150 sections, died in committee in both houses.

The 76th Legislature (1999) created the Select Committee on Constitutional Revision, and Speaker of the House James Laney appointed Representative Joe Driver as chair. This committee held hearings in various locations in the state and made suggestions for changes that could be characterized as elimination of deadwood and updating of wording. The committee saw no need for a general revision of the document or the calling of a constitutional convention or commission.

The piecemeal process of amending the constitution every two years will likely continue for several reasons. First is a lack of support for reform by significant political forces in the state. Strong political leadership from someone like the governor would be necessary. Neither Rick Perry nor his successor, Greg Abbott, has indicated any interest in supporting reform efforts; supporting controversial issues such as revision of the constitution has little appeal or payoff. Currently, no statewide leader has been particularly vocal about supporting revision. In short, the political will to significantly change the constitution does not exist.

Second, the political culture of the state and the basic conservative nature of state politics do not support broad change. The current constitution supports the traditionalistic/individualistic political culture of the state. The document serves select groups of people and protects their interests and privileges, and these groups have the resources to maintain those protections. Senator Ratliff's and Representative Junell's 1999 proposal avoided many of the major controversies by leaving intact important interests that are well protected by the constitution; however, not all were protected.

Third, strong opposition from powerful lobby groups whose interests are currently protected by the document would make change difficult, if not impossible. In his opening address to the constitutional convention assembled in 1974, the vice chairman of the convention, Lt. Governor William Hobby, made the following observation:

> The special interests of today will be replaced by new and different special interests tomorrow, and any attempt to draft a constitution to serve such interests would be futile and also dishonorable.[46]

This convention adjourned without approving a new, rewritten constitution to be submitted to the voters. The special interests in the state had prevailed. The entire effort was, indeed, "futile and also dishonorable."

Fourth, one could cite a general lack of interest and support for change among the citizens of the state. Constitutional revision is not a subject that excites most citizens. The average Texan probably does not see the need for revision. Some proud Texans would take offense at the suggestion that the state document is flawed. The document drafted at the end of Reconstruction in the 1870s will probably continue to serve Texans for many years. The prospects for general revisions do not seem great. Evidence of this can be found in the 1999 election. In that year, the voters rejected three amendments that might be considered mildly progressive. Two of these amendments would have provided that the adjutant general of the national guard and the commissioner of health and human services were to serve at the pleasure of the governor. Another would have created a Judicial Compensation Commission providing procedures that are standard in most state constitutions today.

The American Federal System of Government

Learning Objective: Explain the American federal system of government.

Texas and the other 49 states operate within what is called a **federal system of government**. Broadly, this system provides for a sharing of powers between the national (federal) government and respective state governments. It provides for a balance of power and responsibilities between the national and state governments.

Although the United States is not unique among nations for having a federal system, most nations of the world have what is called a **unitary system of government**. Under a unitary government, power is centralized in a national government, and regional and local governments operate within powers granted by the national government. For example, in England the central government, through Parliament, governs the nation. Regional governments are subservient to the national government. In the United States, state governments have some powers reserved to them by the Constitution, and they can act independently of the national government within those areas.

Under a **confederal system of government**, most of the power rests with the regional and local governments, and the national government has only limited powers. Under the Confederate States of America, the national government found it impossible to compel state governments to contribute troops or supplies to the war effort. This lack of authority hampered the war effort during the American Civil War. Each state acted independently of the others and the national government.

In many respects, a federal system falls in between the unitary and confederal systems of government, as illustrated in Figure 2.2. Power is divided between the central government and between geographic units of government. In the U.S. system, these geographic units are called states. In other countries, such as Canada, these units of government are called provinces. The national government has powers and duties in assigned areas, and the regional governments have powers in assigned areas. In some cases, powers may overlap, and in other

federal system of government
The division of powers between a national government and regional governments

unitary system of government
A system of government where all functions of government are controlled by the central/national government

confederal system of government
A system of government that divides power between a weak national government and strong, independently sovereign regional governments

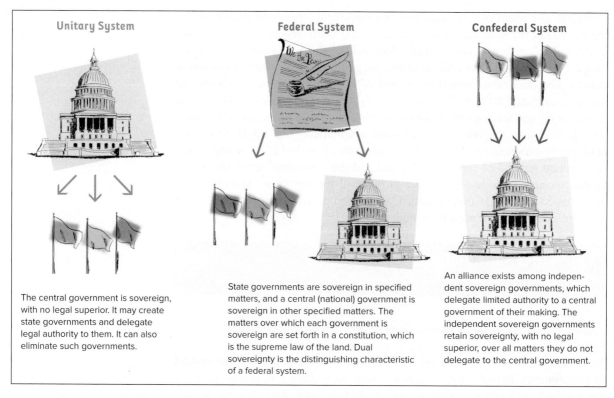

Unitary System

The central government is sovereign, with no legal superior. It may create state governments and delegate legal authority to them. It can also eliminate such governments.

Federal System

State governments are sovereign in specified matters, and a central (national) government is sovereign in other specified matters. The matters over which each government is sovereign are set forth in a constitution, which is the supreme law of the land. Dual sovereignty is the distinguishing characteristic of a federal system.

Confederal System

An alliance exists among independent sovereign governments, which delegate limited authority to a central government of their making. The independent sovereign governments retain sovereignty, with no legal superior, over all matters they do not delegate to the central government.

FIGURE 2.2   Systems of Government

areas both governments may possess similar powers. For example, both the federal and state governments have the power to tax and to spend money.

A federal system has a number of advantages. A key one, as Supreme Court Justice Louis Brandeis noted in 1932, is that states can be "laboratories" of democracy. In particular, he argued, "It is one of the happy incidents of the federal system that a single courageous state may, if its citizens choose, serve as a laboratory; and try novel social and economic experiments without risk to the rest of the country."[47] Another advantage, as the Supreme Court argued in *Bond v. United States* (2011), is that "By denying any one government complete jurisdiction over all the concerns of public life, federalism protects the liberty of the individual from arbitrary power."[48] Other advantages, as one law professor has pointed out, are that federalism can accommodate a diversity of preferences in a heterogeneous society, that the most appropriate level of government can be utilized for a particular purpose, and that the states can compete and their citizens can move to places that have an attractive particular mix of public policies.[49]

Constitutional Distribution of Powers

The U.S. Constitution distributes power between the national and state governments. It grants and denies powers. In some cases, powers are granted exclusively to the national government and in other cases exclusively to the states. There are also instances where powers are granted to both the national and the state governments. The same can be said for denied powers. Some are denied to the national government, others are denied to the states, and some are denied to both.

Division of Powers between National and State Governments

Figures 2.3 and 2.4 present a clear summary of the division of powers between the national and state governments. Although the division of powers may seem straightforward, these figures belie the true complexity of our federal system of government. It is complicated, and the meaning of each power has been subject to interpretation by the federal courts. If we examine four areas of the Constitution and the courts' interpretations, we gain a much better understanding of American federalism. These four areas are the Necessary and Proper Clause versus the Tenth Amendment; the Interstate Commerce Clause; Equal Protection and Due Process Clause of the Fourteenth Amendment; and the power to tax and spend to promote the general welfare.

The "Necessary and Proper" Clause and the Tenth Amendment

Article 1, Section 8, paragraph 18 of the United States Constitution states that Congress shall have the power "To make all Laws which shall be necessary and proper for carrying into Execution the foregoing Powers, and all other Powers vested by this Constitution in the Government of the United States, or in any Department or Officer thereof." This seems to grant considerable power to the national government. However, the **Tenth Amendment** states: "The powers not

Tenth Amendment
Amendment of the U.S. Constitution that delegates or reserves some powers to the state governments or to the people

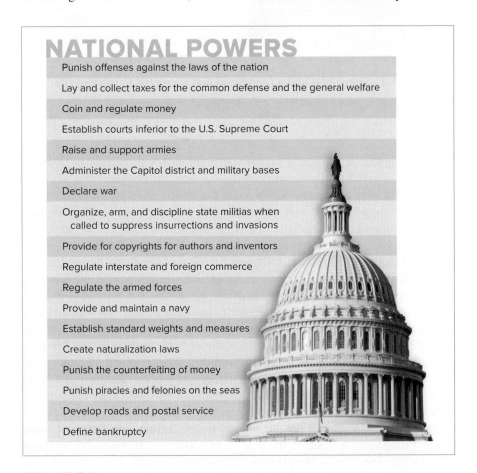

NATIONAL POWERS

Punish offenses against the laws of the nation

Lay and collect taxes for the common defense and the general welfare

Coin and regulate money

Establish courts inferior to the U.S. Supreme Court

Raise and support armies

Administer the Capitol district and military bases

Declare war

Organize, arm, and discipline state militias when called to suppress insurrections and invasions

Provide for copyrights for authors and inventors

Regulate interstate and foreign commerce

Regulate the armed forces

Provide and maintain a navy

Establish standard weights and measures

Create naturalization laws

Punish the counterfeiting of money

Punish piracies and felonies on the seas

Develop roads and postal service

Define bankruptcy

FIGURE 2.3   Enumerated Powers of the National Government

© iStockphoto.com/Greg Cooksey

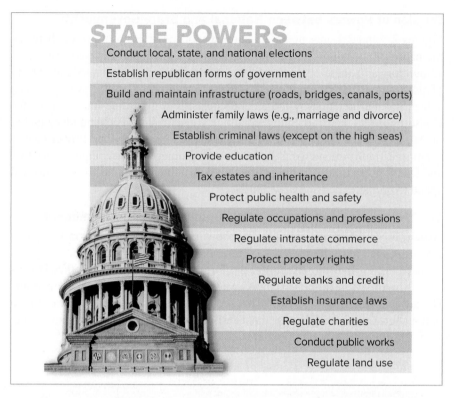

FIGURE 2.4   Constitutionally Delegated and Reserved Powers of the State

© Harvey Loyd/Stockbyte/Getty Images

delegated to the United States by the Constitution, nor prohibited by it to the States, are reserved to the States respectively, or to the people." This seems to grant most powers not expressly granted to the federal government to the states, or that they would remain with the people. The meanings of these two sections of the Constitution were the cause of conflict early in the history of the Republic.

In 1790, Congress created a national bank under the advice of Secretary of the Treasury Alexander Hamilton. Although Article 8 of the Constitution does not grant Congress the right to create a national bank, it does grant it the power to borrow money, regulate commerce, and coin money. Hamilton thought that one could imply that Congress has the power to establish a bank into which money borrowed and coined could be deposited and commerce regulated. Thomas Jefferson objected to the creation of a national bank, fearing it could lead to centralization of power in the federal government. The argument basically came down to defining what exactly was "necessary and proper." Jefferson felt "necessary" meant "indispensable," whereas Hamilton felt "necessary" meant any manner that is deemed appropriate by Congress.

In 1819, the question of the meaning of the **Necessary and Proper Clause** reached the Supreme Court in the case of *McCulloch v. Maryland* (4 Wheaton 316 [1819]). The state of Maryland decided to tax a branch of the national bank located in Baltimore, Maryland. The Court accepted Hamilton's interpretation of the clause, and Justice Marshall, writing for the Court, stated, "Let the end

Necessary and Proper Clause (Elastic Clause)

Statement in Article 1, Section 8, paragraph 18 of the U.S. Constitution that says Congress can pass any law necessary and proper to carry out other powers

be legitimate, let it be within the scope of the Constitution, and all means which are appropriate, which are plainly adopted to that end, which are not prohibited but consistent with the letter and spirit of the Constitution are constitutional." This provides a very broad interpretation to the meaning of this clause, and it came to be called the "Elastic Clause" of the Constitution because it allowed Congress to decide the means to carry out ends, thus "stretching" its powers to meet its needs.

In addition, the McCulloch case also contributed to definitions of national supremacy. The Maryland law, taxing the bank, was found to be in conflict with the federal law establishing the bank. Article 6 of the Constitution says that federal law shall be the "supreme Law of the Land." State laws in conflict with national law are thus unconstitutional, and federal law would prevail over state laws. Without this interpretation, any state could choose to ignore national policy and go its own way. The supremacy clause provided for the creation of national policy with which states must comply.

Interstate Commerce Clause

Another troubling area was the question of interstate commerce. During the nineteenth century and most of the twentieth, the Supreme Court placed a very narrow interpretation on interstate commerce and applied it only to goods that were transported across state lines, leaving most regulation of commerce to the states. In the 1930s, during the Great Depression, the courts came under fire for their narrow view. Because of political pressure and changes in court membership, the meaning of interstate commerce came to be anything that had a substantial effect on national commerce. During the 1960s, the **Interstate Commerce Clause** was used to prohibit hotels and restaurants from being segregated by race. Georgia provides one example. In 1964, Lester Maddox, who would be governor from 1967 to 1971, refused to serve African Americans in a restaurant he owned. He felt he was not engaged in interstate commerce because he owned only one facility in one state. The court's interpretation was that, one, the food he served was shipped across state lines, and two, his establishment served people who potentially traveled across state lines. Therefore, he was engaged in interstate commerce.

Interstate Commerce Clause
Article in U.S. Constitution that gives Congress the exclusive power to regulate commerce between the states; Congress and the courts determine what is interstate commerce

Another question concerns when a state can prohibit the shipment of goods into that state. For example, in the past many states prohibited cattle from Texas to be shipped into their states because they were often infected with a tick fever. In another case, California prohibited citrus fruit from being imported because of infected crops in other states. Texas once prohibited California oranges from coming into Texas because of a fruit fly infection. All these cases address the issue of the legitimacy of trade barriers. If the prohibition on the importation of an item is truly to protect health, morals, and safety, and not a barrier imposed to restrict trade, it will be allowed. For example, if the reason for the barriers is to protect the health of cattle or oranges, then states may erect such barriers. Again, determination is up to the court. The courts decide when barriers have been erected for legitimate purposes and when it is a restraint on interstate trade.

There are many areas of seeming contradiction when it comes to interstate commerce. From the narrow view to the expansion in interpretation during the Great Depression (enshrined in cases such as *Wickard v. Filburn* [1942] where the Court found that a farmer's growing of wheat for personal on-farm use was illegal because it exceeded a federally mandated limit), the interpretation of the Interstate Commerce Clause has continued to evolve case by case. Similarly, some industries are regulated and others are not. The conclusion is that interstate commerce has become largely whatever the courts say it is. Critics of an expansive view of the commerce clause charge that it undermines the notion of the Constitution establishing a government of specific enumerated powers while strengthening the federal government at the expense of the states and individual liberty.

Equal Protection and Due Process Clause of the Fourteenth Amendment

The U.S. Bill of Rights provides for the protection of civil liberties and individual rights. Initially, the Bill of Rights applied only to actions of the national government that affected citizens. For example, the First Amendment states, "Congress shall make no laws respecting an establishment of religion. . . ." It says Congress—not Congress and the states.

In the aftermath of the Civil War, Congress passed and the states approved the Fourteenth Amendment, which for the first time ascribed rights to national as well as state citizenship, and extended some of the basic protections outlined in the Bill of Rights to African American freed men that even state and local governments had to respect:

> "No State shall make or enforce any law which shall abridge the privileges or immunities of citizens of the United States; nor shall any State deprive any person of life, liberty or property, without due process of law, or deny to any person within its jurisdiction the equal protection of the law."

Equal Protection Clause

Clause in the Fourteenth Amendment of the U.S. Constitution that requires states to treat all citizens equally

Due Process of Law Clause

Clause in the Fifth and Fourteenth Amendments of the U.S. Constitution that requires states to treat all citizens equally and that the state must follow certain rules and procedures

The **Equal Protection Clause** and the **Due Process Clause** mean that state and local governments must treat people equally and in accordance with established rules and procedures.

After World War I, the federal courts gradually began to apply the basic rights provided in the Constitution to the states. There were three primary areas where states were required to provide protection for citizens: civil liberties, criminal proceedings, and election laws.

Civil liberties include such things as freedom of speech and religion. States may no longer require prayer in public schools or allow segregated schools. Criminal procedures include such things as protection against self-incrimination (so-called Miranda warnings) and the right to legal counsel in criminal procedures. Election laws overturned restrictive voter registration laws and white primaries. States were also forced to apportion legislative districts equally by population. (These issues are covered in more detail in later chapters.)

This gradual expansion of basic rights also expanded the role of the national government into areas that had traditionally been reserved to the states. Although state power may have been reduced, individual rights and liberties were expanded.

Power to Tax and Spend to Promote the General Welfare of Citizens

Article 1, Section 8, grants Congress the right to tax and spend to promote general welfare. The national government lacks the power to provide many basic services to citizens. Congress cannot, for example, operate schools and hospitals, build roads, or do many things state governments can. These powers are reserved to the states. The national government has only interstate police powers;

however, the national government may provide money to state and local governments to provide these basic services.

In this area, the national government has had great impact on state and local authority. Congress can provide money to state and local governments and set standards for how the money can be spent. Congress supplies money to state governments to build and maintain roads and highways. When states accept this money, they must agree to some standard. Most college students might be aware of these standards as applied to highway funds: states must agree to set a drinking age of 21 if they accept federal money. At the time Congress passed this requirement, most states (30) already had 21 as the drinking age, 4 had the age of 20, 13 had the age of 19, and only 3 had the age of 18. However, many citizens felt that this was an unfair exercise of national authority and an intrusion into an area reserved to the states. Similar requirements applied to the 55-mile-per-hour speed limit in the 1970s, and some states initially refused to comply or enforce the rule.

The attitude of many state and local officials is that the national government should provide funds and then end its involvement in state affairs. They believe that the rules are often burdensome, inflexible, and unnecessary. There are probably cases where this is true; however, the positive side of these requirements is that they have led to improved uniformity in standards. For example, if you drive on an interstate highway anywhere in the United States (including Hawaii) there is a uniformity of highway signs and rules. Also, national requirements have led to improvements in accounting standards. State and local governments that accept federal money must comply with generally accepted accounting principles (GAAPs).

Some argue that the national government has eroded state power through the use of federal grants. In some cases the argument portrays the national government as an uncontrollable Leviathan preying upon the poor defenseless states. Nevertheless, Congress is not an independent force but consists of officials elected from states. When the federal government provides money to states for programs, those programs are passed by a majority vote of Congress, with the approval of the president.

In reaction to the criticism of federal encroachments into state powers, Congress has moved from **categorical grants** for specific purposes to grants that are much broader in scope, generally called **block grants**. This allows Congress to set general rules for how money can be spent and at the same time allows state and local officials to decide specific details. Over the past 50 years, states have been given much more control over how federal money is spent.

categorical grants
Grants that may be used to fund specific purposes as defined by the federal government

block grants
Grants that may be used for broad purposes that allow local governments greater discretion in how funds are spent

CORE OBJECTIVE

Being Socially Responsible . . .

Considering the argument that the national government has eroded state power, to what extent should the government "promote general welfare"? What does promoting general welfare mean to you? In developing an understanding of state and local political systems and their relationship with the federal government, who do you think should play a greater role—the states or the federal government?

© Editorial Image, LLC/Alamy

The Evolution of American Federalism

The real strength of the American federal system is flexibility. The relationship between the national government and state governments has altered and changed with time and political trends, and there is no reason to expect that this will not continue. Several models are used to describe this changing relationship over the past 230 years.

During most of the nineteenth and early twentieth centuries, a system called dual federalism operated. Under this model, there were rather specific areas of influence. The national government had primary delegated powers as defined in the Constitution, and the state governments provided most basic services to citizens. There was little financial assistance from the national government to states. Some have compared this to a layer cake with clearly defined areas of influence. Although this is called dual federalism, for much of the nineteenth century states were dominant. After the Civil War, the idea of states' rights over national power began to decline.

The second model used to describe federal–state relations is often called cooperative federalism. This relationship began in the 1930s with the Great Depression. The federal government began to supply more money to state and local governments to provide assistance to citizens. A cooperative relationship existed between the national and state governments to provide services to citizens.

During the 1960s, some saw a changed relationship with what came to be called creative federalism. President Johnson sought to create a Great Society through a massive expenditure of money to end poverty and lift all citizens in society. Under President Nixon, the system was referred to as new federalism. It involved giving state governments more discretion in program administration and so-called revenue sharing. President Reagan sought to give the states more power in spending grant money while reducing the amount of money available to state and local governments. Some viewed this as a return of both power and responsibilities to the states.

Under President Clinton, with emphasis from the Republicans in Congress, federal–state relations were described as undergoing a devolution of power. This basically means that states were given even greater authority on both program construction and administration.

When it comes to decisions about spending money, the evolution in the United States has been from one where the national government specified programs and provided money to support them to one where state and local governments are given greater power and authority to determine how federal programs are administrated in their states. Whereas federal grants to states declined as a percentage of federal expenditures during the Reagan administration, they grew under both Bush presidents and Clinton. Federal grants are a form of financial assistance from a federal agency for a specific program or purpose. For example, the Texas Railroad Commission receives money annually from the Federal Recovery and Reinvestment Fund. About 24 percent of state expenditures are from the federal government. Of course, while states have greater power now than previously, they can still be coerced. Some grants, called categorical grants, have federal strings attached which specify to states where the money can and cannot be spent. This phenomenon is called coercive federalism. (We examine state financing more closely in Chapter 13.)

Relations between States in the Federal System

It is also important to understand the relations that exist between states, and between states and individuals. Article 4, Section 1, of the Constitution states, **"Full Faith and Credit** shall be given in each state to the public Acts, Records and Judicial Proceedings of every other state." For example, if your last will and testament is probated in a Texas court, other states must recognize that court action.

This seems like an obvious requirement, because it enables citizens to know that the rights they enjoy in their home state will be honored in another. However, this is not as simple as it seems. There are three good examples in the past 50 years where this clause in the Constitution was tested. The first is divorce. In the 1950s, it was difficult, in most states, to obtain a divorce. The state of Nevada was an exception. It granted divorces very easily. At first, some states refused to accept what were often called "quickie divorce mill" decisions, but eventually all states had to recognize these divorces. Second, in the 1980s, some states refused to enforce child custody and support payments following divorce. There were cases where one parent in a divorce would move to another state and refuse to abide by the child custody or payment agreements. Eventually, federal courts forced all states to enforce these court decrees from other states.

A more recent example is the issue of gay marriage. The U.S. Congress passed, and President Clinton signed into law, the federal Defense of Marriage Act (DOMA) in 1996. When DOMA was signed into law, the argument that gay men and women should be allowed to marry was fringe opinion. Yet, over the following decade and a half, more and more states were legalizing gay marriage of their own accord, including the District of Columbia. Unfortunately, however, Section 3 of DOMA "prevented the federal government from recognizing any marriages between gay or lesbian couples for the purpose of federal laws or programs, even if those couples are considered legally married by their home state."[50] Advocates of gay marriage argued that states were violating the full faith and credit clause by refusing to recognize gay marriages performed in other states. Congress, in Section 2 of DOMA, addressed this issue by stating that no state must accept another state's definition of marriage.

Several cases challenging DOMA and Proposition 8 in California, which banned gay marriage, were up for review in the 2012–13 term. In June 2013, the Supreme Court, in *U.S. v. Windsor*, struck down Section 3 of DOMA as unconstitutional. At the same time the Court dismissed Proposition 8 on procedural grounds instead of ruling on its constitutionality. This effectively left the previous lower district court ruling on the

Full Faith and Credit Clause

Clause in Article 4 of the U.S. Constitution that requires states to recognize the judgements, legislation, and public records of other states

David Wegner, center left, and Molly Ryan Butterworth, center right, hold an enlarged copy of their recent marriage license during a rally at the Utah State Capitol in support of gay marriage in 2014.

© Steve C. Wilson/AP Images

proposition intact (originally *Perry v. Schwarzenegger* in 2010), a ruling which did overturn the proposition on constitutional grounds. Later in 2013, a U.S. district court dismissed Pennsylvania's argument that gay marriage is a state issue rather than a federal one, clearing the way for the Supreme Court to weigh in on the constitutionality of Pennsylvania's gay marriage ban. Similar cases were also concurrently underway in other states.

All of this back and forth led to a landmark decision by the Supreme Court on June 26, 2015. In *Obergefell v. Hodges,* the Court determined that the Fourteenth Amendment not only protected marriage as a fundamental right but also "extend[ed] to certain personal choices central to individual dignity and autonomy, including intimate choices that define personal identity and beliefs."[51] As a result, marriage as a federally protected institution can no longer be defined as between one man and one woman. Any law, state or federal or otherwise, requiring such is now unconstitutional and rendered defunct.

The U.S. Constitution, in Article 4, section 2, Clause 2, says that in some areas a state must treat citizens of other states the same way as it treats its own citizens. This is more formally known as the **Privileges and Immunities of Citizenship**. States cannot violate basic rights or protected privileges of any individual federal citizen who happens to be a nonresident or a citizen of other states.[52] When the Supreme Court, for example, struck down both Section 2 and 3 of DOMA in the decisions *U.S. v. Windsor* and *Obergefell v. Hodges,* it meant that all states must both recognize and permit marriage licenses for same-sex couples regardless of their residency. If a state must now recognize and permit marriages between its own same-sex citizens, it must also do so for citizens of other states.

It is understood, however, that in other areas, residents and nonresidents *can* be treated differently. One particularly relevant example is out-of-state tuition at public universities. Differential rates can be charged for residents of Texas and residents of other states. The justification for different rates is that because state universities are publicly funded, residents of Texas rightfully should pay a lower tuition rate because they have been subsidizing higher education through taxes. This also applies to driver's licenses, hunting licenses, law licenses, and professional licenses.

Of course, it can be difficult to determine what falls under the privileges and immunities of citizenship and what does not. It can also be unclear who has the right to decide. There is a long history spanning the judicial and legislative branches, from colonial times to today and onward.[53]

Privileges and Immunities Clause

Clause in Article 4 of the U.S. Constitution that prevents states from discriminating against citizens of other states and requires those citizens to be treated in like manner

CORE OBJECTIVE

Source: United States Department of Agriculture Agricultural Research Service

Taking Personal Responsibility. . .

As a resident of Texas and a citizen of the United States, identify and discuss examples that reinforce the Full Faith and Credit Clause and the Privileges and Immunities Clause of the U.S. Constitution. What examples in your opinion, violate these principles?

Conclusion

As we have seen, one of the real strengths of the American federal system is its flexibility and ability to change with the times. This is obvious if you examine the U.S. Constitution and observe how little the document has been altered in the past 200-plus years (see Table 2.5). A few of the structural amendments are often pointed to as examples. The Sixteenth Amendment gave the national government great financial resources and led to greater national influence over state spending decisions and policies. Many of the civil and voting rights amendments have had a greater impact on federal–state relations. The Fourteenth Amendment applied many of the first eight amendments to the states. Amendments were aimed at ending violations of civil and voting rights practiced by the states (for example, women's right to vote, poll tax).

Admittedly some changes were more profound than others. However, most were evolutional in nature and are not major structural changes. American federalism is a flexible system that will allow for change to meet future needs and challenges.

TABLE 2.5

Amendments to the Federal Constitution

Civil Liberties and Voting Rights		Structural Amendments	
Number	**Subject Matter**	**Number**	**Subject Matter**
1–8	Various civil liberties	10	Reserved powers
9	Other liberties that may exist	11	Sovereign immunity
13	End to slavery	12	Electoral College voting
14	Equal protection, due process of law	20	When the president takes office—lame duck amendment
15	Race and voting	22	Two terms for president
16	Income tax	25	Presidential disability
17	Direct election of senators	27	Congressional pay
19	Women's right to vote		
23	D.C. vote for president		
24	End poll tax as requirement for voting		
26	18-year-old right to vote		
18 & 21	Prohibition and repeal of prohibition on sale of alcohol		

Summary

LO: Describe the principles of constitutional government.

History, culture, traditions, basic principles, and ideas have an impact on constitutions. Several important principles specifically underpin the general idea of constitutional government. The first is the idea of popular sovereignty. This idea holds that, at root, power rests with the people and, theoretically, legitimate constitutions should articulate the will of the people. Second, constitutions are contracts or compacts between the citizens and the government and cannot be violated, i.e social contract theory. Third, constitutions structure government, divide and assign power, and place limitations on government's power.

LO: Describe the characteristics common to state constitutions.

All state constitutions embrace the idea of separation of powers provided in the U.S. Constitution. Most state constitutions have very strong statements on civil liberties that secure basic freedoms. In addition, a constitution should be brief and explicit, embody only the general principles of government, and provide the broad outlines of government subject to interpretation, Constitutions should not be too detailed and specific, but should be broad and flexible. They should provide broad grants of power to specific agencies and hold government officials accountable for their actions. Formal amendments to the constitution should be infrequent, deliberate, and significant.

LO: Describe the development of Texas's constitutions before and after 1876.

During this period, there are four main constitutions to take note of: the Constitutions of 1824 (Republic of Mexico), 1836 (Republic of Texas), 1845 (Texas, as a new state in the Union), and 1875 (Texas, as a state in the Union, post-Reconstruction, current). The first governed Anglos in Texas and was federalist in concept, dividing governing authority between the nation and the states. It designated Catholicism as the state religion and did not recognize slavery. The second constitution (1836) was a composite of the U.S. Constitution and the constitutions of several southern states, providing for a unitary form of government and limiting the president to one 3-year term with prohibitions against consecutive reelection. It also included freedom of religion and property rights protection, that had been absent before. Slavery was legalized. The third constitution (1845) included a few adaptions of Spanish law such as women being granted property rights equal to those of men and also provided for limited executive authority, biennial sessions of the legislature, and two-year terms for most officials. The fourth and current Texas Constitution (1875) reimposed shorter terms of office, reestablished many statewide and local elected offices, and severely restricted the government's authority to act. Otherwise, it maintains many of the characteristics of the 1845 constitution.

LO: Describe how political culture drives institutions.

The various Texas constitutions have all reflected the political climate of the state, demonstrating how political culture drives institutions. For example, during the annexation period, many Texans distrusted government. Their political culture was influenced by their attitudes about the former Mexican government, as well as their deep-rooted southern traditional beliefs. Consistent with that, the 1845 constitution provided for limited government with little centralized power.

LO: Explain how state constitutions, including Texas's, are amended and revised.

All state constitutions allow the legislature to propose changes. A second method of proposing amendments to constitutions is by voter initiative. Initiative requires the collection of a prescribed number of signatures on a petition within a set time. Texas does not have initiative. Most states, including Texas, allow the legislature to submit to the voters the question of calling a constitutional convention to propose amendments. These commissions usually submit a report to the legislature recommending changes. All amendments to the Texas Constitution have been proposed by a two-thirds vote of each house of the state legislature. General voter turnout on these proposals have been traditionally low.

LO: Discuss common criticisms of Texas's constitution.

Common criticisms include length, wording, unclear organization, excessive detail, inflexibility, and constant change. The Texas Constitution is the second longest state constitution in the nation, with much of its length in the form of amendments. The inflexibility comes from the excessive detail. Constant change comes from the frequent adoption of amendments. In addition, broad statements allow for a wider use of discretion in interpreting and implementing constitutional provisions.

LO: Explain the American federal system of government.

The federal system of government provides for a sharing of powers between the national (federal) government and respective state governments. It provides for a balance of power and responsibilities between the national and state governments. In some cases, powers are granted exclusively to the national government and in other cases exclusively to the states. In some cases, powers are granted to both the national and the state governments. The same can be said for denied powers. Some are denied to the national government, others are denied to the states, and some are denied to both.

Key Terms

ballot wording	earmarked	popular sovereignty
bill of rights	Equal Protection Clause	Privileges and Immunities of
block grants	federal system of government	Citizenship
categorical grants	Full Faith and Credit	separation of powers
checks and balances	initiative	social contract theory
confederal system of government	Interstate Commerce Clause	statute
constitution	Necessary and Proper Clause	supremacy clause
constitutional convention	ordinances	Tenth Amendment
Due Process Clause	plural executive system	unitary system of government

Notes

[1] Donald S. Lutz, "Toward a Theory of Constitutional Amendment," *American Political Science Review* 88 (June 1994): 355–370.

[2] Texas Constitution, art. 1, sec. 3a.

[3] Cincinnati v. Baskin, 112 Ohio St.3d 279, 2006-Ohio-6422. Retrieved Feb. 29, 2016 from http://www.supremecourt.ohio.gov/rod/docs/pdf/0/2006/2006-Ohio-6422.pdf

[4] Texas Department of Public Safety. (2016). "Texas License to Carry a Handgun Laws and Selected Statues." Retrieved February 27, 2016 from https://www.txdps.state.tx.us/internetforms/Forms/CHL-16.pdf

[5] Fehrendbach, *Lone Star,* 146–147.

[6] del la Teja, Jesus (1991). *A Revolution Remembered: The Memoirs and Selected Correspondence of Juan N. Seguin.* Austin, TX: State House Press: 88; Vazquez, Josefina Zoraida (1997). "The Colonization and Loss of Texas: A Mexican Perspective". In Rodriguez O., Jaime E.; Vincent, Kathryn. Myths, Misdeeds, and Misunderstandings: The Roots of Conflict in U.S.–Mexican Relations. Wilmington, DE: Scholarly Resources Inc.: 50.

[7] Fehrendbach, *Lone Star,* 206.

[8] Ibid., 222–23.

[9] People & Events: Jose Antonio Navarro (1795-1871). (2004, January 30). Retrieved February 25, 2016, from http://www.pbs.org/wgbh/amex/alamo/peopleevents/p_navarro.html

[10] People & Events: Jose Antonio Navarro (1795-1871). (2004, January 30). http://www.pbs.org/wgbh/amex/alamo/peopleevents/p_navarro.html

[11] *Handbook of Texas Online,* Stanley E. Siegel, "Navarro, Jose Antonio." (2010, June 15). http://www.tshaonline.org/handbook/online/articles/fna09.

[12] People & Events: Jose Antonio Navarro (1795-1871). (2004, January 30). http://www.pbs.org/wgbh/amex/alamo/peopleevents/p_navarro.html

[13] McDonald, David R. (2013) *José Antonio Navarro: In Search of the American Dream in Nineteenth-Century Texas.* Watson Caufield and Mary Maxwell Arnold Republic of Texas Series. (pp. 1765). [Google Books version]. http://books.google.com/books?id=mbwLIze2vEAC

[14] People & Events: Jose Antonio Navarro (1795-1871). (2004, January 30). http://www.pbs.org/wgbh/amex/alamo/peopleevents/p_navarro.html

[15] Webster, David J. *Foreigners in Their Native Land: Historical Roots of the Mexican Americans.* UNM Press, 2003, pp. 83–84.

[16] Ibid.

[17] People & Events: Jose Antonio Navarro (1795-1871). (2004, January 30). http://www.pbs.org/wgbh/amex/alamo/peopleevents/p_navarro.html

[18] Ibid.

[19] Ibid.

[20] Ibid.

[21] Ibid.

[22] Handbook of Texas Online, Stanley E. Siegel, "Navarro, Jose Antonio." (2010, June 15). http://www.tshaonline.org/handbook/online/articles/fna09.

[23] Ibid.

[24] Fehrendbach, *Lone Star,* 411–14.

[25] Constitutional amendments ballot general election, 7 November 1978, tax relief amendment, H.J.R. 1.

[26] Book of the States 2015. http://knowledgecenter.csg.org/kc/system/files/1.1_2015.pdf.

[27] *Texas Constitution,* art. 1, sec. 17. http://www.statutes.legis.state.tx.us/Docs/CN/htm/CN.1.htm.

[28] *Texas Constitution,* art. 1. sec. 32. http://www.statutes.legis.state.tx.us/Docs/CN/htm/CN.1.htm.

[29] McGaughy, Lauren. "Court affirms same-sex marriage nationwide; Texas stay lifted." Houston Chronicle. June 26, 2015. Retrieved May 13, 2016 from http://www.chron.com/news/politics/texas/article/Supreme-Court-legalizes-same-sex-marriage-6341493.php.

[30] *Texas Constitution,* art. 2, sec. 1.

[31] *Texas Constitution,* art. 4, sec. 8(b).

[32] *Texas Constitution,* art. 5, sec. 2(b).

[33] Lutz, "Toward a Theory," 359.

[34] Book of the States 2015. http://knowledgecenter.csg.org/kc/system/files/1.1%202015.pdf.

[35] Book of the States, 2015, Table 1.2. http://knowledgecenter.csg.org/kc/content/book-states-2015-chapter-1-state-constitutions

[36] Mary Lucia Barras and Houston Daniel, "Constitutional Convention of 1974," Texas State Historical Association, *Handbook of Texas Online.* http://www.tshaonline.org/handbook/online/articles/mjc07

[37] Lutz, "Toward a Theory," 359.

[38] Ibid.

[39] Ibid., 360.

[40] Ibid.

[41] These figures are as of the general election in November 2015.

[42] Texas Secretary of State Voter Turnout. http://www.sos.state.tx.us/elections/historical/70-92.shtml.

[43] Constitutional amendments ballot general election, 7 November 1978, tax relief amendment, H.J.R. 1.

[44] Book of the States 2015. http://knowledgecenter.csg.org/kc/system/files/1.1_2015.pdf.

[45] *Texas Constitution* through 2015. http://www.tlc.state.tx.us/pubslegref/TxConst.pdf.

[46] *Houston Chronicle,* 8 January 1974.

[47] New State Ice Co. v. Liebmann, 285 U.S. 262 (1932), in http://caselaw.lp.findlaw.com/scripts/getcase.pl?navby=CASE&court=US&vol=285&page=262.

[48] http://www.law.cornell.edu/supct/html/09-1227.ZO.html.

[49] Alexander T. Tabarrok, "Arguments for Federalism," Hastings Law School, University of California, San Francisco, September 20, 2001.

[50] http://www.glaad.org/marriage/doma

[51] Supreme Court of the United States. Syllabus: Obergefell et al. v. Hodges, Director, Ohio Department of Health, et al. http://www.supremecourt.gov/opinions/14pdf/14-556_3204.pdf

[52] "Congress's Power to Define the Privileges and Immunities of Citizenship," Harvard Law Review (Feb. 10, 2015). http://harvardlawreview.org/2015/02/congresss-power-to-define-the-privileges-and-immunities-of-citizenship/

[53] Ibid.

CHAPTER 3

The Texas Legislature

Judge Gideon Tucker of New York wrote in an 1866 court decision, "No man's life, liberty, or property is safe while the legislature is in session." Although Tucker spoke these words within a narrow context, his statement has since been applied more broadly and can aptly describe generalized American distrust of government. This thought has been expressed by many others across the country, including some here in Texas. Its logic suggests the importance of the Texas legislature in state politics and the fear people have of government. The framers of the 1876 constitution distrusted government generally, but they were especially leery of executive authority and gave more power to the legislature than to the executive. (This sentiment harkens back to the drafters of the U.S. Constitution.) This does not mean that the office of governor is insignificant in state politics; governors play an important role. However, what power the governor of Texas possesses is derived primarily from informal sources. Courts and state agencies are also important, but the legislature is the most important institution in state government.

Legislative action is essential for many things. Money cannot be spent, taxes cannot be levied, state laws cannot be enacted or changed, and, in most states, the constitution cannot be amended without the approval of the legislature. Simply put, without actions by the legislature, most state governments would quickly come to a halt. In recent years, the federal government has shifted more responsibility to state governments in some areas while reducing their power in other areas, most notably in health care policy due to passage of the federal Affordable Care Act and in defining marriage due to recent Supreme Court rulings. State governments have also taken the lead on some issues. State legislatures, therefore, continue to fulfill an important policymaking role in the American system.

Chapter Learning Objectives

- Describe the structure, size, and general characteristics of the Texas legislature.

- Explain legislators' qualifications and member demographics.

- Describe reapportionment and redistricting issues in Texas.
- Explain how legislators are elected, including the single-member district method of election.
- Discuss various leadership positions in the Texas legislature.
- Describe the Texas legislature's functions and procedures.

The Structure and Size of the Texas Legislature

Learning Objective: Describe the structure, size, and general characteristics of the Texas legislature.

bicameral

Legislative body that consists of two houses

The Texas legislature is **bicameral**, meaning it consists of two houses: the senate and the house of representatives. The Texas Senate has 31 members elected for four-year overlapping terms; half the membership is elected every two years. In the election that follows reapportionment (essentially the second year of each decade), all seats in the senate are up for election. Lots are then drawn to determine who will stand for reelection in another two years (half of the senate) or in another four years (the other half). The most recent year in which the entire senate stood for election was 2012.

Texas State Capitol Building, Austin, TX

© Mike Norton/Purestock/Superstock

The Texas House of Representatives now consists of 150 members elected for two-year terms. The first house, elected following the adoption of the 1876 constitution, consisted of 93 members. After 1880, a new house seat was added for every 50,000 inhabitants until the membership reached 150 representatives.[1]

State legislatures vary in size. Alaska has the smallest senate, with 20 members, and Minnesota has the largest, with 67 senators. Lower house membership ranges from 40 in Alaska to 400 in New Hampshire. The New Hampshire House of Representatives is unusually large; the next largest house is Pennsylvania's, at 203.[2] The median size for state senates is 38; for the lower houses it is 100.

The Texas House and Senate are both quite small relative to the state's population. As of 2010 (the date of the most recent official census), there were about 811,147 constituents per state senate district and 167,637 constituents for each house district. Only California had more constituents per senator. In terms of the house, only California, New Jersey, and Arizona had more constituents per district. As of 2010, a Texas state senator represented more people than does a U.S. congressman from Texas![3] Population increases in Texas have only increased the number of people represented by each senator and house member.

The size of legislatures raises several issues. Large bodies might better promote the representation of local concerns and diverse interests within the state. However, statewide interests might go unrepresented. Another downside of large legislatures is that they can become inefficient at decision making or, in part because of that inefficiency, be dominated by a few members (especially legislative leaders). This could certainly be said of Texas, where the relatively small senate is considered to be genteel and historically free of individual domination, and the relatively large house is less genteel and has historically been dominated by the speaker. Yet larger bodies would ensure that the senate and especially the house would be more democratic and closer to the people because each state legislator would represent fewer constituents and a smaller geographical area. As one member of the United States's founding generation noted, smaller constituencies might also allow a wider array of people to participate in state politics, rather than just the "rich" or "well born."[4] Debates about this subject at the state level are likely to follow many of the same arguments that the Federalists (such as James Madison of Virginia) and the Anti-Federalists (such as Robert Yates of New York, who is believed to be the author of the famous "Brutus" essays) utilized in their classic battle over the size of the federal legislature.

CORE OBJECTIVE

Communicating Effectively . . .

It has been argued that smaller constituencies might allow a wider array of people to participate in state politics, rather than just the "rich" or "well born." How would you argue in favor of or against this statement?

© George Lavendowski/USFWS

General Characteristics of the Legislature

Learning Objective: Describe the structure, size, and general characteristics of the Texas legislature.

Sessions and Session Length

The Texas legislature meets in **biennial sessions** (every two years) for 140 days in odd-numbered years, beginning in January. Although the national trend has been moving away from biennial sessions toward annual sessions, Texas (along with Montana, Nevada, and North Dakota) has resisted that trend.[5]

biennial session
Legislature meets every two years

©JayJanner/AustinAmerican-Statesman/
AP Images

sine die
Legislature must adjourn at
end of regular session and
cannot continue to meet

extraordinary session
A specially called meeting of
the legislature, outside the
regular session, to discuss
specified matters

special sessions
In Texas, sessions called by
the governor to consider
legislation proposed by the
governor only

Voters in Texas rejected a proposed change to annual sessions in 1969 and again in 1972. In keeping with the traditionalistic/individualistic political culture of the state (see Chapter 1), there is some concern that the more often the legislature meets, the more damage it can do. One political wag once joked that there was a typographical error in the original Texas Constitution and that the founders had actually intended the legislature to meet for two days every 140 years.

At the end of the 140-day session, the Texas legislature must adjourn (**sine die**). It cannot call itself into special session (sometimes called **extraordinary session**) or otherwise extend a session. This lack of ability to call special sessions makes the limit on the regular session even more meaningful. The legislature must finish its work in the prescribed time and then adjourn. Texas is quite typical in limiting the number of days the legislature can stay in session; only 11 states do not limit the length of legislative sessions.[6] However, the Texas legislature's inability to call itself into special session differs from the national trend. Special sessions can be called by either the governor or the legislature in 35 states.[7]

In Texas, only the governor may call **special sessions**. These sessions may not last more than 30 days each. However, there is no limit on the number of special sessions the governor may call. In Texas, the governor determines the subject matter of the session, thus limiting the range of topics the legislature can consider. This gives the governor tremendous power to set the legislature's agenda during special sessions, as well as a bargaining chip to persuade the legislature to do what the governor wants.

The Texas legislature's inability to call itself into special session also gives the governor stronger veto powers. If the governor vetoes a bill after the legislature has adjourned, the veto stands. This, in part, helps to explain why so few gubernatorial vetoes are overridden.

States like Texas that limit the number of regular session days are often forced to resort to special sessions. Budgetary problems, reapportionment issues, school finance, and prison funding have forced the governor to call special sessions in past decades. The most recent special sessions were held in 2013 during the 83rd Legislature. Those three sessions focused on abortion, redistricting, reforming sentencing guidelines for 17-year-olds convicted of capital murder, and funding transportation infrastructure. The first of these sessions was noteworthy for Senator Wendy Davis's long filibuster of a bill that proposed restrictions on abortion. This vaulted Davis into the public eye across the state and nation, although the limitations under consideration in the first special session were ultimately passed during the second special session. Many critics of Texas's biennial sessions point to the frequency of special sessions as evidence that the state needs to change to annual sessions. However, this would not come without trade-offs.

As we will see in Chapter 13, the tax structure in Texas is closely tied to economic conditions in the state. Predicting state revenues for two-year periods is extremely difficult. However, biennial sessions help the legislature avoid

TABLE 3.1	

Advantages and Disadvantages of Annual and Biennial Legislative Sessions

Arguments in Favor of Annual Sessions	Arguments in Favor of Biennial Sessions
The biennial format is unsuitable for dealing with the complex and continuing problems which confront today's legislatures. The responsibilities of a legislature have become so burdensome that they can no longer be discharged on an alternate-year basis.	There are enough laws. Biennial sessions constitute a safeguard against precipitate and unseemly legislative action.
More frequent meetings may serve to raise the status of the legislature, thereby helping to check the flow of power to the executive branch.	Yearly meetings of the legislature will contribute to legislative harassment of the administration and its agencies.
Continuing legislative oversight of the administration becomes more feasible with annual sessions, and that administrative accountability for the execution of legislative policies is more easily enforced.	The interval between sessions may be put to good advantage by individual legislators and interim study commissions, since there is never sufficient time during a session to study proposed legislation.
States may respond more rapidly to new federal laws which require state participation.	The biennial system affords legislators more time to renew relations with constituents, to mend political fences, and to campaign for reelection.
The legislature cannot operate effectively in fits and starts. Annual sessions may help make the policy-making process more timely and orderly.	Annual sessions inevitably lead to a spiraling of legislative costs, for the legislators and other assembly personnel are brought together twice as often.
Annual sessions would serve to diminish the need for special sessions.	

Source: Table reproduced from National Conference of State Legislatures. See (http://www.ncsl.org/legislatures-elections/legislatures/annual-vs-biennial-legislative-sessions.aspx). Credit: William Keefe and Morris Ogul.

reacting rashly in any particular situation because there is often time to reflect on a problem. Moreover, the nature of the perceived problem may change, especially in the economic realm. Therefore, biennial sessions may insulate politicians from being pressured to chase yesterday's economic news, given the lag before policy can be developed and have a meaningful impact. The advantages and disadvantages of annual and biennial sessions are presented in Table 3.1.

Salary

Some citizens believe that, because the legislature meets for only 140 days every two years, it is part-time, and members should be paid accordingly. Legislative pay reflects this attitude. Texas pays the 181 members of the legislature $7,200 a year, plus an additional $150 per day while in session. In years when the legislature meets, the total compensation is $7,200 in salary plus $21,000 in per diem pay, for a total of $28,200. The Texas Ethics Commission sets the per diem rate.[8] Because most legislators must have a second residence in Austin while the session is going on, the per diem pay is not high. Housing and lodging costs in Austin are among the highest in the state. In years when the legislature is not in session, legislators receive their $7,200 in salary and may receive some additional per diem pay for off-session committee work.

Texas legislators' salaries have not been increased since 1975.[9] As Table 3.2 indicates, of the 10 most populous states, Texas legislators are paid the least.

TABLE 3.2

Legislative Salaries in the 10 Most Populous States

State	Base Salary, 2014
California	$90,526
Texas	$ 7,200
Florida	$29,697
New York	$79,500
Illinois	$67,836
Pennsylvania	$84,012
Ohio	$60,584
Georgia	$17,342
North Carolina	$13,951
Michigan	$71,685

Source: National Conference of State Legislatures. See http://www.ncsl.org/research/about-state-legislatures/2014-ncsl-legislator-salary-and-per-diem-table.aspx.

Several attempts to change the state constitutional limit have been rejected by voters, and the low pay contributes to the small number of legislators who consider themselves full-time. Obviously, most legislators have other sources of income. Many are attorneys or successful business people. Low monetary compensation is very much in keeping with the traditionalistic political culture of the state, according to which only the elite should serve in the legislature. Other southern states (Florida, Georgia, and North Carolina) also have relatively low salaries.

Pay in other states varies greatly. The states with the lowest salaries are New Mexico, where there is no pay but a per diem expense based on federal policy ($159 per day), New Hampshire ($100 per year), and Alabama ($10 per day). At the high end is California at $90,526 per year; 16 other states pay a salary of $30,000 or more per year. Per diem expenses also vary greatly among the states. Texas, at $150 per diem, is higher than average.[10] Five states pay no expenses, and some provide a fixed amount for the year. Most states also provide additional expenses and income to people in leadership positions, such as committee chairs and presiding officers. Most states, including Texas, provide money to legislators for office and staff expenses, although there is great variation among the states.

Most citizens are effectively excluded from being legislators because they would not be able to devote the large amount of time that legislative work requires and still earn a living. In reality, it is difficult to serve in the Texas legislature unless one is independently wealthy, employed in some line of work with a flexible schedule (such as consulting), or otherwise financially supported while in the legislature. In Texas, attorney-legislators with cases in court during the legislative session can postpone their cases until the legislature adjourns. In fact, some clients seek out attorney-legislators to represent them expressly because they want to delay court action.

Many states provide retirement benefits for legislators. In Texas, legislators' retirement pay is linked to the salary of state district judges. Somewhat circularly, the salary of district judges is set by the Texas legislature. Therefore, legislators are able to increase their own retirement pay by voting to raise district judges' pay.[11] Legislators may retire at 50 years of age with 12 years of service or at 60 years of age with 8 years of service. According to the current formula, the pension provides $3,220 for every year in office; therefore, a retired lawmaker who served 8 years would receive $25,760 in benefits annually.[12] This relatively high level of pay may prompt some members to retire after achieving the minimum time requirement. They can count on cost-of-living pay raises as the legislature increases the salaries of district judges. Some increase can also come from cost-of-living adjustments given to all state retirees. In short, as an active member of the legislature, you are worth only $600 per month. Retire, and your pay increases substantially. A potential benefit of this system—whether intended or not—is that turnover is incentivized.

Staff and Facilities

The Texas legislature provides generous support for staff assistance. According to the most recent figures available, Texas trailed only two states (Pennsylvania and New York) in the total number of permanent and session-only staff.[13] Most members keep offices open on a full-time basis in their district, and many do so in the state capital as well. At the beginning of each session, senators and representatives establish their monthly allowance for salary and office expenses. During the 84th Legislature (which met in 2015), the maximum amount each senator could spend on staff salaries and travel expenses was $40,000 per month.[14] The monthly allowance for representatives was set at $13,250 while in session and $12,500 while out of session.[15] In addition, standing committees have staff salary support during and between legislative sessions. The Texas Legislative Council has a large professional staff to assist the legislature. It has produced a very informative website (http://www.tlc.state.tx.us/) that provides easy access for citizens during and between legislative sessions. The house also has the House Research Organization, which provides professional assistance to the legislature. The relatively recent renovations of the state capitol building have provided each senator and house member with excellent office and committee hearing space.

Qualifications for Legislators and Member Demographics

Learning Objective: Explain legislators' qualifications and member demographics.

Setting aside for a moment the politics of state legislatures, let us examine the formal and informal qualifications for membership. Formal qualifications include age, citizenship, state residency, district residency, and qualified voter status. Among the 50 states, the lowest minimum age for state house membership is 18 years and the highest minimum age is 25. Many states require candidates seeking office as a state senator to be slightly older (minimum age ranging from 18 to 30).[16] Most states require U.S. citizenship, residency in the state from one to five years, and district residency for a year or less.

A Texas House member must be a U.S. citizen, at least 21 years of age, and must have lived in the state for at least two years and for a minimum of 12 months in the district he or she will represent. To be a Texas state senator, a person must be a U.S. citizen, at least 26 years old before the date of the general election, and must have been a Texas resident for at least five years and a district resident for at least 12 months. In order to stand for office, candidates do not have to be registered to vote; however, they must be "qualified voters."[17] The Texas Constitution specifically states that individuals who have been "convicted of bribery, perjury, forgery, or other high crimes" are not allowed to vote.[18] Therefore, candidates for the state legislature cannot have been convicted of a felony (unless they have been pardoned or had their rights restored by the governor, which is a rare occurrence).

Formal requirements are minimal and do not constitute much of a barrier to holding office. More important are the informal qualifications that may influence who is elected. These include income, education, occupation, knowledge of state politics and current events, communication skills, a desire for public service, and the ability to raise money for campaigns. State legislators tend to be less diverse than the general population. According to a recent study of state legislatures across the country, legislators tend to be older, male, well educated, and professionals (often employed in business).[19]

Cultural changes in the state over recent decades have increased the diversity of the Texas legislature. The number of officeholders who are members of ethnic minority groups has grown, both in Texas and across the nation, due in part to reapportionment and redistricting (see the later section in this chapter for an explanation of these). However, ethnic minority groups are still underrepresented in the Texas

FOCUS ON

The First Hispanic Woman in the Texas Legislature

Hispanic men have served in leadership roles since Texas was a Mexican province and an independent republic. The first Hispanic woman to serve in the Texas state legislature was elected in 1976. Irma Rangel, a Democrat, represented her district for 26 years and became a champion of educational opportunity for her native region of South Texas.

Born in 1931 in Kingsville, along Texas's Gulf Coast, Irma Rangel was the daughter of small-business owners. After graduating from college she began her career in education, first as a teacher, then as a principal. Rangel subsequently obtained a law degree, and her legal career was marked by several milestones: she was one of the first Hispanic women to clerk for a federal district judge, one of the first Hispanic women to serve as an assistant district attorney in Texas, then (after returning to her hometown) became the first female Hispanic attorney to practice in Kingsville.[21]

During her tenure as a member of the Texas House of Representatives, Rangel's primary focus was education. She chaired the House Committee on Higher Education. She secured more than $450 million in funding for border-area colleges and universities, as well as funding

© Texas House of Representatives

for the first professional school in the South Texas region—a College of Pharmacy that now bears her name.[22] In 1997, she co-authored and spearheaded the effort to pass HB 588, which came to be known as the "Top Ten Percent Plan." This legislation "guarantees admission to Texas public universities and colleges for all Texas high school students who graduate in the top ten percent of their class."[23] Rangel favored the policy because it would increase admissions for poor and minority students at Texas universities.

Rangel died in 2003. The many honors bestowed for her work on behalf of South Texas and the Hispanic community include being named to the "Texas Women's Hall of Fame"[24] and having the Public Policy Institute at the University of Texas at Austin posthumously renamed for her in 2009.[25]

Critical Thinking Questions

1. How did Rangel's "Top Ten Percent Plan" impact poor and minority students in terms of college admissions?

2. What are some reasons for and against the idea that it is important for legislators to share the demographic characteristics of their constituents?

legislature when compared with their proportions of the state population. In 2014, Hispanics made up 38.6 percent of Texas's population, yet Hispanic legislators held just 23 percent of legislative seats at the start of the 2015 session. In the same session, African American legislators held 10.7 percent of legislative seats, whereas African Americans composed 12.5 percent of the Texas population. Asian Americans, with 4.5 percent of the state's population, made up 1.7 percent of the legislature. White non-Hispanic legislators filled 64.6 percent of legislative seats in 2015; at that time, white non-Hispanics made up 43.5 percent of total state population.[20]

The number of female lawmakers has also grown dramatically. Though the first U.S. women to serve in a state legislature were elected to the Colorado General Assembly in 1894 (following Colorado's passage of women's suffrage in 1893),[26] Texas women did not gain full voting rights until 1920, when the Nineteenth Amendment to the U.S. Constitution took effect. Because they were not "qualified voters," women could not be elected to the Texas legislature prior to 1920.[27] The first woman elected to the state legislature was Edith Wilmans of Dallas, who served one term in the Texas House starting in 1923.[28] From that point on, few women served until the 1970s.

In 1971, only 344 women (4.5 percent of all legislators nationwide) served in state legislatures. As of 2016, a total of 1,808 state senators and house members, or 24.5 percent of all state legislators nationwide, were women; this represents an increase of more than five times in the number of female legislators since 1971.[29] Map 3.1 ranks the 50 states in terms of percentage of female legislators. In Texas, the number of women legislators has increased

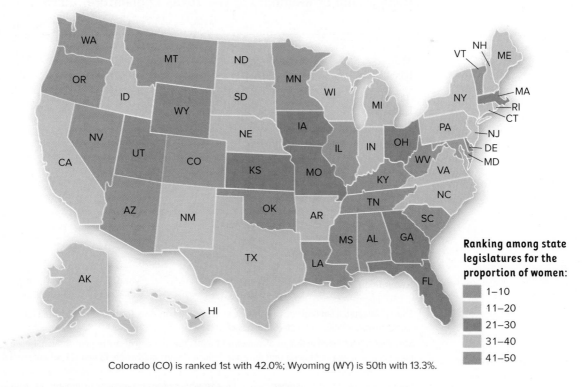

Ranking among state legislatures for the proportion of women:
- 1–10
- 11–20
- 21–30
- 31–40
- 41–50

Colorado (CO) is ranked 1st with 42.0%; Wyoming (WY) is 50th with 13.3%.

MAP 3.1   Percentage of Women Legislators by State

SOURCE: Adapted from Center for American Women and Politics, Women in State Legislatures 2016. http://www.cawp.rutgers.edu/women-state-legislature-2016.

from one woman in each chamber in 1971 to a total of 36 in 2015. This constitutes 20 percent of all seats in the state legislature. At the start of the 84th Legislative Session, 8 of Texas's female legislators were senators, and 28 were state representatives.[30]

Most legislators do not report "legislator" as their full-time occupation, and a recent survey by the National Conference of State Legislatures showed that the number who describe themselves as full-time legislators has been declining nationwide (perhaps due to popular contempt for politicians).[31] Some professions, especially law, allow a person time to devote to legislative duties. The percentage of attorneys in the Texas legislature is much higher than the national average. According to a recent study, 14 percent of legislators nationwide were lawyers, whereas roughly one-third of Texas legislators were lawyers.[32] A higher-than-average percentage of business people are in the Texas legislature, and a lower-than-average percentage of schoolteachers. This is because in Texas, unlike some other states, a state legislator may not hold other compensated public employment. Texas teachers can be paid to teach while also being paid to serve on the "governing body of a school district, city, town, or local governmental district," but they cannot be paid to serve in the state legislature.[33] Table 3.3 provides a demographic breakdown of the 84th Legislature.

TABLE 3.3

Background of Members of the Texas Legislature, 2015

	House	Senate
Sex		
Male	120	23
Female	28	8
Age		
Under 30	0	0
30–39	28	0
40–49	46	3
50–59	35	12
60–69	31	14
70+	8	2
Incumbency		
Incumbents (and previously elected)	124	23
Freshmen	24*	8*
Party Affiliation		
Democrat	51	11
Republican	97	20

Source: Adapted from Legislative Reference Library of Texas. See: (http://www.lrl.state.tx.us/legeLeaders/members/memberStatistics.cfm).

Statistics reflect membership as of January 13, 2015, the first day of the regular session. House membership numbered 148 on that date due to vacant seats in Districts 13 and 123, where special elections were pending.

*Figures include 2 house members and 3 senators whose terms began prior to January 13, 2015, but had served less than one year in that capacity and had not previously participated in a regular session as a member of that legislative body.

Single-Member Versus Multimember Districts

Learning Objective: Explain how legislators are elected, including the single-member district method of election.

Members of legislative bodies are most often elected from **single-member districts**. Under this system, each legislative district has one member in the legislative body. In Texas there are 31 senatorial districts and 150 house districts. The voters living in these districts elect one senator and one congressperson. This system allows for geographical representation—all areas of the state choose representatives to the state legislature. Maps 3.2 and 3.3 show the senate and house districts for the entire state.

In a single-member district system, a party or a candidate need win only a plurality of the vote in a district to win one seat, and districts can be drawn to the advantage of ethnic and political minorities within the county. In countywide districts with multiple seats, a majority of the voters in the county can control all the seats. **Multimember districts** promote majority representation or domination, and single-member districts can promote geographical representation.

single-member districts
Districts represented by one elected member to the legislature

multimember districts
Districts represented by more than one member elected to the legislature

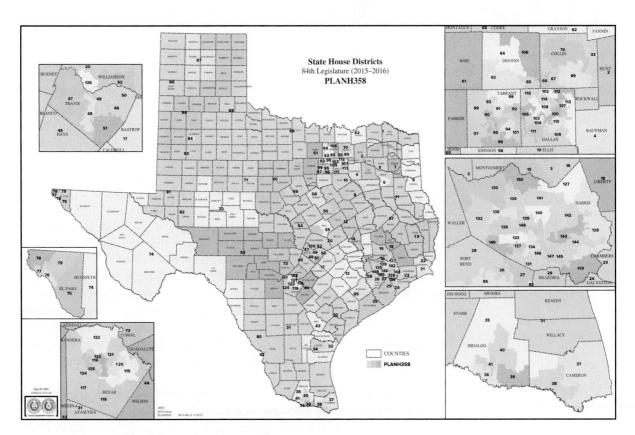

MAP 3.2   Texas State House Districts, 2016

SOURCE: Based on Texas Legislative Council, http://gis1.tlc.state.tx.us/download/House/PLANH358.pdf

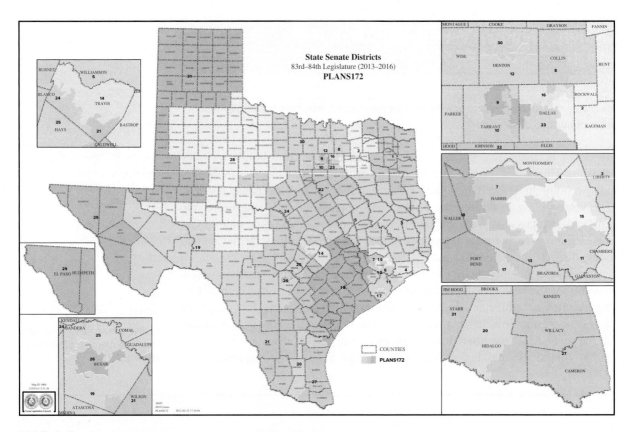

MAP 3.3   Texas State Senate Districts, 2016

SOURCE: Based on Texas Legislative Council, http://gis1.tlc.state.tx.us/download/Senate/PLANS172.pdf.

Depending upon how district lines are drawn, they can also promote racial and ethnic minority representation.

Texas's most recent use of multimember districts was in larger urban counties during the 1970s. In 1971 the Legislative Redistricting Board, which is discussed later in this chapter, drew up a plan after the Texas legislature's plan for house apportionment was found to be unconstitutional. The board created 11 multimember districts with a total of 60 state representatives. (The other 90 state representatives were elected from single-member districts.) For example, Dallas County had 18 representatives elected by ballot place (Place 1 through Place 18). Candidates filed for a ballot place, and voters cast one vote in each of the 18 legislative races. Minority groups contested the plan, pointing out that the system allowed for a majority to elect all the representatives and for minorities to be frozen out. In 1972, a federal court invalidated multimember districts in Texas. Subsequently a new plan, composed entirely of single-member districts, was adopted.

Although Texas no longer uses multimember districts, 10 other states still use them for some legislative elections. In some cases, all electoral districts are represented by more than one officeholder per legislative chamber (such as in the Arizona House); in other cases, only a portion of the districts fill multiple seats in the legislative body (as with the Maryland House).[34] Although multimember

TABLE 3.4

Multimember State Legislative Districts

State	Legislative Body	Number of Multimember Districts	Largest Number of Seats in a District
Arizona	House	30 of 30	2
Idaho	House	35 of 35	2
Maryland	House	43 of 67	3
New Hampshire	House	99 of 204	11
New Jersey	House	40 of 40	2
North Dakota	House	47 of 47	2
South Dakota	House	33 of 35	2
Vermont	Senate	10 of 13	6
	House	46 of 150	2
Washington	House	49 of 49	2
West Virginia	Senate	17 of 17	2
	House	20 of 67	5

Source: Adapted from National Conference of State Legislatures, 2012. See (http://ncsl.typepad.com/the_thicket/2012/09/a-slight-decline-in-legislatures-using-multimember-districts-after-redistricting.html).

election methods vary widely, the most common method is to elect two or three members per district. Voters cast one vote for each seat in the multimember district, and more than one state representative represents each voter. Table 3.4 shows the various multimember district systems used in other states.

Reapportionment and Redistricting Issues

Learning Objective: Describe reapportionment and redistricting issues in Texas.

In Texas, the number of state senators is constitutionally set at 31; therefore, there are 31 (single-member) state senate districts. Likewise, the Texas Constitution stipulates there shall be 150 members in the House of Representatives; therefore, there are 150 (single-member) state house districts. How those representatives are divvied up and what determines the boundary lines for each district are highly controversial matters.

The U.S. Constitution requires that Congress reapportion the seats in the U.S. House of Representatives among the states following each federal census, every 10 years. In other words, Congress determines how many representatives each state will have in the House, based on current population figures. The Texas Constitution similarly requires the state legislature to reapportion the seats following each federal census.[35] Two terms are usually used to describe this process: **reapportionment** and **redistricting**. The term *reapportionment* refers to the process of allocating representatives to districts; *redistricting* is the drawing of district boundary lines. Table 3.5 presents the number of constituents per legislative district in the five most populous U.S. states, as of 2010. Each of the 150 house members in Texas represents about 167,637 people, and each of the 31 state senators represents approximately 811,147 people.

reapportionment
Refers to the process of allocating representatives to districts

redistricting
The drawing of district boundaries

TABLE 3.5

Constituents per Legislative District

	2010 Population	House	Senate
California	37,253,956	465,674	931,349
Texas	**25,145,561**	**167,637**	**811,147**
New York	19,378,102	129,187	307,589
Florida	18,801,310	156,678	470,033
Illinois	12,830,632	108,734	217,468

Apportioning seats in any legislative body is an extremely political process. Each interest group within the state tries to gain as much as possible from the process. Existing powers, such as the majority party in the legislature, will try to protect their advantages. Incumbent legislators will try to ensure their reelection. The primary issues raised by reapportionment are equity of representation, minority representation, and **gerrymandering**, which is drawing district boundary lines for political advantage.

gerrymandering
Drawing district boundary lines for political advantage

Equity of Representation

The issue of *equity of representation* is not new; it is perhaps as old as legislative bodies. Thomas Jefferson noted the problem in the Virginia legislature in the eighteenth century.[36] During most of the nineteenth century, legislative apportionment most often resulted in equity. In other words, each representative represented an equal number of citizens. Some states had provisions that limited the number of seats a single county could have. In the early twentieth century, population shifted from rural to urban areas, and gradually the rural areas were overrepresented in many state legislatures. In the 1960s, only two states (Wisconsin and Massachusetts) had rural/urban representation in the legislature that accurately reflected population distributions in the state.[37]

From 1876 until the 1920s, the Texas legislature made an effort to reapportion the seats after each census. This process was made easier by the addition of one seat for each increase of 50,000 in the population. (The 1876 Constitution initially set state house membership at 93 but allowed for expansion to bring house membership to a maximum of 150 representatives.)[38] However, in 1930 and 1940, the legislature failed to reapportion legislative seats, and no new seats were added. Thus, by 1948, Texas legislative seats had not changed since 1921 despite the fact that major population shifts from rural to urban areas had occurred.[39] This was especially true during and immediately after World War II. These shifts in population created a serious disparity in representation between rural and urban areas of the state. Most urban counties were vastly underrepresented.

In an attempt to resolve the inequality of representation in the state, the Texas Constitution was amended in 1948 to create the **Legislative Redistricting Board (LRB)**. This board was given the authority to redistrict the seats in the Texas House and Senate if the legislature failed to do so. The LRB is made up of the lieutenant governor, the speaker of the house, the attorney general, the comptroller of public accounts, and the commissioner of the general land office.[40]

Legislative Redistricting Board (LRB)
State board composed of elected officials that can draw new legislative districts for the house and senate if the legislature fails to act

The creation of the LRB and the threat of action forced the legislature to act in 1951 and 1961. Representation shifted from rural to urban areas, but large urban counties were still underrepresented. This underrepresentation was due in part to a 1936 amendment to the Texas Constitution that limited the number of representatives any county could have to seven until the population reached 700,000, and then the county could have one additional representative for each 100,000 population.[41] For example, in 1952, had apportionment been based on population alone, each state representative would have represented about 50,000 people. This means that Dallas County would have increased from 7 to 12 representatives, Harris County (Houston) from 8 to 16, and Bexar County (San Antonio) from 7 to 10. However, the number of citizens within each legislative district remained unequal. The constitution also prohibited any county from having more than one senator, no matter how large the county's population.

In 1962, in ***Baker v. Carr***, the U.S. Supreme Court decided that these inequalities in the apportionment of legislative districts denied voters "equal protection of the law" and said that "as nearly as practicable, one man's vote" should be "equal to another's."[42] Two years later, in ***Reynolds v. Sims***, the Court ruled that both houses of state legislatures had to be apportioned based on population. In addition, state legislative districts needed to be roughly equal in population. The Court rejected the analogy to the U.S. Senate, which is based on geographic units, stating "Legislators represent people, not trees or acres. Legislators are elected by voters, not farms or cities or economic interests."[43]

These two cases forced all states to redistrict based on population and led to the "one person, one vote" rule. Over time, the general rule that developed with regard to reapportionment was that the "maximum population deviation between the largest and smallest [legislative] district" must be "less than 10 percent."[44] As of 2015, the largest and smallest senate districts in Texas deviate from the ideal district population by about 4 percent, for a total range of about 8 percent. The largest and smallest house districts deviate from the ideal district population by about 5 percent, for a total range of just under 10 percent.[45]

In 1965, a federal district court ruled that the provisions in the Texas Constitution that limited a county to seven house seats and one senate seat were unconstitutional.[46] This forced the apportionment of both houses of the Texas legislature to be based on population. The political consequences of these court decisions shifted power from rural to urban areas.

Thanks to technological advancements, the issue of equity of representation has been dormant for many decades. Computers have efficiently handled the task of drawing districts with approximately equal numbers of people. However, a recent case before the U.S. Supreme Court raised this issue once again. In *Evenwel v. Abbott,* the plaintiffs argued that Texas's practice of making legislative districts equal in terms of total population violates the "one person, one vote" rule. They contended that, instead, there should be an equal number of eligible voters in each district.[47] If this alternative view had been upheld, states would have been required to change their apportionment and redistricting practices, because non-citizens and children (among others) would have been excluded from relevant population counts when apportioning representatives.[48] In April 2016, the Supreme Court unanimously rejected this challenge,

Baker v. Carr

Court case that required state legislative districts to contain about the same number of citizens

Reynolds v. Sims

Court case that required state legislative districts for both houses to contain about the same number of citizens asserting that "total-population apportionment promotes equitable and effective representation."[49]

Minority Representation

The second issue raised by redistricting is minority representation. According to current law, not only should legislative districts be approximately equal in population, they should also allow for representation of ethnic minorities. This issue was first raised in Texas when the state used multimember districts in some large urban counties. Multimember districts were invalidated by court decisions in the early 1970s.[50]

The 1981 session of the legislature produced a redistricting plan that advanced minority representation in both houses. However, Bill Clements, the Republican governor, vetoed the senate plan, and the Texas Supreme Court invalidated the house plan. This forced the Legislative Redistricting Board to draw new districts. The new plan was challenged in federal courts and by the U.S. Justice Department, which ruled that the plan violated the federal Voting Rights Act because it did not achieve maximum minority representation. African Americans and Hispanics felt that the plan diluted their voting strength. A new plan, drawn up by federal courts, maximized minority representation by creating districts that contained a majority of ethnic minorities—"majority-minority" districts.

Similar battles took place in the 1990s and into the 2000s. Minority voters became better represented, and minority candidates gained many seats in the state legislature (as did Republicans, who in 1996 managed to take control of the Texas Senate for the first time in more than 100 years). In 2008, there were 16 African Americans in the Texas legislature. This represented 9 percent of the total seats, which was equivalent to the average proportion of African American legislators across all 50 states.[51] In 2009, there were 37 Hispanic state legislators in Texas, composing 20 percent of the total seats—the third highest percentage of any state in the country (after New Mexico and California).[52] The number of Hispanic legislators increased to 41 by 2015. The majority of these were Democrats, with only five Republicans. In 2015, there were 19 African Americans, 17 of whom were Democrats, and three Asian American legislators (2 Democrats and 1 Republican).[53]

Political and Racial Gerrymandering

political gerrymandering
Drawing legislative districts to the advantage of a political party

racial gerrymandering
Legislative districts that are drawn to the advantage of a minority group

Political gerrymandering is the drawing of legislative districts to achieve the political advantage of one political party over another. The term also has been applied to the practice of creating minority districts—**racial gerrymandering**. The practice of gerrymandering dates to the early days of our nation. In 1812, Governor Elbridge Gerry of Massachusetts drew a legislative district shaped somewhat like a salamander. A political cartoonist for a Boston newspaper dressed up the outlines of the district with eyes, wings, and claws and dubbed it a "Gerrymander."

With the rise of the Republican Party, political gerrymandering in Texas has intensified. Until 2003, Republicans repeatedly charged that the Democrats reduced the number of potential Republican districts, especially in suburban areas. In the 1980s, Republicans forged alliances with minority groups. Republicans supported the creation of racially gerrymandered majority-minority districts, and minority groups supported the Republican efforts. As we shall see subsequently, the creation of majority–minority districts has aided the Republicans as well as minorities.

A legal challenge to the practice of racial gerrymandering was reviewed by the U.S. Supreme Court in 1996 in *Bush v. Vera*. This challenge was aimed at U.S. congressional districts, rather than state house and senate districts, but the ruling could be applied to the latter as well. In striking down three newly created majority-minority U.S. congressional districts in Texas, the Supreme Court affirmed a lower court finding that these districts were "formed in utter disregard for traditional redistricting criteria" of compactness and regularity and that the district shapes were "ultimately unexplainable" in terms other than race, resulting in "unconstitutional racial gerrymandering."[54] Justice O'Connor, who drafted the Court's majority opinion, explained that "deviations from traditional districting principles . . . cause constitutional harm insofar as they convey the message that political identity is, or should be, predominantly racial."[55] In a rare concurrence with her own opinion, Justice O'Connor added that while the "Voting Rights Act requires the States and the courts to take action to remedy the reality of racial inequality in our political system . . . the Fourteenth Amendment requires us to look with suspicion on the excessive use of racial considerations by the government."[56] The Court did not object to states' considering race when drawing district lines or to their intentionally creating majority-minority districts; however, using race as the predominant factor in drawing districts, while subordinating other considerations, was found to be unconstitutional.[57]

In April 1999, the U.S. Supreme Court, in ***Hunt v. Cromartie***,[58] allowed the use of political gerrymandering in drawing legislative districts. Having affirmed in an earlier case that race could not be the primary factor in determining the makeup of legislative districts, the Court found that drawing district boundaries based on political affiliation or partisan makeup was justifiable and constitutional. Therefore, creating a "safe" Democratic or Republican seat was permissible.

This was an obvious departure from the past practice of packing minorities into "safe" districts. Although political party affiliation and race are often correlated, it is no longer permissible to create legislative districts based on racial considerations alone. The fine art of gerrymandering has been with us since the development of political parties and will surely remain a part of the political landscape for years to come. How to interpret constitutional guidelines when conducting the redistricting process is a matter of ongoing debate.

The original Gerrymander in Massachusetts, 1812

© *Gilbert Stuart/Bettmann/Corbis*

Hunt v. Cromartie

Court case that ruled while race can be a factor, it could not be the primary factor in determining the makeup of legislative districts

© *Editorial Image, LLC/Alamy*

CORE OBJECTIVE

Being Socially Responsible . . .

To what extent should legislators use race when redistricting? Do you think redistricting is an appropriate tool to increase intercultural competency? Why or why not?

Redistricting in 2001

In 2001, reapportionment had just occurred due to the 2000 census, and Texas had gained two additional seats in the U.S. Congress for a total of 32. The legislature was again faced with the task of redistricting. Both parties hoped to gain seats through the redistricting process, and the fight between Democrats and Republicans over these seats added to the controversy in the legislature.

With seats almost evenly divided between the parties in both the Texas House and Senate, even the shift of a few seats had the potential to change party control in either body. As the session wore on, the battle over redistricting intensified. Republican Party activists were more vocal than the Democrats in their criticism of the plans presented by the House and Senate Redistricting Committees. GOP chair Susan Weddington was especially critical of the house plan. She referred to the plan as a ". . . thinly veiled attempt to protect the careers of Speaker Pete Laney and incumbent politicians." The chair of the House Redistricting Committee, Republican Delbert Jones of Lubbock, denied that this was the committee's intent. Weddington said, "The Republican Party supports a fair redistricting plan that puts the interests of the people of Texas ahead of protecting incumbent politicians."[59] Some house Republicans were pressured by their party and threatened with having to face opponents in primary races if they did not support the GOP position on redistricting.

Some Republican attacks were also aimed at house committee chairs who were Republicans. These committee chairs were charged with supporting a plan that would keep current house speaker Pete Laney in power so they could keep their committee chairs in the next session should Laney be reelected. If a Republican replaced Laney in the next session, these Republican chairs anticipated they would lose their positions. (In fact, Laney was replaced by Republican Tom Craddick as house speaker in 2003.)

At the same time, representatives of ethnic minorities felt that they should gain more seats. The Mexican American Legal Defense and Education Fund and the League of United Latin American Citizens complained that the house committee recommendations did not take into account the growth in minority populations. Part of this dissatisfaction stemmed from the fact that the fastest growing areas of the state from 1990 to 2000 were in the predominantly white/Anglo suburbs of Houston, San Antonio, and Dallas. Although the inner cities of Houston and Dallas gained population, they did not increase as significantly as the surrounding suburban areas. In 1990, each house member represented about 109,000 people; by 2002, the number was approximately 139,000. For the senate, the numbers increased from 550,000 in 1990 to 673,000 in 2002. Harris County lost one of the 25 representatives it had in 1990. The 2000 population of Harris County was 3,400,578. Divide this by 25, and the result is 136,023, which is a deviation of 2.15 percent below the "ideal district" of 139,000. Although this is within the margin of acceptability, the Republican-controlled Legislative Redistricting Board gave the seat to the more Republican-leaning suburban area of Fort Bend County. Dallas and Fort Worth did not lose seats, but the suburban areas gained seats. The suburbs in the Austin (Travis County) area also gained seats.

There is one other important difference in reapportionment in the 2001 session of the legislature. In the 1980s and 1990s, the federal Voting Rights Act required state legislatures to consider racial makeup of districts. Recall that in

April 1999, the U.S. Supreme Court in *Hunt v. Cromartie* had ruled that race can be a factor, but not the predominant factor, in drawing legislative districts. In the same case, the Court again allowed the use of political party affiliation as a factor in drawing district lines (political gerrymandering). As indicated previously, minority groups tend to vote Democratic, and it may be possible to achieve the same results by using party rather than race in drawing district lines.

The Texas House and Senate adjourned the 2001 session without approving new redistricting plans. (At this time, Senate rules required a two-thirds, or 21-member, approval to consider a bill on the senate floor. The plan voted out of committee did not receive enough support for floor consideration, so it died. The senate also failed to consider the house-approved plan.) As a result of this inaction, the Legislative Redistricting Board was then left to establish new districts for the Texas House and Senate. The LRB, consisting of the lieutenant governor, speaker of the house, comptroller, land commissioner, and attorney general, was dominated by Republicans. Only one member of this board was a Democrat: Speaker Laney, who was effectively frozen out of the discussion. Lt. Governor Ratliff objected to the proceeding. The remaining three members, Attorney General Cornyn, Land Commissioner Dewhurst, and Comptroller Rylander, proceeded to draw districts that greatly favored Republicans. This board, however, cannot redistrict U.S. Congressional districts, and Governor Perry refused to call a special session for the legislature to settle that issue. Instead, he said the matter was best left to the courts.

Therefore, the congressional district map used in the 2002 election cycle was drawn by a special three-judge federal court. While this appeared to have favored Republicans in a majority of the districts, five districts that heavily favored Republicans were instead won by Democrats. Democrats managed to win election in 17 of the 32 districts, leaving the Republicans with 15 districts. With these unexpected results, U.S. House Majority Leader Tom DeLay (a Republican from Sugarland, Texas) forwarded a plan to the Texas legislature to redraw the 2001 court-ordered congressional district map during the 2003 session. Redistricting normally takes place every decade following the new federal census. This mid-decade redistricting, or re-redistricting, was unprecedented.

2003 and the Texas Eleven

In the 2003 session, Republicans controlled both houses of the Texas legislature for the first time in 130 years. In part because of redistricting efforts by the Legislative Redistricting Board, Republicans had gained 16 state house seats and 3 state senate seats, for a total of 88 house and 19 senate seats in 2003. They used their newfound control to redistrict the state's 32 U.S. Congressional districts. What follows describes how this happened and is an interesting case study of both the politics of redistricting and how the legislature works.

The Texas House, under the direction of newly elected Speaker Tom Craddick (R), took up the cause, and a new congressional district map was reported out of committee. The Texas Senate, under the direction of newly elected Lt. Governor David Dewhurst (R), did not debate the issue during the regular session because of the senate's two-thirds rule, which required 21 members of the senate to agree to allow a bill to be considered by the whole senate. Senate Democrats, who numbered 12 members, refused to consider any bills.

The Texas House rules state that a quorum is two-thirds of the whole membership, or 100 members. A quorum must be present before the house can act. During the last week of the regular session in 2003, 52 Democratic House members left the state and took up residence in the Holiday Inn in Ardmore, Oklahoma. This boycott by the Democrats effectively prevented the house from acting, and the re-redistricting bill failed to pass. The boycott infuriated most of the state and national Republican leadership. Texas Rangers were sent to try to get the renegades back to Austin, but all efforts failed.

Despite much statewide opposition to continuing the re-redistricting battle, on June 19, 2003, Governor Rick Perry called a special session of the legislature, to begin June 30, to reconsider the re-redistricting proposal. This move only heightened the degree of acrimony developing in the state at the time. For example, Clay Robison, an editorial writer for the *Houston Chronicle,* argued that the special session to examine redistricting was a "waste" of tax money. He also suggested that it showed Perry either had "a stubborn, partisan streak made meaner by his pique over the Democratic walkout" or that "he is a tail-wagging lap dog, eager to play 'go fetch' for the right wing of his party."[60] Despite many misgivings, on July 8, 2003, the Texas House quickly passed a new congressional map by a highly partisan vote of 83 to 62.

In this first special session, Lt. Governor Dewhurst left in place the two-thirds rule required to consider a bill on the senate floor. Because the Democrats held 12 seats in the senate, they could block the senate from considering the house-passed bill; however, several Democrats at first withheld their support for blocking the legislation. Some minority Democratic senators were offered passage of legislation favorable to their districts. Others were offered "safe" congressional seats in exchange for favoring re-redistricting. On July 15, 2003, Senator Bill Ratliff, a Republican from Mount Pleasant, joined 10 Democrats in blocking the re-redistricting bill.

Lt. Governor Dewhurst was pressured to drop the two-thirds rule; however, many senators, both Democratic and Republican, opposed that change. Newspapers across the state urged Dewhurst to hold the line and not change the rules. Statewide polls showed Governor Perry losing support over the redistricting issue.

On July 28, 2003, 11 Texas Senate Democrats fled to Albuquerque, New Mexico. Two things prompted this action. First, they anticipated that the governor was going to adjourn the first special session early and call a second special session immediately thereafter (which he did). The rumor was that the senate sergeant-at-arms had been ordered to lock the senators in the senate chamber as soon as the session was called to keep them from busting (preventing) a quorum. Second, Lt. Governor Dewhurst had stated he would suspend the two-thirds rule for future sessions.

While the Texas governor and lieutenant governor were livid at the actions of these Democratic senators, the Democratic governor and lieutenant governor of New Mexico were delighted and welcomed the 11 runaways (who came to be called the "Texas Eleven") to their state. Texas Republicans and Democrats held dueling press conferences, each accusing the other of wrongdoing.

A few hours after the second special session began and a quorum was present in the house, the Texas House passed the same redistricting bill that had been passed during the first special session. The quick passage of the bill led some

Democrats to question the fairness of the process because no debate or discussion was allowed.

The Republican senators in Austin attempted to force the return of the 11 Democrats by imposing fines. In the end, each of the stray senators was fined $57,000, and they had their parking spaces revoked. Some have questioned the legality of this action because a quorum was not present and, technically, the senate could not take action. The fines were later removed on the condition that there would be no more boycotts until the end of the term in January 2005.

The 11 Democratic senators stayed in New Mexico until the 30-day special session expired on August 26, 2003. They did not immediately return to the state out of fear they would be arrested and taken to Austin for a third special session call. On September 3, 2003, the stalemate was broken when Senator John Whitmire, a Democrat from Houston, broke the boycott and returned to Texas.

On September 10, 2003, Governor Perry called a third special session of the legislature to consider redistricting. Some were surprised that a third session was called because a state poll by Montgomery and Associates, an independent research firm, had indicated that most Texans were opposed to redistricting. In fact, only 47.9 percent of self-identified Republicans supported redistricting. The poll also found the governor had a negative job approval rating.

The house and senate quickly passed different redistricting bills, which went to a conference committee. These differences led to infighting among the Republicans, with the main issue being congressional districts in West Texas. House Speaker Tom Craddick wanted a district dominated by his hometown of Midland, but Senator Robert Duncan, Republican from Lubbock, wanted to keep Midland in a district with Lubbock.

The fight over the West Texas districts became so intense that Governor Perry and U.S. Congressman Tom DeLay got involved. Eventually, Congressman DeLay was seen marching between house and senate chambers in the capitol. He claimed he was there as a diplomat, but most believed he was there as an enforcer. In the end, an entirely new map, unseen before DeLay's arrival, was produced by the conference committee and accepted by both houses in mid-October 2003.

Although many predicted that the DeLay redistricting map would be found in violation of the federal Voting Rights Act because it split minority voters rather than concentrating them into majority–minority districts, this did not occur. U.S. Attorney General Ashcroft issued a one-sentence letter saying that he did not object to the new map. At the time, Democratic Texas House members claimed that the professional staff of the U.S. Justice Department objected to the map, and they asked that the report be made public; however, it was not released. When it was later released, they were proven right.

A three-judge special court consisting of two Republicans and one Democrat approved the map, voting along party lines. The logic that prevailed, in essence, set aside the Voting Rights Act by allowing minority voters to be divided into many congressional districts, providing the intent is to divide Democrats, not to divide minority voters. Partisan gerrymandering is considered legal. Because most minorities vote for Democrats, they can be split into many districts as long as the gerrymandering is partisan in intent. This established a new standard for redistricting.

Governor Perry, Congressman Tom DeLay, and the Republicans were successful in their redistricting efforts. In the 2004 election, the Republicans gained five U.S. Congressional seats and controlled the Texas delegation to Congress (21 to 11). Democrats had entered the decade with a 17 to 15 majority, but all targeted Democrats were either defeated or chose not to run. Only Congressman Chet Edwards won reelection in District 17.

In 2006, the U.S. Supreme Court heard an appeal to the DeLay redistricting in *LULAC v. Perry*. They ruled that nothing in the Constitution prohibited redistricting at mid-decade. They did, however, find that the voting strength of minorities had been diluted in one district. To resolve this problem, the boundary lines of five Congressional districts were adjusted.

It is interesting to note that on the national level, Republicans increased their majority in the U.S. House of Representatives by six seats. Five of these came from the redistricting effort in Texas. Without this redistricting, the Republicans might not have retained control of the U.S. House of Representatives in the 109th Congress, which began in 2005.

Because of the continuing nationwide controversy over redistricting, some states have moved away from allowing state legislatures to develop the new redistricting maps and have placed this task in the hands of an independent commission. Although it is difficult to generalize on the various forms of these commissions, in some states, commissions are appointed and the members are not members of the state legislatures, state employees, or elected officials. These commissions draw district maps that must be accepted by the legislature and are subject to review by the courts. Other states have commissions, but the members are elected or appointed officials. For example, the Texas commission is made up entirely of elected officials. It is doubtful that Texas will move in the direction of a commission independent of the legislature.

Redistricting in 2011 and Beyond

The 2010 census showed that Texas's population had increased by more than four million people since the year 2000.[61] As a result, Texas gained four seats from the 2010 apportionment, for a total of 36 seats in the United States Congress. The necessary redistricting process was put into motion for the 2012 election cycle. Three maps needed to be redrawn in 2011: the Congressional districts of Texas, the state of Texas House of Representative districts, and the state of Texas Senate districts. Redistricting can also have an impact on local election districts. However, because local districts often have their own specific rules, they are not within the scope of this discussion.

Debates in the Texas legislature over the 2011 redistricting were intense. The initial maps drawn by the Texas legislature favored Republicans by creating three additional Republican seats and one additional Democratic seat. Then-Texas Attorney General Greg Abbott submitted the maps to a federal court in an attempt to gain preclearance for them, as was required under Section 5 of the 1965 Voting Rights Act. (Texas was one of a number of southern states required to submit redistricting maps for federal approval, or "preclearance," because of a past history of discrimination in regard to voting and elections.) Under this act, redistricting could not discriminate in purpose or effect against minority populations. Concerns were raised about the maps because the majority of population growth in Texas had occurred in minority, and most notably Hispanic, populations. Thus the maps were potentially discriminatory in nature by not reflecting these demographic shifts. A series of legal battles ensued.

A federal court determined that the new maps were in violation of the Voting Rights Act and redrew the district maps in a way that would increase minority as well as Democratic power to some extent. The state of Texas then took these redrawn maps to the U.S. Supreme Court, whereupon the court determined, in *Perry v. Perez* (2012), that in redrawing the maps the federal court must give additional deference to the desires of state policy and the state legislature.[62] Because they did not, the maps needed to be redrawn. So the federal court drew another set of maps that fell more in line with the Texas legislature's initial redrawn maps. These court-ordered interim maps were known as Plan S172 (Texas Senate), Plan H309 (Texas House), and C235 (Congressional).[63] The Texas legislature also created a new set of maps and sought an order for declaratory judgment by the federal court to enact them.

In August 2012, the federal court determined that the maps drawn by the Texas legislature could not receive preclearance. The state appealed this decision to the U.S. Supreme Court. In the meantime, the court-ordered and court-drawn interim maps were used for the 2012 election cycle. The U.S. Supreme Court denied a request by the League of United Latin American Citizens to stop the implementation of these interim maps on the grounds that the maps continued to violate Section 5 of the Voting Rights Act. In June 2013, in the landmark case *Shelby County v. Holder,* the U.S. Supreme Court struck down a portion of the Voting Rights Act. The Court determined that Section 4, which laid out the formula used to determine which states were subject to the preclearance requirement, was unconstitutional.[64] Without a formula in place to identify it as a jurisdiction subject to preclearance, the state of Texas no longer needed to obtain federal approval for its district maps.

This ruling, however significant, has surely not put a lasting end to all squabbles over redistricting in Texas. The 83rd Legislature—albeit with some changes to the state house plan, now dubbed Plan H358—adopted the interim maps that had been in use since 2012 as the permanent district maps. A panel of federal judges affirmed that those same maps would be used for the 2016 election cycle.[65] Legislation related to redistricting was introduced during the 84th Legislature, including a proposal to establish a "Texas Congressional Redistricting Commission" to redistrict Texas's U.S. Congressional seats, but none of these bills passed.[66]

In addition to the impact that the redrawn maps have on partisan and minority voting, they have had a significant impact on a number of incumbent Texas House members whose districts, once considered safe, became highly contested. For example, in areas of East Texas, some longtime incumbents lost large amounts of district size. Chuck Hopson, from District 11, lost about 40 percent of his district, and Wayne Christian, from District 9, lost about 80 percent of his. In 2012, both incumbents lost in elections to newcomers—Hopson in a runoff election and Christian in a primary election. Some Texas lawmakers believe the legislative redistricting is largely at fault for this result.[67] Because of the numerous legal hurdles encountered during the redistricting process, it may be a number of years before final decisions are made in regard to the Texas redistricting maps.

Getting Elected

Learning Objective: Explain how legislators are elected, including the single-member district method of election.

Now that we know something about who is elected to state legislatures, we'll turn our attention to what it takes to win an election. As will be discussed in Chapter 8, running for office can be costly. Although most candidates for the state legislature face little or no opposition in either the primary or general election, there are exceptions. Even when candidates do not face opposition, they are likely to collect large amounts of money from various groups, especially from **PACs**.

In the 2014 election cycle, 319 candidates competed for 150 seats in the Texas House. Taken together, these candidates raised a total of $65.6 million. In the state senate, only 18 seats were up for grabs. The 68 candidates running for those seats raised approximately $29 million.[68] On average, the latter figure amounts to more than $400,000 in campaign contributions collected by each candidate - much higher than the national average of $148,144 per candidate for state senates.[69]

Members of the Texas legislature are prohibited from accepting campaign contributions during the legislative session (as well as in the 30 days before a session starts and for 20 days after adjournment).[70] Most money comes from contributors who live outside the senator's or representative's district. Races in both the house and senate are financed by PACs and large contributors. In some cases, candidates for state legislature receive contributions from out-of-state sources as well.[71]

political action committee (PAC)

Spin-offs of interest groups that collect money for campaign contributions and other activity

Competition for House and Senate Seats

As previously noted, in the one-party Democratic era in Texas (1870s to 1970s), most of the competition for offices took place within the Democratic Party primary. Today, competition is more likely in the general election, but many seats are still in relatively safe districts. In the 2012 election, 64 candidates ran unopposed for seats in the Texas House. The remaining 86 house races had at least two candidates running. However, some of these contests involved third-party candidates; only 52 of the 150 total house races featured two major party candidates squaring off against each other.[72] In recent decades, the level of competition in Republican Party primary elections has also increased. Some of this competition was related to former house speaker Craddick, who was known to seek opponents for those members who opposed his agenda and threatened his continuation as speaker. Even with this increase in competition, most incumbents still survive election challenges.

Party voting is a measure of the strength of a political party in the legislative district, based on voter support for the party's candidates in previous elections. This measure also indicates the level of party competition. Studies of party competition for seats in the U.S. House and Senate define **noncompetitive districts** as any district in which either party receives 55 percent or more of the votes. A district in which party vote is between 44 and 54 percent is considered competitive.[73] The measure used here to gauge party competitiveness is the combined vote received by either party for all offices/candidates in the district in the previous general election. This is the composite party vote. Thus, a house or senate district in which the Republican Party candidates for statewide

noncompetitive districts

Districts in which a candidate from either party wins 55 percent or more of the vote

office collectively received 55 percent or more of the votes is considered a safe Republican district. Table 3.6 shows the number of competitive and noncompetitive seats in the Texas House and Senate from the 2014 General Election.

After party competition, the second variable we can use to describe districts is racial composition, which is the percentages of minority and nonminority populations in the district. If we compare these two variables (party competition and minority population in the district) using some simple statistics, we can see that most Texas House and Senate seats fall into two categories: noncompetitive Republican Anglo districts and noncompetitive Democratic minority districts. The creation of majority-minority districts results in the creation of safe Republican districts. Because minority support for Democratic candidates is always very high, concentrating minorities in districts also concentrates Democratic Party support in these districts. Many remaining districts are therefore noncompetitive Republican districts. Other studies have found the same is true for U.S. congressional districts.[74]

One reason for the low competition in Texas legislative races is racial and political gerrymandering. Competition in such districts is most likely to occur at the primary level and when there is no incumbent. Competition in the general elections is less likely. Safe Democratic districts exist primarily in two places: South Texas, where there are high concentrations of Hispanics, and East Texas, the traditional Democratic stronghold. Republicans are strong in the Panhandle and the Hill Country. Metropolitan areas of the state also contain both safe Democratic and safe Republican districts, with Democrats in the inner city and Republicans in the suburbs.

TABLE 3.6

Competitive and Noncompetitive Seats in the Texas House and Senate, 2016 Election

	Safe Democratic	Safe Republican	Competitive	Unopposed*
House	20 (13%)	39 (26%)	9 (6%)	82 (55%)
Senate	4 (25%)	5 (31%)	0 (0%)	7 (44%)

Source: Adapted from Texas Secretary of State 2016 General Election, Election Night Returns (https://enrpages.sos.state.tx.us/public/nov08_319.htm) and *The New York Times* (http://www.nytimes.com/elections/results/texas).

*"Unopposed" means a candidate ran without opposition from the other major party but may or may not have been opposed by a third-party candidate; unopposed candidates were also included in the "safe" count for their respective party.

CORE OBJECTIVE

Thinking Critically. . .

Both demographics and voting patterns have changed in Texas, and some districts have become more competitive, especially for Democrats in South Texas and in inner-city districts. Discuss what these shifts mean for future elections and the composition of the Texas House and Senate. Reference Table 3.6 in your answer.

Source: National Park Service

Each election year, only about one-third of House members face opposition in the general election. Most members who seek reelection are reelected. Even fewer face opposition in the primary elections. Unless legislators are in a competitive district, they can generally stay as long as they like. Most voluntarily retire after a few years of service.

Term Limits

Although turnover in state legislatures nationwide is quite high, many states have adopted formal **term limits** for state legislators in order to legally limit long tenures in any particular seat. This trend was particularly pronounced in the 1990s, when many states enacted term limits either by constitutional amendment or by statute, for both house and senate seats. These limits were approved despite the fact that self-limiting of terms was working for many years. For example, "nationally, 72 percent of the house members and 75 percent of the senators who served in 1979 had left their respective chamber by 1989."[75] Currently, 15 states impose term limits on legislators.[76] The Texas legislature is not term limited.

Turnover in State Legislatures

Turnover refers to the number of new members of the legislature each session. One might suspect, based on the general lack of competition for Texas legislative seats, that there would be low turnover of the membership. However, this is not the case. Turnover is high in Texas, as it is in all state legislatures, and normally it is higher for the lower house than for the upper chamber.[77]

In the 1980s and 1990s, some states had very high turnover due to the imposition of term limits. Excluding those years, the average turnover in state legislatures around the country is around 25 percent for the lower house and about 15 percent for the upper house.[78] Table 3.7 lists the number of years of service

TABLE 3.7

Years of Service of Members of the 84th Legislature

	House		Senate	
	Number	**Percent**	**Number**	**Percent**
20+	14	9%	6	19%
14–19	14	9%	2	6%
8–13	29	20%	7	23%
1–7	67	45%	8	26%
1st	24*	16%	8**	26%

Source: Adapted from Texas House of Representatives. See: (http://www.house.state.tx.us/_media/pdf/members/senior.pdf) and Legislative Reference Library of Texas. See: (http://www.lrl.state.tx.us/legeLeaders/members/senior84.pdf)

*Includes 2 house members whose terms began prior January 13, 2015, but who had served less than one year and had not previously participated in a legislative session.

**Includes 3 senators whose terms began prior January 13, 2015, who had served less than one year in the senate, but who had previously served at least one term in the Texas House of Representatives.

for members of the Texas legislature. At the start of the 2015 session, there were 24 freshmen members in the house and 8 new members of the senate.[79] During the previous legislative session in 2013, there were 41 freshmen house members (the largest contingent of new members in several decades) and 6 new senators.[80]

Over time, turnover rates in Texas are very high. Turnover is not due mainly to electoral defeat; most members voluntarily retire from service. Retirement around the country is prompted by generous retirement benefits for eligible members, relatively low pay, the lack of professional staff assistance, redistricting, the requirements of the job, the demands upon one's family, fundraising demands, and the rigors of seeking reelection.[81] Some use the office as a stepping-stone to higher office and leave to become members of Congress or take statewide office. In Texas, the retirement benefits are excellent for those serving a relatively low number of years in the legislature, so leaving office can actually be financially wise.

Why is turnover significant in state legislatures? It can be argued that high turnover contributes to the amateurish nature of state legislatures (which could be good or bad, depending on your view). In recent years, this has been especially significant in those states with term limits. If 20 to 25 percent of the members are new each session, these new members are learning the rules and finding their way. This allows a few "old timers" to control the legislative process.

Leadership Positions in the Texas Legislature

Learning Objective: Discuss various leadership positions in the Texas legislature.

In any legislative body, those holding formal leadership positions possess considerable power to decide the outcome of legislation. In the Texas legislature, power is very much concentrated in the hands of two individuals: the speaker of the house and the lieutenant governor. These two individuals control the output of legislation.

Speaker of the House

The members of the house elect the Speaker of the Texas House of Representatives, by majority vote, for a two-year term. The election of the **speaker of the house** is the members' first formal act in each legislative session. The secretary of state presides over the election, and only occasionally is the outcome of this election in doubt. The identity of the speaker is generally known far in advance of the beginning of the session, and this individual spends considerable time lining up supporters before the session begins. In all but a few cases, the person elected is a long-time member of the house and has support from current members. When one-third of the members are new, the person elected speaker may also have to gain support from some of these new members. It is illegal for candidates

speaker of the house
Member of the Texas house, elected by the house members, who serves as presiding officer and generally controls the passage of legislation

for speaker to formally promise members something in exchange for their vote, but key players in the election of the speaker often receive choice committee assignments.

It should be noted that for many years, the Texas House of Representatives operated on a bipartisan basis. In the 2001 session of the legislature, Democrats controlled the house, and Democrat Pete Laney was speaker. Bipartisanship was much more apparent in committee assignments and the overall tone of the session. In the 2003 through 2007 sessions, much of this bipartisanship disappeared when the Republicans held a majority of the seats in the house and Representative Tom Craddick became speaker. In the 2003 session, partisanship was the order of the day, the tone set by Speaker Craddick. Representative Dawnna Dukes (Democrat from Houston) stated that the Republicans did not feel the need to compromise on issues because they controlled a majority of the seats. However, this sentiment may have reflected partisanship itself and the historic nature of the shift in house leadership as much as anything.

Incumbent speakers are almost always reelected. A new speaker is typically chosen only after the death, retirement, or resignation of a sitting speaker. Traditionally, speakers served for two terms and retired or moved to higher offices. From 1951 to 1975, no speaker served more than two terms. In 1975, Billy Clayton broke with this tradition and served for four terms. Gib Lewis, who succeeded Clayton, served for five terms, as did Laney.[82]

Tom Craddick was first elected speaker for the 2003 session. He was the first Republican speaker since Reconstruction. After serving three terms as speaker, Craddick was not reelected in 2009. In the 2008 election, the Republicans barely held onto a majority (76/74). Before the 2009 session even began, a long-standing "Anybody but Craddick" movement gained momentum and ultimately led to the election of San Antonio-area legislator Joe Straus as the speaker for the 81st Legislature. The move to oust Speaker Craddick began in earnest in early January 2009 when what journalist Ross Ramsey called the "Polo Road Gang" of 11 moderate Republican legislators met at the Austin home of Rep. Byron Cook to discuss a challenge to the speaker and to select an alternative candidate. Straus, a moderate Republican first elected to the House in 2005, was chosen on the fifth ballot as a compromise selection. This Polo Road Gang of Republicans was then joined by a few more Republicans and 65 Democrats to push Craddick out.[83] It did not ultimately require much of a push, because Craddick quickly decided not to seek reelection once the writing was on the wall.[84]

Straus has been speaker since that time. Speaker Straus was a departure from past speakers in that he had served only two terms in the house before being elevated to the role of speaker. He had a shaky start but finished the session with some minor success. In the 2010 elections, the Republicans increased their majority from 78 members to 101, and Straus was reelected to a second term as speaker in 2011. He was subsequently elected to his third and fourth terms as speaker in 2013 and 2015, respectively. However, he has earned the ire of conservative and Tea Party Republicans who would like to see a speaker who they think is more in line with their views.[85]

Many believe that speaker of the house is the most powerful position in Texas government. There is no doubt that the speaker is extremely powerful.

Generally, speakers have the power to direct and decide what legislation passes the house. The speaker gains power from the formal rules adopted by the house at the beginning of each session. These rules allow the speaker to do the following:

1. Appoint the chairs of all committees.
2. Appoint most of the members of each standing committee. About half of these committee seats are assigned based on a limited seniority system. In reality, the backers of the speaker often use their seniority to choose a committee assignment, thus freeing up an appointment for the speaker.
3. Appoint members of the calendar and procedural committees, conference committees, and other special and interim committees.
4. Serve as presiding officer over all sessions. This power allows the speaker to recognize members on the floor who want to speak, generally interpret house rules, decide when a vote will be taken, and decide the outcome of voice votes.
5. Refer all bills to committees. As a rule, bills go to subject matter committees. However, the speaker has discretion in deciding what committee will receive a bill. Some speakers used the State Affairs Committee as their "dead bill committee." Bills assigned to this committee usually had little chance of passing. Also, the speaker can assign a bill to a favorable committee to enhance its chances of passing.

Speaker Joe Straus bangs the gavel to start the 83rd Legislative Session.

© Eric Gay/AP Images

These rules give the speaker control over the house agenda. The speaker decides the chairs of standing committees, selects a majority of the members of all committees, and refers bills to committees. The selected chairs are members of the "speaker's team." Few bills pass the house without the speaker's approval. For example, in the 2005 session of the legislature, House Bill 1348, which would have limited campaign contributions from corporations and labor unions, was being co-sponsored by two-thirds of the members of the house, both Democrats and Republicans. However, the bill was not given a hearing by the Elections Committee because of the speaker's influence.

Lieutenant Governor

Unlike the speaker of the house, the **lieutenant governor** is elected by the voters in a statewide general election and serves a four-year term. The lieutenant governor does not owe his or her election to the legislative body, is not formally a senator, and cannot vote in the senate except in cases of a tie.

lieutenant governor
Presiding officer of the Texas Senate; elected by the voters of the state

One might assume that the office was not a powerful legislative office, and in most states this is true. The lieutenant governor in Texas, however, possesses powers very similar to those of the speaker. Lieutenant governors can do the following:

1. Appoint the chairs of all senate committees.
2. Select all members of all senate committees. No formal seniority rule applies in the senate.
3. Appoint members of the conference committees.
4. Serve as presiding officer of the senate and interpret rules.
5. Refer all bills to committees.

On the surface, it may appear that the lieutenant governor in Texas is even more powerful than the speaker. After all, lieutenant governors do not owe their election to the senate, and they have all powers possessed by the speaker. The reality, however, is different. The powers of the lieutenant governor are assigned by the formal rules of the senate, which are adopted at the beginning of each session. What the senate gives, it can take away. Lieutenant governors must play a delicate balancing role of working with powerful members of the senate, often compromising in the assignment of chairs of committees and committee membership. The same is true for all other powers. Thus, the lieutenant governor must forge an alliance with key senators to effectively utilize these powers.

It is often suggested that if the lieutenant governor and the senate are ever of opposite parties, the powers of the lieutenant governor could be diminished. Until recently, though, divided party control was not an issue. From 1876 to 1999, the Democrats controlled the lieutenant governor's office. They also controlled the senate for most of this period (1876–1997). The 1999 session was the first since Reconstruction where Republicans held the majority of the senate seats and the lieutenant governor's office. Then-Lt. Governor Rick Perry retained the powers usually given to lieutenant governors. As previously stated, retaining those powers depends upon a lieutenant governor's ability to compromise and get along with the majority of the 31 members of the senate. Acting Lt. Governor Ratliff, who filled the position in 2000 when George W. Bush moved to the White House and Perry assumed the governorship, retained these powers. This was not surprising because Ratliff had been a member of the senate and was elected by that body to be lieutenant governor when the post was vacated by Perry. Republican senators ensured that former Lt. Governor David Dewhurst kept these powers when he won the office in 2002.

In most states, the lieutenant governor has not traditionally been a powerful leader. Five states (Arizona, Maine, New Hampshire, Oregon, and Wyoming) do not even have lieutenant governors.[86] More than half of all lieutenant governors serve as the presiding officer in their state senate,[87] though some attend a senate session only when their vote is needed to break a tie. In states without a lieutenant governor, the senate elects one of its members to be the presiding officer, called the pro tempore, president of the senate, or speaker of the senate.[88] In only a few states is the lieutenant governor able to appoint committee members and assign bills to committees.[89] Most lieutenant governors are figureheads who stand in when the governor is outside the state or incapacitated, and if the governor's office is vacated due to death, resignation, or removal, the lieutenant governor succeeds as governor. Thus, the office of lieutenant governor in Texas is quite different from, and is more powerful than, the office in most other states.[90]

In addition to their legislative duties, the speaker and the lieutenant governor have other **extra legislative powers**. They appoint members of other state boards, or they serve as members of such boards. For example, they appoint the members of the Legislative Budget Board, which writes the state budget, and they serve as the chair and vice chair of this board. These are important powers because these boards make policy. The state budget, for instance, is a policy statement in monetary terms. The budget decides what agencies and programs will be funded and in what amounts.

The speaker and the lieutenant governor also serve as members of the Legislative Redistricting Board. This board meets if the legislature fails to redraw house or senate districts. The decision of this board is subject to change only by court action.

The current Lieutenant Governor of Texas is Dan Patrick, who took office in 2015 and previously made a name for himself as a conservative radio talk show host. Though both Patrick and Governor Abbott are Republicans, in Texas the lieutenant governor is elected separately from the governor rather than on the same ticket, as the governor's designated running mate.[91] Therefore, the governor and lieutenant governor may theoretically come from different political parties.

Lt. Governor Dan Patrick
© Eric Gay/AP Images

extra legislative powers
Legislative leaders serve on boards outside of the legislature

Committees in the House and Senate

Learning Objective: Discuss various leadership positions in the Texas legislature.

Most of the work of the legislature is done in **standing committees** established by house and senate rules. Besides the standing committees, there are also subcommittees of the standing committees, **conference committees** to work out differences in bills passed by the two houses, temporary committees to study special problems, and **interim committees** to study issues between sessions of the state legislature.

Of these, the standing committees are the most important. In most sessions, there are 14 standing committees in the senate and 41 in the house. In the recent 84th Legislature, there were 14 in the senate and 38 in the house.[92] These are listed in Table 3.8. The chairs of these standing committees have powers similar to those of the speaker and lieutenant governor at the committee level. They decide the times and agendas for meetings of the committee. In doing so, they decide the amount of time devoted to bills and which bills get the attention of the committee. A chair that strongly dislikes a bill can often prevent the bill from passing. Even if the bill is given a hearing, the chair can decide to give that bill to a subcommittee that might kill the bill. As in most

standing committees
Committees of the house and senate that consider legislation during sessions

conference committees
Joint committees of the house and senate that work out differences in bills passed in each chamber

interim committees
Temporary committees of the legislature that study issues between regular sessions and make recommendations on legislation

TABLE 3.8

Standing Committees of the Texas House and Senate, 84th Legislature

Senate Committees	House Committees
Administration	Agriculture & Livestock
Agriculture, Water & Rural Affairs	Appropriations
Business & Commerce	Business & Industry
Criminal Justice	Calendars
Education	Corrections
Finance	County Affairs
Health & Human Services	Criminal Jurisprudence
Higher Education	Culture, Recreation & Tourism
Intergovernmental Relations	Defense & Veterans' Affairs
Natural Resources & Economic Development	Economic & Small Business Development
Nominations	Elections
State Affairs	Energy Resources
Transportation	Environmental Regulation
Veteran Affairs & Military Installations	General Investigating & Ethics
	Government Transparency & Operation
	Higher Education
	Homeland Security & Public Safety
	House Administration
	Human Services
	Insurance
	International Trade & Intergovernmental Affairs
	Investments & Financial Services
	Judiciary & Civil Jurisprudence
	Juvenile Justice & Family Issues
	Land & Resource Management
	Licensing & Administrative Procedures
	Local & Consent Calendars
	Natural Resources
	Pensions
	Public Education
	Public Health
	Redistricting
	Rules & Resolutions
	Special Purpose Districts
	State Affairs
	Transportation
	Urban Affairs
	Ways & Means

Source: Adapted from Texas Senate. See: (http://www.senate.state.tx.us/75r/senate/Commit.htm) and House of Representatives. See: (http://www.house.state.tx.us/committees/)

legislative bodies, power in Texas is heavily concentrated in the individuals who make up the house and senate leadership, and who control the agendas and actions of the legislature. Few bills can pass the legislature without the support of these individuals.

Taking Personal Responsibility. . .

It has been stated that the success of legislation depends largely on a relative few individuals who make up the leadership in the Texas House and Senate. Do you think the speaker of the house and the lieutenant governor have too much control over the passage of bills? How can you influence legislation? What can individuals do to affect legislation?

Source: United States Department of Agriculture Agricultural Research Service

Functions

Learning Objective: Describe the Texas legislature's functions and procedures.

Lawmaking

The Texas legislature has, as one of its main functions, the responsibility to create, alter, and enact laws for the state; the Texas legislature's two branches carry out these functions. This is the main duty and function of legislative bodies in general.

Budget and Taxation

One of the most essential laws enacted by the Texas legislature is the biennial budget. The Legislative Budget Board submits a recommended budget to the legislature. The governor's office also submits an executive budget. The legislature then uses these two documents to help create and enact the budget that will be in place for the state until the next legislative session. The Senate Finance Committee and House Appropriations Committee begin the process of creating the budget bill for the legislature. The budget bill follows a similar process as other bills in the legislature, but it passes to the state comptroller prior to being sent to the governor.

The Texas legislature establishes the state sales tax, which is the main source of revenue for the state because there is no state income tax. Additional taxes can be established, such as franchise taxes on businesses or "sin" taxes on activities the legislature may want to discourage, such as the purchase of alcohol and tobacco.

Oversight

Another key responsibility of the legislature is to keep track of what state agencies are doing, assess their performance, and determine whether they provide necessary functions. The legislature has a number of mechanisms by which it examines these state agencies in order to fulfill this "oversight" duty. One form of oversight is through the use of committees, whereby a committee may call representatives of agencies to testify at a hearing. Although this tactic is commonly used in the federal government, it is less effective for the Texas legislature because of the limited legislative session. Another means of oversight is through financial mechanisms—for example, the actions taken by the Legislative Budget Board and by the Legislative Audit Committee. A final means of oversight is the Sunset Advisory Commission. The Texas legislature established this commission in 1977 as a major means of oversight of state agencies. The commission reviews about 130 state agencies on a rotating basis to determine whether there is a continued need for the agency under review. This works out to each agency being reviewed, on average, about every 12 years. The commission then makes a recommendation to the legislature regarding whether agencies should be continued or abolished. See Figure 3.1 on how this process works.[93]

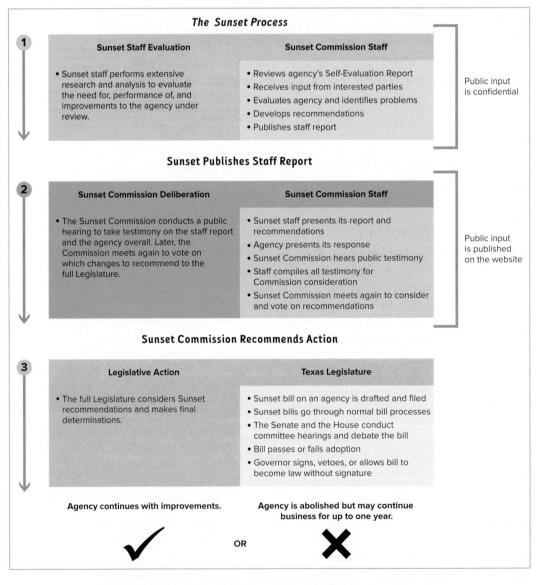

FIGURE 3.1   Sunset Advisory Commission Review Process

Procedures

Learning Objective: Describe the Texas legislature's functions and procedures.

All legislatures have formal rules of procedure that govern their operations. These rules prescribe how bills are passed into law and make the process of passing laws more orderly and fair. These rules also make it difficult to pass laws because a bill must clear many hurdles before it becomes a law. Rules that make it difficult to pass bills have two results: they prevent bills from becoming law without careful review, and they preserve the status quo. In the traditionalistic/individualistic political culture of Texas, these rules protect the ruling elite and enable them to control the legislative process. Thus, it is more important to understand the impact of rules on legislation than to have a detailed understanding of the actual rules. This is the basic approach used here to explain how laws are made in Texas.

Formal Rules: How a Bill Becomes a Law

Figure 3.2 lists the formal procedures in the Texas House and Senate for passing a bill. Each bill, to become law, must clear each step. The vast majority of bills that are introduced fail to pass. Few bills of major importance are passed in any given legislative session. Most bills make only minor changes to existing law.

At each stage in the process, the bill can receive favorable or unfavorable actions. Within each step, a bill can die by either action or inaction. There are many ways to kill a bill, but only one way to pass a bill. To pass, a bill must clear all hurdles.

The rules of the Texas Senate have traditionally had a conserving force on legislation, meaning that they tend to maintain the status quo and deter rapid change. However, a procedural change enacted during the 84th Legislature may make it somewhat easier to pass legislation. During the first 60 days of the regular session, bills on any subject can be introduced in the senate. Once introduced, the bill is referred to a committee whose members analyze the proposed legislation, hold hearings to allow for public testimony, and issue a written report on the bill. At this point, the bill can be brought up for consideration on the senate floor. Figure 3.2 details the subsequent steps in the process.

In practice, relatively few bills complete this process and are passed within the first 60 days. After the sixtieth day of the session, additional restrictions are imposed before a bill can be considered. Technically, after the sixtieth

Texas House of Representatives

© Jay Janner/Austin American-Statesman/AP Images

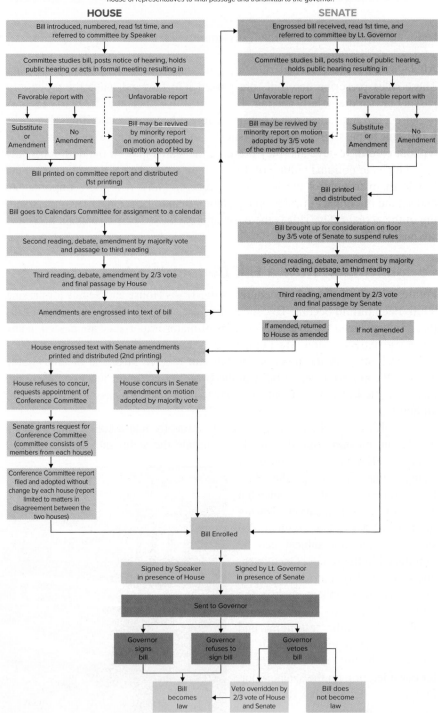

The Texas Legislative Process for House Bills and Resolutions

This diagram displays the sequential flow of a bill from the time it is introduced in the house of representatives to final passage and transmittal to the governor.

FIGURE 3.2 **Basic Steps in the Texas Legislative Process** This diagram displays the sequential flow of a bill from the time it is introduced in the Texas House of Representatives to final passage and transmittal to the governor. A bill introduced in the senate follows the same procedure, flowing from senate to house.

day, senate rules require bills to be considered in the order they are reported out of committee. For a bill to be considered out of order (which, by design, is always the case) the senate must vote to suspend its regular order of business. For the past 70 years, it took the support of two-thirds of the senate to bring up a bill at this point in the process. In other words, 21 senators had to agree to suspend the regular order of business and bring the bill to the floor for debate. This requirement was known as the "two-thirds" rule. Relatively few bills could clear this hurdle and eventually become law. Therefore, this rule played a conserving role in the legislative process.

The 84th Legislature broke with precedent and changed this rule. According to the new rule, three-fifths of the senate must support consideration to bring a bill to the floor.[94] That lowers the threshold to only 19 senators to move legislation forward. Lt. Governor Patrick, a proponent of the rule change, argued it would allow the senate "to pass legislation that has been blocked for many years."[95] Opponents argued that it would make legislation more partisan, as legislators would have less need to reach across the aisle and enlist the support of members of the opposing party in order to get their legislation through.

In some cases, the formal rules can be used to hide actions of the legislature. It is not uncommon in legislative bodies to attach **riders** to appropriations bills. A rider can be a subject matter item (creation of a new state regulatory board) or a money item (money for a park in a legislator's district). In the Texas legislature, the practice adds a new twist. Riders can be attached to appropriations without the knowledge of the public or the media. These are called **closed riders**. They are closed to public inspection and appear only after the appropriation bills have passed the house and senate and go to conference committee. In the conference committee the cloak is removed, and they appear for public inspection for the first time. At this stage, which is always near the end of the session, the likelihood of change is remote. Unless the governor vetoes the bill, these closed riders become law without public comment.

One example of a closed rider dealt with the Bush School at Texas A&M University. In the 1999 session of the legislature, the Bush School (College) was separated from the College of Liberal Arts and made a separate school (college) within the university, and its budget was increased by several million dollars. This move was accomplished by a closed rider on a bill.

rider
Provision attached to a bill that may not be of the same subject matter as the main bill

closed rider
Provisions attached to appropriations bills that are not made public until the conference committee meets

Major and Minor Calendars and Bills

To fully understand the legislative process, we must distinguish between major and minor bills, because state legislators treat them very differently. As political scientist Harvey Tucker noted in his study of calendars and bills, "the major criterion distinguishing major from minor bills is political: the level of conflict the bill is expected to generate within the Legislature."[96] Two organizations, the former Federal Advisory Commission on Intergovernmental Relations and the Citizens Conference on State Legislators, have both recommended that state legislatures use different calendars to distinguish between major, controversial bills and minor, or local bills. By using different calendars, legislatures can better manage their limited time and devote attention to important matters.

According to house rules, there are four different types of calendars, and bills must meet certain criteria to be assigned to each of these calendars. There are

calendars

Procedures in the house used to consider different kinds of bills; major bills and minor bills are considered under different procedures

Committee on Local and Consent Calendars

Committee handling minor and noncontroversial bills that normally apply to only a discrete area

Committee on Calendars

Standing committee of the house that decides which bills will be considered for floor debate by the full house and to which committee they will be assigned

two **calendars** for minor bills—the Local, Consent, and Resolutions Calendar, and the Congratulatory and Memorial Calendar. The Local, Consent, and Resolutions Calendar lists local or noncontroversial bills scheduled to be considered by the house. A local bill "applies only to a discrete community or area rather than to the entire state,"[97] and a noncontroversial bill is one that is not expected to be opposed. To be placed on this calendar, bills must be recommended unanimously by the substantive house committee handling the bill. A bill may be removed from this calendar if five or more members object or if floor debate lasts longer than 10 minutes. If the **Committee on Local and Consent Calendars** determines that a bill is not appropriate for this calendar, it may be sent to the **Committee on Calendars** (regular calendars) for assignment to another calendar. The Local, Consent, and Resolutions Calendar is typically used one day a week during the second half of the regular legislative session.[98]

Two other calendars used by the Texas House are the Daily House Calendar and the Supplemental House Calendar, both of which are prepared by the Committee on Calendars. The Daily House Calendar lists all new bills slated to be considered by the house; the Supplemental House Calendar may include measures scheduled to be considered that day, measures that were read for the third time the previous day, and agenda items that were postponed (or that the members simply did not get to) from a previous day. The Supplemental House Calendar is the main calendar used by the house. Bills are grouped into categories, such as the emergency calendar, the major state calendar, the constitutional amendments calendar, and the general state calendar.[99] Because the Committee on Calendars determines which measures will be scheduled for deliberation on the house floor, it exerts considerable influence over what legislation will ultimately be passed, especially toward the end of the legislative session when time is limited.[100]

Table 3.9 demonstrates the fate of bills in the Texas legislature during a sample 10-year period from 2001-2011. As the table shows, only about 25 percent of all bills introduced in the house and senate made it into law. Most bills died at the committee level, and some were dead on arrival. Some bills were introduced to satisfy a constituency, and the member had no intention of working to pass the bill.

A few similarities and differences exist between major and minor bills. They are identical in three ways:

1. They originate in either chamber.
2. They are equally as likely to be vetoed.
3. They receive final action toward the end of the legislative session.

Major and minor bills are treated differently in six ways:

1. Major bills are introduced earlier in the session than minor bills.
2. Companion bills are introduced in the other chamber more frequently for major bills than for minor bills.
3. Major bills are more evenly distributed across committees; minor bills are more concentrated in a few committees.
4. Major bills are amended more frequently than minor bills.
5. Major bills are more likely to be killed; minor bills are more likely to be passed by the legislature.
6. Final actions to kill major bills occur later in the session than final actions to kill minor bills.[101]

TABLE 3.9

Bill Survival Rate in the Texas Legislature

	77th (2001)	78th (2003)	79th (2005)	80th (2007)	81st (2009)	82nd (2011)
Total Bills	100%	100%	100%	100%	100%	100%
Deliberated by committee in originating chamber	70%	64%	68%	70%	70%	70%
Passed by committee in originating chamber	50%	46%	47%	48%	47%	46%
Floor consideration in originating chamber	41%	37%	35%	40%	34%	36%
Pass originating chamber	40%	35%	33%	37%	33%	34%
Deliberated in second chamber	35%	30%	27%	31%	26%	28%
Passed by committee in second chamber	33%	29%	27%	31%	26%	28%
Floor consideration in second chamber	29%	25%	25%	26%	20%	24%
Pass second chamber	29%	25%	24%	25%	19%	24%
Pass both chambers	29%	25%	24%	25%	19%	24%
Passed into law	27%	24%	24%	24%	19%	23%
Vetoed	1%	1%	<1%	1%	1%	<1%

Source: Adapted from Harvey J. Tucker, "Legislation Deliberation in the Texas House and Senate." Paper presented at Annual Meeting of Midwest Political Science Association, Chicago, Illinois, April 15-18, 2004. Data in this table updated by Harvey Tucker.

Legislative Workload and Logjams

According to much of the literature on state legislatures, most bills pass the legislature in the final days of the session. This scenario gives the impression that the legislature "goofs off" for most of the session and then frantically passes bills just before adjournment, producing laws that are given only "hasty consideration, of poor quality and are confused and inferior."[102]

In Texas, it is true that most legislation—about 80 percent of all bills—is passed in the final two weeks of the session. The question remains: Does this result in poor quality and inferior legislation? The answer is, probably not. Understanding the process of agenda setting makes this more clear.

First, bills may be introduced at any time prior to the session and up until the sixtieth day of the 140-day session. After the sixtieth day, only local bills, emergency appropriations, emergency matters submitted by the governor, and bills with a four-fifths vote of the house may be introduced. Thus, for the first 60 days, the agendas for both houses are being set. After the sixtieth day, the legislature begins to clear these agendas. As indicated, most bills die in committees and are never assigned to a calendar. Killing a bill in committee is an action by the legislature, and it occurs at a regular rate during the session.[103] The bill is dead if it does not make it out of committee. This leaves only about a third of all bills for further consideration late in the session. As Harvey Tucker observes:

> Once the agenda has been set it is cleared at a fairly even rate. Final action on most bills passed occurs at the end of the session by design. Conflicting and complementary bills are reconciled. Bills tied directly or indirectly to the state budget are delayed until the final days of necessity. The legislature

is not able to appropriate funds until the Comptroller of Public Accounts certifies the amount of revenues that will be available. The "certification estimate" is not made until the very end of the legislative session, because, among other reasons, the estimate must be informed by any actions the legislature takes that would affect state revenues.[104]

Thus, the image of the legislature "goofing off" for the first 120 days of the session is not accurate. The nature of the legislative process requires the passage of major legislation near the end of the session. Also, about half the bills that pass toward the end of the session are minor bills, and they are cleared late for different reasons than are major bills.

Thus, the formal rules of the house and senate are very important factors in determining how and what kind of legislation gets passed. These rules have the effect of preserving the status quo. It is very difficult to pass legislation and very easy to kill a bill. Although the Texas legislature is not dramatically different from most other legislatures in this respect, in Texas these rules have historically protected the status quo of the state's traditionalistic/individualistic political culture.

Informal Rules

informal rules

Set of norms or values that govern legislative bodies

In addition to the formal rules, there are also **informal rules**, or legislative norms, that all state legislators must learn if they are to be successful. Political scientists Lee Bernick and Charles Wiggins identified eleven norms that were generally accepted in their study of a sample of state legislatures. These include the following: Legislators should *not*

Conceal the real purpose of a bill or purposely overlook part of it to assure passage.
Deal in personalities during floor debate.
Give first priority to your reelection in all of your lawmaking activities.
Introduce as many bills and amendments as possible.
Be a thorn in the side of the majority by refusing unanimous consent.
Become known as a spokesperson for a special interest group.
Speak on issues you know little about.
Become known as a "loner."
Seek as much publicity as possible to look good to the people back home.
Talk to the press or others about decisions reached in private.
Avoid taking a position on legislation before the final vote or roll call.[105]

Of course, each legislature will have a different set of norms and place different values on them. In fact, only the first norm on the list was accepted in all states examined in the study. However, the next three norms in the list were accepted in at least 10 of the 11 states. Texas was the only state where those three prescriptions did not meet the criteria for a legislative norm. In particular, dealing in personalities during floor debate was viewed as acceptable behavior by a significant number of members in Texas, whereas in the other states only a few members viewed this as appropriate.[106] It is also worth noting that Texas legislators were a lot less concerned with "blabbing" to the press about private deals than those in other states.

Legislators must learn the norms of their legislature and adhere to them, or they might find themselves ineffective or even isolated. The informal rules can be nearly important as the formal rules governing the legislature.

Legislative Roles

Learning Objective: Describe the Texas legislature's functions and procedures.

Members of the legislature are expected to play many roles during legislative sessions. We have already discussed formal leadership roles. Each speaker approaches the job in different ways. Historically, most speakers have exerted very tight control over the house and dominated the legislative process. This was true of Billy Clayton, speaker from 1975 to 1983. However, Gib Lewis, who followed Clayton, exerted much less control. He allowed the members of his team—namely, committee chairs—to control the process, and he himself took a much more "laid back" attitude. Pete Laney was more like Billy Clayton in that he controlled the house. Tom Craddick of Midland followed a role similar to that of Speakers Laney and Clayton.

Great differences can also exist in lieutenant governors' leadership styles. For instance, Bill Hobby, the son of a former governor, served as lieutenant governor for 18 years (1972–90). Hobby, a very quiet, low-key person, seldom forced his will on members of the senate. He preferred to work behind the scenes and forge compromises.

Hobby chose not to run for reelection in 1990, and Bob Bullock succeeded him as lieutenant governor. Bullock had served for 16 years as the state comptroller and had developed a reputation for strong, effective leadership, but he often went out of his way to make enemies. Bullock's leadership style was almost the opposite of Hobby's. Rumors have circulated of shouting matches and angry behavior, sometimes even in open sessions of the senate. The senate seemed to adjust to Bullock's style of leadership, and he managed to get much of his agenda passed. Hobby and Bullock represent contrasting ways of being an effective leader in the senate.

Rick Perry, while serving as the Texas agricultural commissioner from 1995–1999, did not have the reputation of a compromiser; however, judging from all reports, he performed quite effectively as lieutenant governor in the 1999 session. Lt. Governor Dewhurst was something of a political unknown, having served only four years as land commissioner prior to his election. Dewhurst's performance received mixed reviews. He was an effective leader in the regular sessions and was viewed by some as more partisan in the three special sessions. Powerful Republican leaders ensured that he kept the broad powers normally given to lieutenant governors.

Leadership in legislative bodies can take many forms. In addition to formal leadership roles, some members develop reputations as experts in particular areas of legislation and are regarded by other members as leaders in those areas. Being recognized by other members as the expert in some area of legislation obviously increases one's influence. For instance, a person who is a recognized expert on taxation can use this reputation to forge coalitions and pass tax legislation.

Representational Roles

Constituencies have expectations about the roles of their legislators. For centuries, members of legislatures have argued about the representational role of a

delegate
Representational role of member stating that he or she represents the wishes of the voters

trustee
Representational role of a member that states that the member will make decisions on his or her own judgment about what is best for voters

legislator. Whom do legislators represent? Are they **delegates**, sent to reflect or mirror the interests and wishes of voters, or are they **trustees**, entrusted by the voters to make decisions based on their best judgment? The delegate role is perceived as being more democratic—as doing what the people want. The trustee role can be characterized as elitist—as doing what one thinks is best.

In reality, members may play both delegate and trustee roles, depending on the issue before them. For example, in 1981 the Texas legislature passed a bill prohibiting commercial fisherman from catching redfish in some waters in the Gulf of Mexico. The bill was written and advanced by sport fishermen. Representatives from coastal communities in Texas voted as delegates—from the perspective of commercial fishermen and against the bill. Representatives from the Panhandle, however, were free to vote as trustees. In matters affecting the livelihood of Panhandle ranchers but not coastal fisheries, these representatives would reverse their voting roles. Which role representatives play is largely dependent on how the issues affect their district. The problem with this is that local interests can take the forefront, leading legislators to neglect long-term statewide or larger public interests.

Partisan Roles

Party has traditionally not been a strong factor in the Texas legislature. Members of both parties are given committee assignments. Texas differs from states with a tradition of strong partisanship, where party leadership roles are important, formal leadership positions are assigned on the basis of party, and party leaders try to ensure that party members support party positions on issues.

In the past, coalitions in the Texas legislature have organized more around ideology than around party. The 1970s saw the formation of the "Dirty Thirty" coalition of liberal Democratic and conservative Republican house members to fight the conservative Democrats. This uneasy alliance of those excluded from leadership positions was short lived.

In more recent years, conservative Republicans and Democrats organized the Texas Conservative Coalition to fight what they view as liberal ideas. Other caucuses represent Hispanics and African Americans. In 1993, the Republicans formed a caucus to promote the election of Pete Laney as speaker. As a reward, they were assigned several committee chairs. However, partisan factors have played a much larger role in the Texas legislature in recent years.

In 2003 session, this partisanship was evident in the redistricting battles. With the Republicans in control of both the house and the senate in the 2003 session, there was promise of bipartisan cooperation. For example, the new speaker, Tom Craddick, promised to continue bipartisanship and appointed 14 (29.2 percent) Democrats to chair committees. However, there was little evidence of bipartisanship beyond that.

The sessions from 2003 to 2007 were instead marked by deep partisanship by Speaker Craddick. In fact, some members started calling him Speaker Auto-Craddick. He subsequently lost his speakership to Republican Joe Straus from San Antonio in the 2009 session. As discussed earlier, Speaker Straus came to power through a small coalition of Republicans who joined Democrats to wrest the position from Craddick. Key Democrats who helped engineer Straus's victory were given decent committee assignments by the new Republican speaker.[107] Some Democratic members, though, felt the party should have received more committee chairs and thus gave Straus mixed reviews at the start of his term. However, conservative Republicans have never been happy with Straus and have maintained their criticism of him throughout his tenure in the speakership. This led one commentator to describe Straus as "a political piñata for his party's conservatives."[108]

Legislative Professionalism versus Citizen Legislatures: Where Does Texas Stand?

Learning Objective: Explain legislators' qualifications and member demographics.

In this chapter, we have often made comparisons between the Texas legislature and the legislatures of other states. For example, we noted that few states have as many constituents per house and senate district as Texas, and that Texas is one of only four states to have biennial sessions. Political scientists have also compared state legislatures in terms of their level of **legislative professionalism**. According to political scientist Peverill Squire, legislative professionalism can be measured using data on "pay, session length, and staff resources."[109] States with higher legislative pay, longer sessions (such as no limits on the length of regular sessions), and more staff support are deemed more professional. One could say that states with part-time legislators who get lower pay, shorter or biennial sessions, and fewer staff resources are less professional or, more positively, **"citizen legislatures."**[110] Compared to all other states, Texas ranks the fifteenth most professional in the latest Squire Legislative Professionalism Index.[111] New Hampshire has the least professional legislature (or the strongest citizen legislature), and California has the most professional.

legislative professionalism
Legislatures with higher pay, longer sessions, and high levels of staff support are considered more professional

citizen legislatures
Legislatures characterized by low pay, short sessions, and fewer staff resources

Conclusion

Thomas R. Dye comes to three conclusions on state legislatures, all of which could be said to apply to the Texas legislature.[112] First, Dye observes that

> State legislatures reflect socioeconomic conditions of their states. These conditions help to explain many of the differences one encounters in state legislative politics: the level of legislative activity, the degree of inter-party competition, the extent of party cohesion, the professionalism of the legislature . . . [and] the level of interest group activity.[113]

This means that the legislature is greatly influenced by the social and economic conditions in the state and that policies passed by the legislature reflect those conditions. This certainly applies to Texas.

Second, legislatures function as "arbiters of public policy rather than initiators" of policy change.[114] State legislatures wait for others—state agencies, local governments, interest groups, and citizens—to bring issues to them for resolution. Someone other than members of the legislature write most bills introduced. The rules make it much easier to delay legislation than to pass it. Leadership most often comes from others outside the legislature, often the governor. With a few exceptions this applies to Texas.

Third, legislatures "function to inject into public decision making a parochial influence."[115] By this Dye means that state legislatures tend to represent local legislative interests and not statewide interests. Legislators are recruited, elected, and reelected locally. Local interests will always be dominant in determining how legislators vote on proposed legislation. Frequently, no one represents statewide interests. This conclusion certainly applies to Texas. Statewide interests often get lost in the shuffle to protect and promote local interests.

Summary

LO: Describe the structure, size, and general characteristics of the Texas legislature.

The Texas state legislature is bicameral (meaning it consists of two chambers, a senate and a house of representatives). The Texas Senate has 31 members, and the Texas House of Representatives has 150 members. Both chambers are quite small relative to the state's population. The Texas legislature meets biennially (every two years) for a 140-day regular session, and only the governor can call special sessions. Texas legislators receive relatively low pay compared to legislators in other states.

LO: Explain legislators' qualifications and member demographics.

A Texas House member must be a U.S. citizen, at least 21 years of age, and must have lived in the state for at least two years and in the district he or she will represent for a minimum of 12 months. A Texas state senator must be a U.S. citizen, at least 26 years old, and must have been a Texas resident for at least five years and a district resident for at least 12 months. The state legislature is less diverse than the general population. Texas legislators tend to be older, male, well-educated professionals.

LO: Describe reapportionment and redistricting issues in Texas.

Reapportionment is the process of allocating representatives to districts, whereas redistricting is the drawing of district boundary lines. Legislative seats must be reapportioned following each federal census (every 10 years), and district maps often have to be redrawn as a result. Reapportionment and redistricting are highly political matters, as each interest group within the state tries to gain as much as possible from the process. In Texas this process has generated a great deal of controversy, including multiple lawsuits that were ultimately decided by the U.S. Supreme Court.

LO: Explain how legislators are elected, including the single-member district method of election.

Texas uses the single-member district method of election, meaning that each legislative district elects one member to the legislative body. Voters in each of Texas's 31 state senatorial districts and 150 state house districts elect one senator and one congressperson. This system promotes geographical representation, such that all areas of the state choose representatives to the state legislature.

LO: Discuss various leadership positions in the Texas legislature.

In the Texas legislature, power is concentrated in the hands of two individuals: the speaker of the house and the lieutenant governor. The speaker of the house serves as presiding officer in the Texas House of Representatives and generally controls the passage of legislation. The lieutenant governor serves as presiding officer in the Texas Senate. In addition, committee chairs can have a great deal of influence over the legislature's agenda and actions.

LO: Describe the Texas legislature's functions and procedures.

The function of the Texas legislature is to create, alter, and enact laws for the state. Some of the legislature's most important responsibilities are passage of the state budget and oversight of state agencies. The rules of the Texas legislature have traditionally had a conserving force on legislation, meaning that they tend to maintain the status quo and prevent bills from becoming law without careful review.

Key Terms

Baker v. Carr
bicameral
biennial sessions
calendars
citizen legislatures
closed riders
Committee on Calendars

Committee on Local and Consent
  Calendars
conference committees
delegates
extra legislative powers
extraordinary session
gerrymandering

Hunt v. Cromartie
informal rules
interim committees
legislative professionalism
Legislative Redistricting Board
  (LRB)
lieutenant governor

multimember districts
noncompetitive districts
PACs
political gerrymandering
racial gerrymandering
reapportionment

redistricting
Reynolds v. Sims
riders
sine die
single-member districts
speaker of the house

special sessions
standing committees
term limits
trustees
turnover

Notes

[1] *Texas Constitution,* 1876, art. 3, sec. 2.

[2] Council of State Governments, *Book of the States, 2012* (Lexington, Ky.: Council of State Governments, 2012), 118; National Conference of State Legislatures, Number of Legislators and Length of Term in Years. http://www.ncsl.org/research/about-state-legislatures/number-of-legislators-and-length-of-terms.aspx.

[3] National Conference of State Legislatures, 2010 Constituents Per State Legislative District Table. http://www.ncsl.org/legislatures-elections/legislatures/2010-constituents-per-state-legislative-district.aspx.

[4] On this and other points related to the size of the legislature, see Anti-Federalist writings such as Brutus's "III" from the *New York Journal,* November 15, 1787, or Cato's "Letter V" from the *New York Journal,* November 22, 1787. These particular quotations come from Brutus, the pseudonym often attributed to Robert Yates.

[5] At the end of World War II, only four states held annual sessions. By 1966, 20 states met annually, and that number more than doubled by 1974. More recently, Oregon convened its first annual session in 2011. See Rich Jones, "State Legislatures," *Book of the States,* 1944–95, 99; National Conference of State Legislatures, Annual Versus Biennial Legislative Sessions. http://www.ncsl.org/research/about-state-legislatures/annual-versus-biennial-legislative-sessions.aspx.

[6] National Conference of State Legislatures, Legislative Session Length. http://www.ncsl.org/research/about-state-legislatures/legislative-session-length.aspx.

[7] National Conference of State Legislatures, Special Sessions (5/6/2009). http://www.ncsl.org/research/about-state-legislatures/special-sessions472.aspx.

[8] Legislative Reference Library of Texas, Answers to frequently asked questions about the Texas Legislature. http://www.lrl.state.tx.us/genInfo/FAQ.cfm#legPay.

[9] Texas State Historical Association, Texas Legislature. http://www.tshaonline.org/handbook/online/articles/mkt02.

[10] National Conference of State Legislatures, 2014 State Legislator Compensation | Living Expense Allowances During Session. http://www.ncsl.org/research/about-state-legislatures/2014-ncsl-legislator-salary-and-per-diem-table.aspx.

[11] Robert T. Garrett, "Texas lawmakers move to indirectly boost their own pensions," *Dallas Morning News,* May 13, 2013. http://www.dallasnews.com/news/politics/state-politics/20130513-texas-lawmakers-move-to-indirectly-boost-their-own-pensions.ece.)

[12] Ross Ramsey, "Legislators With Benefits, Even When They Stray," *Texas Tribune,* April 12, 2012, http://www.nytimes.com/2012/04/13/us/texas-legislators-with-benefits-even-when-they-stray.html; Employees Retirement System of Texas, Retirement Benefits for Elected State Officials, (January 2016), accessible at https://www.ers.state.tx.us/Employees/Retirement/Types_of_Retirement/.

[13] National Conference of State Legislatures. Size of State Legislative Staff. http://www.ncsl.org/research/about-state-legislatures/staff-change-chart-1979-1988-1996-2003-2009.aspx.

[14] Senate Journal, Eighty-Fourth Legislature - Regular Session, First Day. http://www.journals.senate.state.tx.us/SJRNL/84R/PDF/84RSJ01-13-F.PDF.

[15] House Journal, Eighty-Fourth Legislature - Regular Session, Second Day. http://www.journals.house.state.tx.us/HJRNL/84R/PDF/84RDAY02FINAL.PDF.

[16] National Conference of State Legislatures, Who Can Become a Candidate for State Legislator. http://www.ncsl.org/research/elections-and-campaigns/who-can-become-a-candidate-for-state-legislator.aspx.

[17] Texas Secretary of State, Qualifications for Office. http://www.sos.state.tx.us/elections/candidates/guide/qualifications.shtml.

[18] *Texas Constitution,* art. 6, sec. 1. (see http://www.statutes.legis.state.tx.us/Docs/CN/pdf/CN.6.pdf)

[19] Karl Kurtz, "Who We Elect: The Demographics of State Legislatures," *State Legislatures Magazine* (December 2015). http://www.ncsl.org/research/about-state-legislatures/who-we-elect.aspx.

[20] Alexa Ura and Jolie McCullough, "The 84th Texas Legislature, by the Numbers," Texas Tribune, January 14, 2015, https://www.texastribune.org/2015/01/14

/demographics-2015-texas-legislature/; U.S. Census Bureau, QuickFacts, Texas, http://www.census.gov/quickfacts/table/PST045215/48.

[21] Britney Jeffrey, "Rangel, Irma Lerma," *Handbook of Texas Online.* https://tshaonline.org/handbook/online/articles/fra85.

[22] Sonia R. Garcia, Valerie Martinez-Ebers, Irasema Coronado, Sharon A. Navarro, and Patricia A. Jaramillo, *Politicas: Latina Public Officials in Texas,* (Austin, TX: University of Texas Press, 2008), 48.

[23] Ibid., 44.

[24] Texas Woman's University, Texas Women's Hall of Fame, "Rangel, Irma L." http://www.twu.edu/twhf/tw-rangel.asp.

[25] University of Texas at Austin, Irma Rangel Public Policy Institute, "Irma Rangel." http://www.utexas.edu/cola/ppi/irma-rangel.php.

[26] Laura Chapin, "Colorado Led the Way on Women's Suffrage," *U.S. News & World Report,* August 21, 2010. http://www.usnews.com/opinion/blogs/laura-chapin/2010/08/21/colorado-led-the-way-on-womens-suffrage.

[27] Janice C. May, "Texas Legislature," *Handbook of Texas Online,* accessed April 16, 2016. https://tshaonline.org/handbook/online/articles/mkt02.

[28] Legislative Reference Library of Texas, Women Members of the Texas Legislature, 1923–present. http://www.lrl.state.tx.us/legeLeaders/members/Women.cfm.

[29] Center for American Women and Politics, Women in State Legislatures 2016. http://www.cawp.rutgers.edu/women-state-legislature-2016.

[30] Legislative Reference Library of Texas, Membership Statistics for the 84th Legislature. http://www.lrl.state.tx.us/legeLeaders/members/memberStatistics.cfm.

[31] Karl Kurtz, "Who We Elect: The Demographics of State Legislatures," State Legislatures Magazine, (December 2015), National Conference of State Legislatures. http://www.ncsl.org/research/about-state-legislatures/who-we-elect.aspx.

[32] Karl Kurtz, "Who We Elect: The Demographics of State Legislatures," *State Legislatures Magazine,* (December 2015), National Conference of State Legislatures. http://www.ncsl.org/research/about-state-legislatures/who-we-elect.aspx; Alexa Ura and Jolie McCullough, "The 84th Texas Legislature, by the Numbers," *Texas Tribune,* January 14, 2015. https://www.texastribune.org/2015/01/14/demographics-2015-texas-legislature/.

[33] National Conference of State Legislatures, Dual Employment: Regulating Public Jobs for Legislators (10/1/2015), http://www.ncsl.org/research/ethics/50-state-table-dual-employment.aspx; Texas (State). Legislature. *A joint resolution proposing a constitutional amendment to allow current and retired public school teachers and retired public school administrators to receive compensation for serving on the governing bodies of school districts, cities, towns, or other local governmental districts, including water districts.* H.J.R. 85, 77th Reg. Sess. (May 27, 2001). *The Legislature of the State of Texas,* http://www.lrl.state.tx.us/scanned/sessionLaws/77-0/HJR_85.pdf.

[34] Karl Kurtz, "Changes in Legislatures Using Multimember Districts after Redistricting," The Thicket at State Legislatures, September 11, 2012. http://ncsl.typepad.com/the_thicket/2012/09/a-slight-decline-in-legislatures-using-multimember-districts-after-redistricting.html.

[35] *Texas Constitution,* art. 3, sec. 26.

[36] Leroy Hardy, Alan Heslop, and Stuart Anderson, *Reapportionment Politics* (Beverly Hills, Calif.: Sage, 1981), 18.

[37] Gordon E. Baker, *The Reapportionment Revolution: Representation, Political Power and the Supreme Court* (New York: Random House, 1966).

[38] Texas Legislative Council, "Overview: Texas House Districts 1846–1982," Texas Redistricting. http://www.tlc.state.tx.us/redist/history/overview_house.html.

[39] Wilbourn E. Benton, *Texas: Its Government and Politics,* 2nd ed. (Englewood Cliffs, N.J.: Prentice Hall, 1966), 141.

[40] *Texas Constitution,* art. 3, sec. 28.

[41] Ibid., sec. 26a.

[42] *Baker v. Carr,* 369 U.S. 186 (1962).

[43] *Reynolds v. Sims,* 377 U.S. 533 (1964).

[44] *Evenwel v. Abbott,* 578 U.S. ___ (2016); Opinion accessible at http://www.supremecourt.gov/opinions/15pdf/14-940_ed9g.pdf.

[45] Texas Legislative Council, District Population Analysis with County Subtotals, Senate Districts - Plans 172. http://www.tlc.state.tx.us/redist/districts/senate.html; Texas Legislative Council, District Population Analysis with County Subtotals, House Districts - Plan H358. http://www.tlc.state.tx.us/redist/districts/house.html.

[46] *Kilgarlin v. Martin,* 1965.

[47] SCOTUSblog, *Evenwel v. Abbott.* http://www.scotusblog.com/case-files/cases/evenwel-v-abbott/.

[48] Garrett Epps, "Who Gets to Be Represented in Congress?" *The Atlantic,* December 3, 2015. http://www.theatlantic.com/politics/archive/2015/12/evenwel-supreme-court-districting/418437/.

[49] *Evenwel v. Abbott,* 578 U.S. ____ (2016). http://www.supremecourt.gov/opinions/15pdf/14-940_ed9g.pdf.

[50] *Graves v. Barnes,* 343 F. Supp. 704 (W.D. Tex. 1972); *White v. Register,* 412 U.S. 755 (1973).

[51] National Conference of State Legislatures, African-American Legislators 2009. http://www.ncsl.org/research/about-state-legislatures/african-american-legislators-in-2009.aspx.)

[52] National Conference of State Legislatures, 2009 Latino Legislators. http://www.ncsl.org/research/about-state-legislatures/latino-legislators-overview.aspx.

[53] Alexa Ura and Jolie McCullough, "The 84th Texas Legislature, by the Numbers," *Texas Tribune,* January 14, 2015. https://www.texastribune.org/2015/01/14/demographics-2015-texas-legislature/.

[54] *Bush v. Vera,* 517 U.S. 952 (1996). Accessible at http://www.supremecourt.gov/opinions/boundvolumes/517bv.pdf.

[55] Ibid.

[56] Ibid.

[57] Ibid.

[58] *Hunt v. Cromartie,* 562 U.S. 541 (1999).

[59] R. C. Ratcliffe, "Re-mapping of the Districts Draws Fire: 18 Incumbents Would Square Off," *Houston Chronicle,* 24 April 2001, p. 1.

[60] Clay Robison, "Bush, DeLay in the Lobbying Game," *Houston Chronicle,* June 22, 2003. http://www.chron.com/CDA/archives/archive.mpl/2003_3665599/bush-delay-in-the-lobbying-game.html.

[61] Paul Mackun and Steven Wilson, "Population Distribution and Change: 2000 to 2010," U.S. Census Bureau, 2010 Census Briefs (March 2011). http://www.census.gov/prod/cen2010/briefs/c2010br-01.pdf.

[62] *Perry v. Perez,* 565 U.S. (2012).

[63] Texas Legislative Council, Texas Redistricting, 2010s Cycle. http://www.tlc.state.tx.us/redist/history/2010s.html.

[64] *Shelby County v. Holder,* 570 U.S. ___ (2013).

[65] Ross Ramsey, "Court: Texas Elections Should Proceed with Current Maps," *Texas Tribune,* November 6, 2015. https://www.texastribune.org/2015/11/06/court-texas-elections-should-proceed-current-maps/.

[66] Royce West. *A bill to be entitled an act relating to the reapportionment of congressional districts and the creation, function, and duties of the Texas Congressional Redistricting Commission.* 84(R) SB 127. *Texas State Senate.* http://www.legis.state.tx.us/tlodocs/84R/billtext/pdf/SB00127I.pdf#navpanes=0; Legislative Reference Library of Texas, Redistricting legislation. http://www.lrl.state.tx.us/legis/redistricting/redistrictingBills.cfm.

[67] Longview News Journal. http://www.news-journal.com/news/local/did-new-voting-lines-doom-incumbent-east-texas-legislators/article_16361306-5135-55f5-befa-506fdf5887a6.html.

[68] National Institute on Money in State Politics, Election Overview. http://followthemoney.org/election-overview?s=TX&y=2014.

[69] Ballotpedia, Texas State Senate elections, 2016. https://ballotpedia.org/Texas_State_Senate_elections,_2016.

[70] National Conference of State Legislatures, "Limits on Campaign Contributions During the Legislative Session." http://www.ncsl.org/research/elections-and-campaigns/limits-on-contributions-during-session.aspx.

[71] Ryan Murphy, "Explore 30-Day Report Filings," TRIBPEDIA: Campaign Finance, *Texas Tribune,* October 10, 2014. http://apps.texastribune.org/30-day-reports-general-2014/.

[72] Texas Secretary of State, Race Summary Report, 2012 General Election. http://elections.sos.state.tx.us/elchist164_state.htm.

[73] Gary C. Jacobson, *The Politics of Congressional Elections,* 3rd ed. (New York: HarperCollins, 1992).

[74] Kevin A. Hill, "Does the Creation of Majority Black Districts Aid Republicans? An Analysis of the 1992 Congressional Election in Eight Southern States," *Journal of Politics* 57 (May 1995): 348–401.

[75] *Book of the States, 1994–95,* 27.

[76] National Conference of State Legislatures, The Term-Limited States, March 13, 2015. http://www.ncsl.org/research/about-state-legislatures/chart-of-term-limits-states.aspx.

[77] Samuel C. Patterson, "Legislative Politics in the States," in *Politics in the American States,* 6th ed., eds. Virginia Gray and Herbert Jacob (Washington, D.C.: Congressional Quarterly Press, 1996), 179–186.

[78] *Book of the States, 2004.*

[79] Ibid., 97.

[80] Ross Ramsey, "Texas Lawmakers Put Down Their Swords," *New York Times,* May 26, 2013. http://www.nytimes.com/2013/05/26/us/texas-83rd-legislative-session-characterized-by-agreement.html?pagewanted=all); Jonathan Tilove, "Texas House returns with largest contingent of new members in 40 years," *Austin American-Statesman,* January 5, 2013. http://www.statesman.com/news/news/state-regional-govt-politics/texas-house-returns-with-largest-contingent-of-new/nTnpq/.

[81] Lawrence W. Miller, *Legislative Turnover and Political Careers: A Study of Texas Legislators, 1969–75,* Ph.D. dissertation, Texas Tech University, 1977, 43–45.

[82] *Presiding Officers of the Texas Legislature, 1846–2002* (Austin: Texas Legislative Council, 2002).

[83] Ross Ramsey, "That Old Speaker-Ousting G.O.P. Gang of 11, Down to 4," *New York Times,* September 7, 2013, http://www.nytimes.com/2013/09/08/us/that-old-speaker-ousting-gop-gang-of-11-down-to-4.html; Robert T. Garrett, "Straus era is five years old today," *Dallas Morning News,* January 2, 2014, http://trailblazersblog.dallasnews.com/2014/01/straus-era-is-five-years-old-today.html/.

[84] Gary Scharrer, "Craddick: 'I'm Not Running for Speaker,'" *Houston Chronicle,* January 14, 2009. http://blog.chron.com/texaspolitics/2009/01/craddick-im-not-running-for-speaker/.)

[85] Michael Quinn Sullivan, Shining Light on Texas House Speaker Joe Straus. http://www.breitbart.com/Breitbart-Texas/2014/02/16/Shining-Light-On-House-Speaker-Joe-Straus.

[86] National Lieutenant Governors Association, Roster of Lieutenant Governors. http://www.nlga.us/lt-governors/roster/.

[87] National Lieutenant Governors Association, Responsibilities of the Office of Lieutenant Governor. http://www.nlga.us/lt-governors/.

[88] In Tennessee and West Virginia, the president of the senate simultaneously holds the title of lieutenant governor.

[89] *Book of the States, 1998–99,* 48, table 2.13.

[90] This has not always been the case. J. William Davis, in his book *There Shall Also Be a Lieutenant Governor,* traces the concentration of power in this office to the actions of Allan Shivers and Ben Ramsey during the 1940s and 1950s. Over a period of several years, the office of lieutenant governor gained power in the senate. See J. William Davis, *There Shall Also Be a Lieutenant Governor* (Austin: University of Texas, Institute of Public Affairs, 1967).

[91] National Lieutenant Governors Association, Methods of Election. http://www.nlga.us/lt-governors/office-of-lieutenant-governor/methods-of-election/.

[92] The Senate of Texas, Committees of the 84th Legislature. http://www.senate.state.tx.us/75r/senate/Commit.htm; Texas House of Representatives, House Committees. http://www.house.state.tx.us/committees/.

[93] Sunset Advisory Commission, Sunset in Texas 2015–2017. https://www.sunset.texas.gov/public/uploads/files/reports/Sunset%20in%20Texas_0.pdf.

[94] Texas Legislative Council, Guide to Texas Legislative Information (Revised), March 2015. http://www.tlc.state.tx.us/pubslegref/gtli.pdf.

[95] Aman Batheja, "Without Two-Thirds Rule, Senate Moving Patrick's Priorities," *Texas Tribune,* May 19, 2015. http://www.texastribune.org/2015/05/19/loss-two-thirds-rule-senate/.

[96] Harvey Tucker, "Legislative Calendars and Workload Management in Texas," *Journal of Politics* 51 (August 1989).

[97] Texas Legislative Council, "Guide to Texas Legislative Information (Revised)," (March 2015). http://www.tlc.state.tx.us/pubslegref/gtli.pdf.

[98] Ibid.

[99] Ibid.

[100] Erin Mulvaney, "House Calendars Committee holds sway over bills' fates as Texas Legislature winds down," *Dallas Morning News,* May 11, 2011. http://www.dallasnews.com/news/politics/texas-legislature/headlines/20110511-house-calendars-committee-holds-sway-over-bills_fates-as-texas-legislature-winds-down-.ece.

[101] Harvey J. Tucker, "Legislative Workload Congestion in Texas," *Journal of Politics* 49 (1987): 557.

[102] Ibid.

[103] Ibid., 569.

[104] Ibid., 575.

[105] E. Lee Bernick and Charles W. Wiggins, "Legislative Norms in Eleven States," *Legislative Studies Quarterly* 8.2 (May 1983): 194–195.

[106] Ibid., 194.

[107] Ross Ramsey, "Now It Starts," *Texas Tribune,* February 16, 2009. http://www.texastribune.org/2009/02/16/now-it-starts/.

[108] Ross Ramsey, "Speaker's Original Band of 11 Shrinks to Four," *Texas Tribune,* September 9, 2013. http://www.texastribune.org/2013/09/09/speakers-original-band-11-shrinks-four/.

[109] Peverill Squire. "Measuring State Legislative Professionalism: The Squire Index Revisited." *State Politics & Policy Quarterly* 7:2 (Summer, 2007): 211–227.

[110] William Ruger and Jason Sorens. "The Citizen Legislature." Goldwater Institute Policy Brief. June 22, 2011.

[111] Ibid. 113.

[112] Dye, *Politics in States and Communities,* 192–193.

[113] Ibid., 192.

[114] Ibid., 193.

[115] Ibid.

CHAPTER 4

The Executive Department and the Office of the Governor of Texas

- Explain the structure and function of the executive branch of Texas government.

T he governor is the most salient political actor in state government. Whether the true power center of the state is embodied in the occupant of the office or elsewhere, the office is the focal point of state government and politics. The expectation is that governors will be leaders in their state.

Chapter Learning Objectives

- Summarize the formal and informal qualifications for the governor of Texas.
- Explain the provision for succession of a governor.
- Explain the provision for removal of a governor.
- Explain the governor's formal powers.
- Explain the governor's informal powers.

Qualifications

Learning Objective: Summarize the formal and informal qualifications for the governor of Texas.

Formal Qualifications

In most states the formal qualifications to be governor are minimal. All but three states (Kansas, Massachusetts, and Vermont) set a minimum age requirement, and exactly half of all states require a candidate to be a resident of the state preceding the election. The time period each state specifies varies widely, from no set time to 7 years. Most states also require governors to be U.S. citizens and qualified voters.[1]

In Texas the formal qualifications are simple: One must be at least 30 years of age, a citizen of the United States, and a resident of the state for five years preceding election. There is no requirement to be a registered voter. In fact, in the 1930s, W. Lee O'Daniel ran for governor, stressing that he was not a "professional politician." To prove his point, he made an issue of not being a registered voter.

Informal Qualifications

Experience

informal qualifications
Additional qualifications beyond the formal qualifications required for men and women to be elected governor; holding statewide elected office is an example

Informal qualifications are more important. Nationwide, most governors have held elected office before becoming governor. An examination of the 933 people who have served as governor in the United States between 1900 and 1997 reveals that the most common career path to that office is to begin in the legislature, move to statewide office, and then move to the governor's office. Others who have been elected governor have served as a U.S. senator or representative, and a few have served in local elected offices (such as mayor). Some governors gain experience as appointed administrators or as party officials. Between 1970 and 1999, only 10 percent of all people elected governor had no prior political office experience.[2]

In 2014, *The Washington Post* did a similar, but less exhaustive, survey of all serving governors to identify the positions held immediately preceding governorship. The results line up fairly well with the previous study. Only two held no previous public office. Ten governors were formerly lieutenant governor; 9 served their state in the U.S. Congress; 6 were attorney general; 5 were mayors; 4 served in their state's legislature; and the remaining 14 held other business and political positions.[3] It remains clear that having held elected office is an important informal qualification for becoming governor.

The national statistics generally apply to most Texas governors. Table 4.1 lists the men and women who have served since 1949 and their prior office experience.

TABLE 4.1

Previous Public Office Experience of Texas Governors, 1949–2015

Governor	Term of Office	Previous Offices
Allan Shivers	1949–57	State senate, lieutenant governor
Price Daniel	1957–63	U.S. Senate
John Connally	1963–69	U.S. Secretary of the Navy*
Preston Smith	1969–73	Texas House and Senate, lieutenant governor
Dolph Briscoe	1973–79	Texas House
Bill Clements	1979–83 1987–91	Assistant Secretary of Defense*
Mark White	1983–87	Attorney General
Ann Richards	1991–1994	County office, state treasurer
George W. Bush	1995–2001	None
Rick Perry	2001–2014	State legislature, agricultural commission, and lieutenant governor
Greg Abbott	2015–	Attorney General, Texas Supreme Court Jurist

*Appointed offices. No electoral experience before becoming governor.

Source: James Anderson, Richard W. Murray, and Edward L. Farley. *Texas Politics: An Introduction,* 6th ed. (New York: HarperCollins, 1992), 166-188. Legislative Reference Library, "Governors of Texas, 1846 - present," http://www.lrl.state.tx.us/legeLeaders/governors/govBrowse.cfm.

Only two had not held elected office. The recently retired governor, Rick Perry, followed a rather typical pattern. He served in the state legislature, as agricultural commissioner, and as lieutenant governor prior to becoming governor when George Bush resigned to assume the office of President of the United States. Perry was elected governor in his own right in 2002, 2006, and 2010. He did not run for a fourth term. Current governor Greg Abbott (R) served under Perry as attorney general. He previously served on the Texas Supreme Court, as appointed by George W. Bush, and as a state district judge in Harris County.

Race and Ethnicity

Besides electoral experience, there are many other informal qualifications. Nationwide, most people who have served as governors have been white, wealthy, well-educated, Protestant males. Only three African Americans—Douglas

FOCUS ON

An Hispanic Governor for Texas?

©Tony Gutierrez/AP Images

Absolutely, proclaims *Texas Monthly* magazine. The article, "El Gobernador," written in February 2008, begins with a hypothetical story of Rafael Anchia, currently serving as a state legislator from Dallas, winning the 2018 Texas gubernatorial race. Although the article begins with a look forward, its main focus is on the history of Hispanic politics and the changing demographics of the state.[5] According to the U.S. Census, 38.6% of Texans are Hispanic.[6] Texas will likely have an Hispanic governor some day; the main question is when.

During the 2002 governor's race, the state came very close. Tony Sanchez, a businessman and politician from Laredo, was the first Hispanic to run for governor in the statewide election. Before the election, he served as regent of the board for the University of Texas at Austin and also worked, albeit unsuccessfully, to get an Hispanic to run for president of the UT Health Science Center in

San Antonio. Moving into election season, Sanchez won the Democratic primary with 60 percent of the vote and faced off against Rick Perry, who had been unopposed in the Republican primary.[7]

During the election, many Democrats hoped that the state's Hispanic population would turn out in larger numbers and become a more distinct bloc in favor of the Democratic Party.[8] Unfortunately for Democrats and Sanchez, there was less Hispanic mobilization for their party than desired. Sanchez lost the election, winning only 40 percent of the vote.[9] In addition, although Hispanic turnout improved somewhat from the 2000 election, there was not enough movement to indicate a surge.[10] Hispanic turnout has been historically low as a percentage of its population and remains so.[11] (See Chapter 7 for more information on Hispanic voter turnout.)

Both the Democratic and Republican parties have been making inroads and capturing both votes and candidates from the grassroots up, however. Although voter turnout among Hispanics remains low, Rafael Anchia is part of a rising group of Hispanic politicians who have very real potential to capture the governor's office in the near future. This group also includes current Texas Land Commissioner George P. Bush and Secretary of Housing and Urban Development Julian Castro.

Critical Thinking Questions

1. What do you think it will take to mobilize and expand the Hispanic electorate?

2. In your opinion, why might the Hispanic vote be important for candidates seeking statewide office?

Wilder of Virginia, David Paterson of New York, and Deval Patrick of Massachusetts—have been elected as governor. None currently serve. Several Hispanics have served as state governors, including Tony Anaya, Jerry Abodaca, Bill Richardson, and Susan Martinez (current) in New Mexico; Bob Martinez in Florida; Paul Castro in Arizona; and Brian Sandoval (current) in Nevada. In addition, one Indian-American (Nikki Haley in South Carolina) and one Asian-American (David Ige in Hawaii) currently serve as governor.[4]

Women

More women have served as governor in recent years. In 1924, Wyoming elected the first woman governor, Nellie T. Ross, who served one term. She succeeded her husband, who died in office. Also in 1924, Texans elected Miriam A. Ferguson governor. "Ma" Ferguson was a "stand-in" for her husband, Jim Ferguson, who had been impeached, removed from office, and barred from seeking reelection. Mrs. Ferguson was reelected in 1932. Similarly, in 1968, Lurleen Wallace was elected governor of Alabama as a stand-in governor for her husband, George Wallace, who could not be reelected because of term limits. Although Ferguson and Wallace were stand-in governors for husbands ineligible for reelection, several women have been elected in their own right. Aside from Ferguson, Texas has had one other female governor, Ann Richards. She was elected in 1990 and served from 1991 to 1995.

As of 2016, 27 states have elected a total of 37 women as governor (see Map 4.1). Arizona is the first state where three women have held the office in succession. The number of women serving as governor will undoubtedly increase. As of this writing, 6 women are serving as governors, 12 women are serving as lieutenant governors, and 59 women are serving in other statewide elected executive offices. For women as well as men, service in statewide office is a good stepping-stone to the governor's office.[12]

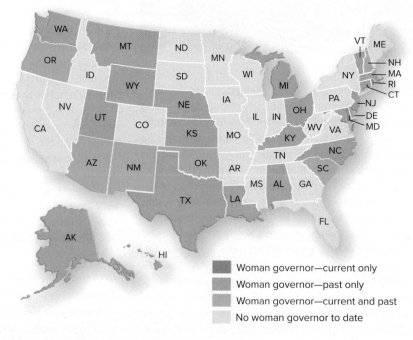

MAP 4.1   Women Governors

CORE OBJECTIVE

Communicating Effectively . . .

Analyze Map 4.1. What inferences can be drawn from the data?

© *George Lavendowski/USFWS*

Wealth

Historically, the men who have served as governor of Texas have generally had one thing in common—wealth. A few, such as Dolph Briscoe and Bill Clements, were very wealthy. If not wealthy, most have been successful in law, business, or politics before becoming governor. Ann Richards was something of an exception to these informal qualifications. She was neither wealthy nor from a wealthy family, and she had no business or law experience. Governor Bush is an example of past governors in terms of background, with a famous family name and family wealth. Governor Perry, while claiming the status of a sharecropper's son, came from a family with a moderate, middle-class background.

Salary

Nationwide, governors receive much higher pay than state legislators. The Council of State Governments notes that "As of 2015, salaries ranged from a low of $70,000 in Maine to a high of $184,632 in Pennsylvania with an average salary of $134,782."[13] The Texas governor's salary of $150,000 per year has been consistently above that average.[14] In addition, Texas also provides the governor with a home in Austin, an automobile with a driver, an airplane, and reimbursement for actual travel expenses. Texas governors also receive a budget for entertaining and for maintaining the governor's mansion. Compared with members of the state legislature, the governor in Texas is extremely well paid. Given the demands and responsibilities of the job, the governor is not overpaid compared with executives of large corporations who earn much more.

Succession to Office and Acting Governor

Learning Objective: Explain the provisions for succession of a governor.

Most states provide for a successor if the governor dies or leaves office. In 45 states, lieutenant governors advance to the office if it is vacant for any reason. In the 5 states without lieutenant governors, another officeholder, usually either the secretary of state or leader of the state senate, succeeds to the governor's office. In 17 states, the lieutenant governor and the governor are separately elected. In 5 states, the lieutenant governor and the governor are jointly elected on a party ticket based on the highest voted candidates in the primary elections. In

Current Lieutenant Governor of Texas Dan Patrick In the 2014 election, Dan Patrick beat out incumbent David Dewhurst in the Republican primary and then won by a wide margin in the general vote in November.[16] Although Texas elects its lieutenant governors separately from its governors, it rarely has a split party executive.

Pat Sullivan/AP Images

acting governor

When a governor leaves a state, the position is held by the lieutenant governor, who performs the functions of the office

21 states, the governor and lieutenant governor are jointly elected.[15] They run as a "team," much as candidates for president and vice president do. In these cases, the candidate for governor picks the lieutenant governor.

In Texas, the lieutenant governor becomes governor if the office is vacated. Following the lieutenant governor, the order of succession is as follows: president pro tempore of the Texas Senate, the speaker of the house, and the attorney general. In the unlikely event that the attorney general is no longer able to discharge the duties of governor, the Texas Constitution stipulates that succession follows the chief justices of the Court of Appeals in ascending order.

When governors leave their states, lieutenant governors become **acting governors**. Sometimes problems arise with this arrangement. For instance, in 1995, Arkansas Governor Jim Guy Tucker had problems with Senate President Pro Tem Jerry Jewell, who was acting as governor in the absence of the lieutenant governor. Jewell "granted two pardons and executive clemency to two prison inmates."[17] Also, the Arkansas lieutenant governor, Republican Mike Huckabee, "signed a proclamation for a Christian Heritage Week after Tucker declined to do so earlier."[18]

In Texas, former Governor Rick Perry may hold the record as serving the most time as acting governor when Governor George W. Bush was campaigning for president outside the state. Lieutenant Governor David Dewherst also served as acting governor for a great deal of time while Governor Perry was out of state running for the Republican presidential nomination in 2012. When serving as acting governor, the lieutenant governor in Texas receives the same pay as the governor.

Postgubernatorial Office

For some governors, the office is a stepping-stone to other offices. Some go on to the U.S. Senate, and several have been elected president of the United States. In Texas, former governor W. Lee O'Daniel served as a U.S. senator from 1941 to 1949, and George W. Bush became president in 2001. Postgubernatorial administrative service in the federal government is also common. Presidents often call upon former governors to head departments. President George H. W. Bush chose former New Hampshire governor John Sununu as his chief of staff. Bill Clinton chose Bruce Babbitt, former governor of Arizona, as secretary of the interior, and he also appointed former governor Richard Riley of South Carolina as secretary of education. Former Texas governor John Connally served as secretary of the treasury under President Richard Nixon. President George W. Bush selected several governors to be in his cabinet, as did President Barack Obama. However, for many governors, the office is the peak of their political careers, and they retire to private life. In a study from the 1980s, over 60 percent did so.[19] More recently, a 2009 study of all states' latest former governors found that 42 percent retired to private life, two-thirds of whom entered into business. Only 20 percent moved on to other forms of public service.[20] This statistic is true for most Texas governors. George W. Bush was the first Texas governor since 1941 to go on to higher elected office.

Removal from Office

Learning Objective: Explain the provisions for removal of a governor.

All states except Oregon have a procedure for removing governors by a process generally called impeachment.[21] Technically, the lower house of the legislature adopts articles of impeachment; then a trial on these articles of impeachment is held in the senate. If the senate finds the governor guilty by a two-thirds vote, he or she is removed from office. Together the two steps—the adoption of articles of **impeachment** and **conviction** by the senate—are commonly called impeachment. Sixteen U.S. governors have had impeachment trials, and 8 have been removed from office.[22] Technically, impeachment is a judicial process, but it is also a very political process. Impeached governors have generally been guilty of some wrongdoing, but they are often removed for political reasons.

Four impeachments illustrate the highly political nature of the process. Governor Jim Ferguson of Texas (1915–1917) is one example. Ferguson was indicted by the Texas House, technically for misuse of state funds, and was convicted and removed from office by the senate. In reality he was impeached because of his fight with the University of Texas board of regents. When Ferguson could not force the board to terminate several professors who had been critical of him, or force the resignation of board members, he used his line-item veto authority to veto the entire appropriations bill for the University of Texas.[23] This veto led to his impeachment. Ferguson tried to prevent his impeachment by calling the legislature into special session. Because only the governor may decide the agenda of a special session, Governor Ferguson told the legislature it could consider any item it wanted, except impeachment. This ploy did not work, and he was removed from office. Courts later upheld Ferguson's impeachment.

A few years after the Ferguson affair in Texas, Oklahoma impeached two consecutively elected governors. These two impeachments were as political as the one in Texas. In 1921, many African Americans were killed in several race riots, the most notable of which occurred in the Greenwood area of Tulsa, Oklahoma. Thirty-five square blocks of this segregated African American community were burned and destroyed, and more than 40 people were killed. The next year, John C. Walton was elected governor as a member of the Farmer-Laborite Party. Walton tried to break up the Ku Klux Klan in the state, and this led to his impeachment. The lieutenant governor, Martin Trapp, served out the remainder of Walton's term but was unable to run for reelection because Oklahoma had a one-term limit at that time. Henry S. Johnson was elected governor in 1926 as a pro-KKK candidate and refused to use his office to quell Klan activity in the state. Johnson used the National Guard to try to prevent the legislature from meeting to consider his impeachment. The legislature was kept out of the state capitol building and had to meet in a hotel in Oklahoma City. Johnson was convicted and removed from office. He had been indicted on 18 counts and found not guilty on all charges but one—"general incompetence"—for which he was impeached.[24]

The impeachment of Evan Mecham in Arizona in 1988 was equally political. Mecham made a number of racist remarks and had become a source of

impeachment

The process by which some elected officials, including governors, may be impeached (accused of an impeachable offense) by the lower house adopting articles of impeachment

conviction

Following adoption of articles of impeachment by the lower legislative house, the senate tries the official under those articles; if convicted, the official is removed from office

James E. Ferguson [D] was the 26th Governor of Texas for three years until his impeachment in 1917. While the judgment technically prevented him from further public office, he would go on to try for both the governorship and the presidency, the former with his wife as the official candidate. They won the governorship in 1924, but did not win reelection.

SOURCE: Library of Congress Prints and Photographs Division LC-B2-3190-1 [P&P]

embarrassment in the state. Technically, he was impeached for misuse of state funds during his inaugural celebration. All these governors had technically committed some malfeasance of office, but they were impeached for largely political reasons.

Nine states also allow **recall** of the governor; Texas does not. Many Texas home-rule cities do allow recall of city councils and mayors. Recall involves having petitions signed by a specific number of voters, followed by an election where, if a majority approves, the governor can be recalled or removed from office. Two governors have been recalled. Lynn J. Frazier of North Dakota was recalled in 1921, the same time when governors were being impeached in Texas and Oklahoma. In 1988, Governor Mecham of Arizona was spared a recall election when impeached by the legislature.[25] In 2003, Gray Davis of California was recalled. In 2011, the voters of Wisconsin voted against recalling Governor Scott Walker. More than 60 percent of voters did not like the idea of using a recall to remove a governor. With so few examples of recall, it is impossible to make any generalizations on the politics of it.

Formal Powers of the Governor

Learning Objective: Explain the governor's formal powers.

Most governors do not have extensive formal powers, but the few they do have can be measured using six variables: election of other statewide executives, tenure of office, appointment powers, budgetary powers, veto powers, and control over party. By examining each of these variables, we can compare the formal powers of governors and, more specifically, assess the powers of the Texas governor.

Election of Other Statewide Executives

The ability of the Texas governor to control administrative functions through formal appointive and removal powers is exceptionally weak. The voters elect many important state administrators. Texas is, therefore, a good example of the **plural executive system** structure. Map 4.2 provides a comparison of the number of elected executive officials in all states. Texas voters elect the lieutenant governor (discussed in Chapter 3), attorney general, comptroller of public accounts, state land commissioner, agricultural commissioner, the railroad commission, and the state board of education.

The election of people to head administrative units of government is a concept dating to the 1820s with the election of Andrew Jackson. Known as Jacksonian statehouse government, the belief is that the ballot box is the best way to select administrators and make them accountable to the public. In the aftermath of Reconstruction in the 1870s, the current constitution reintroduced the idea of electing almost all officeholders and limiting the governor's ability to appoint them.

Office of the Attorney General

This office was created under the 1876 Texas constitution. The **attorney general** serves as the legal counsel to the governor, the legislature, and most of the other agencies, boards, and commissions in state government. Most of the work of

recall
The removal of the governor or an elected official by a petition signed by the required number of registered voters and by an election in which a majority votes to remove the person from office

plural executive system
System in which executive power is divided among several statewide elected officials

attorney general
Chief counsel to the governor and state agencies; limited criminal jurisdiction

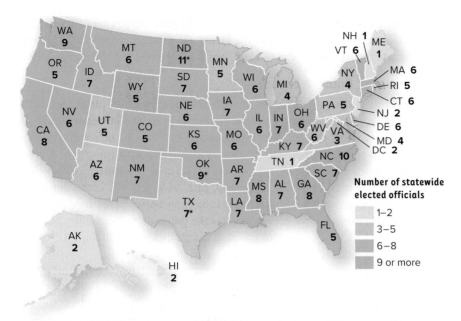

*Some states have Commissions with multiple elected offices therein. For the purposes of this map, we have counted those commissions as a single elected entity.

MAP 4.2   Total Number of Major Statewide Elected Officials for Each State, Executive Branch

the attorney general involves civil law rather than criminal law. The attorney general's office, with some 3,700 state employees, is responsible for representing the state in litigation, enforcing state and federal child support laws, providing legal counsel to state officials, and enforcing state laws. Criminal functions of the office are primarily limited to those cases appealed to federal courts. The most common examples of these criminal cases are death penalty appeals. Occasionally, the attorney general's office may assist local criminal prosecutors when invited to do so. Although the functions of the attorney general are usually civil and not criminal in nature, this does not prevent most candidates who run for the office from emphasizing their commitment to law enforcement and being tough on criminals.

Most of the resources of this office are devoted to collection of child support payments, collection of delinquent state taxes, administration of the Crime Victims' Compensation program, and investigation of Medicare fraud. Despite this rather mundane list of functions, the office has important political functions. The most important of these is to issue so-called AG (attorney general) opinions on legal questions. Many times, when the legislature is in session, the AG will be asked for an opinion on a pending piece of legislation. These AG opinions can have an impact on the course of legislation. Often, a negative AG opinion will kill a bill's chances of passing.

The office of attorney general is also an important stepping-stone to the governor's office. In recent years, several candidates for governor have been former attorneys general (John Hill, Mark White, Jim Mattox, and most recently Greg Abbott who successfully assumed the governorship in 2015). Dan Morales was the first Hispanic to be elected to the office. He did not seek reelection in 1998, and in 2002 he ran and lost a bid to become the Democratic Party nominee for governor. John Cornyn, the AG from 1998 to 2002, was elected to the U.S. Senate in 2002.

Comptroller of Public Accounts

comptroller of public accounts

Chief tax collector and investor of state funds; does not perform financial audits

Another constitutional office created in 1876, the **comptroller of public accounts** has been assigned many additional duties over the years and currently functions as the chief fiscal and revenue forecasting office. In 1966, the office of treasurer was abolished, and the comptroller became responsible for investing state funds.

In many states and in the private sector, the term is "controller," rather than "comptroller" as used in Texas. Generally, in government the controller has a pre-audit responsibility for ensuring that funds can be spent for specific functions. In Texas, the comptroller not only has the pre-audit responsibility but also serves as the chief tax collector (a function normally associated with the office of treasurer), revenue forecaster, and investor of state funds.

The comptroller is responsible for collecting more than 60 taxes and other fees for the state and collects the sales tax for 1,217 cities, 254 counties, and many other special districts.[26] The property tax division also conducts annual audits of property appraisal districts in the state to ensure uniformity in appraisals. This uniformity is important to improve the equity of state aid to local school districts. (See Chapter 6 on local government.)

Former governor Bob Bullock served as comptroller for many years. During his tenure, the office expanded the information and management functions and developed a fiscal forecasting model essential to projecting revenues in a two-year budget cycle. John Sharp, who succeeded Bullock as comptroller, continued and expanded the information management programs of the office. Also under Sharp, the office developed the Texas Performance Review teams to evaluate the effectiveness of government operations and ensure the most efficient use of state funds. These reviews were estimated to have saved the state more than $1.3 billion in the 1998–1999 biennium fiscal years. Similar management information and efficiency audits are available to assist local governments. Most of these programs were kept in place by Sharp's successor, Carole Keeton Strayhorn (1999–2007), as well as Susan Combs (2007–2015) and Glen Hegar (2015-current).

The office also provides assistance to the private sector through the provision of information. The State of Texas Econometric Model is used to forecast state economic growth, keep track of business cycles, and generally provide information on the health of the economy of the state. Finally, the office is responsible for investing state funds.

CORE OBJECTIVE

© Editorial Image, LLC/Alamy

Being Socially Responsible. . .

How does the comptroller promote effective involvement in regional, national, and global communities?

Commissioner of the General Land Office

Texas is one of only four states to have an elected **land commissioner**.[27] In Texas, the office was created under the 1836 constitution to administer state-owned land. When Texas entered the Union in 1845, the agreement between the former republic and the U.S. government was that Texas kept its public debt and its public land. When Texas became a state, most of the land was state owned. Today the state of Texas owns and manages 20.3 million acres, including open beaches and submerged land 10.3 miles into the Gulf of Mexico.

The land commissioner's office is responsible for leasing state lands and generating funds from oil and gas production. The office is also responsible for overseeing the Veterans' Land Board and Veterans' Land Fund, which loans money to Texas veterans to purchase rural land. Finally, the land office is responsible for maintaining the environmental quality of the state's open beaches along the Gulf Coast.

Recent notable land commissioners have been David Dewhurst, the LC from 1999 to 2003 (later lieutenant governor from 2003 to 2015), and George P. Bush, elected LC in 2015 (grandson of former U.S. President George H.W. Bush and nephew of former U.S. President George W. Bush).

land commissioner
Elected official responsible for administration and oversight of state-owned lands and coastal lands extending 10.3 miles into the Gulf of Mexico

Commissioner of Agriculture

The Texas Department of Agriculture (TDA) was created by statute in 1907. A commissioner of agriculture, elected in a statewide election, heads the department. The TDA has the dual, and sometimes contradictory, roles of promoting agricultural products and production and regulating agricultural practices, while also protecting the public health from unsafe agricultural practices. For example, the TDA must both promote cotton production and sales in the state and regulate the use of pesticides.

The TDA has six major functions: marketing of Texas agricultural products, development and promotion of agricultural products, pesticide regulation, pest management, product certification and safety inspection, and inspection and certification of measuring devices (including gasoline pumps, electronic scanners, and scales).

Although the agriculture commissioner is not as publicly visible as the other statewide elected officials, it is an important office to a large section of the state's economy—those engaged in agriculture. Texas's economy has become more diversified in recent years, but agriculture is still a significant player. Major agribusinesses and others in agriculture in the state pay close attention to who serves as the agriculture commissioner.

The Texas Railroad Commission

The **Texas Railroad Commission** (RRC) was created in 1891 under the administration of Governor James S. Hogg to regulate the railroad monopolies that had developed in the state. The commission was also given regulatory authority over terminals, wharves, and express companies. The commission consists of three members who are elected in statewide elections for six-year staggered terms, with one member elected every two years. The member up for election, by convention, always serves as chair of the commission.

In the 1920s, when oil and natural gas production developed in the state, the task of regulating the exploration, drilling, and production of oil and natural gas

Texas Railroad Commission
State agency with regulation over some aspects of transportation and the oil and gas industry of the state

was assigned to the RRC in part because it was the only state regulatory agency at the time. When motor truck transport developed in the state, regulation of the trucking industry was also assigned to the RRC. In part because of federal rules and regulations, the original role of regulating railroads and the later role of regulating trucking have diminished to minor roles, reduced primarily to concern with safety issues. The regulation of the oil and gas industry is the RRC's primary function today.

Many have been critical of the RRC over the years because of close ties between the elected commissioners and the oil and gas industry they regulate. (See Chapter 10 on interest groups.) Large campaign contributions from oil and gas PACs have raised questions about the commission being co-opted by the industry it regulates. Also, like the agriculture commissioner, the RRC has the dual role of promoting oil and gas production in the state and regulating the safety and environmental aspects of the industry (for example, promoting the development of pipelines to carry petroleum products as well as overseeing the safety of such pipelines). A similar conflict may exist between the RRC's task of regulating and promoting the mining of minerals (especially lignite coal) in the state.

The role of the RRC that most directly affects citizens in the state is that of setting the rates charged by local natural gas companies. Those companies must have the rates they charge residential and commercial customers approved by the RRC. The RRC also regulates the safety of natural gas systems.

It has been suggested that the name of this agency be changed to better reflect its function. Proponents of change argue that the present name is confusing to voters and does not reflect its functions.

The State Board of Education

Unlike the other offices discussed in this section, the governing body for public elementary and secondary education in the state has varied greatly in form and structure over the years. Originally, in 1884, an elected school superintendent governed Texas schools. In 1929 an appointed state board was created. In 1949 the Gilmer-Aikin Act created the Texas Education Agency (TEA) with an appointed superintendent of education. An elected state board was added in the 1960s. In 1984 the elected board was reduced from 21 members who were elected from congressional districts in the state to 15 members appointed by the governor. In 1986 the board was again changed, and members were elected from 15 districts. The current board, called the State Board of Education, nominates a person to the governor to be commissioner of education.

In recent years, the authority of the state board has been greatly reduced by actions of the state legislature. The political battle over the power of the state board revolved around social conservatives' (Christian right) success in electing members to the board and the actions taken in setting curriculum standards and textbook selection issues. Public infighting among members of the board diminished its effectiveness. The legislature has removed several functions, most significantly the selection of textbooks, from the state board, in part because of the infighting and control by this faction. One of the main issues has been the teaching of evolution in biology classes. Some members of the board want the curriculum to reflect a creationist approach to human existence.

Taking Personal Responsibility. . .

What can you do to become more actively engaged in the civic discourse about the role of the State Board of Education?

Source: United States Department of Agriculture Agricultural Research Service

Tenure of Office

Tenure of office is both the legal ability of governors to succeed themselves in office and the term length. Historically, the tenure of governors has been less than that for most other statewide elected state officials, in part because of term limits.[28] Term limits for governors have been a fixture since the beginning of the Republic. In the original 13 states, 10 of the governors had one-year terms. States first moved to two-year terms, then four-year terms. In the 1960s, states borrowed from the federal Constitution the idea of limiting governors to two four-year terms.[29] Southern states were the last to move to longer terms. Many southern states once prohibited the governor from serving consecutive terms in office. Today, only Virginia retains this provision. Map 4.3 provides a comparison of gubernatorial term limits.

Tenure is an important determinant of power. If governors can be continually reelected, they retain the potential to influence government until they decide to

tenure of office
The ability of governors to be reelected to office

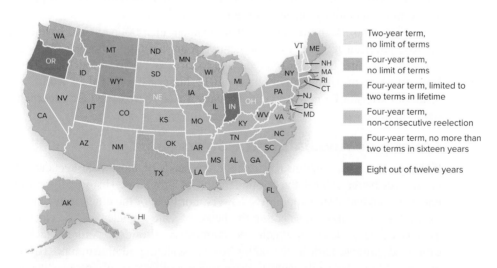

Two-year term, no limit of terms

Four-year term, no limit of terms

Four-year term, limited to two terms in lifetime

Four-year term, non-consecutive reelection

Four-year term, no more than two terms in sixteen years

Eight out of twelve years

*Wyoming had imposed term limits through a ballot measure in 1992, but in 2013 the Wyoming Supreme Court declared it unconstitutional, determining that only a constitutional amendment could legitimately define any such changes.

MAP 4.3   Term Limits for Governors as of 2015

leave office. Only 14 states do not limit how long a person can serve as governor. When prevented from being reelected by term limits, governors suffer as "lame ducks" toward the end of their terms. Long tenure also enables governors to carry out their programs. Short terms (two years) force governors to continually seek reelection and make political compromises. However, the upside is that they have to remain connected to the electorate. Only two states retain the two-year term—Vermont and New Hampshire.

Longer tenure is also an important factor in the governor's role as intergovernmental coordinator. Building up associations with officials in other states and in Washington is important and takes time. Short tenure makes it difficult for governors to gain leadership roles in this area and has the effect of shortchanging the state that imposes them.[30]

The Texas governor has the strongest tenure—four-year terms with no limit on the number of terms. Dolph Briscoe was elected to a two-year term in 1972. In that same election, Texas changed to a four-year term, which became effective in 1975. Briscoe was reelected to serve one four-year term (1975–79). After Briscoe, governors Clements, White, and Richards were limited by voters to one term, although Clements did later regain the governorship. He served from 1970 to 1983, lost to Mark White for one term, and then retook the governorship from 1987 to 1991. George W. Bush was the first governor to be elected to two consecutive four-year terms. However, Bush served only six years because he was elected president in 2000.

Few Texas governors have served more than four years in office. Since 1874, 19 Texas governors have served for four years; most of these (15) were for consecutive two-year terms. Seven served for two years, four served six years, and only one (Allan Shivers, 1949–57) served for eight consecutive years—four two-year terms.[31] Bill Clements served for eight nonconsecutive years. Thus, the history of Texas governors is not one of long tenure. Serving two two-year terms was the norm for most of the state's history. From 1874 until 1953, no person served more than four years as governor in Texas.[32]

Had Governor Bush not been elected president in 2000, he would have been the first governor to serve two consecutive four-year terms. Former Governor Perry was the first governor to be elected to three consecutive four-year terms. Upon finishing his final term in January 2015, he served a total of 14 years. As a result of Governor Perry's long tenure, many Texans have called for gubernatorial term limits.

Governor's Appointment Powers

If the governor can appoint and remove the heads of most state agencies, he or she can better control the administration of programs. Historically, governors have not had strong appointive powers. For most of the nineteenth century, the traditional method of selecting the heads of state agencies was by election. This is called Jacksonian statehouse democracy. President Andrew Jackson expressed ultimate faith in the ballot box for selecting administrators. Toward the end of the nineteenth century, there was a proliferation of agencies headed by appointed or elected boards and commissions. The governor was just one of many elected state officials and had little formal control over state administration.[33] Governors often share power with many other elected individuals. Such arrangements are known as plural executive structures. Figure 4.1 is a diagram

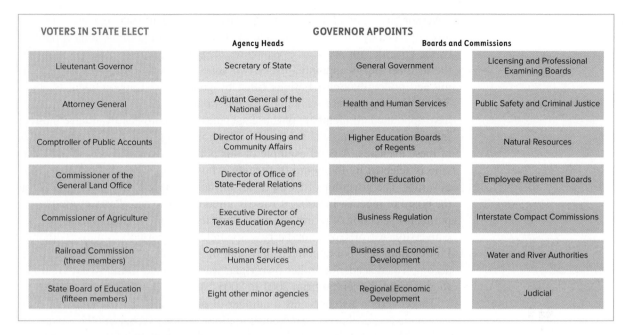

VOTERS IN STATE ELECT	GOVERNOR APPOINTS		
	Agency Heads	Boards and Commissions	
Lieutenant Governor	Secretary of State	General Government	Licensing and Professional Examining Boards
Attorney General	Adjutant General of the National Guard	Health and Human Services	Public Safety and Criminal Justice
Comptroller of Public Accounts	Director of Housing and Community Affairs	Higher Education Boards of Regents	Natural Resources
Commissioner of the General Land Office	Director of Office of State-Federal Relations	Other Education	Employee Retirement Boards
Commissioner of Agriculture	Executive Director of Texas Education Agency	Business Regulation	Interstate Compact Commissions
Railroad Commission (three members)	Commissioner for Health and Human Services	Business and Economic Development	Water and River Authorities
State Board of Education (fifteen members)	Eight other minor agencies	Regional Economic Development	Judicial

FIGURE 4.1   The Administrative Structure of State Government in Texas

of the administrative structure of the Texas state government and is divided into three categories: statewide elected offices, single-head agencies appointed by the governor, and boards and commissions appointed by the governor.

Equally important to the appointive power is the power to remove administrators, which is discussed in a later section of this chapter. Without the power of removal, the appointive powers of the governor are greatly diminished. Beginning in the early twentieth century, the powers of the governor to appoint and remove officials were increased in some states. This expansion of executive authority has increased in the past three decades in many states.[34] This has not been the pattern for much of the South or for the office of governor in Texas. In 2001 the voters in Texas even rejected an amendment that would have made the adjutant general of the Texas National Guard subject to removal by the governor. The traditionalistic political culture does not support the idea of strong executive authority, even for relatively minor offices.

Of the 167 currently active agencies in the Texas[35], the governor appoints a few agency heads; the most significant is the secretary of state, who serves as the chief record keeper and election official for the state. The governor also appoints the executive directors of the departments of Commerce, Health and Human Services, Housing and Community Affairs, and Insurance, and the Office of State-Federal Relations. The governor appoints the head of the Texas National Guard and appoints the executive director of the Texas Education Agency from recommendations made by the elected Texas State Board of Education. The governor also appoints the chief counsels for the Public Utility Commission, the Insurance Commission, and the State Office of Administrative Hearings.

Thus, significant portions of state government are beyond the direct control of the governor because several agency heads are elected. In terms of numbers, most agencies are controlled by independent boards and commissions over which the governor has minimal direct control. These independent state agencies are usually governed by three-, six-, or nine-member boards or commissions appointed by the governor for six-year, overlapping, staggered terms. Usually, one-third of the membership is appointed every two years. In total, the number of governing and policy-making positions filled by gubernatorial appointment is about 3,000.[36] If the governor stays in office for two terms (eight years), she or he will have appointed all members of these agencies and boards and can have indirect influence over them (see Table 4.2). The governing board chooses the heads of these agencies. A good example of this is the president of a state university, who is selected by the board of regents, whose members are appointed by the governor. The governor often exercises influence with his or her appointees on the board of regents. In 2002, it was rumored that Governor Perry strongly supported the selection of retiring Senator Phil Gramm for president of Texas A&M University. All of Governor Perry's appointees supported Gramm. (Although Phil Gramm was not appointed president of Texas A&M, his wife Wendy, an accomplished academic in her own right, was appointed to the A&M Board of Regents, and she served from 2001 to 2005.[37])

The governor also appoints a number of persons to non-policy-making and governing boards that make recommendations to the governor or other state officials. Although not discussed in detail in this chapter, many of these non-policy-making boards recommend changes in policy and programs; others are simply window dressing and allow the governor to reward supporters. Most often, these non-policy-making boards do not require senate approval.

TABLE 4.2

Texas Governor Appointments to Policy-Making and Governing Boards, Commissions, and Agencies

Type of Agency	Number of Agencies	Number of Appointees
General Government	31	244
Health and Human Services	31	366
Higher Education Boards and Regents	12	117
Other Education	16	149
Business Regulation	9	37
Business and Economic Development	24	176
Regional Economic Development	32	276
Licensing and Professional Examining Boards	39	461
Public Safety and Criminal Justice	22	158
Natural Resources	16	156
Employee Retirement Boards	8	53
Interstate Compact Commissions	8	24
Water and River Authorities	18	210
Judicial	18	151
Others	18	251
Totals	302	2,838

Source: Data supplied by the Texas State Governor's Appointment Secretary, Freedom of Information Request, August 2000. Categories for state agencies are by the author. List can be obtained from Governor's Appointment Secretary, State Capitol, Austin, TX (updates to 2010).

Some gubernatorial appointments are subject to approval by a two-thirds vote of the senate. In these cases, the governor must clear his or her appointments with the state senator from the appointee's home district. This limits the discretion of the governor. This process is known as **senatorial courtesy**. If the senator from an appointee's home district disapproves of the appointment, the senate might not confirm the appointee. Senatorial courtesy does not apply to all gubernatorial appointments, especially the non-policy-making boards.

The discretion of the governor is also limited by other factors. For example, some boards require geographic representation. Members of river authority boards must live in the area covered by the river authority. Good examples of this are the Trinity River Authority and the Lower Colorado River Authority. Other boards require specified professional backgrounds. Membership on the Texas Municipal Retirement System, for instance, is limited to certain types of city employees—such as firefighters, police, and city managers.[38]

However, political limits are placed on the governor's ability to appoint people. Interest groups pay close attention to the governor's appointments to these boards and commissions and try to influence the governor's choices. The governor may have to bend to demands from such groups. Chapter 10 discusses this subject in more detail.

In Texas, the appointive power of the governor, even with these formal limitations, allows the governor to indirectly influence policy by appointing people with similar policy views to serve on these boards and commissions. It is unlikely that a governor will select men and women with whom he or she differs on major policy issues. This broad appointive power allows the governor to influence policy even after leaving office, because some of the appointees remain on these boards and commissions after the governor's term ends. Ann Richards used her appointive powers to increase the number of women and minorities serving on these boards and commissions. Richards's successor, George W. Bush, appointed some women and minorities, but tended mainly to appoint white businessmen to these positions. Former Governor Perry, for the most part, appointed white business leaders as well.

In some states, a single person, appointed and serving at the pleasure of the governor, heads most agencies. The structure is much like that of the federal government, where the president appoints members of his own cabinet and they serve at his pleasure. Only a handful of state agencies in Texas meet this model.

Secretary of State

The **secretary of state (SOS)** is a constitutional office, appointed by the governor with approval of the state senate. The constitution and state statutes assign many duties to this office, which can be lumped into three broad categories: elections, record keeping/information management, and international protocol. As the chief election official, the SOS is responsible for overseeing voter registration, preparation of election information, and supervision of elections. The SOS issues rules, directives, and opinions on the conduct of elections and voter registration. These duties allow the secretary some latitude in the interpretation and application of the state election code. For example, the SOS has some latitude in how vigorously he or she encourages citizens to register and vote.

A second duty of the SOS is to serve as the official keeper of state records. This includes records on business corporations and some other commercial

senatorial courtesy
The courtesy of the governor clearing his or her appointments with state senator from the appointee's home district

secretary of state
Chief election official and keeper of state records; appointed by the governor

activities. The office also publishes the *Texas Register,* which is the source of official notices or rules, meetings, executive orders, and opinions of the attorney general that are required to be filed by state agencies. Through the protocol functions of the office, the SOS provides support services to state officials who interact with representatives of foreign countries.

In a few cases, the office of secretary of state has been an important stepping-stone to higher office. It is a highly visible office, and the secretary is often in the public eye, especially with the duties as chief election official. It is without doubt the most important single-head agency appointment that the governor makes. The most noted example is Mark White (1973-1977), who became attorney general and later governor. Former Governor Bush picked his secretary of state, Alberto Gonzales (1998-1999), to become White House counsel in his administration from 2001 to 2005.[39]

Commissioner for Health and Human Services

This office was created in 1991 to coordinate a number of health-related programs and agencies. The governor appoints the commissioner for a two-year term with the approval of the state senate. The commissioner has oversight responsibility over eight separate health and welfare programs, which are directed by boards, councils, or commissions. The commissioner is not directly responsible for the administration of these programs but has oversight and review functions. Those programs include aging; alcohol and drug abuse; the blind, deaf, and hard-of-hearing; early childhood intervention; juvenile probation; mental health and retardation; rehabilitation; and departments of Health, Human Services, and Protective and Regulatory Services. Although this office has little direct administrative control, it can and often does have impact on policy. The commissioner serves as a spokesperson for the governor in health and welfare matters.[40]

Office of State-Federal Relations

The governor appoints the executive director of the Office of State-Federal Relations. As the name suggests, this office coordinates relations between state and federal officials. The office has existed since 1971 and is the primary liaison between the governor's office and federal officials. To some degree this office becomes an advocate for the state in dealing with the Texas congressional delegation and federal agencies.[41]

Adjutant General of the National Guard

This office was created by the Texas Constitution and is responsible for directing the state military force under the direction of the governor. The governor serves as commander-in-chief of the guard. The **military powers** of the governor are quite limited and come into play only in times of natural disaster or civil unrest. The governor appoints the adjutant general of the National Guard and can direct the guard to protect the lives and property of Texas citizens. The most common use of this power is during natural disasters, when the guard is employed to help evacuate people, protect property, and supply food and water to victims. The size of the National Guard (nationwide and in Texas) is determined and funded by Congress as a reserve force to the regular army.

In the 1999 November election, Texas voters rejected a constitutional amendment that would have allowed the governor to appoint and remove the head of

military powers

Powers giving the governor the right to use the National Guard in times of natural disaster or civil unrest

the National Guard. As with other appointees, the governor may appoint the head of the National Guard, but not remove him or her except on approval of the state senate.[42]

Other Single-Head Agencies

The remaining state agencies to which the governor makes a single appointment are not of great significance in terms of policy or politics. This is not to say that they are insignificant, but simply of less importance or visibility. These agencies often receive little or no attention from the average citizen or the press. They include the Department of Housing and Community Affairs, Department of Commerce, State Office of Administrative Hearings, Insurance Commissioner, and Public Utility Commission Council. In addition, five interstate compact commissions govern the rivers in Texas.[43] The governor appoints the executive director of each of these commissions.

Boards and Commissions

In addition to these elected and appointed officials, the governor also appoints about 3,000 members to 302 state **boards and commissions**. These administrative units carry out most of the work of state government. The board or commission usually appoints the head of the agency (e.g., chancellor of a university or executive director of a state agency) and in varying degrees is responsible for policy and administration of the agency. Most operate independently from other agencies of state government, except the legislature.

boards and commissions
Governing body for many state agencies; members appointed by the governor for fixed term

This means state government in Texas is decentralized in nature. For example, some 18 separate agencies provide health and welfare services. In addition to the Department of Agriculture, the General Land Office, and the Railroad Commission—all having some control over environmental and natural resources—at least seven other agencies with independent boards or commissions have some authority in this area. These include the Texas Commission of Environmental Quality, the Texas Parks and Wildlife Department, the Soil and Water Conservation Board, and the Water Development Board.

In this conservative state with a strong belief in the free market there are, nonetheless, no fewer than 38 separate professional licensing and examining boards. Many professions have a state agency that licenses and regulates them. Just a few examples are accountants, architects, barbers, chiropractors, cosmetologists, dentists, exterminators, funeral directors, land surveyors, medical doctors, two kinds of nurses, pharmacists, physical therapists, podiatrists, and veterinarians. Most often a professional group asks for regulation by the state. When such a group advocates government regulation and licensing, it claims its primary interest to be protecting the public from incompetent or dishonest practitioners. This may be partially true; however, regulation also has the added benefit (to interested parties) of the development of rules favorable to the group and limiting entry into the profession that come at a cost to consumers. Two good examples are the water-well drillers and landscape architects. (See Chapter 10 on interest groups.) Also, professionals always make the argument that the people appointed to the boards by the governor should be knowledgeable about the profession they are governing. Knowledge is one factor, but the danger is that these boards and commissions, dominated by members of the profession, will be more interested in making rules and regulations favorable to the group than to protect the public.

Because of this fear, in recent years, the appointment of at least some members of the board from outside the profession has become the norm—for example, non-physicians are on the State Board of Medical Examiners.

Twelve college governing boards oversee the institutions of higher education in the state. These boards are required to coordinate their activities and gain approval for some activities and programs from the State Higher Education Coordinating Board. Within these broad guidelines, each university governing board is relatively free to set policy, approve budgets, and govern their universities. Again, governance is decentralized, with only minimum control from the state and almost none from the governor.

Appointment and Campaign Contributions

Governors have also been known to appoint their campaign supporters to governing boards and commissions. People who were loyal supporters, especially those giving big campaign contributions, are often rewarded with appointment to prestigious state boards and commissions. University governing boards are especially desired positions. Listed in Table 4.3 are the contributions Governor Perry received from individuals who were appointed to state boards and commissions.

Removal Powers

The other side of the power to appoint is the power to remove persons from office. U.S. presidents may remove many of their appointees, but state governors are often very restricted by the state constitution, statutes creating the agency, or term limits set for appointees. Some states allow the governor to remove a person only for cause. This requires the governor to make a case for wrongdoing by the individual. Of course, the governor can force the resignation of a person

TABLE 4.3

Governor Rick Perry Campaign Contributions and Appointments to Boards and Commissions

Appointed Office Category (% of All Appointments)	Average Appointee Contribution	No. of Appointments	Percent Involving Donations	Total Appointee Donations
Education (12%)	$10,616	135	35%	$1,433,093
Humanities (4%)	8,316	45	44%	374,220
Natural Resources (12%)	6,410	133	42%	852,556
Insurance (1%)	6,167	15	20%	92,500
Finance (4%)	3,940	41	32%	161,527
Corrections/Security (9%)	2,673	100	22%	267,278
Other (7%)	2,171	79	27%	171,535
Housing (2%)	1,982	17	29%	7,000
Infrastructure/Transportation (3%)	1,938	39	46%	77,296
Law (7%)	1,501	78	36%	117,080
Health/Human Services (14%)	958	153	16%	146,507
Economy (6%)	840	62	26%	52,070
Licensing (18%)	559	198	25%	110,712
Retirement (2%)	248	28	29%	6,950
Total	$ 3,446	1,123	32%	$3,870,324

Source: TPJ.org "Well-appointed boards." See: (http://info.tpj.org/page_view.jsp?pageid=979.)

without formal hearings, but the political cost of such forced resignations can be quite high and beyond what the governor is willing to pay.

In Texas, the removal power of the governor is very weak. Before 1981, Texas state law was silent on the issue of removal. In 1981 the constitution was amended to allow governors, with a two-thirds vote of the senate, to remove any person they personally appointed. Governors may not remove any of their predecessors' appointees. To date, no person has been formally removed from office using this procedure, but it does provide the governor with some leverage to force an appointee to resign. It might also be used to force a policy change favored by the governor. It does not, however, allow the governor to control the day-to-day administration of state government.

In 2010 Governor Perry became openly involved in the removal of some members of these appointed boards when he demanded the resignation of a member of the Texas Tech Board of Regents who was supporting his rival, Senator Kay Bailey Hutchison, in the Republican primary.

Other evidence that the governor may try to control the decisions of an appointed board occurred when Governor Perry tried to influence the appointment of the chancellor of the University of Texas system. Regents say that Perry called and suggested they support John Munford, a former state senator, over Francisco Cigarroa, a well-qualified academic.[44] Perry also tried to influence appointments of positions at the Texas A&M system where his former chief of staff, Mike McKinney, was chancellor. These include a former president and the vice president of student affairs, General Joe Weber, a roommate of the governor while they were students at Texas A&M University.

Budgetary Powers

Along with tenure of office and appointive/executive authority, **budgetary powers** are an important determinant of executive authority. Control over how money is spent is at the very heart of the policy-making process. Some writers define a budget as a statement of policy in monetary terms. If the governor can control budget formation and development (the preparation of the budget for submission to the legislature) and budget execution (deciding how money is spent), the governor can have a significant influence on state policy. Four kinds of constraints can undercut the governor's budgetary authority:

- The extent to which the governor must share budget formation with the legislature or with other state agencies
- The extent to which funds are earmarked for specific expenditures and the choice on how to spend money is limited by previous actions
- The extent to which the governor shares budget execution authority with others in state government
- The limits on the governor's use of a line-item veto for the budget

In 27 U.S. states, the governor has full responsibility in budget making power; in the other states, responsibility is shared.[45] In those states where the governor is given authority for budget formation, agencies must present their requests for expenditures to the governor's office, which combines them and presents a unified budget to the legislature. In some states, the governor is limited regarding how much he or she can reduce the budget requests of some state agencies. If the governor can change the requests of agencies, this gives him or her tremendous

budgetary powers
The ability of a governor to formulate a budget, present it to the legislature, and execute or control the budget

control over the final form of the budget submitted to the legislature. A common practice of state governments is to earmark revenue for specific purposes. For example, funds received through the gasoline tax are commonly earmarked for state highways. This also limits the discretion of the governor.

Budget execution authority is more complex. Governors and others control budget execution in a variety of ways. If the governor controls the appointment of the major department heads of state government, he or she will have some discretion in how money is spent. The governor may decide not to spend all the money appropriated for a state park, for example. Administrative discretion over how money is spent is a time-honored way to expand executive authority over the budget.

Another area where governors can often exercise control over budgets is veto authority. All but five U.S. governors have a **line-item veto** that allows them to exercise great influence over the budgetary process.[46]

In Texas, the governor's budgetary powers are exceptionally weak, except in the area of the line-item veto. The governor is not constitutionally mandated to submit a budget. This power is given to the **Legislative Budget Board (LBB)**, an agency governed by the speaker of the house and the lieutenant governor. State agencies must present budget requests to the LBB, and the LBB produces a budget that is submitted to the legislature. Historically, governors have submitted budget messages to the legislature, often in the form of reactions to the LBB proposed budget.

In Texas, many funds are earmarked by the previous actions of the legislature. One estimate from the LBB is that more than 80 percent of all funds are earmarked for specific expenditures, such as highways, teachers' retirement, parks, and schools. This is discussed in Chapter 13.

The Texas governor has very limited authority over budget execution. Outside the governor's immediate office, control over the budget rests with other state agencies over which the governor has little or no control. Only in cases of fiscal crisis can the governor exercise any influence. A constitutional amendment approved in 1985 created the Budget Execution Committee, composed of the governor, the lieutenant governor, the comptroller, the speaker of the house, and chairs of the finance and appropriations committees in the senate and house. The Budget Execution Committee can exercise restraints over the budget if there is a fiscal crisis, such as a shortfall in projected revenue.

The one area where the Texas governor does have influence over budget decisions is the line-item veto. The governor can veto part of the appropriations bill without vetoing the entire bill. The legislature determines what a line item is. It can be a department within an agency, or the entire agency. For example, Governor Clements once vetoed the line items appropriating money to operate the systems administration offices of the University of Texas and Texas A&M University. He did not veto all money appropriated to these schools, just the funds for the operation of the systems offices. The governor might line-item veto money for a state park without having to veto the money for all state parks.

The legislature can override this veto by a two-thirds vote of each house. However, as we saw in Chapter 3, appropriations bills generally pass in the last days of the session, so the legislature has adjourned by the time the governor vetoes items. Because the legislature cannot call itself back into session ("extraordinary" sessions), overriding a line-item veto is impossible. The governor may

---

line-item veto

The ability of a governor to veto part of an appropriations bill without vetoing the whole bill

---

Legislative Budget Board

State agency that is controlled by the leadership in the state legislature and that writes the state budget

call special sessions, but he or she controls the agenda. If the governor thought there was a chance of a veto override, this would not be included in the agenda of the special session.

Thus, the line-item veto is a very important power possessed by the Texas governor, but more important than the actual veto is the threat of a veto. Historically, governors have used this threat to discipline the legislature. It is not uncommon for the governor to threaten to veto a local line item, such as an item creating a new state park in a legislator's district. This threat to veto local appropriations can be used to gain legislative support for items important to the governor but unrelated to the park. It should be noted that typically governors do not veto many bills. Although exceptions occasionally occur, as a general rule, threats are more important than the actual veto.

Nationally, the U.S. Congress granted the president of the United States a limited line-item veto. The U.S. Supreme Court declared this act unconstitutional. Although many have advocated that the president needs the line-item veto to control congressional spending, a constitutional amendment will be required to grant this power. If this happens, presidents might use the threat of veto to control members of Congress and gain their support for other programs.

Legislative Powers

The line-item veto can be viewed as a budgetary power, but it is also a **legislative power**. There are also other types of vetoes. All governors possess some form of veto authority, but this varies among the states. (See Table 4.4.) Forty states have formalized **partial vetoes**, where the legislature can recall a bill from the governor so that objections raised by the governor can be changed and a veto avoided.[47] Texas does not have a formal partial veto process; however, the governor can still state objections to a bill before it is passed and thus seek to effect changes in legislation. Formalizing the process would shift some power to the office of governor and give the governor more say in the legislative process.

legislative power
The formal power, especially the veto authority, of the governor to force the legislature to enact his or her legislation

partial veto
The ability of some governors to veto part of a nonappropriations bill without vetoing the entire bill; a Texas governor does not have this power except on appropriations bills

TABLE 4.4	
Veto Authority of State Governors with Override Provisions	
Type of Veto	**No. of Governors**
General veto and item veto: two-thirds legislative majority needed to override	37
General veto and item veto: simple legislative majority needed to override	3
General veto, no item veto: special legislative majority to override*	8
General veto, no item veto: simple legislative majority to override	2

*Most common is three-fifths vote. Not all occurred by three-fifths vote, so depending on the precise method, the data changes slightly.

Source: Thad L. Beyle, "Governors: The Middlemen and Women in Our Political System," in *Politics in the American States,* 8th ed., eds. Virginia Gray and Russell L. Hanson. Washington D.C.: Congressional Quarterly Press, 2004 Book of the States, 2015, Table 4.4.

Requirements for overriding a governor's veto also vary widely among the states. Most states require a two-thirds vote to override, although a few allow a simple majority.[48] In Texas, the governor has very strong veto authority. The office possesses a general veto and line-item veto, with a two-thirds vote of each house required for override. Very few vetoes have been overturned. From 1876 to 1968, only 25 of 936 vetoes were overridden in the legislature. Most of these vetoes occurred before 1940. This low number of veto overrides is primarily due to late passage of bills and adjournment of the legislature. Only one veto has been overturned in recent years, and it was not a significant bill. In 1979, during his first term, Bill Clements vetoed 52 bills. The legislature, in an attempt to catch the governor's attention, overrode the veto on a bill that limited the ability of county governments to prohibit hunters from killing female deer.[49] Since 1979, no vetoes have been overridden by the legislature.

In 15 other states besides Texas, the legislature may not call a "special" session. These are usually called *extraordinary sessions* to distinguish them from *special sessions,* which are called by the governor. States where the legislature cannot call extraordinary sessions add to the power of the governor to veto bills. In the 2001 session of the Texas legislature, Governor Perry set a new record by vetoing 82 bills. If the Texas legislature could have called an extraordinary session, there is little doubt that it would have happened and that some vetoes would have been overridden.

Thus, the veto authority of the Texas governor is significant. Accomplishing a two-thirds override (in both house and senate) is very difficult. If the legislature has adjourned, it is impossible. For these reasons, there have been few overrides.

Some governors have a pocket veto, meaning that they can veto a bill by not signing it. The governor just "puts the bill in a pocket" and forgets about it. The Texas governor does not have a pocket veto. If the legislature is in session, the governor has 10 days to sign a bill or it becomes law without his or her signature. If the legislature has adjourned, the governor has 20 days to sign a bill or it becomes law without a signature. Sometimes governors do not like a bill but do not want to veto it. Letting the bill become law without a signature can be a way of expressing displeasure short of an actual veto.

In recent years, some U.S. governors have used the line-item veto to eliminate more than a line item in an appropriations bill. In Arizona, the Republican-controlled legislature twice sued Democratic governor Janet Napolitano, claiming that she misused her line-item veto authority. The most recent case involved Napolitano's veto of a bill involving a state employee pay plan. The governor vetoed a section of the bill that exempted employees making more than $47,758 from the state merit pay plan. The Republicans contend that this is a misuse of her constitutional authority.

Governor's Control over Party

Governors are expected to be leaders of their political party and in most states are recognized as such. In the one-party era in Texas, the Democratic candidate for governor picked the state party chair and controlled the state party organization. Often such control was based on a personal following rather than a well-organized party structure. Governor Bill Clements, a Republican, made use of his election to build the party in the state, especially during his second term. He managed enough control over the Republican Party and its elected house members to thwart Democratic control of the legislature on some issues.

Today, governors might influence the choice of party leadership, but they do not control the party. George W. Bush found himself in the uncomfortable position of having to work with a state party chair chosen by the social conservatives. Governor Bush would probably have made a different choice for party chair. He did not attend the meeting of the Republican Party convention in 2000. He claimed to be very busy campaigning for president. This may have been the first time a sitting governor did not attend his or her state's party convention. It indicated the level of disagreement between the governor and the party leaders. As the two-party system matures in Texas, party leadership by the governor will have to become more of a fixture in state politics. Except when he was in a primary election with a tough opponent, Governor Perry did not embrace the social conservatives' program or the party platform, in part because of personal beliefs and in part because it is a popular idea in the state.

Administrative Agencies of State Government

In addition to the office of governor, a number of state agencies make up what might be called the state bureaucracy. The term *bureaucracy* often implies a hierarchy of offices with levels of power leading to a centralized controlling authority. This term does not describe the overall structure of state government in Texas, because there is no overall central governing, controlling authority. Government authority in Texas is very decentralized and resides within many independent state agencies. In addition, many independent boards, commissions, and agencies operate independently of the governor. Power is decentralized among many officials. This decentralized structure of power is in keeping with the traditionalistic and individualistic political culture of the state.

State Employees

Most of the funds appropriated by the state legislature go to pay for personnel. This is the largest single expenditure for all state governments. Figure 4.2 shows a breakdown of the four largest state agency categories in Texas by total number of full-time-equivalent employees. Texas has no general civil service system or central personnel agency. Each agency creates its own set of rules and regulations regarding personnel practices and procedures. Most states, however, have a central personnel system and some form of civil service system that formulates personnel policies and procedures. In keeping with the decentralized nature of state government, the personnel system in Texas is also decentralized. Over three quarters of Texas state employees work in the five major functional areas of state government: corrections, highways, public welfare, hospitals, and higher education.

The number of state employees has declined slightly in recent years due in part to the performance review audits conducted by former Comptroller John Sharp. Still, as of March 2014 , Texas has the second highest number of full-time state government employees (278,324), superseded only by California (333,083).[50] It is not surprising, then, that the state of Texas is the largest single employer in Texas.

Legislative Agencies

In addition to the executive agencies, there are also several legislative agencies. These are units controlled by the leadership in the Texas House and Senate. Their purpose is to provide legislative oversight of the executive agencies and to assist the legislature in its lawmaking functions.

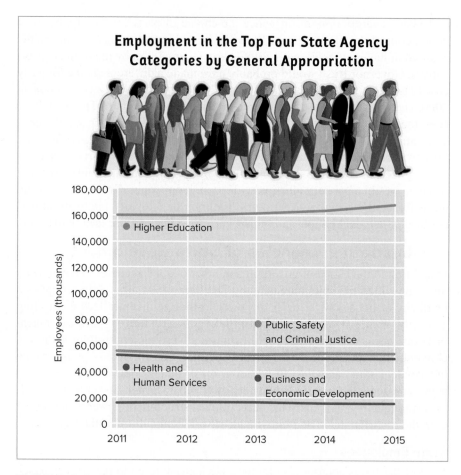

FIGURE 4.2   Employment in the Top Four State Agency Categories by General Appropriation

Legislative Budget Board

The Legislative Budget Board (LBB) is primarily responsible for preparing the state budget. It is composed of the lieutenant governor, the speaker of the house, four senators, and four representatives. All agencies that receive state funds from the state budget must submit their requests for appropriations to the LBB. The LBB reviews these requests and proposes a budget to the state legislature. Unlike most other states, in Texas the governor plays a very limited role in budgeting.[51]

Texas Legislative Council

The speaker of the house, the lieutenant governor, four senators, and four state representatives control this agency and appoint the executive director. The agency was created in 1949 to assist the legislature in drafting bills, conducting research on legislation, producing publications, and providing technical support services. This is a highly professional agency that produces information for the legislature, which is made available to the public in various ways.[52]

Legislative Audit Committee and State Auditor's Office

The Legislative Audit Committee consists of the lieutenant governor, the speaker of the house, and the chairs of the senate finance committee and state affairs committee, and the house appropriations committee and ways and means committee. This committee appoints the state auditor, who is responsible for auditing state agencies and assisting the legislature in its oversight functions.[53]

Legislative Reference Library

This organization assists the legislature in doing research and serves as a depository of records for the legislature. Located in the state capitol, the library is open to other state agencies and members of the public also engaged in legislative research.

Judicial Agencies

Several agencies, which can be called judicial agencies, are under the supervision of the state supreme court (civil matters). Except for bud-

The Texas Legislative Reference Library was originally created in 1909 as the Legislative Reference Division of the Texas State Library. In 1969, the Reference Division was separated out into its own library directly under the authority of the Texas Legislature. The library houses an extensive collection of print and online media, including documents going back to the 1850s.

© Matthew Bollom.

geting of money by the legislature, these agencies are relatively free of legislative oversight. The state bar, which licenses attorneys, receives no state appropriations. The remaining agencies are responsible for court administration (Office of Court Administration), operations of the state law library, and certification of legal licenses and specializations.

Judicial Powers

Governors are also given limited **judicial powers** to grant pardons, executive clemency, and parole. Historically, governors have misused this power. This has led to the creation of some checks on governors' ability to exercise this authority. In Texas, James "Pa" Ferguson was accused of misusing this power, especially during the second term of his wife, "Ma" Ferguson (1933–35). It was charged that Jim Ferguson sold pardons and paroles to convicted felons.[54] These charges led to the creation of the Texas Board of Pardons and Paroles. Today this seven-member board[55], appointed by the governor, recommends the action the governor can take in such matters and serves as a check on the process. Independent of board action, the governor may grant only one 30-day stay of execution for any condemned prisoner. This board must recommend all other actions by the governor.

In the Fergusons' defense, many of the pardons were given to people who were in prison because they had violated the Prohibition laws. Former Lt. Governor Hobby put it this way: "Prohibition's laws filled the prisons and ruined lives . . . The Fergusons may have rightly concluded that the state was better served by these men . . . supporting their families."[56]

In 2010, Governor Haley Barber of Mississippi attracted national attention by pardoning some 200 individuals as he was leaving office. This has led to much discussion about limiting a governor's power to pardon.

judicial powers
The ability of a governor to issue pardons, executive clemency, and parole of citizens convicted of a crime

Ex Officio Boards and Commissions

A number of state agencies are headed by boards whose membership is completely or partially made up of designated state officials who are members because of the position they hold. Examples of these officials are the statewide elected officials—governor, lieutenant governor, speaker of the house, attorney general, and land commissioner. Examples of these agencies are the Bond Review Board, the Legislative Redistricting Board, and the Budget Execution Committee.

Multi-Appointment Boards

Finally, some state agencies have governing boards whose members are appointed by more than one elected official. This is to prevent any one individual from dominating the selection process and the outcome of decisions. An example of such an agency is the Texas Ethics Commission, which has four members appointed by the governor, two by the lieutenant governor, and two by the speaker of the house, and which oversees campaign contributions and lobbying activities.

Democratic Control and Bureaucratic Responsiveness

The concept of democratic control requires that state agencies be responsible to the people—that is, that state agencies respond to demands placed on them by citizens. With Texas state administrative agencies operating quite independently of each other, and overall administrative control being absent from state government, agencies are often able to respond only to clientele groups they serve and not the public generally. (See Chapter 10 on interest groups for a more complete discussion of agency capture.)

In other states, accountability in a more general sense is ensured by giving the governor broader power to appoint agency heads (rather than independent boards and commissions) who serve at the pleasure of the governor. Also, some states have given the governor broad budgetary control over state agencies. Agencies are required to submit budget requests to the governor, who produces a state budget that is submitted to the state legislature. As discussed previously, in Texas the governor plays a small role in the budgetary process; the Legislative Budget Board performs this function.

State government in Texas is so fragmented and responsibility so divided that holding anyone responsible for state government is impossible. Although citizens may blame the governor when things go wrong, and governors may claim credit when things go right, in truth the governor is responsible for very little and deserves credit for much less than most claim. An example of this is a governor who claims to have created hundreds of jobs in the state when, in fact, a governor has very little to do with the economy or job creation.

Sunset Advisory Commission

Agency responsible for making recommendations to the legislature for change in the structure and organization of most state agencies

Sunset Review

Given the lack of overall, central control in state government and the limited and weak authority of the governor, in 1977 the Texas legislature created the 10-member **Sunset Advisory Commission** to review most state agencies every 12 years and recommend changes. This commission consists of five state senators, five representatives, and two public members.

The sunset process is the "idea that legislative oversight of government operations can be enhanced by a systematic evaluation of state agencies."[57] The process works by establishing a date on which an agency of state government is abolished if the legislature does not pass a law providing for its continuance. The act does not apply to agencies created by the Texas Constitution, and some state agencies are exempt, such as state universities. Sunset asks the basic question: "Do the policies carried out by an agency need to be continued?"[58]

In the years of sunset review in Texas, 37 state agencies have been abolished. Most were minor state agencies with few functions. Most notable were the Boll Weevil Commission, the Battleship Texas Commission, and the Stonewall Jackson Memorial Board. More important than abolition is the review process. By forcing a review of an agency every 12 years, the legislature is given the opportunity to recommend changes to improve the efficiency and effectiveness of state government. In many cases, functions of state agencies are transferred to other agencies, and agencies are combined or merged. Sunset review has also forced many agencies that operate much out of the public's attention into the limelight. This is especially true of those agencies that license professions. Sunset review resulted in the appointment of nonprofessionals to these agencies in an effort to promote the broader interests of the public over the narrower interests of the agency and its clientele. Table 4.5 lists the activities of the Texas Sunset Advisory Commission over the past 30 years.

TABLE 4.5

Overview of Sunset Activities in Texas, 1979–2015

Year	Session	Reviews	Agencies Continued	Agencies Abolished	Functions Transferred
1979	66	26	13	7	6
1981	67	28	23	3	2
1983	68	32	29	3	0
1985	69	31	23	6	1
1987	70	20	17	1	1
1989	71	30	22	3	2
1991	72	30	20	3	5
1993	73	31	22	1	5
1995	74	18	14	0	2
1997	75	21	18	0	2
1999	76	25	22	1	1
2001	77	25	19	1	1
2003	78	29	23	1	2
2005	79	29	21	2	4
2007	80	20	14	1	1
2009	81	27	20	2	2
2011	82	29	19	2	4
2013	83	24	19	0	1
2015	84	20	14	0	4
	Total	495	372	37	46
			75%	7.5%	9%

Source: Texas Sunset Advisory Commission, Past Review Cycles, July 2015. See: (http://www.sunset.texas.gov/review-cycles)

Powers of the Texas Governor in Comparative Context

If we take the six indicators of power—election of other statewide executives, tenure of office, governor's appointment powers, budgetary powers, veto powers, and governor's control over party—and compare the Texas governor with the other 49 U.S. governors, the Texas office is comparatively weak in formal powers because of the limitations placed on administrative and budgetary powers, although the office is strong on tenure and veto authority (see Table 4.6.) The formal weakness in the office of governor is very much in keeping with the traditionalistic/individualistic political culture of the state. As was discussed earlier, the present constitution was written in a time when limited government was very much on the minds of the framers of the constitution. Having experienced strong executive authority during Reconstruction, these framers wanted to limit the governor's ability to act, especially in budgetary and administrative matters. They succeeded. In recent years the powers of the Texas governor have been increased somewhat, but the office is still very weak on the budgetary and administrative dimensions. Given this formal weakness, Texas governors must use all their informal powers of persuasion and their political skills if they are to be successful. Also, in recent years the voters have rejected constitutional amendments that would have expanded the governor's ability to appoint and remove agency heads.

TABLE 4.6
Summary of Institutional Powers of Governors by State

State	Score	State	Score
Alabama	2.8	Montana	3.5
Alaska	4.1	Nebraska	3.8
Arizona	3.4	Nevada	3.0
Arkansas	3.6	New Hampshire	3.2
California	3.2	New Jersey	4.1
Colorado	3.9	New Mexico	3.7
Connecticut	3.6	New York	4.1
Delaware	3.5	North Carolina	2.9
Florida	3.6	North Dakota	3.9
Georgia	3.2	Ohio	3.6
Hawaii	3.4	Oklahoma	2.8
Idaho	3.3	Oregon	3.5
Illinois	3.8	Pennsylvania	3.8
Indiana	2.9	Rhode Island	2.6
Iowa	3.8	South Carolina	3.0
Kansas	3.3	South Dakota	3.0
Kentucky	3.3	Tennessee	3.8
Louisiana	3.4	**Texas**	**3.2**
Maine	3.6	Utah	4.0
Maryland	4.1	Vermont	2.5
Massachusetts	4.3	Virginia	3.2
Michigan	3.6	Washington	3.6
Minnesota	3.6	West Virginia	4.1
Mississippi	2.9	Wisconsin	3.5
Missouri	3.6	Wyoming	3.1
		50 average	**3.5**

Source: Thad L. Beyle, "Governors," in *Politics in the American States,* 9th ed., eds. Virginia Gray and Russell L. Hanson. Washington D.C.: Congressional Quarterly Press, 2008.

CORE OBJECTIVE

Source: *National Park Service*

Thinking Critically. . .

The six factors that influence the strength of the power of the governor are the number of elected statewide executives, tenure of office, the governor's appointive powers, the governor's budgetary powers, the governor's veto powers, and the extent to which the governor controls his or her political party. What can you conclude about the powers of the governor?

Informal Powers

Learning Objective: Explain the governor's informal powers.

Although the office of Texas governor is formally very weak, the office can be strong politically. The governor's primary political resource is the ability to exert influence. The governor is the most visible officeholder in the state and can command the attention of the news media, holding press conferences and announcing new decisions on policy issues. Such news conferences usually are well covered and reported by the press and other media. This enables the governor to have an impact on the direction of state government. The governor can also stage events that are newsworthy to emphasize things she or he is interested in changing.

The popularity of the governor in public opinion polls is also an important aspect of informal leadership. Governors who consistently rank high in popularity polls can use this fact to overcome opposition to their policies and reduce the likelihood of opposition, both to policies and electoral challenges. A governor who is weak in public opinion polls becomes an easy target for political opponents.

In very general ways, governors are judged on their leadership abilities. Some governors develop reputations as being indecisive, whereas others become known as effective, decisive leaders. The characterization attached to the governor will affect his or her ability to be effective. The media will begin to repeat the reputational description of the governor, and if this happens often enough, the reputation will become "fact." Therefore, developing a good image is very important.

The power and respect accorded to governors have varied greatly over time. During the colonial period, there was very little; some have argued that the American Revolution was a war against colonial governors. The experiences of southern states following Reconstruction led to a return of weak governors in the South. An old Texas saying states, "The governor should have only enough power to sign for his paycheck." In recent times, the power and prestige of the office have increased, as evidenced by recent presidential politics. In both Democratic and Republican parties, many presidential candidates have been former governors. In the past 40 years, only presidents George H. W. Bush, Barack Obama, and Donald Trump have not served as governors prior to being elected president. Today the office of governor has assumed new significance because of a change in attitude toward the role of the federal government. In the past 50 years, every Congress promised to return power and responsibility to state governments and to allow states more flexibility in administering programs funded by the federal government. Even without the renewed significance of the office, and even though many governors have little formal power, governors are important players in state politics.

Roles

Citizens expect governors to play many roles. First, the governor is expected to be the **chief legislator**, formulating long-term policy goals and objectives. In this capacity the governor recommends policy initiatives to state legislators and coordinates with state agencies that administer programs and implement policies. Although governors do not formally introduce bills, passing legislation requires the support of legislative leaders to carry their program forward. Often governors spend considerable time and energy developing these relationships. If the governor is of one party, and the other party dominates the legislature, it is more difficult to pass legislation.

The governor must act as **party chief**. As the most important party official in the state, the governor leads the party and aids its development and growth. This role is important in promoting the party's position on political issues and shaping its policy initiatives. The governor is the most visible member of the party, helping legislators and other elected officials in their reelection efforts, raising money for the party, and creating a favorable image of the party in the state.

In addition, the governor serves as the ceremonial leader of the state. The **ceremonial duties** can be demanding. The governor receives many invitations to speak, make presentations, and cut ribbons. Some governors become trapped in the safe, friendly environment of ceremonial duties and neglect or avoid the other duties of their office. For governors with an agenda for action, getting caught in a "ceremonial trap" is a diversion from more important and difficult objectives. Governors can, however, use ceremonial duties as communication opportunities to promote their programs. They must carefully choose which invitations to accept and which to delegate to others or decline. Ceremonial appearances, such as a commencement speaker, provide an opportunity to generate favorable press coverage and support for one's programs. Former Governor Bush used these opportunities to promote his state programs and his race for the presidency.

In recent years, a new role for the governor has been added to that list—**crisis manager**. Governors are expected to react to crises, such as natural or man-made disasters. How well the governor reacts to these situations may very well have an impact on reelection chances. For example, during Hurricane Katrina in Louisiana, Governor Blanco was not viewed as a strong leader, thus influencing her decision not to seek reelection in 2007.

Finally, the governor is expected to be the chief **intergovernmental coordinator**, working with federal officials and officials in other states. The governor must also work with the state congressional delegation of U.S. senators and representatives, the president, and cabinet officials to promote the interests of the state.

In Texas, like many other states, the formal powers of the governor are very weak. Without explicit authority, the governor must develop and use the power and prestige of the office to persuade others to accept his or her legislative agenda. This informal leadership trait, the power to persuade others, is perhaps the most important and necessary "power" the governor must develop. Governor Perry used his considerable charm and tenure to persuade the legislature to go along with his programs; over time, his influence and power in the office increased.

---

chief legislator

The expectation that a governor has an active agenda of legislation to recommend to the legislature and works to pass that agenda

---

party chief

The expectation that the governor will be the head of his or her party

---

ceremonial duties

The expectation that a governor attends many functions and represents the state; some governors become so active at this role that they get caught in a ceremonial trap and neglect other duties

---

crisis manager

The expectation that the governor will provide strong leadership in times of a natural or man-made disaster

---

intergovernmental coordinator

The expectation that a governor coordinates activities with other state governments

The Governor's Staff

In Texas, the trend in recent years has been to expand the staff of the governor's office. In 1963, when he became governor, John Connally made the first use of a professional staff of advisors. Previous governors often appointed only a handful of individuals who were loyal to them politically, but not necessarily highly professional. Other governors since Connally have added to the governor's staff. Today an organizational chart is necessary to maintain lines of authority and responsibility. Currently, the governor has a staff of about 200.

Each governor is going to make different use of her or his staff. In recent years most have used their staff to keep track of state agencies over which the governors themselves have little or no direct control. The staff also gathers information and makes recommendations on changes in policy that impact most areas of state government. A message from a member of the governor's staff to a state agency is taken seriously. A report issued by the governor's office automatically attracts the attention of significant state leaders and the news media. Often the governor must use the information gathered to wage a public relations war with the legislature or state agencies. In Texas, the increases in the size, professionalism, and complexity of the governor's staff have become necessary to offset the limited formal control the governor has over state government.

Conclusion

Even though governors in most states do not have much formal power, the office has great importance in state politics. In recent years, the importance of the office has increased. Of the past five U.S. presidents, three have been state governors before their move to the White House (Ronald Reagan in California, Bill Clinton in Arkansas, and George W. Bush in Texas). The office has become increasingly visible in both state and national politics. The need for strong leadership in this office will continue to increase.

Texas is now the second-largest state in population and one of the leading states in industrial growth. The governor's lack of formal power makes the task of governing this large, diverse, and economically important state challenging. Some reform of the powers of the governor is still needed, but it is doubtful that such changes will occur. The political culture of the state does not support that change. Leadership will have to come from force of will and personality, not from formal changes in structure. Interest groups are not supportive of transferring power from state agencies they can dominate to agencies under the control of a single individual appointed by the governor. Although the Sunset Advisory Commission has had a positive impact on some agencies, general reorganization of state government is not likely anytime soon.

Key Terms

acting governor	impeachment	partial veto
attorney general	informal qualifications	party chief
boards and commissions	intergovernmental coordinator	plural executive system
budgetary powers	judicial powers	recall
ceremonial duties	land commissioner	secretary of state (SOS)
chief legislator	Legislative Budget Board (LBB)	senatorial courtesy
comptroller of public accounts	legislative power	Sunset Advisory Commission
conviction	line-item veto	tenure of office
crisis manager	military powers	Texas Railroad Commission

Summary

LO: Summarize the formal and informal qualifications for the Governor of Texas.

While there are certain formal qualifications including citizenship, age, and residency, required by law in Texas, gubernatorial candidates are subject to a much broader range of informal qualifications that can sway the electorate. Political experience, race and ethnicity, gender, and wealth all factor into a candidate's electability.

LO: Explain the provisions for succession of a governor.

Each state elects and provides for the succession of its executive officials according to its own rules. Texas elects the governor and lieutenant governor separately and could, therefore, have a split executive, though this seldom happens. If a governor leaves the state or is removed from office, Texas and most other states dictate that the lieutenant governor move into the governorship.

LO: Explain the provisions for removal of a governor.

Outside of an election, a governor can be removed by either impeachment or recall. Impeachment is the more common (possible in all states except Oregon) whereas recall is only allowable in 15 states, Texas not included. While impeachment is inherently a political process, the state must prove real wrongdoing on the part of the governor in a court of law. Recall, however, is a special vote where the electorate can remove a governor from office.

LO: Explain the governor's formal powers.

While most governors do not have extensive formal powers, the few they do have can be measured using six variables: election of other statewide executives, tenure of office, appointment powers, budgetary powers, veto powers, and control over party. The Texas governor has relatively weak appointive powers but does enjoy four-year terms and no term limits. Texas governors' budgetary powers are exceptionally weak, except in the area of the line-item veto, which is considered a legislative power and is very strong in Texas. Governors also have very limited judicial authority via pardons and other similar actions. Overall, the office of governor in Texas is relatively weak with a few strong abilities.

LO: Explain the governor's informal powers.

The governor's primary political resource is the ability to exert influence. The governor is the most visible officeholder in the state and can command the attention of the news media, holding press conferences and announcing new decisions on policy issues. Of course, this also means the governor is vulnerable to political attacks and can be subject to electoral disapproval.

Notes

[1] *Book of the States,* 2015, Table 4.2.

[2] Thad L. Beyle, "Governors: The Middlemen and Women in Our Political System," in *Politics in the American States,* 6th ed., eds. Virginia Gray and Herbert Jacob (Washington, D.C.: Congressional Quarterly Press, 2004), 197.

[3] Schwarz, Hunter, "What jobs you should have if you want to be elected governor," *The Washington Post,* September 12, 2014, from https://www.washingtonpost.com/blogs/govbeat/wp/2014/09/12/what-jobs-you-should-have-if-you-want-to-be-elected-governor/.

[4] Center on the American Governor, Eagleton Institute on Politics, "Fast Facts about American Governors," Rutgers, The State University of New Jersey, http://governors.rutgers.edu/on-governors/us-governors/fast-facts-about-american-governors/.

[5] Paul Burka,. "El Gobernador: The question isn't whether we'll elect a Hispanic to lead Texas. It's whom, and from which party, and how quickly Jai Alai's loss will be our gain," February 2008. *Texas Monthly.* http://www.texasmonthly.com/politics/el-gobernador/.

[6] United States Census Bureau, "QuickFacts: Texas," http://www.census.gov/quickfacts/table/PST045215/48.

[7] Ballotpedia, "Texas gubernatorial election, 2002," https://ballotpedia.org/Texas_gubernatorial_election,_2002.

[8] Melissa del Bosque, "The Race for the Hispanic Vote," April 26, 2011. *Texas Observer,* https://www.texasobserver.org/the-race-for-the-hispanic-vote/.

[9] Ballotpedia, "Texas Gubernatorial election, 2002," https://ballotpedia.org/Texas_gubernatorial_election,_2002; Elizabeth Cruce Alvarez, editor. *Texas Almanac,* 2004–2005, 2004, Texas State Historical Association, 399, http://texashistory.unt.edu/ark:/67531/metapth162511/m1/399/.

[10] James G Gimpel, "Latinos and the 2002 Election: Republicans Do Well When Latinos Stay Home," January 2003, Center for Immigration Studies, http://cis.org/2002Election-Latinos%2526Republicans.

[11] Melissa del Bosque, "The Race for the Hispanic Vote," April 26, 2011, *Texas Observer,* https://www.texasobserver.org/the-race-for-the-hispanic-vote/.

[12] Center for American Women and Politics (2016), *Statewide Elective Executive Women 2016* (Fact Sheet), http://www.cawp.rutgers.edu/women-statewide-elective-executive-office-2016.

[13] Jennifer Burnett, "Governors' Salaries, 2015," The Council of State Governments: Knowledge Center, http://knowledgecenter.csg.org/kc/content/governors-salaries-2015.

[14] *Book of the States,* 2015, Table 4.3, 169, http://knowledgecenter.csg.org/kc/system/files/4.3%202015.pdf.

[15] Ballotpedia, "Lieutenant Governor," https://ballotpedia.org/Lieutenant_Governor.

[16] Office of the Secretary of State, Texas. 1992 - Current ELECTION HISTORY. Retrieved May 25, 2016 from http://elections.sos.state.tx.us/.

[17] *Book of the States,* 1994–95, 66.

[18] Ibid.

[19] Thad L. Beyle, "Governors," in *Politics in the American States,* 4th ed., eds. Virginia Gray, Herbert Jacob, and Kenneth N. Vine (Boston: Little Brown, 1983), 217.

[20] Todd Donovan, Daniel A. Smith, Christopher Z. Mooney, "Governors and Their Careers," in *State and Local Politics: Institutions and Reform,* Cengage Learning, 2012, p. 290.

[21] *Book of the States,* 2015, Table 4.8. Oregon is the only state without any such provisions. The District of Columbia, Guam, and the U.S. Virgin Islands can only use the recall procedure where citizens can remove an official before the end of their term.

[22] Ann Bowman and Richard C. Kearney, *State and Local Government* (Boston: Wadsworth Cengage Learning, 2011), 206.

[23] Benton, *Texas,* 222–224.

[24] Victor E. Harlow, *Harlow's History of Oklahoma,* 5th ed. (Norman, Okla.: Harlow, 1967), 294–315.

[25] Daniel R. Grant and Lloyd B. Omdahl, *State and Local Government in America* (Madison, Wis.: Brown & Benchmark, 1987), 260.

[26] Texas Comptroller of Public Accounts, "Overview of Public Accounts," http://comptroller.texas.gov/taxes/; Texas Almanac, "Facts," http://texasalmanac.com/topics/facts-profile.

[27] Ballotpedia, "Natural Resources Commissioner," https://ballotpedia.org/Natural_Resources_Commissioner_(state_executive_office).

[28] S. M. Morehouse, *State Politics, Parties and Policy,* (New York: Holt, Rinehart & Winston, 1981), 206.

[29] Beyle, "Governors: The Middlemen and Women in Our Political System," 230.

[30] Ibid., 231.

[31] Allan Shivers was elected lieutenant governor in 1946. Governor Beauford H. Jester died in July 1949. Shivers then became governor, and he was reelected in 1950, 1952, and 1954.

[32] *Texas Almanac* 1994–95, 519.

[33] Beyle, "Governors: The Middlemen and Women in Our Political System," 221.

[34] Ibid., 231.

[35] Texas State Library and Archives Commission, "State Agency List: TRAIL List of Texas State Agencies," https://www.tsl.texas.gov/apps/lrs/agencies/index.html.

[36] Office of the Governor, "Governor's Appointment Responsibility," http://gov.texas.gov/appointments.

[37] Governor Perry's Patronage, Texas for Public Justice, September 2010, www.tpj.org.

[38] Ibid.

[39] For more information, visit http://www.sos.state.tx.us/about/index.shtml.

[40] For more information, visit http://www.hhsc.state.tx.us/about_hhsc/index.shtml.

[41] For more information, visit http://gov.texas.gov/osfr.

[42] For more information, visit https://tmd.texas.gov/office-of-the-adjutant-general.

[43] Texas Commission on Environmental Quality, "Interstate River Compact Commissions," https://www.tceq.texas.gov/permitting/compacts/interstate.html.

[44] Kevin Kiley, "Reign of the Politician-Chancellor: Former lawmakers in public-university leadership roles show Gov. Rick Perry's influence in shaping Texas' higher education institutions," *Inside Higher Ed,* https://www.insidehighered.com/news/2011/08/23/reign-politician-chancellor.

[45] *Book of the States,* 2015, Table 4.4.

[46] Ibid.

[47] *Book of the States,* 2015, Table 3.16.

[48] Ibid.

[49] Anderson, Murray, and Farley, Texas Politics, 122.

[50] United States Census Bureau, "State Government: Employment and Payroll Data by State and by Function: March 2014," from the *2014 Annual Survey of Public Employment and Payroll,* http://www2.census.gov/govs/apes/14stall.xls.

[51] For more information, visit http://www.lbb.state.tx.us/history.aspx.

[52] For more information, visit http://www.tlc.state.tx.us/about.

[53] For more information, visit https://www.sao.texas.gov/About/.

[54] Deborah K. Wheeler, *Two Men, Two Governors, Two Pardons: A Study of Pardon Policy of Governor Miriam*

Ferguson, Unpublished copyrighted paper, presented at State Historical Society Meeting, March 1998, Austin.

[55] Texas Board of Pardons and Paroles. "Board Member Responsibilities," http://www.tdcj.state.tx.us/bpp/brd_members/brd_members.html.

[56] Bill Hobby, "Speaking of Pardons, Texas Has Had Its Share," *Houston Chronicle,* 18 February 2001, 4c.

[57] *Fiscal Size-Up* 2002–03, 242.

[58] Texas Sunset Advisory Commission, *Guide to the Texas Sunset Process,* 1997, Austin, 1991, 1.

CHAPTER 5

The Court System in Texas

Texas Learning Outcomes

- Describe the structure and function of the judicial branch of Texas government.

Texans share with citizens in the rest of the United States a conflicting view of how courts should function in a democratic society. In part, this conflicted understanding arises from the two primary sources of law: legislatures and courts.

When we say "law" in the context of a legislature, we mean a present, binding requirement imposed on all citizens in a given category, such as all minors under the age of 21, or all divorced parents, or all people who drive vehicles, or all people who work. The law in this sense applies to all people in a category of citizens, without exceptions. It embodies majority rule, or *majoritarianism*.

Courts also create law, but they do so by evaluating individuals on a case-by-case basis. Under our common law system, each opinion that a court hands down enjoys equal status with a statute as "law." But the courts ask a different question than the legislature does: Given that a statute has created a general requirement, are there special circumstances that should lead the court to deal with a particular individual differently? For example, a party could argue that if a general law was applied to them, it would violate their constitutional rights. Courts, therefore,

Solicitor General Ted Cruz presents the state's position in the Texas Supreme Court on Wednesday, July 6, 2005, in Austin, Texas. Supreme Court justices, at left, heard oral arguments from both sides in the ongoing court battle over how Texas pays for public education.

© Harry Cabluck/AP Images

write decisions that will later apply to everyone who is in the same category of citizens as the party in court, but they analyze the law in a way that accounts for individual circumstances or that take into account a higher law. Legal scholars sometimes refer to this approach to the law as *countermajoritarianism:* where special circumstances exist that make the application of the general law to a specific individual illegal. In these situations, courts carve out an exception despite the will of the majority expressed in the statute.

These two conflicting roles of the law translate into contradictory views of how law should function, both in Texas and in the country. First, citizens think the court system should be above politics. Courts are expected to act in nonpolitical ways, interpreting our nation's Constitution as individual challenges arise. That is, regardless of generally applicable legislation that theoretically embodies the majority will, the courts should evaluate each case without preexisting assumptions about who should prevail in a specific case. This is the countermajoritarian role of the courts. Justice is often portrayed as a blindfolded woman holding the scales of justice in her hand. Most Americans firmly believe that courts should be blind to political bias. Fairness, it would seem, requires neutrality.[1]

Second, Americans want state courts to be responsive to the electorate, "especially if they play prominent roles in molding and implementing public policy."[2] But how can courts be simultaneously above politics and responsive to the electorate?

Surprisingly, most citizens do not see a conflict between these two ideas. They think that courts should both dispense pure justice and do so according to the wishes of the electorate. Courts are placed in this position because they make decisions on matters ranging from domestic and family law to criminal law, and they serve as the final arbitrator of highly political decisions. In playing the dual roles of decision maker and policy maker, courts function very differently from other institutions.

Some conservative judges and legal scholars, though, would argue that even if courts frequently are playing this dual role in practice, they really should not be engaging in the policy making role. Instead, they should focus on interpreting the law based on the original text and its meaning. For example, recently deceased U.S. Supreme Court justice Antonin Scalia frequently argued against judges engaging in policy making from the bench, properly leaving this role to the legislature.

Chapter Learning Objectives

- Explain the courts' approach to decision making.
- Discuss judicial federalism.
- Explain the structure of state courts, including trial and appellate courts.
- Describe judicial selection in Texas, including the "appointive-elective" system.
- Describe ways in which judges are disciplined and removed.
- Distinguish between civil and criminal legal system branches.
- Discuss crime and punishment in Texas.

Court Decision Making

Learning Objective: Explain the courts' approach to decision making.

The courts' approach to decision making is quite different from that of the executive and legislative branches.[3] Unlike the legislature or governor, who can initiate policy changes, courts evaluate individual disputes that arise in cases that parties file with them. Cases that Texas courts decide may have an important impact on different sectors of the state's population. All school children, all property taxpayers, and all landowners, for example, may be affected by a single decision involving school-specific children, taxpayers, or landowners. Most cases do not involve policy questions, however, but deal only with controversies between individuals. Another way of expressing the role of the courts is that they resolve individual conflicts by interpreting and enforcing existing rules and laws. But in doing so they may create law that plays an important role in the lives of far more people than the individuals who actually participated in the case.

Parties who want a court to resolve their dispute must satisfy *strict rules of access*.[4] Although any citizen may approach the legislature or the governor, courts have rules that limit access to them. Individuals must have "standing." This means that the case must involve real controversies between two or more parties, and someone must have suffered real damage. Courts do not deal in hypothetical or imaginary controversies. In short, they do not play "what if" ("What if I hit this person? What will the court do?").

Courts are governed by *strict procedural rules* that determine when and how facts and arguments can be presented.[5] These rules prevent the introduction of some evidence in a criminal case. For example, evidence gathered by the police in an illegal search may not be allowed.

Generally, a court's decisions affect only the cases being considered by the court and not other cases before other courts.[6] However, a court's decision serves as precedent for parties in the future with a similar dispute. For example, if a trial court rules that a city ordinance in one city is invalid, this does not invalidate all similar ordinances in other cities. Another year later, however, someone in another city may challenge a similar ordinance on similar legal grounds, in which case the earlier decision will serve as legal precedent for invalidating the ordinance in the second case. The court must evaluate each case separately and then decide whether earlier decisions apply to the present case.

The rulings of appellate and supreme courts serve as especially important precedents for future legal decisions. Under the principle of **stare decisis**—"to stand by that which was decided before"—courts must follow principles announced in former cases and diverge from these only when they can show good cause for doing so. In this way, appellate courts affect how trial courts make decisions; however, each case in a lower court might be affected slightly differently.

stare decisis
Court decisions depending on previous rulings of other courts

Courts also differ from other branches of government in that, to the extent possible, they seek to evaluate cases with **objectivity**.[7] Unlike governors and legislators, courts may not appear to be political in their decision making, even though judges' decisions might be affected by political considerations. Judges must base their decisions on the federal and state constitutions, statutes, and earlier court decisions. A court's decision may have unintended or even deliberate

objectivity
The appearance that courts make objective decisions and not political ones

political consequences, but the law binds a court's decision-making process to a greater extent than in the executive and legislative branches.

Thus, courts differ from governors and legislators in the way they make decisions. They must maintain a passive role, enforce rules that restrict access to the courts, uphold strict rules of procedure, confine their decisions to the specifics of the cases before them, and maintain the appearance of objectivity. By doing this, courts help to reinforce the legitimacy of their decisions and their place as the final arbitrators of conflict. This in turn reinforces the concept that the rule of law, not the rule of arbitrary actions by individuals, governs.

Judicial Federalism

Learning Objective: Discuss judicial federalism.

Article III of the United States Constitution established the Supreme Court and gave Congress the authority to create other lower federal courts. Article VI of the U.S. Constitution makes federal law the *supreme law of the land.* Any direct conflicts between federal and state law must be resolved in favor of federal authority.

States create their own courts. As a result, 50 separate jurisdictions have complete court systems that exist side by side with the federal courts. Federal courts hear cases involving federal laws, and state courts hear cases involving state laws. Although some cases might be held in either state or federal court, most cases go to state courts rather than federal courts. There are two high-profile examples, however, of cases that were tried in federal rather than in state courts. One is the 1995 bombing of the Alfred P. Murrah Federal Building in Oklahoma City. Although murder is a crime in Oklahoma, a bombing of a federal facility that results in the death of a federal government employee is a federal crime. Another example is the case of the "Unabomber," in which persons were injured or murdered by a series of bombs, most of which were sent through the U.S. mail, from the late 1970s to the mid-1990s. Both of these cases were tried in federal court. Initially, state prosecutors indicated that they might also file state murder charges against the Unabomber suspect. This did not happen.

Few other countries have dual court systems. Ours developed because of the United States' federal system of government. State courts existed during the colonial period and continued after the adoption of the U.S. Constitution in 1789. State courts act primarily in areas where the federal government lacks authority to act.

The Structure of State Courts

Learning Objective: Explain the structure of state courts, including trial and appellate courts.

Most states provide for three levels of courts: trial courts, appellate courts, and a supreme court. The structure of courts in Texas is more complicated, as shown in Figure 5.1. Texas has several levels of trial courts and appellate courts. Trial courts include the justices of the peace, municipal courts, county courts, district

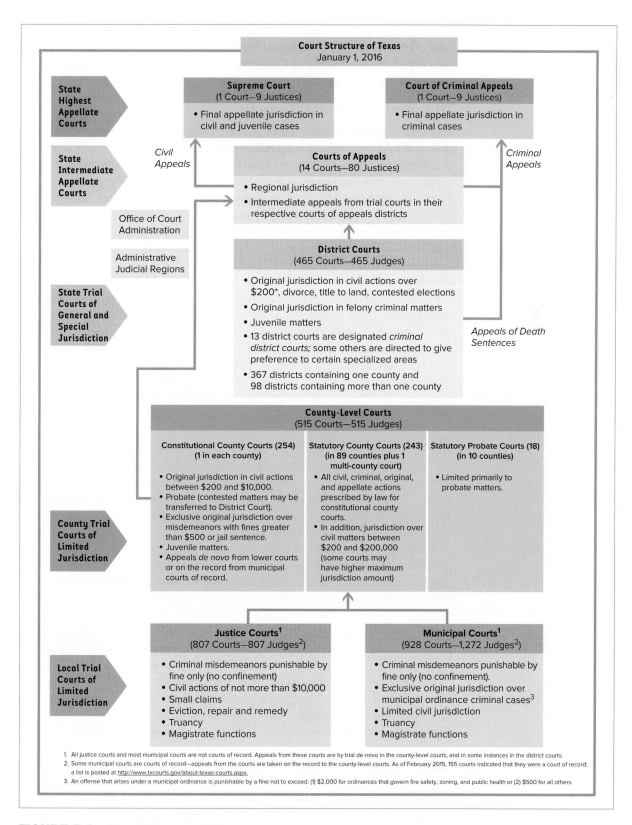

FIGURE 5.1   Court Structure of Texas

SOURCE: Adapted from Texas Courts Online. (http://www.txcourts.gov/media/1244897/Court-Structure-Chart-Jan-2016.pdf)

courts, and special purpose courts, such as probate, juvenile, and domestic relations courts. Texas has 14 intermediate appellate courts and 2 "supreme" appellate courts: one for civil cases (Supreme Court) and one for criminal cases (the Court of Criminal Appeals).

Trial and Appellate Courts

There are two kinds of state courts: trial courts and appellate courts. They differ in several important ways. First, **trial courts** are localized. Jurisdiction is limited to a geographic area, such as a county.[8] Second, only one judge presides over a trial court, and each court is considered a separate court. Third, citizens participate in trial court activity. They serve as members of juries and as witnesses during trials. Fourth, trial courts are primarily concerned with establishing the facts of a case (such as a determination that a person is guilty). Fifth, trial courts announce decisions immediately after the trial is finished.[9]

Appellate courts, on the other hand, are centralized, often at the state level. More than one judge presides, citizen participation is virtually absent, and, of most importance, appellate courts decide points of law, not points of fact. An appeal of a murder conviction from a trial court to a higher court is not based on points of fact (Is the person guilty?) but on points of law (Were legal procedures followed?). Trial courts establish guilt; appellate courts decide whether proper procedures have been followed. For example, in Texas, all death penalty cases are automatically appealed to the Texas Court of Criminal Appeals. The issue is not the guilt or innocence of the person but whether all procedures were properly followed in the trial court and whether the defense adequately defended the person charged.

Magistrate or Minor Courts

All states provide for some type of minor or magistrate court, usually called the justice of the peace. These courts hear cases involving misdemeanors, most often traffic violations and minor civil cases. In Texas there are two courts at this level. The Texas Constitution creates justices of the peace (JPs), and the state legislature creates municipal courts by statute.

Municipal court judges are either appointed by city councils or elected. Some jurisdictions require municipal court judges to be attorneys; others do not. Further, some municipal courts are so-called "courts of record," which means that a court reporter transcribes all the court's hearings and trials. As a result, appeals to county courts from these "courts of record" have a transcript the higher court can review for errors. Most municipal courts create no such record, however, so that the county court considers any case brought up on appeal "de novo": the appeal starts with a blank slate, as if no court has heard the claim before.

Municipal courts hear all cases involving violations of city ordinances, most often traffic violations. Along with JP courts they can hear other misdemeanor offenses. These courts also have magistrate functions involving preliminary hearings for persons charged with a serious offense. These persons are informed of the charges against them, told of their rights, and bail is set. As magistrates, municipal judges can issue arrest warrants.

JPs are not required to be attorneys, and these courts do not create a record of their proceedings for a county court to review. All appeals from a JP court are "de novo." JPs in small communities without coroners can perform essential coroner functions, and they can also issue search-and-arrest warrants. JP courts also

trial courts
Local courts that hear cases; juries determine the outcome of the cases heard in the court

appellate courts
Higher-level courts that decide on points of law and not questions of guilt or innocence

perform these **magistrate functions** and hear minor criminal cases, most of which involve traffic tickets issued by the Texas Highway Patrol or county deputy sheriffs. JP courts also serve as small claims courts in Texas. Municipal courts do not.[10] Jurisdiction in small claims is limited to a maximum of $10,000. Of the cases in the JP courts in Fiscal Year 2015 (September 2014 to August 2015), 84 percent were criminal misdemeanor cases, most of those being traffic cases (77 percent), whereas only 16 percent were civil cases.[11] This rate is on par with most years.

magistrate functions
Preliminary hearings for persons charged with a serious criminal offense

CORE OBJECTIVE

Communicating Effectively . . .
Analyze Figure 5.1. Describe the appeals process for a civil case filed in county court.

© George Lavendowski/ USFWS

Another interesting difference between JP and municipal courts is that JPs can perform marriages, whereas municipal court judges cannot. Although municipal judges have tried to have this changed, they have not been successful. The reason is that JPs charge a fee for performing marriages, and they have challenged competition from municipal judges.

County Courts

In Texas there are two kinds of county courts: constitutional county courts and county courts at law. The state constitution creates a county court in each of the 254 counties in the state, and the state legislature has created 243 statutory county courts at law and 18 probate courts.[12] County courts at law are created in large urban counties. In those counties, the constitutional county court ceases to function as a court, and the "county judge" becomes almost exclusively an administrative officer or county executive but retains the title of judge and some limited judicial functions. The state constitution determines the jurisdiction of constitutional county courts. The jurisdiction of county courts at law is set by the act passed by the legislature creating the court and varies from court to court. The general levels of jurisdiction are shown in Figure 5.1.

County courts primarily hear intermediate criminal and civil cases. Most criminal cases are misdemeanors. On average, more than one million cases are pled in Texas county courts each year. The most common type of cases are driving while intoxicated (DWI), worthless checks, violation of drug laws, and traffic appeals cases from city and justice courts.

County courts also serve as appellate courts for cases heard by JP and municipal courts. All JP and most municipal courts in Texas are trial de novo courts and not courts of record. In **trial de novo courts**, no record of the proceeding is kept, and cases may be appealed for any reason. It is a common practice in Texas to appeal traffic tickets to the county court, where, due to heavy caseloads, they are buried. If a person has the resources to hire a lawyer, there is a good chance the ticket will be "forgotten" in case overload.

trial de novo courts
Courts that do not keep a written record of their proceedings; cases on appeal begin as new cases in the appellate courts

District Courts

In most states, major trial courts are called district or superior courts. These courts hear major criminal and civil cases. Examples of major criminal cases (felonies) are murder, armed robbery, and car theft. Whether a civil case is major is generally established by the dollar amount of damages claimed in the case.

In Texas as of January 2016, there were 465 district courts. These courts are created by the state legislature. Large urban counties generally have several district courts. In rural areas, district courts may serve several counties. The jurisdiction of these courts often overlaps with county courts, and cases may be led in either court. Other cases must begin in district courts.

Appellate Courts

Nine states, in addition to the District of Columbia, do not have courts of appeal, and 35 states have only one court of appeal.[13] The other states, primarily large urban states, have several courts of appeal.[14] Texas has 14 courts of appeal with 80 judges elected by districts in the state.[15] Only California has more judges and courts at this level. These courts hear all civil appeals cases and all criminal appeals except those involving the death penalty, which go directly to the Court of Criminal Appeals.

Supreme Courts

All states have a supreme court, or court of last resort. Oklahoma, like Texas, has two supreme courts.[16] Oklahoma copied the idea from Texas when it entered the Union in 1907. The highest court in Texas for civil matters is the Texas Supreme Court, and the highest court in Texas for criminal cases is the Court of Criminal Appeals. Each court consists of nine judges who are elected statewide for six-year overlapping terms.

Judicial Selection

Learning Objective: Describe judicial selection in Texas, including the "appointive-elective" system.

partisan election

Method used to select all judges (except municipal court judges) in Texas by using a ballot in which party identification is shown

merit system, or Missouri system

A system of electing judges that involves appointment by the governor and a periodic retention election

Under the U.S. Constitution, all federal judges are appointed by the president and serve for life. A lifetime appointment means that a judge continues to serve during good behavior and can be removed only for cause. Among the states, a variety of methods are used to select judges. Seven of the original 13 states allow some judges to be appointed by the governor and serve for life. Four states (plus Puerto Rico), also among the original 13, allow the legislature to elect judges.[17] Some states use **partisan elections** to select certain judges. Candidates must run in a primary and in a general election. Still other states elect particular state judges in nonpartisan general elections. And finally, some states use the **merit system, or Missouri system**. Under this plan, the governor appoints judges from a list submitted by a screening committee of legal officials. After appointment, a judge serves for a set term and is then subjected to a retention election in which the voters decide whether the judge retains the office.

The method of selection also varies between courts within some states. For example, in some states, appellate court judges are chosen by a merit system while the voters elect trial court judges. Table 5.1 and Figure 5.2 show the

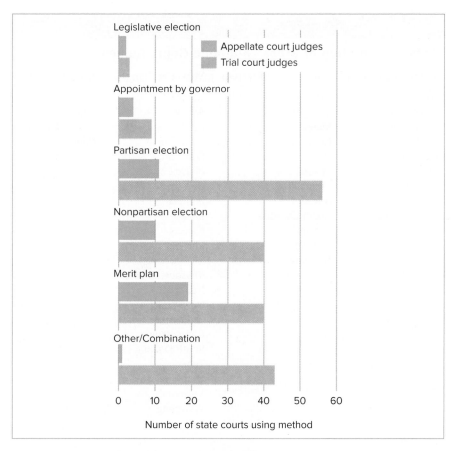

FIGURE 5.2 **Method of Selecting Judges**

Methods of Selecting Judges

Method of Selecting Judges	Number of State Courts Using Method
Appellate Court Judges	
Legislative election	2
Appointment by governor	4
Partisan election	11
Nonpartisan election	10
Merit plan	19
Other/Combination	1
Trial Court Judges (including municipal level)	
Legislative election	3
Appointment by governor	9
Partisan election	56
Nonpartisan election	40
Merit plan	40
Other/Combination	43

Source: Adapted from Council of State Governments, *The Book of the States,* 2015 (Lexington, KY: Council of State Governments, 2015), Tables 5.6 and 5.7.

TABLE 5.2

Judicial Selection of State* Supreme Court Judges

Partisan Election	Nonpartisan Election	Missouri Plan	Appointment
Alabama	Arkansas	Alaska	California
Illinois	Georgia	Arizona	Maine
Louisiana	Idaho	Colorado	New Hampshire
Michigan	Kentucky	Connecticut	New Jersey
New Mexico	Minnesota	Delaware	Puerto Rico
Ohio	Mississippi	Florida	
Pennsylvania	Montana	Hawaii	
Texas	Nevada	Indiana	
West Virginia	North Carolina	Iowa	
	North Dakota	Kansas	
	Oregon	Maryland	
	Washington	Massachusetts	
	Wisconsin	Missouri	
		Nebraska	
		New York	
		Oklahoma	
		Rhode Island	
		South Dakota	
		Tennessee	
		Utah	
		Vermont	
		Wyoming	

*Including Puerto Rico.

Table shows how judges are normally selected. Some judges in partisan and nonpartisan systems may get their initial seat by appointment of the governor. Note that South Carolina and Virginia elect supreme court judges legislatively.

Source: Adapted from Council of State Governments, *The Book of the States,* 2015 (Lexington, KY: Council of State Governments, 2015), Table 5.6.

number of state appellate and trial courts using each selection method. Many states have moved away from partisan election of supreme court and appellate court judges and use either a nonpartisan election or a merit system. However, partisan elections are still a large percentage of the selection process in trial courts, particularly when taking all levels of state trial courts into account.

Table 5.2 shows how states initially select judges to the supreme court in that state. Some states use different methods to select appellate court judges.

Is There a Best System for Judicial Selection?

Learning Objective: Describe judicial selection in Texas, including the "appointive-elective" system.

The debate in Texas over judicial selection will continue in future sessions of the legislature. Judicial selection revolves around three basic issues. Citizens expect

TABLE 5.3			
Strengths and Weaknesses of Judicial Selection Methods			
		Issue	
Method of Selection	**Competence**	**Independence**	**Responsiveness**
Election by legislature	Mixed	Strong	Weak
Appointment by the governor	Strong	Strong	Weak
Partisan election	Weak	Weak	Strong
Nonpartisan election	Mixed/Weak	Mixed/Weak	Strong
Merit/Missouri Method	Moderate	Moderate	Weak

Source: Ann O. Bowman and Richard C. Kearney, *State and Local Government* (Boston: Houghton Mifflin, 1990), 286–297.

judges to be (1) competent, (2) independent and not subject to political pressures, and (3) responsive, or subject to democratic control.[18] Each method used by the states to select judges has strengths and weaknesses regarding each of these issues (see Table 5.3).

Election by the Legislature

Election by the legislature is a system left over from colonial America when much power rested with the state legislature. It is used only in South Carolina and Virginia.[19] This system tends to select former legislators as judges. In South Carolina, the number of judges who were former legislators was traditionally very close to 100 percent, with appointment is viewed as a capstone to a successful legislative career.[20]

Stemming from within-state discontent over questions of judicial independence, attempts at reform in South Carolina culminated in 1996 with an amendment to the state constitution instituting a Judicial Merit Selection Commission. The commission functions as an intermediary between judicial candidates and the General Assembly (the term used for South Carolina's legislature). Instead of direct General Assembly review and appointment,

> a Judicial Merit Selection Commission reviews the qualifications of all applicants and nominates the three most qualified candidates. These three nominees are then voted on by the General Assembly, and the nominee with the highest votes is appointed to the bench.[21]

The result has been an increase in judicial independence from the legislature evidenced by an increase in cases in which the Court has overruled itself. In addition, rules were put into place including a required one-year separation between legislative service and nomination for appointment to the Judiciary.[22]

The establishment of the Judicial Merit Selection Commission in South Carolina created a quasi-hybrid method of judicial selection that infused legislative selection with a merit component.

Appointment by the Governor

When judicial selection is by gubernatorial appointment, there is great potential for selection of judges who are competent, but the process itself does not ensure competence. Governors can use judicial appointments to reward friends and repay political debts. All U.S. presidents, some more than others, have used their judicial appointive powers to select federal judges with political philosophies similar to their own. Governors do the same thing. In such cases, questions of judicial competence are sometimes raised.

Governors are not likely to select unqualified people for judicial appointments; however, governors might not be able to convince the best candidates to agree to serve. The appointive system probably rules out the completely incompetent, but it does not necessarily result in the appointment of the most competent people to serve as judges. Once appointed, judges are not as responsive to voters and can exercise great independence in their decisions.

Partisan Election

In partisan elections of judges, party identification is shown on the ballot. Texas, as will be discussed more in the next section, uses this system. Originally— that is, during the founding and up until the mid-1800s—judges (federal and state) were appointed by the executive and subject to legislative confirmation/ oversight. But as the idea of judicial accountability began to grow in popularity[23], states began to move to elections as their primary method of selection. A problem soon developed, however. All these elections were partisan, and judges, therefore, were potentially subject to political demands.[24]

In response, states began to branch out, either returning to appointive measures or developing other methods: nonpartisan elections and the merit plan.[25] Still, partisan elections were not completely abandoned. They remain the most used system for trial judges (See Table 5.1). Indeed, in states with this system, judges are strongly responsive to the citizenry,[26] though this responsiveness can come at the cost of independence in their interpretation of the law.

Nonpartisan Election

Nonpartisan election is one system being given serious consideration in Texas. This system would reduce the cost of campaigns and eliminate the problem of straight ticket voting. Voters would have to base their decisions on something other than party label. It would not necessarily result in the selection of more competent judges, but it would prevent the kind of large-scale changes in judgeships that happened in Harris County in 1994 and Dallas County in 2008. As indicated earlier, it has also been suggested that Texas prohibit straight ticket voting for judicial candidates, requiring voters to mark the ballot for each judicial race.

The Merit, or Missouri, Plan

The merit, or Missouri, plan is also being given consideration as a method of selecting judges. Under this system, the governor would appoint judges from a list of acceptable (and, it is to be hoped, competent) candidates supplied by a judicial panel and perhaps ranked by the state bar association. Once appointed, the judge would serve for a set term and stand for retention in an election. In this retention election, voters could choose to either retain or remove the judge from office. The system is used by many states; 21 states use it for appellate judges, and 15 for trial judges.

It would seem that the merit plan would be strong on the issues of competency and responsiveness; however, there is little evidence that it results in the selection of more competent judges.[27] There is also evidence that it is weak on responsiveness. In retention elections, the judge does not have an opponent.[28]

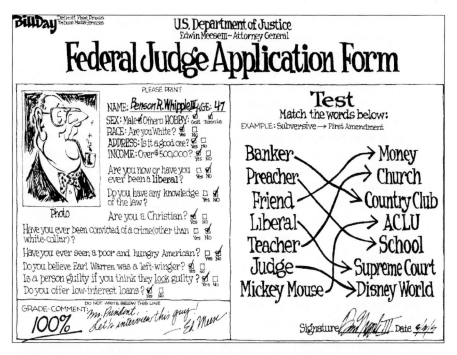

Some methods of selecting judges do not always result in the selection of qualified individuals. Bill Day.
Reprinted by permission of United Features Syndicate, Inc.

Voters vote to retain or remove. Several writers have pointed out that it is difficult to defeat someone with no one.[29] In the states that use this system, most judges are retained; fewer than 1 percent are ever removed.[30] One study showed that between 1964, when the system was first used, and 1984, only 22 of 1,864 trial judges were defeated.[31] When judges are removed, it is usually because of either an organized political effort to remove them from office or gross incompetence.

Some states have variations on these plans. In Illinois, judges are elected using a partisan ballot, but they must win 60 percent of the vote in a retention election to remain in office. In Arizona, judges in rural counties are elected in nonpartisan elections, but judges in the most populous counties are appointed. These variations might also be considered in Texas.

In short, no perfect system exists for selecting judges. All methods have problems. Also, there is no evidence that any one of these judicial selection methods results in the selection of judges with "substantially different credentials."[32] The only exception is that in the states where the legislature elects judges, more former legislators serve as judges.

Judicial Selection in Texas

Learning Objective: Describe judicial selection in Texas, including the "appointive-elective" system.

In Texas, trial court judges are elected in **partisan elections** for four-year terms, and all appellate court judges are elected in partisan elections for six-year terms.

partisan election
Method used to select all judges (except municipal court judges) in Texas by using a ballot in which party identification is shown

The only exceptions to this are municipal court judges who are usually appointed by the mayor or the city council.

The question of judicial selection has been an issue in Texas for almost two decades. In 1995, the Texas Supreme Court established the Commission on Judicial Efficiency to make recommendations on the method of judicial selection, and other issues, to the 1997 session of the Texas legislature, but the legislature took no action on the recommendations. In the 1999 session of the legislature, several bills were introduced to change judicial selections, but none passed. In 2001, seven bills were introduced that called for the appointment or **nonpartisan election** of some judges in Texas. None passed. Again in 2003, six more such bills were introduced, and none passed. In 2005, 2007, 2009, and 2011, session bills were led to move to nonpartisan elections or the merit system; none passed.

Although the election of judges can be problematic, most Texans do not like the idea of giving up their right to elect judges. Other issues in Texas judicial selection include voting by familiar name rather than qualifications, voting by straight ticket, judicial campaign contributions, and lack of minority representation in judicial elections. Indeed, in 2015, a bill was introduced to try to prevent straight ticket voting for judges, forcing voters to manually select their desired candidate, but the bill was left pending in committee.[33]

nonpartisan election
Election in which party identification is not formally declared

CORE OBJECTIVE

© Editorial Image, LLC/Alamy

Being Socially Responsible . . .
What impact, if any, do you think partisan election of judges has on judicial outcomes?

Familiar Names Can Skew Judicial Elections

Several events have brought the issue of judicial selection to the forefront in Texas today. The first of these is electoral problems. Although elections are at the very heart of any democracy, they are imperfect instruments for deciding the qualifications of the persons seeking office. This is especially true for judicial offices, for which qualifications are extremely important. The average voter in Texas will be asked to vote for judges for the Texas Supreme Court and the Court of Criminal Appeals and, in large urban counties, several district judges, county judges, and JPs. Most voters go to the election booth with scant knowledge about the qualifications of judicial candidates, and they often end up voting by **name familiarity**.

There are two good examples of this happening in Texas. In 1976 voters elected Don Yarbrough to the Texas Supreme Court. Yarbrough was an unknown attorney from Houston who won nomination as the Democratic candidate and claimed after the election that God had told him to run. Many voters had thought he was Don Yarborough, who had run unsuccessfully for governor. Still others thought he was Ralph Yarborough, who had served in the U.S. Senate for two terms. Judge Don Yarbrough was forced to resign after about six months because criminal charges were filed against him. He was later convicted of perjury and sentenced to five years in jail, but he jumped bond.

name familiarity
Practice of voting for candidates with familiar or popular names; a significant issue in Texas judicial elections

In 1990 there was a similar case of voting based on name familiarity. Gene Kelly won the Democratic Party primary for a seat on the Texas Supreme Court. Some citizens thought he was the famous dancer and film star from the 1950s and 1960s. However, this Gene Kelly was a retired Air Force judge with little nonmilitary experience. Kelly lost to Republican John Cornyn after extensive television commercials questioned his competency.

Straight Ticket Voting

Another electoral problem that has surfaced in recent years is straight ticket voting. Texas is one of nine states allowing straight ticket voting. (The others are Alabama, Indiana, Iowa, Kentucky, Oklahoma, Pennsylvania, South Carolina, and Utah.)[34] The **straight ticket voting system** allows a voter to vote for all candidates in a party by making a single mark. In 1984, many incumbent Democratic judges lost their seats in large urban counties to unknown Republican challengers because of Republican straight ticket voting. In Harris County in 1994, only one incumbent Democrat was reelected, and Republicans defeated 16 Democrats because of straight ticket voting. In 2008, voters reversed this and returned Democrats to most judicial offices in Harris County. Many of the Republicans elected lacked judicial experience, and some had no courtroom experience.

straight ticket voting system
System that allows voters to vote for all candidates of a single political party by making a single mark and that has resulted in an increase in the number of Republican judges

Also in 1994, Steve Mansfield, an individual who had very limited legal experience and no experience in criminal law, was elected to the Texas Court of Criminal Appeals, the highest court for criminal matters in Texas. After the elections, questions were raised about Mansfield's qualifications. In his state bar application, he had failed to acknowledge that he was behind in his child support payments. This raised the possibility that he could be disbarred and therefore be ineligible to serve. Some statewide officials called for his resignation.

A similar case occurred in the 2002 election. Steven W. Smith, the chief litigant behind the 1996 *Hopwood v. Texas* case that limited the use of racial quotas in selecting law school students at the University of Texas, won election to the Texas Supreme Court. Despite being a Republican, he had little support from statewide party officials and few endorsements from state bar associations; he still managed to win election because of straight ticket voting. He received about the same percentage of votes as other Republican candidates for statewide judicial office. A study by Richard Murray at the University of Houston demonstrated that about 54 percent of the votes cast in Harris County in both 1998 and 2002 were straight ticket votes. A Republican running for countywide office had a 14,000 vote head start.[35]

These incidents, along with more recent cases of straight ticket voting, have caused some to call for nonpartisan election of state judges. In every session since 1995, bills have been introduced that called for the nonpartisan election of district judges and a merit system for appellate judges. Yet another suggestion is to prohibit straight ticket voting in judicial races, which has been considered in past sessions. This would force voters to mark the ballot for each judicial race. Given the recent success of Republicans in gaining control of the legislature and the judiciary, this idea might lack strong support in the legislature.

Campaign Contributions

Another electoral issue is campaign contributions. Under the Texas partisan election system, judges must win nomination in the party primary and in the general election. Two elections, stretching over 10 months (January to November), can

Does money influence the judiciary?

© spxChrome/E 1 /Getty

be a costly process. In 1984, for example, Chief Justice John L. Hill spent more than $1 million to win the chief justice race.[36] More recently in 2014, Chief Justice Nathan Hecht and justices Brown, Boyd, and Johnson spent in excess of 3.6 million dollars to secure their reelection.[37]

Money often comes from law firms that have business before the same judges who receive the money. Other money comes from interest groups, such as the Texas Medical Association, which has an interest in limiting malpractice tort claims in cases before the courts. The Public Broadcasting System's *Frontline* television series ran a program titled "Justice for Sale," about the Texas courts and money. This report detailed how eight justices on the supreme court in 1994 received more than $9 million, primarily from corporations and law firms. In the 2014 election cycle, the majority of contributions came from business (energy, finance, insurance, and real estate), lawyers, and lobbyists.[38]

Since the mid-1990s, corporate donations have steadily grown, often matching or outpacing contributions made by lawyers and other interests. Many of these special interests had cases pending in the courts. According to a report published in 2011 by the Center for American Progress, a majority of cases held by the Texas Supreme Court between 1992 and 2010 were found in favor of corporate defendants.[39]

The basic question raised by these contributions is their impact on judicial impartiality. Do these contributions influence judges' decisions? A 1999 poll conducted by the Texas Supreme Court found that 83 percent of Texans think money influences judges.[40] In 2006, a Texans for Public Justice study found that the Texas Supreme Court is more likely to hear cases filed by large contributors. Because of the volume of cases, the high court accepted only about 11 percent of all petitions filed, but they were seven and a half times more likely to hear cases filed by contributors of $100,000 and ten times more likely from contributors of $250,000.[41] Respect for the law declines when people lose confidence in the courts. This should be of concern to all citizens.

Gender and Minority Representation in the Texas Judiciary

Texas Supreme Court Justice Eva A. Guzman, sworn into office at the Texas Capitol on Jan. 11, 2010, is a well-respected law judge who grew up in an impoverished Houston home. She recently won another six-year term in the November 2016 election.

© Erick Schlegel/AP Images

When asking how the gender, race, or ethnicity of Texas judges compares with these same traits in the state's general population, it is important to remember why the question is relevant. Many studies have asked whether such differences between judges and citizens appearing in their courts result in biased decisions.[42] We will never know the extent to which such bias exists or what forms it takes.

When we consider the racial, ethnic, and gender composition of Texas judges, we have a general sense that our constitutional right to a fair trial prohibits courts from biasing their results based on characteristics that should not influence how a court decides. We don't know when or if these forms of bias creep into the process, but our general sense of fairness suggests that electing judges from a diverse array of backgrounds will lessen whatever bias may exist.

Approximately 50.6 percent of the state's general population is male.[43] However, over 60 percent of Texas judges are male.[44] Despite this disparity, the number of female judges in the state is significant and growing. Even as early as

FOCUS ON

The First Hispanic Justice on the Texas Supreme Court

In March of 1940, Raul A. Gonzalez, Jr., was born to two migrant farm workers from Mexico in Weslaco, Texas. From an interview in 2004, he remembers the following:

As children, we worked out in the fields along with our parents, and my grandfather, and my aunts and uncles, and nieces and nephews harvesting crops. We harvested everything that they grew in the Valley: tomatoes, onions, cabbage, and cotton.[53]

He noted that his parents, particularly his mother, instilled in him the importance of education.

Well before I graduated high school, when I was probably about 12, 13, or 14 years old, my Mom planted in all of our heads that if we were ever going to break the cycle of poverty, it was going to be through education. So she really encouraged us to do as best we could in school.[54]

After graduating from high school and spending the subsequent summer harvesting tomatoes and apricots in California, Gonzalez moved to Austin to study government at the University of Texas at Austin. He became intensely involved with the Texas Young Democrats student club, picketing, participating in marches, and other forms of civil rights activism. He graduated in 1963 and, from there, moved on to the University of Houston to study law where he earned a juris doctorate in 1966.[55]

Over the next several years, he worked as an assistant city attorney in Houston, an attorney for the Houston Legal Foundation, an assistant U.S. attorney for the Southern District of Texas in Brownsville, and as a Diocesan attorney for the Catholic Diocese in Brownsville. He also maintained a private practice for several years while serving in these other positions.[56]

In 1978, however, his career as an attorney shifted to a career in the judiciary when Texas Governor Dolph Briscoe appointed him as a judge to the 103rd Judicial District. In rapid succession, subsequent Texas governors Clements and White appointed Gonzalez to increasingly high positions within the Texas Judiciary. In 1984, Gonzalez was appointed as associate justice to the Texas Supreme Court. Because Texas elects its judges, Gonzalez won the following elections that secured these judicial positions.[57]

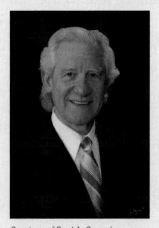

Courtesy of Raul A. Gonzalez

As the first Hispanic to be elected to the Texas Supreme Court, Gonzalez served for 14 years, from 1984 to 1998.[58] In the early years of his tenure, he was, many times, the lone voice of dissent. Although all justices in 1984 were Democrats, most did not share his worldview. He notes, in the same interview from 2004:

When I came to the Court, the members were all Democrats and by and large, were of a different philosophy than me. They were more progressive and liberal than I am. And there were some who didn't know what to make of me, like 'Who is this guy, and where did he come from?' I was very honored to be there. I never dreamed I would be a justice of the Texas Supreme Court. I saw it as a calling or vocation and I was going to do the best I could and speak my mind.[59]

In later years, he would to go on to write both majority and dissenting opinions and, as the court changed over time, his dissents drew more support from other judges.[60]

One of the major issues during his time on the court was a controversy over the possible "buying" of judges. After the Texas Supreme Court ruled to uphold a lower court ruling in 1985 in favor of Pennzoil against Texaco, "granting the largest damage award in history - $10.53 billion, plus interest,"[61] there were accusations of partiality, particularly in light of how judges are selected in partisan elections. In a 1987 *60 Minutes* episode titled "Is Justice for Sale in Texas," host Mike Wallace investigated the issue, noting that many of the "biggest [judicial nominee] campaign contributors are the lawyers who practice before the very judges they helped elect."[62]

Gonzalez has been supportive of the more recent push toward merit selection of judges, even desiring a constitutional amendment in Texas to allow its application.[63] Texas, however, remains firmly committed to the partisan election of judges.

Since retiring from the Texas Supreme Court in 1998 after many successful years, Gonzalez returned to private life but remains active in private practice and consulting.[64]

1995, some major metropolitan areas in Texas saw a significant increase in the number of female judges. At that time, for example, almost half of the 59 sitting district court judges in Harris County were female.[45] As of 2015, 44 percent of justices serving on Texas Courts of Appeals were female,[46] and women have filled two or three of the nine seats on the Texas Supreme Court at different times in recent history.[47] Two women serve on the Texas Supreme Court, and 4 of the 9 justices on the Texas Court of Criminal Appeals are women as of the November 2016 election. Approximately 34 percent of all Texas judges are female.[48]

In 2015, despite the fast-growing Hispanic population in the state, only 23 percent of all Texas judges identify as non-White.[49] Fifteen percent of all judges in the state are identified as Hispanic.[50] In the general population, by comparison, 43.5 percent of Texans identified themselves as white and non-Hispanic.[51] Even more sharply, 38.6 percent of the Texas population identified itself as Hispanic or Latino.[52]

Perhaps the most striking disparity between the composition of Texas judges and the state's general population can be seen among African Americans, who constitute 12.5 percent of the Texas population.[65] Only 4.2 percent of all Texas judges are black.[66]

> Though recent appointments to the Supreme Court have increased the visibility of African American judges, the racial make-up of the defendants and judges in the criminal court system continues to draw criticism.[67]

CORE OBJECTIVE

Source: National Park Service

Thinking Critically . . .

Reflecting on the discussion about representation of minorities and women in the Texas judicial system, do you think it is important to have a judiciary that is representative of the general population? Why or why not?

The "Appointive-Elective" System in Texas

Learning Objective: Describe judicial selection in Texas, including the "appointive-elective" system.

appointive-elective system

In Texas, the system of many judges gaining the initial seat on the court by being appointed and later standing for election

Reformers, some of whom were elected through the current partisan system, have called for change to Texas's judicial selection process. Both nonpartisan and merit systems have been suggested. Some have pointed out that the state already has an **appointive-elective system**. The Texas governor can fill any seat for district or appellate court that becomes vacant because of death or resignation, or any new district court position created by the legislature. Vacancies in the county courts and justice of the peace courts are filled by the county governing body, the

TABLE 5.4

Texas Judges Serving in 2015 Who Were Appointed to Their Initial Seat on the Court

	Appointed		Elected	
	Number	Percent	Number	Percent
Supreme Court	7	78%	2	22%
Court of Criminal Appeals	1	11%	8	89%
Court of Appeals	46	58%	34	43%
District Courts	162	36%	287	64%
Criminal District Courts	2	15%	11	85%
County Courts at Law	54	22%	188	78%
Probate Courts	4	22%	14	78%
Constitutional County Courts	44	17%	210	83%
Justice of the Peace Courts	204	25%	600	75%
Municipal Courts	1,560*	125%*	17	1%

*This is as written in the official report.

Source: Adapted from Office of Court Administration, *Annual Statistical Reports, Fiscal Year 2015.* See Profile of Appellate and Trial Judges, (http://www.txcourts.gov/media/1097007/Judge-Profile-Sept-15.pdf).

County Commissioners Court. Persons appointed to fill vacancies serve until the next regular election for that office, when they must stand for regular election.

Historically, many judges in Texas initially receive their seats on the courts by appointment. The data are not complete for all time periods, but enough is available to show that this is a common practice. Between 1940 and 1962, about 66 percent of the district and appellate judges were appointed by the governor to their first term on the court. In 1976, 150 sitting district court judges were appointed.[68] Table 5.4 shows data on appointments of sitting judges in 2015.

Removing and Disciplining Judges

Learning Objective: Describe ways in which judges are disciplined and removed.

Most states provide some system to remove judges for misconduct. Impeachment, a little-used and very political process, is provided for in 43 states, including Texas. Five states allow for recall of judges by the voters. One state, New Hampshire, allows the governor to remove a judge after a hearing. In five states, the legislature can remove judges by a supermajority (most commonly two-thirds) vote. In recent years, the trend in the states has been to create a commission on judicial conduct to review cases of misconduct by judges and remove them from office. To date, 49 states have established judicial conduct commissions. Also, the method of removal of judges can depend on the level of the judgeship—for instance, trial judges versus appellate judges.

The discipline or removal of judges from the bench can take several routes in Texas. First and foremost in practical terms is the State Commission on Judicial Conduct, which receives complaints about judges at all levels in the judiciary.

This 13-member commission conducts hearings and decides whether "the judge in question is guilty of willful or persistent conduct that is inconsistent with the proper performance of a judge's duties."[69] The commission can privately reprimand, publicly censure, or recommend that the state supreme court remove the judge. One observer has noted that sometimes "the commission persuades judges to resign voluntarily in lieu of disciplinary action."[70]In fiscal year 2009, citizens filed 1,204 cases with the commission, from which the commission issued 70 disciplinary actions. Of the judges the commission reprimanded in 2009, 41 percent were justices of the peace.

In addition, Article 15 of the Texas Constitution creates avenues to remove judges from office and empowers the Texas legislature to create other such processes by statute. The Texas Supreme Court can remove a judge for "partiality, or oppression, or official misconduct," or if his "habits . . . render him unfit to hold . . . office." By two-thirds vote of the Texas legislature, the governor can remove a judge from office for "neglect of duty," "habitual drunkenness," or "oppression in office." A two-thirds vote of the state senate can remove a judge in an impeachment process. District judges may remove county judges and justices of the peace.

The State Commission on Judicial Conduct provides a real check on the actions of judges. Furthermore, if Texas adopts the merit, or Missouri, plan, this commission would probably increase in importance.

CORE OBJECTIVE

Source: United States Department of Agriculture Agricultural Research Service

Taking Personal Responsibility . . .

Given what you read in this section, it would seem that citizens have little impact in disciplining and/or removing judges. What do you think is a citizen's responsibility in this matter? How can individuals take greater personal responsibility to ensure that judges perform properly?

The Legal System

Learning Objective: Distinguish between civil and criminal legal system branches.

The American legal system can be broadly divided into civil and criminal branches. Civil cases are those between individual citizens and involve the idea of responsibilities, not guilt. Criminal cases are those cases brought against individuals for violations of law—crimes against society. Figures 5.3 and 5.4 present a breakdown of caseloads by type for both district and county courts in Texas.[71]

Under civil law, all individuals who believe they have cause or have been injured by others may file a civil lawsuit. Courts decide whether the case has validity and should be heard in the court.

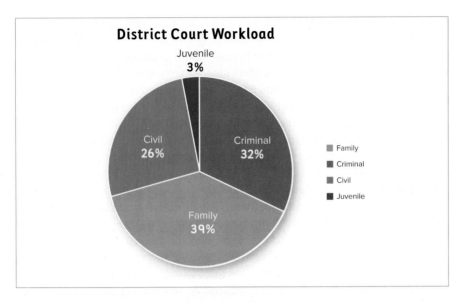

FIGURE 5.3   District Court Workload, 2015

SOURCE: Adapted from Office of Court Administration, *Annual Statistical Reports, Fiscal Year 2015.*
See: Activity Details for District Courts (http://www.txcourts.gov/).

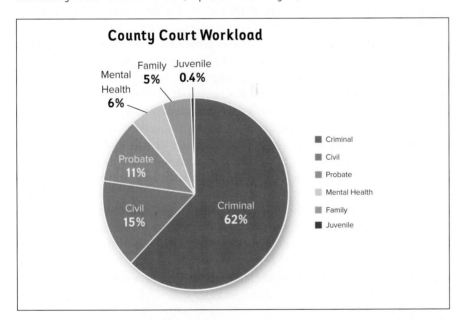

FIGURE 5.4   County Court Workload, 2015

SOURCE: Adapted from Office of Court Administration, *Annual Statistical Reports, Fiscal Year 2015.*
See: Activity Details for Statutory County Courts and Activity Details for Constitutional County
Courts (http://www.txcourts.gov/).

Grand Jury

Although any citizen may file a civil suit in court, a citizen who may face criminal prosecution can require allegations to be screened by a body that reviews
criminal cases. The U.S. Constitution requires the use of **grand juries** to serve
as a screening mechanism to prevent arbitrary actions by federal prosecutors.

grand juries
Juries of citizens that
determine if a person will be
charged with a crime

information or administrative hearing
A hearing before a judge who decides if a person must stand trial; used in place of a grand jury

Some states use the grand jury system for some criminal cases, although in recent years the use of a formal hearing before a judge, which is called an **information or an administrative hearing**, has become more common. The judge reviews the facts and decides whether enough evidence exists to try the case.

Texas uses both grand juries and administrative hearings. A citizen may waive his or her right to review by a grand jury and ask that a judge review the charges. In Texas, grand juries consist of 12 citizens chosen by district judges in one of two ways. The district judge may appoint a grand jury commission that consists of three to five people.[72] Each grand jury commissioner supplies the judge with three to five names of citizens qualified to serve on a grand jury. From these names, the judge selects 12 citizens to serve as a grand jury. In the other method, the district judge can have 20 to 75 prospective grand jurors summoned in the same manner used for petit juries (described in the next section). From this group, the district judge selects 12 citizens who are called grand jurors.[73]

Most grand juries serve for six months. They often screen major criminal cases to decide whether enough evidence exists to go to trial. Grand juries are supposed to serve as filters to prevent arbitrary actions by prosecuting attorneys, but they do not always serve this function. The district attorney often dominates grand juries. Most grand jury members are laypeople who have never served before, and they frequently follow the advice of the prosecuting attorney. Although grand juries may conduct investigations on their own, few do. Those that do conduct investigations are sometimes termed "runaway grand juries" by the media.

A 2002 study by the *Houston Chronicle* presented evidence that some judges in Harris County had been given names of citizens for the grand jury by prosecutors from the district attorney's office. The study also demonstrated that many of the same citizens serve on grand juries year after year. Judges justified the repeated use of the same people for grand juries based on the difficulty of finding people to serve. Often, older, retired citizens volunteer to serve.[74]

Thus, a grand jury might not always serve the function of protecting citizens from arbitrary action by prosecutors. For this reason, a person may ask for an administrative hearing before a judge. During grand jury proceedings, the accused may not have an attorney present during the hearing; during an administrative hearing, however, the attorney is present and can protect the accused.

In Texas the prosecuting attorney leads minor criminal cases in county courts. The county court judge, who determines whether the case should proceed to trial, holds an "administration" hearing. Criminal cases in the county court are generally less serious than those led in district courts. They consist of DWI/DUI, minor theft, drug, assault, and traffic cases.

Petit Jury

petit juries
Juries of citizens that determine the guilt or innocence of a person during a trial; pronounced *petty* juries

Both criminal and civil cases can be decided by a petit (pronounced *petty*) jury. For **petit juries**, the Texas Government Code allows jurisdictions to draw upon two sources for jury selection. A jury pool may be selected randomly from voter registration lists or from a list of licensed drivers.[75] In criminal and civil cases, the defendant has the right to a trial by jury but may waive this right and let the judge decide the case.

Most people charged with a crime plead guilty, often in exchange for a lighter sentence. On average in Texas, over a million cases are filed in county courts each year, and fewer than 5,000 result in jury trials. Less than one-third of cases in the district courts are criminal cases. Most cases end in a plea bargain and never go to trial. The person charged agrees to plead guilty in exchange for a lesser sentence. The judge hearing the case can accept or reject the agreement.

If all criminal cases were subject to jury trials, the court system would have to be greatly expanded. Many additional judges, prosecuting attorneys, and public defenders would be needed. In addition, many more citizens would have to serve on juries. The cost of this expanded process would be excessive, and even though citizens support "getting tough on criminals," they would balk at paying the bill.

Crime and Punishment in Texas

Learning Objective: Discuss crime and punishment in Texas.

For a long time, we heard a lot about crime and rising crime rates. Political candidates often used—and still do use—the crime issue as a campaign strategy to prove to voters they will be "tough on criminals." It is a safe issue that offends few voters. However, there has been more talk lately at both the federal and state levels of reforming the criminal justice system that had become—often through well-intentioned policies—dysfunctional. Perhaps surprising in this age of political gridlock and intense partisanship, there has been strong agreement on the need for reform among key figures on both the left and right sides of the political spectrum. Indeed, the conservative Texas Public Policy Foundation located in Austin has become a national leader in the criminal justice reform movement.

But how much crime is there nationally and in Texas? What factors seem to contribute to higher crime rates? Who commits most of the crimes? What impact does punishment have on crime rates? What is the cost of crime and punishment?

Crime has decreased in the United States over the past several decades, although less in Texas than in the United States as a whole (see Figure 5.5). Texas still ranks fifth among the 15 most populous states in total crime per 100,000 population.

Many factors contribute to the crime rate. Most crimes are committed in larger cities. If we compare the 50 states, we find a strong correlation between the percentage of the population living in urban (metropolitan) areas and crime rates. This in part explains the crime rate in Texas; more than 80 percent of the population lives in metropolitan areas.

A strong relationship also exists between age, sex, and criminal arrests. Twenty percent of people younger than 18 years of age are arrested for crimes, and 73 percent of all persons arrested for crimes are male. Race appears to be determinant in criminal arrests. African Americans constitute about 13 percent of the U.S. population, yet, as shown in Table 5.5, constitute almost 30 percent of persons arrested for crimes.

To find out more on the criminal justice system in both Texas and the nation as a whole, see Chapter 12. There is discussion on current crime rates as well as incarceration and recidivism rates over the past few decades. In particular, there is significant discussion on the impact of income and poverty on the ability to obtain legal representation.

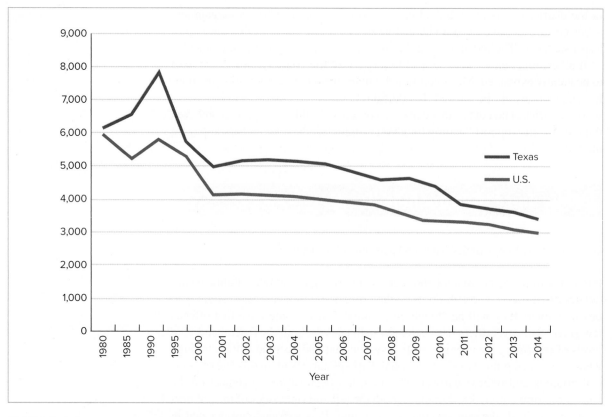

FIGURE 5.5   **Crime Rates per 100,000, 1980–2014**

SOURCE: Adapted from The Disaster Center, *United States Population and Rate of Crime per 100,000 People 1960 - 2014;* Texas Population and Rate of Crime per 100,000 People 1960 - 2014. See: Uniform Crime Rate 1960 - 2014 for USA and Texas (http://www.disastercenter.com /crime/index.html).

TABLE 5.5	
Persons Arrested for Crime by Sex, Race, and Age in 2014	
	Percentage of Arrests
Sex	
Male	73.3%
Female	26.7%
Race	
White*	69.4%
Black	27.8%
Others	2.8%
Age	
Under 18 years of age	20.6%
Over 18 years of age	79.4%

*Includes Hispanics

Source: Adapted from Federal Bureau of Investigation, *Crime in the United States,* 2014, Tables 41, 42, 43 (https://www.fbi.gov/about-us/cjis/ucr/crime-in-the-u.s/2014/crime-in-the-u.s.-2014 /tables).

Conclusion

In the twenty-first century, the court system in Texas faces many challenges. Methods of selecting judges will continue to be controversial. Texas has a partisan election system but utilizes an "appointive-elective" process where the governor can fill any seat for district or appellate court that becomes vacant because of death or resignation, or any new district court position created by the legislature. Some change in these methods will probably occur. Texans may want to think about their approach to dealing with the high crime rates in the state. Although voters seem anxious to approve bonds for the construction of more prisons, they are often reluctant to consider other approaches to crime control. However, recent reform efforts suggest that this may be changing. For more on criminal justice policy, see the discussion in Chapter 12.

Summary

LO: Explain the courts' approach to decision making.

Courts evaluate disputes between individuals not involving policy questions and resolve them by interpreting and enforcing existing rules and laws. But in doing so they may create law that plays an important role in the lives of far more people than the individuals who actually participated in the case. Courts are governed by strict procedural rules that determine when and how facts and arguments can be presented.

LO: Discuss judicial federalism.

Article III of the United States Constitution established the Supreme Court and gave Congress the authority to create other lower federal courts. Article VI of the U.S. Constitution makes federal law the supreme law of the land. Any direct conflicts between federal and state law must be resolved in favor of federal authority. States create their own courts. As a result, 50 separate jurisdictions have complete court systems that exist side by side with the federal courts. Federal courts hear cases involving federal laws, and state courts hear cases involving state laws.

LO: Explain the structure of state courts, including trial and appellate courts.

Most states provide for three levels of courts: trial courts, appellate courts, and a supreme court. Trial courts are local courts that hear cases; juries determine the outcome of the cases heard in the court. Appellate courts are higher-level courts that decide on points of law and not questions of guilt or innocence. Texas has several levels of trial courts and appellate courts. Trial courts include the justices of the peace, municipal courts, county courts, district courts, and special purpose courts, such as probate, juvenile, and domestic relations courts. Texas has 14 intermediate appellate courts and 2 "supreme" appellate courts: one for civil cases (Texas Supreme Court) and one for criminal cases (the Court of Criminal Appeals).

LO: Describe judicial selection in Texas, including the "appointive-elective" system.

In Texas, trial court judges are elected in partisan elections for four-year terms, and all appellate court judges are elected in partisan elections for six-year terms. The only exceptions to this are municipal court judges who are usually appointed by the mayor or the city council. Texas has an appointive-elective system where many judges gain their initial seat on the court by being appointed and later stand for election.

LO: Describe ways in which judges are disciplined and removed.

Most states provide some system to remove judges for misconduct. Impeachment, a little-used and very political process, is provided for in 43 states, including Texas. Five states allow for recall of judges by the voters. One state, New Hampshire, allows the governor to remove a judge after a hearing. In five states, the legislature can remove judges by a supermajority (most commonly two-thirds) vote. To date, 49 states have established judicial conduct commissions. Also, the method of removal of judges can depend on the level of the judgeship—for instance, trial judges versus appellate judges.

LO: Distinguish between civil and criminal legal system branches.

Civil cases are those between individual citizens and involve the idea of responsibilities, not guilt. Criminal cases are those cases brought against individuals for violations of law—crimes against society. Any citizen may file a civil suit in court. Citizens who may face criminal prosecution can require allegations to be screened by a body that reviews criminal cases. These cases must go before a grand jury (as required by the U.S. Constitution). But it is becoming common for people to request a formal administrative hearing before a judge. In these hearings, the judge reviews the facts and decides whether enough evidence exists to try the case.

LO: Discuss crime and punishment in Texas.

Crime has decreased in the United States over the past several decades, although less in Texas than in the United States as a whole. Texas still ranks fifth among the 15 most populous states in total crime per 100,000 population. Many factors contribute to the crime rate. Most crimes are committed in larger cities. Also, a strong relationship also exists between age, sex, race and criminal arrests.

Key Terms

appellate courts
appointive-elective system
grand juries
information or an administrative
    hearing
magistrate functions

merit system, or Missouri system
name familiarity
nonpartisan election
objectivity
partisan election
nonpartisan

petit juries
stare decisis
straight ticket voting system
trial courts
trial de novo courts

Notes

[1] Herbert Jacob, "Courts: The Least Visible Branch," in *Politics in the American States,* 6th ed., eds. Virginia Gray and Herbert Jacob (Washington, D.C.: Congressional Quarterly Press, 1996), 254.

[2] Ibid.

[3] Dye, *Politics in States and Communities,* 8th ed., 227.

[4] Ibid.

[5] Ibid.

[6] Ibid.

[7] Ibid., 228.

[8] Jacob, "Courts," 253.

[9] Ibid., 256–258.

[10] Office of Court Administration, Texas Judicial Council, *Texas Judicial System Annual Report* (Austin: Office of Court Administration, 1994), 31–33.

[11] Office of Court Administration, Texas Judicial Council. 2015 Annual Statistical Report: Justice Courts Activity Detail (Austin: Office of Court Administration, 2015), http://www.txcourts.gov/media/1252949/3-Justice_Court_Activity_Detail-2015.pdf.

[12] Office of Court Administration, "Court Structure Chart as of January 1, 2016," Texas Judicial Branch, http://www.txcourts.gov/media/1244897/Court-Structure-Chart-Jan-2016.pdf.

[13] Council of State Governments, *The Book of the States, 2015* (Lexington, Ky.: Council of State Governments, 2015), Tables 5.6.

[14] Ibid.

[15] Office of Court Administration, Texas Judiciary Council. "Court Structure of Texas," http://www.txcourts.gov/media/1244897/Court-Structure-Chart-Jan-2016.pdf.

[16] Council of State Governments, *The Book of the States, 2015* (Lexington, Ky.: Council of State Governments, 2015), Tables 5.6.

[17] Delaware, Maine, Massachusetts, New Hampshire, New Jersey, New York, and Vermont have some judges who are appointed by the governor and can be removed only for cause. Connecticut, Rhode Island, South Carolina, and Virginia have legislative elections; judges serve for life with good behavior. See Jacob, "Courts," 268, Table 7.2. Also see *Book of the States,* 1994–95, 190–193, Table 4.4. There are some slight variations between the Jacob table and the table in *Book of the States.* This is probably due to interpretations by the writers. Because of minor variations among states, classification differences are possible. Updated information up to 2015 from *Book of the States, 2015,* Tables 5.6 and 5.7.

[18] Ferraro, Francesco, "Ajudication and Expectations: Bentham on the Role of Judges," in *Utilitas,* Vol 25 (2), 2013, pp 140–160.; Gibson, James. *Electing Judges: The Surprising Effects of Campaigning on Judicial Legitimacy,* Chicago Studies in American Politics, 2012.

[19] American Judicature Society, "Judicial Selection in the States: Appellate and General Jurisdiction Courts,"

(2013), https://web.archive.org/web/20141208194400 /http://www.judicialselection.us/.

[20] Herbert Jacob, "The Effect of Institutional Differences in the Recruitment Process: The Case of State Judges," *Journal of Public Law* 33, no. 113 (1964): 104–119.

[21] Petillo, Kimberly C. "The Untouchables: The Impact of South Carolina's New Judicial Selection System on the South Carolina Supreme Court, 1997-2003." *Albany Law Review,* 67: 937-963. pp 8. Retrieved April 10, 2016 from https://web.archive.org/web/20120113053528/ http://www.albanylawreview.org/archives/67/3/ SouthCarolinaHighCourtStudy.pdf.

[22] Ibid.

[23] This occurred for a number of reasons. Matthew J. Streb writes that, "Scholars have put forth several reasons behind the surge in state-elected judiciaries, including concern over an independent judiciary after the Supreme Court's controversial ruling in Marbury v. Madison, resistance to English common law, imitation by the states, the fact that impeachment was difficult to enact, the belief that judges at the local level should be responsive to their communities, and the legal profession's belief that the judiciary needed more independence from state legislatures." (Matthew J. Streb. 2007. "The Study of Judicial Elections," in Running for Judge: The Rising Political, Financial, and Legal Stakes of Judicial Elections, Matthew J. Streb (ed.). New York: New York University Press: 9.)

[24] Ibid, 9–10.

[25] Ibid, 10.

[26] Michael DeBow, Diane Brey, Erick Kaardal, John Soroko, Frank Strickland, Michael B. Wallace, "The Case for Partisan Judges," January 1, 2003, The Federalist Society for Law & Public Policy Studies, http://www.fed-soc.org /publications/detail/the-case-for-partisan-judicial-elections.

[27] Bradley Canon, "The Impact of Formal Selection Processes on Characteristics of Judges"Reconsidered,? *Law and Society Review* 13 (May 1972): 570–593.

[28] Richard Watson and Rondal G. Downing, *Politics of the Bench and Bar: Judicial Selection under the Missouri Nonpartisan Court Plan* (New York: John Wiley, 1969).

[29] Dye, *Politics in States and Communities,* 8th ed., 236.

[30] William Jenkins, "Retention Elections: Who Wins When No One Loses," *Judicature* 61 (1977): 78–86; Gill, R.D., "Beyond High Hopes and Unmet Expectations: Judicial Selection Reforms in the States," *Judicature* 96 (2013): 278–295.

[31] William K. Hall and Larry T. Aspen, "What Twenty Years of Judicial Retention and Elections Have Told Us," *Judicature* 70 (1987): 340–347.

[32] Craig F. Emmert and Henry R. Glick, "The Selection of Supreme Court Judges," *American Politics Quarterly* 19 (October 1988): 444–465.

[33] Langford, Terri (2015 , March 24), Proposed Change to Election of Judges Gets Cool Reception, *The Texas Tribune,* https://www.texastribune.org/2015/03/24 /straight-ticket-election-judges-ban-meets-oppositi/; Texas Legislative Guide: House Bill 25, (2015), *The Texas Tribune,* http://txlege.texastribune.org/84/bills/HB25/

[34] National Conference of State Legislatures, "Straight Ticket Voting States," http://www.ncsl.org/research/elections-and-campaigns/straight-ticket-voting.aspx.

[35] *Houston Chronicle,* "A Closer Look at Harris County's Vote," 14 November 2002, 32A.

[36] Anthony Champagne, "Campaign Contributions in Texas Supreme Court Races," *Crime, Law, and Social Change* 17 (1992): 91–106.

[37] Scott Greytak, Alicia Bannon, Allyse Falce, Linda Casey, and Laurie Kinney, "Appendix A: State Profiles," in *Bankrolling the Bench: The New Politics of Judicial Elections 2013–2014.* The New Politics of Judicial Elections, a collaboration between Justice at Stake, The Brennan Center, and National Institute on Money in State Politics: 2015, http:// newpoliticsreport.org/app/uploads/JAS-NPJE-2013-14.pdf.

[38] Ibid.

[39] Billy Corriher, "Big Business Taking over State Supreme Courts: How Campaign Contributions to Judges Tip the Scales Against Individuals," Center for American Progress. August 2012, https://www.americanprogress.org /wp-content/uploads/issues/2012/08/pdf/statecourts.pdf.

[40] Texans for Public Justice, *Courtroom Contributions Stain Supreme Court Campaigns,* http://info.tpj.org/reports /courtroomcontributions/courtroomcontributions.pdf.

[41] Texans for Public Justice, "Billable Ours: Texas Endures Another Attorney Financed Supreme Court Race," http://info.tpj.org/reports/supremes06/supremes06.pdf.

[42] See, for example, Sherrilyn A. Ifill, "Judging the Judges: Racial Diversity and Representation on State Trial Courts," 39 Boston College Law Review 95 (1998), http:// lawdigitalcommons.bc.edu/bclr/vol39/iss1/3.

[43] Quickfacts, "States," http://www.census.gov /quickfacts/table/PST045215/48.

[44] Texas Politics: 2 Oct 2012: "Profiling Texas Judges," Liberal Arts Instructional Technology Services, University of Texas at Austin, 3rd Edition—Revision 6, http://texaspolitics. utexas.edu/archive/html/just/features/0403_01/judges.html.

[45] Sherrilyn A. Ifill, "Judging the Judges: Racial Diversity and Representation on State Trial Courts," 39 Boston College Law Review 95 at p. 96, note 7 (1998), http:// lawdigitalcommons.bc.edu/bclr/vol39/iss1/3.

[46] Texas Judicial Branch, Office of Court Administration. "Profile of Appellate and Trial Judges As of September 1, 2015," http://www.txcourts.gov/media/1097007/Judge-Profile-Sept-15.pdf.

[47] Texas Office of Court Administration, "Texas Supreme Court," http://www.supreme.courts.state.tx.us/court/justices.asp (three female justices 2001–2005).

[48] Texas Office of Court Administration, *Annual Statistical Reports, Fiscal Year 2015,* Profile of Appellate and Trial Judges As of September 1, 2015, http://www.txcourts.gov/media/1097007/Judge-Profile-Sept-15.pdf.

[49] Ibid.

[50] Texas Office of Court Administration, *Annual Statistical Reports, Fiscal Year 2013.*

[51] Quickfacts, "States," http://quickfacts.census.gov/qfd/states/48000.html.

[52] Ibid.

[53] Robert B. Gilbreath and D. Todd Smith, An Interview with Former Justice Raul A. Gonzalez, XVII(1) The Appellate Advocate 25–33 (Summer 2004), http://www.hptylaw.com/media/article/24_rob.pdf.

[54] Ibid.

[55] Robert B. Gilbreath and D. Todd Smith, An Interview with Former Justice Raul A. Gonzalez, XVII(1) The Appellate Advocate 25–33 (Summer 2004), http://www.hptylaw.com/media/article/24_rob.pdf; Jamail Center for Legal Researach, "Raul A. Gonzalez, Jr. (b. 1940)," in *Justices of Texas 1836–1986,* Tarlton Law Library, University of Texas School of Law, https://tarlton.law.utexas.edu/justices/profile/view/38.

[56] Jamail Center for Legal Researach, "Raul A. Gonzalez, Jr. (b. 1940)," in *Justices of Texas 1836–1986,* Tarlton Law Library, University of Texas School of Law, https://tarlton.law.utexas.edu/justices/profile/view/38.

[57] Ibid.

[58] Ibid.

[59] Robert B. Gilbreath and D. Todd Smith, An Interview with Former Justice Raul A. Gonzalez, XVII(1) The Appellate Advocate 25–33 (Summer 2004), http://www.hptylaw.com/media/article/24_rob.pdf.

[60] Ibid.

[61] Lewin, Tamar (1987), Pennzoil-Texaco Fight Raised Key Questions, *The New York Times,* http://www.nytimes.com/1987/12/19/business/pennzoil-texaco-fight-raised-key-questions.html?pagewanted=all.

[62] Wallace, Mike (1987), Is Justice for Sale in Texas? [Television Broadcast]. In *60 Minutes.* New York, CBS Broadcasting.

Retrieved from a copy of the broadcast uploaded to YouTube: [Hawthorne, Blake] (2015, May 6), 1987 60 Minutes Is Justice For Sale in Texas. [Video File], https://www.youtube.com/watch?v=ob3_-Ilf6Vw.

[63] Robert B. Gilbreath and D. Todd Smith, An Interview with Former Justice Raul A. Gonzalez, XVII(1) The Appellate Advocate 25–33 (Summer 2004), http://www.hptylaw.com/media/article/24_rob.pdf.

[64] Jamail Center for Legal Research, "Raul A. Gonzalez, Jr. (b. 1940)," in *Justices of Texas 1836–1986,* Tarlton Law Library, University of Texas School of Law, https://tarlton.law.utexas.edu/justices/profile/view/38.

[65] Quickfacts, "States," http://quickfacts.census.gov/qfd/states/48000.html.

[66] Texas Judicial Branch, Office of Court Administration, "Profile of Appellate and Trial Judges As of September 1, 2015," http://www.txcourts.gov/media/1097007/Judge-Profile-Sept-15.pdf.

[67] University of Texas at Austin, Liberal Arts Instructional Technology Services, "Characteristics of the Judiciary," last updated 6 Sept 2016, http://www.laits.utexas.edu/txp_media/html/just/0403.html.

[68] Kramer and Newell, *Texas Politics,* 3rd ed. (New York: West, 1987), 281.

[69] Commission on Judicial Conduct, *Annual Report,* 1994 (Austin: Commission on Judicial Conduct, State of Texas, 1994); The Texas Tribune, "TRIBPEDIA: State Commission on Judicial Conduct," https://www.texastribune.org/tribpedia/state-commission-on-judicial-conduct/about/. Accessed 6 Sept 2016.

[70] Diane Jennings, "State Commission on Judicial Conduct has the job of judging Texas' judges," *The Dallas Morning News,* djennings@dallasnews.com. Published: 14 December 2009 02:32 AM Updated: 26 November 2010 03:29 PM).

[71] Office of Court Administration, *Annual Statistical Reports, Fiscal Year 2015,* http://www.txcourts.gov/statistics/annual-statistical-reports/.

[72] Interview with District Court Judge John Delaney, Brazos County Courthouse, November 1995.

[73] *Texas Code of Criminal Procedure,* arts. 19.01–20.22.

[74] *Houston Chronicle,* "Murder Case Testing Grand Jury Selection," 2 March 2002, 1A and 16A.

[75] Texas Family Code section 51.041(a).

CHAPTER 6

Local Governments in Texas

Texas Learning Outcomes

• Describe local political systems in Texas.

L ocal governments in Texas and throughout the United States are hiding in plain sight. Evidence of local government is all around us: paved streets, sidewalks, clean water, fire stations, police cars, parks, and schools. Yet many citizens are either unaware of or uninterested in the operations and procedures of local governments and local government elections. Most citizens show as little interest in the former as the latter. Voter turnout in local government elections is consistently the lowest year in and year out when compared to federal and state elections.

Nearly 85 percent of Texans live in urban areas and rely on local governments for a host of services, and they have been increasing their demands for a greater range of services. Local governments, in short, provide some of the services that make our modern lives possible. Even the roughly 15 percent of Texans who live

Austin City Hall
© Peter Tsai Photography/Alamy

in rural areas rely on services from county governments and special districts. It is important for us, as Texans, to understand how local governments work and affect our lives.[1]

Chapter Learning Objectives

- Define types of local government.

- Define general law cities and home rule cities.

- Explain municipal elections in Texas, including a discussion of voter turnout.

- Describe county governments in Texas, including weaknesses and possible reforms.

- Discuss special purpose districts.

Federalism Revisited

Learning Objective: Define types of local government.

The United States is characterized by its highly decentralized system of government. This lack of centralization has its roots in the historic fear of a strong national government and the principles of federalism enshrined in the U.S. Constitution. Federalism is the political principle that assigns different functions to different levels of government. In Chapter 2 we focused on the relationship between the central government and the various state governments in our federalist structure. Local governments add another layer. Decentralization and the lack of intergovernmental coordination are trends in Texas government and throughout the United States. Nationwide, there are approximately 89,000 local government units, and Texas has a little over 5,000 of them. Counts for 2012 on the number of local governments by category are presented in Table 6.1.

TABLE 6.1

Number of Local Governments in the United States and Texas, 2012

	United States	Texas
Counties	3,031	254
Cities	19,522	1,214
Townships	16,364	—*
School districts	12,884	1,079
Special districts	37,203	2,600
Totals	89,004	5,147

*Texas does not have townships.

Source: U.S. Census Bureau, *2012 Census of Governments: The Many Layers of American Government.* Note that the next Census of Governments will occur in 2017.

Creatures of the State

Learning Objective: Define types of local government.

In a federal system in which multiple governments share authority over the same territory, states possess police powers—the authority to regulate the health, safety, and morals of their citizens. These powers, granted under the Tenth Amendment, are exercised through the enactment and enforcement of statutes. Enforcement here includes not just what we more commonly think of as "police" power (actual police forces; the people in uniform) but also legal sanctions and other methods of nonphysical coercion. States are allowed to form local governments to aid the states in the performance of their police powers. Constitutionally, municipalities and other local governments are legal **creatures of the states**. This means municipal and other local governments are constrained by the same legal limits as are states and lack any legal existence independent of state action. On the other hand, unitary governments, while also able to form creatures of the state, strictly dictate what those governments can and cannot do. Unlike in a federal system where states are granted all those powers not expressly given to the national government, unitary systems are much more centralized. State-level governments receive only those powers expressly granted by the central governing authority. The same principle goes for municipalities and other local governments.

The states, in our federal system, have substantial discretion in the authority they grant their local governments, and local governments within each state have different types of authority. We can categorize local governments by the amount of authority granted to them by the states; there are general-purpose and limited-purpose local governments. General-purpose governments are granted broad discretionary authority to act on a range of issues; to control their own spending, revenue, and personnel; and to establish and modify their own governmental structures. Conversely, limited-purpose governments are granted rather narrow authority to act and have little leeway over revenue, spending, and personnel; the structure of their governments is set by the state.[2]

Examples of limited-purpose government in Texas include school districts and counties. A school district has but one function—education. Its taxing authority is limited to the property tax, and many personnel issues are controlled by a state agency. Texas counties are also limited-purpose governments. State law severely restricts county authority and revenue sources, and all 254 Texas counties share the same government structure.

Municipalities are the most visible example of general-purpose governments in Texas. Home rule Texas cities (see the following section) are granted the authority to pass any ordinance not expressly forbidden by the state constitution or state laws, and they have multiple sources of revenue. Texas home rule cities have greater discretion in deciding their government structure, and the state has limited authority over cities' personnel decisions. Consequently, not all local governments are created equal, although all are legal creatures of their states. Cities, counties, special districts, and school districts all have their unique aspects.

creatures of the state
Local governments are created by state government, and all powers are derived from the state government; there are no inherent rights for local governments independent of what the state grants to them

General Law Cities and Home Rule

Learning Objective: Define general law cities and home rule cities.

general law city
Cities governed by city charters created by state statutes

home rule city
Cities governed by city charters created by the actions of local citizens

City governments are municipal corporations, granted a corporate charter by their state. The term *municipality* derives from the Roman *municipium,* which means a "free city capable of governing its local affairs, even though subordinate to the sovereignty of Rome."[3] A city's charter is its constitution, which provides the basic organization and structure of the city government and outlines the general powers and authority of its government and officials. Cities in Texas are chartered as either a **general law city** or a **home rule city**. The charters for general law cities are spelled out in state statutes, and those cities must choose from the seven charters provided in these statutes.[4] According to the Texas Municipal League, roughly 75 percent of all Texas cities are under general law with only 368 cities under home rule.[5]

After the approval of a state constitutional amendment in 1912, Texas cities with populations of at least 5,000 may be chartered as home rule cities.[6] Most cities with such populations choose to be home rule cities. Home rule affords local citizens a greater range of governmental structure and organization and allows such cities the authority to pass ordinances not prohibited by state law. Although there is no specific grant of power to cities in the state constitution, cities can pass any ordinance that does not conflict with state law or violate the state constitution. For example, no state law establishes the number of city council members, but the state constitution does establish a ceiling of four years for terms of office.

Prohibitions on local government action can be implicit or explicit. For example, there is no explicit prohibition against cities passing an ordinance banning open alcohol containers in vehicles. Several Texas cities passed such ordinances in the 1980s before there was a state law against open containers. However, state courts ruled that the regulation of alcohol was a state function and, by *implication,* Texas cities could not pass ordinances banning open alcohol containers in vehicles.

The home rule provisions of the Texas Constitution allow great latitude in governing local affairs. Once adopted, home rule charters may be amended solely with the approval of the city voters. Usually a charter review commission or the city council proposes amendments; however, "under Section 9.004 of the Local Government Code, citizens can force the city council to call an election on a proposed charter amendment by simply filing a petition signed by five percent of the qualified voters or 20,000, whichever is less."[7] Yet, at times, state law allows home rule councils to amend their charters, without the vote of their citizens, on specific issues. For example, the Texas legislature periodically passes a law permitting city councils a calendar window to change their municipal election date to November. In the fall of 2004, the San Marcos city council, in response to such a state law, changed the city election month from May to November despite the City of San Marcos Charter provision that explicitly granted that authority to its citizens voting on the proposed charter amendment.

Incorporation: The Process of Creating a City

The process of establishing a city is known as **incorporation** because, legally, cities are municipal corporations. Local citizens need to petition the state and ask to be incorporated as a city. Second, an election is held, and a simple majority of the voters need to approve the establishment of a city with explicitly drawn territorial boundaries. Then the state issues a municipal corporate charter.

In Texas, for incorporation to proceed, first, a minimum population of 201 citizens must be living within a two-square-mile area. Second, 10 percent of the registered voters and 50 percent of the property owners in the area to be incorporated must sign petitions asking that an election be held. If the petition is deemed valid, the county judge calls an election. If a simple majority of the voters approve incorporation, the city is granted a general law charter, and a second election is held to elect city officials.[8]

There are some limits regarding where cities can be established. By Texas law, all cities have **extra-territorial jurisdiction** (ETJ) that extends beyond the city limits.[9] General law cities have only one-half mile of ETJ, but the distance increases as the cities' populations increase, and may extend for five miles for cities with populations above 250,000. ETJ is important because it provides a city some measure of regulatory control over the growth (zoning, construction, etc.) of surrounding areas. It is illegal for a city to be incorporated within the ETJ of an existing city unless the existing city approves. This provision was intended to prevent smaller towns from impeding the growth of existing cities within their own ETJs.

Annexation

Cities may expand by annexing land within their ETJ. Annexation is the process by which cities legally add adjoining unincorporated territory to the total land area of the city. Texas cities have broad annexation powers. The city council, by majority vote, can unilaterally annex land, and the residents living in the area being annexed have no voice or vote in the process. This provision in state law, coupled with the ETJ provisions, provides Texas cities with room to expand. In every session of the Texas legislature, many bills are introduced to restrict Texas cities' ability to annex land. Though some restrictions have been placed on home rule cities in the past, Texas cities still have broad annexation authority when compared to many other states.

Annexation has become an increasingly contentious issue in Texas and elsewhere. Cities annex for a number of reasons. First, cities annex so that they will not be surrounded by other incorporated cities. Annexation of one city by another requires the consent of the annexed city, which happens rarely, so encirclement means the end of growth. Second, and connected to the first, cities annex to protect and enhance their tax base. New land means new property taxes, new sales taxes, and larger population. Finally, cities annex to become more important politically. Larger populations mean greater political clout, more federal grant money, and more representatives elected to the state legislature and the U.S. Congress.

The rapid growth in Texas cities created counter pressure from people who had been enjoying the benefits of a nearby city without paying for those benefits before their property was annexed. A new annexation law was passed by the Texas legislature in 1999 that required cities to give a three-year notice before annexation formally begins, to create a service plan and deliver those services within two and a half

incorporation
Process of creating a city government

extraterritorial jurisdiction
City powers that extend beyond the city limits to an area adjacent to the city limits

years, and to arbitrate with the residents of the proposed annexed area.[10] However, in 2009, the attorney general issued an opinion stating that the three-year requirement does not pertain to "sparsely populated areas."[11] Even in the face of these limitations, it is inevitable that cities will be even more important to Texas in the future.

Types of City Government

Learning Objective: Define types of local government.

Cities in the United States use two basic forms of city government: mayor-council and council-manager, 33 and 59 percent respectively.[12] Additionally, the mayor-council system has two variations: the strong mayor system and the weak mayor system. A third form of local government, the commission, is used by only a few cities nationwide. It is not used by any city in Texas, but the commission form is discussed later in this chapter because it once played an important role in the development of local government in Texas.[13]

Council-Manager Government

council-manager form
Form of government where voters elect a mayor and city council; the mayor and city council appoint a professional administrator to manage the city

The **council-manager form** of government is the most popular form of government in Texas today. It arose during the Progressive Era (1901–1920) out of concern about the corruption and inefficiency of large cities dominated by political machines. Figure 6.1 outlines the structure of the council-manager form. Amarillo was the first city to adopt it in 1913, and Phoenix, Dallas, and San Antonio are the largest adopter cities today. Except for Houston, all major cities in Texas use the council-manager form of government.[14] Under this system, the

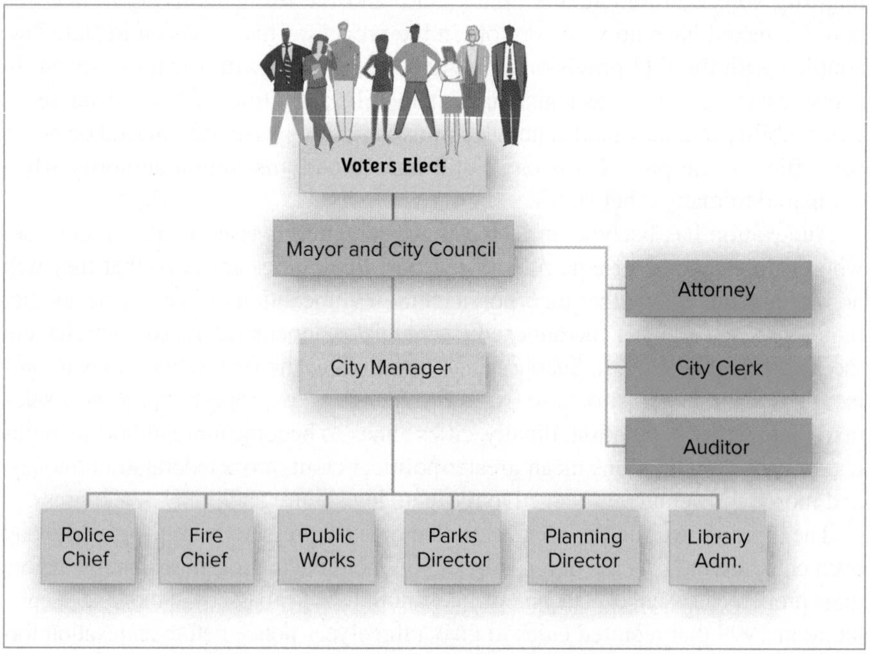

FIGURE 6.1   Council-Manager Form of City Government

voters elect a small city council (usually seven members), including a mayor. The council hires a city manager, who has administrative control over city government. The city manager appoints and removes the major heads of departments of government and is responsible for budget preparation and execution.

The mayor and city council are responsible for establishing the mission, policy, and direction of city government. More specifically, the mayor and council generate policy while all administrative authority rests with the city manager. The mayor and council roles in administration and management are greatly reduced. Figure 6.2 shows the roles of the council and mayor on the four dimensions of city government: mission, policy, administration, and management. In Figure 6.2, the curved line illustrates the division between the council's and the manager's spheres of activity (the council's tasks to the left of the line, the manager's to the right). This division roughly approximates a "proper" degree of separation and sharing; shifts to the left or right would indicate improper incursions. The council and mayor dominate the areas of mission and policy, and the city manager dominates the areas of administration and management.

Role of the Mayor

The role of the mayor in city governments is often misunderstood because of the variations in the roles of the office. The mayor is the presiding officer of the

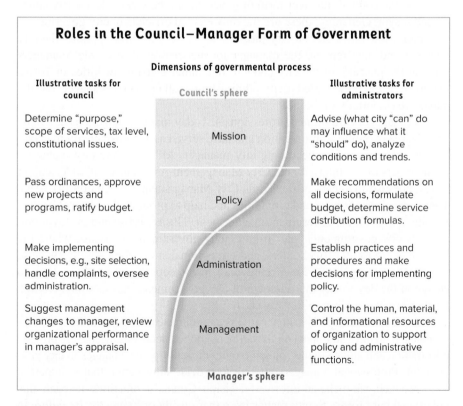

FIGURE 6.2   Roles in the Council-Manager Form of Government The curved line suggests the division between the council's and the manager's spheres of activity (the council's tasks to the left of the line, the manager's to the right). This division roughly approximates a "proper" degree of separation and sharing; shifts to the left or right would indicate improper incursions.

council and most often has a vote on all issues. (A small number of cities have the mayor vote only in case of a tie vote.) The mayor usually lacks any type of veto, though a few cities such as El Paso do extend veto power to the office. Laws are passed by a majority vote of the total council membership, not just a majority of those present. The mayor in this form is the "head of state," the symbolic leader and the embodiment of his or her city, but is not the head of government.

The council, including the mayor, selects only four city government officials: the manager, the attorney, the clerk (sometimes called secretary), and the municipal judge. (Some cities elect the municipal judge.) The city council passes ordinances (also called laws), sets policies for the government, and provides guidelines to the city staff on such issues as the budget, taxes, and fees and spending. The council is considered part-time, so members are paid only a nominal salary or none at all.

Role of the City Manager

city manager

Person hired by the city council to manage the city; serves as the chief administrative officer of the city

Because so many cities in Texas use the council-manager form of government, some understanding of the role of the **city manager** is essential. Texas has always been a leader in the use of this form of government. O. M. Carr, the first city manager in Amarillo, strongly influenced the formation of the International City Managers (Management) Association.[15]

Under the council-manager form of government, the voters elect a city council and mayor. Generally, these are the only elected officials in city government, although a few cities elect a city judge. The council, in turn, appoints the city manager and may remove the manager for any reason at any time; managers serve at the pleasure of the city council. In smaller general law cities in Texas, the position might be called a city administrator rather than a manager, but the duties are essentially the same.

Most managers are trained professionals. Today many managers have a master's degree in public administration and have served as an assistant city manager for several years before becoming city manager. All but a few city managers are members of the International City Management Association (ICMA) and, in Texas, are also members of the Texas City Management Association (TCMA). These organizations have codes of ethics and help to promote the ideas of professionalism in the local government management. This expertise and professionalism sets city governments apart from county governments in Texas, where the voters elect most all officeholders, and professionalism is often absent. Because city managers appoint and can remove all major department heads and are in charge of the day-to-day management of city government, they can instill a high level of professionalism in the city staff.[16]

Although the manager's primary role is to administer city government, managers can and do have an impact on the councils' policy decisions. Managers provide information and advice to the council on the impact of policy changes in city government. Professional managers attempt to provide information that is impartial so the council can make an informed decision. Councils sometimes delegate this policy-making process to city managers, either openly or indirectly, by failure to act. When this happens, councils are neglecting their duty of office and are not serving the citizens who elected them. Over the past 100 years, the council-manager form of government has functioned well in Texas. Texas cities have a national reputation of being well managed and highly professional in their operations.

Weaknesses of the Council-Manager Form

The council-manager form has some weaknesses. First, the council members are part-time and usually serve for a short amount of time. Second, because the city manager is not directly answerable to the voters, citizens may believe he or she lacks influence. Third, owing to political coalitions on a council, a city manager may be able to ignore large parts of the community when it comes to provision of simple city services such as sidewalks and serviceable streets. Finally, a powerful city manager can skew and hide information from the council so as to control council policy decisions before they are even made.

Mayor-Council Government

Mayor-council government is the more traditional form that developed in the nineteenth century. There are two variations of mayor-council government—weak executive and strong executive (see Figures 6.3 and 6.4). Under the **weak mayor form of government** (also known as the weak executive form), the formal powers of the mayor are limited in much the same way that the Texas governor's formal powers are limited. First, the mayor shares power with other elected officials and with the city council. Second, the mayor has only limited control over budget formation and execution. Third, the number of terms the mayor can serve is limited. Fourth, the mayor has little or no veto authority.[17]

Under a strong executive or **strong mayor form of government**, the mayor can appoint and remove the major heads of departments, has control over budget formation and execution, is not limited by short terms or term limits, and can veto actions of the city council.

weak mayor form
Form of government where the mayor shares power with the council and other elected officials

strong mayor form
Form of local government where most power rests with the mayor

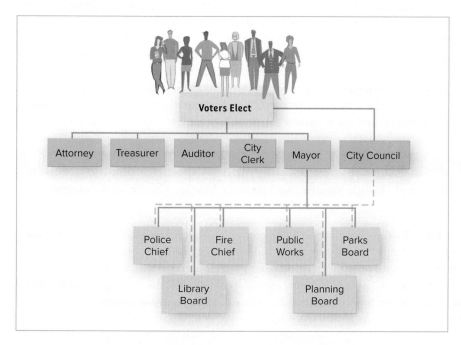

FIGURE 6.3   Weak Mayor-Council Form of City Government

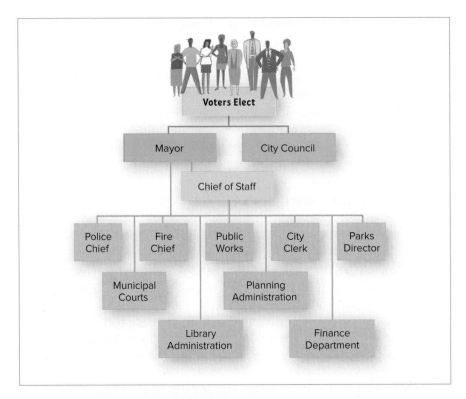

FIGURE 6.4   Strong Mayor-Council Form of City Government

Houston and nearby Pasadena are the two largest home rule cities using the mayor-council form.[18] Many home rule cities in Texas blend strong and weak mayoral powers. The Houston mayor, for example, can appoint and remove department heads and is responsible for budget formation and execution. However, the office has no veto authority, has a short term (two years), and is limited to three terms. Many more mayor-council forms exist in the general law cities in Texas than in the home rule cities. Formally, however, all have very weak mayors. Their powers are provided in the state statutes, and no form provided in the state laws can be classified as a strong executive. A comparison of the council-manager, weak-mayor, and strong-mayor forms of government is provided in Table 6.2.

TABLE 6.2

Comparison of Council-Manager, Weak-Mayor, and Strong-Mayor Forms of Government

Council-Manager Form	Weak-Mayor Form	Strong-Mayor Form
A city manager hired by city council is responsible for administration. City manager appoints and removes department heads. City manager is responsible for budget preparation and execution.	Power of the mayor is limited and divided among city council and other elected officials. Mayor has limited control over budget. Mayor has term limits. Mayor has no veto authority.	Mayor can appoint and remove major department heads. Mayor controls budget. Mayor is not restricted by term limits. Mayor has veto power.

CORE OBJECTIVE

Communicating Effectively . . .

Compare Figures 6.1, 6.3, and 6.4 with Table 6.2. Discuss the fundamental differences between weak mayor, strong mayor, and council-manager forms of government. Which do you prefer and why?

© George Lavendowski/ USFWS

FOCUS ON

Hispanic Representation in Local Government

In terms of political representation, there are, broadly, two types: descriptive and substantive. Descriptive representation means that a representative body *looks* like its constituency, i.e. the demographics of a population are mirrored in the demographics of its government officials. Substantive representation means constituents' interests, however expressed (voting, polls, letters, emails, phone calls, etc.), are *reflected* in the political and policy decisions of their local, state, and nationally elected representatives.[19]

Much of the debate surrounding representation in local government has focused on descriptive representation, with the hope that it will then lead to substantive representation. Research in this area supports that notion.[20] One problem, however, is how few Hispanics (and other minority groups) attain positions of executive authority within municipal governments. Austin's city council, for example, like most city councils in the United States, has been dominated by white males for most of its history. It was in 1975 that the city elected its first Hispanic council member, John Treviño, and there have been only a handful of Hispanic members since.[21] In

Mayor of San Antonio from 2009 to 2014, Julian Castro is a rising star in American politics. He served on the city council for a number of years before attaining the position, becoming only the fifth Hispanic to do so in Texas history. Castro stepped down in 2014 to become the 16th United States Secretary of Housing and Urban Development.

© Erich Schlegel/Alamy

Houston, there is currently only one Hispanic council member for a city that is nearly one-third Hispanic.[22]

In terms of city mayors, there have been well-known Hispanics elected in Texas, such as Henry Cisneros and Julian Castro of San Antonio. But a 2013 study points out that "only 4.6 percent of cities that have 30,000 people or more have Latino mayors."[23] There have been few studies on Hispanic public managers in the United States, but descriptive representation also falls short when compared to overall population percentages.[24]

Still, representation is improving. The number of elected Hispanic officials grows every year. The National Association of Latino Elected Officials (NALEO) found that between 2004 and 2014, Hispanics in elected offices nationwide grew by 25 percent.[25]

Critical Thinking Questions

1. What is the difference between descriptive and substantive representation?

2. Why might executive-level descriptive representation of Hispanics in municipal governments be lagging behind overall population numbers?

Commission Form of Government

The **commission form** of government is not used by any home rule city in Texas, but it deserves mention because of its impact on local Texas governments. The city of Galveston popularized this form of government in the early part of the twentieth century. In 1901, a major hurricane destroyed most of Galveston and killed an estimated 5,000 people. At the time, Galveston was the only major port on the Texas Gulf Coast and was a kingpin in the cotton economy of the state. It was in the interests of all Texans to have the city and port rebuilt. A delegation of Galveston citizens approached the Texas legislature for funds to help in the rebuilding effort. Then-Governor Joseph D. Sayers was opposed to state funding without some state control. The governor proposed that he be allowed to appoint five commissioners to oversee the rebuilding of the city, and he threatened to line-item veto any appropriations without this control. The legislature balked at the idea of locally appointed officials because of the experiences during Reconstruction under the administration of Edmund J. Davis. John Nance Garner, who served as vice president for two terms under Franklin Delano Roosevelt, was speaker of the Texas House at that time and said that without the threat of a line-item veto, it would be impossible to find five men in Galveston who supported the commission form of government. The governor and legislature compromised; initially, the governor appointed three commissioners, and the voters elected two. Later, all were elected.[26]

The new commission in Galveston worked in a very expeditious manner and quickly rebuilt the port city. This efficiency attracted nationwide attention. Many other cities adopted this new form of government, assuming that its form had caused the efficiency. It was a very simple form (see Figure 6.5) when compared to the older weak mayor system and the attendant long ballot of elected officials. In most commission forms, the voters elected five commissioners. Each commissioner was elected citywide by the voters as the head of a department of city government and was also a member of the city commission (the legislative

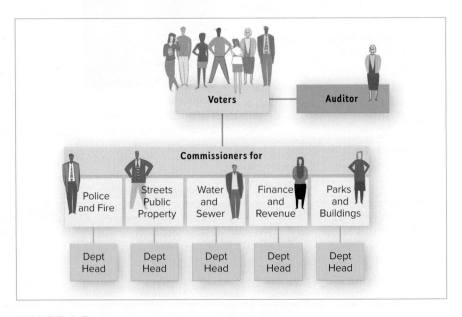

FIGURE 6.5   Commission Form of City Government

body). Thus, the system combined both executive and legislative functions into a single body of government.

This combination seemed to allow for quick action, but it also created many problems. Between 1901 and 1920, many cities adopted the commission form of government, but after 1920, very few cities adopted it, and many began to abandon the form. By the end of World War II, few commission governments remained. Even Galveston abandoned the form in the 1950s.[27] These abandonments were caused by several fundamental weaknesses in the form.

Weaknesses of the Commission Form of Government

The first weakness was that voters did not always elect competent administrators. Citizens voted for candidates based on apparent qualifications. For example, a failed banker might run for finance commissioner and stress his banking experience.[28] Voters might have no way of knowing that his banking experience had been a failure and would, instead, vote based on his apparent qualifications. The failed banker's bank might be happy to see him depart and not challenge his qualifications.

Second, the combination of legislative and executive functions, although efficient, eliminated the separation of powers and its checks and balances. Commissioners were reluctant to scrutinize the budget and actions of other commissioners for fear of retaliation. Logrolling (exchanging political favors) set in: "You look the other way on my budget and programs, and I will on yours."

Third, initially the commission had no leader. The commissioners rotated the position of mayor among themselves. This "mayor" presided over meetings and served as the official representative of the city but was not in a leadership position. This lack of a single, strong leader was a major shortcoming in the commission government. One writer describes it as a ship with five captains.[29] Later variations called for a separately elected mayor with budget and veto authority. Tulsa, Oklahoma, one of the last larger cities to use the form, gave the mayor these powers.[30]

Impact on the Evolution of Local Government

The major contribution of the commission form of government was that it served as a transition between the old weak mayor form, with many elected officials and a large city council, and the council-manager form, with no elected executives and a small city council. Many cities altered their charters, stripping the administrative power from the commissioners and assigning it to a city manager. Many Texas cities retained the term *commission* as a name for the city council. Lubbock retained the five-member commission until the 1980s, when it was forced to increase the size of the council and use single-member district elections.

Municipal Elections

Learning Objective: Explain municipal elections in Texas, including a discussion of voter turnout.

The two most common municipal election types are at-large election systems and single-member district systems. Two additional systems used in Texas are cumulative voting and preferential voting.

At-Large Election Systems

In the beginning of the twentieth century, many cities, led by early commissions, chose to move away from the single-member district system and began to elect council members at large, by all voters in the city. There are several variations of the **at-large election system,** which are summarized in Figure 6.6.

At-large by place is the most common form of at-large voting in Texas. In this system, candidates file for at-large ballot positions, which are usually given a number designation—Place 1, Place 2, and so on. Voters cast one vote for each at-large ballot position, and the candidate with a majority is elected to that place on the city council.

At-large by place with residence wards required is a system by which candidates file for a specific place, just as in at-large by place. However, each place on the ballot is assigned to a specific geographic area, and a candidate must live within that section, area, or ward of the city to file for a specific place. Abilene, Texas, uses this form. The city is divided into two wards with three council seats

at-large election system

System where all voters in the city elect the mayor and city council members

---

At-large by place

This is the most common such system used in Texas. In this system, candidates file for at-large ballot positions, which are usually given a number designation—Place 1, Place 2, and so on. Voters cast one vote for each at-large ballot position, and the candidate with a majority is elected to that place on the city council.

At-large by place with residence wards required

In this system, candidates file for a specific place as in an at-large by place system; however, these candidates must live in a section, area, or ward of the city to file for a specific place. Mayors can live anywhere in the city. All voters in the city elect them at large.

At-large no place

This is the least common system used in Texas. In this system, all candidates seeking election to the council have their names placed on the ballot. If there are ten candidates seeking election and five open seats, each voter is instructed to cast one vote each for five candidates. The top five vote getters are elected. With this method, it is not uncommon for a candidate to win with only a plurality (less than a majority) of the vote.

FIGURE 6.6 **Variations of At-Large Voting Systems**

© Image Source/Getty Images

in each ward. The mayor can live anywhere in the city, and the mayor and council are elected at-large by all city residents.[31]

At-large no place is the least common system in Texas. Under this system, all candidates seeking election to the council have their names placed on the ballot. If 10 candidates are seeking election for five open seats, each voter is instructed to cast one vote each for five candidates. The top five candidates with the most votes win. With this method, it is not uncommon for a candidate to win with only a plurality (less than a majority).[32]

Last, some cities use a combination of at-large and single-member district systems. Houston is a prime example. Voters elect 11 council members from single-member districts while five council members and the mayor are elected at large by all voters within the city.[33]

Single-Member District Election Systems

In **single-member district** elections, each city council seat is assigned to a specific district. The city is divided into election districts of approximately equal populations, and the voters in these districts elect a council member. In a true single-member district system, only the mayor is selected at large. Usually, candidates for a particular council seat must reside within the district for which they are running. Though some municipalities use multimember district systems, all district elections in Texas are single-member district systems.

Prior to 1975, almost no Texas cities used the single-member district (SMD) system. When the 1965 Voting Rights Act took effect, the language surrounding racial discrimination in polls was targeted at specific districts in specific states with known problems. Section 4, for example, targeted those election sites with disenfranchising tactics (such as literacy tests) and required federal intervention.[34] Section 5, the centerpiece of the legislation, subjected those targeted states and counties to preauthorization requirements for any election-related legislation and to federal monitors during election time.[35] But going into the 1970s, with southern states attempting to circumvent the law with at-large voting (to limit the concentration and effect of black votes), Congress began to make changes. One of the outcomes was the growth of single-member districts across the United States. At the federal level, it was believed that in a single-member district a minority group could be the majority, thereby electing their desired candidate.[36] Since the Voting Rights Act was amended in 1975 and applied to Texas, many cities have changed from an at-large system to single-member districts. Most of the major cities have been forced to change to SMD for at least some of the city council seats. Though section 4 of the Voting Rights Act has since been struck down in a Supreme Court decision in 2013 (*Shelby County v. Holder*), SMDs remain.

In cities that have changed from at-large to SMD systems, the number of minority candidates elected to the city council has increased substantially. There is some evidence that SMD council members approach their role differently than at-large council members do. A study of council members in Houston, Dallas, San Antonio, and Fort Worth found that council members from SMDs showed greater concern for neighborhood issues, engaged in vote trading, increased their contacts with constituents in their districts regarding service requests, and became more involved in administrative affairs of the city.[37]

Although SMD council members might view their job as representing their districts first and the city as a whole second, no evidence shows that the

single-member district

A system where the city is divided into election districts, and only the voters living in that district elect the council member from that district

distribution of services changes dramatically. District representation may be primarily symbolic. Symbolism is not insignificant, though, because support for local governments can be increased as minority groups believe they are represented on city councils and feel comfortable contacting their council member.

CORE OBJECTIVE

Being Socially Responsible . . .

Compare at-large election systems and single-member district systems. An argument in favor of single-member district systems is that they increase minority representation in local government. In your opinion, does increased minority representation increase intercultural competency? Why?

© Editorial Image, LLC/Alamy

Cumulative and Preferential Voting Systems

cumulative voting

A system where voters can concentrate (accumulate) all their votes on one candidate rather than casting one vote for each office up for election

In a **cumulative voting system**, each voter has votes equal to the number of seats open in the election. If five seats are open, each voter has five votes and may cast all five votes for one candidate (cumulating their votes), one vote each for five candidates, or any combination or variation. Several cities and school districts have adopted this system as an alternative to single-member districts. This system is preferred by voting rights activists as a means of increasing minority representation. The Amarillo Independent School District adopted the method in 2000[38] and, in May 2005, became the largest government body using the system in Texas.[39] It remains so with 4,282 employees as of May 2015.[40]

preferential voting

A system that allows voters to rank order candidates for the city council

The **preferential voting system** is also referred to as the instant-runoff system. It allows voters to rank their candidates for city council. All candidates' names are listed on the ballot, and the voter indicates the order of his or her preferences (first, second, third, and so on). Using a complicated ballot-counting system, the most-preferred candidates are elected. Although no city in Texas uses this form today, Gorman and Sweetwater used it in the past.

Advocates of the cumulative voting system and the preferential voting system argue that they allow minority interests to vote for candidates without having to draw single-member districts and possibly risk the accompanying gerrymandering (see Chapter 3). Some evidence shows, as in the case of the Amarillo Independent School District, that these alternative systems result in more minority candidates being elected.[41]

Regardless of the system used to elect city council members, some city charters allow for a person to be elected with a plurality of the vote—less than a majority. In Texas, if the city council term of office is longer than two years, a majority vote is required. This may necessitate a runoff election if no one has a majority.

nonpartisan election

Election in which party identification is not formally declared

Nonpartisan Elections

Another facet of municipal elections in Texas is that they are all technically nonpartisan. In **nonpartisan elections**, candidates run and appear on the ballot without any party designation. The Texas Election Code allows home rule cities to conduct partisan elections, but no city in Texas does so.[42]

Nonpartisan elections were a feature of the reform movement in the early part of the past century and were aimed at undercutting the power of partisan big-city political machines. Reformers said that there is no Democratic or Republican way to collect garbage, pave streets, or provide police and fire protection, so partisanship should not be a factor in city decisions.

Texas cities adopted the nonpartisan system largely because the state was a one-party Democratic state for over 100 years, and partisanship, even in state elections, was not a factor as long as candidates ran as Democrats. However, it should be noted that the use of a nonpartisan ballot does not eliminate partisanship from local politics. Partisanship simply takes new forms and new labels are applied.

For decades in several Texas cities, "nonpartisan organizations" successfully ran slates of candidates and dominated city politics. Most noted among these organizations were the Citizens Charter Association in Dallas, the Good Government League in San Antonio, and the Business and Professional Association in Wichita Falls and Abilene.[43] The influence of these groups has declined, but slate making is not unknown today in Texas politics. Partisanship has been a factor in city elections recently in San Antonio, Houston, and Dallas, especially in mayoral races. Without a doubt, partisanship will be a factor in city politics in the years ahead. Although the Tea Party is not a political party, its social conservative views most closely align with the Republican Party. Since the Tea Party's inception, many candidates in local elections run as "Tea Party approved." Although local elections are explicitly nonpartisan, it is quite easy, especially in large cities such as Dallas, Houston, and San Antonio, for voters to glean a candidate's political leanings.

Voter Turnout in Local Elections

Voter turnout in Texas municipal elections is varied but tends to be low for several reasons. One reason is that some cities conduct local elections in off years. This means that some city elections are held when no state or federal legislative or executive elections are being held (off-off-year elections—e.g., 2011, 2013, 2015), some are held when state elections and U.S. House of Representative elections are being held (off-year elections—e.g., 2014), and only one out of four municipal elections are held the same year as presidential elections (e.g., 2016). A second reason is that many Texas cities hold their elections in May, rather than in November when most people expect elections to be held. Voter turnout rates in the City of Austin municipal elections, which are held in May, usually hover around 15 percent.[44] In the May 2016 municipal elections, early votes were at 11 percent and day-of votes were at just below 7 percent.[45] In comparison, voter turnout rates in the City of Dallas, which holds local elections in November, was about 60 percent in 2012 and 34 percent in 2014.[46] A third reason is that many times the candidates' races are not contested. This has happened so often that a state law went into effect in 1991 allowing cities and school boards to cancel elections if no seat was contested. A fourth reason is the lack of media coverage in city elections. Most election news coverage of city races concentrates on mayors' races, and both electronic and print media of major cities ignore suburban city elections. Even local small-town or suburban newspapers virtually ignore city elections in their home communities, arguing that readers are not interested in local issues and races.

The lack of interest in municipal elections is disturbing because city government has such authority over so many aspects of people's daily lives, including streets and sidewalks, police and fire departments, building codes, speed limits, noise ordinances, and zoning and land use designations.

CORE OBJECTIVE

Taking Personal Responsibility . . .

Local government directly impacts people in their daily lives. What can you do to improve local governance?

Source: United States Department of Agriculture Agricultural Research Service

County Governments

Learning Objective: Describe county governments in Texas, including weaknesses and possible reforms.

county government

Local unit of government that is primarily the administrative arm of a state government, in most states, it does not provide urban-type services

The oldest type of local government in the United States is **county government**, an adaptation of the British county unit of government that was implemented in this country. County governments exist in all states except Connecticut, which abolished them in 1963, and Rhode Island (which never needed them). Louisiana calls counties "parishes," from the French influence, and Alaska calls them "boroughs." The number of counties varies greatly among the states. Of those states with counties or their equivalent, Delaware has the fewest (3) and Texas has the most (254).[47]

County governments were originally intended to be a subdivision, or an "arm," of state government to perform state functions at the local level. For example, voter registration, which is a state function, is handled at the county level. Most commonly, the county tax office handles voter registration, although in some large counties a separate elections department may handle this function. Similarly, county governments issue marriage licenses, birth certificates, automobile registrations, and operate state courts. County governments act as an arm of the state in all these activities.

Besides performing state functions, county governments also provide local services. The level of services provided varies from state to state; counties in some states provide many local services. In Texas, however, counties provide only very limited local services. Generally, Texas counties provide road construction and repair and police protection through the sheriff's department. Some urban county governments operate hospitals or health units, libraries, and parks.

In some states, urban counties are major providers of urban services. In Texas, city governments usually provide these services. Urban services include

TABLE 6.3

The 10 Largest Counties in Texas, 2015

County and (Major City)	2015 Population
Harris (Houston)	4,538,028
Dallas (Dallas)	2,553,385
Tarrant (Fort Worth)	1,982,498
Bexar (San Antonio)	1,897,753
Travis (Austin)	1,176,558
Collin (Plano)	914,127
Hidalgo (McAllen)	842,304
El Paso (El Paso)	835,593
Denton (Denton)	780,612
Fort Bend (Sugar Land)	716,087
Total	16,236,945
Percentage of total population of Texas in the 10 largest counties	59%

Source: U.S. Census Bureau, *Annual Estimates of the Resident Population: April 1, 2010 to July 1, 2015 (by County).*

water supply, sewage disposal, planning and zoning, airports, building codes and enforcement, mass transit systems, and fire protection. With few exceptions, Texas counties cannot perform these functions. Texas counties most closely resemble the traditional rural county governments that perform functions for the state: recording vital statistics, operating state courts and jails, administering elections, and maintaining roads and bridges. Texas counties can also assist in the creation of rural fire protection districts. In Harris County, the government may assist in the creation of master water and sewer districts to combine many smaller ones.

The distinguishing feature of county government is population. Of the 3,031 counties in the United States, most are rural with small populations; 671 counties have populations of less than 10,000; and 230 have populations of more than 250,000.[48] In Texas, 59 percent of the population lives in the 10 largest urban counties (see Table 6.3).

Urban Texans tend to identify with city governments rather than with county government. People think of themselves as residents of Houston, not Harris County. Some city residents might not be able to name the county where they reside. This stems in part from their identification with a service being provided, such as police protection. Residents of rural areas are more likely to identify with the county rather than the city, for many of the same reasons.

The Structure of County Government

All Texas county governments have the same basic structure, regardless of the county's size. This structure mirrors the fragmented structure of state government. It can most accurately be described as weak or plural executive. Voters elect the heads of major departments of county government (see Figure 6.7). These provisions appeared in the constitution of 1876. The writers of this document distrusted appointive authority and trusted the electorate to choose administrators.[49]

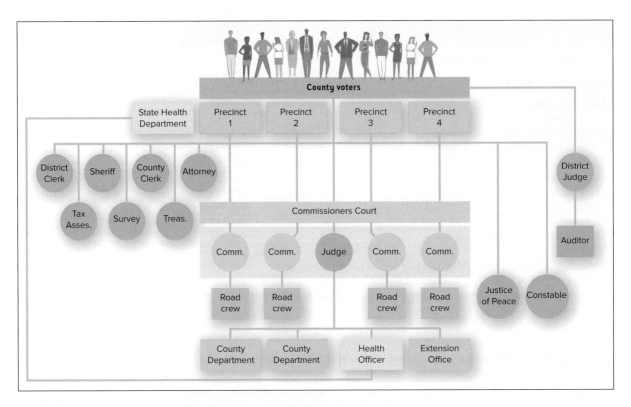

FIGURE 6.7   **Structure of County Government in Texas**

The County Commissioner's Court

commissioner's court

Legislative body that governs a Texas county

In Texas, the governing body of county government is the county **commissioner's court**, composed of the constitutional county judge and four county commissioners. The county judge is elected at large, and each commissioner is elected from a single-member district called a commissioner precinct. Like most other state officeholders, these officials are elected for four-year terms in partisan elections. Even though this body is termed the commissioner's court, it is not a court but a legislative body. Its duties include passing local ordinances, approving budgets and new programs, and oversight of county government.

The county judge presides as the chair of the commissioner's court, participates as a full member in deliberations, and has a vote on all matters. The constitution assigns judicial duties to this office, but the occupant does not have to be a licensed attorney; the constitution states that the constitutional county judge must be "well informed in the law." In urban counties where the state legislature has created county courts of law, the constitutional county judge performs only very limited judicial functions. The judicial functions of constitutional county courts (described in Chapter 5) are transferred to the county courts of law, and the constitutional county judge acts as the primary administrative officer of the county.

Like other legislative districts, commissioner precincts eventually became malapportioned. In 1968, the U.S. Supreme Court ruled that the one-person-one-vote rule applied to these election districts. The Commissioner's Court in Midland County claimed it was a court and not a legislative body, and therefore the one person, one vote rule did not apply. The U.S. Supreme Court disagreed and ruled that it was a legislative body and not a court, and that election districts had to be equally apportioned.[50] This means that each district should comprise roughly the same number of residents, or potential voters.

There are seven constitutionally prescribed county officers elected by the voters: sheriff, district attorney, county attorney, tax assessor/collector, district clerk, county clerk, and county treasurer. These officials act as heads of departments of government. Some counties also have other minor elected officials, such as county surveyor and inspector of hides and wools (which was created to reduce cattle and sheep theft).

The County Sheriff

The **county sheriff** is elected countywide for a four-year term and serves as the law enforcement officer for the county. Sheriffs can appoint deputy sheriffs. In rural counties, the sheriff may be the primary law enforcement officer. In urban counties, city police departments carry out most of these duties, and the sheriff's primary duty may be to operate the county jail. In the smaller counties (fewer than 1,800 residents), state law allows the sheriff to act as the tax assessor/collector.[51] Some have suggested that combining sheriff and tax collector is a frightening leftover from Anglo-Saxon law, inspiring visions of Sherwood Forest, the Sheriff of Nottingham, and Robin Hood.

The voters also elect constables, who serve as law enforcement officers. Their primary function is to serve as court officers for the justice of the peace courts—delivering subpoenas and other court orders. Constables may also provide police protection in the precinct they serve.

county sheriff
Elected head of law enforcement in a Texas county

The County and District Attorneys

The county and district attorneys are the chief prosecuting attorneys for criminal cases in the county, the county attorney at the county court level and the district attorney at the district court level. Each county has a county court and usually several district courts that reside in the constituent districts that make up a given county. Not all counties have county attorneys. In counties with a county attorney, this office usually prosecutes the less serious criminal offenses before county courts, and the district attorney prosecutes major crimes before the district courts.

The County Tax Assessor/Collector

The tax assessor/collector is responsible for collecting revenue for the state and county. Before 1978, this office also assessed the value of all property in the county for property tax collection purposes. In 1978, these functions were transferred to a countywide assessment district. There are 254 of these tax appraisal districts in the state, and they are governed by a board elected by the governing bodies of all governments in the jurisdiction—counties, cities, school districts, and special districts. Although this office still has the title of assessor, few occupants serve in this capacity today. Most still collect county property taxes, sell state vehicle licenses and permits, and serve as voter registrars. The voter registration function is a carryover from the days of the poll tax.[52]

The County and District Clerk

The county clerk is the chief record keeper for the county; the clerk keeps track of all property records and issues marriage licenses, birth certificates, and other county records. Although normally the function of voter registration rests with the tax assessor/collector, in some counties this function has been transferred to the county clerk, who in all counties is responsible for conducting elections.

The district clerk is primarily a court official who maintains court records for county and district courts. The clerk schedules cases in these courts and maintains all records, acts, and proceedings of the court, along with keeping a record of all judgments. The district clerk also administers child support payments and maintains accounts of all funds derived from fines and fees collected by the office.[53]

The County Treasurer

The county treasurer is responsible for receiving, maintaining, and disbursing all county funds, including general revenue and special revenue funds. The county treasurer is the chief liaison between the commissioner's court and the depository banks, and the treasurer is responsible for maintaining a record of all deposits, withdrawals, and reconciling all bank statements. The county treasurer may also at times be designated as the chief investment officer for the county.[54]

The County Auditor

The district judge or judges in the county appoint the county auditor. The county auditor's responsibility is to oversee the collection and disbursement of county funds. The auditor reports to the district judge or judges. Counties with populations of fewer than 10,000 are not required to have auditors. In larger counties (with populations greater than 250,000), the auditor acts as a budget officer unless the commissioner's court appoints its own budget officer.[55]

Weaknesses of County Government in Texas

West Texas volunteer firefighters clean a fire unit at their headquarters on Friday, April 19, 2013. Only two days prior, the West Fire Dept. responded to a fertilizer company explosion that caused several fatalities and extensive damage to the community.

© Ron T. Ennis/Fort Worth Star–Telegram/AP Images

The weaknesses in Texas county government can be broadly divided into two kinds: (1) inherent weaknesses in the plural executive form of government and (2) the inability of county governments to confront many problems in urban areas.

As we have already seen, the plural executive structure of county government in Texas is a product of the nineteenth century and the general distrust of centralized executive authority. The plural executive structure lacks centralized authority, and the elected officials can, and often do, act quite independently of each other. Although the county commissioner's court does exercise some control over these department heads, it is primarily limited to budgetary matters. After a budget is approved, elected officials can make many independent decisions.

Elected officials also hire their own staffs. After each election, personnel at the county courthouse can change dramatically. For example, new sheriffs hire their own deputy sheriffs. The patronage ("spoils") system in some courthouses results in a less professional staff.

As indicated in our discussion of the judiciary in Chapter 5 and in the discussion of the commission form of city government in this chapter, elections are imperfect instruments for determining the qualifications of candidates, and voters do not always select the most competent person to administer departments. The appointment of department heads is more likely to result in the selection of competent persons. A lack of professionalism and competence is a frequently noted problem with officials in some counties.

In most (201 of 254) Texas counties, each county commissioner is responsible for road repair within the boundaries of the precinct in which the commissioner is elected.[56] As a result, there are four separate road crews, each under the direction of a commissioner. Although there is some sharing of equipment, duplication and inefficiencies are common. Commissioners have also been known to use their road crews to reward supporters with more favorable attention to road repairs that affect them directly.

County government was designed to meet the needs of and provide services to a rural population. In rural areas of the state, it still functions adequately. However, in large urban counties, this form of government has many weaknesses.

Inability to Provide Urban Services

The first of these weaknesses is the inability to provide urban-type services. Dense urban populations demand and need services that are unnecessary in rural areas. Usually, county governments are powerless under state law to provide even the most basic services common to city governments, such as water and sewer services. In the 1999 session of the legislature, Harris County was given limited authority to assist in the formation of "master" water and sewer districts by consolidating many small suburban districts.

Citizens living on the fringe of cities are forced to provide these services themselves or to form other governments, such as a water district, to provide these services. In recent years, garbage (solid waste) collection and disposal have become a problem in the urban fringe areas. Many citizens must contract with private collectors for this service. Some counties help residents by providing collection centers, often operated by private contractors. In the area of fire protection, counties often help rural residents to establish volunteer fire departments. However, counties are not permitted to operate fire departments. Each rural fire department goes its own way, and there is often a lack of coordination between departments. Training and equipment are generally below the standards of full-time city fire departments. Counties sometimes contract with city governments to provide fire protection for the county, although this practice has declined in recent years because the state has made it easier to form and finance rural fire districts.

Lack of Ordinance Authority

County governments also lack general ordinance authority. City governments in Texas may pass any ordinance not prohibited by state law, but county governments must seek legislative approval to pass specific ordinances. For example, county governments may not pass ordinances on land use (zoning) or building codes that regulate construction standards. A citizen buying a home in a rural area is largely dependent upon the integrity of the builder.

Even where counties have been given the authority to regulate activities, they often fall short. For example, counties were given the authority to pass ordinances regulating the construction of septic systems. Some counties failed to pass such ordinances, and many failed to adequately inspect the installation of septic systems. In some counties, this function was transferred to the state health department in 1992.

Inequity of Financial Resources

Finally, a related problem with county governments is the inequity of financial resources and expenditures. A few counties have a sales tax, but most rely almost exclusively on the property tax. Most of this tax is paid by citizens living inside cities and not in the unincorporated, rural areas of the county. For example, in the tax year 2010 in Brazos County, the total taxable property was $13.7 billion. Most of this value ($10.8 billion) was located within the cities of Bryan and College Station, leaving only $1.2 billion in rural Brazos County.[57] Thus, most (79 percent) of the cost of county government was paid for with property tax money from the two cities. Although county residents pay little of the cost to operate county governments, they receive many services from them (such as road construction and repair and police protection) that are not provided to city residents by the county. City residents receive these services from their city and pay city taxes. City residents are paying twice for services they receive only once. This financial inequity goes unnoticed by most citizens.

Possible Reform of County Government

Since the 1930s, there have been suggestions to reform county government in Texas. The rhetoric often called for county government to be "brought into the twentieth century." In Texas, apparently all such reforms skipped the twentieth century and must wait for sometime in the twenty-first century. Whereas other states have modernized county governments, Texas has steadfastly refused all efforts for change. One suggestion that has been a frequent agenda item over the past 70 years is to allow for county home rule, which would allow the voters in each county to adopt a local option charter.[58] Voters could then approve any form of government not prohibited by state law; no county would be forced to change its form of government. This might result in the adoption of a strong executive form of government similar to the strong-mayor or council-manager forms popular with Texas cities. Even though this suggestion seems quite reasonable, it has been strongly opposed by the many county elected officials in Texas who see this as a threat to their jobs.

The Texas Association of Counties (TAC) is an umbrella organization that represents elected county officials—sheriffs, tax collectors, treasurers, judges, commissioners, and so on. The TAC has opposed granting county governments home rule. This group is politically powerful and has many supporters throughout the state. One group within the TAC, the Conference of Urban Counties (CUC), has shown mild support for home rule. The CUC represents 36 metropolitan county governments in Texas where home rule would have the greatest impact. The CUC is not pushing home rule issues and is more concerned with representing the unique interests of urban counties.

County officials often have very provincial attitudes about the role of county government. The idea of expanding county services is foreign to many county officials. They seem content with the status quo. Prospects are dim for any great change in Texas county government in the short run. Urban counties will continue to face many problems that have only a mild impact on rural counties and will have to seek solutions to their problems that do not involve the major structural changes home rule would bring. Improving the professionalism of the staff might prove difficult because each elected county official can hire his or her own people. In some counties, officials place great emphasis on professionalism. Other officials reward faithful campaign workers with appointments. In rural counties, these jobs are often well paid and much sought after by supporters.

CORE OBJECTIVE

Thinking Critically . . .

Identify some of the problems facing county governments. What solutions would you propose?

Source: National Park Service

Special District Governments

Learning Objective: Discuss special purpose districts.

The biggest increase in government in Texas and the United States generally in the past 30 years or so has been in **special purpose districts** (not including school districts). Special purpose districts (also known as special purpose governments) have been referred to as shadow governments because they operate out of the view of most citizens. As the name implies, a special purpose district is a type of local government that is created to perform a specific set of duties or functions. Some districts are single function (e.g., fire) and others are multipurpose (e.g., water, sewer, street repair). Some special districts (such as metropolitan transit districts) cover several counties, and others (such as the municipal utility districts) are very small, covering only a few acres.

Texas has approximately 2,600 special purpose districts; only California and Illinois have more.[59] The primary reason special purpose districts are created is to provide services when no other unit of government exists to provide that service. Sometimes the need extends beyond the geographical boundaries of existing units of government. For example, flood control may transcend the municipal boundaries of any one city in particular, and the ability to coordinate among multiple city and county governments may be very difficult. Another good example is mass transportation. Dallas/Fort Worth, Houston, San Antonio,

special purpose district
Form of local government that provides specific services to citizens, such as water, sewage, fire protection, or public transportation

Austin, El Paso, and other metropolitan areas have created transit districts that serve several counties. Sometimes the service involves natural boundaries that extend over county lines.

In still other cases, the need for a service may be confined to a single county, but no government unit exists to provide the service. An excellent example of this is municipal utility districts (MUDs). These are multifunction districts generally created outside cities to provide water, sewage treatment, and other services. In Texas, these MUDs are created because county governments cannot provide these services. Finally, some districts are created for political reasons, when no existing unit of government wants to solve the service problem because of potential political conflicts. The creation of another unit of government to deal with a hot political issue is preferable. The Gulf Coast Waste Disposal Authority, created to clean up water pollution in the Houston area, is a good example.

Special purpose districts are often an efficient and expedient way to solve a problem, but they can also generate problems. One problem for citizens is keeping track of the many special districts that provide services to them. For example, a MUD, a soil and water conservation district, a flood control district, a fire protection district, a metropolitan transit authority, a hospital district, and a waste disposal district can govern a citizen living in the Houston suburbs. Most citizens have trouble distinguishing among a school district, a county, and a city. Dealing with seven or more units of government is even more complicated and can lead to a lack of democratic control over local governments.

The governing boards of special purpose districts in Texas are selected in two ways. Multicounty special purpose districts (such as DART in Dallas and METRO in Houston) are governed by boards appointed by the governmental units (cities, counties) covered by the district. Single-county special purpose districts (such as MUDs and flood control districts) usually have a board of directors elected by the voters.

Many special purpose districts have taxation authority and can raise local property taxes. The remoteness of these districts from the electorate, their number, and their potential impact on the lives of citizens raise questions of democratic control. The average citizen cannot be expected to know about, understand, and keep track of the decisions made by these remote governments. The alternatives are to consolidate governments, expand cities through the annexation of land, or expand the power of county governments. None of these alternatives is generally acceptable. Citizens demand and expect local governments to be decentralized. This is true even if they have only limited ability to watch and control the actions of local government and the government is ineffective. Big government is something most Texans want to avoid.

School Districts

Article 7 of the Texas Constitution vested in the legislature the authority to "establish and make suitable provision for the support and maintenance of an efficient system of public free school."[60] Although schools are subject to state control, especially in the areas of curriculum and financing, the administration of public education is largely the responsibility of the 1,079 school districts operating in the state.[61] Officially, all but one of the school districts in Texas are **independent school districts** (ISDs), which means that they operate independently of any city or county.

independent school district

School districts that are not attached to any other unit of government and that operate schools in Texas

School districts are governed by a board of trustees who are elected to staggered terms of office (varying from two, three, four, and six years) in nonpartisan elections. The board of trustees is made up of no more than seven members and, although school districts may choose under certain circumstances to have trustees elected from single-member districts, trustees in Texas school districts generally are elected at large. The trustees set policy for the district and approve the budget, set tax rates, make personnel decisions, and approve construction and renovation contracts. The board is also responsible for hiring the superintendent, who may serve on contract for no more than five years.[62]

The superintendent is the chief executive officer of the school district and is responsible for planning, operation, evaluation of education programs, and annual performance appraisals of personnel. The superintendent reports to the board of trustees and is expected to provide policy and planning recommendations. The role of the school district superintendent is similar to the role of the city manager in the council-manager system of local government. Although the superintendent is the primary administrator who is responsible for the day-to-day operations of the district, he or she reports to elected officials.

School districts have a profound impact on all citizens and as expected, issues in education can be highly polarizing. Many school boards are politicized, which increases the pressure on the superintendent. Issues facing school districts are discussed in Chapter 11.

Conclusion

Although local governments do not generate the same degree of interest that national and state governments do, they have extremely important effects on the daily lives of citizens. Without the services provided by local governments, modern life would not be possible.

In Texas, city governments are the principal providers of local services. Council-manager governments govern most major cities, a system that has brought a degree of professionalism to city government that is often lacking in county and some other units of local government. In many respects, the contrast between county and city government is remarkable. County governments have resisted change and seem content to operate under a form of government designed by and for an agrarian society. It is a paradox that council-manager city government and plural executive county government could exist in the same state, given the political culture. Economy, efficiency, and professionalism are not values supported by the traditionalistic political culture of the state, yet they are widely practiced in council-manager government. It has been suggested that strong support from the business community in the state is one reason for the acceptance of council-manager government. Business leaders see the economy and efficiency of this form.

Summary

LO: Define general law cities and home rule cities.

City governments are municipal corporations, granted a corporate charter by their state. A city's charter provides the basic organization and structure of the city government and outlines the general powers and authority of its government and officials. Cities in Texas are chartered as either a general law city (charter) or a home rule city. The charters for general law cities are spelled out in state statutes whereas charters for home rule cities are created by their citizens.

LO: Define types of local government.

There are two basic forms of city government: mayor-council and council-manager. The mayor-council system has two variations: the strong mayor system and the weak mayor system. A third form of local government, the commission, is used by only a few cities nationwide; it is not used by any city in Texas, but did play an important role in the development of local government in Texas. In the council-manager form, voters elect a mayor and city council; the mayor and city council appoint a professional administrator to manage the city. In the weak mayor-council form, the mayor shares power with the council and other elected officials. In the strong mayor-council form, most power rests with the mayor.

LO: Explain municipal elections in Texas, including a discussion of voter turnout.

The two main local election systems in Texas are at-large election systems and single-member district systems. Cumulative voting and preferential voting also occur in some areas. In an at-large system, all voters in the city elect the mayor and city council members. In SMDs, the city is divided into election districts and only the voters living in that district elect the council member from that district. In a cumulative voting system, each voter has votes equal to the number of seats open in the election. In a preferential voting system, voters rank order candidates for the city council. Voter turnout in Texas municipal elections is varied but tends to be low, especially when there are no national or state elections occurring at the same time.

LO: Describe county governments in Texas, including weaknesses and possible reforms.

County governments are local units of government and are primarily the administrative arms of a state government. In most states, they do not provide urban-type services. The level of services provided varies. In Texas, counties provide only very limited local services. There are major problems: (1) inherent weaknesses in the plural executive form of government, and (2) the inability of county governments to confront many problems in urban areas. One suggested fix has been to allow for county home rule, which would allow the voters in each county to adopt a local option charter.

LO: Discuss special purpose districts.

Special purpose districts are a form of local government that provides specific services to citizens, such as water, sewage, fire protection, or public transportation. Independent school districts are one example. Many special purpose districts have taxation authority and can raise local property taxes. They can be seen as undemocratic because of their perceived distance from the voter, but they do provide much needed local services.

Key Terms

at-large election system	creatures of the state	nonpartisan election
city manager	cumulative voting system	preferential voting system
commission form	extra-territorial jurisdiction	single-member district
commissioner's court	general law city	special purpose district
council-manager form	home rule city	strong mayor form of government
county government	incorporation	weak mayor form of government
county sheriff	independent school district	

Notes

[1] U.S. Department of Commerce, "Table 1. Population: Earliest Census to 2010; and Housing Units: 1950 to 2010," In *2010 Census of Population and Housing,* CPH-2-45, September 2012, https://www.census.gov/prod/cen2010/cph-2-45.pdf.

[2] Federal Advisory Commission on Intergovernmental Relations, *State and Local Rates in the Federal System: A-88* (Washington, D.C.: US Government Printing Office, 1982), 59.

[3] Terrell Blodgett, *Texas Home Rule Charters* (Austin: Texas Municipal League, 1994), 1.

[4] *Vernon's Texas Statutes and Codes Annotated,* vol. 1, 5.001–5.003.

[5] Texas Municipal League, *Handbook for Mayors and Councilmembers* (Austin: Texas Municipal League, 2015:10,14).

[6] *Vernon's Texas Statues and Codes Annotated,* "Local Government," vol. 1, 9.001–9.008.

[7] Texas Municipal League, *Handbook for Mayors and Councilmembers* (Austin: Texas Municipal League, 2015:13).

[8] *Vernon's Texas Statutes and Codes Annotated,* "Local Government," vol. 1, 7.005.

[9] David L. Martin, *Running City Hall: Municipal Administration in the United States* (Tuscaloosa: University of Alabama Press, 1990), 21–22; Scott Houston. "Municipal Annexation in Texas: Is it really that complicated?" Texas Municipal League. Last updated in March 2012, http://www.tml.org/legal_pdf/ANNEXATION.pdf.

[10] Scott Houston, "Municipal Annexation in Texas: Is it really that complicated?" Texas Municipal League, Last updated in March 2012, http://www.tml.org/legal_pdf/ANNEXATION.pdf.

[11] Attorney General of Texas, Opinion GA?0737, https://www.oag.state.tx.us/opinions/opinions/50abbott/op/2009/pdf/ga0737.pdf.

[12] International City/Council Management Association (ICMA), "2011 Municipal Form of Government Survey Summary," http://icma.org/en/icma/knowledge_network/documents/kn/Document/303954/ICMA_2011_Municipal_Form_of_Government_Survey_Summary.

[13] Texas Municipal League, *Handbook for Mayors and Councilmembers* (Austin: Texas Municipal League, 2015:14).

[14] National League of Cities, "Forms of Municipal Government," http://www.nlc.org/build-skills-and-networks/resources/cities-101/city-structures/forms-of-municipal-government.

[15] Richard Stillman, *The Rise of the City Manager: A Public Professional in Local Government* (Albuquerque: University of New Mexico Press, 1974), 15.

[16] For more information, go to icma.org and tcma.org.

[17] James A. Svara, *Official Leadership in the City: Patterns of Conflict and Cooperation* (New York: Oxford University Press, 1990), chaps. 2 and 3.

[18] Blodgett, *Texas Home Rule Charters,* 30–31.

[19] Rebekah Herrick and Samuel H. Fisher, III, *Representing America: The Citizen and the Professional Legislator in the House of Representatives,* Lexington Books, 2007: 7.

[20] Tim R. Sass, "The Determinants of Hispanic Representation in Municipal Government," *Southern Economic Journal,* Vol. 66, No. 3 (Jan., 2000), pp. 609–630: 612; Nicholas O. Alozie and Cherise G. Moore, "Blacks and Latinos in City Management: Prospects and Challenges in Council-Manager Governments," *Intl Journal of Public Administration,* 30: 47–63, 2007:50.

[21] W. Gardner Selby, "Few Hispanic residents elected to Austin City Council through history," PolitiFact, June 6, 2014, http://www.politifact.com/texas/statements/2014/jun/06/mike-martinez/few-hispanic-residents-elected-austin-city-council/.

[22] Alice Barr, "Fort Worth Hispanic Leaders Pushing for New City Council Seats to Start Now." NBC DFW, May 19, 2016, http://www.nbcdfw.com/news/local/Fort-Worth-Hispanic-Leaders-Want-New-City-Council-Seats-to-Start-Sooner-380194421.html.

[23] Adriana Maestas, "Underrepresented in city hall: a look at U.S. Latino mayors," NBC Latino. 11/2/2013, http://nbclatino.com/2013/11/02/underrepresented-in-city-hall-a-look-at-the-latino-mayors-in-the-united-states/.

[24] Nicholas O. Alozie and Cherise G. Moore, "Blacks and Latinos in City Management: Prospects and Challenges in Council-Manager Governments," *Intl Journal of Public Administration,* 30: 47–63; Abraham David Benavides, "Hispanic City Managers in Texas: A Small Group of Professional Administrators," *State & Local Government Review,* 1/1/2006, Vol. 38, Issue 2, p. 112–119.

[25] NALEO Education Fund, "Latino Elected Officials in America," http://www.naleo.org/at_a_glance.

[26] Bradley Robert Price, *Progressive Critics: The Commission Government Movement in America, 1901–1920* (Austin: University of Texas Press, 1977), 12.

[27] Ibid., 109.

[28] Ibid., 85.

[29] Ibid., 52.

[30] *Tulsa City Charter,* June 1954, 6.

[31] For more information on Abilene's City Council, go to: http://www.abilenetx.com/city-hall/departments/general-government/city-council.

[32] For a good discussion of electoral systems in American cities, see Joseph Zimmerman, *The Federal City: Community Control in Large Cities* (New York: St. Martin's Press, 1972), chap. 4.

[33] Blodgett, *Texas Home Rule Charters,* 46–47; City of Houston, "City Council," http://www.houstontx.gov/council/index.html.

[34] Abigail Thernstrom, "Redistricting, Race, and the Voting Rights Act, *National Affairs,* Issue 3 (Spring 2010), http://www.nationalaffairs.com/publications/detail/redistricting-race-and-the-voting-rights-act.

[35] Ibid.

[36] Joseph F. Zimmerman, "The Federal Voting Rights Act and Alternative Election Systems,? *William and Mary Law Review,* Vol 19 Number 4 (Summer 1978), http://scholarship.law.wm.edu/cgi/viewcontent.cgi?article=2413&context=wmlr.

[37] Svara, *Official Leadership in the City,* 136.

[38] Amarillo Independent School, "Cumulative Voting," http://p1cdn4static.sharpschool.com/UserFiles/Servers/

Server_18929979/File/board/Elections/Cumulative%20
Voting%202015.pdf.

[39] https://www.amaisd.org/index.php?hard=board/about.php.

[40] City of Amarillo, Community Development Department,
Analysis of Impediments of Fair Housing Choice May 2015,
http://comdev.amarillo.gov/wp-content/uploads/2015/08
/Analysis-of-Impediment-2015-Updated-6-5-15-
COMPLETE.pdf.

[41] Fairvote.org, "History of Cumulative Voting in Amarillo,"
http://archive.fairvote.org/?page=247.

[42] *Vernon's Texas Statutes and Codes Annotated,* "Elections,"
41.003.

[43] For a discussion of San Antonio, see David R. Johnson,
John A. Booth, and Richard J. Harris, *The Politics of
San Antonio: Community Progress and Power* (Lincoln:
University of Nebraska Press, 1983).

[44] Travis County Clerk, www.traviscountyclerk.org/eclerck
/cotennt/images/election_results.

[45] Travis County Clerk. May 7, 2016 Joint General and Special
Elections, Official Results, Cumulative Results for the City of
Austin, http://traviscountyclerk.org/eclerk/content/images
/election_results/2016.05.07/Final/20160507coacume.pdf.

[46] Dallas County Elections Department, Historical Election
Results: 2012 General Election - Presidential -
BS,CH,DA,RI,SE,CHISD 11/06/2012, General Election
Results, 11/04/2015, http://www.dallascountyvotes.org
/election-results-and-maps/election-results/historical-
election-results/.

[47] U.S. Department of Commerce, Bureau of the Census, 2012
Census of Governments: Government Organization, Table
13, https://www.census.gov/govs/cog/.

[48] United States Census Bureau, County Governments by
Population-Size Group and State: 2012 - United States—
States 2012 Census of Governments, https://www.census
.gov/govs/cog/.

[49] Gary M. Halter and Gerald L. Dauthery, "The County
Commissioners Court in Texas," in *Governing Texas:
Documents and Readings,* 3rd ed., eds. Fred Gantt Jr., et al.
(New York: Thomas Y. Crowell, 1974), 340–350.

[50] *Avery v. Midland County,* 88 S. Ct. 1114 (1968).

[51] Robert E. Norwood and Sabrina Strawn, *Texas County
Government: Let the People Choose,* 2nd ed. (Austin:
Texas Research League, 1984).

[52] Ibid., 24. Also see John A. Gilmartin and Joe M. Rothe,
*County Government in Texas: A Summary of the Major
Offices and Officials,* Issue No. 2 (College Station: Texas
Agricultural Extension Service).

[53] Texas Association of Counties, "District and County Clerk,"
https://www.county.org/texas-county-government/texas-
county-officials/Pages/District-And-County-Clerk.aspx.

[54] Texas Association of Counties. "County Treasurer," https://
www.county.org/texas-county-government/texas-county-
officials/Pages/County-Treasurer.aspx.

[55] Texas Association of Counties, "County Auditor, https://
www.county.org/texas-county-government/texas-county-
officials/Pages/County-Auditor.aspx.

[56] Information supplied by the Texas Association of Counties,
Austin.

[57] Property tax records of the Brazos County Central Appraisal
District, 1673 Briarcrest Dr., Bryan, TX.

[58] For an extensive explanation of the county home rule efforts
in Texas, see Wilborn E. Benton, *Texas: Its Government
and Politics,* 2nd ed. (Englewood Cliffs, N.J.: Prentice
Hall, 1966), 317–381.

[59] United States Census Bureau, "Table 2. Local Governments by
Type and State, 2012," https://www.census.gov/govs/cog/.

[60] *Texas Constitution,* Article 7, sec. 1.

[61] United States Census Bureau, "Table 2. Local Governments by
Type and State: 2012," https://www.census.gov/govs/cog/.

[62] *Texas Education Code,* Chapter 11 School Districts, sec. 11.052.

CHAPTER 7

Voting and Political Participation in Texas

Texas Learning Outcomes

• Identify the rights and responsibilities of citizens.

O ne of the hallmarks of life in a democracy is people's ability to participate in politics. Voting is the most obvious way that citizens play a part in collective governance in a democracy. However, this is just one of many ways that people can participate in the public square. While people engage in politics to varying degrees, most people are not participating that actively in state and local politics, either here in Texas or around the country. So although men and women are certainly social beings, it might be too optimistic to argue—as the ancient Greek philosopher Aristotle did—that we are naturally political animals.

Then-candidate Ted Cruz speaks with reporters during his campaign for U.S. Senate. Cruz won the 2012 General Election and assumed office in 2013. Following a failed presidential bid in 2015–2016, he continues to serve a 6-year term as the junior U.S. Senator from Texas.

© Pat Sullivan/AP Images

This chapter explores the ways in which Texans participate in politics, with special emphasis on voting behavior. It also examines why voter turnout in Texas is so low today and has been in years past.

Chapter Learning Objectives

- Explain political participation.
- Discuss voter turnout in Texas, including citizens' rights and responsibilities.
- Describe ways in which the state of Texas has, historically, restricted access to voting.
- Describe forms of political participation other than voting.

Political Participation

Learning Objective: Explain political participation.

political participation
All forms of involvement citizens can have that are related to governance

Political participation refers to taking part in activities that are related to governance. Table 7.1 lists some common forms of such participation and the percentage of adults who took part in them during a 12-month period, according to the most recent national survey on this topic conducted by the Pew Research Center.

TABLE 7.1

Civil and Political Participation in America

Activity	Percentage of Adults Surveyed Who Participated During the Previous 12 Months
Took part in some sort of political activity in the context of a social networking site (e.g., Facebook/Twitter)	39%
Worked with fellow citizens to solve a problem in your community	35%
Attended a political meeting on local, town, or school affairs	22%
Signed a paper petition	22%
Contacted a national, state, or local government official in person, by phone call, or by letter about an issue	21%
Contributed money to a political candidate or party, or any other political organization or cause	16%
Been an active member of any group that tries to influence public policy or government, not including a political party	13%
Attended a political rally or speech	10%
Worked or volunteered for a political party or candidate	7%
Attended an organized protest of any kind	6%
Sent a letter to the editor of a newspaper or magazine	3%

Source: Pew Research Center's Internet & American Life Project, Civic Engagement Tracking Survey 2012. Based on an adult sample (n = 2,253). Margin of error is +/− 2%. Available online at http://www.pewinternet.org/datasets/august-2012-civic-engagement/.

Researchers found that almost three-fourths (72 percent) of adults surveyed had participated in at least one of the activities about which they inquired. (The activities listed in Table 7.1 are not an exhaustive list.) Some respondents took part in more than one such activity within the year. Conversely, a significant proportion (more than one-fourth) of survey respondents had not participated in any of these activities. Another big takeaway from the survey was the rising use of online methods to engage in political activity—though this is a fairly passive means of participation. Indeed, the *Washington Post* recently noted that less burdensome or demanding "forms of advocacy, particularly those related to social media, are often derisively referred to as 'slacktivism' or 'armchair activism.'"[1]

In addition to looking at involvement in specific activities, participation can also be conceptualized in terms of levels and types of activities. Sidney Verba and Norman H. Nie, in their classic book *Participation in America*,[2] divide the population into several groups based on the types of participation and the intensity of involvement that citizens can have in the political process (see Figure 7.1).

- Inactives, who take no part in politics
- Voting specialists, who confine their efforts to voting in elections
- Parochial participants, who become active in politics when the issue has a direct effect on them
- Campaigners, who like the activity and the controversial and competitive nature of political campaigns
- Communalists, who, while being active voters, avoid the combat and controversy of partisan campaigns and are attracted to other kinds of nonpartisan, noncontroversial community activity
- Complete activists, who get involved in all levels and kinds of activity, including voting, campaigning, lobbying officials, and participating in community affairs

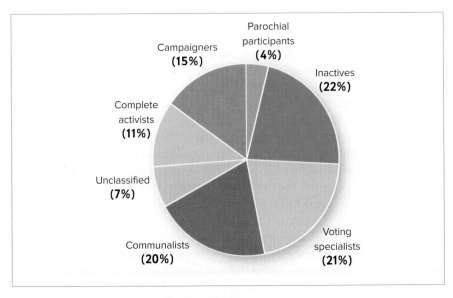

FIGURE 7.1   Types of Political Activists

SOURCE: Sidney Verba and Norman Nie, *Participation in America: Political Democracy and Social Equality.* (Chicago: University of Chicago Press, 1987), 79.

CORE OBJECTIVE

Taking Personal Responsibility . . .

What activities do you engage in that are related to governance? Which forms of political participation do you think are the most effective?

Source: United States Department of Agriculture Agricultural Research Service

Voting in Texas

Learning Objective: Discuss voter turnout in Texas, including citizens' rights and responsibilities.

One of the most common forms of participation in politics is voting in elections. Amendments to the U.S. Constitution stipulate that the right to vote cannot be denied on the basis of race, color, sex, failure to pay a **poll tax** (or any other tax), or age (as long as individuals are at least 18 years old).[3] Apart from these stipulations, states have considerable discretion to determine who is eligible to vote as well as what election system will be used within their borders.

Current Voting Requirements

In Texas today, any individual who is at least 18 years of age, a U.S. citizen, and a resident of the state may vote. The Texas Constitution excludes convicted felons and those formally judged to be "mentally incompetent" from voting. Furthermore, the Texas Constitution states that voters must register prior to voting in an election.[4] As defined by the U.S. Census Bureau, **voter registration** is "the act of qualifying to vote by formally enrolling on an official list of voters."[5] Texans are required to register at least 30 days in advance to vote in a given election.

There are several ways to register in Texas. In general, it involves completing a paper form. Voter registration applications are available at libraries, high schools, post offices, and some state and county offices. Official applications can be requested, but not submitted, online. Applicants must provide either a driver's license number, personal identification number issued by the Texas Department of Public Safety, or partial Social Security number on the form. Applicants may then mail their completed form, with postage prepaid by the state, or personally deliver it to their local registrar's office.[6]

Alternatively, Texans may register to vote when they apply for or renew their driver's license. In 1993, the U.S. Congress passed the National Voter Registration Act (also known as the "Motor Voter Act") to facilitate voter registration. Though the law's provisions apply only to federal elections, they impact state elections as well because states use the same registration systems for both federal and state elections. Individuals applying for a driver's license can

poll tax

In place from 1902 until 1966 in Texas, a tax citizens were required to pay each year between October and January to be eligible to vote in the next election cycle

voter registration

The act of qualifying to vote by formally enrolling on an official list of voters

simultaneously submit an application to register to vote (or update their address for purposes of voter registration, if applicable).[7]

After their application is processed, individuals receive a voter registration certificate or card. This card specifies the precinct in which that individual will vote, based on the person's address. Voters are automatically sent a new card every two years; the post office is instructed not to forward it if an individual has moved. If the card cannot be delivered to the addressee at the address on the card, it is returned to the voter registrar, and the voter's name is removed from the registration list. Individuals who move must re-register at their new address. Movers can change their address online only if they have relocated within the same county. Otherwise, they are required to submit a new paper form.[8]

On Election Day voters who have a government-issued photo ID must present it when they go to their polling place to vote.[9] (This requirement stems from the state's relatively new voter ID law, which is discussed later in this section.) Even if individuals are listed on the voter registration roll, they must still provide this identification. Texans can present one of seven kinds of ID, including an election identification certificate that is available free of charge from the Department of Public Safety.[10] Subsequent to a 2016 court order, the state also provides an accommodation for individuals who have been unable to get one of the seven forms of ID. Such individuals are not required to show a photo ID; instead, they can sign a declaration stating they had a "reasonable impediment" to obtaining a photo ID, then show an alternate form of identification such as a birth certificate, paystub, utility bill, or bank statement. If a voter still does not have any of the approved forms of identification, a provisional ballot may be cast that is counted if that individual reports to the county registrar's office within six days of the election with proper ID.[11]

There have been some attempts to make voting easier in Texas. For example, Texas allows early voting, either in person or by mail. With early voting, individuals go to their polling location, which is typically open between 17 and 4 days before an election, and vote as usual. Alternatively, individuals who expect to be away from their county of residence on Election Day are encouraged to vote early by mail. This process is sometimes called **absentee voting**. Although this practice began as a way to allow members of the military who were stationed outside of Texas to vote, it has since been extended to other individuals. Such voters must request or apply for their mail-in ballot before in-person early voting begins (that is, more than 17 days prior to the election). Marked ballots must be returned to the voting clerk and received by 7 p.m. on the date of the election (or, if mailed from outside the U.S., by the fifth day after the election). Military voters and citizens living overseas may use the regular vote-by-mail process; however, there is also a special process available only to military and overseas voters.[12]

Ongoing Controversies with Voting

Texas's voter ID law, which requires voters to show a government-issued picture ID in order to vote, has generated a great deal of controversy since its inception. Advocates of voter ID laws argue that these requirements ensure the integrity of elections by reducing voter fraud, while opponents counter that the need to obtain proper identification effectively restricts the right to vote and imposes a burden on would-be voters and government officials. Following heated debate

absentee voting
A process that allows a person to vote early, before the regular election; applies to all elections in Texas; also called early voting

that stretched over three separate legislative sessions and a span of six years, state legislators passed SB 14 (the voter ID law) in 2011.[13] However, the controversy did not end there.

Having been identified as a state with a history of discriminatory election practices, Texas was at that time subject to certain provisions of the federal Voting Rights Act. Under Section 5 of the Act, certain states could not change their voting laws without prior approval of either the U.S. Attorney General (Justice Department) or the U.S. District Court for the District of Columbia.[14] Therefore, Texas needed federal approval (or "preclearance") before its voter ID law could go into effect. In March 2012, the U.S. Justice Department denied preclearance of the Texas voter ID law because the data submitted by the state demonstrated that minority groups would be adversely affected by the law. Then-Attorney General Greg Abbott appealed this decision, arguing there was no evidence of discrimination against minorities in Texas at that time and that Section 5 of the Voting Rights Act exceeded the enumerated powers of Congress and conflicted with both Article IV of the Constitution and the Tenth Amendment. However, the U.S. District Court for the District of Columbia denied the state's application for court reconsideration in August 2012.[15] Abbott then filed a brief with the U.S. Supreme Court. On June 25, 2013, the Supreme Court declared Section 4 of the Voting Rights Act (which laid out the formula for identifying which states or jurisdictions would be subject to the preclearance requirement) unconstitutional. With this key portion of the Act struck down, Section 5 was rendered unenforceable. Texas no longer required federal approval for its voter ID law.[16] As a result, the voter ID law went into immediate effect.[17] The November 2013 election was the first in which Texans were required to show a photo ID in order to vote.

Legal challenges to the voter ID law continued. In August 2015, a panel of three federal judges rejected a portion of Texas's voter ID law as discriminatory but said it did not amount to an unconstitutional poll tax. This ruling allowed the law to remain in effect.[18] In July 2016, the full federal appeals court ruled that the law violated Section 2 of the Voting Rights Act and ordered that a "temporary fix" be put in place before the November 2016 election. As of August 2016, the agreed-upon solution allowed prospective voters who were unable to present a photo ID to sign a declaration regarding that difficulty and present alternate documentation. However, this issue may be far from a final resolution: a spokesman for Attorney General Ken Paxton's office said they would "continue evaluating all options moving forward."[19]

Another area of continuing controversy relates to the "motor voter" law. State compliance with the law requires the Texas Department of Public Safety (or DPS, which handles driver's licenses) to transmit voter information to the office of the Texas Secretary of State, which then forwards it onto a local voter registrar. In 2015, the state agreed to investigate complaints from residents that their voter registration applications submitted through DPS had not been processed properly, resulting in their inability to vote and a need to repeat the registration process.[20] In addition, a lawsuit recently filed against the state alleged that individuals who conducted their driver's license business online were subject to different voter registration procedures than those who went to a DPS office in person. The suit alleged that such disparate treatment constituted a violation of the law and of prospective voters' rights.[21] As of August 2016, this case had not been resolved.

CORE OBJECTIVE

Thinking Critically. . .

How do you think the Texas voter ID law impacts voter turnout in Texas? Where do you stand on the issue? Explain why you favor or oppose voter ID laws.

Source: National Park Service

In Comparison with Other States

Most states impose some restrictions on voting. Preregistration is one example of such a restriction. In most states, prospective voters must register by a certain deadline, typically ranging from 8 to 30 days, prior to an election. However, eleven states currently have no pre-election registration requirements and allow "same-day" registration (also known as "Election Day registration").[22] In states with **same-day registration**, voters show up at their polling place on Election Day, register on the spot (usually by providing identification and proof of residency), and are allowed to vote. Research has shown that same-day registration results in greater turnout; states that have implemented same-day registration have turnout levels above the national average.[23] North Dakota, for its part, has no voter registration whatsoever.[24]

Other factors related to voting restrictions include registration methods and identification requirements. All states provide paper registration forms upon request, but for added convenience, 31 states also offer online voter registration. Four more states have legalized but not yet implemented online systems.[25] As of 2016, 34 states including Texas had adopted voter ID legislation. These laws range from a strict requirement that voters show a photo ID to non-strict requirements that allow voters to provide some means of identification without a photo (like a bank statement). The remaining states require no documentation to vote.[26]

Texas requires registration 30 days in advance of an election, does not offer online voter registration, and requires some form of identification to vote. Therefore, despite the recent weakening of its voter ID law, Texas appears to be fairly demanding in terms of voting requirements. But do these additional requirements actually deter people from coming to the polls and casting a ballot? Let's turn our attention now to the available data on how many Texans vote in elections.

Voter Turnout in Texas

There are several ways to calculate **voter turnout**, or the proportion of people who cast ballots in an election. One measure is the percentage of **registered voters** who cast a ballot. This statistic is commonly reported because it is simple to calculate and readily available to state elections divisions. However, there are drawbacks to using the percentage of registered voters to assess voter turnout. As discussed previously, registration requirements vary greatly among the states. These varying requirements (preregistration/same-day registration/no registration) make it difficult to compare turnout rates across states using this method. In same-day registration states, for example, anyone who is eligible to vote can cast a ballot, whereas in other states voters must have been proactive enough to register ahead of time

same-day registration

Voters are allowed to register on Election Day; no preregistration before the election is required.

voter turnout

The proportion of people who cast ballots in an election

registered voters

Citizens who have formally gone through the process of getting their names on the voter registration list

Voters waiting in line to cast ballots

© Hill Street Studios/Getty Images RF

voting-age population

The number of people age 18 and over

voting-eligible population

The voting-age population, corrected to exclude groups ineligible to vote, such as noncitizens and convicted felons

in order to participate. Furthermore, voter registration lists are not completely accurate and up-to-date; most contain "deadwood," or the names of individuals who are registered at a certain address but no longer live there.[27] This inaccuracy in the rolls distorts the count of registered voters in a precinct area.

A second measure is the percentage of the voting-age population that votes. **Voting-age population** (VAP) is defined as the number of people age 18 and over. To calculate turnout using VAP, the number of people casting votes in an election is divided by the number of residents 18 years of age and older.[28] VAP is generally the preferred measure (and the one most often used by political scientists) because it discounts variations in state voting and registration requirements and makes it easier to compare states. However, there are problems with using VAP to express voter turnout as well. The voting-age population includes a sizable number of people who have met the age requirement but are nonetheless unable to register and vote. Reasons a person may be excluded from voting include not being a U.S. citizen, having committed a felony, having been declared mentally incapacitated, or not having met the state and local residency requirements for registration.[29] Measuring turnout by using VAP is distorted because these ineligible persons are counted in the figure, even though it is impossible for them to vote.

The United States Election Project presents yet a third measure of voter turnout, based on the **voting-eligible population** (VEP). VEP is calculated by correcting VAP to eliminate ineligible groups, such as noncitizens and convicted felons.[30] Michael McDonald, the political scientist who pioneered the VEP measure, claims that "the most valid turnout rates over time and across states are calculated using voting-eligible population."[31] Using the VEP turnout rate (which, for the data shown here, is calculated by dividing the number of ballots cast for highest office by VEP), participation in recent presidential elections appears higher than previously determined using the VAP measure. (In fact, McDonald has argued that "the much-lamented decline in voter participation" since 1971, based on VAP, is "entirely explained by the increase in the ineligible population."[32]) Some other political scientists have also recommended the use of VEP turnout rates but acknowledge that VEP data is not universally available at this time.[33] Table 7.2 compares voter turnout rates calculated according to these three methods. Note that using the percentage of registered voters who voted produces higher turnout rates than the other two methods; using the percentage of voting-age population (VAP) who voted yields the lowest figures.

How does Texas fare in terms of voter turnout rates? In general, Texans are not avid voters. As shown in Table 7.3, Texas consistently falls below the national

TABLE 7.2

Comparison of Percentage of Registered, Voting-Age, and Voting-Eligible Voters Voting in Texas Elections, 1988–2016

Year	Percent of Registered Voters Who Voted	Percent of VAP Who Voted	VEP Highest Office Turnout Rate
Presidential Election Years			
1988	66.2	44.3	50.1
1992	72.9	47.6	54.2
1996	53.2	41.0	46.5
2000	51.8	44.3	49.2
2004	56.6	46.1	53.7
2008	59.5	45.6	54.1
2012	58.6	43.7	49.7
2016	59.4	46.5	51.1*
Congressional and Statewide Election Years			
1990	50.6	31.1	35.3
1994	50.9	33.6	37.5
1998	32.4	26.5	29.9
2002	36.2	29.4	34.2
2006	33.6	26.4	30.9
2010	38.0	27.0	32.1
2014	33.7	25.0	28.3

*VEP based on total number of ballots counted rather than ballots cast for highest office.

Source: Texas Secretary of State, *Turnout and Voter Registration Figures* (1970–current). http://www.sos.state.tx.us/elections/historical/70-92.shtml; Michael P. McDonald (2015), "1980–2014 November General Election," and (2016), "2016 November General Election Turnout Rates," *United States Election Project.* (See http://www.electproject.org/.)

TABLE 7.3

Texas Rank as a Percentage of Voting-Eligible Population in National Elections, 1988–2016

Year	Texas Rank	National Turnout	Texas Turnout
Presidential Election Years			
1988	37	52.8	50.1
1992	40	58.1	54.2
1996	43	51.7	46.5
2000	41	54.2	49.2
2004	48	60.1	53.7
2008	48	61.6	54.1
2012	47	58.2	49.7
2016	47	58.8	51.1
Congressional/Statewide Election Only Years			
1990	41	38.4	35.3
1994	42	41.1	37.5
1998	47	38.1	29.9
2002	46	39.5	34.2
2006	48	40.4	30.9
2010	50	41.0	32.1
2014	48	36.0	28.3

Source: Michael P. McDonald (2015), "1980–2014 November General Election," and (2016) "2016 November General Election Turnout Rates," *United States Election Project.* (See http://www.electproject.org/.)

average in terms of percentage of the voting-eligible population participating in elections during the past 30 years. Texas's voter turnout also ranks at or near the bottom when compared to other states (see also Figure 7.2). In fact, for the 2010 congressional and statewide races, Texas had the lowest voter turnout of all 50 states. Data from subsequent elections suggest a continuation of this low-turnout trend. The Texas Secretary of State reported that 4.7 million people, or 33.7 percent of registered voters, cast a ballot in the 2014 general election (which included a gubernatorial contest).[34] According to the U.S. Election Project, slightly more than a quarter of the VEP voted.[35] Voter turnout is typically lower for midterm elections than in years when there is a presidential election at stake.

The 2016 presidential primary season was marked by record-breaking turnout in state after state across the nation. (These primary elections provided proof, as discussed later in this chapter, that high levels of competition drive high voter turnout. The hotly contested Republican field, led by Donald Trump, started out with no less than 17 announced candidates, 12 of whom were still in the race when primary voting began. On the Democratic side, the race between Hillary Clinton and Bernie Sanders was more contentious than many had anticipated.[36]) Texas was no exception to the high turnout trend, where 2.8 million voters turned out for the Republican primary, and another 1.4 million voted in the Democratic primary. In all, 4,272,383 Texans participated in presidential primary voting in March 2016—a

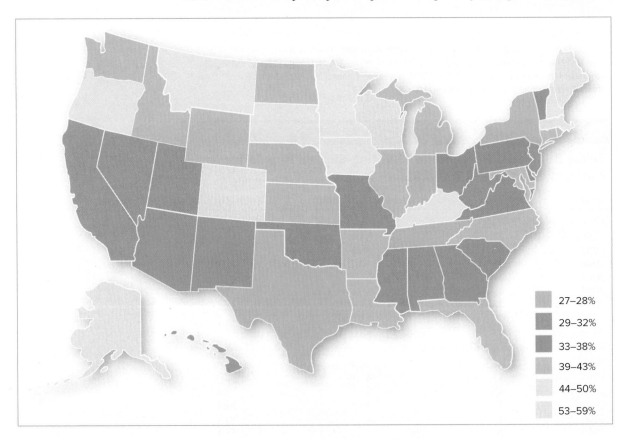

27–28%

29–32%

33–38%

39–43%

44–50%

53–59%

FIGURE 7.2   **Percentage of Eligible Voters Voting in 2014 General Election**

SOURCE: Michael P. McDonald (2015), "2014 November General Election Turnout Rates," *United States Elections Project,* http://www .electproject.org/2014g.

number that exceeded the previous record for participation set in the 2008 presidential primaries.[37] Nonetheless, compared to most other states, Texas's turnout (14.7% of VAP for Republicans; 7.4% of VAP for Democrats) was still quite low.[38] As is typical, turnout for the primaries was lower than for general elections.

Despite the contentiousness and historic nature of the 2016 presidential contest, turnout for the general election was consistent with recent trends. As shown in Tables 7.2 and 7.3, barely more than half of the voting-eligible population cast a ballot in Texas, and the national average for turnout failed to crack 60 percent. Texas again ranked among the lowest of all 50 states in terms of voter turnout.

It is also worth noting that voter turnout at the national level is lower in the United States than in most other industrialized nations. Moreover, participation in state politics is lower than at the national level and still lower at the local levels.

Explaining Voter Turnout

Learning Objective: Describe ways in which the state of Texas has, historically, restricted access to voting.

How can we explain the relatively low levels of voting among Texans? For one thing, a significant portion of the state's population (namely, noncitizens and convicted felons) is not eligible to vote. Including these ineligible groups in Texas's VAP inflates that figure and negatively exaggerates commonly cited turnout levels based on VAP. Even if we correct for this problem by using VEP to calculate turnout, however, the state's level of voter participation is still low. So what else accounts for low voter turnout in Texas?

Many other factors are involved. The political culture discourages participation. There is a legacy of restricted access to the ballot for many groups, and other social, economic, and political factors play a role. Of course, many of the factors that impact voter turnout in Texas are also connected to turnout levels across the country, and even around the world.

The Legacy of Restricted Ballot Access in Texas

Like other southern U.S. states, Texas has a history of restrictive voter registration laws. In the past, these laws made it difficult to qualify to vote and limited avenues of political participation. The state's history of restricting access to voting is very much in keeping with its traditionalistic political culture.

In 1902 the Texas legislature adopted, with voter approval, payment of a poll tax as a requirement for voting. This law primarily targeted the Populist movement, which had organized low-income white farmers into a political coalition that threatened the establishment within the Democratic Party.[39] This tax ($1.75) was a large amount of money for poor farmers in the early 1900s.[40] The poll tax also restricted ballot access for African Americans and Hispanics, who were disproportionately poor as a group. The poll tax had to be paid each year between October 1 and January 31 for a person to be allowed to vote in the next election cycle. Figure 7.3 shows an original poll tax receipt.

The poll tax was in effect in Texas for about 60 years. In 1964, passage of the Twenty-Fourth Amendment to the U.S. Constitution eliminated the poll tax

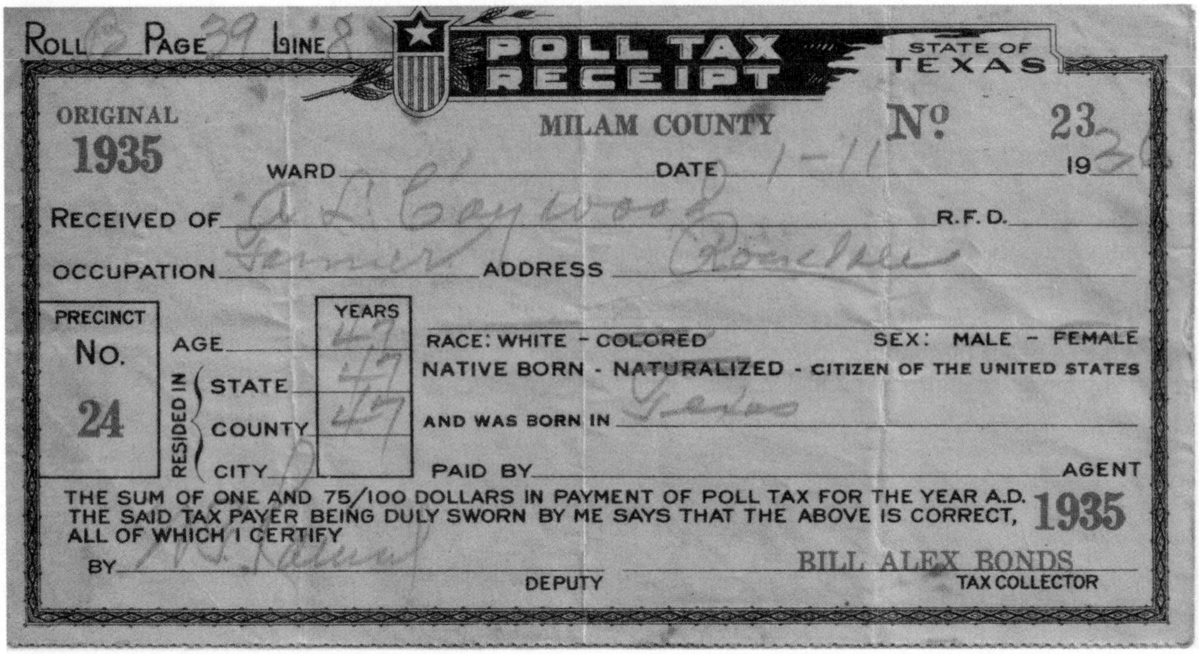
ROLL PAGE 39 LINE 8

POLL TAX RECEIPT

STATE OF TEXAS

ORIGINAL 1935

MILAM COUNTY

Nº 23

WARD DATE 1-11 19

RECEIVED OF R.F.D.

OCCUPATION ADDRESS

PRECINCT No. 24

AGE YEARS 47

RESIDED IN STATE 47

COUNTY 47

CITY

RACE: WHITE - COLORED SEX: MALE - FEMALE

NATIVE BORN - NATURALIZED - CITIZEN OF THE UNITED STATES

AND WAS BORN IN Texas

PAID BY AGENT

THE SUM OF ONE AND 75/100 DOLLARS IN PAYMENT OF POLL TAX FOR THE YEAR A.D. 1935

THE SAID TAX PAYER BEING DULY SWORN BY ME SAYS THAT THE ABOVE IS CORRECT, ALL OF WHICH I CERTIFY

BY DEPUTY

BILL ALEX BONDS

TAX COLLECTOR

FIGURE 7.3 Original Poll Tax Receipt

© Jerry Caywood

as a requirement for voting in federal elections. However, Texas retained the poll tax as a requirement for voting in state elections.[41] In 1964–65, 2.4 million Texans still paid the tax. In 1966, the U.S. Supreme Court invalidated Texas's poll tax entirely.[42] The very next election cycle proved how successful the poll tax had been in reducing the number of qualified voters. In 1968, the number of registered voters jumped by more than 1 million from the previous presidential election year, an increase of about 35 percent.[43]

annual registration
A system that requires citizens to reregister to vote every year

Even after the poll tax was eliminated in 1966, Texas retained a very restrictive system of voter registration. It had an **annual registration** system, meaning voters were required to register each year between October 1 and January 31. Individuals were required to register at the courthouse, where they had also been required to pay the poll tax. (In most Texas counties, even today, the county tax collector is also the voter registrar.) For minorities, the trip to the courthouse could be an intimidating experience, and many avoided it.

permanent registration
A system that keeps citizens on the voter registration list without their having to reregister every year

Following a 1971 court decision prohibiting annual registration systems,[44] the Texas legislature passed a very progressive voter registration law that eliminated annual registration and replaced it with a permanent registration system. **Permanent registration** is a system that keeps citizens on the voter registration list without requiring them to reregister every year. Easy voter registration procedures have been shown to increase the number of registered voters. In 1972, the first year Texas used a permanent registration system, voter registration increased yet again, by another 1 million (or nearly 28 percent) over the 1968 figure.[45]

white primary
From 1923 to 1945, Democratic Party primary that excluded African Americans from participating

Another past practice used by many southern states, including Texas, to block participation by African Americans was the **white primary**. In 1923, the Texas legislature passed a law prohibiting African Americans from participating in Democratic Party primaries. The U.S. Supreme Court declared this law unconstitutional.[46] In 1927, the legislature granted the executive committee of each political

party the right to determine voter eligibility for primaries, thereby allowing the Democratic Party to exclude African Americans.[47] In response, the U.S. Supreme Court again declared the legislature's role unconstitutional.[48] In 1932, bypassing the legislature entirely, the state Democratic Party convention adopted a resolution to hold a white primary.[49] This action prompted yet another U.S. Supreme Court challenge.[50] The issue before the Court at this point was whether a political party was an agent of the government or a private organization. The Supreme Court's 1935 ruling stated that political parties were in fact private organizations and therefore could decide who was permitted to participate in primary elections. This

National Anti-Suffrage Association Headquarters, 1911

Source: Library of Congress Prints and Photographs Division [LC-USZ62-25338]

allowed the Democrats to exclude African Americans from participating in the party primary. Because, at this time, the Republicans presented no real competition in the general election, the primary effectively became the "general election." Thus, from 1932 until 1945, African Americans in Texas were denied the right to vote by the rules of the Democratic Party, rather than by state law.

In 1944 the U.S. Supreme Court outlawed all-white primaries in southern states in *Smith v. Allwright,* a case that originated in Texas.[51] This ruling overturned earlier rulings that political parties were private organizations. In *Smith,* the Supreme Court held that political parties were agents of the state and therefore could not exclude people from participating in primary elections because of race. Thus, federal court actions finally ended the practice of the white primary after it had been used for two decades to deny the vote to African Americans.

As was common in many states, property ownership was also used to restrict the right to vote in Texas. These restrictions applied mostly to local elections, particularly bond elections. The reasoning behind limiting voting to property owners was that property taxes provided the primary source of revenue for local governments, and renters supposedly did not pay property tax. However, enforcement of the property ownership requirement was difficult. Property ownership requirements were eliminated in the 1970s when permanent registration took effect in Texas.

Women were also disenfranchised in Texas. By 1915, 11 states (not including Texas) had granted women the right to vote.[52] During the 1915 session, the Texas legislature considered granting women the right to vote, but the measure failed. In 1918, women were given the limited right to participate in primary elections. In 1919, Texas voters rejected a proposed amendment to the state constitution that would have granted women full suffrage. The following month, however, the state legislature ratified the Nineteenth Amendment to the U.S. Constitution, which outlawed any citizen from being denied the right to vote based on their sex. Texas was the first southern state to approve the amendment, which took effect in 1920.[53]

All these restrictions combined to prolong the state's tradition of limiting or even discouraging participation in elections. Although past restrictions have been removed from law, and current access to voter registration is comparatively easy (and has increased the number of registered voters in the state), there are persistent and lingering effects of Texas's legacy of restricted ballot access. Texas still has low levels of participation in the political process. As shown in Table 7.3, Texas recently ranked at or near the bottom of all states on voter turnout in elections. In time, the residual effect of restrictive practices may decline, but there are other factors influencing voter turnout.

Social and Economic Factors

socioeconomic factors

Factors such as income, education, race, and ethnicity that affect voter turnout

Rates of participation are also strongly affected by **socioeconomic factors**, such as educational level, family income, and minority status. Well-educated people (those with a college education and/or post-graduate degree) are more likely to vote than are less well-educated people (those with a high school degree or less).[54] People of higher socioeconomic status are likely to be more aware of elections and to perceive themselves as having a high stake in election outcomes; therefore, they are more likely to vote. They are also more likely to contribute financially to political campaigns and become actively involved in elections and party activity.

Age is another factor that contributes to turnout. Young voters, particularly those aged 18 to 29, are less likely to vote than older adults.[55] They often have other interests, are more mobile, and may not perceive themselves as having an important stake in political outcomes. Although still lower than the turnout rate for the population as a whole, youth voting rates have increased recently, especially during the 2008 and 2012 elections.[56]

Race is yet another factor in voting. Nationwide, minority groups have historically voted and registered to vote in smaller proportions than non-Hispanic whites. However, a notable exception to this pattern emerged in recent years with regard to voting among African Americans. In 2008, blacks both registered and voted at about the same level as whites.[57] Because this is not normally the case, the higher levels of black participation may have been attributable to President Obama being on the ballot. Black turnout remained relatively strong in the 2010 midterm elections (although as usual, absolute voting levels fell off compared to the numbers in a presidential election year). Voting patterns in Texas tracked with this national trend. In the 2012 election, the percentage of black citizens who voted in Texas surpassed the percentage of white non-Hispanics who voted (63 versus 61 percent)[58] (see Figure 7.4). Again, this atypically high black turnout may have been due to President Obama's bid for reelection.

According to Census Bureau data on the 2012 election, both voter registration and turnout among Hispanics was significantly lower than for the non-Hispanic white population. Only about 39 percent of voting-age Hispanics in Texas are registered to vote. In the 2012 election, just over one-quarter (28 percent) of Hispanic Texans over the age of 18 cast a ballot. By comparison, about 60 percent of all non-Hispanic whites of voting age participated in the same election. When considering only those who are citizens, however, the number of Hispanics in the state who were registered and voted increases to 55 percent and 39 percent, respectively.[59] Turnout rates among Texans of Asian descent are also lower than those of non-Hispanic whites and blacks. Although nearly 60 percent of Asian citizens are registered to vote, only 42 percent cast a ballot in the 2012 presidential election.[60] Table 7.4 provides a breakdown of voter turnout and voter registration rates by gender and ethnicity.

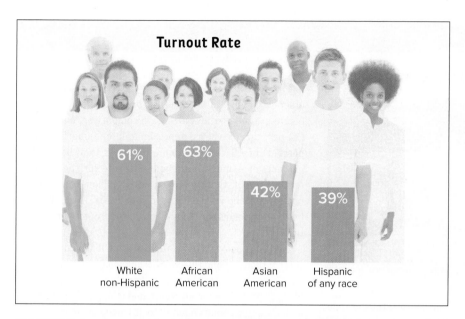

FIGURE 7.4 Voter Turnout in Texas in the 2012 Presidential Election, by Race
© Ryan McVay/Getty Images RF

TABLE 7.4

Registration and Voter Participation by Race and Sex in Texas, 2012

	Total Voting Age Population (VAP)	Total Citizen Population	Total Registered	Percent Registered (Total)	Percent Registered (Citizen)	Total Voted	Percent Voted (Total)	Percent Voted (Citizen)
Total	18,642	16,062	10,749	57.7	66.9	8,643	46.4	53.8
Male	9,046	7,719	4,977	55.0	64.5	3,925	43.4	50.8
Female	9,596	8,344	5,772	60.1	69.2	4,719	49.2	56.6
White alone	15,029	12,989	8,643	57.5	66.5	6,900	45.9	53.1
White non-Hispanic alone	8,512	8,360	6,101	71.7	73.0	5,087	59.8	60.9
Black alone	2,213	2,144	1,569	70.9	73.2	1,352	61.1	63.1
Asian alone	900	506	299	33.2	59.1	214	23.8	42.4
Hispanic (of any race)	6,831	4,867	2,652	38.8	54.5	1,890	27.7	38.8
White alone or in combination	15,200	13,144	8,749	57.6	66.6	6,968	45.8	53.0
Black alone or in combination	2,293	2,207	1,606	70.0	72.8	1,380	60.2	62.5
Asian alone or in combination	909	515	305	33.5	59.2	220	24.2	42.8

VAP = Population 18 years and older, in thousands.

Source: U.S. Census Bureau. Voting and Registration in the Election of November 2012 Detailed Tables. Table 4b. Reported Voting and Registration by Sex, Race and Hispanic Origin, for States: November 2012. http://www.census.gov/hhes/www/socdemo/voting/publications/p20/2012/tables.html.

Focus On

Low Voter Turnout among Hispanics

© Erich Schlegel/Getty Images

Hispanics constitute a burgeoning share of the national vote. According to an estimate by Pew Research Center, a record-breaking 27.3 million Hispanics nationwide were eligible to vote in the 2016 election.[61] Moreover, the Hispanic electorate is projected to increase to 40 million by the year 2030. This massive increase will be fueled primarily by large numbers of young Hispanics reaching voting age (and secondarily by naturalizations).[62] In Texas, growth in the number of eligible Hispanic voters is expected to mirror that national trend.

Although the Hispanic population continues to grow, Hispanics play a much smaller role in shaping the state's politics than their numbers might suggest. Analysis of election data shows that, historically, Hispanics have voted at much lower rates than blacks and non-Hispanic whites. National data provides some explanation for this. About half (52 percent) of all Hispanics nationwide are not eligible to vote, either because they are too young or they are not citizens. In comparison, one-fifth (20 percent) of whites, approximately one-quarter (28 percent) of African Americans, and less than half (44 percent) of Asians are ineligible to vote for the same reasons.[63] Of the remaining 23.3 million Hispanics nationwide who were eligible to vote in 2012, only about half (48 percent), or 11.2 million, turned out to vote in the election.[64]

Several socioeconomic factors contribute to lower voter turnout among Hispanics, including generally lower education levels and incomes. Young people are less likely to participate in elections, and millennials (defined in one study as adults aged 18 to 35) made up 44 percent of eligible Hispanic voters in 2016.[65] In addition, lower political interest may account for lower turnout among Hispanics. Texas is generally not considered to be a key battleground state in presidential elections — something that can generate considerable interest in voting and the political process.[66] Other possible factors include the number of Hispanic candidates running for office and candidates' efforts to engage the Hispanic community, including making campaign materials available in Spanish.[67]

Critical Thinking Questions

1. Discuss the factors involved in low voter turnout among Hispanics.
2. What do you think the future will bring with regard to Hispanic participation in elections?

Felony Conviction and Voting

Most states limit the voting rights of people convicted of a felony. Maine and Vermont are the only states that allow felons to vote, even while they are in prison.[68] Texas prohibits persons convicted of a felony, as well as those on probation or parole, from voting. However, felons in Texas may register to vote after they have served out their sentence and completed their time on probation and parole.[69] According to U.S. Elections Project, in 2014 there were 486,110 ineligible felons (2.4 percent of the voting age population) in Texas who could not vote.[70] This proportion was nearly twice the national average for felony disenfranchisement.

Being Socially Responsible . . .

Considering the discussion of the socioeconomic factors that affect voter turnout, identify effective ways to increase civic knowledge in culturally diverse communities.

© Editorial Image, LLC/Alamy

Party Competition

The lack of party competition in Texas for more than 100 years also contributes to the state's overall lower voter turnout. Studies have shown that party competition and closeness of elections are important factors in voter turnout. (However, the effect of the latter is smaller in comparative perspective than one might think.)[71] When there is party competition in a district, voters believe that their votes will actually "count," so they are more likely to show up at the polls and to participate in grassroots political organizations. Moreover, in competitive districts, both parties have a big incentive to increase voter turnout.[72] Texans elected Republicans to all statewide offices from 2002 through 2014.[73] The state has also been solidly Republican in U.S. presidential elections. Furthermore, Texas has many noncompetitive seats, especially in the state legislature. It remains to be seen if this domination of state politics will be permanent. Although party competition has increased in recent years, the state has a long history of being a one-party state; consequently, voter turnout is lower than it might be with greater competition.

Other Factors Affecting Voter Turnout

Other factors can affect voter turnout in some elections. One is the timing of the election. Voter turnout is higher in November presidential elections than in midterm elections when we do not elect a president or other statewide or national officeholders. For the most part, turnout for primary elections is even lower than for general elections. Also, local elections for city councils and school boards are generally not held in conjunction with general elections; in Texas these are commonly held in May. However, efforts are currently being made to move these local contests to the fall. In 2012, Austin voters approved a proposition to move city elections from May to November.[74] Turnout in local elections is always lower than in other elections (despite the fact that the odds of being the marginal voter increase as the number of people voting goes down). There are several reasons for this: local elections are less visible and receive less attention by the media; voters do not perceive these elections as being important; and many of these races are not contested. In 1995 the Texas legislature proposed a constitutional amendment, which the voters approved, to change state law to allow cities and school boards to cancel elections if all races are uncontested. The governing body certifies the uncontested candidates as "winners." (Chapter 6 has more information on local elections.)

The day of the week an election is held can also affect voter turnout. Tuesday is the most common day for elections in the United States. This tradition dates back to 1845, when the U.S. Congress set the date for federal elections as the

Texas delegates at a convention

© McGraw-Hill Education/Jill Braaten, photographer

first Tuesday after the first Monday in November.[75] Local city and school board elections are often held on Saturday, which might appear to be a better day to hold elections than Tuesday because many people are off work and have time to vote. However, Saturday is also a departure from one's regular workday routine, and people might forget to vote or choose to devote the day to other activities, such as recreation or errands, that they believe will provide greater utility than participation in political life. Also, elections in the United States are generally held on a single day, with the polls typically being open for 12 hours. In contrast, many European countries hold elections over an entire weekend.

Longer election periods, early voting opportunities, and other ways that voting (and registration) can be made easier (such as voting by mail and more numerous polling places) might increase voter turnout. As political scientist Andre Blais notes, "It makes sense to assume that people are more prone to vote if it is easy."[76] Empirical evidence generally supports this intuition. However, a recent University of Wisconsin study of early voting offers a caveat. Kenneth Mayer, one of the study authors, found in this particular instance that early voting "actually causes voter turnout to go down."[77] Co-author Donald Downs surmised that the existence of early voting might make voting on Election Day seem less important. It is not clear, though, whether this finding will be confirmed in other studies, because scholars have generally found the opposite impact when it comes to making voting easier.

Rationalist Explanations for Low Voter Turnout

A last reason for low voter turnout may be the realization by a number of voters that, at least in their individual cases, individual voting is irrational because (1) it does not meet the requirements of "strategic" or "instrumental" rationality (in the sense of voting being a purposeful act to influence an election), given the low probability of any single individual being the "marginal," "pivotal," or "deciding" voter in large-scale elections; and (2) the "consumption" or "expressive" value of voting does not outweigh the costs of participation (especially the cost of one's time). In other words, duty doesn't call, nor is the act of voting all that valuable relative to the costs for some segment of the population.

There is a long tradition of literature in political science and economics, starting with the path-breaking work of Anthony Downs, that makes these "rational choice" points. Scholars of voting often wonder, as Nobel Prize–winning economist Kenneth Arrow did, "Why an individual votes at all in a large election, since the probability that his vote will be decisive is so negligible."[78] But since so many do—thus creating the so-called paradox of voting—we may want to ask not why so many don't vote but why so many people do vote! This is undoubtedly a more complicated question than we can fully answer here. However, one answer might be that individuals, like people who clap at the end of a movie or cheer in a football stadium full of people, gain expressive value from the act of voting.[79] It simply makes them feel better to express their preference for one candidate (or against another). An individual may also, consciously or not, want to signal to others that he or she is a "good citizen" or a "serious person" by being seen voting or wearing the voting sticker we can easily obtain only at the voting facility. Or it could be that some individuals believe they have a real duty to participate in elections or to be concerned about the "social good," especially given the price they believe others have paid to secure that civil right.[80] There could be any number of honestly good reasons why people might vote, apart from narrowly strategic reasons. However, it is worth seriously considering that some people might choose not to vote for rational reasons. And it is worth asking why individuals pay less attention to and vote less often in local elections where they have a statistically greater chance of influencing the election.

Another rational reason some people may not vote is that they are satisfied with (or alienated from) the political system in general and do not feel the need to express themselves in favor of (or against) any particular candidate. Last, an admittedly small number of eligible citizens may be principled nonvoters who do not want to provide legitimacy to what they believe is an illegitimate system.

CORE OBJECTIVE

Communicating Effectively . . .
Write a one-page summary of the rationalist explanations for low voter turnout.

© George Lavendowski/USFWS

Other Forms of Political Participation

Learning Objective: Describe forms of political participation other than voting.

Although voting in an election is the most common form of political participation, people participate in politics in many other ways. As noted at the beginning of this chapter, participation types and the extent of involvement vary widely. In fact, one could be "involved" in politics quite intensely by becoming a candidate for public office or quite superficially by signing a petition or writing a short letter to the editor of the local newspaper. Other forms of participation seen in Texas and the rest of the country include donating money to a campaign, volunteering for a campaign, supporting an advocacy group, contacting an elected official, attending a rally or protest, or even using online social networks to support a candidate or group. A common goal of all these types of participation is to affect the decisions made by the government, either by electing certain people to office or by influencing those who are already in office.

A 2009 survey of Texas adults by the University of Texas at Austin (see Table 7.5) sheds more light on the ways Texans participate in politics. Although voting is far and away the most common form of political participation, just over half of survey respondents reported encouraging others to vote for a particular candidate. More than one-third of respondents reported supporting a candidate through such actions as displaying a bumper sticker, and the same number reported forwarding an email from a political candidate or group. Thirty percent reported contacting an elected official to express an opinion, and 20 percent reported connecting with a candidate or political group through an online social network such as Facebook or Twitter. The least popular forms of political participation cited were attending a rally or protest (13 percent) and volunteering for a campaign (9 percent).[81]

Thanks to a greater reliance on the Internet by campaign fundraising efforts, donating to a campaign has become one of the easiest ways to participate in politics. About 22 percent of respondents to the University of Texas poll reported making a political donation. According to OpenSecrets.org, a website run by the Center for Responsive Politics that tracks political contributions, individual Texans donated more than $68 million to presidential candidates during the 2012 election.[82] This placed Texas second in the nation for the amount of individual contributions to presidential campaigns. Republican candidates were the largest beneficiaries of these individual contributors, claiming about 78 percent of all political contributions.[83]

TABLE 7.5

Popular Forms of Political Participation in Texas

"Please think back over the past year and indicate if you have done any of the following."

Political Activity	%
Voted in an election	80
Encouraged others to vote for a particular candidate	51
Publicly supported a political candidate (e.g., bumper sticker)	35
Forwarded an email from a political party, candidate, or interest group	35
Contacted an elected official to express an opinion	30
Donated money to a political candidate	22
Joined an online social network group supporting a political candidate	20
Attended a political rally, protest, or event	13
Volunteered for a political campaign	9

Source: University of Texas at Austin Department of Government, N = 800 Adults, Feb 24–Mar 6, 2009.

However, political participation as a whole is still relatively low in the United States, and especially in Texas. Why don't more people participate in politics? Political scientists Henry Brady, Sidney Verba, and Kay Schlozman answer, "Because they can't, because they don't want to, or because nobody asked."[84] Participation in politics requires free time, expendable income, and political interest. The cost of participation in terms of time, in particular, is a crucial constraint. Involvement in social networks such as civic associations and churches, which enable people to interact and mobilize, also promotes political participation. These kinds of social networks also help people to develop "civic skills," or the ability to communicate and organize, which are important to political activity. Many Americans lack some or all of these resources for political participation. As a result, they either "can't" or "don't want to" participate, or perhaps they would accept that they do not belong to a social network and so "nobody asked" them to participate.

Does low political participation threaten American democracy? Although turnout in presidential elections has increased slightly in recent years (and, as political scientist Michael McDonald has argued, the supposed decline in voter participation since 1971 may not be as significant as once thought), it is still lower than in the 1950s and 1960s.[85] Other types of participation are also in decline. In his book *Bowling Alone,* Robert Putnam cites declining involvement in traditional civic associations as contributing to a loss of "social capital" in America. Social capital refers to the sense of shared purpose and values that social connection promotes, which Putnam and many others cite as necessary for a thriving democracy. Still others are less pessimistic. Russell Dalton, for example, argues that the decline in traditional civic associations is accompanied by a rise in other types of participation that reflect the changing values of a younger generation.[86]

Volunteers at "Battleground Texas" campaign headquarters call voters on Election Day.
© Tamir Kalifa.

Tea Party activists head to a rally at the Texas State Capitol.
© Tamir Kalifa.

Conclusion

The Lone Star State has chronically low levels of voter turnout in elections and low levels of participation in the political process in general. Many factors influence participation in voting and other political activities. Individual states determine who is eligible to vote within their borders, and some states, like Texas, have relatively strict requirements for voting. Some states, mostly southern and including Texas, also have a legacy of restricting access to the ballot and discouraging voter participation. Despite the removal of these restrictions and increases in voter turnout, voter turnout has not surged as much as some might have expected or hoped, suggesting that other factors may play an important role in political participation. Social and economic factors, level of party competition, and other variables including the rational calculations of individuals are also involved. Moreover, political behavior can persist for generations (especially if there is a "habit component" to voting).[87] Demographic changes and increased party competition may impact voter turnout levels in the state at some future time. However, currently low levels of participation are consistent with the traditionalist political culture of Texas.

Summary

LO: Explain political participation.

Political participation refers to all the ways in which citizens can be involved in governance. Voting in elections is the most obvious way (but not the only way) that citizens take part in politics. Participation can be conceptualized in terms of types of activities and degree or level of involvement.

LO: Discuss voter turnout in Texas, including citizens' rights and responsibilities.

Voter turnout is the proportion of people who cast ballots in an election. Regardless of the method used to calculate it, Texas has low voter turnout. Over the past 30 years, Texas has consistently fallen below the national average in terms of percentage of the population participating in elections. The state's voter turnout also ranks at or near the bottom when compared to other states. In Texas today, any individual who is at least 18 years of age, a U.S. citizen, and a resident of the state may vote. Texans must register 30 days before an election and provide some form of identification in order to vote.

LO: Describe ways in which the state of Texas has, historically, restricted access to voting.

For part of its history, Texas required citizens to pay a poll tax each year to be eligible to vote in the next election cycle. After the poll tax was eliminated, Texas had an annual registration system, which required citizens to reregister to vote every year. Another restrictive practice was the white primary. From 1923 to 1945, the Democratic Party in Texas prohibited African

Americans from participating in primary elections. All these practices were invalidated by court decisions.

LO: Describe forms of political participation other than voting.

Although voting in an election is the most common form of political participation, other forms include include

donating money to a campaign, volunteering for a campaign, supporting an advocacy group, contacting an elected official, attending a rally or protest, or using online social networks to support a candidate or group. Alternatively, individuals might try to influence governmental decisions by running for public office, signing a petition, or writing a letter to the editor of the local newspaper.

Key Terms

absentee voting
annual registration
permanent registration
political participation
poll tax

registered voters
same-day registration
socioeconomic factors
voter registration
voter turnout

voting-age population
voting-eligible population
white primary

Notes

[1] Aaron Smith, "Civic Engagement in the Digital Age," Pew Research Center, April 25, 2013, http://www.pewinternet.org/2013/04/25/civic-engagement-in-the-digital-age/. For raw data, see http://www.pewinternet.org/datasets/august-2012-civic-engagement/; Laura Seay, "Does slacktivism work?" *Washington Post,* March 12, 2014, https://www.washingtonpost.com/news/monkey-cage/wp/2014/03/12/does-slacktivism-work/.

[2] Sidney Verba and Norman H. Nie, *Participation in America* (Chicago: University of Chicago Press, 1987).

[3] These prohibitions are laid out in Amendments 15, 19, 24, and 26. See Constitution of the United States, Amendments 11-27, http://www.archives.gov/exhibits/charters/constitution_amendments_11-27.html.

[4] Texas Constitution art. 6, sec. 1-2. See http://www.statutes.legis.state.tx.us/Docs/CN/htm/CN.6.htm.

[5] U.S. Census Bureau, Voting and Registration (revised February 10, 2016), http://www.census.gov/topics/public-sector/voting/about.html.

[6] Texas Secretary of State, Texas Voting, http://www.sos.state.tx.us/elections/pamphlets/largepamp.shtml.

[7] Texas Department of Public Safety, Application for Texas Driver License or Identification Card, http://dps.texas.gov/internetforms/Forms/DL-14A.pdf.

[8] Texas Secretary of State, Texas Voting, http://www.sos.state.tx.us/elections/pamphlets/largepamp.shtml; VoteTexas.gov, Your Voter Registration Card, http://www.votetexas.gov/register-to-vote/550-2/.

[9] VoteTexas.gov, Required Identification for Voting in Person, accessed September 3, 2016, http://www.votetexas.gov/register-to-vote/need-id/.

[10] Texas Department of Public Safety, Election Identification Certificate (EIC), http://www.txdps.state.tx.us/driverlicense/electionid.htm.

[11] Ibid., 217.

[12] Texas Secretary of State, Early Voting, http://www.votetexas.gov/voting/when/#early-voting; Texas Secretary of State, Military and Overseas Voters, http://www.votetexas.gov/voting/#military-and-overseas-voters.

[13] "Tribpedia: Voter ID," *Texas Tribune,* https://www.texastribune.org/tribpedia/voter-id/about/.

[14] U.S. Department of Justice, The Voting Rights Act of 1965, http://www.justice.gov/crt/about/vot/intro/intro_b.php.

[15] For the court's opinion, see *State of Texas v. Holder,* available online at http://electionlawblog.org/wp-content/uploads/texas-voter-id.pdf.

[16] Adam Liptak, "Supreme Court Invalidates Key Part of Voting Rights Act," *New York Times,* June 25, 2013, http://www.nytimes.com/2013/06/26/us/supreme-court-ruling.html?pagewanted=all&_r=0; For the Supreme Court's ruling, see Shelby County, Alabama v. Holder, available online at http://www.supremecourt.gov/opinions/12pdf/12-96_6k47.pdf.

[17] Todd J. Gillman, "'Texas voter ID law will take effect immediately,' says Attorney General Greg Abbott," *The Dallas Morning News,* June 25, 2013, http://trailblazersblog.dallasnews.com/2013/06/texas-voter-id-law-could-start-now-attorney-general-greg-abbott.html/.

[18] Jim Malewitz, "Court: Texas Voter ID Law Violates Voting Rights Act," *Texas Tribune,* August 5, 2015, https://www.texastribune.org/2015/08/05/ruling-offers-texas-voter-id-critics-narrow-victor/.

[19] Jim Malewitz, "Texas Voter ID Law Violates Voting Rights Act, Court Rules," *Texas Tribune,* July 20, 2016, https://www.texastribune.org/2016/07/20 /appeals-court-rules-texas-voter-id/; Khorri Atkinson, "Federal Judge Approves Plan to Weaken Texas Voter ID Law," *Texas Tribune,* August 10, 2016, https://www.texastribune.org/2016/08/10 /fed-judge-approves-plan-weaken-texas-voter-id-law/.

[20] Lise Olsen, "State to review thousands of motor voter registration complaints," *Houston Chronicle,* July 3, 2015, http://www.houstonchronicle.com/politics /election/state/article/State-to-review-thousands-of-motor-voter-6365671.php.

[21] Chuck Lindell, "Texas sued over 'motor-voter' law compliance," *Austin American-Statesman,* March 14, 2016, http://www.mystatesman.com/news/news /texas-sued-over-motor-voter-law-compliance/nqkfY/.

[22] Three states—California, Hawaii, and Vermont—have legalized same-day registration, but as of April 2016 those laws had not yet gone into effect. See NationalConference of State Legislatures, Same Day Voter Registration (6/2/2015), http://www.ncsl.org /research/elections-and-campaigns/same-day-registration.aspx.

[23] Barry C. Burden, David T. Canon, Kenneth R. Mayer, and Donald P. Moynihan, "Election Laws, Mobilization, and Turnout: The Unanticipated Consequences of Election Reform," *American Journal of Political Science* 58:1 (January 2014).

[24] North Dakota Secretary of State, North Dakota. . . . The Only State Without Voter Registration (revised July 2015), https://vip.sos.nd.gov/pdfs/portals/votereg.pdf.

[25] National Conference of State Legislatures, Online Voter Registration (4/6/2016), http://www.ncsl.org/research /elections-and-campaigns/electronic-or-online-voter-registration.aspx#table

[26] National Conference of State Legislatures, Voter Identification Requirements | Voter ID Laws (4/11/2016), http://www.ncsl.org/research/elections-and-campaigns/voter-id.aspx.

[27] Michael P. McDonald, "Why not calculate turnout rates as percentage of registered voters?" Voter Turnout FAQ, *United States Elections Project,* http://www.electproject .org/home/voter-turnout/faq/reg.

[28] Thomas Holbrook and Brianne Heidbreder, "Does Measurement Matter? The Case of VAP and VEP in Models of Voter Turnout in the United States," *State Politics & Policy Quarterly,* 10:2 (Summer 2010): pp. 157–179.

[29] U.S. Census Bureau, "Voting, people eligible to register," *Current Population Survey (CPS), Subject Definitions,* https://www.census.gov/programs-surveys/cps /technical-documentation/subject-definitions.html#voting.

[30] Ibid., 220.

[31] Michael P. McDonald. (2016). "Why should I care if turnout rates are calculated as percentage of VAP or VEP?" Voter Turnout Frequently Asked Questions, *United States Elections Project,* http://www.electproject.org/home /voter-turnout/faq/vap-v-vap.

[32] Michael P. McDonald (2016), "Voter Turnout," *United States Elections Project,* http://www.electproject.org/home /voter-turnout.

[33] Ibid., 218.

[34] Texas Secretary of State, Turnout and Voter Registration Figures (1970–current), http://www.sos.state.tx.us /elections/historical/70-92.shtml.

[35] Michael P. McDonald (2015), "2014 November General Election Turnout Rates," *United States Election Project,* http://www.electproject.org/2014g.

[36] Drew DeSilver, "So far, turnout in this year's primaries rivals 2008 record," Pew Research Center, March 8, 2016, http://www.pewresearch.org/fact-tank/2016/03/08 /so-far-turnout-in-this-years-primaries-rivals-2008-record/.

[37] Ibid., 222.

[38] Ibid.; Jolie McCullough, Texas Near Bottom Among States in Primary Turnout This Year, *Texas Tribune,* March 8, 2016, https://www.texastribune.org/2016/03/08/ despite-record-turnout-texas-ranks-low-among-other/.

[39] Calvert and DeLeon, *History of Texas,* 212.

[40] The state tax was $1.50. The county was permitted to add 25 cents, and most county governments did so. See Article 7, Section 3 of the Texas Constitution, 1902.

[41] Calvert and DeLeon, *History of Texas,* 387.

[42] *Texas v. United States,* 384 U.S. 155 (1966).

[43] Texas State Historical Association, "Voter Participation in Texas," *Texas Almanac,* http://texasalmanac.com/sites /default/files/images/topics/prezturnout.pdf.

[44] *Beare v. Smith,* 321 F. Supp. 1100.

[45] Ibid., 43.

[46] *Nixon v. Herndon et al.,* 273 U.S. 536 (1927).

[47] Sanford N. Greenberg, "White Primary," *Handbook of Texas Online,* published by the Texas State Historical Association, http://www.tshaonline.org/handbook/online /articles/wdw01.

[48] *Nixon v. Condon et al.,* 286 U.S. 73 (1932).

[49] Ibid., 47.

[50] *Grovey v. Townsend,* 295 U.S. 45 (1935).

[51] *Smith v. Allwright,* 321 U.S. 649 (1944). Also, in *United States v. Classic,* 313 U.S. 299 (1941), the U.S. Supreme Court ruled that a primary in a one-party state (Louisiana) was an election within the meaning of the U.S. Constitution.

[52] George McKenna, *The Drama of Democracy: American Government and Politics,* 2nd ed. (Guilford, Conn.: Dushkin, 1994), 129.

[53] A. Elizabeth Taylor, "Woman Suffrage," *Handbook of Texas Online,* http://www.tshaonline.org/handbook/online /articles/viw01.

[54] Michael P. McDonald, "Voter Turnout Demographics," *United States Election Project,* http://www.electproject.org /home/voter-turnout/demographics.

[55] Ibid. (See http://www.electproject.org/home/voter-turnout/ demographics.)

[56] Stacy Teicher Khadaroo, "Youth vote decides presidential election – again. Is this the new normal?" *Christian Science Monitor,* http://www.csmonitor.com/USA /Elections/President/2012/1107/Youth-vote-decides- presidential-election-again.-Is-this-the-new-normal.

[57] Ibid., 226.

[58] U.S. Census Bureau, "Voting and Registration in the Election of 2012—Detailed Tables," Table 4b, Reported Voting and Registration by Sex, Race and Hispanic Origin, for States: November 2012, http://www.census. gov/hhes/www/socdemo/voting/publications/p20/2012 /tables.html.

[59] Ibid., 226.

[60] Ibid., 226.

[61] Jens Manuel Krogstad, Mark Hugo Lopez, Gustavo Lopez, Jeffrey S. Passel, and Eileen Patten, "Millennials Make Up Almost Half of Latino Eligible Voters in 2016," Pew Research Center, January 19, 2016, http://www .pewhispanic.org/2016/01/19/millennials-make-up-almost- half-of-latino-eligible-voters-in-2016/.

[62] Ibid.; Paul Taylor, Ana Gonzalez-Barrera, Jeffrey S. Passel and Mark Hugo Lopez, "An Awakened Giant: The Hispanic Electorate is Likely to Double by 2030," Pew Research Center, November 14, 2012, http://www .pewhispanic.org/2012/11/14/an-awakened-giant-the- hispanic-electorate-is-likely-to-double-by-2030/.

[63] Ibid., 228."

[64] Mark Hugo Lopez and Ana Gonzalez-Barrera, "Inside the 2012 Latino Electorate," Pew Research Center, June 3, 2013, http://www.pewhispanic.org/2013/06/03 /inside-the-2012-latino-electorate/.

[65] Ibid., 228.

[66] Ibid.

[67] Matt Stiles and Zahira Torres, "Texas Still Waiting for Latinos to Show Power at Polls," *Texas Tribune,* July 26, 2010, https://www.texastribune.org/2010/07/26 /texas-still-waiting-for-latinos-to-vote/.

[68] National Conference of State Legislatures, Felon Voting Rights (1/4/2016), http://www.ncsl.org/research/elections- and-campaigns/felon-voting-rights.aspx.

[69] Texas Secretary of State, Effect of Felony Conviction on Voter Registration, http://www.sos.state.tx.us/elections /laws/effects.shtml.

[70] Michael P. McDonald, 1980–2014 November General Election, *United States Election Project,* http://www .electproject.org/home/voter-turnout/voter-turnout-data.

[71] See Andre Blais, "What Affects Voter Turnout?" *Annual Review of Political Science* 9 (2006), 119.

[72] See ibid., and G. Bingham Powell, Jr. "American Voter Turnout in Comparative Perspective," *American Political Science Review,* 80:1 (March 1986), pp. 17–43.

[73] Texas Secretary of State, Historical Election Results (1992–Current), http://elections.sos.state.tx.us/index.htm.

[74] Ballotpedia, Municipal elections in Austin, Texas (2014), https://ballotpedia.org/ Municipal_elections_in_Austin,_Texas_(2014).

[75] Peter Grier, "Election Day 2010: Why we always vote on Tuesdays," *Christian Science Monitor,* November 2, 2010, http://www.csmonitor.com/ USA/DC-Decoder/Decoder-Wire/2010/1102/ Election-Day-2010-Why-we-always-vote-on-Tuesdays

[76] Blais, 116.

[77] Julia Van Susteren, "Early Voting Has Little Effect," *Badger Herald,* October 2, 2012, http://badgerherald.com /news/2012/10/02/early_voting_has_lit.php.

[78] Kenneth Arrow, "The Organization of Economic Activity: Issues Pertinent to the Choice of Market versus Non- market Allocation," 1969, http://msuweb.montclair.edu /lebelp/PSC643IntPolEcon/ArrowNonMktActivity1969. pdf. I first saw this quoted in a draft paper by David P. Myatt titled, "On the Rational Choice Theory of Voter Turnout." There is an enormous amount of research on this question, starting with key works such as Anthony Downs, *An Economic Theory of Democracy* (New York: Harper and Row, 1957); Gordon Tullock, *Toward a Mathematics of Politics* (Ann Arbor: University of Michigan Press, 1967); and William Riker and Peter Ordeshook, "A Theory of the Calculus of Voting." *American Political Science Review* 62:1(1968): 25–42.

[79] For a review of the literature on "expressive" voting, see Alan Hamlin and Colin Jennings, "Expressive Political

Behaviour: Foundations, Scope and Implications," *British Journal of Political Science* (2011).

[80] See Arrow.

[81] Texas Statewide Survey, University of Texas at Austin, *Texas Tribune,* March 2009.

[82] Center for Responsive Politics, Top States Funding Candidates. http://www.opensecrets.org/pres12/pres_stateAll.php?list=all

[83] Center for Responsive Politics, Fundraising By Party. http://www.opensecrets.org/pres12/states.php

[84] Henry Brady, Sidney Verba, and Kay Schlozman, "Beyond SES: A Resource Model of Political Participation," *American Political Science Review* 89:2 (June 1995).

[85] See graph of "Presidential Turnout Rates 1948–2012," Michael P. McDonald, "Voter Turnout," *United States Election Project,* http://www.electproject.org/home/voter-turnout.

[86] Russell Dalton, *The Good Citizen: How a Younger Generation Is Reshaping American Politics,* (Washington, D.C.: CQ Press, 2008).

[87] Many scholars have found this to be the case. See Blais, 123.

CHAPTER 8

Campaigns and Elections in Texas

Texas Learning Outcomes

- Analyze the state and local election process in Texas.

Elections are the heart of any democratic system and perform a number of important functions that make government work. Elections bestow legitimacy upon government; without them, all actions of governments are questionable. Elections provide for an orderly transition of power from one group to another where, most importantly, the public perceives the newly elected government as legitimate. One of the great stabilizing forces in the American system of government has been this orderly transfer of power. Elections also allow citizens to express their opinions about public policy choices. By voting in elections, citizens express what they want the government to do. Elections are still the most essential element of any democracy, despite the fact that many citizens do not participate in them.

Delegates to the Texas GOP Convention cheer for outgoing Gov. Rick Perry after his speech in Fort Worth, Texas on Thursday, June, 5, 2014. In his address, the longest-serving governor in the state's history focused more on the future and national issues than his political legacy at home.

© Rodger Mallison/Fort Worth Star-Telegram/MCT/Getty Images

Elections occur at regular intervals as determined by state and federal laws. All states conduct elections on two-year cycles. The date established by federal law for electing members of the U.S. Congress and the president is the first Tuesday after the first Monday in November of even-numbered years. States must elect members of Congress and vote for the president on this date. Most states also use this November date to elect governors, state officials, state legislators, and some local offices.

Texas holds **general elections** every two years. During nonpresidential years, voters elect candidates to statewide offices: governor, lieutenant governor, attorney general, land commissioner, agricultural commissioner, comptroller, some members of the Texas Railroad Commission and the Texas State Board of Education, and some members of the Texas Supreme Court and the Court of Criminal Appeals.[1] Before 1976, all nonjudicial

general elections
Regular elections held every two years to elect state officeholders

officeholders served two-year terms. In 1977 the state constitution was amended, and in 1978, four-year terms were first used.

Every two years, voters also elect all 150 members of the Texas House of Representatives (for two-year terms), one-half of the members of the Texas Senate (for four-year terms), many judges to various courts, and local county officials.[2]

Chapter Learning Objectives

- Discuss ballot forms in Texas.

- Discuss ballot access in Texas.

- Describe primary elections.

- Explain special elections.

- Describe the federal Voting Rights Act.

- Discuss absentee and early voting.

- Discuss ways in which the nature of elections has changed.

- Describe political campaigns in Texas, including the use of consultants and the role of money.

Ballot Form

Learning Objective: Discuss ballot forms in Texas.

ballot form

The forms used by voters to cast their ballots; each county, with approval of the secretary of state, determines the form of the ballot

party column format

Paper ballot form where candidates are listed by party and by office

Each county in Texas decides the **ballot form** and method of casting ballots. The method used to cast votes must be approved by the secretary of state's office. Some systems are precleared by the secretary of state's office, and counties can choose any of these systems.

Texas counties formerly used paper ballots with a **party column format**, where candidates were listed by party and by office. The party that holds the governor's office was the first party column on the ballot. Being first on the ballot is an advantage—voters often choose the first name when all candidates are unfamiliar to them. The party column ballot also encouraged straight-ticket voting and was advocated strongly by the Democratic Party for many years. In recent years, straight-ticket voting has worked to the advantage of the Republicans in some elections, especially judicial offices.

Since the 2008 election, all 254 counties in Texas have used electronic voting systems. These systems were purchased with federal funds provided by the Help America Vote Act of 2002. The secretary of state must approve all electronic voting systems before counties can purchase them. Three systems are currently approved by the secretary of state's office. The Premier Election System (formerly called Diebold) is used by seven counties in Texas; the Electronic Systems Software (ES&S) is used by 146 counties; and the Hart e-slate systems are used by 101 counties.[3]

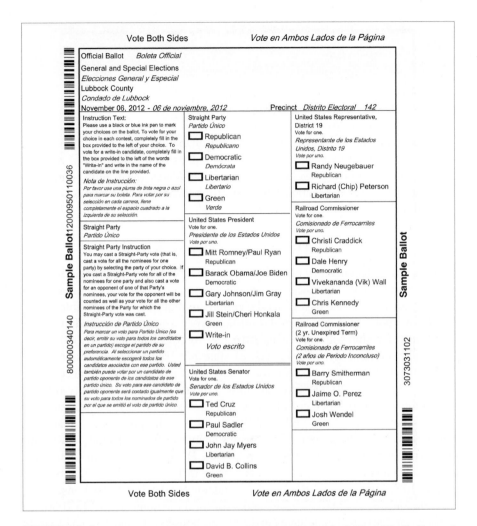

FIGURE 8.1   A Sample Texas General Election Ballot in Office Block Format

SOURCE: Adapted from Sidney Verba and Norman Nie, *Participation in America: Political Democracy and Social Equality* (Chicago: University of Chicago Press, 1987), 79.

© *Courtesy of Texas Secretary of State*

Most computer ballots are in **office block format** (see Figure 8.1). This ballot form lists the office (e.g., president), followed by the candidates by party (e.g., Republican: Donald Trump, Democrat: Hillary Clinton). The ballot for each county system in Texas can be found on individual county websites or the Texas Secretary of State website prior to each election.

The office block format is often advocated as a way of discouraging straight-ticket voting, the impact of which is discussed in Chapter 9. However, Texas law allows computer-readable ballots to enable voters to vote a straight ticket. By marking a single place on the ballot, the voter can vote for all candidates for that party. The voter can then override this by voting in individual races. For example, a voter could vote a straight Republican ticket, but override this and vote for the Democratic candidate for selected offices.

office block format

Ballot form where candidates are listed by office with party affiliation listed by their name; most often used with computer ballots

Ballot Access to the November General Election

Learning Objective: Discuss ballot access in Texas.

To appear on the November general election ballot, candidates must meet criteria established by state law. Each state has its own unique set of requirements. These criteria prevent the lists of candidates from being unreasonably long. The Texas Election Code specifies three ways for names to be on the ballot.[4]

Independent and Third-Party Candidates

To run as an independent, a candidate must file a petition with a specified number of signatures. For statewide office, signatures equal to 1 percent of the votes cast for governor in the past general election are required.[5] For example, in the 2014 governor's race, a total of 4.7 million votes were cast.[6] An **independent candidate** for statewide office in 2016 had to collect at least 47,000 signatures. For multicounty offices, such as state representative, signatures equal to 5 percent of the votes cast for that office in the past election are needed. On average, 30,000 to 40,000 votes are cast in house races.[7] For county offices, signatures equal to 5 percent of votes cast for those offices are needed. This might seem like a large number of signatures, but the process is intended to weed out people who do not have a serious chance of being elected. Few candidates file for statewide office as independents. However, it is not uncommon to have independents for house and senate races. In 1996, 13 people filed by petition as Libertarians and 2 filed as independents for the 150 Texas house seats. In 1998, only 3 people filed as independents for these house seats.[8] In 2000, the Libertarian Party had candidates in 22 of 150 house seats and 1 senate seat. In 2002, the Libertarian Party fielded 12 candidates for the state senate and 29 for the state house. Even if these candidates declare a party, such as Libertarian, they may still be considered independents under the state election code.

Obtaining signatures on a petition is not easy. Each signer must be a registered voter and must not have participated in the primary elections of other parties in that electoral cycle. For example, persons who voted in either the Democratic or the Republican Party primary in 1996 were not eligible to sign a petition to have Ross Perot's Reform Party placed on the 1996 ballot. Signing the petition is considered the same as voting. This provision of state law makes it all the more difficult for independents to gather signatures and be placed on the ballot.

The 2006 governor's race in Texas was an exception to this. Carole Keeton Strayhorn, then comptroller, and Kinky Friedman, a country-western singer and mystery writer, qualified for positions on the ballot as independents. Friedman and Strayhorn suffered the same fate as most independent and minor party candidates: they did not win, but they pulled enough votes away from the Democratic candidate to upset the election outcome. Governor Perry won with a plurality of 38.1 percent while Friedman won 12.6 percent and Strayhorn 18

independent candidate
A person whose name appears on the ballot without a political party designation

percent. Chris Bell, the Democratic candidate, did better than expected with 30 percent. The role of these independent candidates was to help reelect the Republican governor who, after six years in office, managed to capture less than 40 percent of the votes.

Candidates who were defeated in the primary election may not file as independents in the general election for that year. This is the **"sore loser" law**. Write-in candidates are sometimes confused with people who file and are listed on the ballot as independents. The process of filing as a write-in candidate is a separate procedure. To be "official" **write-in candidates**, individuals must file their intention before the election. This is true for all elections, including local, city, and school board elections. If a person does not file before the election, votes for that person are not counted. For some state offices, a filing fee may be required to have a person's name listed on the ballot as a write-in candidate. The amount varies from $3,750 for statewide office to as little as $300 for members of the State Board of Education.[9] People sometimes write in things such as "Mickey Mouse" and "None of the above." These are recorded but not counted. In 1990, nineteen write-in candidates filed for governor. Bubbles Cash, a retired Dallas stripper, led the pack with 3,287 out of a total of 11,700 write-in votes.[10]

"sore loser" law
Law in Texas that prevents a person who lost the primary vote from running as an independent or minor party candidate

write-in candidate
A person whose name does not appear on the ballot; voters must write in that person's name, and the person must have led a formal notice that he or she was a write-in candidate before the election

---

CORE OBJECTIVE

Thinking Critically. . .

Explain the challenges that hinder minor party candidates from succeeding in statewide elections.

Source: National Park Service

Party Caucus

The state election code defines a **minor party** (sometimes called a *third party*) as any political organization that receives between 5 and 19 percent of the total votes cast for any statewide office in the past general election. In the past 50 years, there have been four minor parties: the Raza Unida Party in South Texas in the 1970s,[11] the Socialist Workers Party in 1988, and the Libertarian Party and the Green Party in the 1990s and 2000s. Parties that achieve minor-party status must nominate their candidates in a **party caucus** or convention and are exempt from the petition requirement discussed previously. Currently, only the Libertarian Party and the Green Party qualify as minor parties in Texas.[12]

The Texas Election Code defines a *major party* as any organization receiving 20 percent or more of the total votes cast for governor in the past election. Only the Democratic and Republican parties hold this status today. By law, these party organizations must nominate their candidates in a **primary election**.

minor party
A party other than the Democratic or Republican Party; to be a minor party in Texas, the organization must have received between 5 and 19 percent of the vote in the past election

party caucus
A meeting of members of a political party to nominate candidates (used only by minor political parties in Texas)

primary election
An election used by major political parties in Texas to nominate candidates for the November general election

Former gubernatorial candidate Bill White served three full terms as the 60th Mayor of Houston (2004–2010). Previously, he served as the U.S. Deputy Secretary of Energy from 1993 to 1995 under President Bill Clinton.

© Duane A. Laverty/Waco Herald Tribune/AP Images

open primary system

A nominating election that is open to all registered voters regardless of party affiliation

closed primary system

A nominating election that is closed to all voters except those who have registered as a member of that political party

semi-closed primary system

A nominating election that is open to all registered voters, but voters are required to declare party affiliation when they vote in the primary election

semi-open primary system

Voter may choose to vote in the primary of either party on Election Day; voters are considered "declared" for the party in whose primary they vote

By definition, Texas has an **open primary system**, but this is a bit misleading because there can also be an argument for it having a semi-open system, as discussed shortly. Open primaries allow the voter to vote in any primary without a party declaration. The voter can vote as a Democrat and attend the Republican precinct convention or participate in any activity of the opposite party.

A **closed primary system** is currently used in 15 states. This system requires voters to declare their party affiliation when they register to vote. They may vote only in the primary of their party registration. Most of these states have a time limit after which a voter may not change part affiliation before the election.

There are several important variations of open and closed primaries (see Table 8.1). A **semi-closed primary system** allows voters to register or change their party registration on Election Day. Independents may vote in the primary of their choice, but otherwise, registered members may only vote in their party's primary. In a **semi-open primary system**, the voter may choose to vote in the primary of either party on Election Day. After they request a specific party ballot, however, voters are considered "declared" for the party in whose primary they vote. If you vote in the Republican Party primary, you are in effect declaring that you are a member of that party. You may not participate in any activity of any other party for the remainder of that election year. For example, if you vote in the Republican primary, you may not attend the precinct convention of the Democratic Party. This also limits the voter in other ways.

Texas is, perhaps confusingly, also commonly labeled as having a semi-open system (see Table 8.1). Although Texas does have an open primary system, the state also restricts voters to a certain degree (though not to the extent of a more by-the-book semi-open system). Voters in Texas do not have to declare a party, but when attending a primary, they must choose a ticket and pick only from the candidates in that party. After the primary is over, however, voters can cross party lines. In addition, when the next year begins, voters receive a new registration card and are free to vote however they choose. Texas might be best labeled as having a (semi-) open system.

In the past, Alaska, California, and Washington used a **blanket primary**. This system allowed voters to switch parties between offices. A voter might vote in the Republican primary for the races for governor and U.S. House, and in the Democratic primary for the U.S. Senate race. These have been ruled unconstitutional by the U.S. Supreme Court (*California Democratic Party v. Jones*, 2000). Alaska currently uses a closed primary with voter registration by party, whereas California has adopted an open primary system. Washington has adopted Louisiana's system of a nonpartisan primary for all statewide and U.S. House and Senate races. Under this system, all candidates are listed on the ballot by

TABLE 8.1

Primary Systems Used in State Elections

Closed Primary: Party Registration Required before Election Day

Alaska	Kentucky	New Mexico
Connecticut	Maine	New York
Delaware	Nebraska	Oklahoma
Florida	Nevada	Pennsylvania
Idaho*	New Jersey	South Dakota

Semi-closed Primary: Voters May Register or Change Registration on Election Day

Arizona	Massachusetts	Utah
Colorado	New Hampshire	West Virginia
Iowa	North Carolina	Wyoming
Kansas	Oregon	
Maryland	Rhode Island	

Semi-open Primary: Voters Required to Request Party Ballot

Alabama	Mississippi	Virginia
Arkansas	Ohio	
Georgia	South Carolina	
Illinois	Tennessee	
Indiana	Texas	

Open Primary: Voters May Vote in Any Party Primary

California	Montana
Hawaii	North Dakota
Michigan	Vermont
Minnesota	Wisconsin
Missouri	

Nonpartisan: Voters May Switch Parties between Races

Louisiana	Washington

Source: John R. Biddy and Thomas M. Holbrook, "Parties and Elections," in *Politics in American States: A Comparative Analysis,* 8th ed., edited by Virginia Gray and Russell L. Hanson (Washington, D.C.: Congressional Quarterly Press, 2004).

In the original chart from 2004, Idaho had an open primary system. In 2011, its legislature passed House Bill 351 in response to a court case finding the open primary system unconstitutional as applied to the state's Republican party. As a result, the state moved to a closed system.[13]

© Pat Sullivan/AP Images

office. The voter can choose one candidate per office. If no person receives a majority, the top two candidates face each other in a runoff. This can result in two candidates from the same party facing each other in a runoff election.

blanket primary system
A nominating election in which voters could switch parties between elections

Political Differences between Open and Closed Primary Systems

Learning Objective: Describe primary elections.

The primary system used in a state may affect the party system in the state. Advocates of the closed primary system say that it encourages party identification and loyalty and, therefore, helps build stronger party systems. Open primary systems, they say, allow participation by independents with no loyalty to the party, which weakens party organization. There is no strong evidence that this is the case.

Open primaries do allow **crossover voting**. This occurs when voters leave their party and vote in the other party's primary. Occasionally voters in one party might vote in the other party's primary in hopes of nominating a candidate from the other party whose philosophy is similar to their own. For example, Republicans have been accused of voting in the Democratic primary in Texas to ensure that a conservative will be nominated. This occurred in the 1970 U.S. Senate race when Republicans voted for the more conservative Lloyd Bentsen over the liberal Ralph Yarborough. Many voting precincts carried by Bentsen in the Democratic primary voted for Republican George H. W. Bush in the general election.

From 1996 to 2002, more Texans voted in the Republican primaries than in the Democratic primaries. Republicans claimed that this was evidence that their party was the majority party. Democrats suggest that these differences in turnout are explained by the low levels of opposition in the Democratic primaries. For instance, President Bill Clinton did not have any opposition in his primary election, whereas Bob Dole and Pat Buchanan were still actively seeking the Republican nomination. Some Democratic Party leaders claim that many traditional Democratic Party voters, therefore, crossed over and voted in the Republican primary in an attempt to affect the Republican outcome. As it turned out, the Democrats' explanation may be the more accurate.

Party raiding occurs when members of one political party vote in another party's primary; it is difficult to orchestrate. What distinguishes party raiding from crossover voting is that whereas crossover voting may be genuine (another party's candidate appeals to voters), party raiding is intentional and designed to nominate a weaker candidate or split the vote among the strongest contenders. Although there are often accusations of such behavior during primary elections, it is difficult to prove. Additionally, although there have been attempts to organize party raids, it is unclear whether they are effective. A notable example during the 2008 primary was Operation Chaos, in which popular conservative talk radio host Rush Limbaugh encouraged Republicans to vote in Democratic primaries for Hillary Clinton in order to weaken then-candidate Obama.[14] More recently, in 2012, voters in Michigan attempted to disrupt the Republican primary by voting for Rick Santorum over front-runner Mitt Romney.[15] In both cases, efforts were ineffective in changing the outcome.

Runoff primaries are held in 11 states: Alabama, Arkansas, Georgia, Louisiana, Mississippi, North Carolina, Oklahoma, South Carolina, South Dakota, Texas, and Vermont.[16] A **runoff primary** is required if no candidate receives a majority in the first primary. Until recently in the South, winning the Democratic Party primary was the same as winning the general election, and the runoff primary became a fixture, supposedly as a way of requiring the winner to have "majority" support. In reality, voter turnout in the runoff primary is almost always lower than in the first primary, sometimes substantially lower. The "majority" winner often is selected by a small percentage of the electorate—those who bother to participate in the runoff primary.

---

crossover voting
Occurs when voters leave their party and vote in the other party's primary

party raiding
Occurs when members of one political party vote in another party's primary in an effort to nominate a weaker candidate or split the vote among the top candidates

runoff primary
Election that is required if no person receives a majority in the primary election; primarily used in southern and border states

The Federal Voting Rights Act

Learning Objective: Describe the federal Voting Rights Act.

In 1965, under the leadership of President Lyndon Johnson, the U.S. Congress passed the Voting Rights Act. As previously mentioned in Chapters 6 and 7, this act has had extensive effects upon the state of Texas and the conduct of elections. After being passed in 1965 and extended to Texas in 1975, the **Voting Rights Act**

Voting Rights Act
A federal law aimed at preventing racial discrimination in the operation of voter registration and elections at the state level

Focus On

The Hispanic Population and Bilingual Ballots

© Niyazz/Shutterstock

When the Voting Rights Act was amended in 1975, one of the included special provisions prohibited discrimination against or denial of voting rights to members of "language minorities." This provision covers speakers of Spanish, Asian, Native American, and Alaskan Native languages. These groups in particular were singled out because Congress determined that they had "suffered a history of exclusion from the political process."[19] Prior to this, some jurisdictions had imposed a literacy test, in English, as a prerequisite for voting.

As a result of this law, localities must provide all election-related information—including ballots (regular, absentee, and sample), voter registration forms, voter instruction pamphlets, official notices of elections and polling place locations, candidate qualifying information, website information, and frequently asked questions at polling places—"in the language of the applicable minority group as well as in the English language."[20] This provision applies to all elections—federal, state, and local—from general and primary elections to school board elections and bond referenda. In addition, polling places are

required to employ bilingual poll workers on Election Day, and bilingual employees must be available to answer voting and election-related questions in government offices. A precinct must comply with these requirements if it contains a significant number of minority language voters, which is defined as more than 5 percent of its voting-age citizens, or more than 10,000 voting-age citizens within the precinct, who speak a single minority language.[21]

Texas has been printing ballots in both English and Spanish statewide, as well as providing bilingual voting clerks in certain precincts, since 1975.[22] Texas election code specifies the method for identifying voters of Spanish origin or descent, using census data to determine the percentage of voters within each precinct who have Hispanic surnames. Precincts are required to provide bilingual election workers if 5 percent or more of their voters have Hispanic surnames.[23] (Incidentally, due to Voting Rights Act requirements, a few counties in Texas must offer materials in a third language, in addition to English and Spanish. Harris County, for example, must also provide election materials in Vietnamese.[24])

The legal requirement for bilingual ballots has generated controversy. Supporters have argued that such accommodations are necessary to give all citizens the opportunity to vote, while opponents have pointed to the cost, borne by local governments, of complying with these regulations, even when many jurisdictions are facing budget constraints.[25]

Critical Thinking Questions

1. What are bilingual ballots and how does the provision requiring them relate to Texas and its Hispanic population?

2. Why might this legal requirement be generating controversy?

required preclearance by the U.S. Justice Department of all changes in the election procedures, including such things as ballot reform, the time and place of an election, and the method of electing legislators.[18]

Until 2013, the Voting Rights Act allowed the federal government to oversee the operation of elections at a state level. The greatest impact had been felt in southern states, where racial and ethnic minorities were formerly barred from participating in elections (see Chapter 6). When the U.S. Supreme Court struck down Section 4 of the Voting Rights Act in *Shelby County v. Holder* in late June 2013, certain states identified within the law no longer had to receive federal approval before changing any in-state voting procedure. Indeed, Texas and other states had been trying to legislate voter identification laws for several years without success. Once Section 4 no longer applied, Texas immediately put its voter identification laws into effect. They applied from November 2013 forward, though a court order modified their implementation for the 2016 election (see Chapter 7). The other sections of the Voting Rights Act are still functioning.

CORE OBJECTIVE

© George Lavendowski/USFWS

Communicating Effectively . . .

Do you think the Voting Rights Act requirement that Texas provide a bilingual ballot increases voter turnout? Construct an argument in favor or against this provision of the Voting Rights Act.

Absentee and Early Voting

Learning Objective: Discuss absentee and early voting.

absentee voting
A process that allows a person to vote early, before the regular election; applies to all elections in Texas; also called early voting

All states allow some form of **absentee voting**. This practice began as a way to allow members of the U.S. armed services who were stationed in other states or overseas to vote. In all but a few states, it has been extended to other individuals. In most states, persons who will be out of the county on Election Day may file for absentee voting.

In Texas before 1979, to vote absentee, voters had to sign an affidavit saying they would be out of the county and unable to vote on Election Day. They could also file for an absentee ballot to be sent to them if they were living out of state or confined to a hospital or nursing home. In 1979, the state legislature changed the rules to allow anyone to vote absentee without restrictions. In Texas this is called "early voting." Early voting now begins 17 days before an election and closes four days before the election.[26] During that period, polls are typically open from 7 a.m. to 7 p.m. Voters simply go to an early polling place and vote as they would on Election Day.

The Changing Nature of Elections

Learning Objective: Discuss ways in which the nature of elections has changed.

If you go back 30 to 40 years, you will find that social issues were rarely a facet of state and national politics. The civil rights movement was an exception. Today, such issues as abortion, gay rights, women's rights, gun control, the environment, and health care dominate elections. All these issues excite passions in the minds of voters. To some degree, this is why politics have become so partisan. Many people have very strong feelings about these issues and maintain their positions on these issues throughout their lives. Some individuals believe that their views are endorsed by God; often these "value voters" consider people who don't agree with them to be valueless. Other individuals feel strongly that human rights should never be dictated by religion or majority opinion. Most of the time, neither side will compromise on such wedge issues. For example, in the 2004 presidential election, 14 states had antigay marriage propositions on the ballot. This turned out an impressive number of so called "value voters" and infuriated supporters of gay rights.

Three other changes in elections are also worth noting. First, labor unions have declined in the United States as a voice in elections because of manufacturing jobs being shipped overseas and southern states that have antiunion (right-to-work) statutes, including Texas. Second, the Catholic and male votes, which used to be overwhelmingly Democratic, have migrated over to the Republican Party because of such issues as abortion and gay rights. Many Catholics have formed alliances with Christian fundamentalist groups, and many traditional old-line males have gravitated further to the right. And third, changes in the media have had an enormous impact on politics. Influential 24-hour news networks such as CNN and Fox News, as well as email campaigns and political activity through social networking websites, have changed the way election campaigns are run and often have undue influence on the outcome of elections (see Chapter 14).

Campaigns

Learning Objective: Describe political campaigns in Texas, including the use of consultants and the role of money.

Campaign activity in Texas has changed considerably in the past two or three decades. These changes are not unique to Texas but are part of a national trend. Norman Brown, in his book on Texas politics in the 1920s, describes the form of political campaigning in the state as "local affairs."[27] Candidates would travel from county seat to county seat and give "stump" speeches to political

The Texas legislature's incumbent Republican Speaker of the House, Joe Straus, campaigns for re-election during the 2016 election season.

© Scott Ball

rallies arranged by local supporters. Brown devotes special attention to the campaigns of governors Jim and Miriam Ferguson ("Pa" and "Ma" Ferguson). Jim Ferguson, when campaigning for himself and later for his wife, would travel from county to county, telling each group what they wanted to hear—often saying different things in different counties. Brown contends that, unlike candidates today, Ferguson and other candidates could do this because of the lack of a statewide press to report on these inconsistencies in such political speeches.

The Role of the Media in Campaigns and Elections

In modern-day Texas, the media play a significant role in political campaigns. Reporters often follow candidates for statewide office as they travel the vast expanses of Texas. Political rallies are still held but are most often used to gain media attention and convey the candidate's message to a larger audience. Candidates hope these events will convey a favorable image of them to the public.

Heavy media coverage can have its disadvantages for the candidates. For instance, in 1990 Clayton Williams, the Republican candidate for governor, held a media event on one of his West Texas ranches. He and "the boys" were to round up cattle for branding in a display designed to portray Williams as a hardworking rancher. Unfortunately for Williams, rain spoiled the event and it had to be postponed. Resigned to the rain delay, Williams told the reporters, "It's like rape. When it's inevitable, relax and enjoy it." The state press had a field day with this remark, and it probably hurt Williams's chances with many voters. The fact that his opponent was a woman (Ann Richards) helped to magnify the significance of the statement.[28]

Similarly, in 1994, George W. Bush was the Republican candidate for governor running against incumbent Ann Richards. In Texas, the opening day of dove season is in September, and the event marks the beginning of the fall hunting season. Both Bush and Richards participated in opening-day hunts in an attempt to appeal to the strong hunting and gun element in the state. Unfortunately for Bush, he shot a killdeer by mistake rather than a dove. Pictures of Bush holding the dead bird appeared in most state papers and on television. He was fined for shooting a migratory bird. A Texas Democratic group in Austin produced bumper stickers reading: "Guns don't kill killdeer. People do." In 1998, Governor Bush did not have a media event for the opening day of dove season. He was so far ahead in the polls that even opening the issue could result in nothing but a painful reminder.

Most campaign events are not as disastrous as the cattle-branding and dove-hunting incidents. Some gain attention and free media coverage for the candidate; however, free media attention is never enough. Candidates must purchase time on television and radio and space in newspapers. In a state as large as Texas, this can be quite costly. The media and its role in both national and state elections are discussed in much more detail in Chapter 14.

Being Socially Responsible. . .

What responsibility do you think the media have in covering campaigns and elections? Are the media living up to your expectations?

Political Consultants

The use of professional campaign consultants is common in almost all races. Most candidates find it necessary to have such professionals help run their campaigns. If their opponents use professionals, candidates might be disadvantaged by not having one. Professional campaign consultants use many techniques. They take public opinion polls to measure voter reaction to issues so the candidate knows what stands to take. They run **focus groups** in which a panel of "average citizens" is asked to react to issues or words. Consultants also help the candidate in the design of written and visual advertisements and generally "package" the candidate to the voters. In 2002, David Dewhurst filmed a TV spot for his consulting firm, praising its effectiveness in making him look professional. Public opinion polling is further discussed in Chapter 14.

focus group
Panel of "average citizens" who are used by political consultants to test ideas and words for later use in campaigns

Money in Campaigns

Using media advertisement, professional consultants, and a full-time paid campaign staff increases the cost of running for state office. The cost can run into the millions, even for a race for the Texas House of Representatives.

The amount of money spent in campaigns is increasing each election cycle. Most of this money comes from political action committees (PACs). Table 8.2 shows the increase in the total amount of money contributed by PACs 2006 to 2014. Only at the start of the new decade was there any decrease and that was only in the ideological sector. The business sector continues to increase and makes up a significant majority of total PAC campaign contributions.

As shown in Table 8.3, statewide races can be quite costly, and costs have continued to increase. Most of the money is coming from PACs, which obviously want something from government for their contributions. A few candidates, such

TABLE 8.2

Total PAC Money in State Campaigns from 2006 to 2014

Sector	2006 Cycle	2008 Cycle	2010 Cycle	2012 Cycle	2014 Cycle	Growth
Business	$57,034,732	$ 62,741,376	$ 68,235,849	$ 70,399,948	$ 81,135,492	15%
Ideology	$37,003,210	$ 50,403,265	$ 57,847,226	$ 47,292,862	$ 65,225,862	38%
Labor	$ 5,116,613	$ 6,307,456	$ 7,032,134	$ 8,173,262	$ 12,085,061	48%
Unknown	$ 13,099	$ 109,764	$ 330,977	$ 501,388	$ 868,218	73%
Totals	$99,167,654	$119,561,860	$133,446,187	$126,267,460	$ 159,314,633	26%

Source: Texas PACs: 2014 Election Cycle Spending. February 2016. See (www.tpj.org).

TABLE 8.3

Total Contributions Raised by Major Party Candidates by Office in 2010

Office	Loser Total	Primary Loser Total	Winner Total	Candidates
Governor	$26,298,865	$16,565,395	$39,328,540	8
Attorney General	$ 910,779	NA	$ 5,828,869	2
Comptroller	NA	NA	$ 2,716,730	1
Land Commissioner	$ 98,758	$ 2,270	$ 863,307	3
Lieutenant Governor	$ 949,944	$ 56,772	$10,635,480	4
Texas House	$15,367,175	$ 5,328,930	$56,155,371	271
Texas Senate	$ 110,780	$ 897,362	$10,951,410	44

Source: Texans for Public Justice, Money in PoliTex: A Guide to Money in the 2010 Texas Elections (http://info.tpj.org/reports/politex2010/Introduction.html).

Source: Library of Congress Prints and Photographs Division [LC-USZ62-25338]

as Tony Sanchez in 2002, are able to self-finance their campaigns. In that year, Sanchez self-financed $27 million (89 percent of the total) and received campaign contributions totaling $3.5 million.[29] In that same election year, former governor Rick Perry raised $31,402,362 from political action committees.[30]

Money in campaigns has increased dramatically in recent years. With the 2010 Supreme Court decision in *Citizens United v. Federal Election Commission*, campaign advertising by corporations and labor unions cannot be prohibited or restricted at the federal level.[31]

Money supplied by PACs obviously has an impact on elected officials. At the least, PAC money buys the group access to the official. At the worst, PAC money buys the vote of the elected official. Distinguishing between the two is almost impossible. Most states, including Texas, have passed laws designed to regulate campaign finances. Many other states have passed laws limiting the amount of money that could be spent on campaigns, but these laws have been invalidated by the U.S. Supreme Court. (See Chapter 10 on interest groups.)

Candidates sometimes loan themselves money that they can later repay with what are often called "late train" contributions. Special interest groups usually will not retire the debt of losers. The law limits the amount of money that a candidate can collect to retire personal campaign debts for each election (primary, runoff, general) to $500,000 in personal loans. In 2002, several candidates far exceeded this amount in personal loans. The leaders were gubernatorial candidate Tony Sanchez with $22,262,662 in personal loans and Lieutenant Governorelect David Dewhurst with $7,413,887 in outstanding debt.[32]

Today the regulation of campaign finances in Texas is limited to requiring all candidates and PACs to file reports with the Texas State Ethics Commission. All contributions over $50 must be reported with the name of the contributor (see Map 8.1). An expenditure report must also be filed. These reports must be filed before and after the election. The idea behind the reporting scheme is to make public the sources of the funds received by candidates and how the candidates spend their funds. Sometimes these reports are examined closely by the news media and are given significant media coverage, but this is not common. The best source for Texans' funds is Texas for Public Justice (www.tpj.org). For the most part, citizens are left to find out such information on their own, which is difficult for the average citizen. Texas has no limit on the amount of money candidates can spend on their statewide races.

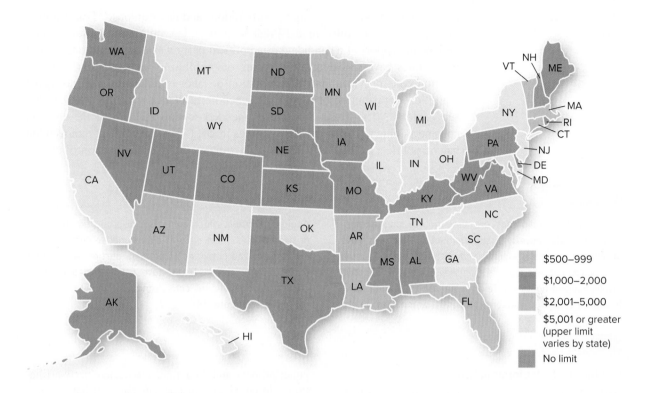

	$500–999
	$1,000–2,000
	$2,001–5,000
	$5,001 or greater (upper limit varies by state)
	No limit

MAP 8.1   Limitations on PAC Contributions in Statewide Races, 2015-2016 Some states differentiate between types of statewide office, typically separating gubernatorial, legislative and 'other' candidates. House and senate candidates may also be differentiated. For the purposes of this map, gubernatorial candidate limits were chosen if there was any differentiation whatsoever.

SOURCE: National Conference of State Legislatures. "State Limits on Contributions to Candidates 2015-2016 Election Cycle." May 2016. See (www.ncsl.org).

CORE OBJECTIVE

Source: United States Department of Agriculture Agricultural Research Service

Taking Personal Responsibility. . .

If you choose to contribute to a candidate's campaign, to what extent is the candidate obligated to you as a contributor? Should your contribution influence public policy? What about corporate contributions?

Impact of *Citizens United* Decision

The 2010 decision in *Citizens United v. Federal Election Commission* established that the federal government cannot prohibit or limit direct spending on campaign advertising by corporations or labor unions. Although the case applied to federal elections, it did leave the question unresolved as to the status of 24 states that have laws prohibiting such spending by corporations and labor unions.[33] For example, the Supreme Court ruled in 2012 that Montana's law limiting corporate contributions in support of a candidate or a political party was unconstitutional. Eight other states have repealed laws limiting or prohibiting such spending. Texas's election code provides that "a corporation or labor organization may not make a political contribution or a political expenditure that is not authorized by this subchapter."[34] The Texas legislature amended section 253.094 of the election code pertaining to corporate contributions in 2011. The amendment removed the ban on political expenditures and solely regulated direct campaign contributions.

Conclusion

Elections and campaigns are essential to any democracy. The rules governing the conduct of elections have an impact on who is elected and on the policies enacted by government. For reasons discussed in Chapter 7, active involvement in politics in Texas is limited to a small number of citizens. The electoral process is dominated by the Anglo population, which controls a disproportionate share of state offices. Most citizens choose not to participate in elections or the activities of political parties. As in other states, campaigns in Texas have become media affairs dominated by political consultants, sound bite ads, and money (see Chapter 14).

Summary

LO: Discuss ballot forms in Texas.

Ballot forms are the forms used by voters to cast their ballots; each county, with approval of the secretary of state, determines the form of the ballot. Texas counties formerly used paper ballots with a party column format, where candidates were listed by party and by office. This encouraged straight-ticket voting. Since the 2008 election, however, all Texas counties have used electronic voting systems, most of which use the office block format. This ballot form lists the office (e.g., president), followed by the candidates by party.

LO: Discuss ballot access in Texas.

To appear on the November general election ballot, candidates must meet criteria established by state law. The Texas Election Code specifies three ways for names to be on the ballot. To run as an independent, a candidate must file a petition with a specified number of signatures. A subset of independents, write-in candidates must pay a filing fee to legitimize their status. Major party candidates access the ballot through their party's primary election. Primaries can be open or closed, or a mixture of both. Texas has a semi-open primary.

LO: Describe primary elections.

Primaries are elections used by major political parties in Texas to nominate candidates for the November general election. They can be open (voters can vote in either primary and do not need to declare party affiliation), closed (voters must declare party affiliation when registering and can only vote in that party's primary), or a mixture of both. Open primaries, by nature, allow crossover voting. This occurs when voters leave their party and vote in the other party's primary. Party raiding can occur when this happens. Whereas crossover voting may be genuine (another party's candidate appeals to voters), party raiding is designed to nominate a weaker candidate or split the vote.

LO: Explain special elections.

By Texas law, elections may be held in January, May, August, and November. Any election that takes place in January, May, or August is considered a special election. There are three types. The most common is selection of city council members and mayoral elections if they are not held in November. A second type of special election may be called to decide on amendments to the state constitution. A third type of special elections occurs when only one contest is on the ballot.

LO: Describe the Federal Voting Rights Act.

The Federal Voting Rights Act is a federal law aimed at preventing racial discrimination in the operation of voter registration and elections at the state level. It required preclearance by the U.S. Justice Department of all changes in the election procedures, including such things as ballot reform, the time and place of an election, and the method of electing legislators. When the U.S. Supreme Court struck down Section 4 of the Voting Rights Act in late June 2013, the primary method of enforcement, Section 5, was rendered useless and Texas immediately put voter identification laws into effect.

LO: Discuss absentee and early voting.

Absentee voting is a process that allows a person to vote early, before the regular election. It applies to all elections in Texas and is also called early voting. Early voting begins 17 days before an election and closes four days before the election. During that period, voters can either mail in a ballot or simply go to an early voting polling place.

LO: Discuss ways in which the nature of elections has changed.

Issues such as abortion, gay rights, women's rights, gun control, the environment, and health care dominate elections. Labor unions have declined. The Catholic and male votes, which used to be overwhelmingly Democratic, have migrated over to the Republican Party because of such issues as abortion and gay rights. Influential 24-hour news networks as well as email campaigns and political activity through social networking websites have also changed the way election campaigns are run and often have undue influence on election outcomes.

LO: Describe political campaigns in Texas, including the use of consultants and the role of money.

Political campaigns are large undertakings, requiring constant publicity, media expertise, and a lot of money. Reporters often follow candidates for statewide office as they travel. Political rallies are still held but are most often used to gain media attention. Professional campaign consultants help candidates in the design of written and visual advertisements and generally "package" the candidate to the voters. Most campaign money comes from political action committees (PACs), with few legal limitations on what they can donate. Indeed, the regulation of campaign finances in Texas is limited to requiring all candidates and PACs to file reports with the Texas State Ethics Commission.

Key Terms

absentee voting	independent candidate	runoff primary
ballot form	minor party	semi-closed primary system
blanket primary system	office block format	semi-open primary system
closed primary system	open primary system	"sore loser" law
crossover voting	party caucus	Voting Rights Act
filing fee	party column format	write-in candidate
focus group	party raiding	
general elections	primary election	

Notes

[1] The office of treasurer was also a statewide elected office. In 1996, the voters abolished this office by constitutional amendment. The functions of this office have been taken over by the state comptroller and other state agencies.

[2] Texas House of Representatives, "Frequently Asked Questions," http://www.house.state.tx.us/resources/frequently-asked-questions/.

[3] Texas Secretary of State, "Voting System Equipment by County (PDF)," updated as of October 2014, http://www.sos.state.tx.us/elections/laws/votingsystems.shtml.

[4] The Texas Election Code can be found in full here: http://www.statutes.legis.state.tx.us/?link=EL.

[5] Texas Secretary of State, "Independent Candidates," http://www.sos.state.tx.us/elections/candidates/guide/ind.shtml#a.

[6] Texas Secretary of State, "Turnout and Voter Registration Figures (1970–current)," http://www.sos.state.tx.us/elections/historical/70-92.shtml.

[7] Texas Secretary of State home page, http://www.sos.state.tx.us.

[8] Ibid.

[9] Texas Secretary of State, "Write-In Candidates," http://www.sos.state.tx.us/elections/candidates/guide/writein.shtml.

[10] James A. Anderson, Richard W. Murray, and Edward L. Farley, *Texas Politics: An Introduction,* 6th ed. (New York: HarperCollins, 1992), 34.

[11] The Raza Unida Party did not receive enough votes to qualify as a minor party but challenged this in court. The federal court sustained the challenge, and they were allowed to operate as a minor party.

[12] Texas Secretary of State, Votesmart.gov, "FAQ," http://www.votetexas.gov/faq/registration/.

[13] Idaho Secretary of State, "Idaho Primary Election, The Purpose of Primary Elections," http://www.sos.idaho.gov/elect/primary_election.htm; Idaho Republican Party v. Ysursa. Case No. 1:08-CV-165-BLW, Memorandum Decision and Order, Document 97, Filed 3/2/11, http://www.sos.idaho.gov/ELECT/ClosedPrimaryOrder.pdf.

[14] *Rush Limbaugh Show,* transcript March 12, 2008, "Rush the Vote: Operation Chaos," http://www.rushlimbaugh.com/daily/2008/03/12/rush_the_vote_operation_chaos.

[15] Maggie Haberman, Politico, "Romney also said he voted in Dem primaries to influence the race (Updated)," February 2012, http://www.politico.com/blogs/burns-haberman/2012/02/romney-also-said-he-voted-in-dem-primaries-to-influence-115774.html.

[16] National Conference of State Legislatures, "Primary Runoffs," (May 2014), http://www.ncsl.org/research/elections-and-campaigns/primary-runoffs.aspx.

[17] Texas Secretary of State, "Republican or Democratic Party Nominees," http://www.sos.state.tx.us/elections/candidates/guide/demorep.shtml.

[18] A court case in 1971 ended the early registration procedures in Texas (*Beare v. Smith,* 31 F. Supp. 1100).

[19] U.S. Department of Justice, "Minority Language Citizens: Section 203 of the Voting Rights Act," https://www.justice.gov/crt/minority-language-citizens.

[20] Voting Rights Act of 1965, Pub. L. 89-110, (see http://library.clerk.house.gov/reference-files/PPL_VotingRightsAct_1965.pdf).

[21] U.S. Department of Justice, "Minority Language Citizens: Section 203 of the Voting Rights Act," https://www.justice.gov/crt/minority-language-citizens; U.S. Department of Justice, "About Language Minority Voting Rights," https://www.justice.gov/crt/about-language-minority-voting-rights.

[22] Texas Secretary of State, Election Advisory No. 2015-05, http://www.sos.state.tx.us/elections/laws/advisory2015-04.shtml.

[23] Texas Election Code, Chapter 272, Bilingual Requirements, http://www.statutes.legis.state.tx.us/Docs/EL/htm/EL.272.htm.

[24] U.S. Census Bureau, "Voting Rights Act Amendments of 2006, Determinations Under Section 203," *Federal Register,* October 13, 2011, https://www.census.gov/rdo/pdf/2011_26293.pdf.

[25] "Federal Government Orders Bilingual Ballots in 25 States Ahead of Elections," *FoxNews.com,* October 14, 2011, http://www.foxnews.com/politics/2011/10/14/federal-government-orders-bilingual-ballots-in-25-states-ahead-elections.html.

[26] Texas Secretary of State, votetexas.gov, "Who, What, Where, When, How: When: Early Voting," http://www.votetexas.gov/voting/when/#early-voting.

[27] Norman D. Brown, *Hood, Bonnet, and Little Brown Jug: Texas Politics, 1921–1928* (College Station: Texas A&M University Press, 1984).

[28] *The New York Times,* "Texas Candidate's Comment About Rape Causes Furor," March 26, 1990, http://www.nytimes.com/1990/03/26/us/texas-candidate-s-comment-about-rape-causes-a-furor.html.

[29] Texans for Public Justice, "Tony Sanchez's War Chest: Who Gives to a $600 Million Dollar Man?" www.tpj.org/docs2002/10reports/sanchez/page3.html.

[30] Texans for Public Justice, "Governor Perry's War Chest: Who Said Yes to Governor No?" www.tpj.org/docs/2002/10/reports/perry/page3.html.

[31] *Citizens United v. Federal Elections Commission* 558 U.S. 310 (2010).

[32] Lobby Watch, "Texas Loan Stars Incurred $48 Million in Political Debts," http://info.tpj.org/Lobby_Watch/latetrain.html.

[33] National Conference of State Legislatures, " *Citizens United* and the States," July 2016, http://www.ncsl.org/legislatures-elections/elections/citizens-united-and-the-states.aspx.

[34] *Texas Election Code,* Title 15, Chapter 253, sec. 253.094.

CHAPTER 9

Political Parties in Texas

• Evaluate the role of political parties in Texas.

Political parties are integral to government and politics in the nation and states, even though they are not mentioned in either the U.S. Constitution or the Texas Constitution. A **political party** is an organization that acts as an intermediary between the people and government, with the goal of having its members elected to public office. Traditionally, parties have vetted candidates, run campaigns, informed the populace on policy issues, and organized their members who are serving in office to ensure a measure of accountability.[1] As political scientists frequently note, parties play an important role in aggregating and articulating the preferences of citizens. Today, our representative government would not function without political parties.

political parties
Organizations that act as an intermediary between the people and government with the goal of getting their members elected to public office

The Founding Fathers did not favor parties, calling them "factions," because they saw these entities as pursuing special parochial interests instead of the interests of the country as a whole. While acknowledging the natural tendency to affiliate with others who share similar interests, George Washington, in his farewell address, warned of the potentially ruinous effects of parties on liberty and government. He referred to the spirit of party as the "worst enemy" of governments and argued that it leads to "despotism," "kindles the animosity of one part against another," and "foments occasionally riot and insurrection."[2]

Despite Washington's warning, parties developed in this country, largely due to political expediency and the useful functions they provide in democratic politics. As early as the drafting of the U.S. Constitution, groups of like-minded political leaders and concerned citizens joined together in an effort to promote their ideas and influence those voting at ratifying conventions; these groups were known as the Federalists and Anti-Federalists. Following ratification, factions continued to work together as politicians sought to influence the direction of the fledgling government.[3] The first party system in the U.S. emerged during Washington's presidency, when a division emerged between one group including Thomas Jefferson and James Madison (which ultimately became the Democratic-Republicans) and another that included Alexander Hamilton and John Adams (which maintained the Federalist name). This division centered largely on issues related to the proper role of the federal government vis-a-vis the states, financial policy, and foreign affairs. The U.S. has had parties ever since; they have remained because they serve many purposes.

Political parties in the United States have never been strongly centralized. Throughout history, U.S. parties have consisted of coalitions of state parties. The most powerful party leaders arose from leadership positions in important states. Today, Texas and the United States do not have strong parties, although partisan polarization has been increasing. Most candidates within parties self-select to run for office; once elected, they tend to toe the party line, as evidenced by their voting patterns. In Texas, neither party has a strong party organization or a strong grassroots organization. Candidates can act quite independently of either party.

Chapter Learning Objectives

- Describe the evolution of the political party system in the United States and in Texas.

- Explain the history of party realignment, one-party Republican dominance, and party dealignment in Texas.

- Describe third-party movements in the United States and in Texas.

- Explain political party organization in Texas, including caucus and primary delegate selection systems.

How Parties Have Operated in the United States

Learning Objective: Describe the evolution of the political party system in the United States and in Texas.

In the past, parties performed many different activities and functions. They also played a much more central role in our political system, which gave parties a great deal of power. There have been two primary modes of party activity: labor-intensive politics and capital-intensive politics. Parties still do some of the former, but the latter has become more prominent over time.

Labor-Intensive Politics

From the 1790s until roughly the 1970s, parties relied on members and volunteers to perform a number of tasks related to elections and campaigns. These traditional party functions are sometimes described as *labor-intensive politics* because, historically, the lack of communication and printing technologies (such as radio, television, the photocopier, and the personal computer) meant that parties had to enlist a lot of people or expend a lot of labor to accomplish these tasks.

First, the parties selected candidates to run for office. Party leaders (usually, but not always, elected officials) decided who would be put forward as candidates. The infamous Tammany Hall was the first urban party organization that successfully selected candidates for office. In reality, Tammany was the executive committee of the New York City Democratic Party, which put together slates of candidates for city and county offices. The organization was so powerful that it not only controlled New York City elections but also (due to the city's large population) influenced state and national elections from 1790 until well into the twentieth century. Tammany leaders through the years represented a Who's Who of important American political figures, including Aaron Burr and "Boss" William Tweed. A competing Whig-Republican machine in upstate New York was headed by Thurlow Weed from the early 1830s to the late 1860s. In Illinois, the Cook County Democratic Party slated candidates for city and county offices and was influential in determining statewide Democratic candidates from the 1930s until the present. Richard J. Daley served as both mayor of Chicago and Chair of the Cook County Democratic Party. Holding these offices allowed him to dominate both city and county and had a significant effect on Illinois and even national politics, by virtue of Daley's selection of candidates and his ability to "get out the vote." In Texas, the Democratic Party had its own powerful political machine. Before ascending to national prominence as a confidential adviser to President Woodrow Wilson, "Colonel" Edward House earned the reputation of "kingmaker" in Texas. House handpicked Democratic gubernatorial candidates and stewarded their campaigns to victory from 1892 to 1904; he and his "crowd" then controlled the governorship by advising the newly elected executive on political appointments and other matters.[4]

Second, parties were also important to organizing candidates' campaigns. In the past, candidate campaigns were completely controlled by the parties, which sent party workers into neighborhoods to knock on doors and inform potential voters about the candidates and issues. Many times, the entire party slate would share the platform and speak at the same event.

This 1874 Thomas Nast cartoon is considered the origin of party symbols still in use today: here, an elephant represents the Republican Party and a donkey (wearing a lion's skin) represents the Democratic Party.

Source: Library of Congress

Third, parties could raise money directly and then distribute it to different candidates' campaigns. By controlling the purse strings, the party could keep its candidates in line and under control.

Fourth, the party organized campaign rallies to facilitate candidate and voter interaction. Before candidates campaigned for themselves, the party would produce campaign literature, arrange speakers on behalf of the candidates, and, from the early 1900s on, arrange speaking tours for the candidates.

Fifth, inconceivable as it may be today, the parties—not local governments—printed election ballots.

Sixth, starting in the 1930s, parties hired pollsters to conduct survey research for their candidates. Candidates were beholden to the party for such poll data.

Finally, the parties ran the governments to which their candidates were elected. This was especially true after the introduction of the spoils system (or patronage system) circa 1830. The spoils system is a practice in which the victorious political party gives government jobs to party supporters. When Andrew Jackson won the presidency in 1828, government positions were filled by recognized party members; the higher the office, the more important the party member chosen to fill it.

The role of parties in our political system has changed in many ways. For one thing, parties no longer designate a slate of candidates for office; rather, candidates self-select to run. Candidates generally assemble their own team to manage their campaigns (or hire professional political consultants to perform this function). While parties still provide funding for campaigns, candidates might receive money directly from **PACs** and donors and/or fund themselves. In addition, local governments now prepare official ballots according to state specifications (although primary ballots are still prepared by the party holding the primary)[5], and the merit system has, for the most part, replaced the spoils system. As a result of these changes, the influence of parties on the election process has declined.

political action committees (PACs)
Spin-offs of interest groups that collect money for campaign contributions and other activity

Capital-Intensive Politics

Recently, there has been a shift from labor-intensive politics, dominated by political parties, toward more capital-intensive politics. These are activities for which campaigns must use money (or capital) to purchase non-human resources (such as information and communication technology and media services) to reach voters. The introduction of new technologies has revolutionized how political campaigns operate, but these technologies are costly.

Mass communication allows candidates to reach an exponentially greater number of voters than they could at rallies or by going door-to-door. The importance of broadcast media to campaigns began with radio in the 1930s, and that importance increased substantially with the introduction of television in most U.S. homes by the early 1960s. According to one media research firm, a total of $3.8 billion was spent on political ads for television during the 2012 election cycle.[6] That amount was projected to increase in 2016, with the majority of political ad spending going toward broadcast TV and cable TV ads, and the remaining amount spent on radio, online, newspaper, telephone, direct mail, and other advertising.[7]

Previously, television ads cast a wide net, reaching all television viewers rather than just those who might be persuaded to support a particular candidate. Because television ad buying is relatively expensive, this was an inefficient use of media budgets. However, recent technological developments allow campaigns to target their television advertising with remarkable precision. A technique called "microtargeting" involves "gathering information about individuals, and using it to serve up personalized messages to prospective voters."[8] Applied to television, this technique pairs lists of undecided or pivotal voters with actual, real-time data about television viewing behavior. Using this data, media firms can direct a political ad to a TV set-top box in a specific household. In fact, neighboring households watching the same program might see different political ads during commercial breaks.[9] Not surprisingly, the fee for this service is exorbitant—ranging from tens of thousands to millions of dollars—and therefore prohibitively expensive for many campaigns.[10]

Another crucial element of capital-intensive politics is the Internet. Successful campaigns utilize email and websites to communicate their message to voters, at a fraction of the cost of television and even direct mail.[11] Like television advertising, online or digital advertising can now be incredibly targeted: firms can send a personalized political ad to voters based on their Internet history (including websites they visited, news articles they read, and Google searches they conducted).[12] However, research has shown that a "digital divide"—the finding that younger, better educated, higher-income households are more likely to own computers and have Internet access than are older, less educated, lower-income households—still exists.[13] Therefore, campaigns that rely too heavily on online communication risk ignoring substantial numbers of the potential electorate.

Polling or survey research is also essential to campaigns. Without good polling data, a modern campaign might have difficulty gauging the effectiveness of its message or the mood of the electorate. Survey workers ask potential voters questions about party affiliation, candidate preferences, issue preferences (pro-choice or pro-life, for example), and issue salience or intensity (the relative importance of an issue to a voter). With the information obtained from polling data, a phone bank can be set up. This generally involves campaign volunteers calling targeted voters, providing information about a candidate, and asking for a donation or other form of candidate support, such as displaying a yard sign. During early voting and on Election Day, phone bank callers remind previously identified supporters of a particular candidate to go to the polls. Information from survey research can also be used for direct mail, in which specific campaign literature is mailed to targeted likely voters. For example, if a survey respondent indicated that education was the most important issue for her, a direct-mail piece detailing the candidate's stance on education would be sent to her. This process of using poll data to isolate subsets within subgroups within groups to target campaign and candidate messages is sometimes called "salami-slicing the electorate."

Professional campaign consultants have replaced the parties when it comes to running campaigns. Many times, these firms have different departments that are able to produce television and radio advertisements, direct mail pieces, phone banking, email communication and web design, and write and conduct polls. Sometimes political consultants will contract out some or all of the services associated with capital-intensive campaigns, providing the large themes and overall campaign direction while reserving the right to veto or modify any of the campaign products being developed by these specialized companies. Because of the more specialized skill sets necessary for professional polling, many campaign companies contract out their polling needs to an independent company whose sole function is to construct and conduct polls.

Political Reforms and the Weakening of Political Parties

Learning Objective: Describe the evolution of the political party system in the United States and in Texas.

In general, parties are weaker today than at any other time during their history. This trend seems unlikely to change anytime soon. To a large extent, parties have been weakened by political reforms, many of which came about during the Progressive Era (1890–1920). This was a time when reformers were very concerned about corruption and the influence of large urban political machines, led by powerful men who controlled government jobs, contracts, and regulations. In an attempt to reduce the power of the machines, reformers introduced measures that compromised the strength of political parties.

One way that parties traditionally maintained their power was through the voting system. Early in our country's history, some states used voice voting. According to this practice, eligible voters appeared at the courthouse, were called upon by name, then vocally announced their chosen candidate in front of onlookers. The lack of privacy and anonymity inherent in this voting system made it easy for party members to intimidate or coerce voters. Those in a position of power (such as employers, landlords, and public officials) could pressure their subordinates to vote a certain way, then witness their ballot casting to ensure compliance.[14] In states where printed ballots were used, the parties themselves printed them, and they employed a number of techniques to identify how a ballot was cast or otherwise influence voters. Often, the parties each used a different color of paper to make their ballots, and voters had to choose a ballot based on which party they wanted to support. As a result, voting was not private, as onlookers could easily determine which party's ballot had been selected and deposited in the ballot box. Again, party members had ample opportunity to intimidate and threaten retaliation for noncompliance.[15]

The advent of the "Australian" ballot subdued this type of abuse by parties and guaranteed that the voting process was both secret and uniform. With this system, ballots were produced by the government, rather than by parties; all ballots were identical; and each ballot listed all candidates running for office, not just those affiliated with a certain party.[16] Consequently, voters could mark and submit their choice in private, without fear of retribution. As an added benefit of this system, voters could also (if they wished) engage in "split-ticket" voting. In other words, they could vote for one party's candidate for one office and a different party's candidate for another office, all on the same ballot.[17] The Australian ballot gained widespread use in the U.S. during the 1880s. Thus, ballot reforms decreased the influence of political parties on the voting process.[18]

Another party stronghold existed in the nominating process, because party bosses selected candidates for office. To combat this aspect of party control, reformers introduced the concept of the direct primary. In direct primaries, all members of the party vote in an election, called a primary, to determine the party's nominee for an office. This practice was first adopted in Wisconsin in 1904.[19] Initially it was difficult for candidates to gain access to primary ballots,

The Spoils System Under Siege: This Currier & Ives image argues for civil service reform by depicting Ulysses S. Grant with party supporters clamoring for government patronage.

Source: Library of Congress

but in the wake of the disastrous 1968 Democratic National Convention in Chicago (characterized not only by party divisiveness but also outright violence between protesters and police), the Democratic Party instituted substantial reforms. The Republican Party soon followed suit, and by 1972, the vast majority of delegates to party presidential nominating conventions were allocated as a result of primary elections. Party primaries are now used to select the nominees for all types of elected government positions, from justice of the peace to U.S. senator. As a general rule, delegates to party nominating conventions are allocated to candidates proportionally, based on results of the popular vote in primary elections. Some states use a caucus system to determine party nominations instead of conducting a primary. A caucus is a gathering at which party members publicly declare which candidate they will support and select delegates to attend the nominating convention.

Another way parties consolidated their power was through the spoils or patronage system, which involved the appointment, by elected officials, of faithful party members to government jobs. Reforms in this area gained wide support in the United States in the wake of the assassination of President James Garfield in 1881. Garfield was shot by a disappointed office seeker who had previously campaigned on Garfield's behalf, and the president's wounds ultimately led to his death.[20] The Pendleton Act of 1883 established a class of federal government positions, called the "civil service," that would be filled as a result of competitive examinations instead of political appointments.[21] In addition, this employment continued regardless of which party held the White

House.[22] Initially, only a small percentage of government positions were designated as civil service (nonpartisan) jobs and awarded by merit. However, Chester Arthur, the Republican vice president who succeeded to the presidency after Garfield's death, added more positions to the civil service rolls, as did each president thereafter through the end of the nineteenth century. By 1900, a majority of federal government positions were protected by the Pendleton Act. As the merit system replaced the spoils system, it undermined the connection parties had with government workers.

Reformers brought about other changes as well. For example, based on a theory of technocratic governance, they pushed for nonpartisan local elections to remove "political" considerations from municipal policy. They also championed the manager-council form of municipal government. In this form of government, a professional city manager, rather than a mayor, is typically hired by an elected city council to administer the departments and employees of the city.[23] (See Chapter 6 for a fuller discussion of this form of city government.) In the past, city governments had been a breeding ground for party talent development. Grover Cleveland began his career in elective office by being elected mayor of Buffalo, New York, and Theodore Roosevelt began as police commissioner of New York City.

More recently, campaign finance laws have also lessened the influence of parties, albeit without achieving their intended goal of dampening the role of money in elections.

CORE OBJECTIVE

© George Lavendowski/USFWS

Communicating Effectively . . .

Explain how political reforms have weakened political parties.

Fifty States, Fifty Party Systems

Learning Objective: Describe the evolution of the political party system in the United States and in Texas.

The United States does not have strong national parties; rather, it has 50 state party systems. One factor that determines the strength of national parties relative to state parties is the number of national offices. In the United States, there are few officeholders who are elected on a nationwide basis; only the president and vice president are elected by voters across the country. (In fact, even presidential and vice presidential elections are essentially state elections, because voters in each state elect members to the Electoral College, who in turn elect the president and vice president.) This lack of national offices weakens national parties and shifts power to state parties. Another factor in the strength of national parties is the level of activism or visibility of the national party organization. Although the labels "Democrat" and "Republican" are used constantly by the news media, the only time we see anything resembling a national party organization is every four years, when Democrats and Republicans hold national conventions to nominate their candidates for president. (The leadership, or national committee, of both major parties also meets in between conventions, but these meetings receive little notice from the news media and the average citizen is generally unaware of them.) Each of the 50 state party organizations can act independently of the others and of the national party organization.

A clear distinction exists between federal and state office holders. At the federal level, Texas elects two U.S. senators and 36 U.S. representatives. These members of Congress spend most of their time in Washington, focusing on national, not state, policy. At the state level, Texans elect 31 state senators and 150 representatives to the state legislature. These state legislators focus on state issues. Occasionally, federal and state legislators might come together on common ground, but most often they have different interests, agendas, and priorities. Thus, although state-elected officials might carry the Democratic or Republican label, little interaction occurs between state and national parties or officials.

Years ago, political scientist V. O. Key, Jr. observed this about the state party system:

> The institutions developed to perform functions in each state differ markedly from the national parties. It is an error to assume that the political parties of each state are but miniatures of the national party system. In a few states that condition is approached, but . . . each state has its own pattern of action and often it deviates markedly from the forms of organization commonly thought of as constituting party systems.[24]

Professor Key's observation is as valid today as it was in the 1950s. State party systems vary widely, and often the only common link is the name *Democrat* or *Republican*.

The Strength of State Party Organizations

Learning Objective: Describe the evolution of the political party system in the United States and in Texas.

States can be classified according to the strength of party organization within the state. In Texas, the Democratic Party dominated state politics for roughly 100 years following Reconstruction. During that period, the Republican Party was essentially absent except on a few occasions. In many elections there was not even a Republican candidate on the ballot. However, the Republican Party in Texas has gained strength over the past 50 years. It now controls both houses of the Texas legislature, and it has captured the governor's office without interruption since 1994. Today, Republicans hold all statewide elected offices.[25]

Note that the Democratic and Republican party labels do not necessarily indicate ideology.[26] **Ideology** is the basic belief system that guides political theory and policy, and different political ideologies are generally classified along a

ideology
Basic belief system that guides political theory and policy; typically conceptualized as falling along a conservative/ moderate/liberal continuum

spectrum of conservative, moderate, and liberal. The Democratic Party in one state, for example, can be quite different ideologically from the Democratic Party in another state. For many years in Texas, the Democratic Party had very strong conservative leanings. The Democratic Party in Massachusetts, on the other hand, has a strong liberal orientation.

Even when the Democrats still controlled statewide offices and the state legislature, Texans had a tendency to support Republican candidates for president (see Table 9.1). In the past 17 presidential elections, Texas has voted Democratic only four times. In two of these cases, a native-son Democrat (Lyndon Johnson, who ran as Kennedy's vice president in 1960 and for president in his own right in 1964) was on the ballot. Hubert Humphrey, who had served as Johnson's vice president, won the state in 1968. Texans supported Jimmy Carter in 1976, partly because he was a southerner and partly due to backlash from the Watergate scandal. This strong support for Republican presidential candidates, even in times of Democratic dominance, reflects ideological differences that existed between the more conservative Texas Democratic Party and the more liberal national Democratic Party organization.

It may be that the common thread running through the state's political and electoral history is a generally consistent ideology. Despite the relative waxing and waning of the two major parties in Texas, the party offering a more conservative ideology has more often won the day. Even today, about twice as many Texans, when surveyed, describe themselves as conservative rather than liberal.[27]

TABLE 9.1

Presidential Candidates Winning the Popular Vote in Texas (1952–2016)

Year	Candidate	Party
1952	Dwight Eisenhower	Republican
1956	Dwight Eisenhower	Republican
1960	John Kennedy*	Democratic
1964	Lyndon Johnson	Democratic
1968	Hubert Humphrey*	Democratic
1972	Richard Nixon	Republican
1976	Jimmy Carter	Democratic
1980	Ronald Reagan	Republican
1984	Ronald Reagan	Republican
1988	George H. W. Bush	Republican
1992	George H. W. Bush	Republican
1996	Bob Dole	Republican
2000	George W. Bush	Republican
2004	George W. Bush	Republican
2008	John McCain	Republican
2012	Mitt Romney	Republican
2016	Donald J. Trump	Republican

Source: Texas Secretary of State, Presidential Election Results, http://www.sos.state.tx.us/elections/historical/presidential.shtml.

*Won the state by a margin of less than 50,000 votes

CORE OBJECTIVE

Taking Personal Responsibility . . .

Examine your political values and compare them to the expressed values of both parties. Do your ideas about the role of government, politics, and policy align with one particular party?

Source: United States Department of Agriculture Agricultural Research Service

Evolution of Political Parties in Texas

Learning Objective: Describe the evolution of the political party system in the United States and in Texas.

We have seen that political parties in the United States are not particularly strong, either at the national or the state level. We have also seen that, in Texas, the two major parties have alternated in terms of their relative positions of dominance and weakness over time. So what happens in a political system in which parties are fairly weak?

Many political scientists believe that weakened parties lead to what is called *candidate-centered politics.* According to political scientists Jeffrey Cohen and Paul Kantor, with candidate-centered politics, prospective officeholders "emphasize their own talents, backgrounds, and characteristics rather than their association with either major party when running for office."[28] Indeed, the political history of Texas could be viewed as a chronological parade of personalities, intertwined with their respective ideologies and political parties.

Politics of the Republic of Texas

When the Republic was founded, the party system as we know it did not yet exist in Texas. Still, politics at the time were highly competitive. The politics and government of the Republic were dominated by two men, Sam Houston and Mirabeau Buonaparte Lamar. Houston advocated for annexation and peaceful relations with the Native American tribes of Texas, whereas Lamar envisioned a Texas empire stretching to the Pacific and initiated hostilities against the Native tribes. During the years of the Republic, Houston, Lamar, and their supporters competed for control of the Texas government. Because the Republic's constitution did not permit presidents to serve consecutive terms, elections revolved around the personalities of the two men and their surrogates. Texas politics of this era were dominated by strong political leaders instead of issues and public policy differences. This characteristic of Texas politics is still present today.

Annexation and the Civil War Era

Texas's state politics from U.S. annexation until the end of the Civil War clearly established a pattern of Democratic Party dominance. The Anglo settlers of

Sam Houston, Governor of Texas, 1859–1861; U.S. (Democratic) Senator from Texas, 1846–1859; President of Texas, 1836–1838, 1841–1844; Texas House of Representatives, 1839–1841; Governor of Tennessee, 1827–1829; U.S. Representative from Tennessee, 1823–1827.

© Library of Congress Prints and Photographs Division [LC-USZ62-110029]

pre-Civil War Texas were predominantly from the U.S. South; many were either slaveholders or sympathetic toward slaveholders, distrustful of the federal government, and convinced of the legitimacy of state sovereignty. During this period, Texas experienced a substantial expansion of its plantation economy.[29]

As a rule, Texas Democratic officeholders supported the southern position on issues dominating the United States during the Civil War era. The conspicuous exception to this was Sam Houston, who represented Texas in the U.S. Senate from 1846 to 1859 and served as governor from 1859 to 1861 as a Union Democrat. Houston voted for establishing Oregon as a free territory in 1848, and he argued successfully for the Boundary Act, a part of the Compromise of 1850, whereby Texas sold its right to territory now in New Mexico, Oklahoma, Kansas, Wyoming, and Colorado to the United States.

Houston's opposition to slavery deepened the cleavages between pro- and anti-Houston groups in the Texas Democratic Party that had existed since the early 1850s. Two factions arose in Texas: the pro-Houston faction, or "Jacksonians," and the newer, radical anti-Houston faction who called themselves the Constitutional Democrats. By 1857, the latter completely controlled the party. Houston ran for governor and lost that year, but in 1859 he ran for governor as an independent in an attempt to build up a Union Party, and he won. Houston campaigned against secession, but the people of Texas voted for it by more than a 3-to-1 margin in a popular referendum. Houston refused to take the oath of allegiance to the Confederacy, at which point the convention declared the governorship vacant and appointed the lieutenant governor to replace him. The Democratic Party would remain the sole party in Texas for the duration of the Civil War.

The only period of one-party Republican dominance in Texas before the 1990s was during Reconstruction, when Edmund J. Davis was governor. Davis, a native of Florida, moved to Texas in 1848 and opposed secession in 1861. In 1869 he was elected governor in an election in which less than 50 percent of registered white citizens voted because of federal Reconstruction laws and a boycott by Conservative Democrats.[30] The party was divided between the Conservative Republicans and the Radicals under Davis. His administration was controversial for Democrats and Republicans alike and was a source of acrimony for former Confederates.[31] V. O. Key, Jr. observed that following the Civil War and the experiences of Reconstruction, southerners felt a very strong resentment toward the rest of the nation and the party that dominated it after the Civil War. This resentment bonded the South together as a unit, and it voted uniformly against all Republicans.[32]

The One-Party Democratic Era in Texas

Reconstruction ended in Texas in 1874. For roughly the next 100 years, Texas was a one-party Democratic state. When Davis lost his bid for reelection in 1873, the switch from Republican to Democratic control was almost immediate and absolute. From 1874 until 1961, no Republican was elected to statewide office, and only a few were elected to other offices. In 1928, the state did vote Republican, casting its Electoral College votes for Herbert Hoover. Notably, however, Hoover's opponent was Al Smith, a Roman Catholic from New York, whose candidacy suffered from anti-Catholic sentiment as well as opposition to the Democratic machine politics of Tammany Hall.

Certain factors were influential in deflecting Republican challenges and allowing the Democratic Party to dominate. Several third-party movements arose during the last three decades of the nineteenth century, and the conservative Democrats who controlled the party effectively destroyed all competition.

In 1877, the Greenback Party (initially, Greenback clubs) formed in the South and West in reaction to declining farm prices. In Texas, the Greenbackers recruited from the more radical farmers. They demanded currency expansion ("greenbacks") to drive up agricultural prices, an income tax, the secret ballot, direct election of U.S. senators, better schools, and reduced railroad freight rates. In 1878, Greenbackers won 12 seats in the Texas legislature and even won a U.S. House seat. In 1880, the Greenback Party received about 12 percent of the vote in the governor's race and reelected its member to the U.S. Congress.[33] However, the party was already in decline. By 1886, the organization had faded out of existence and its reform agenda was taken up by the People's Party, or "Populists"—a party that fused together different groups and ultimately had a significant impact on U.S. politics. Also formed at this time was the Texas Farmers' Alliance, which became known as the Grange. This organization also represented small farmers and made an uneasy alliance with African Americans, who were the primary supporters of the Republican Party in Texas and in the rest of the South.[34]

The People's Party—or Populists—had a large impact on the national Democratic Party (as depicted in the political cartoon below) and the U.S. system as a whole, despite its short life. Formed in the early 1890s from the remnants of other agrarian reform groups, the Populists were primarily a farm movement but expanded its membership to include urban labor voters. The Populists were anti-elite and stood for bimetallism, a graduated income tax, direct election of senators, an eight-hour work day, and government ownership of the railroad.[35] In Texas, the Populists were a "coalition of Anglo small farmers, blacks, and labor," and currency issues predominated.[36] The national party had its greatest electoral success in the presidential election of 1892, when Populist candidate James B. Weaver of Iowa won four states and 22 Electoral College votes. Weaver and Texas gubernatorial candidate Thomas Nugent won about a quarter of the vote in the state. Despite its successes early in the decade, Populism waned as an independent force in the country and in Texas, as the Democratic Party adopted many of its planks and the national economy improved.[37] In 1896, the Populists supported the Democratic Party presidential nominee William Jennings Bryan, and as one historian put it, "in effect, abolished themselves."[38] It also did not help that William Jennings Bryan was defeated in successive presidential elections by Republican William McKinley.

As the Populists declined, the Progressives gained steam as the key reform movement. Despite its differences with the Populists, the Progressive movement did take up some Populist causes and carried them across the goal line in the early twentieth century. However, the Progressives did not share the anti-elitism and anti-centralism of the Populists. In fact, the Progressives embodied "a faith that educated and civilized individuals can, through the use of reason, determine what is best for society as a whole."[39] Thus it is not surprising that the Progressives favored elite (and national) management of government and

Swallowed! Political cartoon showing a python with the head of William Jennings Bryan, as the Populist Party, swallowing the Democratic Party donkey, 1900.

© Library of Congress Prints and Photographs Division [LC-USZC4-1473];

the economy to lead the country forward. More specifically, Progressive causes included both political and economic reforms, such as women's suffrage, prohibition, direct election of senators, anti-monopoly efforts and greater regulation of business, as well as progressive taxation and other egalitarian reforms.[40] One could argue that this activist view of government came to dominate American politics for much of the twentieth century, especially in the presidencies of Republican Theodore Roosevelt and Democrats Woodrow Wilson and Franklin D. Roosevelt. However, in Texas, it met with limited favor owing to the state's basic conservatism. Prohibitionism, though, did strike a chord with certain segments of the Texas population, and the state eventually ratified the prohibition amendment to the federal Constitution and passed a state prohibition amendment.[41]

The state Democratic Party successfully destroyed these smaller party movements and continued to control state politics until the 1960s. In fact, the lack of competition from outside the party rendered general elections in November irrelevant; the earlier Democratic Party primary election determined outcomes. The party's conservative element, made up of business people, oilmen, wealthy farmers, and cattle ranchers, dominated the party for decades and kept it in power. The period from 1940 to 1960 might even be characterized as an era of nonpartisan politics, dominated by the conservative business community. Writing about Texas political parties in 1949, V. O. Key, Jr. observed: "In Texas the vague outlines of a politics are emerging in which irrelevancies are pushed into the background and the people divided broadly along liberal and conservative lines." This division, according to Key, was due to "personal insecurity of men suddenly made rich who are fearful lest they lose their wealth. . . . The Lone Star State is concerned about money and how to make it, about oil and sulfur and gas, about cattle and dust storms and irrigation, about cotton and banking and Mexicans."[42] Until the late 1960s, Texas politics revolved almost exclusively around personality and economic issues.

Though there was no effective challenge to Democratic hegemony from outside the party, all was not smooth sailing within the party itself. Infighting among the different factions—the pro-business conservatives, liberals (including progressives, who were more critical of business and championed civil rights), and moderates—increasingly divided the party. Though minority groups joined the ranks of the Democratic Party more and more over time, the party's conservative element eventually found more in common with religious groups and those newly settled in Texas for economic reasons. This set the stage for major changes in the Texas party system.

Party Realignment in Texas

Learning Objective: Explain the history of party realignment, one-party Republican dominance, and party dealignment in Texas.

Though it seemed absolute, the long-running Democratic Party dominance of Texas politics did not last forever. The party system is susceptible to changes in voting behavior and can be transformed by them. Without question, Texas has undergone a significant change in the voting behavior of its citizens over the past 50 years. This change is referred to as party realignment.

Realignment is "a lasting shift of party loyalty and attachment" in voting citizens.[43] V.O. Key, Jr. defined one type of realignment as "a movement of the members of a population category from party to party that extends over several presidential elections and appears to be independent of the peculiar factors influencing the vote at individual elections."[44] Another political scientist, Gerald Pomper, classified "realigning elections" as those "in which one party displaces the other as the majority party."[45] Regardless of the particular definition used, the term "realignment" does not apply to a temporary deviation in voting behavior, such as when a life-long party member crosses over to vote for the opposing party in a single election. Rather, realignment is a long-lasting change occurring on a large scale that literally changes the party landscape, as well as the relationship of the parties to each other. As the political landscape evolved from one of Democratic Party dominance to one of Republican Party dominance, such a change took place in Texas.

realignment
"a lasting shift of party loyalty and attachment" (as defined by James L. Sundquist in *Dynamics of the Party System: Alignment and Realignment of Political Parties in the United States*, p. 4.)

The Beginning of Change

In the 1952 and 1956 presidential elections, many Yellow Dog Democrats (individuals who strongly identify as Democrats regardless of the party's ideological position) broke with tradition and voted for the Republican presidential candidate, Dwight D. Eisenhower. The leader of this movement was Governor Allan Shivers, the leader of the conservative faction of the Texas Democratic Party. This faction chose to dissociate from the New Deal/Fair Deal element of the national Democratic Party and from any candidate it might put forward.

Allan Shivers, Governor of Texas, 1949–1957.

© Photo by John Dominis/The LIFE Picture Collection/Getty Images

---

straight-ticket voting

Casting all your votes for candidates of a single party

In the fall of 1952, at the state Democratic Party convention, Governor Shivers persuaded the state delegates to endorse Eisenhower. The Texas Republican Party convention also nominated Shivers and most statewide Democratic candidates as the Republican nominees. Thus, Shivers and most statewide office seekers were candidates for *both* political parties in 1952. This group became known as the "Shivercrats." The liberal faction of the Texas Democratic Party, still aligned with the national party, became known as the "Loyalists."[46]

This action, and a similar action in 1956, initiated the Texas tradition of supporting Republican presidential candidates while retaining Democratic Party dominance over state offices. Presidential politics in 1952 broke the tradition of **straight-ticket voting**, in which voters select candidates from the same party for all offices on the ballot—at least for the top offices on that ticket.

The Election of John Tower

In 1960, Lyndon Johnson, the Democratic senior senator from Texas, ran for reelection to the U.S. Senate and won. At the same time, however, he was also John F. Kennedy's vice presidential running mate. Johnson's presence on the Democratic ticket temporarily stayed Texas's movement toward the Republican Party. In 1961, after the Kennedy-Johnson victory, a special election was held to fill Johnson's seat. John Tower won this election, becoming not only the first Republican U.S. Senator from Texas since Reconstruction but also the first Republican statewide officeholder in Texas since Reconstruction. Tower had won a plurality against a huge field of candidates in the initial round of voting, then claimed victory with a slight majority in the runoff election.

Tower's election seemed to herald the beginning of a new era of two-party politics in the state. In the 1962 elections, Republicans managed to field candidates for many statewide, congressional, and local races. There were, for a variety of reasons, few successes. Some of these candidates were very weak, and some proved an embarrassment for the Republicans. Tower won reelection in 1966, 1972, and 1978, but it would be 17 years after Tower's first victory before a different Republican won statewide office.

The Election of Bill Clements

For a time, Republicans had limited success in electing legislators and local officeholders. However, the election of Republican Bill Clements as governor in 1978 marked the real beginning of two-party politics in Texas. Governor Clements used his power to make appointments to boards, commissions, and judgeships, and to recruit people who would publicly declare their Republicanism. Some referred to these new converts as "closet Republicans" who had finally gone

Campaign literature from Tower's election.

© Image courtesy of Jimmy Tyler/Senator John G. Tower Archives, Southwestern University, Georgetown, TX

public. These appointments helped build the Republican Party in Texas and promote party realignment.

Clements's 1982 loss to Democrat Mark White was a blow to the Republicans because the party also had little success in winning other high offices. That year, the Democrats elected to statewide office included Ann Richards as state treasurer, Jim Hightower as agriculture commissioner, Gary Mauro as land commissioner, and Jim Mattox as attorney general. Republican fortunes improved in 1986 when Clements returned to the governor's office. He defeated White in what many termed a "revenge match," and he used his return to resume building the Republican Party in Texas.

The "Conversion" and Election of Phil Gramm

After four terms in office, John Tower announced he would not seek reelection to the U.S. Senate in 1984. Phil Gramm, the Democratic representative from Texas's Sixth Congressional District, used Tower's retirement to advance from the U.S. House to the Senate. Gramm had first been elected to the U.S. House of Representatives in 1978 as a Democrat. By early 1981, he had gained some national prominence for his work on the federal budget under Republican President Ronald Reagan. Gramm, who served as a member of the House Budget Committee, was accused of leaking Democratic strategy to the White House Budget Office. David Stockman, budget director under Reagan, confirmed that Gramm had in fact done this.[47] Because of his disloyalty to the party and because of House rules, Gramm was not reappointed to another term on the Budget Committee.

In a smart political move, Gramm used the loss of his committee seat as an excuse to convert to the Republican Party. In 1983 Gramm resigned his seat in the U.S. House. Outgoing Republican Governor Clements called a

Former Senator Gramm, with wife Wendy by his side.

© Kenneth Lambert/AP Images

special election, which was held one month after Gramm's resignation, to fill Gramm's seat. Because no other candidate could possibly put together a successful campaign in so short a time and due to the fit between his views and the state's conservative majority, Gramm easily won reelection to the same seat he had just vacated—this time as a Republican. In 1984, "fully baptized" as a Republican, Gramm won election as U.S. Senator, thereby filling the seat previously held by John Tower. This allowed the Republican Party to retain one of Texas's two seats in the U.S. Senate. Gramm easily won reelection in 1990 and 1996 but chose not to run for reelection in 2002, thus ending a long career in Texas politics.

The Move toward Parity with the Democrats

In 1988, the Republican Party in Texas made significant gains, aided by Bill Clements's return to the governor's mansion and George H. W. Bush's election to the presidency. The party won four statewide offices. Three Republicans won election to the Texas Supreme Court, and Kent Hance was elected to the Texas Railroad Commission.

In 1990, Republicans captured the offices of state treasurer and agriculture commissioner and another seat on the state supreme court. The big setback for the Republicans in 1990 was the loss of the governor's office. Bill Clements did not seek reelection. Clayton Williams, a political newcomer, used his considerable wealth to win the Republican nomination. His campaign for governor was something of a disaster, and he lost to Democrat Ann Richards. Williams's loss, in a way, aided George W. Bush's 1994 gubernatorial and 2000 presidential victories. If Williams had won and served two terms, Bush could not have been elected governor until 1998, and this would have made it less likely for him to make a legitimate bid for the presidency in 2000.

Ann Richards, Governor of Texas, 1991–1995.
© Bettmann/Corbis

In 1992, after serving as U.S. Senator from Texas for 20 years, Democrat Lloyd Bentsen resigned to become Secretary of the Treasury under President Clinton. His resignation allowed Texas Republicans to capture their second seat in the U.S. Senate with the election of Kay Bailey Hutchison. (Phil Gramm, in the meantime, had been reelected to his seat in the U.S. Senate.)

The One-Party Republican Era in Texas

The 1994 election marked the year that Texas went from its brief two-party system to a one-party Republican system. In 1994, the Republicans captured all three seats on the Railroad Commission as well as a majority of the seats on the state supreme court, and they retained control of the agriculture commissioner's office. They gained three additional seats on the state board of education, for a total of eight. In addition, George W. Bush was elected governor. When the dust cleared, Republicans controlled 23 of a total 27 statewide offices. Subsequent elections only solidified their position. After the 1998 elections, the Republicans held all statewide offices. After the 2000 elections, Republicans held all statewide offices and were in the majority in both the Texas House and Senate (see Table 9.2). These victories substantially changed Texas party politics.

For realignment to have occurred, the shift in party affiliation must be enduring and of considerable magnitude. Therefore, party realignment cannot be confirmed unless a significant amount of time has passed, and the observed change was large in

TABLE 9.2

Total Offices Held by Republicans, 1974–2016

Year	U.S. Senate (2)	U.S. House (36)	Statewide Office (27)	Texas Senate (31)	Texas House (150)	County Office	Board of Education (15)
1974	1	2	0	3	16	53	—
1976	1	2	0	3	19	67	—
1978	1	4	1	4	22	87	—
1980	1	5	1	7	35	166	—
1982	1	5	0	5	36	270	—
1984	1	10	0	6	52	377	—
1986	1	10	1	6	56	504	—
1988	1	8	5	8	57	608	5
1990	1	8	6	8	57	717	5
1992	1	9	7	13	58	814	5
1994	2	11	13	14	61	900	8
1996	2	11	13	17	68	950	8
1998	2	11	18	16	71	973	9
2000	2	11	18	16	71	1,231	9
2002	2	15	27	19	88	1,327	10
2004	2	22	27	19	87	1,390	10
2006	2	22	27	19	81	1,410	10
2008	2	22	27	19	76	1,345	6
2010	2	26	27	19	101	1,356	6
2012	2	23	27	19	100	n/a	11
2014	2	25	27	20	97	n/a	10
2016	2	25	27	20	95	n/a	10

The number in parentheses at the top of each column represents the current total number of offices in that category. State Board of Education was not elected until 1988.

scope.[48] In retrospect, it seems clear that such a realignment has occurred in Texas. More than 20 years after the state converted to Republican dominance, Republicans still hold all statewide offices and the majority of state legislative seats. Today the state is as solidly one-party Republican as it had been one-party Democratic.

The Current Party System in Texas

Learning Objective: Explain the history of party realignment, one-party Republican dominance, and party dealignment in Texas.

With Republican dominance firmly established in Texas, the state party system has remained fairly stable for several decades. After George W. Bush's rise to the presidency in 2000, his Republican lieutenant governor, Rick Perry, succeeded him in the governor's office. Perry was subsequently reelected for three full terms and became the longest-serving governor in Texas history (as well as the second longest-serving state governor in U.S. history). After more than 14 years in office, Perry was succeeded by current Governor Greg Abbott. Texas politicians have continued to attain prominence on the national stage as well; Perry and fellow Texans Ron Paul and Ted Cruz have all thrown their hats in the ring as Republican Party presidential candidates in recent years.

An Update on the Republicans

The Republican Party in Texas, like most dominant parties, is currently characterized by multiple, sometimes overlapping, wings with differing agendas. Two of the primary wings are the social conservatives and the more pro-market, libertarian Republicans. However, traditional establishment and pro-business conservatives (some of whom might more accurately be called moderates in contemporary Texas politics), such as Speaker of the House Joe Straus, are also well-represented in the diverse Republican caucus.

Traditionally, pro-business conservatives have been at the core of the Texas establishment. Their priorities were to keep spending and taxes low while limiting state government regulation of the economy. Their goal has been to foster a pro-business climate, even when a general free-market outlook was compromised by active government support of business. This has meant support for government spending on infrastructure, such as roads, highways, and port development and maintenance. But it has also meant more active efforts, such as special subsidies for companies like the Texas Enterprise Fund and the Texas Emerging Technology Fund.[49] Of course, some due consideration is also given to the basic economic liberalism shared by the pro-market, libertarian Republicans. This economic liberalism is centered on a belief in the existence of an efficient, largely self-regulating market that functions best when government strongly defends property rights. But either because of the power of special interests or a principled position that sometimes the business climate needs a helping hand, the pro-business establishment Republicans have not generally been too particular about adhering strictly to the creed of economic liberalism. This, in turn, drives the more pure free-market libertarian Republicans to call some of the pro-business efforts "crony capitalism," inconsistent with true capitalism.[50]

The social conservatives focus on "culture war" issues and are troubled by a perceived decline of morality in Texas and the United States in general. These conservatives stress their pro-life stance against abortion, oppose gay civil rights (including same-sex marriage), support prayer in public schools (although this is not a consensus view, even among social conservatives), and have pushed for teaching alternatives to evolution (such as creationism or intelligent design) in the public schools. The strength of these conservatives was seen in the Texas Republican primary in July 2012, when Tea Party and social conservative candidate Ted Cruz defeated the pro-business conservative and establishment candidate (and then-lieutenant governor) David Dewhurst in the race for U.S. Senate (57 percent to 43 percent). Dewhurst's defeat was also a defeat for then-governor Rick Perry, who had supported Dewhurst.

Governor Greg Abbott.
© Tony Gutierrez/AP Images

There is also a rising force in the GOP—the more pro-market, libertarian Republicans who are as committed to personal liberty as they are to economic freedom and who challenge both the party establishment and the social conservatives. Indeed, Wayne Slater of the *Dallas Morning News* argues that the "real divide within the Texas GOP is between Christian conservatives who have been dominant in recent years and 'liberty' groups with a more secular view—those who believe government should set a moral agenda and those who want as little government as possible."[51] Some, including supporters of Kentucky Senator and recent Republican presidential candidate Rand Paul (son of long-time Texas Republican Congressman Ron Paul) believe at the national level that these libertarian types represent the future of the Republican Party if it is to compete with the Democrats. It is unclear whether they can make serious inroads in the still relatively conservative Texas GOP or find a way to live together with more socially conservative Republicans in a "fusionist" party that somewhat mirrors the one that Ronald Reagan put together in the 1980s.[52]

Finally, it should be noted that the "Tea Party" includes both some of the pro-market libertarian Republicans and the social conservative Republicans. Indeed, some members fuse (in more or less consistent ways) the libertarian freedom agenda with a number of social conservative positions. The group also includes a fair number of anti-establishment or more populist tenants who rage against the many problems they see coming from the political and cultural power centers on both coasts. It is unclear at the time of this writing what impact Donald Trump's presidential campaign will have on the GOP nationally and in the state of Texas.

An Update on the Democrats

In contrast with twentieth-century Texas Democrats, the state Democratic Party today has less factional infighting because the vast majority of conservative Democrats have stampeded to the Republican Party. Nevertheless, the party has struggled to win elections; no Democrat has been elected to statewide office since 1994.[53] In fact, in recent years, there have been numerous races at both the state and county levels for which the Democrats have not even fielded a candidate.

In an effort to revitalize their standing in the state, Democratic Party operatives recently launched an initiative called "Turn Texas Blue." (The name plays on the common media reference to Republican-dominated states as "red" states and Democratic states as "blue" states.) This Democratic movement is alternatively known as "Battleground Texas" and refers to efforts to return Texas to Democratic dominance. Wendy Davis's 2014 campaign for governor was seen as key to that effort. Even though she lost in her unlikely campaign against heavily favored Greg Abbott, Davis's candidacy was seen as critical to the long-term Democratic Party effort, given her ability to raise money and inspire the grass-roots.[54] Fundraising, grassroots inspiration, and building party infrastructure are seen as important to the long-term success of this initiative.

In addition, the Democrats have two talented young Hispanic politicians to aid in this effort: the Castro brothers. Former San Antonio mayor and Obama administration Secretary of Housing and Urban Development, Julián Castro, and his twin brother, U.S. Congressman Joaquín Castro (representing Texas's 20th district), are likely to be key players in the future of the Democratic Party in Texas and in Washington. Democrats could also benefit from the influx of in-migrants from other states that could change the state's political culture (though these migrants may also consider themselves "refugees" from more liberal states).

Democrats have long viewed demographic realities in the state cutting in their favor, particularly the relative increase in the size of the Hispanic population. *Texas Monthly* recently explained this logic:

> Demography is the driver of this runaway freight train. The 2010 census found that the state's population had increased by 4.3 million over the previous decade and that more than 3.3 million of the new inhabitants were minorities. Of these, an astounding 2.8 million were Hispanic, historically a reliable constituency for Democrats. These numbers conveyed a new reality: the Texas political landscape was getting friendlier for Democrats and tougher for Republicans.[55]

However, there are a few caveats to a Democratic destiny that some see as inevitable. First, some liberal Democrats—including Davis herself, given her strong support of abortion rights—may not be attractive to more socially conservative

Wendy Davis, flanked by Julian Castro (left) and Joaquin Castro (right).
© LeAnn Mueller

Hispanics. This can be seen in Davis's inability to perform well in many parts of south Texas during the 2014 primary.[56] Second, as the *New Republic* argues, "Latinos in Texas are disproportionately ineligible to vote. Too many either aren't citizens or are too young to upend the state in the next few election cycles."[57] Third, the Republican Party also gets a vote in this war for the future. More specifically, the Republicans aren't likely to hold pat and allow Texas to turn blue without a fight. They have already begun greater outreach efforts toward minorities. This fight for Hispanic voters will also be impacted by whether the current Republican governing majority is successful in maintaining Texas's general economic growth, as well as providing opportunities for the Hispanic community in particular. However, it is unclear if the state's Republicans can be successful in attracting Hispanics to their cause, especially if national Republican policies (for instance, those regarding immigration) or the rhetoric of Republican national leaders (such as Donald Trump) cut against those efforts.

Focus On

The Political Affiliation of Hispanics

© VikingIllustrations/Alamy

Hispanic Texans are more likely to be affiliated with the Democratic Party than with the Republican Party. According to Gallup survey data from 2013, 46 percent of Hispanics living in Texas either identify as or lean Democratic, whereas 27 percent were Republican or leaning Republican. This sizable Democratic advantage among Hispanics tracks with the national trend; however, Hispanics in Texas were somewhat less likely to prefer the Democratic Party (and somewhat more likely to prefer the Republican Party) than Hispanics living in all other states.[58] (Viewed from another perspective, Hispanic Texans are more likely to describe themselves as conservative or moderate than Hispanics in California.[59])

This apparent preference for the Democratic Party among Hispanics has not translated into across-the-board support for Democratic candidates or into Democratic victories at the polls. Exit poll data from 2014 showed that Democratic gubernatorial candidate Wendy Davis won the Hispanic vote in Texas (55 percent to 44 percent), even though she lost the election to Republican Greg Abbott. In Texas's U.S. Senate race that year, the Hispanic vote was basically evenly split between the Democratic and Republican candidates (47 percent to 48 percent).[60] Republican incumbent John Cornyn was reelected easily.

Many eyes are trained on how the Hispanic population will impact the future political balance in Texas. In nationwide polling, about half (49 percent) of Hispanic voters have said the most important issue to them is the economy, followed by health care (24 percent) and illegal immigration (16 percent).[61] Therefore, Republican handling of the state's economy could be crucial to that party's ability to secure the Hispanic vote. The Republican Party of Texas has made specific efforts to appeal to Hispanics, such as the formation of interest groups to recruit Hispanic candidates for office and the promotion of Hispanic leadership within the GOP. Texas Democrats, for their part, have outlined a strategy of increasing voter registration and turnout among Hispanics in the state, and they face the challenge of engaging increasing numbers of Hispanic youth as they reach voting age.[62]

Critical Thinking Questions

1. Thinking back on what we have learned about voting patterns in Texas, what are the challenges each party faces in terms of recruiting Hispanic voters to their cause?

2. In light of anticipated demographic changes in the state, what do you think the outcome will be with regard to Texas's party system?

If the Democrats are successful in turning Texas "blue," the national political ramifications could be huge. Indeed, it could cinch Democratic dominance at the presidential level and perhaps beyond. As recent U.S. Trade Representative and former Dallas mayor Ron Kirk noted in 2010: "When Texas turns blue, this country's going to turn blue and it's going to stay blue."[63] Republican Ted Cruz was even more dour about the future of the Republican Party if Texas goes Democratic, arguing: "No Republican will ever again win the White House . . . If Texas turns bright blue, the Electoral College math is simple . . . The Republican Party would cease to exist."[64] Clearly, the success or failure of these efforts will have big national and state ramifications.

CORE OBJECTIVE

© Editorial Image, LLC/Alamy

Being Socially Responsible . . .

What impact, if any, do factions have on enhancing or diminishing civic engagement?

In your opinion, do factions promote acceptance of diverse opinions?

Party Dealignment

Learning Objective: Explain the history of party realignment, one-party Republican dominance, and party dealignment in Texas.

In analyzing voter behavior, political scientists define "dealignment" as voters "moving away" or distancing themselves from both of the major political parties.[65] In contrast with realignment, the connection with one party is not merely replaced with connection to a different party. Rather, in a dealigned system, voters remain unaffiliated.

party dealignment

View that a growing number of voters and candidates do not identify with either major political party but are independents

Many political scientists believe that an era of **party dealignment** began at the national level in the late 1960s or early 1970s[66] and reached Texas a decade or so later. There is evidence that this trend toward dealignment has persisted. First, as discussed in Chapter 7, voter turnout is low. When former governor Rick Perry was reelected to his final term in office in 2010, only 27 percent of the voting-age population participated in the election.[67] Low voter turnout is thought to be a symptom of dealignment, as a result of apathy toward the two major parties.[68] However, this lack of participation might also be expected in a one-party state with a traditionalistic political culture.

In further support of the dealignment theory, voters have increasingly engaged in split-ticket voting—that is, voting for candidates from different parties, instead of just one party, within the same election. In the past, straight-ticket voting was much more prevalent and indicated party loyalty. In addition, campaigns have become increasingly candidate-centered. To connect directly with voters, candidates distance themselves from parties and try to establish themselves as brand names. Many candidates do not put their party affiliation on their billboards, yard signs, and campaign literature. Their goal is to achieve name recognition rather than promote the party. By using mass media in campaigns, candidates attempt to reach a broad swath of the electorate, rather than directing their message only to party members.[69]

Perhaps the most direct assessment of dealignment comes from simply asking voters about their party affiliation. Based on polling data, the number of people across the United States who identify themselves as a member of either major party appears to have declined. According to the most recent national figures from Gallup (an independent polling firm), in April 2016, the number of Americans surveyed who identified as either Democrat or Republican was at or near historic lows (31 percent and 25 percent, respectively). On the other hand, 44 percent of respondents considered themselves "independent." Since 2011, Gallup polls have consistently shown independent identification to be above 40 percent nationally, and this figure is higher than in previous years. However, survey respondents who initially identified as independent were subsequently asked whether they leaned toward one party or the other. When these follow-up responses were included, a total of 49 percent of Gallup's sample identified as either Democrat or leaning Democrat, and 41 percent identified as Republican or leaning Republican.[70]

This is roughly consistent with data specific to Texas. According to 2015 data from Gallup, 37 percent of Texans identified as either Democratic or leaning Democratic, whereas nearly 43 percent identified as Republican or leaning Republican.[71] Another poll conducted in February 2016 by the University of Texas and the *Texas Tribune* found 44 percent of those surveyed identified as Democrat, 42 percent as Republican, and 14 percent as independent.[72] In other words, the state was split about evenly in terms of identification with the two major parties, and relatively few considered themselves independent. These newer figures suggest that the Democratic Party may be gaining steam in Texas and that the ranks of the independents may be thinning. However, this data, combined with national polling, calls into question the conventional wisdom regarding independents. Namely, it is unclear whether most self-identified independents were ever truly free of party leanings in the first place. Indeed, political scientists and journalists have suspected for some time that so-called independents actually harbor allegiance to one party or the other, even if they do not outwardly admit such an affiliation.[73]

Therefore, though there is some support for dealignment theory, other evidence suggests that, deep down, most Americans do in fact maintain a connection with one of the two major political parties.

Third-Party Movements

Learning Objective: Describe third-party movements in the United States and in Texas.

Although the story of Texas politics is generally one of two major political parties, third-party movements develop in Texas from time to time. Some are national, whereas others have been state based. At a national level, segregationist George Wallace used the American Independent Party to run for president in

Raza Unida (United Race)
Minor party that supported election of Hispanic Americans in Texas in the 1970s

1968 and managed to gain nearly 19 percent of the vote in Texas.[74] In the 1970s, the **Raza Unida** (United Race) Party ran candidates for several state and local offices, especially in south Texas. As a Raza Unida candidate, Ramsey Muniz managed to gain 6 percent of the vote for governor in 1972.[75]

The Libertarian Party has put forth candidates for statewide office in Texas for many years. It adheres to the principles of respect for individual rights, constitutionalism and the rule of law, personal responsibility, and limited government.[76] In general, Libertarian Party (LP) candidates do not receive more than a small percentage of the vote, especially because many Republicans also espouse the same principles. It is also the case that not all philosophical libertarians belong to the LP, and some of these are principled non-voters. Nobel Prize-winning economist Milton Friedman, for example, famously noted he was a "small-l" libertarian and a "large-R" Republican—meaning his party of choice was the Republican Party even though his principles were largely libertarian. The most successful Libertarian candidate for governor of Texas was Jeff Daiell, who received 3.3 percent of the vote in 1990.[77] The LP has consistently maintained its status as a minor party in Texas and guaranteed its candidates' appearance on the ballot by garnering at least 5 percent of total votes cast in the previous election.[78] Currently, Libertarians hold five elected offices in Texas: three city council seats and two town mayorships, and the party had 88 candidates for statewide and local offices on the ballot in 2016.[79] Despite its staying power, it is highly unlikely the LP will ever be a major electoral force in the state.

Texas industrialist Ross Perot ran as an independent candidate for president in 1992; he received about 22 percent of the statewide vote in Texas (see Table 9.3) as well as an impressive 19 percent of the national vote. In 1996, the Natural Law Party gained enough signatures to have its name placed on the ballot in Texas. This organization promoted the idea of transcendental meditation as a way to reduce crime and strongly supported environmental protection, clean energy, and health issues. This party is no longer active in Texas.[80] However, the Green Party of Texas, which advocates social justice, ecological sustainability, nonviolence, and political reform (including public financing of election campaigns), has been more active in recent years (see Table 9.4).[81] It, too, is unlikely to occupy a prominent place in state politics.

TABLE 9.3

Texas General Election Results for President, 1992–2016

Year	Candidate	Percentage of Vote
1992	**Republican**	
	George Bush/Dan Quayle	40.56%
	Democrat	
	Bill Clinton/Al Gore	37.07%
	Independent	
	Ross Perot/James Stockdale	22.01%
	Libertarian	
	Andre Marrou/Nancy Lord	0.32%
1996	**Republican**	
	Bob Dole/Jack Kemp	48.75%

	Democrat	
	Bill Clinton/Al Gore	43.83%
	Independent	
	Ross Perot/James Campbell	6.74%
	Libertarian	
	Harry Browne/Jo Jorgensen	0.36%
2000	**Republican**	
	George W. Bush/Dick Cheney	59.29%
	Democrat	
	Al Gore/Joe Lieberman	37.98%
	Green	
	Ralph Nader/Winona LaDuke	2.15%
	Libertarian	
	Harry Browne/Art Olivier	0.36%
2004	**Republican**	
	George W. Bush/Dick Cheney	61.08%
	Democrat	
	John F. Kerry/John Edwards	38.22%
	Libertarian	
	Michael Badnarik/Richard V. Campagna	0.52%
2008	**Republican**	
	John McCain/Sarah Palin	55.45%
	Democrat	
	Barack Obama/Joe Biden	43.68%
	Libertarian	
	Bob Barr/Wayne A. Root	0.69%
2012	**Republican**	
	Mitt Romney/Paul Ryan	57.16%
	Democrat	
	Barack Obama/Joe Biden	41.38%
	Libertarian	
	Gary Johnson/Jim Gray	1.10%
	Green	
	Jill Stein/Cheri Honkala	0.30%
2016	**Republican**	
	Donald Trump/Mike Pence	52.23%
	Democrat	
	Hillary Clinton/Tim Kaine	43.24%
	Libertarian	
	Gary Johnson/William Weld	3.16%
	Green	
	Jill Stein/Ajamu Baraka	0.80%

Source: Office of the Secretary of State, 1992-Current Election History, See: (http://elections.sos.state.tx.us/elchist.exe).

To date, third parties have not had much impact on Texas politics. The rules governing elections in Texas, as in many other states, do not make it easy for third parties to gain access to the ballot. Even if third parties do gain access, they still face an uphill battle to secure the financial resources necessary to run a successful high-dollar media campaign. Often the best a minor party can hope to do is to have its ideas picked up by a major party. Ross Perot is credited with

TABLE 9.4

Texas Election Results for Governor, 1994–2014

Year	Candidate	Percentage of Vote
1994	**Republican**	
	George W. Bush	53.47%
	Democrat	
	Ann W. Richards	45.87%
	Libertarian	
	Keary Ehlers	0.64%
1998	**Republican**	
	George W. Bush	68.23%
	Democrat	
	Garry Mauro	31.18%
	Libertarian	
	Lester R. "Les" Turlington, Jr.	0.55%
2002	**Republican**	
	Rick Perry	57.80%
	Democrat	
	Tony Sanchez	39.96%
	Libertarian	
	Jeff Daiell	1.46%
	Green	
	Rahul Mahajan	0.70%
2006	**Republican**	
	Rick Perry	39.02%
	Democrat	
	Chris Bell	29.78%
	Independent	
	Carole Keeton Strayhorn	18.11%
	Independent	
	Richard "Kinky" Friedman	12.44%
	Libertarian	
	James Werner	0.60%
2010	**Republican**	
	Rick Perry	54.97%
	Democrat	
	Bill White	42.29%
	Libertarian	
	Kathie Glass	2.19%
	Green	
	Deb Shafto	0.39%
2014	**Republican**	
	Greg Abbott	59.27%
	Democrat	
	Wendy R. Davis	38.90%
	Libertarian	
	Kathie Glass	1.41%
	Green	
	Brandon Parmer	0.39%

Source: Office of the Secretary of State, 1992–Current Election History. See: (http://elections.sos.state.tx.us/elchist.exe).

focusing on the need to balance the federal budget in his 1992 campaign. Few other good examples of third-party movements that have had an impact on state or national policy can be found in the late twentieth century to early twenty-first century. Instead, we have seen groups like the "Tea Party" emerge as a faction within a major party and attempt to influence that party. Indeed, the Tea Party has explicitly tried to fight within the Republican Party to reshape or focus the party on Tea Party policy preferences. This strategy has met with mixed electoral results, but it has certainly led to a fight on "the Right" about the future of conservatism and the Republican brand. A recent manifestation of this fight occurred in 2014 in Virginia, where a relatively obscure Tea Party-backed candidate (David Brat) defeated the incumbent U.S. House majority leader (Eric Cantor) in a primary race. Brat went on to win the general election and currently represents Virginia in Congress.

A number of reasons have been suggested to explain the failures of third parties in the United States at the federal and state levels. First, some scholars point to the political cultural consensus in our country and state. The United States operates within a narrower ideological range than has most of the world in the past couple of centuries. Our political range is rather limited, and most people agree on the foundations of our political order. Second is the issue of voter identification. Most people grew up with the two major parties. They know them and identify themselves politically in reference to those parties.

Third is the lack of proportional representation in our state and national legislatures. Many countries elect representatives based on the percentage of the national and provincial (state) vote that the parties receive. For example, if in Germany 35 percent of the votes are cast for a Christian Democratic candidate, then 35 percent of the seats in the national or provincial/state legislature will be held by Christian Democrats. In the United States, we have single-member districts. A candidate is elected if he or she receives more votes than any other candidate, regardless of any other election outcome. Therefore, if people vote for a candidate who comes in third, their votes do not result in any seats in the legislature.

Another factor that hurts third parties is the fact that candidates can be elected to office by a plurality (winning the most votes, not necessarily more than 50 percent) rather than a majority (winning with more than 50 percent of the votes). Currently, Texas law requires that to win a primary election, a candidate must win a majority of the vote. But candidates in general elections for positions in the executive, judicial, and legislative branches in the United States and Texas need to win only a plurality of the vote. If a majority was required, it is possible that would increase the bargaining leverage of third parties and their candidates, thereby raising the profile of both and leading to increased support and interest in those third parties.

The difficulty of third parties in single-member districts with plurality election rules is not surprising given **Duverger's Law**. This scientific law tells us that the electoral system strongly conditions the type of party system that will result. Therefore, an electoral system in which candidates in single-member districts only need to win a plurality incentivizes parties to develop broad pre-election coalitions and disincentivizes more narrow parties that cannot win a large vote share (and thus consistently fail to win any elections). Likewise, in proportional representation systems, there is little disincentive for smaller parties, because they can win seats without winning pluralities or majorities and even play a key role in coalition governments.

Duverger's Law
A scientific law indicating that the electoral system strongly conditions the type of party system that will result

A fifth reason for third-party failure is that the two major parties legally limit access to the ballot. Republicans and Democrats are automatically on the ballot, but other parties need petitions signed by 5 to 10 percent of registered voters who did not vote in any of the primaries. Third parties must spend large amounts of money merely to qualify their candidates for the ballot. The two major parties have no such costs, so they are free to spend more money on the actual campaigns. Finally, the perception of third-party failure also contributes to the weakness of third parties. Many people think that a vote for a third party is wasted. Past failures reinforce the belief in future failures. No third-party candidate has ever won the U.S. presidency or the Texas governorship.

CORE OBJECTIVE

Source: National Park Service

Thinking Critically . . .

For a variety of reasons, third parties do not currently have much impact on Texas politics. What measures might be taken to level the playing field for third parties and improve their competitiveness in elections?

Party Organization in Texas

Learning Objective: Explain political party organization in Texas, including caucus and primary delegate selection systems.

© Republican Party of Texas

© Texas Democratic Party

Political parties in all states have both permanent and temporary organizations. Their structure is partly determined by federal and state law, but parties have some discretion in deciding specific arrangements. Additionally, rules established by the national Democratic and Republican party organizations might dictate state party actions in selected areas, such as the number of delegates to the national convention and how those delegates are selected.

Texas Election Code determines many aspects of party activity, especially the conduct of primary elections. Earlier we discussed the white primaries in Texas, which excluded African Americans from voting in Democratic Party primary elections and which were eventually outlawed by the U.S. Supreme Court. This is a good example of party activity being restricted by national or state laws. Parties are not free agents or purely private organizations, but quasi-public agents.

Each county in Texas is divided into election precincts. Also known as voting districts or election districts, precincts are the smallest political subdivisions in the state. According to Texas Election Code, each precinct must contain between 100 and 5,000 registered voters, although exceptions to this minimum standard may be granted for rural areas.[82] Statewide there are just under 8,000 election precincts.[83] When voters register, they are assigned to a precinct-based polling place near their home. Polling places are normally located in public buildings (schools, city halls, churches) but may be located in private buildings when no public building is available.

Permanent Party Organization

The **permanent party organization** within the state consists of a hierarchy of elected party officials who handle party business on a regular basis. At the lowest level is the precinct chair, whereas the highest level is the state chair.

The Precinct Chair

In March of even-numbered years, the Democrat and Republican parties in Texas each hold a primary election. In addition to selecting which of their party's candidates will run in the general election in November, primary voters also elect a **precinct chair** and a county chair. The role of the precinct chair is to organize the precinct, identify party supporters, make sure they are registered to vote, turn out voters on Election Day, and generally promote and develop the interests of the party. In the one-party Democratic era in Texas, few precinct chairs actually performed these duties; generally their only job was to serve as an election judge (the person who supervises the conduct of an election at a polling place) during primary and general elections. If Texas develops into a two-party state, the role of the precinct chair may change from election judge to party organizer at the grassroots level. In some counties this has already occurred, but neither party is well organized at the grassroots level.

The precinct chair serves a two-year term. Any registered voter who lives in the election precinct may file as a candidate for precinct chair, and his or her name will be placed on the ballot. Occasionally these races are contested, but often candidates for precinct chair are unopposed. Write-in votes are allowed if a declaration of write-in candidacy has been filed.

The County Chair

The next office in the party hierarchy is **county chair**. Similar to that of the precinct chair, the role of the county chair is to organize the party at the county level. This includes voter registration, fundraising, candidate recruitment and education, and facilitating the election of candidates in the general election. Informally, the county chair's duties consist of representing the party in the county, serving as the official spokesperson for the party, maintaining a party headquarters (in some counties), and serving as a fundraiser. Formally, the county chair is responsible for receiving formal filings from persons seeking to have their names placed on the party's primary election ballot, conducting the primary election, filling election judge positions, giving official notice of precinct and county conventions, and officially counting the ballots in the primary election.

The position of county chair is filled during the primary election for a two-year term. In large urban counties, the county chair is often a full-time employee of the party. Any registered voter who is a resident of the county may file for the office. In large urban counties, the race for this office is usually contested.

permanent party organization
Series of elected officials of a political party that keep the party organization active between elections

precinct chair
Party official elected in each voting precinct to organize and support the party

county chair
Party official elected in each county to organize and support the party

The County Executive Committee

county executive committee

Committee made up of a county chair and all precinct chairs in the county; serves as the official organization for the party in each county

The **county executive committee** is the next level in the permanent party organization. It is composed of a county chair and all precinct chairs within that county. The degree of organization of this committee varies greatly from county to county. In some counties, the executive committee is an active organization that works to promote the party's interests. In many counties, especially in rural areas, this committee is more an organization on paper that fulfills the formal duties of canvassing the election returns and filling vacancies in party offices when they occur. Occasionally, the committee might be called upon to fill a vacancy on the general election ballot if a nominee has died or has become ineligible to run between the time of the primary and the general election.

Many large metropolitan counties use, instead of the county executive committee, a district executive committee for these functions. This is an organizational convenience because these counties would otherwise have very large county committees. District committees are established based on the electoral districts from which federal and state officeholders are elected.

The State Executive Committee

state executive committee

Committee, made up of one man and one woman from each state senatorial district as well as a chair and vice-chair, that functions as the governing body of the party

The next level of permanent party organization is the **state executive committee**. The state executive committee consists of 62 members: one committeeman and one committeewoman from each of Texas's 31 state senatorial districts. Members of the state executive committee are elected at the state convention and serve two years; delegates to the convention gather by senatorial district and recommend representatives.

The state executive committee, guided by the chair and vice-chair, provides leadership for the party. Its duties are very similar to those of the county chair and county executive committee in terms of organizing the party and overseeing primary elections. However, the state executive committee is also a policy-making body. It establishes rules, orchestrates the state convention, and communicates with the national party organization. Both parties in Texas have permanent, full-time, paid professional staffs that do most of the work at the state level.

Being selected to serve on the state executive committee is considered an honor, usually reserved for those who have strong political ties and who have supported the party for many years. Occasionally a maverick group will surface and take control of the party and elect its people, who might not be the longtime party faithful.

The State Chair

state party chair

Heads the state executive committee and provides leadership for the party

The **state party chair** and state vice-chair, one of whom must be a man and the other a woman, are also elected at the state convention. These officers are chosen by a majority vote of all the delegates in attendance. Historically in the Democratic Party, the state chair and vice-chair were chosen by the governor or gubernatorial candidate, and the office of state chair was often filled by the governor's campaign manager. With the rise of the Republican Party and control of the governorship by the GOP, the state chair is no longer automatically chosen by the governor; however, the party's candidate for governor still has influence in the selection of the state party chair.

Temporary Party Organization

temporary party organization

Series of meetings or conventions that occur every two years at the precinct, county, and state levels

The **temporary party organization**, for both parties, consists of a series of conventions held in even-numbered years. These are the precinct, county or senatorial district, and state conventions. These conventions are not limited to elected party officials; rather, they are attended by a greater number of party supporters. Because these meetings last for only a brief period of time, they are referred to as the "temporary" party organization.

Precinct Convention

The precinct convention is usually held on the same day as the party primary in March. Only individuals who voted in that party's primary are eligible to attend; all those who attend are considered delegates to the precinct convention. The polls usually close at 7:00 p.m., and the precinct convention begins shortly thereafter, typically between 7:00 and 7:30 p.m. The precinct chair acts as temporary chair of the convention, verifying that attendees have voted in that party's primary, calling the meeting to order, and directing the election of permanent officers to run the remainder of the meeting. Sometimes, especially during presidential election years, there is contention over control of the convention's offices. In non-presidential-election years, though, attendance is usually very low, and control of the convention is generally not an issue.

After officers are elected, the convention's most important function is the selection of delegates to attend the county convention (or the senatorial district convention, in large metropolitan counties). The number of delegates a precinct sends to the county convention is based on party support in the precinct; the higher the party support, the larger the number of delegates. For years, Democrats awarded one county convention seat for every 25 votes cast for the party's candidate for governor in the past election. During presidential election years, many people are interested in attending the county convention, and seats can be hotly contested. In odd years, finding enough volunteers to attend the county convention can be difficult. Precinct conventions may also adopt resolutions in hopes of having them included in the party platform.

County or Senatorial District Convention

The county convention (or senatorial district convention), which is held on the third Saturday after the primary election and precinct convention, is similar to the precinct convention. Again, its most important function is to select delegates to attend the next higher convention level (in this case, the state convention). The number of delegates a county sends to the state convention depends on the county's support for the party's gubernatorial candidate in the previous election.

State Convention

The state convention normally takes place in June of even-numbered years. Generally, the convention is held in a major city. During presidential election years, the most important event is the selection of delegates to the national convention, at which the party's candidate for president will be nominated. During presidential election years, the convention also selects representatives (or electors) to serve in the Electoral College in the event their party's candidate wins the popular vote in Texas. At the state convention, Democratic delegates break into separate meetings by state senatorial district and choose their elector. Republicans caucus by U.S. congressional district. These decisions are ratified by the convention as a whole. The party that wins the statewide popular vote sends its electors to meet in the state senate chamber in Austin on the

Texas Republican Party State Convention.
SOURCE: © LM Otero/AP Images

first Monday after the second Wednesday in December following the election. At 2 p.m. on that date, they cast their vote for their party's nominee for president.[84] Those chosen to serve in the Electoral College are generally longtime party supporters.

Even in non-presidential election years, the state convention handles important party business, including choosing state party officers and adopting a platform. In addition, the convention elects individuals to serve on the national committee for either the Democratic or Republican Party. This committee provides leadership for the party at the national level.

Caucus and Primary Delegate Selection Systems

Learning Objective: Explain political party organization in Texas, including caucus and primary delegate selection systems.

Both major parties hold national conventions every four years to nominate a candidate for president. These conventions are perhaps the best-known institutions of American political parties. They attract national media attention and are usually covered from gavel to gavel.

Primary versus Caucus

The nominating process is complex, and the party's nominee is ultimately determined by the number of delegates supporting each candidate. Each state is allocated a certain number of delegates to the national convention based on party rules. (In 2016, Texas Republicans were allowed to send 155 delegates to the Republican National Convention, and Texas Democrats were allowed 252 delegates to the Democratic National Convention.[85]) To determine the delegates who will be sent to the national convention (where they will vote to determine the party's nominee), states hold a caucus, a **presidential primary election**, or a combination of the two.

Texas uses a primary system to determine most of the state's delegates to the national party conventions. Democratic and Republican primaries are held every four years in March. In a **primary**, voters go to their polling place (as they would in a general election) and cast a ballot for the candidate they prefer as their party's nominee. In very general terms, delegates are awarded to candidates based on the proportion of the popular vote they receive in their party's primary. However, delegate allocation is complicated, and not all delegates are allocated based on the statewide outcome. For the Democrats, a large number of delegates are allocated based on the primary outcome in each state senatorial district; the Republicans allocate many of their delegates by primary outcomes in each of the state's 36 U.S. congressional districts.[86] In addition, in the Democratic Party some delegates are "unpledged" or not committed to any candidate; these delegates may vote for any candidate they choose at the national convention.[87] (These Democratic delegates are called "superdelegates.")

Until 2016, the Democratic Party in Texas used both a primary and a caucus to determine delegates to the national convention. In what was called the "Texas Two-Step," about three-fourths of Democratic delegates were allocated based on the outcome of the Democratic primary, while the other one-fourth was allocated based on caucuses.[88] After primary voting closed, primary voters could return to participate in their precinct convention (also called a **caucus**). A caucus is a town hall-style meeting of party members. Delegates were distributed based on the number of supporters for each candidate who were in attendance. The more supporters of a particular candidate who were present, the more delegates that candidate would receive.[89] Therefore, a candidate's ability to mobilize and turn out large numbers of people was crucial for success at these caucuses. The national leadership for the Democratic Party deemed the Two-Step confusing to voters, so the state party eliminated the caucus.[90]

Without presidential primary elections, all delegate preferences would be decided at conventions or caucuses. In states without presidential primaries, like Iowa, these meetings take on great significance. Delegates selected at the precinct level go on to participate in the county level convention and, eventually, at the state and national conventions. A well-organized group can dominate these meetings. In 2008, Arkansas Governor Mike Huckabee developed a strong grassroots organization and worked with local churches to win the most delegates in the Iowa caucuses. Churches were used as a rallying point before the evening caucus. Incentives such as potluck dinners, child-care services, and church buses that delivered voters to precinct conventions generated high turnout in support of the candidate.

Thus, a caucus system is a way of securing convention delegates that harkens back to the era of labor-intensive politics. It requires an organization of active

presidential primary election
Election held every four years by political parties to determine voters' preferences for presidential candidates

primary
An election used by major political parties in Texas to nominate candidates for the November general election

caucus
A meeting of members of a political party to nominate candidates (now used only by minor political parties in Texas)

volunteers to produce results. If a candidate inspires large numbers of voters to attend their precinct conventions, he or she can win enough delegates to move on and prevail at the county level. Win enough counties, and your delegation will dominate at the state level. If you are able to control the state, then your delegates will go on to the national convention. Control enough states, and you might win the nomination for president.

If Texas were to change from a primary system to using caucuses, different campaign organization and strategies would be required. Presidential primaries are mass media events that require big money and professional consultants. On the other hand, caucus systems require grassroots organization and dedicated volunteers. This demonstrates how important electoral rules are in impacting political behavior and outcomes. In Texas Republican state conventions since 1996, some Christian organizations have called for an end to primaries and a shift to the caucus system of selecting delegates. Because of religious groups' ability to organize and mobilize supporters, a caucus system would benefit them and allow them to control many delegates to the national convention. If this caucus were held early enough in the election process, it might affect the direction of the Republican presidential race, or at least give the winner some early exposure.

2008 Democratic Party Caucuses

One of the last iterations of the Democratic Party caucus in Texas was also one of its most chaotic. In 2008, Hillary Clinton and Barack Obama were in a very tight race for delegates, and the Texas primary was widely anticipated. Although in most election years, few people attended precinct conventions, the situation was quite different in 2008. That year, precinct conventions were attended by tens of thousands of people statewide, and party organizers were taken by surprise. Massive crowds of participants overwhelmed most convention chairs. Sign-in sheets, used to show candidate support, were in short supply. In some cases, people wrote on campaign signs to register attendees.

Confusion reigned throughout the evening. Crowds were often too large for the size of the rooms reserved. News reports described the meetings as attended by rowdy mobs. In a few cases, police were summoned. Many meetings began late and lasted until late in the evening. Most attendees had never attended a precinct meeting before and were unaware of why they were there and what the meeting would accomplish. The media had described the activity as a chance to vote twice, and many showed up thinking they were going to vote again.

Subsequent conventions were nearly a repeat of what had occurred at the precinct level. The county and district conventions held two weeks after the precinct meetings were equally well attended. Many attendees were first-timers who did not know the rules. Often these meetings ran from noon until late in the evening, with many attendees leaving before the convention had officially concluded. Some suggested that the whole process proved the old saying by Will Rogers, "I am not a member of any organized political party. I am a Democrat."

In the end, Clinton won the popular vote in the Texas primary, yet Obama secured the majority of the state's precinct convention delegates in the caucus. This allowed him to edge out Clinton in the total delegate count for the state (99 to 94).[91]

Conclusion

U.S. political parties are not nearly as strong today as they were in the past. That may seem counter-intuitive, given the frequency with which we hear the labels "Democrat" and "Republican" bandied about in the media. Political reforms during the Progressive Era significantly reduced the influence of parties. Yet, they still play a vital role in our democracy. The political history of Texas has basically been a tale of two major parties, marked by an earlier period of Democratic Party dominance, then, following a major realignment, a more recent period of Republican Party dominance. Although Texas is today a solidly Republican state, both major parties are well established.

The average citizen has little awareness of party organization at the state and local levels. The few active elite of the parties control this element of American politics. However, it is not very difficult to become part of this group. Any citizen with available time to devote to the party can become active at the precinct, county, and state levels. Most positions are not paid.

In the past, the state executive committees of both parties were likely to be part-time organizations with limited staff. Today, both parties have permanent headquarters, full-time paid professional staffs, and financial resources to help party development. They are actively engaged in organizing and building the party through voter identification and registration, candidate recruitment, candidate education, get-out-the-vote drives, and supporting candidates during the general election.

Summary

LO: Describe the evolution of the political party system in the United States and in Texas.

The United States has both national and state political party systems, which function fairly independently of each other. The United States does not have strong political parties. In fact, parties in the U.S. and Texas are weaker today than previously in our nation's history, thanks mainly to political reforms that took place during the Progressive Era. Due to this weakness, politics revolve primarily around candidates and their personalities.

LO: Explain the history of party realignment, one-party Republican dominance, and party dealignment in Texas.

For approximately a century after the end of Reconstruction, Texas was a one-party Democratic state. Then, following a realignment (or shift in party loyalty among voting citizens), Texas became a one-party Republican state. Republicans currently hold all statewide offices and the majority in both the Texas House and Senate. There is some evidence that a dealignment (or distancing of voters from both of the major political parties) has occurred, but opinions on this vary.

LO: Describe third-party movements in the United States and in Texas.

Third-party movements develop in the United States and Texas from time to time, but typically they are not very successful. Often the most a third party can hope to achieve is to have its issues adopted by one of the major parties.

LO: Explain political party organization in Texas, including caucus and primary delegate selection systems.

Political party organization in Texas includes both permanent (consisting of elected party officials) and temporary (consisting of a series of conventions) organizations. State party organization has become more professional over time. Major parties in Texas use a primary (or election), rather than a caucus (or meeting of members of a political party), to nominate candidates for the November general election.

Key Terms

caucus	party dealignment	Raza Unida
county chair	permanent party organization	realignment
county executive committee	political parties	state executive committee
Duverger's Law	precinct chair	state party chair
ideology	presidential primary election	straight-ticket voting
political action committees (PACs)	primary	temporary party organization

Notes

[1] Theodore J. Lowi, Benjamin Ginsberg, Kenneth A. Shepsle, and Stephen Ansolabehere, *American Government: Power and Purpose,* brief 12th ed. (New York: W.W. Norton Company, 2012), 354.

[2] Washington's Farewell Address to the People of the United States, https://www.gpo.gov/fdsys/pkg/GPO-CDOC-106sdoc21/pdf/GPO-CDOC-106sdoc21.pdf.

[3] Library of Congress, Creating the United States, Formation of Political Parties, https://www.loc.gov/exhibits/creating-the-united-states/formation-of-political-parties.html.

[4] Charles E. Neu, *Colonel House: A Biography of Woodrow Wilson's Silent Partner* (New York: Oxford University Press, 2015), 21–48.

[5] Texas Election Code Section 52.002, http://www.statutes.legis .state.tx.us/Docs/EL/htm/EL.52.htm.

[6] Danielle Kurtzleben, "2016 Campaigns Will Spend $4.4 Billion On TV Ads, But Why?" NPR, August 19, 2015, http://www.npr.org/sections/itsallpolit ics/2015/08/19/432759311/2016-campaign-tv-ad-spending.

[7] Robin Respaut and Lucas Iberico Lozada, "Some US ad firms could win big in the 2016 elections," *Business Insider,* April 14, 2015, http://www.businessinsider.com/r-slicing-and-dicing-how-some-us-firms-could-win-big-in-2016-elections-2015-4.

[8] Meta S. Brown, "Big Data Analytics and the Next President: How Microtargeting Drives Today's Campaigns," *Forbes,* May 29, 2016, http://www.forbes.com/sites /metabrown/2016/05/29/big-data-analytics-and-the-next-president-how-microtargeting-drives-todays-campaigns/#776b4ac31400.

[9] Patrick O'Connor, "Political Ads Take Targeting to the Next Level," *Wall Street Journal,* July 14, 2014, http://www .wsj.com/articles/political-ads-take-targeting-to-the-next-level-1405381606; Robin Respaut and Lucas Iberico Lozada, "Some US ad firms could win big in the 2016 elections," *Business Insider,* April 14, 2015, http://www .businessinsider.com/r-slicing-and-dicing-how-some-us-firms-could-win-big-in-2016-elections-2015-4.

[10] Rebecca Berg, "GOP Candidates Track Voter TV Preferences to Target Ads," RealClearPolitics.com, February 1, 2016, http://www.realclearpolitics.com/articles /2016/02/01/gop_candidates_track_voter_tv_preferences_ to_target_ads_129507.html.

[11] Robin Respaut and Lucas Iberico Lozada, "Some US ad firms could win big in the 2016 elections," *Business Insider,* April 14, 2015, http://www.businessinsider. com/r-slicing-and-dicing-how-some-us-firms-could-win-big-in-2016-elections-2015-4; Patrick O'Connor,

"Political Ads Take Targeting to the Next Level," *Wall Street Journal,* July 14, 2014, http://www.wsj.com/articles/ political-ads-take-targeting-to-the-next-level-1405381606.

[12] Robin Respaut and Lucas Iberico Lozada, "Some US ad firms could win big in the 2016 elections," *Business Insider,* April 14, 2015, http://www.businessinsider.com/r-slicing-and-dicing-how-some-us-firms-could-win-big-in-2016-elections-2015-4.

[13] White House Council of Economic Advisers, "Mapping the Digital Divide" (July 2015), https://www.whitehouse.gov /sites/default/files/wh_digital_divide_issue_brief.pdf; U.S. Census Bureau, Computer and Internet Use in the United States: 2013 (November 2014), http://www.census.gov /content/dam/Census/library/publications/2014/acs /acs-28.pdf.

[14] Donald Ratcliffe, "The Right to Vote and the Rise of Democracy, 1787–1828," *Journal of the Early Republic* 33 (Summer 2013): 234–235, http://jer.pennpress.org /media/26167/sampleArt22.pdf.

[15] John Kenneth White and Daniel M. Shea, *New Party Politics: From Jefferson and Hamilton to the Information Age* (Boston: Bedford/St. Martin's, 2000), 58.

[16] Ibid.

[17] Ibid.

[18] Jamie L. Carson and Jason M. Roberts, *Ambition, Competition, and Electoral Reform: The Politics of Congressional Elections Across Time* (Ann Arbor: University of Michigan Press, 2013), 53–54.

[19] John Kenneth White and Daniel M. Shea, *New Party Politics: From Jefferson and Hamilton to the Information Age* (Boston: Bedford/St. Martin's, 2000), 59–60.

[20] Frank Freidel and Hugh Sidey, "James Garfield," *The Presidents of the United States of America,"* White House Historical Association, http://www.whitehouse.gov/about /presidents/jamesgarfield.

[21] Pendleton Act (1883), http://www.ourdocuments.gov/doc. php?doc=48.

[22] John Kenneth White and Daniel M. Shea, *New Party Politics: From Jefferson and Hamilton to the Information Age* (Boston: Bedford/St. Martin's, 2000), 60.

[23] Ibid., 63–64.

[24] V. O. Key Jr., *Politics and Pressure Groups,* 4th ed. (New York: Thomas Y. Crowell, 1958), 331.

[25] Texas Secretary of State, Statewide Elected Officials, http:// www.sos.state.tx.us/elections/voter/elected.shtml.

[26] That being said, the current relationship between party and ideology is fairly robust. According to 2014 Gallup polls, a high percentage (70 percent) of U.S. Republicans identify

themselves as conservative, whereas only 19 percent of Democrats consider themselves conservative. On the other hand, 44 percent of Democrats call themselves liberal, while only 5 percent of Republicans identify with that moniker. See http://www.gallup.com/poll/180452/liberals-record-trail-conservatives.aspx.

[27] A 2015 Gallup poll found that 39.9 percent of Texans identified themselves as conservative, compared to 20.1 percent who described themselves as liberal. See http://www.gallup.com/poll/125066/State-States.aspx. Also, the Texas Statewide Survey, conducted by the University of Texas and the Texas Tribune in February 2016, found that 43 percent of Texans surveyed described themselves as extremely, somewhat, or leaning conservative, while 17 percent identified as extremely, somewhat, or leaning liberal. See https://texaspolitics.utexas.edu/sites/texaspolitics.utexas.edu/files/201602_poll_uttt_topline.pdf.

[28] Jeffrey E. Cohen and Paul Kantor, "The Places of Parties in American Politics," in *American Political Parties: Decline or Resurgence?* edited by Jeffrey E. Cohen, Richard Fleisher, and Paul Kantor (Washington, D.C.: CQ Press, 2001), 1–8.

[29] Randolph B. Campbell, "Antebellum Texas," *Handbook of Texas Online,* http://www.tshaonline.org/handbook/online/articles/npa01.

[30] Dale Baum, "Chicanery and Intimidation in the 1869 Gubernatorial Race," *Southwestern Historical Quarterly* 97 (April 1994), 34–54.

[31] Carl H. Moneyhon, "Davis, Edmund Jackson," *Handbook of Texas Online,* http://www.tshaonline.org/handbook/online/articles/fda37.

[32] V. O. Key Jr., *Southern Politics in State and Nation* (New York: Knopf, 1949), 7.

[33] Jack W. Gunn, "Greenback Party," *Handbook of Texas Online,* http://www.tshaonline.org/handbook/online/articles/wag01.

[34] Robert A. Calvert, Arnoldo De León, and Gregg Cantrell, *History of Texas* (Wheeling, Ill.: Harlan Davidson, 2002), 201–207.

[35] Jack M. Balkin, "Populism and Progressivism as Constitutional Categories—Part II," *Yale Law Journal* (1995).

[36] Donna A. Barnes, "People's Party," *Handbook of Texas Online,* http://www.tshaonline.org/handbook/online/articles/wap01.

[37] Ibid.

[38] Paul Johnson, *A History of the American People* (New York: Harper Collins, 1997), 599.

[39] Jack M. Balkin, "Populism and Progressivism as Constitutional Categories—Part II," *Yale Law Journal* (1995), http://www.yale.edu/lawweb/jbalkin/articles/popprog2.htm.

[40] John Halpin and Conor P. Williams, *The Progressive Intellectual Tradition in America,* Center for American Progress (April 2010), http://americanprogress.org/issues/progressive-movement/report/2010/04/14/7677/the-progressive-intellectual-tradition-in-america/.

[41] Lewis L. Gould, "Progressive Era," *Handbook of Texas Online,* http://www.tshaonline.org/handbook/online/articles/npp01; K. Austin Kerr, "Prohibition," *Handbook of Texas Online,* http://www.tshaonline.org/handbook/onlline/articles/vap01.

[42] V. O. Key, Jr., *Southern Politics in State and Nation,* 225.

[43] James L. Sundquist, *Dynamics of the Party System: Alignment and Realignment of Political Parties in the United States* (Washington, D.C.: Brookings Institute, 1983), 4.

[44] V. O. Key, Jr., "Secular Realignment and the Party System," in John Kenneth White and Daniel M. Shea, *New Party Politics: From Jefferson and Hamilton to the Information Age* (Boston: Bedford/St. Martin's, 2000), 148.

[45] James L. Sundquist, *Dynamics of the Party System: Alignment and Realignment of Political Parties in the United States* (Washington, D.C.: Brookings Institute, 1983), 9.

[46] Douglas O. Weeks, *Texas Presidential Politics in 1952* (Austin: University of Texas, Institute of Public Affairs, 1953), 3–4.

[47] David A. Stockman, *The Triumph of Politics: How the Reagan Revolution Failed* (New York: Harper & Row, 1986).

[48] James L. Sundquist, *Dynamics of the Party System: Alignment and Realignment of Political Parties in the United States* (Washington, D.C.: Brookings Institute, 1983), 5–6.

[49] Erica Grieder, "The Revolt Against Crony Capitalism," *Texas Monthly,* February 18, 2014, http://www.texasmonthly.com/story/revolt-against-crony-capitalism?fullpage=1.

[50] Ibid.

[51] Wayne Slater, "Texas GOP Splits between Social Conservatives, Libertarians," *Dallas Morning News,* June 7, 2014, http://www.dallasnews.com/news/politics/headlines/20140607-texas-gop-splits-between-social-conservatives-libertarians.ece.

[52] Frank S. Meyer, *In Defense of Freedom,* (Indianapolis: Liberty Fund, 1996).

[53] Aman Batheja, "Republicans Extend Statewide Streak to 16 Years," *Texas Tribune,* November 4, 2014, https://www.texastribune.org/2014/11/04/republicans-extend-statewide-streak-16-years/.

[54] Manny Fernandez, "For Wendy Davis, Filibuster Goes Only So Far in Race to Be Governor of Texas," *New York Times,* June 28, 2014, http://www.nytimes.com/2014/06/29/us/for-davis-filibuster-goes-only-so-far-in-race-to-be-governor-of-texas.html.

[55] Robert Draper, "The Life and Death (and Life?) of the Party," *Texas Monthly,* August 2013, http://www.texasmonthly.com/story/life-and-death-and-life-party?fullpage=1.

[56] Manny Fernandez, "For Wendy Davis, Filibuster Goes Only So Far in Race to Be Governor of Texas," *New York Times,* June 28, 2014, http://www.nytimes.com/2014/06/29/us/for-davis-filibuster-goes-only-so-far-in-race-to-be-governor-of-texas.html.

[57] Nate Cohn, "These Eight Charts Explain Why 'Blue Texas' Won't Happen," *New Republic,* August 11, 2013, http://www.newrepublic.com/article/114145/blue-texas-eight-charts-show-why-it-wont-happen.

[58] Andrew Dugan, "Texan Hispanics Tilt Democratic, but State Likely to Stay Red," Gallup, February 7, 2014, http://www.gallup.com/poll/167339/texan-hispanics-tilt-democratic-state-likely-stay-red.aspx.

[59] Jay Root, "Against the Grain, G.O.P. Dominated on Election Day," *New York Times,* November 8, 2012, http://www.nytimes.com/2012/11/09/us/gop-dominated-in-texas-on-election-day.html.

[60] Jens Manuel Krogstad and Mark Hugo Lopez, "Hispanic Voters in the 2014 Election: Democratic Advantage Remains, but Republicans Improve Margin in Some States," *Pew Research Center,* November 7, 2014, http://www.pewhispanic.org/2014/11/07/hispanic-voters-in-the-2014-election/.

[61] Ibid.

[62] Andrew Dugan, "Texan Hispanics Tilt Democratic, but State Likely to Stay Red," Gallup, February 7, 2014, http://www.gallup.com/poll/167339/texan-hispanics-tilt-democratic-state-likely-stay-red.aspx; Jason Margolis, "Could Latino Voters Turn Deep-Red Texas Democratic by 2020?" *The Atlantic,* May 29, 2012, http://www.theatlantic.com/politics/archive/2012/05/could-latino-voters-turn-deep-red-texas-democratic-by-2020/257738/.

[63] Alexander Burns, "Democrats Launch Plan to Turn Texas Blue," *Politico,* http://www.politico.com/story/2013/01/democrats-launch-plan-to-turn-texas-blue-86651_Page2.html.

[64] Tim Wigmore, "The Republicans' Worst Nightmare: Losing Texas and Becoming Extinct. Could It Really Happen?" *The Telegraph,* May 23, 2013, http://blogs.telegraph.co.uk/news/timwigmore/100218460/the-republicans-worst-nightmare-losing-texas-and-becoming-extinct-could-it-really-happen/.

[65] John Kenneth White and Daniel M. Shea, *New Party Politics: From Jefferson and Hamilton to the Information Age* (Boston: Bedford/St. Martin's, 2000), 152.

[66] David G. Lawrence, "On the Resurgence of Party Identification in the 1990s," in *American Political Parties: Decline or Resurgence?* ed. Jeffrey E. Cohen, Richard Fleisher, and Paul Kantor (Washington, D.C.: CQ Press, 2001), 54.

[67] Office of the Secretary of State, Race Summary Report, 2010 General Election, http://elections.sos.state.tx.us/elchist154_state.htm; Texas Secretary of State, Turnout and Voter Registration Figures (1970-current), http://www.sos.state.tx.us/elections/historical/70-92.shtml.

[68] White and Shea, New Party Politics: *From Jefferson and Hamilton to the Information Age,* 152.

[69] Richard Fleisher and Jon R. Bond, "Evidence of Increasing Polarization Among Ordinary Citizens," in A*merican Political Parties: Decline or Resurgence?* ed. Jeffrey E. Cohen, Richard Fleisher, and Paul Kantor (Washington, D.C.: CQ Press, 2001), 55–56.

[70] Gallup, "Party Identification,"http://www.gallup.com/poll/15370/party-affiliation.aspx; Jeffrey M. Jones, "Democratic, Republican Identification Near Historical Lows," *Gallup,* January 11, 2016, http://www.gallup.com/poll/188096/democratic-republican-identification-near-historical-lows.aspx.

[71] Gallup, "State of the States," http://www.gallup.com/poll/125066/State-States.aspx.

[72] University of Texas at Austin, The Texas Politics Project, Texas Statewide Survey (February 2016), https://texaspolitics.utexas.edu/sites/texaspolitics.utexas.edu/files/201602_poll_uttt_topline.pdf.

[73] For example, see Bruce E. Keith, David B. Magleby, Candice J. Nelson, Elizabeth A. Orr, Mark C. Westlye, and Raymond E. Wolfinger, *The Myth of the Independent Voter* (Berkeley: University of California Press, 1992); Alan I. Abramowitz, "The Myth of the Independent Voter Revisited," *Sabato's Crystal Ball,* August 20, 2009, http://www.centerforpolitics.org/crystalball/articles/aia2009082001/); and Amy Walter, "The Myth of the Independent Voter," *Cook Political Report,* January 15, 2014, http://cookpolitical.com/story/6608).

[74] Texas Secretary of State, Presidential Election Results, http://www.sos.state.tx.us/elections/historical/presidential.shtml.

[75] Teresa Palomo Acosta, "Raza Unida Party," *Handbook of Texas Online,* http://www.tshaonline.org/handbook/online/articles/war01.

[76] Libertarian Party of Texas, https://www.lptexas.org/).

[77] Ross Ramsey, "Analysis: Democrats Found Candidates, if Not Voters," *Texas Tribune,* June 4, 2014, http://www.texastribune.org/2014/06/04/analysis-democrats-found-candidates-if-not-voters/).

[78] Texas Secretary of State, Nominee of New Party or Party or Nominee of a Party Without Ballot Access in 2016, http://www.sos.state.tx.us/elections/candidates/guide/newparty.shtml.

[79] Libertarian Party, Elected Officials, http://www.lp.org
/candidates/elected-officials; Libertarian Party, 2016
Candidates, https://lptexas.org/candidates).

[80] Natural Law Party, Main Issues, http://www.natural-law.org
/platform/index.html).

[81] Green Party of Texas, Green Party of Texas State
Platform, http://www.txgreens.org/platform.

[82] Texas Election Code Sec. 42.006, http://www.statutes.legis
.state.tx.us/Docs/EL/htm/EL.42.htm.

[83] "Texas Primary Results," *New York Times,* June 2,
2016, http://www.nytimes.com/elections/results/texas.

[84] Benton, *Texas Politics,* 80–81.

[85] Eric Opiela, "Texas Delegate Selection Process to Republican
National Convention," https://www.texasgop.org
/wp-content/uploads/2013/10/Texas-Delegate-Selection-
Process-to-GOP-Convention.pdf; Texas Democratic Party,
"Texas Delegate Selection Plan for the 2016 Democratic
National Convention," September 23, 2015, http://www
.txdemocrats.org/act/be-a-delegate.

[86] Ibid.

[87] Texas Democratic Party, "Texas Delegate Selection
Plan for the 2016 Democratic National Convention,"
September 23, 2015, http://www.txdemocrats.org/act/
be-a-delegate.

[88] Ally Mutnick, "Texplainer: What's the 'Texas Two-Step' and
Why is it Gone?" *Texas Tribune,* July 7,
2015, https://www.texastribune.org/2015/07/07/
texplainer-whats-texas-two-step-and-why-it-gone/.

[89] Carolyn Feibel, "A Guide to Texas' Electoral Two-step,"
Houston Chronicle, March 1, 2008, http://www.chron.
com/news/politics/article/A-guide-to-Texas-electoral-two-
step-1653159.php.

[90] Ally Mutnick, "Texplainer: What's the 'Texas Two-Step'
and Why is it Gone?" *Texas Tribune,* July 7, 2015, https://
www.texastribune.org/2015/07/07/texplainer-whats-
texas-two-step-and-why-it-gone/.

[91] "Election 2008," *New York Times,* http://politics.nytimes.com/
election-guide/2008/results/states/TX.html.

CHAPTER 10

Interest Groups and Lobbying in Texas

Texas Learning Outcomes

- Evaluate the role of interest groups in Texas.

hapter 7 discussed various forms of participation in the political process. Being an active member of an interest group is yet another form of political participation and a way to exert influence on the government. Chapter 7 also demonstrated that voter participation in Texas is relatively low. This lack of citizen involvement in elections leads to a corresponding increase in the importance and influence of interest groups in Texas politics. Indeed, it is frequently not the individual, or even the more broadly defined "public opinion," that influences government, but rather these interest groups that have the ear of public officials. However, interest groups are not necessarily "others" but are often "us" as we act in concert with like-minded or similarly interested citizens.

An **interest group** is an organization of individuals sharing common goals that tries to influence governmental decisions. This term is often used interchangeably with the term "lobby group," although lobbying is a specific activity or technique (discussed later) whereby interest groups attempt to influence legislation. Sometimes the term PAC is also used to refer to interest groups. **Political action committees (PACs)** are organizations that collect and distribute money to candidates and, as such, are a more specialized kind of interest group. Often, broad-based interest groups have PACs associated with them. Interest groups are distinct from political parties in the sense that their members are not trying to gain election to public office.

Interest groups play an important role in a democratic society. They are capable of exerting both positive and negative effects on political processes and outcomes. Public attention is often drawn to the negative influences; however, interest groups and their activities are protected by the First Amendment to the U.S. Constitution, which provides for the people's right "peaceably to assemble, and to petition the Government for a redress of grievances."

interest group
An organization of individuals sharing common goals that tries to influence governmental decisions

political action committees (PACs)
Spin-offs of interest groups that collect money for campaign contributions and other activity

James Madison, c. 1821
© Courtesy National Gallery of Art, Washington

Early observers of American politics realized the importance of these political associations. In 1787, James Madison, writing under the name Publius in *Federalist No. 10*, predicted that interest groups or factions would play a significant role in American politics. Madison believed that the diversity of economic and social interests in an "extended republic" would be so great, and so many factions would form, that no one group would be able to dominate. Madison's observation regarding the diversity of national interests applies to most individual states as well—especially large and populous states such as Texas. Alexis de Tocqueville, writing in 1835, commented on the formation of interest groups in American politics and their importance in increasing individual influence.[1] De Tocqueville's observation to some degree confirmed Madison's predictions.

Chapter Learning Objectives

- Describe interest group typology.

- Discuss the various techniques interest groups use, including lobbying.

- Explain how interest groups are regulated.

- Describe the factors that influence interest groups' strength.

Interest Group Typology

Learning Objective: Describe interest group typology.

Considering the great diversity of economic and social interests in the country and the state, it would not surprise Madison that a vast array of interest groups exists throughout the United States and in Texas. Interest groups may be formed for any reason and may represent any interest. Many of these groups have both national and state organizations. The National Rifle Association (NRA), the U.S. Chamber of Commerce, Mothers Against Drunk Driving (MADD), and the National Education Association (NEA) are all examples of interest groups that are active on both the national and state levels.

The diversity of interest groups applies not just to the range of topics they address, but also to their form of organization and other characteristics. For instance, some groups are permanent organizations with full-time, well-financed professional staffs; others are temporary organizations that fade out of existence after their issue is resolved. Groups advocating property tax reform, insurance reform, and amendments to state constitutions are examples of such temporary groups. Groups can represent a single person, a large number of people, a private company, an entire industry, or even government employees and officials.

There are three broad categories of interest groups (see Table 10.1). **Membership organizations** are private groups whose members are individual citizens or businesses. **Nonmembership organizations** represent individuals, single corporations, businesses, law firms, or freelance lobbies; their membership is not open to the general public. **Government organizations** represent local government

membership organizations
Interest groups that have individual citizens or businesses as members

nonmembership organizations
Interest groups that represent corporations and businesses and do not have broad-based citizen support

government organizations
Interest groups that represent state and local governments; also called SLIGs, for state and local interest groups

TABLE 10.1

Interest Group Typology

Type	Examples
Membership Organizations	
Business/Agriculture	
Peak business organizations	Texas Association of Business
	State Chamber of Commerce
Trade associations	Texas Oil and Gas Association
	Good Roads Transportation Association
Agricultural trade groups	Texas Farm Bureau
	Corn Producers Association of Texas
Retail trade associations	Texas Apartment Association
	Texas Automobile Dealers Association
Professional Associations	
Private sector organizations	Texas Medical Association
	Texas Trial Lawyers Association
Public sector organizations	Texas State Teachers Association
	Association of Texas Professional Educators
Organized Labor Unions	Texas AFL-CIO
Noneconomic Membership Organizations	
Racial and ethnic groups	NAACP
	League of United Latin American Citizens
Religious groups	Christian Coalition of America
	Interfaith Alliance
Public interest groups	MADD
	American Civil Liberties Union
	AARP
	National Rifle Association
Nonmembership Organizations	
Representing individuals or single businesses	Halliburton Company
	American Airlines
	United Airlines
Government Organizations	
State and local interest groups (SLIGs)	Texas Municipal League
	Texas Police Chiefs Association

Source: Charles Wiggins, professor emeritus of political science at Texas A&M University, class handout, 1999.

(city, county, school board, special districts) as well as state and federal agencies. Membership in these organizations ranges from local elected officials (such as mayors and council members) to government employees (police officers, firefighters, and federal and state employees).[2] This type of group is also called a state and local interest group, or SLIG, and is discussed later in the chapter.

Membership Organizations

Membership organizations within the state represent a wide range of both economic and noneconomic interests. One kind of membership organization, a peak business association, is an interest group devoted to statewide business interests.

These groups primarily try to promote their members' interests, through a variety of means. While these groups favor policies conducive to maintaining the state's "good business climate," they also present a united front against policies they view as harmful to business and business owners. Examples of peak business associations include the state Chamber of Commerce (which merged with the Texas Association of Business in 1995), the Texas Association of Manufacturers, and the National Federation of Independent Business. These groups are often most active at the state level and are generally well financed.

trade associations
Interest groups that represent more specific business interests

Trade associations differ from peak business associations in that they represent more specific business interests. Texas has many such groups. Two trade associations often considered among the more powerful are the Texas Oil and Gas Association, representing oil and gas producers, and the Good Roads Transportation Association, which represents highway contractors.

CORE OBJECTIVE

Source: National Park Service

Thinking Critically . . .

Review Table 10.1. Are you a participant in a membership organization? If so, how does the organization represent your interests? If not, how are your interests represented at the state and federal levels of government?

Given the importance of agriculture to the Texas economy, it is not surprising that there are multiple types of agricultural interest groups. First are those that represent general farming interests. The Texas Farm Bureau, the largest farm organization in the state, represents large agricultural producers, whereas the Texas Farmers Union, the oldest farm organization in the state, represents family farms and ranches. The second type are organizations that represent commodity groups, such as cotton growers, cattle raisers, chicken raisers, and mohair producers. The third type of agricultural interest group represents suppliers to the above-mentioned producers. These groups include, for example, cotton ginners, seed and fertilizer producers, and manufacturers and sellers of farm equipment.

retail trade associations
Organizations seeking to protect and promote the interests of member businesses involved in the sales of goods and services

Retail trade associations are another type of trade group. The primary goal of these groups is to protect their trades from state regulations that the groups deem undesirable and to support regulation and policies favorable to the groups' interests (what some would consider "rent seeking" behavior, as we discuss later in the chapter). Examples of retail trade groups are the Texas Apartment Association, the Texas Automobile Dealers Association, the Texas Restaurant Association, and the Beer Alliance of Texas.

professional associations
Organizations promoting the interests of individuals who generally must hold a state-issued license to engage in their profession

Professional associations differ from trade associations in two ways: (1) members typically hold a professional license issued by the state, and (2) the state regulates their scope of practice. Some of the most well-known groups in this category represent physicians (the Texas Medical Association) and attorneys (the Texas Trial Lawyers Association). In addition, there are other organizations representing the interests of architects, landscape professionals, engineers, surveyors, plumbers, tax preparers, librarians, cosmetologists, funeral directors, athletic trainers, hearing aid dispensers, dentists, nurses, chiropractors, optometrists, pharmacists, podiatrists, psychologists, veterinarians, and many other professions.

Although medical, legal, and other aforementioned professions generally fall under the private sector, public school educators (who, ultimately, are government employees) are part of the public sector. There are multiple interest groups related to education. One such group is the Texas State Teachers Association (TSTA), the oldest (and formerly the largest) educators' association in the state. TSTA is the state affiliate of the National Education Association (NEA), a national teacher's union.[3] The Association of Texas Professional Educators (ATPE) has no affiliation with any national organization and is currently the largest educators' group in the state.[4]

The Texas High School Coaches Association (THSCA) is an example of a specialized "educational" association. In a state where football is a Friday night tradition, this organization has some political clout. In 1984, the Texas legislature enacted the "no-pass/no-play" law, requiring students to pass their classes or be barred from participating in athletic and other extracurricular events.[5] The THSCA formed a PAC to combat this rule, earning them the moniker "Flunk-PAC."[6] Despite strong opposition, the legislation passed and remains in effect to this day.

In other states, groups representing state and local employees are classified as public-sector labor unions. However, Texas does not give public employees the right to bargain collectively. **Collective bargaining** is a process of negotiation "between an employer and a group of employees so as to determine the conditions of employment."[7] If collective bargaining existed in Texas, organizations representing government workers would be able to force the government to enter into such negotiations and reach an agreement. Because Texas lacks collective bargaining, public-sector employee organizations are merely professional associations rather than labor unions.

In many industrialized states, organized labor unions have traditionally been important and powerful interest groups, although their influence has declined in recent years. In Texas, private sector labor unions do exist; however, they are not powerful and represent only a small fraction of workers. Except in a few counties on the Texas Gulf Coast, where organized labor represents petrochemical workers and longshoremen, organized labor in Texas is very weak. According to the Bureau of Labor Statistics, only 4.5 percent of wage and salaried employees in Texas belonged to labor unions in 2015.[8] As in most of the South, strong anti-union feelings are very much a part of the traditionalistic/individualistic political culture.

Texas is one of 26 states with **right-to-work laws**.[9] According to these laws, "a person cannot be denied employment because of membership or nonmembership in a labor union or other labor organization."[10] Among other things, these laws prohibit union shops where all workers are required to join the union within 90 days of beginning employment as a condition of keeping their jobs (see Map 10.1). Compare this map with the political culture map in Chapter 1.

As previously stated, interest groups are not limited to focusing on economic interests; they can address social issues as well. One type of noneconomic organization relates to the special interests of minorities or ethnic groups. These organizations are primarily concerned with advancing their views on civil rights, discrimination, government services, and economic and political equality for

collective bargaining
Negotiations between an employer and a group of employees to determine employment conditions, such as those related to wages, working hours, and safety

right-to-work laws
Legislation stipulating that a person cannot be denied employment because of membership or nonmembership in a labor union or other labor organization

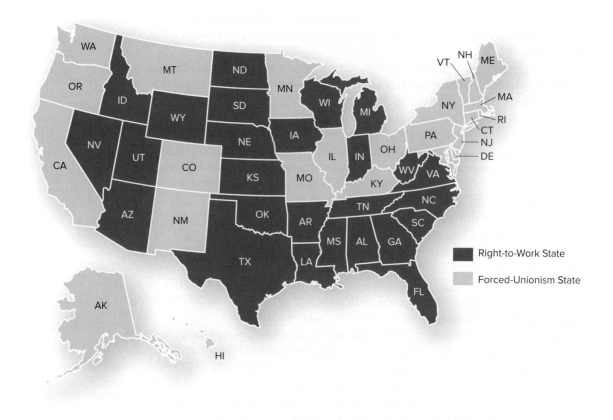

MAP 10.1   States with Right-to-Work or Anti-union Laws

League of United Latin American Citizens (LULAC)

The oldest organization representing Latinos in Texas, established in 1929

those they represent. Hispanics are represented by a variety of groups including the **League of United Latin American Citizens (LULAC)**, the oldest such group in the state. Other Hispanic organizations active in Texas include the Mexican American Legal Defense and Education Fund (MALDEF), the Mexican American Democrats (MAD), the Republican National Hispanic Assembly (RNHA), and the National Council of La Raza (NCLR). The National Association for the Advancement of Colored People (NAACP) played a significant role in the civil rights movement in Texas and continues to represent African Americans in the state and throughout the country.[11]

Another type of social interest group focuses on religious issues. Religious groups have a long history in Texas. In the nineteenth century, fundamentalist Protestants in Texas, believing alcohol consumption to be immoral, supported the nationwide temperance movement to prohibit the production and sale of alcohol. They formed organizations such as the United Friends of Temperance and the Woman's Christian Temperance Union.[12] These religious groups advocated the passage of local option laws, allowing communities to vote on whether alcohol sales would be legal in their area. These local option elections persist to this day. As of November 2015, seven Texas counties were completely "dry," not permitting alcoholic beverage sales anywhere in the county.[13]

In recent years, too, fundamentalist Christian groups have been quite visible on the national stage as well as in Texas. Organizations such as the Christian

Coalition of America oppose abortion and seek to end taxpayer funding of abortion and stem cell research.[14] Similar groups promote abstinence-based sex education, homeschooling, school prayer, and traditional marriage, among other issues. These groups have been somewhat successful in using government to promote their agenda. The Texas State Board of Education, which oversees some aspects of school policy statewide, including textbook selection and curriculum, is composed of 15 elected members. At one point, fundamentalist Christians were thought to control a majority of seats on the board. In fact, in 2009 and 2010, the board generated controversy by approving changes to the science and social studies curricula consistent with more conservative or religious views. However, by 2011, the number of "conservative Christians" on the board had declined to six.[15]

Over the past several decades, the Catholic Church has become active in Texas state politics. This activity, primarily among Hispanic Catholics, is motivated by concerns about economic advancement, local services, and abortion. In San Antonio, the Catholic Church was a driving force behind the creation of Communities Organized for Public Service (COPS) in the 1970s.[16] This coalition of interest groups successfully challenged the Good Government League, a political machine that had dominated city elections for decades, and secured millions of dollars in funding for infrastructure and public services for low-income, primarily Hispanic areas of the city.[17] In the Rio Grande Valley, the Catholic Church was a driving force in the formation of Valley Interfaith. In the El Paso area, the Interreligious Sponsoring Organization was created to advance Hispanic interests. In 2012, the Catholic Church sued the federal government over the Affordable Care Act (also called "Obamacare"), alleging the new health care law violated religious freedom by mandating coverage of contraceptives and other drugs.[18] Several dioceses in Texas were among those filing suit. Although the future of the Affordable Care Act is uncertain, a recent case at the Supreme Court (*Zubik v. Burwell*) suggested a path forward in which the concerns of religious groups would be accommodated while the objective of the law in terms of contraceptive coverage would also be met.[19]

Public interest groups represent causes or ideas rather than economic, professional, or governmental interests. Many of these Texas organizations have national counterparts—for instance, Mothers Against Drunk Driving (MADD), the National Organization for Women (NOW), the National Right to Life Committee, the Sierra Club, the American Civil Liberties Union (ACLU), the Institute for Justice (IJ), Common Cause, and the League of Women Voters. These groups usually limit their support or opposition to a narrow range of issues.

Demonstrators gather outside the Capitol building to protest the passage of President Barack Obama's health care reform bill. With the Democratic Party in control after the 2008 election, conservatives became more outspoken in exercising their right to protest.

© Tom Williams/CQ Roll Call/Getty Images

Nonmembership Organizations

Nonmembership organizations (which do not have active members but rather represent a single company, organization, corporation, or individual) form the largest category of interest groups. Even a cursory glance at the list of organizations registered with the Texas Ethics Commission in Austin reveals nearly 2,000 of these groups (see https://www.ethics.state.tx.us/dfs/paclists.htm). For example, Bank of America and Valero Energy Corporation are both registered as active political committees (PACs) with the Ethics Commission. Many law firms, including Locke Lord, also can act as "hired guns" available to represent a variety of interests in the state.

Government Organizations

state and local interest groups (SLIGs)

Interest groups that represent state and local governments, such as the Texas Association of Counties

In this typology, government organizations are considered separately from membership groups, even though some government organizations have active members. The members of these **state and local interest groups (SLIGs)** are government employees and officials; however, the interest groups represent the organization, not the interests of individual members.

The goal of these groups is to protect local government interests from actions of the state legislature, the governor, and state agencies. Examples include the Texas Municipal League, the Texas Police Chiefs Association, the Combined Law Enforcement Association of Texas, the Texas Association of Fire Fighters, the Texas City Attorneys Association, the Texas Association of Counties, and the Texas Association of School Boards.

Techniques Used by Interest Groups

Learning Objective: Discuss the various techniques interest groups use, including lobbying.

For interest groups to accomplish their goals, they must have an influence on government and public policy decisions. How do they exert this influence? Interest groups use a variety of techniques to further their agendas; the type of technique employed depends on the type of group and the resources available to that group. The primary techniques used by interest groups are lobbying, electioneering, public education and grassroots lobbying, and litigation. Other tactics (not discussed in detail here) include petitions, protests, marches, and demonstrations.

Lobbying

lobbying

The practice of trying to influence members of the legislature, originally by catching legislators in the lobby of the capitol

Perhaps the best known and most common technique used by interest groups is **lobbying**. According to the Texas Ethics Commission, lobbying involves "'direct communications' with members of the legislative or executive branch of state government to influence legislation or administrative action."[20] The term "lobbying" likely originated from the fact that commonly, in the past, legislators did not have their own private offices; their workspace was a desk on the floor of the house or senate chamber. Because access to the chamber floor was limited to members of the legislature, those wanting to speak with legislators had to catch them in the lobby of the capitol building. Thus, it is believed the term "lobbying" grew out of this practice of waiting in the lobby of the legislative chamber.

An ACLU worker distributes literature.

© Brad Doherty/The Brownsville Herald/AP Images

Today, lobbying involves much more than this ambush-style meeting. Because lobbying is regulated by state and federal laws, it refers to a strictly defined set of activities. For instance, having a casual conversation with a member of the legislature does not constitute lobbying.[21] However, if that conversation "is intended to generate or maintain goodwill for the purpose of influencing potential future legislation or administrative action, the communication is a lobby communication."[22] Likewise, publishing a newsletter to keep members of an interest group informed about legislative activities is not considered lobbying (even though legislators may read the group's newsletter).[23] The following activities, all aimed at convincing legislators to promote an interest group's agenda, are included in lobbying efforts:

- Contacting members of the legislature (in person or by phone, written letter, or electronic communication) to express support for or opposition to legislation
- Convincing members of the legislature to propose legislation (file a bill) favorable to the group
- Working with members of the legislature to draft legislation
- Testifying before a committee hearing about the effect of proposed legislation
- Encouraging members of an interest group to contact legislators (email or phone campaigns, discussed later) regarding legislation[24]
- Issuing press releases and buying newspaper and television ads
- Providing written material to members of the legislature

This last activity serves a particularly important function in Texas politics. Interest groups often provide research findings to members of the legislature and their staffs. This information can obviously be self-serving, but it is often accurate and can be an important resource for busy state legislators. An interest group that produces good, high-quality research and information can have a positive impact on public policy. Over the years, several business-sponsored groups in Texas have developed a reputation for providing quality research and information to the Texas legislature. A Texas lobbyist recently confided to one of this book's authors just how important such a reputation is and how well it must be guarded. This desire to maintain integrity acts as a much-needed self-check on lobbyists' behavior.

Lobbying efforts take place throughout the year, although there are periods of particularly intense activity. Because the Texas legislature meets every two years for 140 days, most lobbying efforts are concentrated during the regular legislative session. However, lobbying does not stop when the legislature adjourns. All legislatures, including the one in Texas, perform some activities between regular sessions, and interest groups attempt to influence interim committees and other special activities of the legislature. Lobbyists also try to build knowledge and political capital between sessions. As two Texas lobbyists, Jim Grace and Luke Ledbetter, noted in the *Houston Lawyer,* "The session is simply too busy to build long-standing relationships while it is in progress. Only through continued hard work in the interim can you understand the personalities of the members, the unique needs of the constituents in their districts, and the issues about which they are passionate."[25] See Table 10.2 for Grace and Ledbetter's advice to fellow lobbyists.

Though lobbying is often thought of in conjunction with the legislature, the executive branch can also be lobbied. After a bill is passed, the governor has the option to sign it, veto it, or take no action (in which case the bill becomes

TABLE 10.2

Grace and Ledbetter's Rules and Tricks of the Lobbying Trade

1. NEVER lie to a member of the legislature.
2. Preparation. Preparation. Preparation.
3. Know what you don't know and be willing to admit it.
4. There are some things you can't control.
5. Information is the currency of the realm.
6. "Only speak when it improves the silence."[26]
7. Don't write it down (and especially don't put it in an email) unless you are comfortable waking up and seeing it as the headline on the front page of the *Houston Chronicle.*
8. The "Reply to All" button is not your friend.
9. Be prepared to forge strange alliances.
10. Compromise when you can; hold firm when you must.
11. Never ask members for a vote you know they can't take back to the district.
12. Be ever-present at the Capitol during session.
13. Know the calendar rules better than anyone else.
14. Money will never buy you a vote.
15. Treat everyone with respect.
16. Legislation (like water) takes the path of least resistance: do everything possible to make a staffer's life easier.
17. And finally, remember that "[n]o man's life, liberty, or property are safe while the legislature is in session."[27]

Source: Jim Grace and Luke Ledbetter, "The Lobbyist," *Houston Lawyer* (September/October 2009), 10. Available online at http://www.thehoustonlawyer.com/aa_sep09/page10.htm.

law without a signature).[28] Therefore, persuading the governor either to sign or veto a bill can be an important part of lobbying activity. One example in which interest groups sought a gubernatorial veto occurred during the 2013 session. The legislature passed a bill which would have allowed employees alleging they had been subject to wage discrimination to sue their employers in state court. The *Houston Chronicle* reported that several major interest groups in the state, including the Texas Association of Business, the National Federation of Independent Business, and the Texas Retailers Association (along with some of its member businesses), had sent letters to the governor opposing the bill.[29] The governor vetoed the bill and issued a proclamation explaining the basis for his objection. He argued that such legislation would compromise Texas's favorable business climate and that this particular bill duplicated a federal law already in effect, which allows employees with this type of complaint to file a claim with the U.S. Equal Employment Opportunity Commission.[30] It is difficult to determine whether the negative letters influenced the governor's decision, but this is one avenue interest groups pursue in service of their goals.

After a bill goes into effect, a regulatory agency (typically part of the executive branch) must enforce the new law. As a result, lobbying can also be directed toward how much discretion or leeway an agency exercises in enforcing the law. Interest groups expend a great deal of effort to influence how agencies interpret and enforce regulations. If individuals friendly to the interest group are appointed to governing boards and commissions, enforcement of the law can be eased considerably.

Lobbyists can be classified into five types:

1. Professional lobbyists are hired to represent a client (an individual, group, or organization) and to try to influence the legislative process on behalf of that client. Many of these lobbyists represent more than one client.

2. In-house lobbyists are employees of a particular business or association, and they engage in lobbying as part of their job.

3. Governmental lobbyists and legislative liaisons work for a governmental organization and lobby as part of their job. They might not be required to register formally as lobbyists.

4. Citizen or volunteer lobbyists are nonpaid volunteers representing citizen groups and organizations. A good example is volunteers for Mothers Against Drunk Driving (MADD).

5. Finally, there are private individuals, usually with a pet project or issue. Sometimes called "hobbyists," these individualists act on their own behalf and do not officially represent any organizations.[31]

Lobbying is often looked down upon by people worried about special interests taking precedence over the greater good. This is not a novel sentiment, as evidenced by Supreme Court Justice Noah Swayne's remark in *Trist v. Child* (1874) about such "infamous" employment: "If any of the great corporations of the country were to hire adventurers who make market of themselves in this way, to procure the passage of a general law with a view to the promotion of their private interests, the moral sense of every right-minded man would instinctively denounce the employer and employed as steeped in corruption, and the employment as infamous."[32] However, lobbyists (and interest groups in general) would counter that their actions are protected by the First Amendment to the U.S. Constitution, which guarantees "the right of the people peaceably to assemble, and to petition the Government for a redress of grievances."[33]

CORE OBJECTIVE

Source: United States Department of Agriculture Agricultural Research Service

Taking Personal Responsibility . . .

Socrates suggested "know thyself," and Shakespeare's Hamlet admonished "to thine own self be true." It is important to know what your interests are and how they are represented in government. Consider what you have read in this chapter and determine how interest group efforts align with your personal interests. If they do not, what can you do to ensure that government addresses your interests or the interests of those who share similar values?

Electioneering

In addition to lobbying political leaders, interest groups devote considerable time and effort to try to influence the outcome of elections. Their goal is to help candidates who are sympathetic to the group's cause win public office. This type of activity is called **electioneering**. In pursuit of electioneering, an interest group's most important resource is money, usually contributed to campaigns

electioneering
Various activities in which interest groups engage to try to influence the outcome of elections

TABLE 10.3

PAC Spending from 1998 to 2014

Election Cycle	No. of Active PACs	PAC Spending	Spending Increase from Previous Cycle	Percent Spending Increase
1998	893	$ 51,543,820	$ 8,461,274	20%
2000	865	$ 53,996,975	$ 2,453,155	5%
2002	964	$ 85,320,226	$31,323,251	58%
2004	850	$ 68,904,524	($16,415,702)	(19%)
2006	1,132	$ 99,167,646	$30,263,122	44%
2008	1,209	$119,561,861	$20,394,215	21%
2010	1,302	$133,466,187	$13,904,326	12%
2012	1,364	$126,367,460	($ 7,098,727)	(5%)
2014	1,421	$159,314,633	$32,947,173	26%

Source: Texans for Public Justice, "Texas PACs: 2008 Cycle Spending," April 2009 (http://info.tpj.org/reports/txpac08/chapter1.html); "Texas PACs: 2010 Election Cycle Spending," August 2011 (http://info.tpj.org/reports/pdf/PACs2010.pdf); "Texas PACs: 2012 Election Cycle Spending," October 2013 (http://info.tpj.org/reports/pdf/PACs2012.pdf); "Texas PACs: 2014 Election Cycle Spending," February 2016 (http://info.tpj.org/reports/pdf/PACs2014.pdf).

and funneled to candidates through PACs. Some interest groups prefer to give money to other groups who, in turn, funnel the money to campaigns. At the national level, PACs—whether or not they are connected to a corporation, trade association, or labor union—are required to register with the Federal Election Commission at the time they are formed.[34] Historically, there were limits on how much money PACs could receive and distribute in a single year or election cycle, but those restrictions were lifted subsequent to the *Citizens United* ruling by the Supreme Court (the section titled "Regulation of Interest Groups" discusses this in more depth).[35] See Table 10.3 for the amount of money contributed by the major PACs in Texas during recent election cycles. Note that the total amount of money spent by general purpose PACs in the 2006 spending cycle was double the amount spent in 1998. During that period, PAC spending grew from $51 million to $99 million.[36] Table 10.4 shows PAC spending broken down by major interest category.

Some writers have observed that PAC money has undermined party loyalty and weakened political parties in this country. Candidates no longer owe their loyalty to the party that helped elect them but to interest groups that funded them. Political action committees buy access in "an intricate, symbiotic relationship involving trust, information exchange, pressure and obligations. The inescapable fact is that resources, and especially money, are at least three-fourths of the battle in building and maintaining good relations and in securing the other essential elements that lead to access and influence."[37] But many political observers would argue that money doesn't guarantee outcomes in elections or in public policy debates. For example, Jeb Bush—and the PACs supporting him— was tops in money spent during the 2016 Republican presidential campaign but dropped out of the race fairly early due to lack of voter support in the primaries and caucuses. As David Keating of the Center for Competitive Politics asked in an MSNBC article, "Has there ever been a better example than Jeb Bush of the fact that voters decide the outcome of elections, not money?"[38]

TABLE 10.4

2014 PACs by Interest Category

Interest Category	No. of Active PACs	2014 PAC Spending	Share of 2014 Spending	'12-'14 Change
Agriculture	27	$ 2,820,091	2%	18%
Communications/Electronics	25	$ 2,455,506	2%	−2%
Construction	99	$ 8,350,849	5%	18%
Energy/Nat'l Resources	76	$ 12,199,625	8%	3%
Finance	39	$ 7,302,181	5%	25%
Health	80	$ 10,467,095	7%	5%
Ideological/Single Issue	650	$ 65,225,862	41%	38%
Insurance	20	$ 3,472,351	2%	−6%
Labor	153	$ 12,085,061	8%	48%
Lawyers & Lobbyists	56	$ 10,207,560	6%	−9%
Miscellaneous Business	72	$ 4,842,111	3%	18%
Other/Unknown	54	$ 868,218	1%	73%
Real Estate	39	$ 15,602,970	10%	69%
Transportation	31	$ 3,415,154	2%	32%
TOTALS	1,421	$159,314,634	100%	26%

Source: Texans For Public Justice, "Texas PACs: 2014 Election Cycle Spending," February 2016, (http://info.tpj.org/reports/pdf/PACs2014.pdf).

CORE OBJECTIVE

Communicating Effectively . . .

Review the data presented in Table 10.4. Identify the interest group category that spent the most money in 2014. Discuss the impact that PAC spending has on government.

© George Lavendowski/USFWS

Money may be among the most important tools for interest groups trying to influence an election, but it is by no means the only tool. The process of election-eering begins with candidate recruitment. Interest groups work to recruit candidates for office many months before an election. They encourage individuals who will be sympathetic to their cause to seek nominations in party primaries. This encouragement takes the form of promises of support and money in both the primary and general elections. Some interest groups might encourage both Democratic and Republican candidates to seek nomination in their respective parties. This covers their bets: regardless of which candidate wins, the interest group will likely have access and influence.

A number of other activities constitute electioneering. Interest groups can make a public endorsement, signaling to potential voters that a particular candidate is aligned with the group's interests. They can run television and newspaper ads detailing the records of officials or the virtues of a nonincumbent, or they can undertake voter registration drives and get-out-the-vote campaigns. Interest

What point does this cartoon make about the nature of 2008 political campaign contributions?

Reprinted with permission of Joe Heller

groups might also aid candidates by helping to write speeches and organize rallies and by staging political events such as fundraisers. Some groups keep track of legislators' voting records and circulate "good guy/bad guy score cards" to members of the organization, suggesting members vote for or against certain candidates.

Public Relations: Public Education and Grassroots Lobbying

Interest groups also attempt to influence policy through public relations activities. The goal of these efforts is twofold: to influence public opinion regarding a particular issue and to create a favorable public image for the group. In service of this goal, organizations might sponsor an educational program or other forum where policy issues are discussed. In addition, they might publish and disseminate educational literature.[39] Obviously, information prepared and distributed by an interest group can be very self-serving and in some cases might even be called propaganda. Not all such information is wrong, but some filtering of the information by the public is necessary. Some interest groups might counter the information provided by a competing interest group. In a mass media society, characterized by constant public scrutiny, an interest group's credibility with the public can be compromised if the group provides inaccurate or misleading information.

Interest groups also try to mobilize their supporters to advocate on behalf of the organization, using a technique called *grassroots lobbying*. Grassroots lobbying is defined as a communication with the general public that attempts to influence specific legislation by expressing a view about that legislation and urging the public to act.[40] Such a "call to action" can take several forms, including asking individuals to contact their elected officials, providing names and contact information for pertinent representatives, or providing a means of communicating with representatives such as a postcard that can be mailed or an email link that can be used to send a message to a representative.[41] The goal of such email or phone campaigns is to generate a public response of sufficient magnitude that elected officials will act in accord with the group's wishes.

Aside from efforts to create a favorable opinion of themselves with the public, interest groups also try to curry favor with public officials. Inviting public officials to address organizational meetings is one strategy used to advance the group's standing in the eyes of these officials. Giving awards to officials at such gatherings, thanking them for their public service, is also a common technique.

FOCUS ON

Hispanic Groups Lobbying the Courts

©James Steidl/Shutterstock

Hispanic interest groups have used Texas courts to advance the interests of their members. One notable example of this was in the case *Delgado v. Bastrop ISD*. In the early twentieth century, many communities in Texas operated three separate, segregated school systems: one for white children, one for black children, and a third for Hispanic children.[49] Although state laws at that time allowed segregation by race in public schools, children of Mexican descent were considered Caucasian.[50] In 1948, attorneys for the League of United Latin American Citizens (LULAC) filed suit on behalf of Minerva Delgado, the parent of a Hispanic student, against the Bastrop Independent School District and three other districts.[51] The lawsuit claimed that the segregation of Hispanic children based on their national origin was not

justified by any law and that these children were receiving a substandard education.[52] The court agreed and prohibited the segregation of Hispanic students on separate campuses in Texas public schools.[53]

Another lawsuit related to educational opportunity was *Edgewood ISD v. Kirby*. In 1984, the Mexican American Legal Defense and Education Fund (MALDEF) filed a lawsuit on behalf of the Edgewood Independent School District in San Antonio.[54] (The lawsuit named William Kirby, in his official capacity as Texas's Commissioner of Education, as the defendant.) Because the main source of funding for public education in Texas is property taxes, school districts in wealthier areas were able to generate higher revenues, and therefore had more money available for education, than school districts in poorer areas. MALDEF's lawsuit alleged that the state's method of educational funding violated the Texas Constitution and discriminated against students in poor districts.[55] In 1987 (and again in 1989, following appeals) the court "found that the state's public school financing structure was unconstitutional and ordered the legislature to formulate a more equitable one."[56] Though controversy and lawsuits have persisted, the state's current funding arrangement, based on redistribution of property tax wealth (discussed in more detail in Chapter 11), is a legacy of the *Edgewood* decision.

Critical Thinking Questions

1. In what way might litigation be an effective way for interest groups to pursue the goals of their members?

2. What are the advantages and drawbacks of this approach for our system of government?

Another note is warranted here regarding interest groups' attempts to curry favor with public officials: interest group tactics have changed in recent years. In the past, the process was described primarily as "booze, bribes, and broads." Although entertaining members of the legislature remains very much a part of the process, the more unethical aspects of such entertainment occur less frequently today. Bribery of a public official is a felony punishable by 2 to 20 years in prison and a fine of up to $10,000.[42] One lobbyist had this to say regarding "making women 'available' to interested male lawmakers": "'I got hit up for the first time this session by a member wanting me to get him a woman. I told him I have trouble enough getting my own dates.'"[43] Interest groups have moved away from such sexist and unsavory practices and are more likely to rely on other tactics today.

Litigation

The court system provides another means for interest groups to advance their cause and influence policy. Interest groups file lawsuits against individuals, organizations, or government entities "to safeguard the interests of their members [and] promote test cases or class action suits to secure judicial favor for a particular principle."[44] Interest groups sometimes sponsor litigation themselves, orchestrating and funding a lawsuit on behalf of their members. In other instances, groups file *amicus curaie* (literally, "friend of the court") briefs to try to influence court decisions.[45] This occurs when the organization itself is not a party to the litigation but has an interest in the outcome of a case.[46] Research suggests that when they have submitted amicus briefs, interest groups have been quite effective in swaying courts in favor of a particular argument on the relevant legal issue.[47] As political scientists Kim Lane Scheppele and Jack L. Walker, Jr. stated, "Clearly, the courts are an important battleground for interest groups."[48]

Regulation of Interest Groups

Learning Objective: Explain how interest groups are regulated.

Most states have laws regulating two activities in which interest groups engage: lobbying and making financial contributions to political campaigns (also known as "campaign finance"). In terms of lobbying regulations, organizations that have regular contact with legislators are generally required to register and file reports on their activities. Often these reporting requirements are weak, and the reports generated might not reflect the true activities of the organization.

Texas first attempted to regulate the activities of interest groups in 1907.[57] The Lobby Control Act prohibited "efforts to influence legislation 'by means other than appeal to reason' and provided that persons guilty of lobbying were subject to fines and imprisonment."[58] However, the statute was never enforced. In 1957, a new law was passed requiring lobbyists to register and disclose information about their activities; this law had many loopholes and was ineffective. Subsequent amendments to state law have called for increasingly more stringent reporting.

In 1991, the **Texas Ethics Commission** was created to administer and enforce laws related to lobbying, political fundraising and spending, and financial disclosure by state officials (among other duties).[59] Under current rules, an individual, association, or business entity that crosses either the "compensation and reimbursement threshold" or the "expenditure threshold" while engaged in lobbying efforts must register as a lobbyist with the Ethics Commission. In other words, registration is required if a person receives, as pay and in reimbursed expenses for lobbying, a combined amount of more than $1,000 per quarter-year. Alternatively, persons must register if they spend more than $500 per quarter on gifts or other paid expenses for a state official or employee or their immediate families.[60]

The official list of registered lobbyists for 2016 included 1,473 individuals.[61] However, there are many exemptions from the registration requirement. Government employees who lobby in an official capacity (as part of their jobs) are not required to register as lobbyists. Journalists are not considered lobbyists, even though news media outlets may communicate directly with public officials and express opinions on government policy. Some businesses may avoid registration if all of their lobbying activity is reported by a registered individual (for instance, a lawyer who is representing that business). In addition, persons are not required to register if they are paid to lobby for less than 26 hours per quarter.[62] Thus, the total number of persons or entities who actually engage in lobbying is likely much higher than reported.

Regarding campaign finance, most states require some formal registration of PACs. In Texas, PACs must register with the Texas Ethics Commission, designate a treasurer, and file periodic reports regarding the group's contributions and expenditures. These reports must provide the full name and occupation of persons who donate more than $50 to the group during a given reporting period.[63] PACs are prohibited from making a contribution to members of the legislature during the period beginning 30 days before the start of a regular session and ending 20 days after the regular 140-day session.[64] Although corporations and labor unions are prohibited from giving money directly to campaigns, state law does not limit the amount individuals or PACs can contribute to candidates for statewide or legislative office.[65]

In 2010 the U.S. Supreme Court, in *Citizens United v. Federal Election Commission,* removed previous restrictions by the federal government on PACs' ability to spend money on election campaigns. The case stated that "political spending is a form of protected speech under the First Amendment."[66] Therefore, the government cannot prohibit corporations and unions from spending money, through PACS, on "electioneering communications," such as television ads for or against a particular candidate.[67] This ruling opened the door to a greatly expanded role for PACs in elections. The *Citizens United* decision does not affect the Texas law prohibiting direct campaign contributions by unions and corporations; however, it does allow these groups to establish PACS for the purpose of funding election-related advertising.[68]

The Texas Ethics Commission has been criticized in the past for "timid" and ineffective enforcement of the rules, but greater efforts have been made in recent years to ensure compliance.[69] Although reporting systems have improved, it is still somewhat difficult to find and summarize information on interest group activities. The *Texas Tribun*e has compiled a database using the commission's data; available data from 2000 to 2014 can be accessed at the following website: https://www.texastribune.org/library/data/campaign-finance/#corporate.

Texas Ethics Commission

State agency responsible for enforcing requirements for interest groups and candidates for public office to report information on money collected and activities

The ethics of interest group activity varies from state to state, dictated by the political culture of each state. What is considered acceptable in a traditionalistic/individualistic state such as Texas may be viewed as corrupt in a state with a moralistic political culture. The late Molly Ivins, a well-known Texas newspaper writer and observer of Texas politics, once said that in the Texas legislature, "what passes for ethics is if you're bought, by God, you stay bought."[70] Despite Ms. Ivins's deprecating humor, her comment reflects the evolution of Texas lobbying activity over time.

Factors Influencing the Strength of Interest Groups

Learning Objective: Describe the factors that influence interest groups' strength.

Interest groups have a variety of resources available to them. Their resource base depends on the type of group, the number of members in the group, and who those members are. For example, the Association of Texas Professional Educators (ATPE) has strength because it has so many members (more than100,000 according to the group's website).[71] Thus, they represent a large potential voting bloc. On the other hand, the Texas Municipal League (TML), which represents Texas city officials, has a comparatively smaller membership of approximately 16,000.[72] However, the TML's membership includes influential public officials, such as mayors and council members. The TML has lists of representatives and senators keyed with local officials. The TML contacts local officials, asking them, in turn, to contact representatives and senators regarding legislation.[73] Local elected officials can easily contact legislators, and those legislators will listen, even if they do not always agree.

It is important to note, though, that some groups have difficulty recruiting members (or money) to their cause due to the "free-rider problem." All interest groups provide benefits, and individuals may derive benefits from an interest group's efforts regardless of whether they participate in the group's activities. Thus, it is rational for some people not to contribute to or work on the group's behalf because they will still benefit.[74] This can lead to an underprovision of a collective good. The larger the group and the more diffuse the possible benefits, the greater the possibility of the free-rider problem undermining the group's cause. On the other hand, smaller groups that seek more concentrated benefits are less likely to suffer from this problem.[75]

The status and size of an interest group are important determinants of power. Obviously, the presidents of large banks and corporations in Dallas, due to their status, can command the ear of most state senators and state representatives from the Dallas area. Groups with many members can use their numbers to advantage by inciting a barrage of telephone calls and messages to legislators regarding legislative actions.

The total number of groups representing a particular interest may not be a valid indication of strength. For example, in recent years the number of groups representing business interests has multiplied dramatically, whereas the number of groups representing the interests of local government has grown very little. One might take this as a sign that business groups have grown in influence relative to governmental

Dallas teachers protest against an extended school day. Several associations represent Texas teachers, but according to state law, they lack the right to collective bargaining.

© Richard Michael Knittle Sr. /Demotix/Corbis.

groups. However, growing numbers do not necessarily indicate increased influence. Instead, they may indicate the increased diversity of economic interests in Texas over the past several decades. Except for special districts, the number of local governments has not changed in the past 40 years, which explains the more constant number of governmental interest groups. Factors other than sheer numbers—such as leadership, organization, geographic distribution of its membership, and money—determine the strength of an interest group. Other authors point to additional factors, such as economic diversity, party strength, legislative professionalism, and government fragmentation, to help explain an interest group's power.[76]

Leadership and Organization

Leadership quality and organizational ability can be important factors in the power of interest groups. Many interest groups hire former legislators to help them. Some groups are decentralized, with a loose-knit membership, making mobilization difficult. Other groups, such as the Texas Municipal League, are highly organized, monitor legislation being considered, and can easily contact selected members to influence bills while they are still in committee. Between legislative sessions, the TML's policy committees meet to begin formulating a legislative program that will be put in place for the next legislative session.[77] These committees recommend positions on legislation likely to be considered. Their recommendations are then considered by the TML membership at an annual conference, where the organization adopts stands on key items, and finalized by the TML Board. This process gives the group's leadership a firm basis on which to act, and constant contact with all members is not necessary. Key members are contacted only when quick action is required.

Geographic Distribution

Some groups have more influence than others because they have members in all geographic areas of the state and therefore can command the attention of many more legislators. The Texas Municipal League, for example, has city officials in the district of every senator and representative. Texas bankers and lawyers are located throughout the state as well. Legislators might not listen to citizens from other areas of the state, but they certainly will listen to citizens from their own district. Legislators will also listen to local elected officials. Thus, having members that are geographically distributed across the state is a key advantage for interest groups. Obviously, some groups cannot have **geographic distribution**. For instance, commercial shrimp fishermen are limited to the Gulf Coast region of Texas.

geographic distribution
A characteristic of some interest groups in that they have members in all regions of the state

CORE OBJECTIVE

Being Socially Responsible . . .

How can geographic distribution of interest groups improve political awareness between culturally diverse populations?

Editorial Image, LLC/Alamy

Money

As one might guess, interest groups need money to fund their lobbying, electioneering, and public relations efforts. Money is also an important resource for other, less obvious reasons. Interest groups able to hire full-time staff and travel to meet with legislators have more potential influence than those dependent on volunteers and part-time staff. As indicated earlier, some groups have no active members per se, but instead represent individuals, corporations, or businesses. With enough money, groups do not need dues-paying or contributing members to have an impact on government policy. Some of these groups do a very good job of mobilizing nonmember citizens to their cause. For example, through the use of television ads, newspaper ads, and "talk radio," one such group, the Coalition for Health Insurance Choices (CHIC), managed to mobilize opposition to President Clinton's health care proposal. One writer has referred to such non-membership groups, which lack a grassroots (spontaneous, community-based) organization, as "**astroturf** organizations."[78]

astroturf
A political term for an interest group that appears to have many grassroots members but in fact does not have individual citizens as members; rather, it is sponsored by an organization such as a corporation or business association

Economic Diversity

The economic diversity of a state can impact the strength of an interest group operating within that state. Highly industrialized states with a variety of industries generally have a multitude of interest groups. Because of the diversity and complexity of the state's economy, no single industry or group can dominate. The many interests cancel each other out, as Madison predicted they would in *Federalist No. 10.* In other states, a single or a few industries dominate the economy. For example, in Alaska, oil is still dominant. Coal mining dominates Wyoming's economy, providing much of the state's revenues. Copper mining was once the most prominent industry in Montana, and lumbering is still the primary industry in Oregon.

In the past, the Texas economy was dominated by a few industries: cotton, cattle, banking, and oil. Today, the Texas economy is more diversified, and the number of interest groups has grown accordingly. It is much more difficult for one or a few interests to dominate state politics. Nonetheless, the traditional industries still wield a lot of power.

Political Party Competition

The strength of political parties in the state can influence the strength of interest groups. States with two strong, competitive parties that recruit and support candidates for office can offset the influence of interest groups attempting to put their own candidates forward. Legislators in competitive party states might owe their election to, and therefore be more loyal to, their political party and be less influenced by interest groups. In Texas, a history of weak party structure has contributed to the power of interest groups.

Professionalism of the State Legislature

In Chapter 3, we defined a professional legislature as being characterized by higher legislative pay, longer sessions (such as no limits on the length of regular sessions), and more staff support.[79] In theory, well-paid legislators with professional staffs are less dependent upon information supplied by interest groups, and the information exchange between lobbyist and legislator is reduced. The Texas legislature has improved staff quality in recent years; most members have full-time staff in Austin and their local offices. In addition, committee staff has increased. The Texas Legislative Council also provides excellent staff assistance in research and information. This increased level of support has led to a rise in legislative professionalism in Texas; whether this has resulted in a corresponding decrease in the power of interest groups remains to be seen. However, there are potential costs, too; it is not automatically better to have a professional legislature rather than a citizen legislature.

Fragmented Government Structure

As previously stated, interest groups expend much effort trying to influence the administration of state laws. The degree to which interest groups succeed in this endeavor depends in part on the structure of state government. If the government is centralized under a governor who appoints and removes most department heads, interest groups will find it necessary to lobby the governor directly and the agencies indirectly.

Texas has a **fragmented government structure**. The governor of Texas makes few significant appointments of agency heads. Therefore, each interest group tries to gain access to and influence the particular state agency relevant to its cause. Often these agencies were created to regulate the industry that the interest group represents. For example, the Texas Railroad Commission, an agency originally created to regulate railroads, also oversees the state's oil industry. Historically, oil industry lobby groups have had great influence over the agency's three commissioners and their decisions.[80] In 1971, the Texas Almanac contained a full-page ad, paid for by the Texas Independent Producers and Royalty Owners Association and the American Association of Oil Well Drilling Contractors, thanking the Railroad Commission. The ad read: "Since 1891, The Texas Railroad Commission Has Served the Oil Industry." Following public outcry over the impropriety of a state regulatory agency "serving" a private industry, the revised ad in the 1974 edition of the Almanac read as follows: "Since 1891 The Texas Railroad Commission Has Served Our State."[81] In truth, similar relationships exist between many state agencies and interest groups.

The members of most state licensing boards (such as the State Bar of Texas, the Texas Medical Board, and the Texas Funeral Service Commission, formerly the State Board of Morticians) are professionals in those fields and may also be members of a relevant interest group. These licensing boards were ostensibly created to "protect the public interest," but they often spend most of their time protecting the profession by limiting the number of persons who can be licensed and by creating rules favorable to the group.

For example, in Texas, cremation cannot occur until at least 48 hours after the time of death.[82] However, if a body is not buried within 24 hours of death, state law dictates it must be embalmed or refrigerated.[83] Supposedly, the reason for embalming is to preserve the body and protect the public from the spread of diseases. However, others have suggested that embalming prior to cremation is completely unnecessary and merely protects the profit margin of morticians doing the embalming. (In fact, a law took effect in 2015 making it a "deceptive" practice for funeral directors to suggest that embalming is required when

fragmented government structure

A government structure where power is dispersed to many state agencies with little or no central control

refrigeration is available as an alternative.[84]) Still, the way these laws are written, including the waiting period for cremation, creates an opportunity for morticians for charge for additional services.

This situation illustrates how members of a profession or interest group can influence rule making in a way that favors the group, thereby influencing how much money members of the group can make. Another term for this type of practice is **rent seeking**. Rent seeking occurs when individuals or groups try to secure benefits for themselves through political means.[85] Rent-seeking behavior can lead to great costs to society, not only in the obvious senses but also because of the opportunity cost associated with people using scarce resources (time, energy, human capital, money, etc.) to capture political benefits rather than for "productive endeavors."[86]

When the relationship between a state agency and an interest group becomes very close, it is referred to as **capture**. In other words, the interest group has "captured" the agency. However, capture of the agency by the interest group is probably more the exception than the rule. Often, competing interest groups vie for influence with the agency and reduce the likelihood of capture by a single interest group. (The creation of the Public Utility Commission is a good example of this.)

In practice, policy is created through the combined efforts of interest groups, the state agency, and the legislative committee (with oversight of the agency). This process is called the "Iron Triangle." (See Figure 10.1)

rent seeking
The practice of trying to secure benefits for oneself or one's group through political means

capture
The situation in which a state agency or board falls under the heavy influence of or is controlled by its constituency interest groups

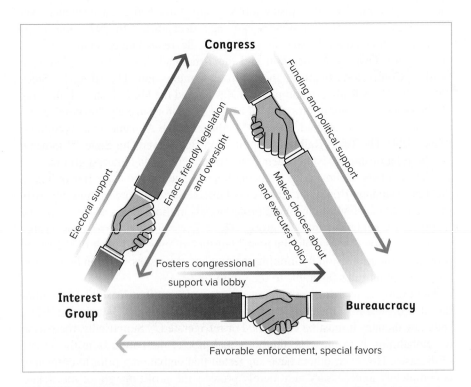

FIGURE 10.1 Often, a close relationship exists between the state agency created to regulate an industry, the legislative oversight committee, and interest groups. This relationship is sometimes called the "Iron Triangle."

Conclusion

Though often criticized (and sometimes rightly so), interest groups play a very important role in state politics. The First Amendment to the U.S. Constitution protects free speech and association, and interest groups are a necessary part of the political process. Government efforts to control interest groups are, and to many observers should be, limited. Knowing the tactics these groups use to influence government helps us understand how politics operate.

There is little doubt that the influence of interest groups, especially PACs, will continue to grow in the years ahead—especially if the size, scope, and budget of government continue to expand, thereby offering greater enticement for getting a piece of the pie or capturing a regulatory agency. In some campaigns, PAC money has essentially replaced the political party as a nominating and electing agent. The recent U.S.

Supreme Court decision in *Citizens United v. Federal Election Commission,* by lifting a previous ban on direct PAC funding of certain types of political communication, has given PACs even more freedom to participate in election campaigns. In a mass-media age, little can be done to suppress the influence of interest groups.

Given the low levels of voter turnout and other forms of political participation in Texas, interest groups will likely continue to dominate state politics. The traditionalistic/individualistic political culture also supports such dominance. The present decentralized administrative structure in the state enhances the ability of interest groups to influence state agencies. Because a reorganization of state agencies into a centrally controlled administration seems unlikely, this situation will persist for many years to come.

Summary

LO: Describe interest group typology.

There are three basic types of interest groups (or organizations of individuals with a shared goal that try to influence governmental decisions). Membership organizations are groups whose members are dues-paying individual citizens or businesses. Nonmembership organizations represent a single company, organization, corporation, or individual; their membership is not open to the general public. Government organizations represent the interests of local government as well as state and federal agencies.

LO: Discuss the various techniques interest groups use, including lobbying.

Interest groups use various techniques to promote their agendas, including lobbying, electioneering, public relations, and litigation. Lobbying involves direct communication with a member of the legislature or the executive branch in an effort to influence legislation or administrative action. Electioneering activities, such as making financial contributions to political campaigns, attempt to influence the outcome of elections. Interest groups engage in public relations activities to influence public opinion regarding a particular issue and to create a favorable image for the group. Groups may also protect their members' interests by filing lawsuits in court.

LO: Explain how interest groups are regulated.

Most states have laws regulating the activities of interest groups. The Texas Ethics Commission administers and enforces laws related to lobbying and campaign finance (or political fundraising and spending). In terms of lobbying, individuals and organizations that have regular contact with legislators are generally required to register with the Ethics Commission and file reports on their activities. With regard to campaign finance, political action committees (or PACs) must register with the Ethics Commission and file reports on the group's contributions and expenditures. The Supreme Court, in *Citizens United v. Federal Election Commission,* held that "political spending is a form of protected speech under the First Amendment"; therefore, corporations and unions cannot be prohibited from funding advertisements that support or oppose candidates.

LO: Describe the factors that influence interest groups' strength.

Many factors influence the strength of interest groups, including their status, the number of members they have, the quality of their leadership, degree of organization, the geographic distribution of their members across the state, money, the economic diversity of the state, the presence of competitive political parties, the degree of professionalism of the state legislature, and whether government structure is fragmented or centralized.

Key Terms

astroturf
capture
collective bargaining
electioneering
fragmented government structure
geographic distribution
government organizations
interest group

League of United Latin American
    Citizens (LULAC)
lobbying
membership organizations
nonmembership organizations
political action committee (PAC)
professional associations
rent seeking

retail trade associations
right-to-work laws
state and local interest groups
    (SLIGs)
Texas Ethics Commission
trade associations

Notes

[1] Alexis de Tocqueville, *Democracy in America,* trans. George Lawrence, ed. J. P. Mayer (Garden City, N.J.: Anchor Books, 1969), 190–191.

[2] Adapted from a typology developed by Charles Wiggins, Professor of Political Science, Texas A&M University, College Station, 1999 (unpublished class handout).

[3] Texas State Teachers Association, http://www.tsta.org /about-tsta/join-tsta.

[4] Association of Texas Professional Educators, "History of ATPE," http://www.atpe.org/en/About-ATPE /History-of-ATPE.

[5] Terrence Stutz, "Texas' school reform law of 1984 still touches millions of students," *Dallas Morning News,* July 7, 2014, http://www.dallasnews.com/news/local-news/20140706-school-reform-law-of-1984-still-touches-millions-of-texas-students.ece.

[6] "Flunk-PAC," *Washington Post,* National Weekly Edition, 30 December 1985, 22.

[7] Cornell University Law School Legal Information Institute, "Collective Bargaining," http://www.law.cornell.edu/wex /collective_bargaining.

[8] U.S. Department of Labor, Bureau of Labor Statistics, "Union Affiliation of Employed Wage and Salary Workers by State, 2014-2015 annual averages," http://www.bls.gov /news.release/union2.t05.htm.

[9] National Right to Work Legal Defense Foundation, Inc., "Right to Work States: Do you work in a Right to Work state?" 2016, http://www.nrtw.org/rtws.htm.

[10] Attorney General of Texas Ken Paxton, "Right-to-Work Laws in Texas," 2016, https://www.oag.state.tx.us/agency /righttowork.shtml.

[11] Michael L. Gillette, "National Association For the Advancement of Colored People," *Handbook of Texas Online,* accessed June 17, 2016, http://www.tshaonline.org /handbook/online/articles/ven01.

[12] K. Austin Kerr, "Prohibition," *Handbook of Texas Online,* accessed June 17, 2016, http://www.tshaonline.org /handbook/online/articles/vap01.

[13] Texas Alcoholic Beverage Commission, "Wet and Dry Counties," 2015, http://www.tabc.state.tx.us/local_option_ elections/wet_and_dry_counties.asp.

[14] Christian Coalition of America, "Christian Coalition of America's Agenda for the 114th Congress," http://www .cc.org/our_agenda.

[15] Gail Collins, "How Texas Inflicts Bad Textbooks on Us," *The New York Review of Books* 21 (June 2012), http:// www.nybooks.com/articles/archives/2012/jun/21 /how-texas-inflicts-bad-textbooks-on-us/?pagination=false.

[16] Robert E. Wright, O.M.I., "Catholic Church," *Handbook of Texas Online,* accessed June 17, 2016, http://www .tshaonline.org/handbook/online/articles/icc01.

[17] Cynthia E. Orozco, "Texas Iaf Network," *Handbook of Texas Online,* accessed June 17, 2016, http://www.tshaonline.org /handbook/online/articles/pqtpp.

[18] Terry Baynes, "U.S. Catholic Groups Sue to Block Contraception Mandate," Reuters, 21 May 2012, http:// www.reuters.com/article/2012/05/21/us-usa-healthcare-contraception-idUSBRE84K19R20120521.

[19] *Zubik v. Burwell,* 578 U. S. _____ (2016), http://www .supremecourt.gov/opinions/15pdf/14-1418_8758.pdf.

[20] Texas Ethics Commission, Lobbying in Texas: A Guide to the Texas Law (September 15, 2015), https://www.ethics.state .tx.us/guides/LOBBY_guide.htm.

[21] National Conference of State Legislatures, How States Define Lobbying and Lobbyist (3/4/2015), http://www.ncsl.org /research/ethics/50-state-chart-lobby-definitions.aspx.

[22] Texas Ethics Commission, Lobbying in Texas: A Guide to the Texas Law (September 15, 2015), https://www.ethics.state. tx.us/guides/LOBBY_guide.htm.

[23] Ibid.

[24] Internal Revenue Service, Lobbying (March 4, 2016), https://www.irs.gov/charities-non-profits/lobbying.

[25] Jim Grace and Luke Ledbetter, "The Lobbyist," *Houston Lawyer* (September/October 2009), 10. Available online at http://www.thehoustonlawyer.com/aa_sep09/page10.htm.

[26] Chris Mathews, *Hardball: How Politics Is Played Told by One Who Knows the Game* (Touchstone Press, 1988), 133.

[27] *Final Accounting in the Estate of A. B.,* 1 Tucker 248 (N.Y. Surr. 1866).

[28] Texas House of Representatives, How A Bill Becomes A Law, http://www.house.state.tx.us/about-us/bill/.

[29] Patricia Kilday Hart, "Perry vetoed wage bill after getting letters from retailers," *Houston Chronicle,* August 5, 2013, http://www.houstonchronicle.com/news/houston-texas/texas/article/Perry-vetoed-wage-bill-after-getting-letters-from-4708525.php

[30] Proclamation by the Governor of the State of Texas, June 14, 2013, http://www.lrl.state.tx.us/scanned/vetoes/83/HB950.pdf.

[31] Clive S. Thomas and Ronald J. Hrebenar, "Interest Groups in State Politics," in *Politics in the American States,* ed. Virginia Gray, Herbert Jacob, and Robert Albritton, 5th ed. (Glenview, Ill.: Scott Foresman/ Little, Brown, 1990), 150–151.

[32] As cited in Luigi Zingales, *A Capitalism for the People: Recapturing the Lost Genius of American Prosperity* (New York: Basic Books, 2012), 183.

[33] U.S. Bill of Rights.

[34] Federal Election Commission, Quick Answers to PAC Questions, http://www.fec.gov/ans/answers_pac.shtml.

[35] SCOTUSblog, *Citizens United v. Federal Election Commission,* http://www.scotusblog.com/case-files/cases/citizens-united-v-federal-election-commission/.

[36] Texans for Public Justice, "Texas PACs: 2008 and 2011 Cycle Spending," www.tpj.org/reports/txpacs02total.html.

[37] Clive S. Thomas and Ronald J. Hrebenar, "Interest Groups in State Politics," in *Politics in the American States,* ed. Virginia Gray, Herbert Jacob, and Robert Albritton, 5th ed. (Glenview, Ill.: Scott Foresman/Little, Brown, 1990), 154.

[38] Benjy Sarlin, "Campaign finance activists try to explain Jeb Bush's $130 million fail," msnbc.com, February 23, 2016, http://www.msnbc.com/msnbc/campaign-finance-activists-try-explain-jeb-bushs-130-million-fail.

[39] Internal Revenue Service, "Lobbying," https://www.irs.gov/charities-non-profits/lobbying.

[40] Nayantara Mehta, "Nonprofits and Lobbying: Yes, They Can!" *Business Law Today* 18:4 (2009), https://apps.americanbar.org/buslaw/blt/2009-03-04/mehta.shtml; Internal Revenue Service, "Direct" and "Grass Roots" Lobbying Defined, https://www.irs.gov/charities-non-profits/direct-and-grass-roots-lobbying-defined

[41] Mehta, "Nonprofits and Lobbying Yes, They Can!"

[42] Texas Ethics Commission, Lobbying in Texas: A Guide to the Texas Law (September 15, 2015) https://www.ethics.state.tx.us/guides/LOBBY_guide.htm#PROHIBITIONS; Texas Penal Code § 36.02, http://www.statutes.legis.state.tx.us/Docs/PE/htm/PE.36.htm.

[43] Keith E. Hamm and Charles W. Wiggins, "The Transformation from Personnel to Information Lobbying," in *Interest Group Politics in the Southern States,* ed. Ronald J. Hrebenar and Clive S. Thomas (Tuscaloosa: University of Alabama Press, 1992), 170.

[44] Kim Lane Scheppele and Jack L. Walker, Jr., "The Litigation Strategies of Interest Groups," In *Mobilizing Interest Groups in America: Patrons, Professions, and Social Movements,* edited by Jack L. Walker Jr., 158 (Ann Arbor: University of Michigan Press, 1991).

[45] Ibid.

[46] "Amicus brief," Legal Dictionary, http://legaldictionary.net/amicus-brief/.

[47] Paul M. Collins, Jr., "Lobbyists before the U.S. Supreme Court: Investigating the Influence of Amicus Curiae Briefs," *Political Research Quarterly* 60:1 (March 2007): 55–70.

[48] Kim Lane Scheppele and Jack L. Walker, Jr., "The Litigation Strategies of Interest Groups," In *Mobilizing Interest Groups in America: Patrons, Professions, and Social Movements,* edited by Jack L. Walker Jr., 158 (Ann Arbor: University of Michigan Press, 1991).

[49] Cynthia E. Orozco, "Del Rio ISD v. Salvatierra," *Handbook of Texas Online,* http://www.tshaonline.org/handbook/online/articles/jrd02.

[50] V. Carl Allsup, "Delgado v. Bastrop Isd," *Handbook of Texas Online,* http://www.tshaonline.org/handbook/online/articles/jrd01.

[51] Ibid.; League of United Latin American Citizens, "LULAC's Milestones," http://lulac.org/about/history/milestones/.

[52] V. Carl Allsup, "Delgado v. Bastrop Isd," *Handbook of Texas Online,* http://www.tshaonline.org/handbook/online/articles/jrd01.

[53] V. Carl Allsup, "Hernandez v. Driscoll Cisd," *Handbook of Texas Online,* http://www.tshaonline.org/handbook/online/articles/jrh02.

[54] Teresa Palomo Acosta, "Edgewood ISD v. Kirby," *Handbook of Texas Online,* http://www.tshaonline.org/handbook/online/articles/jre02.

[55] Ibid.

[56] Ibid.

[57] Janice C. May, "Texas Legislature," *Handbook of Texas Online,* http://www.tshaonline.org/handbook/online/articles/mkt02.

[58] Keith E. Hamm and Charles W. Wiggins, "The Transformation from Personnel to Information Lobbying,"

in *Interest Group Politics in the Southern States,* ed. Ronald J. Hrebenar and Clive S. Thomas (Tuscaloosa: University of Alabama Press, 1992), 152.

[59] Texas Ethics Commission, "A Brief Overview of the Texas Ethics Commission and its Duties" (September 22, 2009), https://www.ethics.state.tx.us /pamphlet/B09ethic.htm.

[60] Texas Ethics Commission, Lobbying in Texas: A Guide to the Texas Law, (September 15, 2015), https://www.ethics.state .tx.us/guides/LOBBY_guide.htm#COMPENSATION AND REIMBURSEMENT THRESHOLD.

[61] Texas Ethics Commission, "2016 List of Registered Lobbyists" (April 7, 2016), https://www.ethics.state.tx.us /tedd/2016RegisteredLobbyists.pdf.

[62] Texas Ethics Commission, "Lobbying in Texas: A Guide to the Texas Law," (September 15, 2015), https://www .ethics.state.tx.us/guides/LOBBY_guide.htm# EXCEPTIONS_REGISTRATION.

[63] Texas Ethics Commission, Campaign Finance Guide for Political Committees (June 22, 2016), https://www.ethics .state.tx.us/guides/pac_guide.pdf.

[64] Texas Election Code, Title 15 Sec. 253.034, http://www .statutes.legis.state.tx.us/Docs/EL/htm/EL.253 .htm#253.034.

[65] National Conference of State Legislatures, "State Limits on Contributions to Candidates: 2015–2016 Election Cycle," http://www.ncsl.org/Portals/1/documents/legismgt/elect /ContributionLimitstoCandidates2015-2016.pdf.

[66] SCOTUSblog, *Citizens United v. Federal Election Commission,* http://www.scotusblog.com/case-files/cases /citizens-united-v-federal-election-commission/.

[67] Cornell University Law School Legal Information Institute, Supreme Court, http://www.law.cornell.edu/supct/html/08- 205.ZS.html.

[68] National Conference of State Legislatures, Life After *Citizens United.* http://www.ncsl.org/research/elections-and- campaigns/citizens-united-and-the-states.aspx.

[69] Matt Stiles, "TX Ethics Commission Cracking Down," Texas Tribune, Nov. 10, 2009, https://www.texastribune .org/2009/11/10/tx-ethics-commission-cracking-down/.

[70] Molly Ivins, *Molly Ivins Can't Say That, Can She?* (New York: Random House, 1991), 58.

[71] ATPE, "Educators who do their homework choose ATPE," http://www.atpe.org/ATPE/media/ATPE/PDF/15_ MC_ComparisonBoxstuffers_1516-02_TSTANEA_ WEB_1.pdf.

[72] Texas Municipal League, "About the Texas Municipal League," http://www.tml.org/about.

[73] Texas Municipal League, "How the League Implements Organizational Policy" (June 11, 2015), http://www.tml .org/p/LeagueOrganizationalPolicy2015.pdf.

[74] Tyler Cowen, "Public Goods," *Library of Economics and Liberty,* 2012, http://www.econlib.org/library/Enc /PublicGoods.html.

[75] Mancur Olson, *The Logic of Collective Action,* (Cambridge, MA: Harvard University Press, 1971).

[76] Thomas R. Dye, *Politics in States and Communities,* 7th ed. (Englewood Cliffs, N.J.: Prentice Hall, 1991), 112–113.

[77] Texas Municipal League, "2015–2016 TML Legislative Policy Development Process," http://www.tml.org/p/2015_ TML_Policy_Process.pdf.

[78] Molly Ivins, "Getting to the Grass Roots of the Problem," *Bryan-College Station Eagle,* 13 July 1995, A4. Copyright Molly Ivins. Reprinted by permission.

[79] Peverill Squire, "Measuring State Legislative Professionalism: The Squire Index Revisited," *State Politics & Policy Quarterly* 7:2 (Summer, 2007), 211–227.

[80] David F. Prindel, *Petroleum Politics and the Texas Railroad Commission* (Austin: University of Texas Press, 1981).

[81] Richard H. Kraemer and Charldean Newell, *Texas Politics,* 2nd ed. (St. Paul: West, 1984), 79. Also see *The Texas Almanac and State Industrial Guide, 1970–71* (Dallas: A.H. Belo, 1970), 425; and *The Texas Almanac and State Industrial Guide, 1974–75,* (Dallas: A.H. Belo, 1974), 19.

[82] Texas Health and Safety Code, Sec. 716.004, http://www .statutes.legis.state.tx.us/Docs/HS/htm/HS.716.htm.

[83] Texas Administrative Code §181.4, https://tex.reg.sos.state .tx.us/public/readtac$ext.TacPage?sl=R&app=9&p_ dir=&p_rloc=&p_tloc=&p_ploc=&pg=1&p_ tac=&ti=25&pt=1&ch=181&rl=4.

[84] Texas Administrative Code §203.48, https://texreg.sos.state .tx.us/public/readtac$ext.TacPage?sl=T&app=9&p_ dir=N&p_rloc=174025&p_tloc=&p_ploc=1&pg=5&p_ tac=&ti=22&pt=10&ch=203&rl=48.

[85] David R. Henderson, "Rent Seeking," *Library of Economics and Liberty,* 2012, http://www.econlib.org/library/Enc /RentSeeking.html. Also see the pioneering works by Gordon Tullock and Anne Krueger, especially the latter's "The Political Economy of the Rent-Seeking Society," *American Economic Review* 64 (1974), 291–303.

[86] Tyler Cowen and Alex Tabarrok, "The Opportunity Costs of Rent Seeking," http://mason.gmu.edu/atabarro /TheOpportunityCostsofRentSeeking.pdf. Also see Kevin M. Murphy, Andrei Scheifer, and Robert W. Vishny, "Why Is Rent-Seeking So Costly to Growth?" AEA Papers and Proceedings (May 1993).

CHAPTER 11

Public Policy in Texas

- Analyze important public policy issues in Texas.

What is public policy? This seems like a simple question. However, political scientists have wrestled with it and offered a variety of answers. Thomas Dye, in one of the most popular books on **public policy**, defines it quite simply as, "Whatever governments choose to do or not to do." Scholars Marc Eisner, Jeffrey Worsham, and Evan Ringquist are even more minimalist, defining public policy as "patterns of governmental action and inaction." A scholar outside the field of political science, psychiatrist and crime victim rights advocate Dean Kilpatrick, provides one of the more detailed definitions, arguing that public policy is "a system of laws, regulatory measures, courses of action, and funding priorities concerning a given topic promulgated by a governmental entity or its representatives."[1]

public policy
"Whatever governments choose to do or not to do."
—Thomas Dye

Each of these three definitions offers a clue as to what the realm of public policy encompasses. But they all imply that the public policy world is fairly huge and touches nearly all aspects of our lives. For good or for bad, justly or unjustly, our state and local governments here in Texas impact us from the time we wake up in the morning until we go to bed at night. They affect us when we turn on the lights (utility regulation), when we take a shower (water policy), when we get in the car and drive to work or school (the Department of Motor Vehicles, among others), when we are at the office or the university (business regulations and education policy), and so on throughout the day. In this chapter, we examine some of the most important areas of governmental action at the state and local levels. These include regulatory policy, welfare policy, education policy, social policy, water policy, and policies affecting immigrants and veterans. But first we discuss the steps involved in the policy-making process and how Texas compares to other states in terms of its overall policy ideology.

Chapter Learning Objectives

- Discuss the steps in the policy-making process.

- Explain policy liberalism indices and what they can tell us.

- Discuss public policy areas in Texas state government.

Steps in the Policy-Making Process: The "Policy Cycle"

Learning Objective: Discuss the steps in the policy-making process.

Political scientists have for some time been interested in explaining the process by which public policy is formulated and implemented. In his book *Public Policymaking,* James Anderson published one of the first comprehensive attempts to define policy making as a process. In particular, he refers to this process as a "policy cycle."[2] He outlined the primary stages of the policy cycle as follows: problem identification and agenda setting; policy formulation; policy adoption; policy implementation; and policy evaluation (see Figure 11.1).

Of course, not all policy-making efforts include each step in the process. The cycle, instead, represents the ideal. In actuality, there is often no policy evaluation, which consists of an attempt to assess effectiveness after a policy has been implemented and then to make possible adjustments. Often policies are passed with no consideration of this need for review and change in the future. In some cases, reversing a policy would be quite costly, requiring funding that would put pressure on the budget (and necessitate either cuts elsewhere or tax increases). For example, the Texas state legislature has decided to fund less and less of the cost of public education. It is not likely that this policy will be reversed unless tax revenues increase substantially, because reversing this policy would probably require a tax increase.

The policy formulation stage may also lack critical analysis of the impact of the proposed policy or any alternatives (not to mention failure to consider the likely unintended consequences of any policy proposal). This is due in part to the nature of legislative work: constituents complain and legislators react. Indeed,

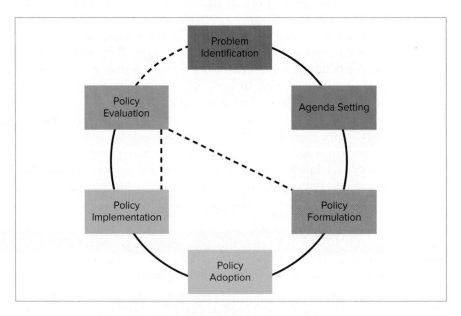

FIGURE 11.1   The Policy-Making Cycle

responding to constituent complaints is a time-honored role for legislators—and something that many citizens expect of state and local decision makers. In some cases, legislators may propose legislation to correct a perceived problem based on anecdotal evidence from a single constituent. Legislators may react, not with great forethought, but instead because they know their constituents expect them to take some action. This is not a recipe for careful policy design, especially in moments of crisis when the urge to "do something, do anything" is strong. However, the Texas legislature's biennial sessions help to mitigate somewhat the problem of reacting under pressure without thinking.

In some cases, the policy implementation stage of the policy cycle is skipped altogether because the new policy is largely symbolic. Some would argue that state bans on gay marriage were examples of such policies, because these laws required little substantive implementation when the state already restricted marriage to heterosexual couples. Instead, these laws often were ways for some legislators to show symbolic support for the conservative and religious beliefs of their key constituencies.

CORE OBJECTIVE

Taking Personal Responsibility . . .

How can you impact public policy decisions? At what point in the policy cycle could you voice your preferences?

Source: United States Department of Agriculture Agricultural Research Service

Policy Liberalism Index

Learning Objective: Explain policy liberalism indices and what they can tell us.

"Policy liberalism" is a common measure of state policy ideology that can be used to compare the 50 states. Political scientists have identified policy liberalism as a key component underlying variation in state policy. In other words, policy differences in the American states are understood to reflect differences in ideology that run along a left-right, or liberal-conservative, spectrum. Policy liberalism also tracks well with public opinion ideology. However, as political scientists Jason Sorens, Fait Muedini, and William Ruger have cautioned in their own study of state policy ideology, "It is also important to recognize that most policy variation in the states is not a reflection of mere ideological differences." Instead, a variety of factors specific to each state accounts for a lot of the policy differences we see. These include the fact that each state has specific policy problems it is trying to solve (and policies that will reflect those particular conditions and needs) as well as different historical "legacies" and institutional arrangements.[3]

However, rigorous policy liberalism indices have been developed that help us measure how liberal or conservative a state is on some state policies and compare the 50 states in terms of those policies. Despite possible connotations of the term "policy liberalism," these indices are *not* judgments about state policies from a particular political stance or ideology. Instead, they are simply scientific measures that help us understand state policy and how the states compare to each other along a liberal-conservative dimension. Most of these indices utilize only a few policies but are still able to construct accurate and informative measures that capture the underlying concept. For example, political scientist Virginia Gray has constructed a policy liberalism index using five policy indicators: gun control laws, abortion laws, conditions for receiving Temporary Assistance to Needy Families (TANF) benefits, tax progressivity, and right-to-work laws.[4] However, Sorens, Muedini, and Ruger's "State Policy Index" (SPI) contains a **policy liberalism index** constructed from more than 200 policies in the fiscal, regulatory, and social policy realms. Sorens and Ruger have updated the original index to reflect the most recent data for 2008 and 2012.

policy liberalism index
A measure of how liberal or conservative a state is on some state policies

Table 11.1 compares the updated SPI and Gray rankings for all 50 states. Despite their different constructions, the Gray and SPI indices are remarkably consistent in their findings for many states. For example, California, New York, and New Jersey were the most liberal and the top three in the same order in both SPI and Gray (2011); likewise, many of the same states were the most

TABLE 11.1

State Rankings on Policy Liberalism

State	SPI Policy Liberalism Ranking (2012)	SPI Policy Liberalism Score (2012)	Gray Policy Liberalism Ranking (2011)	SPI Policy Liberalism Ranking (2008)	Gray Policy Liberalism Ranking (2005)
California	1	−14.3521	1	1	1
New York	2	−11.5009	2	2	3
New Jersey	3	−10.0342	3	3	5
Hawaii	4	−9.05985	6	5	2
Massachusetts	5	−9.04744	11	4	8
Maryland	6	−8.90795	7	6	11
Rhode Island	7	−7.06503	8	7	10
Connecticut	8	−6.99311	5	9	6
Illinois	9	−6.63467	18	8	13
Washington	10	−3.99201	15	10	18
Delaware	11	−3.16527	21	13	16
Maine	12	−2.4372	10	11	9
Iowa	13	−1.91866	25	14	24
Vermont	14	−1.80142	4	12	4
Minnesota	15	−1.78163	12	16	14
Oregon	16	−1.00876	9	17	7
Michigan	17	−0.56489	22	15	25
Colorado	18	−0.18053	23	18	28
Pennsylvania	19	0.295057	24	20	20
Nevada	20	0.37851	31	24	30
New Hampshire	21	0.487105	19	19	23
New Mexico	22	0.527307	16	23	15
North Carolina	23	0.708056	30	21	37
Wisconsin	24	0.709303	13	22	21
West Virginia	25	0.904698	17	30	19

Montana	26	1.111977	14	25	12
Ohio	27	1.216359	28	26	26
Alaska	28	1.306331	20	29	17
Florida	29	1.486236	46	31	40
Nebraska	30	1.843856	33	28	29
Louisiana	31	1.926403	49	27	36
Missouri	32	2.01637	27	33	22
Indiana	33	2.219354	35	32	33
Texas	34	2.794667	48	36	41
Tennessee	35	3.002842	39	35	34
Arizona	36	3.015639	38	34	35
Kansas	37	3.03307	29	37	31
Utah	38	3.139452	37	41	39
Kentucky	39	3.357733	26	42	27
Arkansas	40	3.393507	50	39	43
Georgia	41	3.39765	32	45	46
North Dakota	42	3.511446	40	49	48
Wyoming	43	3.541751	45	44	50
South Dakota	44	3.643725	44	43	49
Virginia	45	3.845109	36	40	38
Alabama	46	4.041639	41	38	44
Oklahoma	47	4.075824	43	47	45
South Carolina	48	4.154134	34	46	32
Idaho	49	4.167597	42	48	42
Mississippi	50	4.431663	47	50	47

Sources: Jason Sorens, Fait Muedini, and William Ruger, "U.S. State and Local Public Policies in 2006: A New Database," *State Politics and Policy Quarterly* 8:3 (Fall 2008): 309–326. The rankings used in the text are based on Sorens and Ruger's updated data that are available at http://www.statepolicyindex.com/the-research/; Virginia Gray, "The Socioeconomic and Political Context of States," in *Politics in the American States: A Comparative Analysis,* 9th ed., ed. Virginia Gray and Russell Hanson (Congressional Quarterly Press, 2008); Virginia Gray, "The Socioeconomic and Political Context of States," in *Politics in the American States: A Comparative Analysis,* 10th ed., ed. Virginia Gray, Russell L. Hanson, and Thad Kousser (Congressional Quarterly Press, 2011).

conservative in both indices. Differences between the two are likely due to the greater range of policies examined in the SPI index as well as policy changes over time. It is also worth comparing how some states have changed over time.

It is important to note that some states rank high on some particular indicators of policy liberalism and near the bottom on others. For example, Vermont is one of the states with the most laissez-faire gun laws in the country, despite being a relatively liberal (in the modern sense) state on many other issues. In the Gray index (2011), Washington state ranks second on abortion rights and sixth in terms of fewest conditions for receiving TANF benefits, but ranks at the bottom on regressivity of taxes and near the middle on gun control. Some states (especially those that are more liberal on social policies such as civil unions but economically more conservative) fit the standard left-right, liberal-conservative pattern less well than others.

Texas ranks as one of the more conservative states in the country. It comes in at #34 in the most recent SPI ranking from 2012 and #48 in the most recent version of Gray's policy liberalism index from 2011. In terms of the Gray index, Texas ranks roughly in the middle on gun laws (which might surprise many Texans), whereas it is generally conservative on abortion, tax progressivity, and access to TANF (see Map 11.1). Both rankings provide accurate reflections of the political culture of Texas. Texans oppose gun control, are more often than not pro-life/anti-abortion,

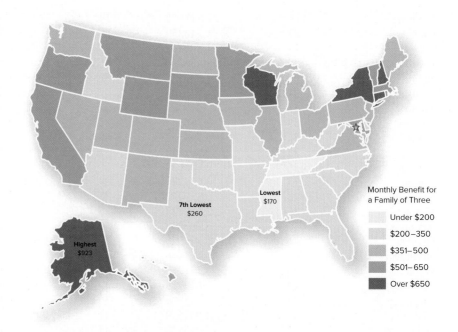

MAP 11.1 Monthly TANF Benefits by State

SOURCE: Ife Finch & Liz Schott, "TANF Benefits Fell Further in 2011 and Are Worth Much Less Than in 1996 in Most States," *Center on Budget and Policy Priorities,* Nov. 2011 (http://www.cbpp.org/files/11-21-11pov.pdf).

and favor regressive consumer taxes. The states ranked near or below Texas are, as one might expect, either Western or Southern states—thus passing a "smell test" of sorts in terms of the validity of the rankings.

These policy liberalism indices can also provide some insight into the kind of policies that can be expected to pass the legislature and be advocated by the governor and other state agencies. They are not intended as critiques of conservative states like Texas, or their policies, but rather as one way of explaining why things are the way they are. Texas ranks in the lower third in both indices because it has very conservative policies, such as relatively limited regulation (for example, right-to-work/anti-union laws), a strict criminal justice system, a very regressive tax structure (meaning that, as economist Dwight Lee notes, such taxes "take a larger percentage of income from those with less income"), and laws limiting some aspects of abortion.[5] The average Texan likely agrees with these policy positions, especially if we assume that legislators are responsive to public opinion (especially the opinion of the average voter!).

Public Policy Areas in Texas State Government

Learning Objective: Discuss public policy areas in Texas state government.

Despite the ever-expanding range of issues over which the federal government has assumed control in the past half-century or so, states still play an important role in legislating in certain policy areas and implementing a wide array of policies set at both the state and federal levels. As we saw in the discussion of state policy liberalism, states vary quite a bit in terms of policy output and outcomes. Chapter 13 focuses specifically on tax policy at the state level, an area in which states differ dramatically and meaningfully. The remainder of this chapter examines a number of other important policy areas in the state of Texas, including regulatory policy, welfare policy, education policy, social policy, water policy, and policies affecting immigrants and veterans.

Regulatory Policy

First, let us consider Texas's regulatory policies toward business and put them in national perspective. In the United States, state governments regulate a range of activities that include the following:

- Life, property, and auto insurance (how much insurance companies can charge consumers, as well as their financial soundness)
- The court system (how friendly the process is to defendants or plaintiffs, often covered by the term "**tort** reform")
- Professions and occupations (requirements for obtaining and maintaining licenses to practice)
- Public utilities (electricity, natural gas, telecommunications, and cable)
- Labor law (minimum wage, workers' compensation, collective bargaining between unions and employers, and so on)
- The environment, including land use (whether and how land can be developed or taken for a public purpose)

tort
"a civil wrong, recognized by law as grounds for a lawsuit, which can be redressed by awarding damages" *Source:* Cornell University Law School, Legal Information Institute, Wex Legal Dictionary

Texas's regulatory policies are usually considered pro-business. In fact, *Chief Executive Magazine* rated Texas the best state for business in 2015 due to its stellar job creation, low taxes, and favorable cost of living for employees.[6] The state's policymakers have fostered this pro-business environment in a number of ways.

For instance, Texas labor law tends to be anti-union and pro-employer. Texas has a right-to-work law that prohibits collective bargaining agreements between employers and unions from including clauses that require employees to pay agency fees to the union as a condition of employment. (See Map 10.1 for all right-to-work states.) Right-to-work laws tend to reduce the power of unions because many employees prefer to opt out of paying the agency fees while still receiving the benefits of collective bargaining. (Agency fees and union dues are slightly different. As one teachers' group explains: "An agency fee is a percentage of dues that the union determines is the amount it costs the union to represent you before your employer in the areas of bargaining, contract administration, and grievances.")[7] Another point supporting Texas's pro-employer reputation is that it is the only state not to mandate that employers purchase workers' compensation insurance in case of employees' injuries. Employers are allowed to opt for a "tort" model instead, in which injured employees can sue their employers for damages. Texas's labor laws have both benefits and costs. They probably raise business investment and levels of employment, but they also reduce the wages of those specific workers who would otherwise be represented by stronger unions.

Texas is also considered to be pro-business because of what state and local governments do to actively recruit and support businesses. Foremost among these are tax abatements and programs for special corporate subsidies, such as

Former Governor Rick Perry holds a sign boasting of Texas's favorable business climate.
© Eric Gay/AP Images

the Texas Enterprise Fund. For example, Texas has no corporate income tax, and the business franchise tax was recently cut by 25 percent.[8] The Texas Enterprise Fund, which awards grants to corporations for locating (or expanding) a business in Texas, was created to attract businesses (and the jobs that come with them) to the state. It has provided companies with more than $580 million in incentives since its inception in 2003. The Office of the Governor notes that this "'deal-closing' fund" has strengthened the state's economy by boosting capital investment and job creation.[9] Meanwhile, Governor Abbott opted to discontinue the Texas Emerging Technology Fund, started by former Governor Rick Perry to bolster early-stage tech companies.[10]

This amalgamation of pro-business policies has drawn the ire of both liberal Democrats and free-market, libertarian Republicans. The former complain that the subsidy programs are, at best, funnels for "corporate welfare" and, at worst, "political slush-funds" for Republican politicians.[11] The latter criticize them on the grounds that they are examples of "crony capitalism" and inconsistent with true capitalism. As Erica Grieder of *Texas Monthly* explained, these skeptics "argue that such subsidies aren't even good for business, because they amount to the government 'picking winners and losers,' thereby distorting potentially efficient markets: companies with a bad product may be artificially buoyed by the grants, and those that might otherwise succeed struggle to outlast their well-funded competitors."[12] Critics also point out that there isn't enough transparency in the incentive rewarding process.[13] Although former Governor Perry was a strong advocate of these programs, Governor Abbott has said he wants the government "out of the business of picking winners and losers," and his decision to eliminate the Texas Emerging Technology Fund may signal his intent to scale back such initiatives.

Texas is one of the least regulated states in the country on land use. The state and most localities within the state place comparatively few restrictions on landowners' ability to subdivide and build on their property. The city of

Houston remains the only major city in the country without zoning, a type of land-use regulation that segregates residential and commercial uses for land. (However, Houston's municipal code regulates land use significantly.) The most recent national study of state and local land-use regulations was conducted by researchers at the University of Pennsylvania's Wharton School of Business. The "Wharton Residential Land-Use Regulation Index" rated Texas as the twenty-first least-regulated state, with many rural states somewhat less regulated. However, Dallas, Fort Worth-Arlington, San Antonio, and Houston were all in the top 10 least-regulated metropolitan areas in the country.[14] A benefit of low land-use regulation is a high supply of housing and therefore low home prices and rents, perhaps the biggest reason Texas has attracted so many new residents in recent years.[15] The costs of few restrictions on development include loss of natural habitat and lower quality of life for residents who oppose development.

Texas has also placed more restrictions on the use of eminent domain than most other states. Eminent domain is the process whereby the government can take private land for a public purpose with compensation. The U.S. Supreme Court case *Kelo v. City of New London* (2005) established that local governments may use eminent domain to transfer private property to other private parties so long as the government envisions public benefits from doing so. This decision was highly unpopular across the country, and many state legislatures rushed to place legal restrictions on this use of eminent domain. In most states, those reforms were mostly symbolic and left significant loopholes. Texas, however, enacted one of the more far-reaching reforms. According to the Sorens, Muedini, and Ruger study, which includes an index of eminent domain reform, Texas is tied for eleventh among the states in the strictness of its restrictions on private-to-private eminent domain transfers, and it is tied for ninth in terms of overall eminent domain reform.[16]

Texas has a history of rather burdensome licensing regulations, but reforms have recently been made in this area. Occupational and professional licensing regulations can be a barrier to employment and small business formation, as job seekers and would-be entrepreneurs must meet requirements in education and training, take examinations, and pay fees before they can get the government's permission to work. Traditionally associated with careers in medicine and law, occupational licenses are now issued for a wide range of workers, from contractors to hair stylists to athletic trainers. Strict requirements for obtaining a license reduce competition, economic opportunities for working-class people, and affordability for consumers, but they are often justified on grounds of public health or ensuring higher quality for the consumer.[17] During his campaign, Governor Abbott promised reforms in this area, and in 2015 he signed legislation eliminating the annual licensing fee for a number of professionals including doctors, lawyers, engineers, and accountants.[18] (This law impacted more than 600,000 Texans and constituted the single largest tax break enacted during the 84th Legislative Session.) Additional legislation reduced licensing requirements for low-income occupations as well. For example, hair braiding—an occupation that previously required 35 hours of training for licensure—was completely deregulated, meaning individuals no longer need to obtain a state license in order to braid hair or teach hair braiding.[19] This is an area of rare left-right agreement at the national level, as both conservative groups and President Obama have argued for the scaling back of occupational licensing requirements that impair economic opportunity.[20]

An area where Texas is not so pro-business is its court system. The U.S. Chamber of Commerce evaluates states on the business friendliness (and, therefore, plaintiff unfriendliness) of their civil liability systems. In the latest survey from 2015, Texas ranked fortieth, indicating that the state is comparatively friendly to plaintiffs who sue businesses for, say, product-liability claims.[21]

Welfare Policy

States are responsible for administering many federally legislated programs providing income support and in-kind benefits to the poor, unemployed, and disabled. In some cases, states have considerable leeway to determine eligibility for these programs. For instance, Medicaid, the public health insurance program for the poor, is run entirely by state governments, but the federal government encourages states to fund the program generously by offering matching grants. Still, because Medicaid expenditures are such a large item in state budgets (looking at the most recent data available across all 50 states, Medicaid accounted for fully one-quarter, or 25.6 percent, of total state spending in 2014[22]), significant variation exists in benefit levels and eligibility requirements among the states, as some states try to keep costs down.

As of June 2015, 15.7 percent of Texas's population was enrolled in Medicaid, compared to a national average of 18.3 percent.[23] Because Texas has a relatively high poverty rate (16.4 percent of Texas's 2014 population lived in households with incomes below the federal poverty threshold, compared with an official poverty rate of 14.8 percent nationwide for that year[24]), these figures suggest that Texas's eligibility criteria for Medicaid are relatively stringent. The state has maintained these stricter standards regarding qualification for benefits despite recent federal pressure to relax them. Under the Affordable Care Act (ACA), states were encouraged to expand their Medicaid programs, or offer Medicaid coverage to more people, by raising the income threshold. If a state has expanded Medicaid, individuals can now qualify for coverage if their income is up to 138 percent of the federal poverty level.[25] As of January 2016, Texas was one of 19 states not to expand Medicaid.[26] Map 11.2 shows which states expanded Medicaid under the ACA (see Map 11.2).

Other evidence suggests that Texas provides lower benefit levels than other states and imposes additional eligibility requirements on those obtaining benefits. Federal food programs include Women, Infants, and Children (WIC), the Supplemental Nutrition Assistance Program (SNAP, formerly known as "food stamps"), and the school lunch program. In fiscal year 2014, Texas had the second highest number of people participating in SNAP of all 50 states. (California had the highest number.) SNAP recipients made up 14.8 percent of Texas's population, similar to the 14.9 percent of the population participating in SNAP nationwide. However, the average monthly benefit per person was $115.30 in Texas, slightly lower than the national average of $125.01.[27] In 2013, the state legislature passed a bill requiring drug testing of some applicants for unemployment, but implementation of that law has been delayed pending receipt of drug testing guidelines from the federal government. Legislators have also considered drug testing of TANF recipients.[28]

When it comes to expenditures classified by the Census Bureau as "public welfare," Texas's state government spent $30.8 billion in fiscal year 2013. That amounts to 28.5 percent of general expenditures being dedicated to welfare, a

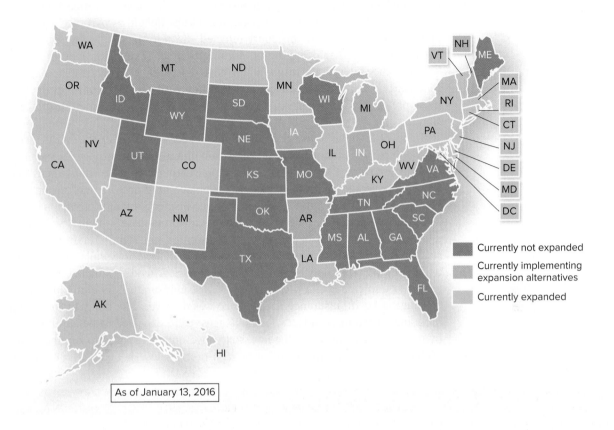

MAP 11.2   Medicaid Expansion by State

SOURCE: National Conference of State Legislatures, "State Decisions on ACA-Related Medicaid Expansion," January 2016, http://www.ncsl.org/research/health/affordable-care-act-expansion.aspx.

figure that is below the national average of 30.8 percent.[29] Nevertheless, "welfare policy" might be thought more broadly to include all spending on health and hospitals in addition to income support, housing, community development, and food programs. If those categories are added together, they total $38.8 billion for Texas in 2013, or 31.1 percent of total state expenditures. The national average for these categories is 32.4 percent.[30] Thus, no matter how one slices the data, Texas spends less than most other states on welfare programs as a share of the state budget.

Health Care Policy

The Affordable Care Act (ACA, also known as "Obamacare") was passed by Congress and signed into law by President Obama in 2010 as an effort to reform health care and extend coverage to more Americans. After weathering multiple legal challenges (the state of Texas was among those who sued the Obama administration), most of the ACA was ultimately upheld by a 5-4 vote of the U.S. Supreme Court in *National Federation of Independent Business v. Sebelius* (2012).[31] The court ruled that although Congress's passage of an individual mandate to buy health insurance could not be justified under the Commerce Clause of the Constitution, it could be upheld as part of Congress's taxing power. However, the court rejected the portion of the law involving expansion of Medicaid eligibility, arguing that this expansion would unduly "coerce" the states. As a result, states have discretion over whether to expand Medicaid benefits to individuals and families with higher income levels than those previously specified. As stated earlier, Texas has not adopted this expansion to date.

Table 11.2 shows some key provisions of the ACA. Under the ACA, insurance companies cannot place an annual or lifetime limit on benefits, nor can they deny coverage to someone with a preexisting condition. Individuals can maintain coverage under their parents' insurance until age 26, and certain preventive services are available at no cost to the insured. A major provision of the law is the requirement—known as the "individual mandate"—that every person purchase and maintain health insurance coverage satisfying certain minimum standards; uninsured individuals are assessed what the IRS calls an "individual shared responsibility payment," or what less officially is called a "fee" or tax.[32] To implement this provision and assist uninsured individuals in finding coverage, a health insurance marketplace was devised. Like many other federal programs, these marketplaces, or exchanges, were expected to be administered by the states. According to the law, state governments can opt to run their own exchange, share a regional exchange with other states, or operate an exchange

TABLE 11.2

Key Provisions of the ACA

Guaranteed Coverage	Health insurers cannot refuse to cover an individual because of current or prior health problems (called "preexisting conditions").
Benefit Standards	Health insurance policies must provide certain benefits, called "minimum essential coverage."
Individual Mandate	Individuals are required to buy health insurance or pay a fee (what critics contend is a tax) for not having coverage.
Health Insurance Exchanges	Individuals who do not have health insurance through their employer or the government must buy coverage through a state or federal exchange (i.e., online "Health Insurance Marketplace").
Low Income Subsidies	Individuals who buy coverage through an exchange and whose income is below a certain threshold are eligible for a government subsidy. In other words, the government pays a portion of that person's insurance premiums.
Medicaid Expansion	The income threshold used to qualify individuals for Medicaid coverage has been raised. (Note: States may opt out of this expansion and continue to use the prior income threshold to determine whether individuals qualify for their state's program.)
Coverage for Young Adults	Children can remain on their parents' insurance plan until age 26.
Annual and Lifetime Limits	Insurance companies cannot limit the dollar amount they would spend for most of an individual's covered benefits, either during a given year or during the entire time a person is enrolled in that insurance plan.

Sources: Mike Patton, "Obamacare: Seven Major Provisions And How They Affect You," *Forbes,* November 27, 2013, http://www.forbes.com/sites/mikepatton/2013/11/27/how-obamacare-will-change-the-american-health-system/#1d8423ab6593; U.S. Department of Health and Human Services, "Key Features of the Affordable Care Act By Year," http://www.hhs.gov/healthcare/facts-and-features/key-features-of-aca-by-year/index.html.

jointly with the federal government.[33] However, if a state refuses to set up an exchange, the federal government will step in and establish one. As of February 2016, only 11 states and the District of Columbia were operating their own exchanges, fully independent of federal assistance. Texas has declined to run its own exchange, meaning that Texans shopping for health insurance in the online marketplace use a federally run exchange.[34] Interestingly, the decision whether or not to set up a state-run exchange has generally aligned with the party affiliation of the governor: the majority of states defaulting to a federally run exchange are led by Republican governors, whereas most states with their own exchanges are governed by Democrats.[35]

According to the U.S. Census Bureau, in 2014, Texas had the highest percentage of uninsured people of all 50 states, at roughly 19 percent of the state's population. This not only exceeded the national average of 10.4 percent of the population without health insurance; it was also higher than the 13.5 percent uninsured rate for states that did not expand Medicaid.[36] Proponents of the ACA anticipate the law will reduce the number of uninsured, therefore guaranteeing access to health care for a greater number of people, and drive down the cost of coverage. Opponents argue the law represents an overreach of federal authority that violates individual rights protected by the U.S. Constitution. Furthermore, they point out that compliance with the law will be very expensive, thus stressing state budgets, and that the federal government has not provided clear information about how the system will work.[37] Texas's past two governors have firmly opposed the health care law. For instance, former Governor Perry denounced the ACA, calling its provisions "brazen intrusions into the sovereignty of our state."[38] Governor Abbott reiterated this objection shortly after he took office, stating "Medicaid expansion is wrong for Texas."[39]

Primary and Secondary Education in Texas
School District Financing

The state of Texas pays for part of the cost of public K–12 (also referred to as primary and secondary) education. Over the past 20 years, the state's share of the cost of education has declined, and local school districts have been forced to pick up a larger part of the cost. For the 2014–2015 school year, the state of Texas paid about 41 percent of the cost of public education; the federal government picked up another 10 percent; and local districts provided the rest through taxes, bonds, and other means.[40] Because the primary source of local funding is the property tax, some school districts have been better able than others to absorb the higher local share. Some school districts have a high per-pupil property tax base (so-called rich districts) and others have a low per-pupil property tax base (so-called poor districts). Although the state does show preference to poor districts with increased funding, this support does not completely alleviate the disparities that exist in the amount of money available to school districts on a per-pupil basis.

These funding disparities became a statewide issue in 1968 when parents in the Edgewood school district in San Antonio filed a lawsuit challenging the financing of schools in Texas (*Rodriguez v. San Antonio Independent School District*). The U.S. Supreme Court found the system of school financing to be unfair but deemed it a state problem and said that resolution should rest with the state. Because of this case, the state did increase aid to poor school districts. However, differences continued. In 1984 another lawsuit brought education finance to the forefront in Texas (*Edgewood v. Kirby*). This case was filed in state district court, and because of the efforts of the Mexican American Legal Defense and Education Fund (MALDEF) and the Equity Center in Austin, the Texas Supreme Court ruled the state's system of school finance unconstitutional in 1989.

Data used in this court case indicated disparities among school districts. The critical variable is the par value. This is an index of the per-pupil/student value of property in a district compared with the statewide average, with an index of 100 being average. If a district is above 100, it has more wealth per pupil; below 100, it has less wealth per pupil. Changes in state law have decreased these disparities, but they have not disappeared. Although state aid makes up for some of these differences, most aid is aimed at providing the basic foundations of education. Wealthier districts can still provide funds for so-called enrichments.

In an attempt to correct these funding disparities, the state legislature in 1991 consolidated property taxes within 188 units called county education districts. These districts collected property taxes to be used for school operations and distributed it to the school districts in their jurisdiction on a per-student basis. This system became known as the **Robin Hood Plan** (named after the character from English folklore who took from the rich and gave to the poor) and was subsequently challenged in court by some high per pupil property tax districts. The courts ruled that the plan violated the Texas Constitution. Although the state legislature proposed a constitutional amendment to make the system legal, voters rejected this amendment in May 1993 by a large margin (63 percent against).[41]

[Incidentally, rejection of this system had political implications for the governor's race at the time. According to the *Dallas Morning News,* the Republican National Committee spent $400,000 to help defeat this amendment and to promote negative views about the Democratic governor, Ann Richards, by linking her to the unpopular amendment in ads.[42] Richards was defeated by George W. Bush in 1994.]

Following the defeat of this amendment, the legislature passed a new law, this one accepted by the courts, giving the so-called rich districts several options. Under this plan, a school district's property tax wealth per pupil is capped at a certain amount. For 2014–2015, that level of property wealth per student was $319,500. When a district meets or exceeds that cap (and a final determination is made, based on a few other factors, that it must reduce and equalize its wealth), a district has several choices. It may send its excess wealth to the state, which will send the money to poor districts. Alternatively, the district can consolidate with another district, send money directly to a poor district, or detach property from the district. Most wealthy districts opt to send money, either to the state or to a poor district. Of the roughly 1,000 independent school districts in Texas, 226 (about 22 percent) had to make payments in order to reduce wealth in 2014. This system was also labeled a Robin Hood plan, and it too was challenged in court. However, the Texas Supreme Court found the school funding system constitutional in May 2016.[43]

Robin Hood Plan

System for funding the state's primary and secondary public school education whereby rich districts send money to the state, which then distributes those funds to poor school districts

Being Socially Responsible . . .

To what extent should the government of Texas be responsible for ensuring equal funding for wealthy school districts and poor school districts?

© Editorial Image, LLC/Alamy

High Stakes Test

Local school districts are required to follow guidelines set by the State Board of Education (SBE) and the Texas Education Authority (TEA). In effect, the TEA is the enforcement body for the SBE and the state in general. According to the TEA's website, its organization is responsible for "assessing public school students on what they have learned and determining district and school accountability ratings."[44] To that end, basic mandatory standardized testing is administered to measure student and school performance. The Texas Assessment of Knowledge and Skills (TAKS) testing was the standard until 2012, when it was replaced by the State of Texas Assessment of Academic Readiness (STAAR) exam. STAAR is given to students starting in third grade and continuing throughout students' public school education. Elementary and middle school students are assessed in the areas of reading, math, writing, science, and social studies, and high school students take end-of-course (EOC) tests in English, math, science, and social studies.[45] Performance is classified as either advanced, satisfactory, or unsatisfactory, and to graduate, students must achieve a cumulative score reflecting satisfactory performance in each subject area. Students are allowed to retake EOC exams for any reason.

Anecdotal evidence suggests that teachers "teach to the test" because of the central role that test scores play in the evaluation of public school districts.

Controversial Curriculum

In school board elections in Texas and across the nation, three curriculum issues have stirred up controversy: sex education, evolution and creationism, and bilingual education. Sex education and creationism are issues primarily driven by "social conservatives," including the Christian Right. Social conservatives have sought to limit sex education to abstinence-based programs and to require teaching of creationism as an alternative to evolution or along with evolution. (See the section titled "Sex Education" for more information on this.)

Teachers at the Texas capitol protest proposed cuts to the education budget.

© Eric Gay/AP Images

Bilingual education has been a controversial issue dating back to the early twentieth century, when Germans and Czechs in Texas wanted to teach their native languages in the schools. Following World War I, anti-German sentiment in the state killed these efforts, and in the 1920s the legislature prohibited the teaching of languages other than English. There is an old story in the lore of Texas politics claiming that when Governor "Ma" Ferguson signed the bill prohibiting teaching in any language other than English, she reportedly said, "If English was good enough for Jesus Christ, it's good enough for the school children of Texas."

Higher Education in Texas

Like other populous states, Texas has a large number of public higher educational institutions serving a diverse population of students. According to the Texas Higher Education Coordinating Board, Texas's public higher education system is composed of a vast network of 38 four-year institutions, 50 community and junior college districts, four technical colleges, three state colleges, and nine

FOCUS ON

Hispanics and Bilingual Education

© Gustavo Frazao/Shutterstock

With the explosive growth of Texas's Hispanic population, bilingual education has again become a salient issue. At one point in time, many Anglo Texans objected to the use of tax dollars for bilingual education, but former governors Bush and Perry both helped soften resistance to these programs and reached out to Hispanic voters in the state. Texas law currently requires that bilingual education, as well as instruction in English as a second language (commonly referred to as ESL), be offered as a means of facilitating English competency in students whose primary language is not English. Over 17 percent

of Texas public school students receive such instruction.[46] According to state code, bilingual education is defined as "a full-time program of dual-language instruction that provides for learning basic skills in the primary language of the students enrolled in the program" in addition to English instruction. (Typically, bilingual education involves students in a self-contained classroom being taught all academic subjects using a mix of Spanish and English.) ESL instruction consists of students being pulled out of mainstream classrooms for brief periods of "intensive instruction in English."[47] Bilingual education and/or ESL is mandated for school districts with at least 20 students designated as English language learners. There is continued debate over which instructional models offer the most effective, cost-efficient way to help non-English speaking students acquire proficiency with the English language, as well as whether students should be required to learn English in an increasingly globalized economy.

Critical Thinking Questions

1. What are some arguments for and against the idea that public school students should achieve competence in the English language?

2. Explain whether current state mandates regarding bilingual education are appropriate and/or sufficient.

health science centers.[48] Just as with K-12 public education, taxpayers pay part of the cost of public higher education. These schools received $18.7 billion in total funds in fiscal year 2014 while enrolling more than 1.6 million students.[49]

Tuition and Fees

For many years, the cost of college tuition and fees in Texas was very low and affordable for most people. In fact, nonresidents of Texas often found it cheaper to come to Texas and pay a small out-of-state fee than to attend college in their own state. In the 1970s, the legislature began to gradually increase tuition, tying the amount students paid to the number of semester hours taken. For most of the 1970s, the cost was $4.00 per semester hour (about $12.00 per course) with a few fees for labs attached to certain courses. Although this cost was very low, most students did not realize what a bargain it was for them.

State universities approached the legislature for more money during the 1980s and 1990s. For most of this time, the legislature prohibited universities from setting their own tuition rates but did allow them to charge additional fees for student services. Such services included computer access, recreation, and transportation.

Texas A&M and the University of Texas at Austin approached the legislature about allowing the two "flagship" universities to charge higher tuition. ("Flagship" is a term used by the University of Texas and Texas A&M to denote their claimed status as the lead universities in the state.) This request to charge higher tuition rates encountered considerable opposition in the legislature. Nonetheless, Texas A&M and the University of Texas continued to press the issue, and during the 2003 legislative session, the newly installed Republican majority and then-Speaker Craddick passed a new policy of **"deregulated" tuition** for all state universities. Deregulating tuition allowed individual colleges and universities to set the tuition rate they charged their students. Because the legislature faced a $10 billion revenue shortfall at the time, increasing tuition seemed an easy way to increase revenue.

In the fall of 2003, the average cost of tuition and fees for 15 credit hours was $1,934. In the spring of 2004, after tuition deregulation took effect, the cost per semester increased to $2,032. Thereafter, from fall 2003 to fall 2011, average tuition charges at Texas public universities jumped 90 percent, to an average of $3,671 per semester.[50] After the policy changed, some constituents began to complain to legislators about the increases.

Much of the state budget is fixed by the state constitution and state and federal law. In other words, the legislature has very little discretion regarding how the money is spent. However, operating funds for higher education are not part of this **budget fix**. Education funds come from the nonrestricted area of the budget and thus can be reduced. Even as tuition costs have risen, the proportion of educational costs covered by state funding (on a per-pupil basis) has gone down. The Texas comptroller's office reported that "from fiscal years 2002 to 2007, the Texas state budget was cut in terms of real dollar, per-student funding for universities by 19.92 percent."[51] Therefore, the cost of higher education has been funded increasingly with tuition and fee hikes, and the burden of paying for higher education has increasingly shifted from taxpayers to the individual student and parents. (In a similar fashion, the cost of elementary and secondary education has been increasingly funded by local property taxes, which now

"deregulated" tuition

A decision by the state legislature to allow state colleges and universities to set the rate of tuition charged to students

budget fix

State laws and constitutional amendments that set aside money to be spent on specific items; the best example is the state gasoline tax being committed to state highways

equal almost half the total taxes collected at the state and local levels in Texas.) In the spring of 2012, the University of Texas at Austin voted to hold tuition rates steady for two years.[52] In the fall of 2012, then-governor Perry proposed that state universities offer incoming freshmen a four-year tuition freeze, thus guaranteeing students a level tuition rate during the time they are pursuing a degree.[53] While parents and students continue to exert pressure on universities to keep costs down, others express concern that educational quality will suffer due to cost-cutting measures. On the other hand, some suggest the costs of education are rightly borne by those who utilize the service and benefit the most, rather than taxpayers in general.

Tuition increases over the years have helped Texas schools stay competitive with institutions in other states. See Table 11.3 for a look at how tuition at these two Texas schools compares with the costs of other state universities. It is worth remembering that there are many Texas state colleges and universities with lower costs than the University of Texas and Texas A&M.

Although tuition costs have increased and may continue to do so, at least part of the cost of higher education is constitutionally protected and covered by the state.

Curriculum and Degree Requirements

In recent years, the Texas legislature has been more active in making laws and rules that impact the curriculum choices of students, faculty, and university officials. The following are a few examples of these decisions.

According to state law, all state universities are required to offer a set number of courses in what is called the core curriculum. As of 2013, the core consists of 36 hours of fundamental component areas identified by the Higher Education Coordinating Board (which includes 6 hours of political science and 6 hours of history) plus an additional 6 hours identified by each institution, provided they

TABLE 11.3

2015–2016 Tuition Costs among Major Public Universities (First-Year Tuition and Fees for Undergraduates)

University	Residents ($)	Nonresidents ($)
University of Illinois - Urbana-Champaign	15,626	30,786
University of California - Los Angeles	12,753	35,631
University of Colorado - Boulder	11,091	34,125
University of Arizona	10,872	30,025
University of Alabama	10,170	25,950
University of Texas at Austin	9,830	34,836
University of Missouri	9,509	25,166
Texas A&M University	9,428	28,020
State University of New York at Buffalo	8,870	22,290
University of North Carolina - Chapel Hill	8,562	33,644
Iowa State University	7,736	20,856
University of Mississippi	7,444	20,674

Sources: Texas A&M University, Scholarships & Financial Aid, Cost of Attendance, http://financialaid.tamu.edu/Undergraduate/Cost-of-Attendance#0-Undergraduate; U.S. News & World Report, National University Rankings, http://colleges.usnews.rankingsandreviews.com/best-colleges/rankings/national-universities.

justify that the courses meet at least 4 core objectives. Students must complete these courses in order to graduate.

The total number of hours required for degree completion is limited to 120 hours for most degrees. Prior to this change (which went into effect in fall 2008), most degrees required at least 128 hours. The justification for this policy change was cost cutting: the legislature wants students to graduate more quickly, thereby reducing the state's cost for higher education. In addition, if a student takes more than 120 hours, the university does not receive any state funding for these extra hours.

Students can receive a rebate of $1,000 if they graduate within three credit hours of the total number of hours required for their degree. The legislature forced this policy on universities but did not appropriate any money to cover the cost. Therefore, rebates are most likely funded by fees.

Undergraduate students pay in-state tuition rates up to a certain number of total hours in their undergraduate degree. After they have exceeded this number of credit hours (set by the legislature), a student must pay the out-of-state tuition rate.

Transferring courses from one university to another has been a source of controversy. If a student earns a "D" in a course at one school, other state schools have to accept this course as transfer credit. Although this benefits students in their ability to transfer credits, some of the major schools object to transfers of such low grades.

Higher Education Funds

Operating budgets for institutions of higher education are part of the regular state budget, but higher education in Texas has other funds available for capital projects. (A capital project is a "long-term investment project requiring relatively large sums" of money, such as constructing a new building on campus.[54]) The **Permanent University Fund (PUF)** was established by the Texas Constitution of 1876 to support the University of Texas and Texas A&M University systems. The original endowment began in 1839 when the Republic of Texas set aside 221,400 acres of land, the income from which was designated to fund higher education. This land was located in East Texas and was rather good farmland. Because this land was so valuable for agricultural purposes, the state legislature later transferred the endowment to approximately 2 million acres of land, thought to be of less value, primarily in West Texas. Ironically, in the early part of the twentieth century, oil was discovered on these new lands, and the income they generated became substantial over time.[55] As of December 31, 2015, the PUF had a market value of $17.4 billion and a book value of $15.1 billion.[56] The University of Texas and some of its branch campuses receive two-thirds of the money generated by the PUF's investments, and Texas A&M, its branches, and divisions receive the remaining one-third.[57]

According to this policy, other colleges and universities in the state did not receive any portion of these funds, and other universities began to pressure the Texas legislature for a share of the PUF fund. In 1984, the legislature proposed an amendment to the state constitution (subsequently approved by the voters) creating the **Higher Education Assistance Fund (HEAF)**. Beginning in 1985, the legislature set aside annual appropriations of $100 million for this fund. This amount was later increased to $175 million. Today this fund provides $262.5 million each year for colleges and universities not supported by the PUF.[58]

Permanent University Fund (PUF)

The PUF is money set aside in the state constitution to benefit the University of Texas at Austin and Texas A&M University

Higher Education Assistance Fund (HEAF)

The HEAF is money set aside for use by those universities not benefiting from the PUF

In 2015, Governor Abbott proposed and the legislature approved the establishment of the Governor's University Research Initiative. According to the Governor's Office, the purpose of this initiative is to help fund the recruitment of "prestigious, nationally-recognized researchers . . . to Texas public universities."[59] By providing matching funds for universities to hire desirable faculty, the governor aimed to elevate the status of Texas higher education and boost the state's economy through research advances. To create this fund, legislators diverted money from the scrapped Emerging Technology Fund.[60]

The authors of the Texas Constitution of 1876 saw a need for higher education in Texas and responded by creating the PUF. Later sessions of the legislature wanted to fund other institutions of higher learning and created the HEAF; Governor Abbott recently created the Governor's University Research Initiative. The establishment of these funds is an example of public policy prioritizing education relative to other ends.

Access to Higher Education

From the 1950s to the 1970s, access to state colleges and universities in Texas was governed by "open enrollment." In other words, all Texas residents who had graduated from high school were automatically admitted without consideration of high school standing or standardized test scores. Nearly all students could enroll in the university of their choice. In the 1980s many schools, particularly Texas A&M and the University of Texas, began to impose higher standards for admittance, using mainly SAT scores and high school class standing to make that determination.

Higher enrollment standards conflicted to some degree with the aim of increasing minority enrollment at state colleges and universities. At the time, Hispanics and African Americans were a growing minority of the state's population, but only about 20 percent were enrolled in colleges and fewer still in the top two state universities. Minority students were also underrepresented in law and other professional schools.

Many colleges and universities began affirmative action programs in an attempt to increase minority enrollment in colleges and universities. These programs prompted a lawsuit regarding admission of minority students to the University of Texas law school. In 1996, the federal court ended affirmative action practices at the University of Texas law school in the ***Hopwood Decision***.[61] Texas Attorney General Daniel Morales, himself a beneficiary of affirmative action programs while a student in Texas, applied the *Hopwood* decision to all state colleges and universities and effectively eliminated affirmative action admission policies across the state. Morales found that ". . . Hopwood's restrictions would generally apply to all internal institutional policies, including admissions, financial aid, scholarships, fellowships, recruitment and retention, among others."[62] Thus, under Morales' interpretation, *Hopwood* was extended to prevent race from being considered in areas beyond admissions. *Hopwood* was overturned in 2003 by a case originating in Michigan. The U.S. Supreme Court, in *Grutter v. Bollinger,* 539 U.S. 306 (2003), ruled that the U.S. Constitution does not prohibit tailoring standards to use race in an admissions decision or policy.

Prior to *Grutter v. Bollinger,* the Texas legislature, in an attempt to solve the problems of minority representation and equal opportunity, changed admission standards at Texas universities and established that admissions decisions and

Hopwood Decision
Decision by federal courts to end affirmative action in Texas schools; these programs had provided for special treatment for minority students in being accepted to colleges and professional schools

ADMISSIONS

IT'S HIS FAULT!

DAUGHTER of ALUM   SON of BIG DONOR   SOCCER PLAYER   RAISED in DISTANT STATE   MINORITY   DIDN'T GET IN

This cartoon points to a number of the factors that colleges consider when making admissions decisions and suggests that minority enrollments are unfairly singled out for criticism. Why is membership in a minority group controversial, whereas other factors—such as the ability to play a certain sport or being the child of a graduate—are not? Should college admission be based on academic merit alone, or should other factors be considered?

financial awards could not be based primarily on standardized test scores such as the SAT, ACT, or GRE. Under the new policy, any student graduating in the top 10 percent of his or her high school class was granted automatic admission to any state college or university, without consideration of other factors such as SAT scores. This rule, known as the "Top Ten Percent Plan," had the greatest impact on the University of Texas, where 81 percent of the 2008 freshman class was admitted under the Top Ten Percent rule.[63]

This Top Ten Percent rule was expected to increase minority enrollment by allowing students from inner-city high schools to attend the top schools in the state. Some evidence suggests that the Top Ten Percent rule has in fact increased minority enrollment, especially at the University of Texas and to a lesser degree at Texas A&M. However, the policy has created a problem for some high-performing students at better high schools in the state. It is not unusual for students at a competitive high school not to place in the top 10 percent of their graduating class, even with a 1500 or higher score on the SAT. Therefore, these students are not guaranteed admission to a Texas institute of higher education under the Top Ten Percent rule. Conversely, some students from small rural schools, who have very low SAT scores, are able to gain admission via the same policy.

The U.S. Supreme Court has considered the issue of race and university admissions in Texas not once, but twice, in recent years. In *Fisher v. University of Texas*, the Court ruled in 2013 that universities can use affirmative action in their admissions policies only if there is no other way to achieve diversity among the student body.[64] This ruling did not change the University of Texas's admissions policy, but the case was sent back to a lower court for consideration of whether the university had met this standard.[65] The case was again argued before the U.S. Supreme Court in 2015. In its 2016 ruling, the Court upheld the university's "consideration of race as part of its [admissions] process" as lawful.[66]

Social Policy

Firearms Policies

Despite being a relatively conservative state, Texas has traditionally had more restrictive gun laws than many other states, including liberal states such as Vermont and Maine. However, some restrictions on the right to carry firearms that did exist have recently been lifted. In January 2016, legislation permitting the "open carry" of firearms went into effect in Texas. Under this new law, licensed gun owners are allowed to carry a loaded or unloaded handgun, in plain view, as long as it is in a holster. Although open carry is still prohibited on college campuses, additional legislation that went into effect later in 2016 allows licensed individuals to carry concealed handguns on the premises of an institution of higher education.[67] Seven other states have enacted similar legislation, presumably in response to campus shootings that have occurred in recent years.[68] In Texas an initial permit to carry a firearm costs $140 plus training course costs, more than most other states.

Gay Rights

Texas was one of the last states to maintain antisodomy laws, which banned particular private sex acts between consenting adults (and were largely aimed at homosexuals). At one time all states had antisodomy laws, but by 2003, when the Supreme Court declared these laws unconstitutional in the case *Lawrence v. Texas,* only Texas and 13 other states still had such laws on the books.[69] Today, though most Americans agree that antisodomy laws were rightly invalidated, whether same-sex marriages should enjoy the same legal status as opposite-sex marriages has been relatively controversial.

Public opinion has been evolving rapidly on the issue of same-sex marriage, and the legal landscape regarding this issue looks radically different than it did just a few years ago. In January 2013, only 9 states and the District of Columbia allowed same-sex couples to marry, and by October 2014, 24 states and the District of Columbia allowed same-sex marriage. In June 2015, the U.S. Supreme Court essentially ended the political and legal debate over this issue, ruling in *Obergefell v. Hodges* that state bans on same-sex marriage were unconstitutional.[70] Therefore, all states are now required to issue marriage licenses to all couples, regardless of sexual orientation.

Prior to the Supreme Court ruling, Texas had a longstanding ban on same-sex marriage. In 1996 the U.S. Congress passed the federal Defense of Marriage Act (DOMA), which defined marriage as the union of one woman and one man and denied federal recognition of same-sex marriage. Texas amended its constitution in 2005 to prohibit same-sex marriage; the ban was initially proposed in the legislature and overwhelmingly approved by voters (76 percent in favor).[71] Many state bans followed the language of the DOMA. Texas's amendment was actually a "Super-DOMA," which not only defined marriage as the union of one man and one woman; it also denied legal status to any other type of relationship that approximated marriage (such as civil unions and domestic partnerships). Therefore, unmarried couples, including same-sex couples, could be (in the words of one legal scholar) "nothing other than complete legal strangers to one another."[72] Nineteen other states had similar amendments. In June 2013, in the case *United States v. Windsor,* the U.S. Supreme Court struck down a portion of DOMA and declared that the federal definition of marriage was unconstitutional.[73] Although this ruling did not necessarily guarantee same-sex couples the right to be married (because individual states regulate marriage within their borders), it opened the door for state laws or constitutional provisions banning same-sex marriage to be challenged in court. In February 2014, the Texas state ban was struck down by a federal judge.[74] Meanwhile, the ability of gay and lesbian couples to marry remained on hold while the state appealed this decision.[75] This was finally resolved in *Obergefell.*

Individuals in Texas are allowed to adopt children without consideration of their sexual orientation. Therefore, gays and lesbians can adopt children; because only one partner in a same-sex couple can be listed on the child's birth certificate,[76] these adoptions tend to be single-parent adoptions and may be followed by a second adoption by a same-sex partner. Some Texas courts have recognized same-sex second parent adoptions, such as in *Hobbs v. Van Stavern* (2006) and *Goodson v. Castellanos* (2007).[77] Finally, there is no statewide antidiscrimination law specifically protecting members of the LGBT community. However, some local governments in Texas, including the cities of Dallas, Fort Worth, Austin, and San Antonio, have passed such laws. In 2015 Houston voters rejected a nondiscrimination ordinance by a vote of 61 to 39 percent.[78] Advocates of the ordinance sought protections for LGBT residents from being fired, evicted, or refused service due to their gender identity or sexual orientation. Opponents voiced religiously inspired arguments in addition to concerns about the rights of business owners and transgender access to bathrooms. Indeed, this last point led the ordinance to be dubbed the "bathroom bill"—which, fairly or not, helped to defeat it.[79]

Abortion Policies

In the 1973 case *Roe v. Wade*, the U.S. Supreme Court ruled that the Texas law banning abortions was unconstitutional.[80] The ruling limits what states can do to prevent a woman from having an abortion. Ever since the ruling, however, states have tried in a variety of ways to limit and restrict abortions. Texas is no exception.

Roe v. Wade
Texas court case that limits what states can legally do to prevent abortions

Some abortion-related regulations previously on the books in Texas include a requirement that abortions be performed by a licensed physician, specify a gestational limit banning late-term abortions (with life and health exceptions as required by the Supreme Court), and include requirements that young women under 18 obtain parental consent before having an abortion (with a judicial bypass required by the Supreme Court). In addition, there is a 24-hour waiting period for abortion, and women must receive an ultrasound from their physician before an abortion can be performed.[81] Texas also prohibits public funding of abortions except in cases of rape, incest, or life endangerment.[82] In 2013, Texas enacted controversial abortion legislation considered strict in comparison with other states. The new law banned abortion after the twentieth week of pregnancy, required abortion clinics to meet the same standards as surgical centers, and required doctors to have hospital admitting privileges near where they perform abortions. Senate deliberation of the bill was marked by intense Democratic opposition, including an 11-hour filibuster by state senator Wendy Davis that initially killed the bill during a special session. However, former Governor Perry called another special session for the bill to be reconsidered, and it was subsequently approved (although the filibuster had gained wide media

Public debate over abortion was not settled by the Supreme Court's 1973 decision in *Roe v. Wade*. Here, a group from Texas demonstrates their pro-life position at a march in Washington, D.C. In the other photo, abortion rights supporters express their dissatisfaction with new legal restrictions inside the State Capitol.

(Left) © *Tom Williams/Getty Images; (Right)* © *Tamir Kalifa/File/AP Images*

attention and vaulted Davis to statewide and national prominence).[83] When this law first went into effect, approximately half of the 41 abortion clinics in the state closed due to the additional requirements, with the prospect of more closures in the future.[84] After it was passed, the law was subject to multiple court challenges. Although it was initially upheld by the Fifth Circuit Court of Appeals, in 2016 the U.S. Supreme Court reversed the lower court's decision, ruling in *Whole Woman's Health v. Hellerstedt* that the provisions relating to admitting privileges and surgical center standards "place a substantial obstacle in the path of women seeking a previability abortion, constitute an undue burden on abortion access, and thus violate the Constitution." With those provisions of the law struck down, abortion clinics in Texas remained in operation, with the possibility that previously closed clinics might reopen at some future date.[85]

CORE OBJECTIVE

© *George Lavendowski/USFWS*

Communicating Effectively . . .

Summarize the legislation that Texas has passed on abortion. Discuss the advantages and disadvantages of state involvement in this policy issue.

Sex Education

Sex education is frequently a controversial component of public school curricula. In their 2009 study of sex education in Texas school districts, Wiley, Wilson, and Valentine found that 94 percent of Texas school districts taught abstinence-only when providing instruction on human sexuality. Their review of actual materials used in classrooms indicated that 2 percent of school districts skipped over sexual education entirely, and only the remaining 4 percent provided information on STD and pregnancy prevention, including contraception. These researchers concluded that "Abstinence-only programs have a stranglehold on sexuality education in Texas public schools."[86] Indeed, the state accepts no federal funding for sex education programs that promote anything beyond celibacy.[87]

Discussions of sexuality are often glossed over because of a desire to avoid controversy.[88] For example, many Texans believe it is not the role of public schools but rather that of parents to provide sex education. These parents express concern that giving students information about sex will encourage them to engage in sexual activity. Nonetheless, these parents believe that if schools are going to venture into this realm, they should teach total abstinence. Other parents favor teaching sex education as a necessary part of health education as well as a way of empowering young people to make good choices about an important aspect of life. Attitudes about these issues have implications not just for education but also for public health initiatives.

At the beginning of the 2007 legislative session, then-governor Perry issued an executive order requiring all Texas schoolgirls to be vaccinated against the human papillomavirus (HPV), a common sexually transmitted infection that can cause cervical cancer.[89] Several members of the house and senate introduced legislation preventing these vaccinations from taking place. They reasoned that if young women were vaccinated, they would be more likely to engage in promiscuous sex owing to the reduced risk of cancer later in life. Other members were skeptical that teen decision making about sex involved such rational considerations. Still others accused Perry of being influenced by donations from the vaccine manufacturer[90] or questioned his attempt to mandate government intervention in the private health care decisions of parents for their daughters, a seemingly inconsistent position for a conservative Republican governor. In the end, the legislature overturned Perry's executive order, and the governor allowed the legislation to stand. Nonetheless, this controversy trailed Perry into his unsuccessful presidential bid in 2011–2012.[91]

Immigration Policy

Immigration has become a highly publicized issue nationally, due in part to the surge of illegal immigrants from Central America in recent years, the widely debated question of whether to accept Middle Eastern refugees in light of the threat of terrorism, and the 2016 presidential campaign. It is important to note that immigration policy is set at the federal level; however, due to its more than 1,200-mile border with Mexico, Texas understandably plays a very prominent role in how our country deals with immigration.

During the period from 2010 to 2014, 16.5 percent of Texas's population was composed of foreign-born persons.[92] Although the Census Bureau counts people who are present both legally and illegally, it is important to distinguish between the two types of immigrants. Legal immigrants go through a process to become lawful permanent residents, also known as Green Card holders. The process for becoming a lawful permanent resident (LPR) differs depending on whether the individual is outside or inside the United States at the time of application, but it generally requires being sponsored by a family member or employer, submitting forms, paying fees, and sometimes even attesting that an individual will have adequate financial support when he or she is in the country.[93] Foreign citizens living outside the United States must first obtain an immigrant visa; the number of immigrant visas issued each year is limited by Congress. Individuals who are already living in the United States (including refugees) must apply for an "adjustment of status" to lawful permanent residency. Upon approval, LPRs have permission from the federal government to live and work in the United States indefinitely.[94] LPRs can subsequently apply for U.S. citizenship, or naturalization. In 2014, 95,295 people in Texas obtained lawful permanent resident status, and 52,879 people were naturalized.[95] Illegal immigrants, on the other hand, are those who have entered or remain in the country without having government permission; these individuals may also be referred to as unauthorized or undocumented (what these individuals should be called has become controversial). According to the most recent figures available, the number of unauthorized immigrants in the United States in 2012 was estimated at 11.4 million, with 1.8 million of that population living in Texas.[96]

The number of unauthorized or illegal immigrants in Texas had been fairly constant for some time. However, there has been a reported surge of illegal immigrants entering the state in recent years. Of particular note was the record number of unaccompanied children from Central America (particularly El Salvador, Guatemala, and Honduras) crossing through Mexico into Texas in 2014. That year, Border Patrol in Texas apprehended 58,000 minors traveling by themselves—more than twice the number from the previous fiscal year and nearly four times as many as in fiscal year 2012.[97] This situation was called a "humanitarian crisis" and garnered national attention, partly because federal detention centers were so overcrowded that it became necessary to transport illegal immigrants caught in Texas to facilities in other states.[98] Data from the early part of fiscal year 2016 suggested another trend toward increased apprehensions might be underway.[99]

How does this large illegal immigrant population impact the state financially? The Texas state comptroller attempted to answer that question in a 2006 report, which found that state revenue generated by undocumented immigrants (primarily from sales tax and other government fees) outweighed what the state government spent on services for this population. However, the report notably excluded the cost of educating illegal immigrants' children born in the United States, because these U.S.-born children are in fact citizens. The report also acknowledged that local governments and hospitals bear a disproportionate share of the cost of educating, incarcerating, and providing health care for illegal immigrants—costs for which localities are not compensated.[100] The comptroller's office has not updated this report in a decade. In 2015, a member of the Texas House proposed a bill requiring such a report be produced each year; that bill was set aside for discussion at a future time.[101]

Illegal immigrants are not eligible for federally funded programs such as TANF, food stamps, or public housing in Texas.[102] However, they are eligible for K-12 education, emergency medical care, and other health services. In the 1981 case *Plyler v. Doe* (which originated in Tyler, Texas), the U.S. Supreme Court ruled that denying any individual the right to an education violated the Equal Protection Clause of the U.S. Constitution. Therefore, all states are required to provide K-12 education for undocumented immigrants and their children.[103] In 2001 the state legislature passed House Bill (HB) 1403, also known as the Texas DREAM Act (which stands for Development, Relief and Education of Alien Minors), and amended this law in 2005 with Senate Bill (SB) 1528. This legislation allows some undocumented students to be classified as residents for the purpose of paying in-state college tuition rates, provided they meet certain requirements (including at least 3 years of prior residence in Texas and a signed statement of intent to apply for lawful permanent resident status as soon as possible).[104]

Statistics on this population are hard to find because the subjects of inquiry are, quite literally, without documentation, and therefore their presence cannot be verified. Most figures are either estimated or not reported at all. For fiscal year 2013, the Texas Health and Human Services Commission (a state agency) estimated the cost of providing medical and domestic violence services to illegal immigrants at $129 million.[105]

Recent federal policy on immigration has primarily been to enforce existing immigration laws by apprehending and deporting people who are in the country illegally. Legislation intended to reform the immigration system has not passed the full U.S. Congress. In the absence of congressional action, in 2014, President Obama issued an executive order that would have allowed certain individuals who are in the country illegally (but who are parents of U.S. citizens or LPRs) to avoid deportation and obtain work permits. This plan, known as "Deferred Action for Parents of Americans and Lawful Permanent Residents," or DAPA, would have applied to 825,000 people living in Texas.[106] Implementation of this program was delayed, however, when 26 states (led by Texas) sued the administration. These states charged the president with overreach of presidential authority and failure to enforce the nation's current immigration laws. In 2016, the U.S. Supreme Court issued a deadlocked decision (4-4) on this case, resulting in blockage of the president's immigration program.[107]

Members of the U.S. Army install part of the fence along the border near Puerto Palomas, Mexico. The federal government is building a 745-mile fence along the U.S.–Mexico border to reduce the flow of illegal migrants into the United States.

© Guadalupe Williams/AFP/Getty Images

Although border security is mainly the responsibility of the federal government, Governor Abbott has expressed his intention to bolster security along the state's border with Mexico. For instance, in 2015 state leaders committed $800 million in state funds (over a two-year period) to border security—approximately double the amount appropriated for equivalent periods of time previously.[108] These funds have been earmarked for new technology, training of law enforcement agents, and the hiring of 250 additional state troopers to guard the border, among other things.

Water Policy

A snapshot of water use in Texas is necessary to understand the state's water policies. The Texas population is projected to grow 82 percent from 2010 to 2060, from 25.4 million in 2010 to 46.3 million in 2060.[109] For purposes of allocating water rights, water is measured in "acre feet," which equals the amount of water needed to cover one acre of land in one foot of water.[110] Employing this unit of measure, total water use in Texas from 2010 until 2060 will increase from approximately 18 million acre feet to approximately 22 million acre feet, representing a jump of 22 percent.[111]

These statistics suggest something puzzling: namely, that water demand will grow at just over one-fourth the rate of population growth. Part of the explanation for this apparent discrepancy concerns how water is used in different sectors of the economy. State policy makers break down the demand for water into six categories: municipal (residential and commercial demand in cities); manufacturing; mining; steam-generated electricity; livestock production; and crop irrigation.[112] Of these categories, between 2010 and 2060, municipal, manufacturing, and steam electricity uses are expected to increase.[113] At the same time, however, livestock and irrigation uses are expected to decline. Geographically, the Dallas-Fort Worth, Austin, San Antonio, and Lower Rio Grande urban areas will experience the greatest increase in demand.[114]

Texas relies on both surface and groundwater to satisfy its tremendous demand for water. The state's fresh water derives from 1 natural lake, 200 man-made reservoirs, 14 major rivers, 3,700 streams, and 30 underground aquifers (a naturally formed underground reservoir) of varying sizes throughout the state.[115] The central region of the Edwards Aquifer, for example (approximately 180 miles long from Del Rio, Texas, to south of Austin, Texas) is one of the state's largest bodies of underground water.[116] Groundwater currently provides approximately 59 percent of the state's water demand; surface water totals 41 percent.[117]

The broadest way to categorize water law relates to quantity and quality: one set of laws and policies determines who has the right to use a given quantity of water. A second set of laws and policies exists to keep water uncontaminated and suitable for human use.

Water rights in Texas are governed by a complex system of laws: both statutes the legislature has enacted and law that courts have created on a case-by-case basis. Taken together, these laws regulate surface and groundwater in different ways. With respect to surface water, the state of Texas owns the water, but citizens can obtain exclusive rights to use a certain quantity of water, expressed in acre feet. Landowners with property adjoining a river have so-called riparian rights to withdraw limited quantities of water. Otherwise, the procedure for obtaining water rights in publicly owned surface water is called "prior appropriation" or "first in time, first in right," the same system used in most of the western United States.[118] The first person to claim water in a stream can obtain a right ("usufruct") over a quantity of water that no one else can use without purchasing the right from the first owner. The person who claims the right to use the water first then "perfects" the right by registering it with a state agency called the Texas Commission on Environmental Quality (TCEQ), which maintains records of who owns how many acre feet of water in different rivers, streams, and lakes of the state.[119] Surface water rights have been perfected for at least 98 percent of the total available water in the state. Individuals, local governments, and businesses now sell surface water rights to one another in a burgeoning market.[120]

Even though the majority of groundwater is connected with bodies of surface water, such as rivers or reservoirs, Texas treats groundwater as if it were a separate source, subject to its own rules. Whereas surface water is publicly owned, Texas treats the water underneath a landowner's property as private property.[121] This leads to strange results. For example, the law would define water in a river as publicly owned, but when the same body of water flows underground, the law defines it as privately owned. A significant percentage of the water in the Edwards Aquifer flows to the surface to feed major springs and rivers, for example.[122] The so-called "rule of capture" provides that, even before the landowner removes the water from the ground, it is private property. Any law that limits the landowner's property-right interest in groundwater could be construed as a regulatory "taking," for which a unit of government might have to provide the property owner with compensation.[123]

Despite the legal definition of groundwater as private property, the Texas legislature has made efforts to regulate groundwater in various ways. On the local level, groundwater conservation districts have limited powers over such issues as the spacing of wells and monitoring the quantity of water pumped.[124] In response to problems that excessive groundwater pumping has caused in particular regions of the state, the legislature has created larger groundwater districts with more authority limited to a specific geographic area. Examples include preventing land subsidence and property damage in the Galveston area,[125] or keeping groundwater levels sufficient to prevent the intrusion of contaminated water into the water supply of roughly 3 million Texans, or preserving habitat for federally endangered plant and animal species.[126]

Recent legislation impacting Hays County illustrates the clash between regulation/conservation efforts and property rights. A Houston-based corporation announced plans to pump 5 million gallons of groundwater a day from wells in the Trinity Aquifer. Because its water well field was in an area not governed by any groundwater conservation district, the corporation could, in exercise of its lawful property right, pump an unlimited amount of water from these wells. Responding to concerns from nearby landowners that this pumping could deplete their own water supply, the legislature enacted HB 3405, which expanded the territory of the Barton Springs-Edwards Aquifer Conservation District to include the well field in question. As a result, any pumping from these wells is now subject to regulation from the appropriate conservation district.[127] It remains to be seen whether the company will challenge the statute on grounds of a violation of its property-right interest.

Texas has created a statewide groundwater planning process under the Texas Water Development Board (TWDB).[128] The TWDB oversees a statewide water planning process for surface and groundwater every five years.[129] The state is divided into 16 regions, each of which has the responsibility for developing a comprehensive plan detailing the total estimated water needs of the region for the next five years and the total water supply from all sources for that region. The regional plans compare their cumulative water demand to a water supply equivalent to the severe drought of the 1950s to plan for contingencies. At the end of each five-year regional water planning cycle, the TWDB synthesizes the 16 regional water plans and other sources to create the State Water Plan. The governor, lieutenant governor, and state legislature then review the final adopted plan and approve it for use in the following five-year planning period.[130]

The second broad category of water law deals with water quality. The TCEQ carries out the Federal Clean Water Act and Safe Drinking Water Act, as well as state water quality statutes, to eliminate water contamination from many sources.[131]

Texas faces a number of water-related challenges in the coming decades. Severe drought conditions in recent years have dealt a blow to surface water supplies. Declining river levels deprive coastal estuaries of fresh water they must have to support multibillion-dollar commercial fishing and tourism industries. Texas water policy makers continue to seek solutions to such problems.[132]

CORE OBJECTIVE

Source: National Park Service

Thinking Critically . . .

Given the water-related challenges facing Texas, what measures would you recommend to ensure all Texans have access to water? What might be some negative or unintended consequences of your recommendations?

Veteran Policy

Texas has one of the largest veteran populations of any state, with an estimated 1.68 million former members of the armed forces living within its borders as of 2014.[133] The main public agency responsible for veterans' issues in the state is the Texas Veterans Commission (TVC), established in 1927. The TVC assists veterans in filing claims for disability benefits and represents them in matters involving the U.S. Department of Veterans Affairs (VA).[134] In addition to traditional public programs for welfare-related assistance, service-connected disability compensation is available for qualified veterans, as are non-service-connected pensions for qualifying veterans with low or no income. In 2009, former Governor Rick Perry directed the TVC to establish a Claims Processing Assistance Team to reduce the number of cases pending in the state's disability and claims system.[135]

The TVC also provides employment and education services through Veterans Employment Services and the Veterans Education Program. Veterans Employment Services addresses such issues as translating military skills to civilian employment, providing career guidance, and connecting veterans with employers. In addition, the TVC oversees delivery of a number of federal programs providing education benefits to veterans in the state of Texas; for example, the Montgomery and Post-9/11 GI Bills both provide financial support for veterans pursuing vocational training or higher education. The Hazlewood Act (also known as the Hazlewood Exemption) is a state program providing exemption from tuition and certain fees (for qualified veterans, spouses, and some children) at higher education institutions in Texas.[136]

The Texas Veterans Leadership Program, established in 2008 under the Texas Workforce Commission, focuses on veterans of the Iraq and Afghanistan wars. It provides resources and referrals for those veterans for services ranging from employment to educational and healthcare needs. Another program established in partnership with the Texas Workforce Commission, the College Credit for Heroes Program, allows institutions of higher education to give veterans college credit for experience, knowledge, and skills earned during their service. In addition, the Texas legislature has provided that qualified veterans, spouses, and children receive veterans' employment and retention preference in state agencies.[137] Recent legislation was passed to help veterans transition to civilian jobs by waiving occupational licensing fees for qualified veterans, allowing military experience to satisfy the requirements for certain teaching certifications, and exempting new veteran-owned businesses from franchise tax for the first five years.[138]

Texas provides a range of other policies and programs for veterans. For example, the Veterans Land Board (VLB), established in 1946, has established Texas State Veterans Homes that provide long-term nursing care, including specialized Alzheimer's units, to veterans and qualified veterans' families. The VLB also provides various types of land, home, and home-improvement loans to veterans. In 2009, HB 8 and HB 3613 were enacted to minimize property appraisal costs and increase exemptions for disabled veteran homeowners.[139] Qualified veterans are able to obtain various state-issued licenses and passes at reduced fees, such as the Texas Parklands Passport[140] for entry and discounts within the state park system; various hunting and fishing licenses, such as the Texas Resident Active Duty Military "Super Combo" Hunting and All-Water Fishing Package[141]; and free driver's licenses.[142]

Conclusion

As this chapter shows, state and local government policy decisions impact a wide range of issues and areas of life. For good or bad, the Texas state government is actively involved in regulating business activity, providing welfare and educational services, attempting to manage natural resource and land use, and restricting certain behaviors or protecting certain rights. Whether or not you are interested in public policy, public policy is interested in you! The legislature, the governor, and many state agencies, including the board of regents of your public college or university, can have a direct effect on your life (including your education). Hopefully, by reading this book, you are more aware of how the government of Texas impacts your life and the community in which you live.

Summary

LO: Discuss the steps in the policy-making process.

Political scientist James Anderson described the process by which public policy is made as a "policy cycle" with the following steps: problem identification and agenda setting; policy formulation; policy adoption; policy implementation; and policy evaluation. Often this process begins with a complaint by a constituent (problem identification), in response to which a legislator proposes legislation to correct the perceived problem (policy formulation). Depending on the specific policy-making effort, steps in this process may be omitted. For instance, there is often no policy evaluation (an attempt to assess effectiveness after a policy has been implemented to then make possible adjustments).

LO: Explain policy liberalism indices and what they can tell us.

"Policy liberalism" is a common measure of state policy ideology that can be used to compare the 50 states. Policy liberalism indices can tell us how liberal or conservative a state is with regard to a selection of state policies. For example, the Gray Policy Liberalism Index uses five policy indicators: gun control laws, abortion laws, conditions for receiving Temporary Assistance to Needy Families (TANF) benefits, tax progressivity, and right-to-work laws. In contrast, the State Policy Index uses more than 200 policies in the fiscal, regulatory, and social policy realms. On both of these indices, Texas ranks as one of the more conservative states in the country.

LO: Discuss public policy areas in Texas state government.

Although the federal government has taken the lead with regard to many issues, states still play an important role in legislating and implementing a wide array of policies. Important policy areas in Texas state government include regulatory policy, welfare policy, health care policy, education policy (both K-12 and higher education), social policy (including gay rights, abortion, and sex education), water policy, and policies affecting immigrants and veterans.

Key Terms

budget fix
"deregulated" tuition
Higher Education Assistance Fund (HEAF)

Hopwood Decision
Permanent University Fund (PUF)
policy liberalism index
public policy

Robin Hood Plan
Roe v. Wade
tort

Notes

[1] See Thomas R. Dye. *Understanding Public Policy,* 7th ed. (Englewood Cliffs, N.J.: Prentice-Hall.1992), 4; Marc Allen Eisner, Jeff Worsham, and Evan J. Ringquist, *Contemporary Regulatory Policy* (Boulder, Colo.: Lynne Reinner, 2000); Dean G. Kilpatrick, "Definitions of Public Policy and the Law." https://mainweb-v.musc.edu /vawprevention/policy/definition.shtml.

[2] For his earliest attempt to do so, see James E. Anderson, *Public Policy-making* (New York: Praeger Publishing, 1975). The most recent edition is James E. Anderson, *Public Policymaking: An Introduction,* 7th ed. (Boston: Wadsworth, Cengage Learning, 2010).

[3] Jason Sorens, Fait Muedini, and William Ruger, "U.S. State and Local Public Policies in 2006: A New Database," *State Politics and Policy Quarterly* 8:3 (Fall 2008), 318, 319, and 321.

[4] Virginia Gray, "The Socioeconomic and Political Context of States," in *Politics in the American States: A Comparative Analysis,* 10th ed., ed. Virginia Gray, Russell L. Hanson, and Thad Kousser (Congressional Quarterly Press, 2011).

[5] Dwight Lee, "Redistribution," *The Concise Encyclopedia of Economics,* http://www.econlib.org/library/Enc /Redistribution.html.

[6] "2015 Best and Worst State Rankings," *Chief Executive,* http:// chiefexecutive.net/best-worst-states-business/.

[7] California Teachers Empowerment Network, "CTEN's Frequently Asked Questions," http://www.ctenhome.org /faq.htm.

[8] Jonathan Tilove, "Greg Abbott: Franchise tax cut will usher in 'new era of job growth,'" *Austin American-Statesman,* June 15, 2015. http://www .statesman.com/news/news/state-regional-govt-politics /abbott-franchise-tax-cut-will-usher-in-new-era-of-/nmdFt/.

[9] Office of the Governor Greg Abbott, "Economic Development and Tourism - Texas Enterprise Fund." http://gov.texas. gov/ecodev/financial_resources/texas_enterprise_fund/.

[10] Matthew Watkins, "Legislature replaces Emerging Technology Fund with university fund," *Dallas Star-Telegram,* June 1, 2015. http://www.star-telegram .com/news/politics-government/state-politics /article22800357.html.

[11] Forrest Wilder, "The Future of? Corporate Welfare" in Texas after Rick Perry,? *The Texas Observer,* April 24, 2014, http://www.texasobserver.org/future-corporate-welfare-texas-rick-perry/; and see Dana Liebelson, "Rick Perry's $487 Million Corporate Slush Fund Doesn't Need Your Stinkin' Audit," *Mother Jones,* March 20, 2013, http:// www.motherjones.com/politics/2013/03/rick-perry-texas-enterprise-fund-audit.

[12] Erica Grieder, "The Revolt Against Crony Capitalism," *Texas Monthly,* February 18, 2014. http://www.texasmonthly. com/story/revolt-against-crony-capitalism?fullpage=1.

[13] Jess Fields (January 2014) "An Overview of Local Economic Development Policies in Texas," Texas Public Policy Foundation. http://old .texaspolicy.com/center/local-governance/reports /overview-local-economic-development-policies-texas.

[14] Joseph Gyourko, Albert Saiz, and Anita Summers, "A New Measure of the Local Regulatory Environment for Housing Markets: The Wharton Residential Land Use Regulatory Index," *Urban Studies* 45 (March 2008), 693–729.

[15] Edward L. Glaeser and Kristina Tobio, "The Rise of the Sunbelt," NBER Working Paper No. 13071, April 2007. http://www.nber.org/papers/w13071.

[16] The data first used in this study were published in Jason Sorens, Fait Muedini, and William Ruger, "U.S. State and Local Public Policies in 2006: A New Database." *State Politics and Policy Quarterly* 8:3 (Fall 2008), 309–326. The rankings used in the text are based on updated data that are available at http://www.statepolicyindex.com /the-research/.

[17] Morris M. Kleiner, *Licensing Occupations: Ensuring Quality or Restricting Competition?* (Kalamazoo: W.E. Upjohn Institute for Employment Research, 2006).

[18] Aman Batheja, "Lawmakers Ditch $200 Fee for Lawyers, Doctors, Brokers," *Texas Tribune,* August 3, 2015. https:// www.texastribune.org/2015/08/03/31-days-professional-fees/.

[19] Texas Department of Licensing and Regulation, "Hair Braiding Deregulation," https://www.tdlr.texas.gov/cosmet /cosmetfaq.htm#braiding.

[20] Nick Sibilla, "Citing Adam Smith And Milton Friedman, Obama's Economic Advisors Back Occupational Licensing Reform," *Forbes,* July 31, 2015, http://www .forbes.com/sites/instituteforjustice/2015/07/31 /citing-adam-smith-and-milton-friedman-obamas-economic-advisors-back-occupational-licensing-reform/#228acabc7a94.

[21] U.S. Chamber Institute for Legal Reform, 2015 Lawsuit Climate Survey: Ranking the States, http://www .instituteforlegalreform.com/states/texas.

[22] National Association of State Budget Officers, State Expenditure Report Examining Fiscal 2013–2015 State Spending. https://www.nasbo.org/sites/default/files /State%20Expenditure%20Report%20%28Fiscal%202013-2015%29S.pdf

[23] Medicaid.gov, April - June 2015 Medicaid MBES Enrollment Report, https://www.medicaid.gov/medicaid-chip-program-information/program-information/downloads /cms-64-enrollment-report-apr-june-2015.pdf; U.S. Census Bureau, Annual Estimates of the Resident Population: April 1, 2010 to July 1, 2015, http://factfinder .census.gov/faces/tableservices/jsf/pages/productview. xhtml?src=bkmk.

[24] U.S. Census Bureau, Current Population Survey Annual Social and Economic Supplement, 2014 Poverty, POV46. Poverty Status by State. https://www .census.gov/hhes/www/cpstables/032015/pov /pov46_001_10050.htm.

[25] HealthCare.gov, "Medicaid expansion & what it means for you," https://www.healthcare.gov/medicaid-chip /medicaid-expansion-and-you/.

[26] National Conference of State Legislatures, "Affordable Care Act Medicaid Expansion," (January 2016), http://www .ncsl.org/research/health/affordable-care-act-expansion .aspx.

[27] U. S. Department of Agriculture Food and Nutrition Service, Supplemental Nutrition Assistance Program State Activity Report, Fiscal Year 2014 (October 2015), http://www.fns .usda.gov/sites/default/files/FY14%20State%20 Activity%20Report.pdf.

[28] Alexa Ura, "Drug Testing for Welfare Benefits Back on the Table," *Texas Tribune,* February 5, 2015, http://www.texastribune.org/2015/02/05 /drug-testing-welfare-benefits-back-table/.

[29] U.S. Census Bureau, 2013 Annual Survey of State Government Finances, "State Government Finances Summary: 2013," http://www2.census.gov/govs/state/g13-asfin.pdf.

[30] U.S. Census Bureau, 2013 Annual Survey of State Government Finances, 2013 Annual Survey of State Government Finances Summary Table, https://www .census.gov/govs/state/.

[31] U.S. Department of Health and Human Services, "Read the Law," http://www.hhs.gov/healthcare/rights/law/index .html.

[32] HealthCare.gov, "The Fee You Pay if You Don't Have Health Coverage," https://www.healthcare.gov/what-if-i-dont-have-health-coverage/.

[33] National Conference of State Legislatures, "State Actions to Address Health Insurance Exchanges," http://www.ncsl.org/research/health/state-actions-to-implement-the-health-benefit.aspx#Exchange_Status_Map.

[34] Ibid.

[35] Sarah Kliff, "It's Official: The Feds Will Run Most Obamacare Exchanges," *Washington Post,* February 18, 2013, http://www.washingtonpost.com/blogs/wonkblog/wp/2013/02/18/its-official-the-feds-will-run-most-obamacare-exchanges/; Drew Desilver, "Most Uninsured Americans Live in States That Won't Run Their Own Obamacare Exchanges," Pew Research Center, September 19, 2013, http://www.pewresearch.org/fact-tank/2013/09/19/most-uninsured-americans-live-in-states-that-wont-run-their-own-obamacare-exchanges/.

[36] U.S. Census Bureau, Health Insurance Coverage in the United States: 2014, "Population Without Health Insurance Coverage by State: 2013 and 2014," https://www.census.gov/content/dam/Census/library/publications/2015/demo/p60-253.pdf.

[37] Robert Pear, "Most Governors Refuse to Set Up Health Exchanges," *New York Times,* December 14, 2012, http://www.nytimes.com/2012/12/15/us/most-states-miss-deadline-to-set-up-health-exchanges.html.

[38] Manny Fernandez, "Perry Declares Texas' Rejection of Health Care Law 'Intrusions,'" *New York Times,* July 9, 2012, http://www.nytimes.com/2012/07/10/us/politics/perry-says-texas-rejects-health-law-intrusions.html.

[39] Edgar Walters, "With Hospital Funds in Question, Abbott Holds Firm Against Medicaid Expansion," *Texas Tribune,* April 20, 2015, http://www.texastribune.org/2015/04/20/hospital-funds-question-abbott-holds-firm-against-/.

[40] Texans for Positive Economic Policy, Texas Public Education Funding, TXSmartSchools.org, http://www.txsmartschools.org/about/funding_and_spending.php.

[41] Secretary of State, State of Texas, *Votes on Proposed Amendments to the Texas Constitution,* 1875–November 1993 (Austin: Secretary of State, 1994), 73.

[42] *Dallas Morning News,* January 12, 1994, 1A.

[43] Texas Education Agency Office of School Finance, "School Finance 101: Funding of Texas Public Schools," September 2014, http://tea.texas.gov/Finance_and_Grants/State_Funding/Manuals/School__Finance_Manuals/; Texas Education Agency, Chapter 41 Wealth Equalization, http://tea.texas.gov/Finance_and_Grants/State_Funding/Chapter_41_Wealth_Equalization/Chapter__41_Wealth_Equalization/; For the Supreme Court of Texas decision, see http://www.txcourts.gov/media/1371141/140776.pdf.

[44] Texas Education Agency, "Student Testing and Accountability," http://tea.texas.gov/Student_Testing_and_Accountability/.

[45] Texas Education Agency, STAAR Resources, http://www.tea.state.tx.us/student.assessment/staar/.

[46] Office of the Governor Greg Abbott, "2016 Report to the People of Texas," http://gov.texas.gov/2016report/?utm_medium=social&utm_source=&utm_campaign=20160202_txgov-p-2016report_02022016_website&utm_con.

[47] Texas Education Code (TEC) §29.051 - 29.064 - Bilingual Education and Special Language Programs, http://www.statutes.legis.state.tx.us/Docs/ED/htm/ED.29.htm#B.

[48] Legislative Budget Board, (February 2013), "Financing Higher Education In Texas: Legislative Primer," http://www.lbb.state.tx.us/Documents/Publications/Primer/690_Higher_Education_Finance.pdf.

[49] Texas Higher Education Coordinating Board, "2015 Texas Public Higher Education Almanac: A Profile of State and Institutional Performance and Characteristics," http://www.thecb.state.tx.us/index.cfm?objectid=A44B548A-E50C-8417-E09BF83FC11EA1EF.

[50] Texas Higher Education Coordinating Board, "Overview: Tuition Deregulation," September 2012, www.thecb.state.tx.us/download.cfm?downloadfile=A199D6C9-C3D9-F563-B8CA6AAE154F324A&typename=dmF . . .

[51] Carole Keeton Strayhorn, Texas Comptroller of Public Accounts, "Texas Where We Stand, https://web.archive.org/web/20120220175031/ http://www.window.state.tx.us/comptrol/wwstand/wws0512ed/wws0512.pdf.

[52] Ralph K.M. Haurwitz, "Regents Freeze In-State Tuition for Two Years at UT-Austin," *Austin American-Statesman,* May 3, 2012. http://www.statesman.com/news/news/local/regents-freeze-in-state-tuition-for-two-years-at-1/nRnTP/.

[53] "Perry Pushing Tuition Freeze, $10,000 Degrees," *Austin American-Statesman,* October 1, 2012, http://www.statesman.com/news/news/state-regional-govt-politics/perry-pushing-tuition-freeze-10000-degrees/nSQ8b/.

[54] "Capital Project," BusinessDictionary.com, http://www.businessdictionary.com/definition/capital-project.html.

[55] Vivian Elizabeth Smyrl, "Permanent University Fund," *Handbook of Texas Online,* published by the Texas State Historical Association, http://www.tshaonline.org/handbook/online/articles/khp02.

[56] UTIMCO, (December 31, 2015), "Permanent University Fund: Report on Certain Specified Data as Required by Art. 4413 (34e) of the Civil Statutes," http://www.utimco.org/Funds/Endowment/PUF/PUFSemiAnnual201512.pdf.

[57] State Constitution, art. 7, sec. 18.

[58] Texas Higher Education Coordinating Board, (October 2014), "Higher Education Fund Allocation Recommendation for Fiscal Years 2016 through 2025," http://www.thecb.state.tx.us/reports/pdf/6084.pdf.

[59] Office of the Governor Greg Abbott, (January 29, 2015), "Governor Abbott Proposes To Eliminate Emerging Technology Fund; Establish New University Research Initiative," http://gov.texas.gov/news/press-release/20479.

[60] Aman Batheja, "Abbott Signs Higher Ed Bill Ending Fund Touted by Perry," *Texas Tribune,* June 4, 2015, http://www.texastribune.org/2015/06/04/abbott-signs-bill-ending-perry-fund-boost-higher-e/; Matthew Watkins, "Legislature replaces Emerging Technology Fund with university fund," *Dallas Star-Telegram,* June 1, 2015, http://www.star-telegram.com/news/politics-government/state-politics/article22800357.html.

[61] *Hopwood v. Texas,* 78 F.3d 932 (5th Cir. 1996), *cert. denied, Texas v. Hopwood,* No. 95–1773 (July 1, 1996).

[62] Ibid.

[63] "81% of U.T.'s Admissions Offers Go to Top 10% Graduates," *Houston Chronicle,* March 20, 2008, p. i.

[64] Amy Howe, "Finally! The Fisher Decision in Plain English," SCOTUSblog, June 24, 2013, http://www.scotusblog.com/2013/06/finally-the-fisher-decision-in-plain-english/.

[65] Manny Fernandez, "Texas University's Race Admissions Policy Is Debated Before a Federal Court," *New York Times,* November 13, 2013. http://www.nytimes.com/2013/11/14/us/texas-universitys-race-admissions-policy-is-debated-before-a-federal-court.html).

[66] *Fisher v. University of Texas at Austin et al.* Supreme Court of the United States. 2016. https://www.supremecourt.gov/opinions/15pdf/14-981_4g15.pdf; SCOTUSblog (Supreme Court of the United States Blog), Fisher v. University of Texas at Austin, http://www.scotusblog.com/case-files/cases/fisher-v-university-of-texas-at-austin-2/.

[67] Texas Department of Public Safety, New laws for Handgun Licensing Program, http://www.txdps.state.tx.us/rsd/chl/legal/newlegislation.htm.

[68] National Conference of State Legislatures, "Guns on Campus: Overview," http://www.ncsl.org/research/education/guns-on-campus-overview.aspx.

[69] Erwin Chemerinsky, *Lawrence v. Texas,* Duke Law, originally at http://web.law.duke.edu/publiclaw/supremecourtonline/commentary/lawvtex; now accessible at https://web.archive.org/web/20130504091256/ http://web.law.duke.edu/publiclaw/supremecourtonline/commentary/lawvtex.

[70] National Conference of State Legislatures, "State Same-Sex Marriage Laws: Legislatures and Courts," December 2012, http://www.ncsl.org/issues-research/human-services/same-sex-marriagelaws.aspx; National Conference of State Legislatures, "Defining Marriage: State Defense of Marriage Laws and Same-Sex Marriage," October 2014, http://www.ncsl.org/research/human-services/same-sex-marriage-overview.aspx; National Conference of State Legislatures, "Same-Sex Marriage Laws," June 2015, http://www.ncsl.org/research/human-services/same-sex-marriage-laws.aspx.

[71] Office of the Secretary of State, Race Summary Report, "2005 Constitutional Amendment Election," http://elections.sos.state.tx.us/elchist117_state.htm.

[72] Daniel R. Pinello, (2009), "Location, Location, Location: Same-Sex Relationship Rights by State," *Law Trends & News,* American Bar Association, http://www.americanbar.org/newsletter/publications/law_trends_news_practice_area_e_newsletter_home/bl_feat5.html.

[73] Supreme Court of the United States, *United States v. Windsor,* http://www.supremecourt.gov/opinions/12pdf/12-307_6j37.pdf.

[74] Manny Fernandez, "Federal Judge Strikes Down Texas' Ban on Same-Sex Marriage," *New York Times,* February 26, 2014, http://www.nytimes.com/2014/02/27/us/texas-judge-strikes-down-state-ban-on-same-sex-marriage.html#.

[75] Edgar Walters, "State Files Notice of Appeal on Gay Marriage Ruling," *Texas Tribune,* February 26, 2014, http://www.texastribune.org/2014/02/26/federal-judge-rules-texas-gay-marriage-ban-unconst/.

[76] Texas Department of State Health Services, "Adoption: Frequently Asked Questions," http://www.dshs.state.tx.us/vs/reqproc/faq/adoption.shtm#question 4.

[77] National Center for Lesbian Rights, "Legal Recognition of Lesbian, Gay, Bisexual, and Transgender (LGBT) Parents in Texas," http://www.nclrights.org/wp-content/uploads/2013/07/TX_custody_pub_FINAL.pdf.

[78] Alexa Ura, Edgar Walters and Jolie McCullough, "Comparing Nondiscrimination Protections in Texas Cities," *Texas Tribune,* November 11, 2015, http://www.texastribune.org/2015/11/11/comparing-nondiscrimination-ordinances-texas/.

[79] Ballotpedia, "City of Houston Anti-Discrimination HERO Veto Referendum, Proposition 1 (November 2015)," https://ballotpedia.org/City_of_Houston_Anti-Discrimination_HERO_Veto_Referendum,_Proposition_1_(November_2015); Jeff Guo, "Houston isn't alone: These are the largest U.S. cities that still allow LGBT discrimination," *Washington Post,* November 4, 2015, https://www.washingtonpost.com/news/wonk/wp/2015/11/04/houston-isnt-alone-these-are-the-largest-u-s-cities-that-still-allow-lgbt-discrimination/; Alexa Ura, "Bathroom Fears Flush Houston Discrimination Ordinance," *Texas Tribune,* November 3, 2015, https://www.texastribune.org/2015/11/03/houston-anti-discrimination-ordinance-early-voting/.

[80] Tex. Code Crim. Proc. arts. 1191–94, 1196.

[81] Texas Department of State Health Services, Woman's Right to Know, http://www.dshs.state.tx.us/wrtk/.

[82] Guttmacher Institute, "State Facts About Abortion: Texas," http://www.guttmacher.org/pubs/sfaa/texas.html.

[83] John Schwartz, "Texas Senate Approves Strict Abortion Measure," *New York Times,* July 13, 2013, http://www.nytimes.com/2013/07/14/us/texas-abortion-bill.html?_r=0.

[84] Adam Liptak and Manny Fernandez, "Supreme Court Allows Texas Abortion Clinics to Remain Open," *New York Times,* June 29, 2015, http://www.nytimes.com/2015/06/30/us/supreme-court-allows-texas-abortion-clinics-to-remain-open.html.

[85] *Whole Woman's Health v. Cole,* Fifth Circuit Court of Appeals, 2015, http://www.ca5.uscourts.gov/opinions%5Cpub%5C14/14-50928-CV0.pdf; *Whole Woman's Health et al. v. Hellerstedt,* Supreme Court of the United States, 2016, https://www.supremecourt.gov/opinions/15pdf/15-274_p8k0.pdf; Manny Fernandez and Abby Goodnough, "Opinion Transforms Texas' Abortion Landscape," *New York Times,* June 27, 2016, http://www.nytimes.com/2016/06/28/us/abortion-rights-supporters-find-ruling-a-practical-and-symbolic-victory.html?action=click&contentCollection=U.S.&module=RelatedCoverage&ion=EndOfArticle&pgtype=article.

[86] David Wiley, Kelly Wilson, and Ryan Valentine (2009), *Just Say Don't Know: Sexuality Education in Texas Public Schools,* Texas Freedom Network Education Fund, http://tfn.org/cms/assets/uploads/2015/11/SexEdRort09_web.pdf.

[87] Gail Collins, "Gail Collins on Texas's Abstinence Sex Education Problems," *The Daily Beast,* June 4, 2012, http://www.thedailybeast.com/articles/2012/06/04/gail-collins-on-texas-s-abstinence-sex-education-problems.html.

[88] David Wiley, Kelly Wilson, and Ryan Valentine (2009). *Just Say Don't Know: Sexuality Education in Texas Public Schools,* Texas Freedom Network Education Fund, http://tfn.org/cms/assets/uploads/2015/11/SexEdRort09_web.pdf.

[89] Centers for Disease Control and Prevention, "Genital HPV Infection–Fact Sheet," http://www.cdc.gov/std/hpv/stdfact-hpv.htm.

[90] Dan Eggen, "Rick Perry and HPV Vaccine-maker Have Deep Financial Ties," *Washington Post,* September 13, 2011, http://www.washingtonpost.com/politics/perry-has-deep-financial-ties-to-maker-of-hpv-vaccine/2011/09/13/gIQAVKKqPK_story.html.

[91] Kate Alexander, "Perry Calls HPV Vaccine Mandate a Mistake," *Austin American-Statesman,* Aug. 15, 2011, http://www.statesman.com/news/news/state-regional-govt-politics/perry-calls-hpv-vaccine-mandate-a-mistake/nRdY7/.

[92] United States Census Bureau, QuickFacts, http://www.census.gov/quickfacts/table/PST045215/00,48.

[93] U.S. Department of State, "The Immigrant Visa Process., http://travel.state.gov/content/visas/english/immigrate/immigrant-process.html.

[94] Randall Monger and James Yankay (May 2014), "U.S. Lawful Permanent Residents: 2013," Department of Homeland Security Office of Immigration Statistics, http://www.dhs.gov/sites/default/files/publications/ois_lpr_fr_2013.pdf.

[95] Department of Homeland Security, Office of Immigration Statistics (August 2016), 2014 Yearbook of Immigration Statistics, https://www.dhs.gov/sites/default/files/publications/ois_yb_2014.pdf.

[96] Bryan Baker and Nancy Rytina (2013), Estimates of the Unauthorized Immigrant Population Residing in the United States: January 2012. Department of Homeland Security, http://www.dhs.gov/sites/default/files/publications/ois_ill_pe_2012_2.pdf.

[97] Department of Homeland Security, U.S. Customs and Border Protection, U.S. Border Patrol Statistics, http://www.cbp.gov/newsroom/media-resources/stats?title=Border+Patrol.

[98] Alexa Ura, "Health Officials: Immigrant Surge is a Medical Crisis," *Texas Tribune,* June 24, 2014, http://www.texastribune.org/2014/06/24/health-officials-docs-raise-concerns-about-immigra/; Gilad Edelman, "Abbott, Cruz Blame Obama for 'Humanitarian Crisis,'" *Texas Tribune,* June 23, 2014, http://www.texastribune.org/2014/06/23/abbott-cruz-blame-obama-humanitarian-crisis/; Rick Jervis, "Immigrant children continue to surge into South Texas," *USA Today,* June 17, 2014, http://www.usatoday.com/story/news/nation/2014/06/17/children-surge-immigration-texas/10643609/.

[99] Department of Homeland Security, U.S. Customs and Border Protection, "Southwest Border Unaccompanied Alien Children Statistics FY 2016," http://www.cbp.gov/newsroom/stats/southwest-border-unaccompanied-children/fy-2016.

[100] Carole Keeton Strayhorn, (December 2006), "Undocumented Immigrants in Texas: A Financial Analysis of the Impact to the State Budget and Economy," Office of the Texas Comptroller.

[101] Morgan Winsor, "Immigration Reform 2015: Texas Lawmaker Proposes Annual Economic Impact Report On Illegal Immigrants," *International Business Times,* March 6, 2015, http://www.ibtimes.com/immigration-reform-2015-texas-lawmaker-proposes-annual-economic-impact-report-illegal-1839082.

[102] U.S. Department of Health and Human Services, Office of the Assistant Secretary for Planning and Evaluation, (March 2012), "Overview of Immigrants' Eligibility for SNAP, Medicaid, TANF, and CHIP," https://aspe.hhs.gov/basic-report/overview-immigrants-eligibility-snap-tanf-medicaid-and-chip#_edn4.

[103] *Plyler v. Doe,* 457 U.S. 202 (1982).

104 Texas Higher Education Coordinating Board, Overview: Residency and In-State Tuition, September 2008, http://www.thecb.state.tx.us/reports/PDF/1528.PDF.

105 Texas Health and Human Services Commission, (December 2014), "Report on Texas Health and Human Services Commission Services and Benefits Provided to Undocumented Immigrants," http://www.hhsc.state.tx.us/reports/2015/hhsc-benefits-provided-undocumented-immigrants.pdf.

106 Mark Hugo Lopez and Jens Manuel Krogstad, (February 11, 2015), "States suing Obama over immigration programs are home to 46% of those who may qualify," Pew Research Center, http://www.pewresearch.org/fact-tank/2015/02/11/states-suing-obama-over-immigration-programs-are-home-to-46-of-those-who-may-qualify/.

107 Adam Liptak and Michael D. Shear, "Supreme Court to Hear Challenge to Obama Immigration Actions," *New York Times,* January 19, 2016, http://www.nytimes.com/2016/01/20/us/politics/supreme-court-to-hear-challenge-to-obama-immigration-actions.html; *United States v. Texas.* Supreme Court of the United States. 2016, https://www.supremecourt.gov/opinions/15pdf/15-674_jhlo.pdf; Adam Liptak and Michael D. Shear, "Supreme Court Tie Blocks Obama Immigration Plan," New York Times, June 23, 2016, http://www.nytimes.com/2016/06/24/us/supreme-court-immigration-obama-dapa.html.

108 Paul J. Weber, "Texas approves $800 million for border security," *PBS Newshour,* June 16, 2015, http://www.pbs.org/newshour/rundown/texas-approves-800-million-border-security/.

109 Texas Water Development Board, "Water for Texas: 2012 State Water Plan," http://www.twdb.texas.gov/publications/state_water_plan/2012/2012_SWP.pdf.

110 www.merriam-webster.com/acrefoot.

111 Texas Water Development Board, "Water for Texas: 2012 State Water Plan, http://www.twdb.texas.gov/publications/state_water_plan/2012/2012_SWP.pdf.

112 Ibid.

113 Ibid.

114 Ibid.

115 Ibid.

116 Ibid.

117 Ibid.

118 Texas A&M University, "Texas Water Law," http://texaswater.tamu.edu/water-law.

119 Texas Commission on Environmental Quality, www.tceq.texas.gov/permitting/water_rights.html.

120 www.texaswatermatters.org/pdfs/articles/powerful_thirst.pdf.

121 *Edwards Aquifer Authority v. Day,* 389 S.W.3d 814 (Tex. 2012).

122 Edwardsaquiferauthority.net/ . . . /san-marcos-and-barton-springs-connection.org.

123 See Private Real Property Rights Preservation Act, www.oag.tx.us/AG_Publications/txts/propertyguide2005.shtml.

124 Chapter 36, Texas Water Code. See also "Spotlight on Groundwater Conservation Districts," (Environmental Defense, Austin, Texas), www.texaswatermatters.org.

125 Harris-Galveston Subsidence District, www.hgsubsidence.org.

126 www.edwardsaquifer.org/display_authority_m.php?pg=mission. See also Louis Rosenberg, Nohl P. Bryant, Cynthia Smiley et al., *Essentials of Texas Water Resources,* ed., Mary Sahs (State Bar of Texas 2012) pp. 4–20 through 4–23.

127 Neena Satija, "Groundwater Wars Brewing in Austin's Suburbs," *Texas Tribune,* January 23, 2015, https://www.texastribune.org/2015/01/23/hays-county-pumping-project/; Neena Satija, "Hays County Groundwater Bill Heads to Governor's Desk," *Texas Tribune,* May 31, 2015, http://www.texastribune.org/2015/05/31/hays-county-groundwater-bill/; Kiah Collier, "New law won't necessarily stop Electro Purification drilling," *San Marcos Mercury,* September 10, 2015, http://smmercury.com/2015/09/10/new-law-wont-necessarily-stop-electro-purification-drilling/.

128 Louis Rosenberg, Nohl P. Bryant, Cynthia Smiley et al., *Essentials of Texas Water Resources,* ed., Mary Sahs (State Bar of Texas 2012) pp.4–11 through 4–19.

129 Texas Water Development Board, http://www.twdb.texas.gov/.

130 Ibid.

131 Texas Commission on Environmental Quality, https://www.tceq.texas.gov/agency/water_main.html.

132 www.mysanantonio.com/news/article/Texas-part-of-growing-drought-in-U.S.-that-rivals-3711733; www.cbbep.org.

133 U.S. Department of Veterans Affairs, "Veteran Population," National Center for Veterans Analysis and Statistics, http://www.va.gov/vetdata/veteran_population.asp.

134 Texas Veterans Commission, "Welcome to the Texas Veterans Commission," http://www.tvc.state.tx.us/Home.aspx.

135 Office of the Governor Rick Perry (Nov. 12, 2009), *Gov. Perry Announces Initiative to Reduce Federal Claims Backlog for Veterans in Waco and Houston,* Office of the Governor Rick Perry, originally located at http://governor.state.tx.us/news/press-release/13928/; now accessible at https://web.archive.org/web/20120220064836/http://governor.state.tx.us/news/press-release/13928/.

136 Texas Veterans Commission, "Veterans Education Program," http://www.tvc.texas.gov/Education.aspx.

137 Texas Government Code, "Title 6, Public Officers and Employees. Subtitle B. State Officers and

Employees. Chapter 657. Veteran's Employment Preferences," http://www.statutes.legis.state.tx.us/Docs/GV/htm/GV.657.htm.

[138] Ryan Poppe, "Gov. Abbott Signs Veterans Bills During San Antonio Visit," *Texas Public Radio,* June 5, 2015, http://tpr.org/post/gov-abbott-signs-veterans-bills-during-san-antonio-visit#stream/0.

[139] Office of the Governor Rick Perry (July 9, 2009), "Gov. Perry: Appraisal Reform Legislation Makes Progress Toward Slowing Pace of Increasing Property Appraisal Rates," originally located at http://governor.state.tx.us/news/press-release/13190/; now accessible at https://web.archive.org/web/20120220065925/http://governor.state.tx.us/news/press-release/13190/.

[140] Texas Parks and Wildlife (n.d), "Texas Parklands Passport," Park Passes, http://tpwd.texas.gov/state-parks/park-information/passes/park-passes#texas-parklands-passport-.

[141] Texas Parks and Wildlife (n.d.), "Licenses: Frequently Asked Questions," Texas Parks and Wildlife. http://www.tpwd.state.tx.us/faq/business/license/.

[142] Texas Department of Public Safety, "Veteran Services." http://www.txdps.state.tx.us/driverlicense/VetServices.htm.

CHAPTER 12

The Criminal Justice System in Texas

Texans' attitudes toward crime and punishment, in many ways, reflect a tradition of "frontier justice," which arose when no formal legal system was in place and people took justice into their own hands. Over time, this informal system of justice has been transformed by Texas's current constitution, amendments to it, and other statutory changes enacted by the legislature into a complex, multilevel court system to address both criminal and civil matters (see Chapter 5). The justice system provides for public safety and the common good not only through the courts but also through the Department of Public Safety, which enforces the law, and the Department of Criminal Justice, which houses and supervises over half a million inmates and parolees, as well as a variety of other local law enforcement agencies.[1] Texas's justice system is large and, from the perspective of the average Texan, can be difficult to navigate.

Texas's criminal justice system is shaped by the sophisticated and challenging nature of providing justice as well as the complicated labyrinth of Texas's multilevel court system. Any large system of this type will at times face difficulty satisfying the underlying, simple philosophy held by most citizens of the state that justice should be swift and equitable. Individuals interact with the criminal justice system in a myriad of ways and for equally numerous reasons. For example, people in Texas might interact with the law enforcement community to report a crime or be subject to policing if suspected of committing one. Others might be involved with the court system when arrested for a crime, to address personal family matters, to settle financial questions arising from economic disputes between individuals or businesses, or to resolve dilemmas over discrimination or even political contests. Citizens expect government to pursue justice on behalf of victims where crimes have been committed, just as they expect judges and juries to deliver fair rulings after weighing arguments and considering evidence and the law. There are, however, many criticisms leveled at Texas's criminal justice system (aside from the difficulty citizens face as they seek to navigate the complex, fragmented, and overlapping jurisdictions within it). These include issues with policing, the number and complexity of laws, the high cost of legal assistance, sentencing, and the perception that justice may not be equal for all.

This chapter expands on the information covered in Chapter 5 through a deeper exploration of the concept of law and a further discussion of punishment and problems associated with the processes of delivering justice in Texas. It examines the state's various policing agencies and how they enforce the law and implement the findings of juries and judges on behalf of citizens. Attention is given to the legal procedures associated with both criminal and civil trials and how Texas deals with juvenile offenders. The chapter also examines the concepts of correction and rehabilitation in Texas—including incarceration, parole, and probation—to understand how the criminal justice system's policies and procedures impact justice and how justice is perceived by society. The chapter concludes with a look at issues with the criminal justice system raised by reformers and whether and how Texas has attempted to deal with them.

Chapter Learning Objectives

- Understand the differences between criminal and civil law and explain criminal justice policy in Texas.

- Describe the state of Texas's juvenile justice system and its procedures.

- Explain the state of Texas's correction system, including its approach to rehabilitation and use of the death penalty.

- Describe the challenges the state of Texas faces in its criminal justice system.

Elements of the Criminal Justice System

Learning Objective: Understand the differences between criminal and civil law and explain criminal justice policy in Texas.

In Texas, as elsewhere, the criminal justice system serves many broad purposes, including promoting public safety, punishing criminal activity, recompensing victims, deterring future criminal action, and rehabilitating offenders so they do not break the law again upon returning to society. The many elements of that system include the courts, policies enacted by the legislature, and correctional facilities and programs. For many individuals, their first (and perhaps only) point of contact with the criminal justice system is through law enforcement or police.

Law Enforcement and Policing

According to the federal Bureau of Justice Statistics (BJS), law enforcement preserves order and ensures compliance with the law, primarily through "the activities of prevention, detection, and investigation of crime and the apprehension of criminals."[2] In 2008 (the most recent year for which BJS has made this data available), Texas had more law enforcement agencies than any other state, and together these agencies employed nearly 100,000 people. This workforce included 244 sworn personnel (officers with the authority to make arrests) per 100,000 residents of the state (which is equivalent to about 1 officer for every 400 residents).[3] Texas law enforcement agencies operate at the state, county, and municipal levels as well as in other special jurisdictions, and law enforcement officers include highway patrol troopers, sheriffs, city police officers, campus police officers, and many others.

The Texas Department of Public Safety (DPS) is the chief law enforcement agency in the state. It is the fourth largest such agency in the United States (after the California Highway Patrol, the New York State Police, and the Pennsylvania State Police) in terms of the number of full-time, sworn personnel.[4] DPS is overseen by the Public Safety Commission, whose five members are appointed by the governor. DPS divisions include the Texas Highway Patrol (which is primarily responsible for supervising vehicular traffic but whose troopers are fully authorized to enforce criminal law throughout the state), the Criminal Investigations Division, the Driver License Division, the Division of Emergency Management, and the Texas Rangers, among others.[5] In addition to coordinating border security, the Texas Rangers investigate major crimes as well as serial and unsolved crimes, charges of public corruption, and shootings involving police officers.[6]

The primary law enforcement agency at the county level is the County Sheriff's Office. As required by the state constitution, each of Texas's 254 counties has a sheriff who is elected by county voters to a four-year term. Additional staff in the sheriff's office might include deputies, reserve deputies, guards, and clerks.[7] While these offices carry out "traditional law enforcement functions," such as making traffic stops, responding to calls for assistance, and patrolling, sheriff's office personnel also provide security for courthouses, serve warrants and other official papers, and run county jails.[8] Although the sheriff's office has authority over the entire county, sheriffs typically do not operate in incorporated areas or within city limits where municipal police departments have jurisdiction.[9]

Texas also has a considerable number of local police departments, most of which are operated by city governments. Some of these, including the Houston, Dallas, and San Antonio police departments, are among the largest in the nation in terms of number of sworn officers.[10] Texas law allows municipalities to establish a police force to maintain public safety; police officers are appointed by the governing body of the city or municipality, and they perform many of the same law enforcement functions as do sheriffs' offices.[11]

Aside from these state and local agencies, additional agencies provide law enforcement for particular jurisdictions or geographic areas. These special jurisdictions include public school districts, public colleges and universities, other state-owned buildings, natural resources (such as parks and wildlife), and transportation systems (including airports, mass transit, and port facilities), all of which may have their own police force.[12]

Of course, police and other law enforcement agents could not do their jobs without an established set of laws to enforce. Thus, the state legislature, in its lawmaking capacity, also plays an important role in the criminal justice system. By enacting and amending state law or code, legislators not only lay out the rules of the state but also specify what constitutes a rule violation, the punishment that will be applied, and the duties law enforcement and the courts have when they address such rule violations.

Criminal Law and Civil Law

The function of courts is to hear matters of legal controversy and deliver justice to the parties involved. In criminal cases, the parties include a government attorney who prosecutes a defendant and seeks punishment on behalf of society or a victim. The government must prove the defendant is guilty of having committed the alleged offense. The defendant enters a plea and generally seeks to be found "not guilty."[13] **Criminal law** applies in cases involving a violation of the **Texas Penal Code**, the statutory law that establishes "a system of prohibitions, penalties, and correctional measures to deal with conduct that unjustifiably and inexcusably causes or threatens harm to those individual or public interests for which state protection is appropriate."[14] The penal code lists and defines the offenses and **graded penalties** associated with offenses against a person, family, society, or public office, in addition to providing guidance for law enforcement to protect against arbitrary treatment of people suspected, accused, or convicted of offenses.

Equally important, however, is the **Texas Code of Criminal Procedure**, which describes the rules associated with the criminal justice process in Texas. Created by the Texas Supreme Court, this code contains specific rights afforded the accused during trial, sentencing, and punishment phases, and details the procedures that must be followed by government representatives taking part in these processes. Anyone who has read the U.S. Constitution would find the first chapter of the Texas Code of Criminal Procedure familiar; there are many similarities to the Bill of Rights. For example, Article 1.04 protects the accused's right to due process, and Article 1.06, like the Fourth Amendment, guarantees Texans the expectation of privacy in their person, papers, and homes, free from governmental intrusion without a search warrant. The Texas Penal Code and the Code of Criminal Procedure, together, form the framework for delivering justice in criminal trials in Texas.

The Texas Penal Code grades offenses, based on severity, into two categories: felonies and misdemeanors. **Felony** offenses are divided into five categories that range from the most serious—capital—to first-, second-, and third-degree felonies and state jail felonies. Felony offenses carry penalties ranging from death (for capital offenses) to a minimum of 180 days confinement in jail (for state jail felonies). **Misdemeanors** are considered less serious crimes, punishable by fine, incarceration, or both. Table 12.1 lists the categories of offenses from the Texas Penal Code, examples of the offenses, and the typical punishment imposed for a guilty verdict.

Because Texas uses enhanced sentencing for repeat and habitual offenders, the accused's prior convictions (both felonies and misdemeanors) can play a major role when a judge or jury imposes punishment. The practice of **enhanced punishment,** applied to defendants who have been convicted previously, involves elevating the charges and increasing the penalty to that associated with the next most serious crime. For example, in 2014, the Third District Court of Appeals affirmed a Hays County jury verdict sentencing a Texas woman to life in prison after her fifth conviction for driving while intoxicated (DWI). Although a first-time DWI offense is typically considered a Class B misdemeanor, Rose Ann Davidson's prior DWI convictions (two misdemeanors and two felonies) resulted in the penalty being increased for subsequent offenses.[15] Laws that allow harsher punishment for repeat or habitual offenders have been called recidivist statutes, habitual offender laws, or three-strikes laws. **Recidivism** refers to the rate at

Margin glossary

criminal law

Statutory law that defines both the violation and the penalty the state will seek to have imposed upon the defendant

Texas Penal Code

The statutory law that defines criminal offenses and punishments in Texas

graded penalties

Punishments that differ based upon the seriousness of the crime

Texas Code of Criminal Procedure

The rules created by the Texas Supreme Court to govern the proceedings of trials in Texas

felony

A serious criminal offense, punishable by death or incarceration

misdemeanors

Less serious criminal offenses, punishable by fine, incarceration, or both fine and incarceration

enhanced punishment

The application of the next most serious penalty for repeat offenders

recidivism

The rate at which criminal offenders commit crime after they leave the state's custody

TABLE 12.1

Categories of Crime and Maximum Punishments

Offense	Example	Maximum Punishment
Capital Felony	Murder of a first-responder; murder of a child under the age of 10; murder for hire; murder during the commission of another crime; mass murder	Life imprisonment without the possibility of parole OR execution
First-degree Felony	Murder; aggravated sexual assault; theft of $200,000+; sale of more than 4 grams of heroin or cocaine	5-99 years imprisonment; $10,000 fine
Second-degree Felony	Manslaughter; sexual assault; arson; robbery; theft of $100,000+	2-20 years imprisonment; $10,000 fine
Third-degree Felony	Kidnapping; tampering with consumer products; theft of $20,000+; drive-by shootings	2-10 years imprisonment; $10,000 fine
State Jail Felony	Criminally negligent homicide; auto theft; theft of $1,500+; forgery; credit or debit card abuse	180 days to 2 years in jail; $10,000 fine
Class A Misdemeanor	Public lewdness; assault; bigamy; burglary of a vehicle; theft of $500+; stalking; theft of cable service	1 year in jail; $4,000 fine
Class B Misdemeanor	DUI; indecent exposure; theft of over $20; prostitution; possession of 4 ounces or less of marijuana	180 days in jail; $2,000 fine
Class C Misdemeanor	Gambling; aiding suicide; leaving a child unattended in a vehicle; theft of less than $20; smoking in a public elevator; attending a dog fight; public intoxication	$500 fine

Source: Texas Penal Code. See http://www.statutes.legis.state.tx.us/docs/PE/htm/PE.12.htm.

which criminal offenders commit another crime after they leave the state's custody. Though the intent of recidivist statutes is certainly to target and discourage repeat offenders,[16] enhanced punishment is typically reserved for violent offenders or serious offenses involving minors. However, Texas does not require any of an individual's prior convictions to be violent in order for enhanced punishment to apply.[17] Some reformers have argued that these types of laws have led to excessive or disproportionate sentencing.

Texas also uses mandatory minimum sentences. The state legislature has passed laws dictating a fixed amount of time in prison for individuals convicted of certain crimes. Many of these mandatory minimum sentences are imposed for nonviolent drug crimes.[18] For instance, an individual possessing between 4 ounces and 5 pounds of marijuana is guilty of a felony in Texas. This crime is punishable by a mandatory minimum sentence of no less than 180 days in jail.[19] Supporters of mandatory minimums argue that these compulsory sentences increase public safety by keeping criminals off the streets for longer periods of time and by discouraging others from committing similar crimes. However, mandatory minimums have been controversial because they take discretion away from judges, who cannot consider other factors (such as an offender's prior record or mitigating circumstances) in these cases, and because they often lead to sentences some consider to be out of proportion to the crime committed.[20] A famous federal case involving mandatory minimums was that of Weldon Angelos, who was convicted of selling about $1,000 worth of marijuana while in possession of a gun. Because the sale of narcotics while in possession of a firearm triggered a mandatory minimum sentence, Angelos (who had no prior record) was sentenced to 55 years in prison. He was released in 2016 after serving 13 years.[21] The reasons for his release are not fully clear, given that his records are sealed. But many reformers campaigned on his behalf, and the prosecutor's office is reported to have worked for this result. It is worth noting that Texas has fewer mandatory minimums than a lot of other states (including large, populous states like California and Florida).

The vast majority of crime in Texas involves property. As part of the FBI's Uniform Crime Reporting program, DPS collects data on the number of certain "index crimes" reported across the state. Of the over 900,000 index crimes reported in Texas in 2014, property crimes (such as burglary and motor vehicle theft) made up 88.1 percent. Violent crime, including murder, rape, and aggravated assault, represented 11.9 percent of reported index crimes in 2014. Overall, the total number of index offenses decreased 5.5 percent from 2013 to 2014.[22] However, because the FBI changed its reporting standards and expanded the definition of rape to include males as victims, reported incidents of rape in Texas increased by more than fifty percent from 2013 to 2014.[23]

Aside from the sheer volume of crimes reported, another way to analyze trends is by looking at the crime rate. This statistic is based on population and is defined as the number of crimes committed for every 100,000 residents. The Texas crime rate for 2014 was calculated as 3,392.2 offenses per 100,000 persons.[24] This represented a 7.2 percent decrease from 2013, which is consistent with the data on crime volume.

civil law

Defines private relationships as well as financial matters or damages to property committed by businesses or other individuals to a person

Civil law has to do with private relationships (rather than violations of the penal code) and can address financial matters, including financial wrongs that citizens or businesses might commit against others. In civil cases, the party who claims to have been harmed by another's conduct and seeks a remedy is referred to as the petitioner or plaintiff. The other party, who is being sued by the plaintiff, is called a respondent or defendant. In civil trials, the plaintiff must prove that the defendant has caused the plaintiff harm.[25] The respondent answers the charges of harm and seeks to be found "not responsible." Just as criminal cases are governed by the Texas Code of Criminal Procedure, civil cases are governed by the Texas Rules of Civil Procedure.

Civil law cases generally fall into one of four categories: family law, tort law, contract law, and property law.[26] Common examples of family law cases decided in civil court are divorces and child custody cases. Another type of civil case, involving tort law, may arise when an individual files suit against another individual or a corporation. An example would be if an individual alleged that a product manufactured by a corporation had caused the individual harm. Contract law would include things like landlord-tenant disputes and other contractual disagreements. For example, if a tenant fails to pay rent or violates the terms of the lease in some other manner, the landlord can serve notice to the tenant to vacate the property. If the tenant fails to vacate, the landlord can file for eviction in the local justice court.[27]

Depending on the amount of money or the value of property in dispute, (see Chapter 5, Figure 5.1), there may be multiple options for filing suit because of concurrent jurisdiction of justice, county, and district courts. For example, in matters involving $200 to $10,000, a suit may be filed in either justice, county, or district court. Moreover, two or more district courts may overlap in terms of the geographic area over which they have jurisdiction, and many courts hear both civil and criminal cases. However, patterns have emerged in terms of the kind of case typically filed in a given court. For example, in 2015, the vast majority of family cases were heard in district courts. Debt cases tended to be handled by county courts, and justice courts were the preferred venue for landlord-tenant disputes.[28]

It is important to note that civil cases can follow from criminal cases. Namely, a guilty verdict in a criminal trial may lead to a subsequent civil trial wherein monetary damages are awarded to a plaintiff. For instance, an individual may be charged with and convicted of assault in a criminal proceeding. The victim of the assault may then seek damages, via a civil proceeding, for medical bills as well as pain and suffering.

Aside from the differences described previously, there are also differences between criminal and civil law in terms of proving a case in court. The standard for providing evidence in support of an argument is called the **burden of proof**. The burden of proof in civil matters requires that the party bringing suit persuade the judge (or in some cases a jury) by only a "preponderance of evidence" in order to prevail. In criminal law, the standard of proof is much higher, but that is because the stakes are higher. The government, after charging an individual with a criminal offense, is required to provide sufficient evidence that demonstrates to a judge or jury "beyond a reasonable doubt" that the individual being accused actually committed the crime. Whereas the plaintiff must prove that the defendant caused the plaintiff harm in a civil trial, in criminal trials, the burden of proving guilt rests on the state. In addition, the rules associated with providing evidence are different for criminal and civil trials. Because the state has significant resources at its disposal, it is required to share with the defense any information or evidence that could assist the accused. The Brady Rule, established by a 1963 U.S. Supreme Court decision, requires the government to disclose to the accused any **exculpatory evidence** that could materially affect the judge's or jury's determination of guilt.[29]

burden of proof
The obligation associated with providing evidence sufficient to support the assertion or claim made by the individual bringing suit in a court of law

exculpatory evidence
Material evidence that could assist the accused in proving that he or she was innocent of the offense charged

CORE OBJECTIVE

Communicating Effectively . . .

Explain the difference between criminal and civil law, including how the standard of proof differs for each. Provide an example of each type of case.

© George Lavendowski/USFWS

Criminal Justice Policy

Texas has a reputation as a "tough on crime" state. That reputation is well-deserved. The strictness of Texas's criminal justice policies is reflected in the state's incarceration or imprisonment rate. (The imprisonment rate is the number of prisoners with longer than one-year sentences who are under the jurisdiction of state and federal correctional authorities, per 100,000 residents.) According to the Bureau of Justice Statistics, Texas's imprisonment rate in 2014 was 584, down slightly from 600 the prior year. Texas's rate was seventh highest of all states and well above the nationwide average of 471. At the other end of the

Focus On

Navigating the Criminal Justice System in Spanish

© ZUMA Press Inc/Alamy

For most people, navigating the criminal justice system is intimidating without the presence of a language barrier. Many Spanish-speaking Texans do not speak English well enough to easily interface with law enforcement and may find it difficult to understand the process or to be understood, especially in court proceedings. Therefore, they depend on interpreters (who work with signed or spoken languages) and translators (who work with written language).[30]

In *Miranda v. Arizona* (1966), the U.S. Supreme Court made it standard operating procedure for law enforcement to inform individuals of their rights (specifically, the right to speak with a lawyer and avoid self-incrimination) when they are in police custody or being interrogated. This instruction is called the Miranda warning.[31] In Texas, Spanish-speaking individuals typically have their

Miranda warning read to them in Spanish. In addition, they may be given a card to read with a Spanish-language translation of the Miranda warning printed on it.[32] However, there is no universally agreed-upon Miranda translation (in fact, the Supreme Court did not provide exact wording for the English version either), and different translations have been found to vary considerably. Cases have been overturned on the grounds that the accused did not have a proper understanding of their rights. As a result, in 2016, the American Bar Association recommended that a standardized Spanish Miranda translation be developed and used nationwide.[33]

Texas law also provides for the use of interpreters in civil and criminal court proceedings. If it is determined that either a party to the proceeding (such as the defendant) or a witness "can hear but does not comprehend or communicate in English," the court will appoint an interpreter for that individual.[34] Interpreters must be licensed to provide real-time, verbatim translations of court proceedings, and they must "give an oath or affirmation to make a true translation."[35]

Critical Thinking Questions

1. In what way does communicating through an interpreter allow individuals to participate effectively in legal proceedings? What are the potential pitfalls?
2. What are the possible positive and negative impacts of a standardized Miranda translation in Spanish?

spectrum, Maine's rate was lowest at 153.[36] This data indicates that, as a percentage of population, Texas locks up more of its residents than other states do.

However, Texas's incarceration rate is high in part because the state's crime rate is high. Texas had the fifteenth highest violent crime rate in the country in 2014.[37] As shown in Table 12.1, violent crimes are typically felonies and carry longer prison sentences. Therefore, a high violent crime rate would be expected to result in a high incarceration rate. To more accurately assess the strictness of a state's sentencing policies, as well as systematic differences in the likelihood of conviction, Ruger and Sorens have adjusted the raw incarceration rate in light of the violent crime rate. Using this method, Texas's adjusted incarceration rate was ninth in the country in 2014, suggesting that the state's sentencing policies and prosecutorial eagerness and success are well above average in terms of their strictness.[38] In other words, more people were incarcerated than would be expected based on the state's high rate of violent crime.

Ruger and Sorens have also examined how police in different states prioritize arrests for drug crimes. They calculated a "drug enforcement rate" (based on the number of arrests for violating drug laws and the number of people who report illegal drug use in surveys). A low rate indicates that fewer people involved with drugs were arrested, whereas a high rate indicates that more people involved with drugs were arrested. For Texas, the drug enforcement rate was 6.8 percent in 2013, higher than the national average of 5.3 percent. Thus, police departments in Texas tend to prioritize arresting people for drug-related offenses more than police in most other states. (In addition, Texas has not legalized marijuana for medical or recreational use; adopting such policies would reduce arrest rates for drug offenses.)[39]

Despite the state's reputation as "tough on crime," Texas has recently witnessed some fairly significant reform efforts and garnered national attention as a leading criminal justice reform state. These reforms included increased use of drug courts (which channel nonviolent drug offenders into treatment programs rather than jail), changes to its juvenile justice system, and shutting down prisons.[40] Perhaps surprisingly, these reforms have been supported by conservative Republicans, such as former governor Rick Perry and state legislator Jerry Madden, as well as conservative groups such as the Texas Public Policy Foundation (whose "Right on Crime" initiative led by Marc Levin has addressed issues such as overcriminalization, civil asset forfeiture, and policing and prison reform) and the Texas Association of Business. These reformers were allied with Democrats, including state senators John Whitmire and Rodney Ellis, both strong proponents of prison reform. Although more elevated motives are certainly at play (namely, concern about the dignity of individuals and the impact of excessive sentencing and high incarceration rates on families and communities), conservative reformers cannot have failed to notice that having a high incarceration rate and being so tough on crime carries a daunting price tag for state taxpayers and negatively impacts labor markets.[41]

Juvenile Justice

Learning Objective: Describe the state of Texas's juvenile justice system and its procedures.

As of 2015, 26.3 percent of the Texas population was under 18 years of age.[42] Both state and federal law in the United States treat juveniles differently from adults. A citizen is a juvenile until he or she reaches the so-called age of majority, which in Texas is age 17 for civil and criminal responsibility before the law.[43] "Juvenile justice" applies not only to those minors charged with civil or criminal wrongdoing, but also those who, through no fault of their own, are wards of the state.

Government's Duties to Minors

Texas state and local governments are charged with at least three general legal duties in cases involving minors. The first is **in loco parentis**, which means that the state must act in the place of the parent to protect the interests of the child,

in loco parentis
Latin for "in the place of a parent"

parens patriae

Latin for "parent of the fatherland"

even without a formal legal relationship.[44] The second is **parens patriae**, which refers to the inherent power of the state to protect persons legally incapable of protecting themselves before the law.[45] The third is the "police powers doctrine," defined as the state's duty to protect the health, safety, and welfare of its citizens.[46] The state acts as a caretaker for the minor, a defender of his or her legal interests, and is at the same time the guardian of public safety.

Because these duties are complex and difficult to carry out, Texas juvenile justice encompasses a large network of state and local authorities charged with meting out justice while also safeguarding the interests of minors. This network includes judges who determine whether a minor faces full criminal responsibility as an adult; state agencies that provide needed detention and living facilities; and caseworkers, lawyers, and other experts who must act in the best interests of minors while also giving consideration to parents or legal guardians and crime victims. The agency responsible for coordinating and overseeing juvenile justice programs in the state is the Texas Juvenile Justice Department.

Until 2011, two separate state agencies bore the responsibility of administering the juvenile justice system: the Texas Youth Commission, which managed detention centers and halfway houses throughout the state, and the Texas Juvenile Probation Commission, which oversaw the entire system at the local level and coordinated state-local communication. Unfortunately, these agencies were plagued by a long-standing record of abuse and misconduct and lost the public's trust. One example of this occurred at the Mountain View State School for Boys, which opened in 1962. In the early 1970s, this facility incarcerated juveniles who had previously been held at the nearby Gatesville State School and were deemed dangerous. Both were run by the Texas Youth Council (the precursor to the Texas Youth Commission).[47] Conditions at the Mountain View School were harsh, and abuse perpetrated by staff members and inmates alike was widespread. Some juveniles had been involuntarily committed to the Council (often without due process), whereupon they were housed in dormitories like Mountain View and largely forgotten.[48]

In 1971, a class-action lawsuit was filed on behalf of the inmates against the Texas Youth Council. In *Morales v. Turman,* Judge William Wayne Justice found that the state schools' operations violated the Eighth Amendment's prohibition against cruel and unusual punishment and ordered Texas to shutter both Gatesville and Mountain View. Additionally, he ordered Texas to establish "a system of community-based treatment alternatives" for juveniles and institutionalize only those not appropriate for some "alternative form of rehabilitative treatment."[49] In his order, Justice cited a quote from *Kent v. U.S.* (1966) that he likened to conditions faced by delinquent children in Texas:

> While there can be no doubt of the original laudable purpose of juvenile courts . . . There is evidence, in fact, that there may be grounds for concern that the child receives the worst of both worlds: that he gets neither the protections accorded to adults nor the solicitous care and regenerative treatment postulated for children.[50]

Mountain View was closed in 1975, and its inmates were transferred to other facilities across the state.[51] In 1983, the Texas Youth Council was renamed the Texas Youth Commission and, under federal supervision that was a condition of its legal settlement, began attempts to overhaul the juvenile justice system in

Texas.[52] However, this effort was unsuccessful, and the system foundered on further allegations of misconduct. Between 2004 to 2008, there was a quelled riot at the Evins Regional Juvenile Center, child sexual abuse scandals at two facilities run by the Texas Youth Commission, and yet another civil rights lawsuit filed against the Commission by students in its care. During the 2011 legislative session, Senator John Whitmire, chair of the Senate Committee on Criminal Justice, proposed SB 653, which abolished both the Texas Youth Commission and the Texas Juvenile Probation Commission and transferred their responsibilities to a newly established agency, the Texas Juvenile Justice Department. The bill passed and was signed into law by Governor Perry.[53] Today, the newly reconstituted Texas Juvenile Justice Department (TJJD) is directed by a thirteen-member board appointed by the governor.[54]

The current juvenile justice system bears the imprint of Judge Justice's orders. Traditionally, Texas has considered juvenile justice to be part of family law. In 1995, the legislature revised and amended the Family Code to create the Juvenile Justice Code (now Title III of the Texas Family Code, Chapters 51 through 61).[55] This revision established a more "localized" approach to handling juveniles, with rehabilitation as the primary goal. When a youth is charged with a violation, the county or local district court generally prosecutes the case. In fact, some counties have dedicated district courts or county courts at law that deal exclusively with juvenile cases. Harris County has three such "juvenile district courts"; Dallas County has two.[56] At that point, the county's juvenile probation department implements any punishment or treatment imposed by the court. Every county provides juvenile probation services, although some juvenile probation departments serve more than one county.[57] Each probation department operates under the guidance of the county's juvenile board, and each board may create an advisory council of citizens who provide guidance to the board, including a prosecuting attorney, mental health and medical professionals, and a representative from the educational community.[58]

In other words, all phases of a juvenile case—including intake, predisposition investigation, prosecution, and possible probation—are handled at the county level to the greatest extent possible. Only those individuals who have "exhausted their options in the county" or "committed the most serious offenses" are sent to TJJD.[59] If a juvenile is found guilty and is to be detained at a TJJD facility, he or she can appeal the court's decision. That appeal proceeds directly to the Texas Supreme Court, as discussed in Chapter 5.

Procedures Involving Juveniles

The Juvenile Justice Code applies only to children aged 10-17; children younger than 10 cannot be prosecuted for a crime.[60] Juveniles who do commit offenses—whether they be misdemeanors or felonies—are arrested and generally referred to juvenile court. Two types of offenses result in a child's referral to juvenile court: conduct indicating a need for supervision (CINS) or delinquent conduct. According to the Texas Juvenile Justice Code, conduct indicating a need for supervision is defined as an act that, if committed by an adult, would either be punishable by a fine or would not be considered a violation at all (such as running away from home). Delinquent conduct, on the other hand, involves a violation of the penal code and would result in imprisonment if committed by an adult.[61] Some examples of these offenses are listed in Table 12.2.

TABLE 12.2

Juvenile Offenses Tried in Court

CINS Offenses	Delinquent Conduct Offenses
Any finable offense	Felonies or jailable misdemeanors
Running away	Contempt of court or violation of a court order
Prostitution or sexting	DUI
School expulsion for conduct code violations	

Source: Texas Family Code 51.03(a) and (b)

Under certain circumstances, juveniles may be tried as adults.

Michael Ainsworth/Dallas Morning News/Corbis

The process associated with a juvenile criminal trial is almost the same as that for an adult. However, one notable difference is that a hearing is held to determine whether or not the juvenile will be tried as an adult. In Texas, the juvenile court must waive its jurisdiction over the case in order for a minor to be tried as an adult. In making this decision, the juvenile court judge can consider whether the crime was committed against a person or property, whether the minor had a prior record, whether the minor's mental state at the time of the crime indicated criminal intent, whether the minor committed several crimes in the same transaction, and similar issues.[62]

Some studies have shown that, in practice, there is not much difference between minors tried as adults versus those tried in juvenile court; the process of distinguishing between the two populations and certifying some minors as adults appears somewhat arbitrary.[63] It is worth noting that minors tried as adults are not necessarily the "worst" offenders in the juvenile system in terms of violent or repeated offenses. Compared to other juvenile offenders, however, those tried as adults do face more serious consequences later in life from long sentences and criminal records that are more difficult to keep confidential.[64]

Even if tried as an adult, a minor cannot be sentenced to life imprisonment without parole or to death if he or she committed the crime before the age of 18.[65] Before 2005, Texas and 19 other states had the dubious distinction of allowing a death sentence for juveniles. In *Roper v. Simmons* (2005), however, the U.S. Supreme Court barred the death penalty for defendants who were under the age of 18 at the time of their crime, thereby resulting in the sentences of 29 juveniles on Texas's death row being commuted to life without parole.[66] In 2012, the Supreme Court ruled in *Miller v. Alabama* that the sentence of life without parole also constituted cruel and unusual punishment for juveniles and could not be applied to those under 18 at the time their crime was committed.[67] Texas applied this ruling retroactively and commuted the sentences of juvenile offenders who had been convicted prior to the *Miller* ruling.

Another difference between adult and juvenile trials involves terminology. The term "adjudication"is used to refer to the trial phase of a juvenile case. It also refers to a finding of guilt or conviction for the alleged offense. Similarly, a "disposition hearing" in a juvenile case is the equivalent of the sentencing phase in an adult trial. In addition, juvenile cases differ from adult cases in the sense that there is often a hard cap or limit on the length of punishment. If a minor is put on probation, that probation must end by the individual's eighteenth birthday. A juvenile sent to a TJJD facility is either released by his or her nineteenth birthday or transferred to an adult facility, depending on the type of sentence imposed and the individual's behavior while in TJJD custody.[68]

During fiscal year 2013, 818 juveniles were placed in the custody of the Texas Juvenile Justice Department, all for committing felony offenses. The vast majority of these (92 percent) were male, most had at least one prior felony adjudication or were on probation at the time they committed their crime (64 percent and 76 percent, respectively), and 82 percent were ethnic minorities. More of these offenders came from Harris County (15 percent) than from any other single county in the state. Statistics indicate a decrease in the number of juveniles committed to state-run correctional facilities over the past several years.[69] Some of this decrease can be attributed to reforms undertaken by state lawmakers to both improve the system and decrease the number of youths detained. For example, a bill passed in 2007 made it illegal for minors convicted of misdemeanors (minor offenses) to be sent to a detention facility. To encourage community-based treatment, the legislature increased funding for juvenile probation departments and cut the budget for state-run facilities. The state was subsequently able to close eight juvenile detention facilities.[70] In 2015, a new law decriminalized truancy (although this change could lead to an increase in criminal charges against parents or guardians).[71] Apart from these reforms, there is also evidence that the juvenile crime rate has decreased in Texas. For instance, the number of referrals to juvenile probation departments fell from 2011 to 2012.[72] Despite the checkered past of juvenile justice in Texas and the uncertainty associated with the newness of the Texas Juvenile Justice Department, these trends suggest there is reason for cautious optimism regarding the future of the new state agency as it carries out wide-ranging and difficult responsibilities.

CORE OBJECTIVE

Taking Personal Responsibility . . .

Currently, at what age does the state of Texas consider a person an adult in criminal and civil proceedings? At what age do you think the state should require individuals to take personal responsibility? Why?

Source: United States Department of Agriculture Agricultural Research Service

Correction and Rehabilitation

Learning Objective: Explain the state of Texas's correction system, including its approach to rehabilitation and use of the death penalty.

The Texas Department of Criminal Justice (TDCJ) is a vast organization with a $3.4 billion dollar budget for fiscal year 2016.[73] TDCJ is responsible for the detention and supervision of over a half-million adult inmates, parolees, and individuals on community supervision (also known as probation). TDCJ is governed

TABLE 12.3

2014 Incarceration Rate per 100,000 Residents by State (Top 10 States)

STATE	Rate
Louisiana	816
Oklahoma	700
Alabama	633
Arkansas	599
Mississippi	597
Arizona	593
Texas	**584**
Missouri	526
Georgia	517
Florida	513

Source: U.S. Department of Justice, Bureau of Justice Statistics, Prisoners in 2014 (http://www.bjs.gov/content/pub/pdf/p14.pdf.) Table 6.

by the gubernatorially appointed, nine-member Texas Board of Criminal Justice, which hires an executive director to run the agency.[74] The department oversees the operation of many types of facilities, including state prisons, state jails, private prisons, transfer and prerelease facilities, as well as medical, psychiatric, and geriatric facilities. As of July 2016, the state had a total of 112 operational units.[75]

The State Prison System

Texas has one of the highest rates of incarceration in the nation; as of 2014, it was 584 per 100,000. (Table 12.3 lists the states with the 10 highest incarceration rates.) There were 166,000 prisoners in Texas in 2014—more than in any other state and second only to the Federal Bureau of Prisons in raw numbers. This represents a 1.4 percent decrease from 2013 (168,300) and a 5.1 percent increase since the year 2000 (157,997).[76]

Having the largest prison population of any state and the seventh-highest incarceration rate comes with challenges. Foremost among those is maintaining enough space to house all the state's inmates. Prison overcrowding has been a chronic problem in Texas, at times reaching crisis levels. In 1980, U.S. District Court Judge William Wayne Justice ruled, in *Ruiz v. Estelle,* that conditions in Texas prisons constituted "cruel and unusual punishment" and thus violated the U.S. Constitution.[77] The court ordered changes to many aspects of the state's prison system. As part of this process, Texas began a massive prison construction program to relieve overcrowding. One journalist called this enterprise "the greatest expansion of prison beds in the history of the free world."[78] According to one estimate by the Urban Institute, the state built 120 prisons from 1980 until 2000. By 2004, it had 137 total units in operation.[79]

However, the prison population continued to outpace the number of prison beds available. The prison population grew from 36,769 inmates in 1983 to a peak of 173,649 inmates in 2010.[80] In light of this staggering increase, it is not surprising that the state explored a number of options to both accommodate its growing prison population and reduce the future need for additional beds.

Managing the Prison Population

Of course, one way to reduce the prison population is to increase the number of individuals on parole. According to the TDCJ, parole is defined as "the release of an offender, by decision of a parole panel, to serve the remainder of his or her sentence under supervision in the community."[81] The Texas Board of Pardons and Paroles is the entity responsible for determining if an offender has been sufficiently rehabilitated to be paroled and, based on a combined score of "static" and "dynamic" factors, rates his or her potential risk to society. Inmates serving life sentences for capital crimes must serve at least 40 years before they are considered eligible for parole. Those who are convicted of other violent offenses must serve at least half their sentence, and those convicted of nonviolent crimes must serve a minimum of one-quarter.[82] Releasing offenders on parole is associated with a considerable cost savings over keeping them in prison. Table 12.4 shows the average costs in 2014 of incarceration versus alternatives to it. (Note that the figures for juveniles, also included here, are significantly more dramatic in terms of cost savings.)

The creation of the "state jail felony" represented another attempt to manage the Texas prison population. In 1993, the state legislature created this new, fifth category of felony offenses.[83] The concept behind the new state jail division was twofold. First, state jails would relieve overcrowding in state penitentiaries. Second, nonviolent drug and property offenders, previously convicted of third-degree felonies, would be separated from more violent offenders in state prisons and offered a greater opportunity for rehabilitation, as "rehabilitation programming [was] meant to be the cornerstone of the state jail system."[84] This rehabilitation program included vocational and educational training as well as substance abuse treatment and community service projects. Unfortunately, while it is a laudable goal, rehabilitation is not often achieved. According to a senate committee report, these programs were plagued by poor participation, accompanied by the fact that jail administrators could not force inmates to participate in rehabilitation activities.[85] While Texas has made great strides since 2007 in reducing recidivism from prison, it has seen much less success with inmates in

TABLE 12.4

Daily Cost per Person for Various Correctional Programs, 2014

Texas Department of Criminal Justice	
Prison	$ 54.89
Parole Supervision	$ 4.04
Community Supervision	$ 3.20
Texas Juvenile Justice Department	
State Residential Facilities	$437.11
Parole Supervision	$ 31.93
Juvenile Probation Supervision	$ 14.52

Source: Legislative Budget Board, Criminal and Juvenile Justice Uniform Cost Report, Fiscal Years 2013-2014, February 2015, http://www.lbb.state.tx.us/Documents/Publications/Policy_Report/1440_Criminal_Juvenile_Justice_Uniform_Cost_Report.pdf.

its state jail facilities, for whom the percentage rearrested and reincarcerated is significantly higher.[86]

Another approach to reducing incarceration, recidivism, and related costs has been the use of "specialty courts." According to TDCJ, nonviolent offenders made up nearly half (44 percent) of Texas's incarcerated population in 2014.[87] Specialty or problem-solving courts are "trial courts with specialized dockets that often hear only nonviolent cases for either certain types of defendants or offenses."[88] Common types of specialty courts are drug courts, prostitution courts, and DWI courts. An offender convicted in one of these specialty courts is diverted from incarceration and given a treatment plan (with required participation) and community supervision. The first such specialty court in the state was a drug court established in 1990.[89] By 2013, there were over 100 specialty courts operating in Texas, the majority of which were drug or DWI courts, but these were soon followed by courts focusing on veterans, prostitutes, and mental health. The sudden proliferation of these nontraditional courtrooms caught the attention of the state legislature, which decided that special statutory language should be written to better capture what these courts were doing and how they were doing it, as well as establish accountability by creating a Specialty Courts Advisory Council. As of mid-2016, Texas had nearly 200 specialty courts, with Houston and Dallas having the disproportionate statewide share.[90] Initial reports suggested that offenders who were processed through drug courts and completed their treatment programs had lower rates of recidivism than similar offenders who either did not complete treatment or were not seen in a specialty court.[91] Other research has shown that specialty courts are associated with lower criminal justice costs.[92]

CORE OBJECTIVE

Being Socially Responsible . . .

Why might the use of special courts to punish crimes like prostitution provide a cost savings for the criminal justice system?

© Editorial Image, LLC/Alamy

Private Prisons

Private prisons emerged as another attempt to address the problem of a growing prison population and limited space in state prisons. Rather than building, staffing, and maintaining new state prisons, Texas opted to contract with for-profit prison corporations. These private corporations then built and operated the new facilities, with oversight provided by the TDCJ. In other cases, private corporations were contracted to operate facilities built for the state. As Table 12.5 illustrates, TDCJ currently provides oversight for a number of private correctional facilities, jails, residential halfway houses, and substance abuse facilities (SAF), among others.[93]

TABLE 12.5

Selected Private Facilities under State Contract, 2015–2016

Type	Contractor	Number of Units (Beds)
Correctional	Management & Training Corp. (formerly Wackenhut)	7 (4,118)
State Jail	CCA Tennessee	4 (5,129)
Halfway Houses	Various	8 (2,043)
Residential Substance Abuse Facilities (SAF)	Various	16 (1,778)

Source: Texas Department of Criminal Justice, Private Facility Contract Monitoring/Oversight Division, Contracted Facilities as of February 02, 2016, http://tdcj.state.tx.us/divisions/pf/pf_unit_list.html.

Beginning in the late 1980s, the state of Texas, like many other states, began negotiating contracts with private prison corporations in an effort to help relieve prison overcrowding and save tax dollars, even as it was still constructing new state-owned prisons. The resulting boom in prison construction produced such an oversupply that prison beds in Texas were rented out for use by inmates from other states.[94] Though not as robust as it was in the 1990s, the private-prison industry continues in Texas today, as many prisoners are housed through contracts with the federal government. (The federal government, specifically Immigration and Customs Enforcement, or ICE, had contracted with several private prison corporations to run immigrant detention centers, some of which are located in Texas. In August 2016, however, the U.S. Department of Justice announced it would decrease, with the eventual goal of terminating, its use of private prisons in the near future.)[95]

Many of these private prisons were built in rural areas. Smaller rural counties, searching for additional revenue sources or opportunities for economic development, partnered with private corporations to construct new prisons. Potential benefits to the county included the creation of new jobs, because members of the community found employment at the prison. These new jobs, in turn, brought growth to established businesses. Such projects also promised a relatively passive revenue stream for the county. The county would offer revenue bonds to finance construction and, once paid off, the county would own a prison facility that would be staffed and operated by an outside contractor. In addition, repairs to infrastructure were included as part of the contracts, along with new construction projects for the community. In fact, rural counties that contracted to build private prisons initially experienced increased revenues, allowing them to expand budgets based on this injection of new money and improving their economic outlook.[96]

Unfortunately, the private-prison industry has not been lacking in scandal and corruption. Allegations of physical abuse, neglect, inhumane conditions, and dangerous understaffing have been made at these prisons. One example is found in Willacy County, which built three detention centers, the largest of which was the Willacy County Correctional Center. This facility, built in 2006 and operated by Management & Training Corporation (MTC), initially generated about $2.5 million a year in revenue for the county. Known as "Tent City" because of its use of Kevlar tents, the prison had space to house up to 3,000 inmates.

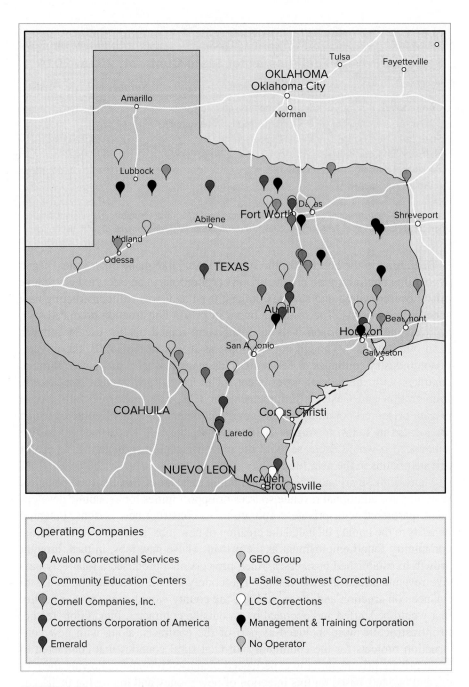

FIGURE 12.1 **Private prisons are located throughout Texas but are largely concentrated in the rural areas that surround major urban city centers.**

SOURCE: © Google, Inc. All rights reserved.

However, it lost its federal contract following a *Frontline* documentary detailing physical and sexual abuse there. After a riot in early 2015 that lasted about five hours, the 2,800 federal prisoners housed there were transferred, and the prison was shut down. When the prison closed, Willacy County faced a budget shortfall due to the loss of prison-related revenue as well as debt payments for construction of the prison, the outstanding balance of which was $128 million. Bond

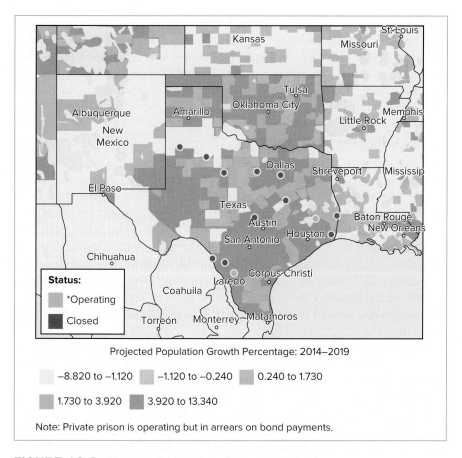

Status:

*Operating

Closed

Projected Population Growth Percentage: 2014–2019

−8.820 to −1.120   −1.120 to −0.240   0.240 to 1.730

1.730 to 3.920   3.920 to 13.340

Note: Private prison is operating but in arrears on bond payments.

FIGURE 12.2   Texas private prison boom goes bust.

SOURCE: Rachael Gleason, ExpressNews.com research

service payments amounted to almost $250,000 a month. Ultimately, the county faced difficult decisions that required layoffs for county government employees, including jail staff, and reductions in operational hours for the courts and other agencies. Willacy County was not alone in this enterprise; more than a dozen private prisons have closed in rural areas across the state, and more closures are expected.[97]

Due to a number of issues, it is difficult to compare private and public prisons in terms of cost and outcomes. According to data provided by the TDCJ and the Legislative Budget Board, the daily cost per inmate is lower for privately operated prisons ($40.88 in 2014) than for state-operated facilities. However, such comparisons are muddied by the fact that certain expenses for privately operated facilities, including inmate medical care and facility repairs, are paid by the state of Texas and are therefore not included in private facilities' cost estimates.[98] Comparing outcomes—including such variables as staff and inmate injuries, escapes, number of inmate complaints, and facility accreditation—is equally problematic. Studies specifically comparing recidivism rates for public and private prisoners have been criticized for design flaws.[99]

Arguments have been made on both sides regarding the use of private prisons. On the one hand, studies have consistently shown that operating costs are lower for private prisons than for public prisons—an average cost savings of 10 to

15 percent. Another important justification for using private prisons is to relieve overcrowding in state facilities. Conversely, critics have questioned whether the profit motive distorts how private prison operators fulfill their duties. For instance, correctional programs focused on rehabilitation and reducing recidivism run counter to the incentive of private prison corporations to keep all of their beds occupied.[100]

Local Government Jails

Although not part of the state penal system, local jails also house and care for prisoners. According to state statute, each county is required to provide a "safe and suitable" jail.[101] County jails house inmates scheduled to serve time in the state system; they also incarcerate people who commit misdemeanors within the county's jurisdiction. The Texas legislature created the Texas Commission on Jail Standards to ensure that counties maintain minimum standards for construction and the custody, rehabilitation, and treatment of inmates in their care. As of July 2016, there were almost 70,000 individuals incarcerated in Texas's county jails; of these inmates, eight percent were federal inmates and another two percent were state jail inmates serving their time or awaiting transfer.[102]

Cities operate detention facilities as well. Municipalities are authorized under the Local Government Code to operate jails,[103] and cities in Texas may use their jails or holding cells to detain state statute violators who are being processed or waiting to be interviewed or interrogated before being transferred to a county jail. Generally, city jails incarcerate individuals for violations of municipal ordinances, which are fine-only penalties, when the individual cannot or chooses not to pay the fines. If cities do not have a facility to do so, they may enter into an agreement with the county to detain individuals who fail to pay fines.

Although privately operated municipal jails are subject to the same standards as county jails, publicly operated municipal jails (of which there are approximately 350 statewide) have no regulatory body to oversee their operations. Moreover, no other state laws or rules govern the operation of city jails. There have been attempts during previous legislative sessions to expand the authority of the Texas Commission on Jail Standards to provide oversight and regulation for all municipal jails, but these bills faced extreme opposition, primarily from city officials who argued that it would be cost-prohibitive to make the necessary improvements to meet current standards.[104]

Recently, local jails have come under increased scrutiny because of inmate deaths while in custody. In Texas, there were 1,111 deaths in city and county jails between 2005 and 2015. Although 54 percent of these deaths were determined to be from natural causes, 27 percent were suicides and 9 percent were due to drug or alcohol intoxication.[105] Other possible causes of death include failure to provide medical care and failure to respond to mental health issues. Several wrongful death suits have been filed in recent years by family members of individuals who died while in custody. Table 12.6 indicates the four cities and counties where the most custodial deaths occurred during this period, according to the Texas Attorney General's Custodial Death Report. During the first half of 2016, 129 people died in the custody of local law enforcement statewide.[106]

TABLE 12.6

Custodial Deaths in City and County Jails in Texas, 2005–2015

City Jails		County Jails	
Houston	205	Harris	202
San Antonio	126	Dallas	91
Dallas	117	Bexar	79
Ft. Worth	58	Tarrant	42

Source: Office of the Attorney General of Texas. Custodial Death Reports 2005–2015. https://www.texasattorneygeneral.gov/criminal/custodial/report_deaths.php CSV Downloaded May 26, 2016.

The "Three R's": Recidivism, Rehabilitation, and Reform

As noted previously, Texas's criminal justice system experienced an unprecedented expansion at the end of the twentieth century. The incarcerated population ballooned, scores of prisons were built, and state spending on corrections skyrocketed from 1980 to 2000. Faced with a dire forecast that even more prison beds would be needed in the future, Texas lawmakers, looking for a solution to their anticipated budgetary woes, analyzed the system with the goal of curbing that trend.[107]

Data indicated that the prison population was growing because of increases in the state's population, rising crime rates, and recidivism. Most offenders who were likely to return to criminal activity did so within three years of being released from some form of criminal supervision (prison, probation, or parole). Most repeat offenders (68 percent in 2001) had committed nonviolent drug or property crimes for their first offense. In terms of prison admissions, about 25 percent of those entering prison each year were being sent back to prison because they had violated their parole. Similarly, 30 percent of prison admissions were attributable to individuals whose sentence of probation (community supervision) had been revoked, and they were being sent to prison instead. Moreover, repeat offenders could have their parole or probation revoked either for commission of a new crime or for mere technical violations of the terms of their parole or probation.[108] Viewed in this light, it is easy to see how Texas prisons had become a sort of "revolving door," especially for large numbers of nonviolent offenders.

The Sunset Advisory Commission made a number of recommendations regarding the criminal justice system, foremost among which involved increased funding for treatment and rehabilitation. The report stated:

> Reducing recidivism through treatment and supervision is highly cost-effective for the State. Programs to reduce recidivism keep people out of prison, reducing the need for new prisons, while also protecting the public by reducing crime. They also help offenders become contributing members to society, maintaining jobs and paying obligations such as taxes, restitution, and child support. Community-based treatment, particularly treatment in response to parole or probation violations, can allow offenders to learn skills while remaining out of prison, at considerably lower costs than if they were incarcerated.[109]

Since 2005, the legislature has enacted a number of reforms focused on rehabilitation and alternatives to incarceration. First, the legislature incentivized probation departments to reduce probation revocations by offering them increased funding. During the 2007 session, the legislature appropriated nearly $250 million for treatment and diversion facilities, including mental illness and substance abuse treatment. This initiative was estimated to have saved the state $2 billion and averted what was projected by TDCJ to be a 17,000-bed shortfall by 2012. Bills passed in 2011 created additional incentives for improvements in the system. For example, individuals under community supervision could reduce their time on probation by demonstrating "exemplary behavior." Another legislative change allowed state jail felons, who previously were not considered for early release, to serve the last few months of their jail sentence on probation if they participated in rehabilitation programs.[110]

The state's shift in approach has had a dramatic effect. The prison population, which peaked in 2010, has declined.[111] The state's incarceration rate, second highest in the country in 2004, has fallen to seventh. In 2011, due to surplus capacity at other facilities, Texas closed a public prison for the first time in the state's history.[112] Recidivism has also decreased. According to one study, the recidivism rate for inmates released in Texas in 2007 (and followed for three years) was 11 percent lower than the rate for inmates released in 2005 and 22 percent lower than the rate for 2000 releases.[113] Parole revocation rates fell from 9.1 percent in 2009 to 6.5 percent in 2014.[114] In addition, the state's crime rate has also fallen. Since 2009 in particular, the crime rate has slowly but consistently declined.[115]

Thanks to legislative reforms, Texas has shown that an increased focus on rehabilitation programs, rather than just expanding prison capacity, can cut costs and decrease incarceration by reducing recidivism. These programs provide many offenders with the skills required to transition to being productive members of society.

Substance abuse treatment is one of the many programs provided in an effort to reduce recidivism. Because many offenders struggle with drug and alcohol addiction, inmates are assessed for substance abuse as part of the intake process. Appropriate inmates are then transferred to units that offer specific programs operated by TDCJ's rehabilitation division. The Substance Abuse Felony Punishment Facility (SAFPF) and the In-Prison Therapeutic Community (IPTC) are both six-month programs, with aftercare and follow-up supervision. The SAFPF is a "diversion" program, operated by TDCJ, to which offenders can be sentenced in lieu of prison. Alternatively, the Board of Pardons and Paroles may require a parolee's participation in the program as a condition of parole.[116]

Another service aimed at reducing recidivism is education. According to the most recent demographic profile of inmates received by the TDCJ, average educational attainment scores among offenders in custody reflected an eighth-grade education. Since 1969, the Windham School District has provided education for inmates at TDCJ facilities. Its purpose is to assist inmates in obtaining their high school diploma or High School Equivalency Certificate (GED) or vocational training, with the goal of easing their transition back into society. Windham was the first school district in the nation expressly for offenders and is still in operation today.

In 1998, a study conducted by the now-defunct Texas Criminal Justice Policy Council found that 86 percent of the 16,205 inmates who participated in Windham educational programs did not reoffend in the first two years after their release. Over the years, more offenders were encouraged to participate, and have participated, and achieved positive results.[117] During fiscal year 2014–15, almost 20 percent of the 70,311 offenders released had attained their GED or high school diploma.[118] In a study conducted by Sam Houston State in 2014, researchers found that offenders who had participated in educational programs offered through Windham were half as likely to reoffend as those who did not participate but were released at the same time.[119]

The Death Penalty

One area in which Texas has remained tough on crime is the death penalty. This form of punishment was effectively suspended in the United States in 1972 (*Furman v. Georgia*) when the U.S. Supreme Court found that many state laws regarding the death penalty were applied in an arbitrary or discriminatory fashion.[120] In 1976, however, the Court established guidelines under which states could reinstate the death penalty (*Gregg v. Georgia*). Since 1976, most executions in the U.S. (81 percent) have taken place in southern states,[121] which is perhaps unsurprising considering the dominant traditionalistic culture of the South.

Texas reinstated the death penalty in 1976 and is currently the leading state in terms of the number of death sentences handed out and the number of prisoners executed. From the time of reinstatement until July 2016, Texas carried out 537 of the nation's 1,437 executions.[122] Although it represents less than 9 percent of the total U.S. population, Texas accounts for 37 percent of the country's executions. As of November 2016, Texas had executed 7 people since the beginning of the year.[123] Table 12.7 shows states with prisoners currently on death row. (Some of these states have a moratorium on executions, have abolished the

TABLE 12.7

Death Row Inmates by State

Total Number of Death Row Inmates as of January 1, 2016: 2,943

State	Number Waiting to Be Executed	State	Number Waiting to Be Executed
California	743	Kentucky	34
Florida	396	Missouri	28
Texas	263	Delaware	18
Alabama	196	Indiana	13
Pennsylvania	180	Kansas	10
North Carolina	155	Nebraska	10
Ohio	143	Idaho	9
Arizona	125	Utah	9
Louisiana	81	Washington	9
Nevada	79	Virginia	7
Georgia	78	U.S. Military	6
Tennessee	71	Colorado	3
U.S. Government	62	South Dakota	3
Oklahoma	49	Montana	2
Mississippi	48	New Mexico	2
South Carolina	43	New Hampshire	1
Arkansas	36	Wyoming	1
Oregon	34		

Source: Death Penalty Information Center. Death Row Inmates by State. See (http://www.deathpenaltyinfo.org/documents/FactSheet.pdf).

Gate to Death Row at the Ellis
Unit in Huntsville

*© Per-Anders Pettersson/Getty
Images*

exoneration
The official absolution of a
false criminal conviction and
release from incarceration

death penalty since these sentences were handed
down, or have otherwise not carried out an execution in several years).

When a Texas jury concludes that a criminal
defendant murdered someone under especially hei-
nous circumstances, as defined by the Texas Penal
Code, that jury can condemn that defendant to death.
Such a crime is called capital murder. Proponents
of the death penalty argue that it deters crime (particularly murder), restores justice when a life has
been taken, provides retribution for society and the
victim's family, and costs less than imprisoning the
convicted person for life. Critics argue that the death
penalty does very little to deter future violent crime,
that it constitutes "cruel and unusual punishment,"
that governments have no moral right to deprive
someone of life, that death penalty cases cost more
to prosecute than life imprisonment, and that inno-
cent people may be put to death when the criminal justice system makes mistakes.

In Texas prior to 2005, a defendant convicted of capital murder could only be
sentenced to death or life imprisonment (which included the possibility of parole
after 40 years). However, in 2005, the legislature passed and then-governor Perry
signed SB 60, which provided juries a third option when assessing punishment
for a capital offense. Juries can now sentence a person to death, life in prison, or
life without parole.[124] This third option allows juries to permanently confine an
individual who might pose a "threat to the community" if released, while allowing them to avoid imposing a death sentence. This may be particularly relevant
to concerns about "irrevocable mistakes" within the system.[125] Reexamination
of older cases has cast doubt on some death penalty convictions, suggesting that
Texas has likely put innocent people to death. One particularly well-publicized
case was that of Cameron Todd Willingham, who was executed in 2004.[126] Since
1973, 13 inmates on Texas's death row have been **exonerated**.[127]

Texas, the Death Penalty, and the Harris County Factor

What factors contribute to the large number of death sentences in Texas, and in
Harris County (Houston) in particular? First, the statutes in Texas for assigning
a death sentence are among the least complicated in the nation. Following a trial
in which guilt is determined, the punishment phase of the trial begins. The jury
must answer two questions: (1) Did the defendant act intentionally; and (2) Is the
defendant a future threat to society? If a person commits murder while committing another crime (such as rape or robbery), kills more than one person, kills a
police officer, firefighter, or child, or is a murderer for hire—and committed any
of these crimes intentionally—that person can receive the death sentence. These
standards make it easy for juries to answer "yes" and render a death sentence.

Second, the Texas Court of Criminal Appeals (to which all death penalty
cases in Texas are appealed) rarely reverses a death sentence. Between 1995 and
2000, only 8 of 270 capital cases considered by this court were reversed or sent
back to lower courts.[128] In 2014, the Court of Criminal Appeals upheld 10 of the

12 death penalty cases brought before it.[129] Judge Sharon Keller has served as presiding justice of the court since 2000. During her election campaign, Judge Keller stated that failure to execute condemned murderers was a violation of human rights.[130] She garnered widespread criticism when, in September 2007, defense attorneys representing convicted murderer Michael Richard (who was scheduled to be executed that night) were attempting to file last-minute paperwork to stay their client's execution but were experiencing technical problems. The attorneys asked for additional time to file the paperwork but were told by Judge Keller: "We close at five." The attorneys missed the deadline, and Richard's execution proceeded hours later.[131]

Third, the U.S. Fifth Circuit Court of Appeals, a federal court that hears appeals from Texas, also rarely overturns cases. The purpose of appellate courts is to check on procedures and processes in lower courts and make sure no mistakes were made.

Finally, the Texas Board of Pardons and Paroles, often the final recourse for those with failed appeals, is even less likely to make sentencing changes when reviewing convictions. During fiscal year 2015, the board reviewed 29 capital cases and recommended clemency (commutation of sentence, pardon, or reprieve of execution) for none.[132] As Table 12.8 shows, even if the board makes a recommendation for clemency, the governor is unlikely to approve. During his first 11 years in office, former governor Perry commuted only 31 capital sentences, 28 of which were due solely to the U.S. Supreme Court's ban on capital punishment for minors.[133]

The governor of Texas has limited authority with respect to his or her powers of pardon, clemency, and parole. Although the governor can choose to grant a **reprieve** for an individual scheduled for execution—providing a 30-day temporary stay of execution—the Board of Pardons and Paroles decides which inmates will be granted parole and makes recommendations to the governor on matters respecting executive clemency. The governor, on the recommendation of the board, may grant a full **pardon** wherein the individual convicted of a crime receives no punishment. The board might also recommend the governor **commute** or reduce the sentence received.

In Texas, Harris County places more defendants on death row than any other. With a population of almost 4.5 million as of 2014, the county forms part of the greater metropolitan area of Houston, the fourth largest city in the nation. The county's huge

reprieve
The temporary 30-day stay of execution the governor may grant

pardon
Grants forgiveness by the state for a conviction and requires that the convicted receive no punishment; does not erase the criminal record

commute
The reduction in punishment for an individual convicted of a crime

TABLE 12.8

Clemency Actions by the Board of Pardons and Paroles, 2010–2015

Clemency Type	Cases Considered by the Board	Cases Recommended for Clemency	Cases Approved by the Governor
Commutations of Sentence	103	2	0
Reprieves of Execution	82	0	0
Conditional Pardons	2	0	0
Total Death Penalty Actions	187	0	0

Source: Texas Board of Pardons and Paroles. Annual Statistical Reports 2010–2015. http://www.tdcj.state.tx.us/bpp/publications/publications.html.

size alone, however, does not seem to explain the large number of people it sentences to death. In fact, Harris County has sentenced more people to death than all other large urban Texas counties combined. Between December 1982 and August 2016, Texas executed 537 individuals; of these, 126 came from Harris County. The next highest counties are Dallas (Dallas) with 55, Bexar (San Antonio) with 42, and Tarrant (Forth Worth) with 38. Below that, the number of executions per county decreases sharply: the next highest county is Nueces (Corpus Christi) with 16.[134]

One explanation for the large number of death sentences in Harris County has to do with financial resources. Death penalty cases are costly; smaller, rural counties often lack the money to prosecute them. Even large urban counties often find that death penalty cases strain their budgets. Harris County is an exception, however, because the annual budget for its district attorney's office in fiscal year 2016–2017 was over $77 million, and it has a staff of nearly 300 assistant district attorneys.[135] Dallas County, the jurisdiction with the next highest number of death penalty convictions, had a 2016 annual budget of about $44 million and roughly 240 assistant district attorneys.[136] Harris County also has a total of 16 criminal courts, whereas Dallas County has eleven.[137] Traditionally, many of the criminal court judges in Harris County are former prosecutors in the Harris County District Attorney's Office.

Concerns exist about the large number of death sentences handed down by Texas courts, including accessibility of legal representation for those accused of capital crimes, the appeals procedure, and prosecution-oriented courts. Nevertheless, a majority of Texans support the death penalty. In the most recent national poll conducted by Gallup, 61 percent of those surveyed approved of the death penalty for convicted murderers; in a 2012 survey specific to Texas, that figure was 73 percent.[138] Table 12.9 provides a breakdown of responses

TABLE 12.9

Public Opinion on the Death Penalty in Texas

Which of the following characterizes your opinion on the death penalty for those convicted of violent crimes?

Strongly support	42%
Somewhat support	31%
Somewhat oppose	11%
Strongly oppose	10%
Don't know	5%

Generally speaking, do you believe the death penalty is applied fairly or unfairly in Texas today?

Fairly	51%
Unfairly	28%
Don't know	21%

If you could choose between the following two approaches, which do you think is the better penalty for murder?

The death penalty	53%
Life imprisonment with absolutely no possibility for parole	37%
Don't know	10%

Source: University of Texas/Texas Tribune Texas Statewide Survey (May 2012) https://texaspolitics. utexas.edu/sites/texaspolitics.utexas.edu/files/201205-summary.pdf.

by Texans polled about the death penalty. Texans favor the death penalty more strongly than the nation as a whole and view the death penalty as a deterrent to crime. Also, Texans indicate they feel safer because of the death penalty.

Whether or not the death penalty is effective in deterring crime is controversial. A fairly recent study by sociologist Kenneth Land and colleagues, which focused on Texas and claimed a small reduction in the number of homicides after executions, set off intense debate.[139] However, this and other studies of the death penalty's deterrent effect have been criticized as seriously flawed (and therefore inconclusive).[140] A 2008 survey of criminologists indicated that 88 percent "[do] not believe that the death penalty is a deterrent" when they were asked to consider their knowledge of the empirical research.[141] One argument against the deterrent value is the long time span between sentencing and execution. In Texas, the average time from sentencing to execution is 10.87 years. David Lee Powell spent the longest amount of time on Texas's death row— 31 years—before being executed in 2010.[142] Therefore, the consequences of homicidal behavior are not immediately apparent to the general public.

Poverty and Access to Legal Services

Some basic statistics illustrate the impact of economic status on the ability to obtain legal representation or participate effectively in the legal system. In 2015, according to the U.S. Census Bureau, 27,469,114 people lived in Texas. Of these, 17.2 percent were estimated to be living below the federally defined poverty threshold.[143] As of 2015, the federal poverty threshold for a single individual under the age of 65 was $12,331; for two people, this figure increased to $15,871.[144] For such individuals, legal and attorneys' fees can represent a significant percentage of annual income.

Anyone, from an infant to an elderly person, may require some form of legal services. For example, issues requiring legal representation may arise from the quality of care given to an infant or health issues related to an elderly person. Moreover, Texans below the poverty line are not the only ones who cannot afford an attorney. Legal aid services for the poor often use 125 percent of the federal poverty threshold as their guideline for free legal services, for example. This means that millions of Texans living below or near the federal poverty threshold have difficulty paying for legal services.

Texas addresses these citizens' need for legal representation with a patchwork of public and private resources at the state and local levels. Through the Interest on Lawyers Trust Accounts (IOLTA) program, money generated from interest-bearing accounts (held by attorneys for their clients) is diverted to provide legal aid for the poor.[145] Free or reduced-fee legal representation is referred to as *pro bono,* short for *pro bono publico,* or "for the public good." Private law firms sometimes require their attorneys to devote a percentage of their time to *pro bono* work, often coordinated through the State Bar of Texas's Legal Access Division or its Care Campaign.[146] University legal clinics and nonprofit organizations provide representation to a small number of indigent clients on a wide range of civil and criminal matters, such as immigration, environmental protection, family and domestic abuse matters, criminal defense, and death penalty defense.[147] The State Bar and local bar associations offer referral services to attorneys who may work for reduced rates if a client is poor.[148] Courts can appoint defense counsel in criminal cases. In 1995, the Texas legislature passed a law requiring that indigent condemned men and women be provided tax-paid attorneys for automatic *habeas corpus* appeals.

The Texas Access to Justice Commission is a state agency that funds indigent legal services for thousands of clients—primarily for problems related to marriage, child custody, domestic abuse, and other issues. This agency, which is supported by the state legislature and its own fundraising efforts, makes grants to fund legal assistance and recruits lawyers to work *pro bono*.[149] Whether in civil or criminal matters, Texas provides little assistance to indigent citizens for their legal needs. The state has relatively low indigent criminal defense spending when compared to other states. In 2012, the top five spending states reported over $100 million each, whereas Texas spent only $27 million.[150] The Texas Indigent Defense Commission reports that Texas spent $28.7 million in 2015.[151] The result is that tens of thousands of low-income Texans likely represent themselves *pro se*—without an attorney—in legal matters that will have an impact on the rest of their lives.[152]

Problems and Reform: Implications for Public Policy

Learning Objective: Describe the challenges the state of Texas faces in its criminal justice system.

Throughout its history, Texas has earned a reputation as a "tough on crime" state, but systems—even those as large as the Texas criminal justice system—can change. Supreme Court rulings, shifting public attitudes, and shrinking budgets are all factors that drive policy changes in states, and Texas is no exception. In an effort to rein in the size of the state's criminal justice system, the Texas legislature has instituted a number of reforms, ranging from the use of specialty courts to channel nonviolent offenders into treatment programs rather than jail, to shutting down prisons, to overhauling the entire juvenile justice system.[153] In general, these policy prescriptions have changed the focus from punishment to rehabilitation.

Despite the successes of recent years, there is still room for improvement. This section details several problem areas where reformers are focusing their attention on both the federal and state levels.

Overcriminalization

Overcriminalization is the notion that laws defining criminal behavior have proliferated to include "vast areas of [nonviolent] conduct," and as such, represent an overreach of criminal justice power.[154] According to one source, there are over 4,000 federal criminal laws, an additional 300,000 federal regulatory offenses, and more than 1,700 state crimes with which Texans can be charged. In addition, in many cases, it is no longer required that the accused have intent or prior knowledge of doing anything wrong (a legal concept called *mens rea*) in order to be convicted of a crime.[155] This phenomenon led attorney Harvey Silverglate to write that the average American commits three felonies in the course of a normal day, without even knowing he or she has done so.[156]

Sentencing Reform

A number of harsh sentencing practices, including mandatory minimum sentences and enhanced punishment for repeat offenses, grew out of efforts to get "tough on crime" during the 1980s and 1990s. Many have argued that such sentences can be disproportionate to the crimes committed and have generated numerous unintended negative consequences (such as growth of the prison population and destruction of families).[157] In the case of Weldon Angelos (discussed previously), the federal judge who imposed the sentence called it "utterly unjust" and wrote to President Obama, asking for a reduction of Angelos's sentence.[158] The Fair Sentencing Act (FSA), passed by the U.S. Congress in 2010, was part of reform efforts in this area. Among other things, the FSA "eliminated the mandatory minimum sentence for simple possession of crack cocaine."[159] Previously, the minimum sentence for this crime was five years for first-time offenders.

Police Militarization

Police militarization refers to the trend for police departments to increasingly use military vehicles, weapons, and gear as well as military tactics (such as violent no-knock raids) in performing their regular duties. This trend has been exacerbated by federal programs that allow state and local law enforcement agencies to obtain surplus military equipment.[160] Proponents argue that such programs, equipment, and tactics provide greater safety for law enforcement officers and allow equipment that might otherwise go unused to be repurposed. Critics of this trend argue that it can lead to feelings of insecurity and a hazardous escalation of violence in communities and contributes to a mindset among police officers that they are "at war" with an enemy, rather than serving and protecting normal citizens.[161]

Civil Asset Forfeiture

According to the ACLU, civil asset forfeiture "allows police to seize—and then keep or sell—any property they allege is involved in a crime."[162] When this mechanism is invoked, the government takes property belonging to an individual citizen or business without benefit of a trial or due process. Initially, law enforcement engaged in this practice to deprive criminal enterprises (such as drug traffickers) of resources, but the practice has since been abused by law enforcement agencies, some of which have allegedly used seized property as a means of funding their own departments' operations.[163]

Mental Illness in Prison

In the latter twentieth century, deinstitutionalization (the movement of mentally ill individuals out of large, state-run psychiatric hospitals), as well as reduced federal and state funding for mental health programs, led to increased numbers of the severely mentally ill living within communities. Evidence suggests that significant numbers of the mentally ill population have since been incarcerated in prisons and jails. This thesis has been called "progressive transinstitutionalism."[164] In 2006, the U.S. Bureau of Justice Statistics issued a special report estimating that, at that time, federal and state prisons and local jails were housing more than 1.2 million mentally ill individuals (94 percent of whom were in state and local jails).[165] This situation led investigative journalist Mary Beth Pfeiffer to call prisons "the de facto custodians of people with mental illness."[166]

The mentally ill come into contact with law enforcement for a number of reasons, ranging from major crimes to petty violations such as vagrancy, panhandling, or other unacceptable behaviors in public. According to a 2007 report, approximately 30 percent of inmates in Texas correctional facilities had previously received mental health care from the state.[167] Moreover, inmates with mental illness have higher rates of recidivism. Many argue that these cases are dealt with more appropriately and effectively by medical and mental health professionals, rather than by incarceration, not to mention the potential for decreased costs. The amount of money spent on corrections **intake** alone for mentally ill detainees has been estimated at $138.7 million annually for six of the state's largest counties.[168]

Thus far, the state has experimented with pretrial diversion programs, which divert the mentally ill to community-based mental health services that not only better serve these individuals' needs but also are more cost-effective. A small number of Texas's specialty courts have been designated as mental health courts.[169] Houston mayor Sylvester Turner quoted a Legislative Budget Board estimate that community mental health services cost about $12 a day per patient, as opposed to $137 a day for incarceration.[170] During the 2013 legislative session, Harris County received $5 million in annual funding to pilot a "jail diversion" program.[171] As of March 2016, the program had diverted over 750 people from the criminal justice system, saving an estimated $3 million a year for Harris County taxpayers.[172] For many years, Bexar County has had its own jail diversion program, which serves as a model for other, similar programs. Since its inception, it has served thousands of mentally ill individuals, diverting them from jail to treatment, and has saved Bexar County millions of dollars.[173]

Some would argue that, in order to fully address this problem, the state needs to spend more on mental health in general. For fiscal year 2013, average per capita spending on mental health care nationwide was $131, but Texas's per capita spending was $40.65, ranking it 48th in the nation.[174] If the thesis of progressive transinstitutionalism is valid, the state's cost savings on mental health care may have merely shifted to the criminal justice system.

Fine and Fee Practices

Many people are detained in local jails simply because they cannot pay the fines and costs associated with misdemeanor offenses (such as traffic tickets). Although it is against state law for people to be jailed for inability to pay fines, evidence suggests this occurs nonetheless. Under Texas law, judges are required to perform a poverty assessment to determine a defendant's financial situation. If the defendant is indigent, the judge may offer a payment plan or, in lieu of fines, impose community service.[175] The judicial system garnered negative publicity in 2015 when an investigative report claimed that 9 out of 20 Texas courts had no record of having conducted poverty hearings. In addition, in 100 cases where defendants had been jailed for five days or more, no poverty hearings were documented by the El Paso municipal court.[176]

A related issue is bail and pretrial release. According to the Texas Commission on Jail Standards, in 2016, 63 percent of inmates in county jails were awaiting trial and had not been convicted.[177] Many are detained because they cannot

---

intake

The procedures involved with the arrest and detention of an individual before a bail hearing

make the bail payment necessary to be released from custody until their trial. The Conference of Chief Justices found that

> . . . defendants who are detained can suffer job loss, home loss, and disintegrated social relationships, and, according to the Bureau of Justice Assistance, "receive more severe sentences, are offered less attractive plea bargains and are more likely to become 'reentry' clients because of their pretrial detention regardless of charge or criminal history."[178]

Supporters of reforms argue that excessive bail and pretrial confinement conflict with the judicial principle of "innocent until proven guilty," not to mention the high cost to taxpayers. Pretrial confinement costs an estimated $63 per day per inmate.[179] Both the legislative and judicial branches are studying this issue. State Senator John Whitmire, head of the Senate's Criminal Justice Committee, said that pretrial release would be his "highest priority" during the 2017 legislative session.[180]

Suicide

From 2000 to 2013, the leading cause of death in local jails was suicide, which accounted for 34 percent of inmate deaths nationwide.[181] In Texas, 27 percent of inmates who died in jail over a 10-year period committed suicide. In contrast, only about 6 percent of state prison deaths during the same period were attributed to suicide.[182] Data from the 4-year period from 2005 to 2009 yielded similar statistics.

Experts propose that the primary reason the suicide rate is higher in jails is the initial "shock of confinement" that detainees experience; they recommend that the best practice to reduce suicide rates would be an initial interview with medical personnel during the intake process.[183] The Texas Commission on Jail Standards amended its rules on admission such that "'health tags' which may identify the inmate as having special medical or mental health needs shall be noted in the inmate's medical record and brought to the attention of health personnel and/or the supervisor on duty."[184] The Texas Commission on Jail Standards maintains a list of noncompliant jails on its website. As of August 2016, two counties were cited for noncompliance related to "health tagging" and monitoring of detainees with potential mental health issues.[185]

A highly publicized suicide in a Texas county jail was that of Sandra Bland in 2015. In July 2015, Bland, a 28-year-old African American female, was pulled over by DPS officer Brian Encinia for failing to signal a lane change. The traffic stop quickly turned into an altercation wherein Bland was thrown to the ground and arrested. Three days after her arrest, Bland was found hanging in her cell in the Waller County jail. Her death was ruled a suicide. The Commission on Jail Standards inspected the Waller County jail and found deficiencies in its procedures. As of September 2016, trooper Encinia had been fired and charged with perjury related to Bland's arrest, and the family of Sandra Bland had negotiated a $1.9 million settlement (pending court approval) in a wrongful death suit

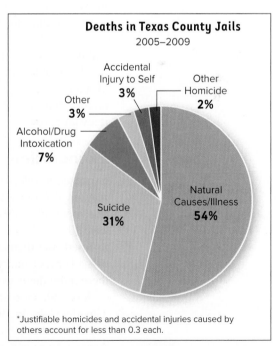

Deaths in Texas County Jails
2005–2009

Accidental Injury to Self **3%**
Other **Homicide 2%**
Other **3%**
Alcohol/Drug Intoxication **7%**
Natural Causes/Illness **54%**
Suicide **31%**

*Justifiable homicides and accidental injuries caused by others account for less than 0.3 each.

Deaths in Texas County Jails, 2005–2009

SOURCE: Daniel Dillon, "A Portrait of Suicides in Texas Jails: Who is at Risk and How Do We Stop It?" *LBJ Journal of Public Affairs* (Fall 2013), 51.

against the county and DPS. Although Waller County did not admit responsibility for Bland's death, terms of the settlement included changes the county agreed to make to its jail practices.[186]

Technology and Crime

American fascination with crime dramas has generated a spate of television programs that stretch the boundaries of belief when compared to the actual processes associated with investigating and prosecuting offenses. In the space of one hour, detectives are able to solve a murder, the district attorney prosecutes, and the case is resolved. In actuality, the investigation and prosecution of a crime, particularly a serious violent crime, can take months or even years. After the initial evidence is gathered, crime labs analyze it. The science and technology associated with doing so evolves quite rapidly.

The Texas Forensic Science Commission—composed of nine members appointed by the governor, seven of whom are scientists—was created in 2005 and ensures the integrity of lab results used in criminal trials. It is responsible for investigating charges of professional negligence or misconduct with regard to forensic analysis. It also accredits crime labs in Texas and establishes the policies and procedures under which crime labs operate.[187] This agency, in collaboration with the FBI Crime Lab, brings together regional state labs for discussion and training to ensure that the most up-to-date scientific knowledge drives the investigation and analysis of evidence. For example, in August 2015, the Texas Forensic Science Commission (TFSC) notified the Texas criminal justice community of concerns about a protocol for interpreting mixed DNA evidence and the fact that forensic errors could impact current and past cases.[188] In response to changes in technology or specific complaints, the TFSC may reexamine cases already decided based on outdated methods of analysis. If a review of the case "identifies potential issues with the laboratory report and/or expert testimony rendered at trial," the TFSC notifies relevant parties.[189]

Exoneration

Exoneration refers to the official absolution of a false criminal conviction and may involve release from prison or jail. Nationwide, there were 1,863 exonerations between 1989 and 2016, with 281 of these in Texas (more than in any other state). In 2015, Texas had the most exonerations of any state, with 54 inmates released after their cases were reopened (many by the Conviction Review Section of the Harris County District Attorney's Office), and review of the case revealed these individuals were wrongly convicted.[190]

A notable case of wrongful conviction and posthumous exoneration is that of Timothy Cole. In 1985, a female student at Texas Tech was abducted and raped. In photo and in-person lineups, the victim identified Timothy Cole, a 24-year-old African American male who was also a student at Tech, as her attacker. She testified against him in court, and even after several of Cole's friends testified that he was at home studying at the time of the rape, he was convicted and received a 25-year sentence. In 1995, Jerry Wayne Johnson, who was serving a life plus 99-year sentence for two rapes, wrote to judges, the Lubbock County prosecutor, and Cole's lawyer claiming that he had in fact committed the rape for which

Cole was serving time. No action was taken based on Johnson's letters. In 1999, Cole died in prison of an asthma attack. In 2000, another letter of confession written by Johnson was dismissed. In 2008, the Innocence Project obtained DNA proving that Johnson committed the rape. Cole was officially exonerated in 2009, and a posthumous pardon was signed by then-governor Perry the next year. The Texas legislature enacted the Timothy Cole Act, which provides $80,000 in compensation to a wrongfully incarcerated individual for each year served; Cole's family received more than $1 million.[191]

Inmate Jerry Wayne Johnson (center) stands next to a picture of Timothy Cole at the hearing conducted to clear Cole's name.

© Harry Cabluck/AP Image

Race, Gender, and the Criminal Justice System

Women are underrepresented in the criminal justice system relative to their percentage of the total state population. According to 2014 data from the TDCJ, women made up only 8.1 percent of the state's prison population, despite the fact that they make up about half of the Texas population overall.[192] Statistics show that women commit crime at a lower rate than men. In Texas, fewer women than men were arrested for index crimes in 2014 (207,250 versus 611,904).[193]

Nationally, racial and ethnic minorities make up a disproportionate percentage of prison and jail populations compared to their numbers in the total population.[194] This is also true in Texas. For fiscal year 2014, TDCJ reported that the state prison population was 31.7 percent white, 34.7 percent African American, and 33.1 percent Hispanic (whereas their proportions in the state population were 43.5 percent white, 12.5 percent African American, and 38.6 percent Hispanic).[195] As noted previously, these racial disparities are also present at the juvenile level, as 82 percent of TJJD detainees in 2013 were members of ethnic minority groups.[196]

Data suggest that minorities, and particularly African Americans, are overrepresented in crime statistics compared to their proportion of the population. For instance, according to Texas's Uniform Crime Report for 2014, African Americans made up 25 percent of all individuals arrested for tracked crimes (twice their percentage of the population), and 36 percent of those arrested for the same crimes were of Hispanic ethnicity.[197] Multiple theories have been put forth to explain the overrepresentation of African Americans in the criminal justice system. Some have argued that African Americans are arrested, convicted, and imprisoned at higher rates due to discrimination and bias throughout the criminal justice system (including policing and the courts).[198] A 2016 Harvard Law School study of counties with a high output of death penalty sentences (which included Harris County, Texas) laid the blame not only on "overzealous prosecutors" and "inadequate defense" but also on racial bias. The study noted that "all 18 men who have been newly sentenced to death in Harris County since November 2004 have been people of color."[199]

Concerns about racial bias in the criminal justice system have been fueled by numerous incidents. In 1999, 39 African Americans—roughly 10 percent of the town's African American population—were arrested in Tulia, Texas, a predominantly white community. Thirty-eight of those arrested were convicted of cocaine distribution based on the testimony of one white officer working undercover. However, there were no records, written or otherwise, no evidence, and no other witnesses to substantiate any of the charges. Detective Tom Coleman, who was accused of racial prejudice, was found to have "submitted false reports, misrepresented his investigative work, and misidentified various defendants during his investigation." Ultimately, then-governor Perry granted pardons to 35 of the convicted and a $5.9 million settlement was paid. Coleman was later convicted on perjury charges; the district attorney who prosecuted the Tulia cases lost his bid for re-election and was subsequently disciplined by the Texas Bar Association. The expense associated with the trials was estimated to have increased county residents' property taxes by about six percent.[200]

Racial tensions have also been evident in the national conversation about police use of deadly force. The 2014 police shooting of Michael Brown in Ferguson, Missouri, along with the accompanying protests and publicity surrounding that incident, focused national attention on this issue. The following year, in 2015, 986 people in the United States were shot and killed by police. The killing of African Americans, in particular, by law enforcement officers generated an immense public outcry and sparked numerous protests.[201] During the summer of 2016, the debate about race as a factor in policing practices again reached a boiling point. The first week of July 2016 marked a particularly violent series of racially charged events. Two African American men—Alton Sterling in Baton Rouge, Louisiana, and Philando Castile in St. Paul, Minnesota—were killed by police within a matter of days. The movement "Black Lives Matter" and other groups organized protests across the country, one of which took place in Dallas. During that protest, five Dallas police officers were killed by a sniper, who was later killed by police. According to Dallas police chief David Brown, the sniper "was upset about the recent police shootings" and "wanted to kill white people, especially white officers."[202] As the Dallas shootings punctuated an exceptionally violent week, they also served as a catalyst for reflection on how minorities, and more specifically African Americans, experience encounters with police officers, as well as on the relationship that law enforcement and the larger criminal justice system have with the communities they serve.

Misconduct in the Justice System

District attorneys serve the state and the people. They bring charges, present evidence, and argue for the conviction of individuals charged with crimes. As prosecutor, they present the state's case to a jury and coordinate with the defense to ensure that the accused receives a fair trial. The Texas Code of Criminal Procedure states that the primary duty of a district attorney is ". . . not to convict, but to see that justice is done." Further, Article 2.01 mandates that prosecuting attorneys ". . . shall not suppress facts or secrete witnesses capable of establishing the innocence of the accused."[203] Unfortunately, instances of misconduct do occur. When prosecutors fail to follow procedure, it is referred to as misconduct. Misconduct can involve many types of wrongdoing, including intentionally denying or hiding evidence from the defense, encouraging witnesses to lie under oath, or using their office to intimidate witnesses for the defense.

One especially prominent and egregious case of prosecutorial misconduct involved Michael Morton, who in 1987 was convicted of murdering his wife and sentenced to life in prison. It was later determined that exculpatory evidence, including a bloody bandana discovered about 100 yards from Morton's house, was withheld from the defense. In 2011, partly due to efforts by the Innocence Project, DNA testing conducted on the bandana proved that another individual (who, in the intervening time had been convicted of a similar murder) had been present at the crime scene.

Michael Morton (center) and his legal team hold a press conference after it was determined that the attorney who prosecuted him withheld evidence.

© Austin American-Statesman, Rodolfo Gonzalez/AP Images

Morton was released and exonerated in 2011 after serving almost 25 years. The district attorney responsible for prosecuting the case was subsequently charged with ethical violations, gave up his licence to practice law, and served ten days in jail.[204] This case caused such uproar that the 2013 legislature passed SB 1611, the "Michael Morton Act," which requires that all evidence pertaining to a criminal case, whether or not it is perceived as relevant to guilt or punishment, is disclosed to the defense.[205]

Though sensational when it is uncovered, prosecutorial misconduct is uncommon. The Texas District and County Attorneys Association, after analyzing 91 suspected cases of misconduct, found only 6 cases of "actual prosecutorial misconduct" during a four-year period, representing less than one percent of all trials in Texas during period studied.[206]

Misconduct can be committed, and errors introduced into cases, by other parties in the legal system. For instance, Houston's crime lab was shut down in 2002 after allegations of lapses in protocols, evidence fabrication and tampering, and faulty DNA testing. In 2007, a final report on the lab's work on over 3,500 cases resulted in the release of four individuals who had been convicted based upon the lab's testimony or testing.[207] The Houston lab experienced a similar scandal in 2013. An analyst who committed misconduct had examined evidence in more than 5,000 cases for 36 counties in Texas. Although thousands of drug convictions were thought to be in jeopardy because of this individual's involvement, the court later established guidelines whereby such evidence could be reconsidered in a retrial.[208]

CORE OBJECTIVE

Thinking Critically . . .

Given the current challenges faced by the criminal justice system, what types of reforms would you recommend? What might be some of the negative or unintended consequences of your recommendations?

© National Park Service

Conclusion

Historically, Texas's criminal justice system has reflected the political culture of the state. In a traditionalistic political culture, citizens expect government to maintain order and the status quo; as a result, there may be a heavy emphasis on punishment and incarceration for those who break the law. In recent years, however, Texas has relied less on incarceration and more on alternatives to imprisonment. This shift in approach from punishment toward rehabilitation has yielded initial success in the form of reduced recidivism, cost savings, and a smaller prison population (not to mention a lower crime rate). Other potential areas of reform still persist.

Summary

LO: Understand the differences between criminal and civil law and explain criminal justice policy in Texas.

Criminal law involves violations of the Texas Penal Code, a system of state laws dealing with conduct that causes or threatens harm to individual or state-protected public interests. Civil law has to do with private relationships (rather than violations of the penal code) and can address financial matters, including wrongs committed by individuals or businesses against others. In criminal law, the standard of proof is higher ("beyond a reasonable doubt") than for civil cases (which require only a "preponderance of evidence"). Historically, Texas has had a "tough on crime" approach to criminal justice policy, primarily focused on punishment through incarceration. More recently, however, it has been the site of some fairly significant reform efforts.

LO: Describe the state of Texas's juvenile justice system and its procedures.

The Texas Juvenile Justice Department is the agency responsible for coordinating and overseeing juvenile justice programs in the state. This system has been overhauled to reflect a focus on rehabilitation as an alternative to incarceration. Juvenile cases are handled locally whenever possible, with county courts and local probation departments shouldering the bulk of the responsibility for them. A distinguishing feature of juvenile cases is that a hearing must take place to determine whether or not the juvenile will be tried as an adult.

LO: Explain the state of Texas's correction system, including its approach to rehabilitation and use of the death penalty.

The Texas Department of Criminal Justice (TDCJ) is a vast organization responsible for the detention and supervision of adult inmates, parolees, and individuals on community supervision (parole). It operates state prisons, state jails, and other facilities in addition to overseeing the operation of private prisons within the state. (Although they are not part of the state correctional system, local jails also detain prisoners.) Recently, Texas has attempted to curb its growing prison population and reduce recidivism by focusing on rehabilitation and alternatives to incarceration. Texas is still tough on crime in its use of the death penalty. It leads all other states in the number of death sentences imposed and number of executions carried out.

LO: Describe the challenges the state of Texas faces in its criminal justice system.

Despite the success of recent reform efforts, Texas continues to face challenges with regard to its criminal justice system. Some areas of continued concern include overcriminalization, excessive sentencing, police militarization, civil asset forfeiture, mental illness and suicide among the incarcerated, fine and fee practices, technological advances in evidence analysis, exoneration, race, and professional misconduct.

Key Terms

burden of proof	exonerated	pardon
civil law	felony	parens patriae
commute	graded penalties	recidivism
criminal law	in loco parentis	reprieve
enhanced punishment	intake	Texas Code of Criminal Procedure
exculpatory evidence	misdemeanors	Texas Penal Code

Notes

1 Danielle Kaeble, Lauren Glaze, Anastasios Tsoutis, and Todd Minton, "Correctional Populations in the United States, 2014," Bureau of Justice Statistics, rev. January 21, 2016, http://www.bjs.gov/content/pub/pdf/cpus14.pdf.

2 Bureau of Justice Statistics, Terms & Definitions: Law Enforcement, http://www.bjs.gov/index.cfm?ty=tdtp&tid=7.

3 Brian A. Reaves, "Census of State and Local Law Enforcement Agencies, 2008," Bureau of Justice Statistics, July 2011, http://www.bjs.gov/content/pub/pdf/csllea08.pdf; Bureau of Justice Statistics, Terms & Definitions: Law Enforcement, http://www.bjs.gov/index.cfm?ty=tdtp&tid=7.

4 Brian A. Reaves, "Census of State and Local Law Enforcement Agencies, 2008," Bureau of Justice Statistics, July 2011, http://www.bjs.gov/content/pub/pdf/csllea08.pdf.

5 Texas Department of Public Safety, http://www.dps.texas.gov/about.htm.

6 Texas Department of Public Safety, Texas Rangers, http://www.dps.texas.gov/TexasRangers/.

7 Texas Constitution, art. 5, sec. 23, http://www.statutes.legis.state.tx.us/Docs/CN/htm/CN.5.htm; Texas Local Government Code Sec. 85.003-85.005, http://www.statutes.legis.state.tx.us/Docs/LG/htm/LG.85.htm.

8 Brian A. Reaves, "Census of State and Local Law Enforcement Agencies, 2008," Bureau of Justice Statistics, July 2011, http://www.bjs.gov/content/pub/pdf/csllea08.pdf; Texas Association of Counties, "Sheriff ," https://county.org/texas-county-government/texas-county-officials/Pages/Sheriff.aspx.

9 William B. Travis, "Message from Sheriff Travis," Denton County, TX, http://dentoncounty.com/Departments/Sheriff/Message-from-Sheriff-Travis.aspx; Comal County Sheriff's Office, Frequently Asked Questions, http://www.co.comal.tx.us/so/Questions.html.

10 Brian A. Reaves, "Census of State and Local Law Enforcement Agencies, 2008," Bureau of Justice Statistics, July 2011, http://www.bjs.gov/content/pub/pdf/csllea08.pdf.

11 Texas Local Government Code Sec. 341.001, http://www.statutes.legis.state.tx.us/Docs/LG/htm/LG.341.htm.

12 Brian A. Reaves, "Census of State and Local Law Enforcement Agencies, 2008," Bureau of Justice Statistics, July 2011, http://www.bjs.gov/content/pub/pdf/csllea08.pdf.

13 United States Courts, Criminal Cases, http://www.uscourts.gov/about-federal-courts/types-cases/criminal-cases.

14 Texas Penal Code, Sec. 1.02.

15 *Rose Ann Davidson v. State of Texas,* No. 03-13-00708-CR (Tex. App.—Austin 2014, n.p.h.) (no pub; 8-1-14); Texas Penal Code Sec. 49.04, http://www.statutes.legis.state.tx.us/Docs/PE/htm/PE.49.htm#49.04.

16 *Rummel v. Estelle,* 445 U.S. 263 (1980).

17 Texas Penal Code, Sections 12.42-12.46, http://www.statutes.legis.state.tx.us/docs/PE/htm/PE.12.htm.

18 Families Against Mandatory Minimums, Primer, http://www.prisonpolicy.org/scans/famm/Primer.pdf.

19 National Organization for the Reform of Marijuana Laws (NORML), Texas Laws & Penalties, http://norml.org/laws/item/texas-penalties-2#mandatory.

20 Derek M. Cohen, Texas' Mandatory Sentencing Enhancements, Texas Public Policy Foundation (June 2016), http://www.texaspolicy.com/library/doclib/Texas-Mandatory-Sentencing-Enhancements.pdf.

21 Byron Pitts, Jackie Jesko, and Lauren Effron, "Former Federal Judge Regrets 55-Year Marijuana Sentence," ABC News, February 18, 2015, http://abcnews.go.com/US/federal-judge-regrets-55-year-marijuana-sentence/story?id=28869467.

22 Texas Department of Public Safety, Crime in Texas 2014, Chapter 2, Texas Crime Analysis, http://dps.texas.gov/administration/crime_records/pages/crimestatistics.htm.

23 Federal Bureau of Investigation Uniform Crime Reporting Program, "Frequently Asked Questions about the Change in the UCR Definition of Rape." December 11, 2014, https://www.fbi.gov/about-us/cjis/ucr/recent-program-updates/new-rape-definition-frequently-asked-questions.

24 Texas Department of Public Safety, Crime in Texas 2014, Chapter 2, Texas Crime Analysis, accessed July 26, 2016, http://dps.texas.gov/administration/crime_records/pages/crimestatistics.htm.

25 United States Courts, Civil Cases, http://www.uscourts.gov/about-federal-courts/types-cases/civil-cases.

26 See Legal Dictionary, "Civil Law," http://legaldictionary.net/civil-law/.

27 Harris County Justice of the Peace Courts, Information about Justice Court Cases, http://www.jp.hctx.net/evictions/filing.htm.

28 Office of Court Administration, Annual Statistical Report for the Texas Judiciary: Fiscal Year 2015, accessed May 24, 2015, http://www.txcourts.gov/media/1308021/2015-ar-statistical-print.pdf.

29 *Brady v. Maryland,* 373 U.S. 83 (1963).

30 Texas Judicial Branch, Interpretation & Translation, http://www.txcourts.gov/lap/.

31 United States Courts, Facts and Case Summary— *Miranda v. Arizona,* http://www.uscourts.gov/educational-resources/educational-activities/facts-and-case-summary-miranda-v-arizona.

32 *Bernabe v. Texas,* No. 03-10-00773-CR (2012), https://cases.justia.com/texas/third-court-of-appeals/03-10-00773-cr.pdf.

33 Richard Rogers, Amor A. Correa, Lisa L. Hazelwood, Daniel W. Shuman, Raquel C. Hoersting, Hayley L. Blackwood, "Spanish Translations of Miranda Warnings and the Totality of the Circumstances," *Law and Human Behavior 33*(1), (February 2009) p. 61–69; Shaun Rabb, "Lawyers want universal Spanish translation for Miranda Rights," Fox4News.com, August 12, 2016, http://www.fox4news.com/news/189600908-story.

34 Texas Government Code, Sec. 57.002, http://www.statutes.legis.state.tx.us/Docs/GV/htm/GV.57.htm; Texas Code of Criminal Procedure, Art. 38.30, http://www.statutes.legis.state.tx.us/Docs/CR/htm/CR.38.htm#38.30.

35 Texas Government Code, Sec. 57.001, http://www.statutes.legis.state.tx.us/Docs/GV/htm/GV.57.htm; Texas Rules of Evidence, Rule 604 (April 1, 2015), http://www.txcourts.gov/media/921665/tx-rules-of-evidence.pdf.

36 E. Ann Carson, "Prisoners in 2014," U.S. Department of Justice Bureau of Justice Statistics (September 2015), http://www.bjs.gov/content/pub/pdf/p14.pdf.

37 Federal Bureau of Investigation, 2014 Crime in the United States, Table 5, Crime in the United States by State, 2014, https://ucr.fbi.gov/crime-in-the-u.s/2014/crime-in-the-u.s.-2014/tables/table-5.

38 Calculations based on methodology of William P. Ruger and Jason Sorens, *Freedom in the 50 States: An Index of Personal and Economic Freedom* 4th ed. (Washington, D.C.: Cato Institute), 2016.

39 William P. Ruger and Jason Sorens, *Freedom in the 50 States: An Index of Personal and Economic Freedom* 4th ed. (Washington, D.C.: Cato Institute), 2016.

40 Editorial Board, "Texas Leads the Way in Needed Criminal Justice Reforms," *Washington Post,* January 28, 2014, http://www.washingtonpost.com/opinions/texas-leads-the-way-in-needed-criminal-justice-reforms/2014/01/28/83919b72-879d-11e3-916e-e01534b1e132_story.html; Office of the Governor Rick Perry, "Drug Courts," https://web.archive.org/web/20140518192648/http://governor.state.tx.us/priorities/security/public_safety/drug_courts/; Olivia Nuzzi, "Prison Reform Is Bigger in Texas," *The Daily Beast,* April 12, 2014, http://www.thedailybeast.com/articles/2014/04/12/prison-reform-is-bigger-in-texas.html.

41 Bill Hammond, "Why Texas Businesses Back Reforming the State's Criminal Justice System," *Dallas Morning News,* January 19, 2014, http://www.dallasnews.com/opinion/latest-columns/20140119-why-texas-businesses-back-reforming-the-states-criminal-justice-system.ece.

42 U.S. Census Bureau, QuickFacts, Texas, http://www.census.gov/quickfacts/table/PST045215/48.

43 Texas Family Code section 51.041(a).

44 See, for example, definition of "in loco parentis" in the Free Legal Dictionary, http://legal-dictionary.thefreelegaldictionary.com/in+loco+parentis.com.

45 See, for example, definition of "parens patriae" in the Free Legal Dictionary, http://legal-dictionary.thefreelegaldictionary.com/prens+patriae.com.

46 See, for example, definition of the police power doctrine in the Free Legal Dictionary, http://legal-dictionary.thefreelegaldictionary.com/Police+powers.com.

47 William T. Field, "Mountain View School For Boys," *Handbook of Texas Online,* http://www.tshaonline.org/handbook/online/articles/jjm01.

48 University of Texas Tarlton Law Library, The William Wayne Justice Papers, Juvenile Incarceration: *Morales v. Turman,* http://tarlton.law.utexas.edu/william-wayne-justice/morales-v-turman; William S. Bush, *Who Gets a Childhood?: Race and Juvenile Justice in Twentieth-Century Texas.* Athens, GA: University of Georgia Press, 2010.

49 *Morales v. Turman,* 383 F.Supp. 53 (1974) Available at https://tarltonapps.law.utexas.edu/exhibits/ww_justice/documents_3/Morales_opinion_3_1974.pdf.

50 Ibid.

51 Ibid., 374.

52 Laurie E. Jasinski, "Texas Youth Commission," *Handbook of Texas Online,* http://www.tshaonline.org/handbook/online/articles/mdt35.

53 Texas Legislature Online, History, SB653, http://www.legis.state.tx.us/billlookup/History.aspx?LegSess=82R&Bill=SB653.

54 Texas Juvenile Justice Department, TJJD Board Members, http://www.tjjd.texas.gov/aboutus/board_members.aspx.

55 Texas Family Code, Chapter 51, http://www.statutes.legis.state.tx.us/Docs/FA/htm/FA.51.htm.

56 Harris County District Courts, http://www.justex.net/courts/Juvenile/JuvenileCourts.aspx; Dallas County Court System, http://www.dallascounty.org/department/courts/juvenile.php.

57 Texas Juvenile Justice Department, Texas Juvenile Probation Departments, http://www.tjjd.texas.gov/publications/other/alljuveniledepartments.aspx.

58 Texas Human Resources Code, Sec. 152.0010, http://www.statutes.legis.state.tx.us/Docs/HR/htm/HR.152.htm.

59 Texas Juvenile Justice Department, Overview of the Juvenile Justice System in Texas, http://www.tjjd.texas.gov/about/overview.aspx.

60 Texas Family Code, Sec. 51.02, http://www.statutes.legis.state.tx.us/Docs/FA/htm/FA.51.htm.

61 Texas Family Code, Sec. 51.03, http://www.statutes.legis.state.tx.us/Docs/FA/htm/FA.51.htm; Texas Juvenile Justice Department, Overview of the Juvenile Justice System in Texas, http://www.tjjd.texas.gov/about/overview.aspx.

62 Texas Family Code Section 54.02.

63 Michele Deitch, *Juveniles in the Adult Criminal Justice System in Texas,* LBJ School of Public Affairs, University of Texas at Austin, Special Project Report, March

2011, http://www.utexas.edu/lbj/sites/default/files/file/news/juvenilestexas—final.pdf.

[64] Ibid. See also provisions relating to expunging or keeping confidential the criminal records of minors: Texas Government Code section 411.081 (orders of nondisclosure), Texas Family Code section 58.003 (sealing juvenile records); Texas Family Code section 58.203 (automatic restriction of access to juvenile records except by law enforcement officers).

[65] Death penalty: see Tarlton Law Library, Jamail Center for Legal Research, Texas Death Penalty Law: Resources and Information about the Death Penalty Law in Texas, http://www.tarltonguides.law.utexas.edu/texas-death-penalty. See also Texas Penal Code section 8.07(c). Life sentence: see *Miller v. Alabama,* United States Supreme Court, June 2012.

[66] *Roper v. Simmons* (03-633) 543 U.S. 551 (2005); Charles Lane, "5-4 Supreme Court Abolishes Juvenile Executions," *Washington Post,* March 2, 2005, http://www.washingtonpost.com/wp-dyn/articles/A62584-2005Mar1.html.

[67] *Miller v. Alabama,* 567 U.S. _____ (2012); accessible at https://www.supremecourt.gov/opinions/11pdf/10-9646g2i8.pdf.

[68] Texas Juvenile Justice Department, Overview of the Juvenile Justice System in Texas, http://www.tjjd.texas.gov/about/overview.aspx.

[69] Texas Juvenile Justice Department, New Commitment Profile Fiscal Years 2006–2013, http://www.tjjd.texas.gov/research/profile.aspx.

[70] Tony Fabelo, Nancy Arrigona, Michael D. Thompson, Austin Clemens, and Miner P. Marchbanks III, "Closer to Home: An Analysis of the State and Local Impact of the Texas Juvenile Justice Reforms" (January 2015), Council of State Governments Justice Center and the Public Policy Research Institute, https://csgjusticecenter.org/wp-content/uploads/2015/01/texas-JJ-reform-closer-to-home.pdf.

[71] Eva-Marie Ayala, "Texas Senate approves measure to decriminalize truancy," *Dallas Morning News,* April 15, 2015, http://www.dallasnews.com/news/politics/state-politics/20150415-texas-senate-approves-measure-to-decriminalize-truancy.ece; Patrick Svitek, "Abbott Signs Bill Decriminalizing Truancy," *Texas Tribune,* June 19, 2015, https://www.texastribune.org/2015/06/19/texas-decriminalize-truancy-after-abbott-signs-bil/.

[72] Texas Juvenile Justice Department, The State of Juvenile Probation Activity in Texas: Statistical and Other Data on the Juvenile Justice System in Texas for Calendar Year 2012 (September 2014), https://www.tjjd.texas.gov/publications/reports/RPTSTAT2012.pdf.

[73] Texas Board of Criminal Justice, Operating Budget for Fiscal Year 2016 (December 1, 2015), http://tdcj.state.tx.us/documents/finance/Agency_Operating_Budget_FY2016_Governor.pdf.

[74] Texas Department of Criminal Justice, Texas Board of Criminal Justice Overview, http://www.tdcj.state.tx.us/tbcj/index.html.

[75] Texas Department of Criminal Justice, Unit Directory, http://tdcj.state.tx.us/unit_directory/.

[76] U.S. Department of Justice, Bureau of Justice Statistics, Prisoners in 2014, (http://www.bjs.gov/content/pub/pdf/p14.pdf.); U.S Department of Justice, Bureau of Justice Statistics, Prisoners in 2000, (http://www.bjs.gov/content/pub/pdf/p00.pdf).

[77] *Ruiz v. Estelle* 503 F. Supp. 1265 (S.D. Tex. 1980) Opinion available at https://tarltonapps.law.utexas.edu/exhibits/ww_justice/documents_3/Ruiz_opinion_1_1980.pdf.

[78] Robert Draper, "The Great Texas Prison Mess," *Texas Monthly,* May 1996, http://www.texasmonthly.com/articles/the-great-texas-prison-mess/.

[79] Fox Butterfield, "Study Tracks Boom in Prisons and Notes Impact on Counties," *New York Times,* April 30, 2004, http://www.nytimes.com/2004/04/30/us/study-tracks-boom-in-prisons-and-notes-impact-on-counties.html.

[80] Paul M. Lucko, "Prison System," *Handbook of Texas Online,* http://www.tshaonline.org/handbook/online/articles/jjp03; Jolie McCullough, "Dip in Texas Prison Population Continues Trend," *Texas Tribune,* Sept. 25, 2015, https://www.texastribune.org/2015/09/25/slight-dip-in-texas-prisoner-population-trend/.

[81] Texas Board of Pardons and Paroles and Texas Department of Criminal Justice Parole Division, Parole in Texas: Answers to Common Questions (2005), http://www.tdcj.state.tx.us/bpp/publications/PIT_eng.pdf.

[82] Texas Board of Pardons and Paroles, Revised Parole Guidelines, accessed May 27, 2016, http://www.tdcj.state.tx.us/bpp/parole_guidelines/parole_guidelines.html.

[83] Texas Penal Code, Sec. 12.35, http://www.statutes.legis.state.tx.us/docs/PE/htm/PE.12.htm.

[84] Texas Senate Committee on Criminal Justice, Charge 5, Interim Report to the 77 th Legislature, http://www.lrl.state.tx.us/scanned/interim/76/c868_5.pdf.

[85] Ibid.

[86] Legislative Budget Board, "Statewide Criminal and Juvenile Justice Recidivism and Revocation Rates," Report to the 84 th Legislature, http://www.lbb.state.tx.us/Documents/Publications/Policy_Report/1450_CJ_Statewide_Recidivism.pdf.

[87] Texas Department of Criminal Justice, Fiscal Year 2014 Statistical Report, https://www.tdcj.state.tx.us/documents/Statistical_Report_FY2014.pdf.

[88] Legislative Budget Board, Specialty Courts, http://www.lbb.state.tx.us/Documents/Publications/Issue_Briefs/3015_Specialty_Courts_0701.pdf.

[89] Ibid.

[90] For a comprehensive list, see Texas Specialty Courts, http://gov.texas.gov/files/cjd/Specialty_Courts_By_County_May_2016.pdf.

[91] Texas Department of Criminal Justice, Texas Drug Courts, March 3, 2003, https://www.tdcj.state.tx.us/documents/cjad/CJAD_Texas_Drug_Courts_Fact_Sheet.pdf; Alma I. Martinez and Michael Eisenberg, "Initial Process and Outcome Evaluation of Drug Courts in Texas," Texas Criminal Justice Policy Council, January 2003.

[92] Skyler Stuckey, Marc Levin, and Kate Murphy, "Enhancing Public Safety and Saving Taxpayer Dollars: The Role of Mental Health Courts in Texas," Texas Public Policy Foundation, April 2015, http://www.texaspolicy.com/library/doclib/PP-The-Role-of-Mental-Health-Courts-in-Texas.pdf.

[93] Texas Department of Criminal Justice, Private Facility Contract Monitoring/Oversight Division, Contracted Facilities as of February 02, 2016, http://tdcj.state.tx.us/divisions/pf/pf_unit_list.html.

[94] John MacCormack, "Private prison boom goes bust: In state, more than a dozen of the lockups have failed," San Antonio Express News, August 22, 2015, http://www.expressnews.com/news/local/article/Private-prison-boom-goes-bust-6459964.php.

[95] John Burnett, "Texas Judge Refuses To License Child Care Facility In Immigrant Detention Center," NPR, May 6, 2016, http://www.npr.org/sections/thetwo-way/2016/05/06/476976133/texas-judge-refuses-to-license-childcare-facility-in-immigrant-detention-center; Matt Zapotosky and Chico Harlan, "Justice Department says it will end use of private prisons," Washington Post, August 18, 2016, https://www.washingtonpost.com/news/post-nation/wp/2016/08/18/justice-department-says-it-will-end-use-of-private-prisons/?utm_term=.86e2c9baee71.

[96] John MacCormack, "Private prison boom goes bust: In state, more than a dozen of the lockups have failed," San Antonio Express News, August 22, 2015, http://www.expressnews.com/news/local/article/Private-prison-boom-goes-bust-6459964.php.

[97] Sarah Childress, "'Predictable' Riot at Texas Prison Followed Years of Complaints," Frontline, February 25, 2015, http://www.pbs.org/wgbh/frontline/article/predictable-riot-texas-prison-willacy-years-complaints/; John MacCormack, "Private prison boom goes bust: In state, more than a dozen of the lockups have failed," San Antonio Express News, August 22, 2015, http://www.expressnews.com/news/local/article/Private-prison-boom-goes-bust-6459964.php.

[98] Legislative Budget Board, Criminal and Juvenile Justice Uniform Cost Report, Fiscal Years 2013 and 2014, February 2015, http://www.lbb.state.tx.us/Documents/Publications/Policy_Report/1440_Criminal_Juvenile_Justice_Uniform_Cost_Report.pdf.

[99] Sasha Volokh, "Are private prisons better or worse than public prisons?" Washington Post, February 25, 2014, https://www.washingtonpost.com/news/volokh-conspiracy/wp/2014/02/25/are-private-prisons-better-or-worse-than-public-prisons/?utm_term=.09cedd6c6d9c.

[100] Adrian T. Moore, Private Prisons: Quality Corrections at a Lower Cost, Reason Policy Study No. 240, http://reason.org/files/d14ffa18290a9aeb969d1a6c1a9ff935.pdf; Joseph Margulies, "This Is the Real Reason Private Prisons Should Be Outlawed," Time, August 24, 2016, http://time.com/4461791/private-prisons-department-of-justice/.

[101] Texas Local Government Code, 351.001-002, http://www.statutes.legis.state.tx.us/Docs/LG/htm/LG.351.htm.

[102] Texas Commission on Jail Standards. County Jail Population, July 1, 2016, http://www.tcjs.state.tx.us/docs/POPSUMCurrent.pdf.

[103] See Local Government Code 341.902 and 361.

[104] Brandi Grissom, "City Jails Unregulated Despite Deaths, Complaints," Texas Tribune, September 17, 2010, https://www.texastribune.org/2010/09/17/city-jails-unregulated-despite-deaths-complaints/.

[105] Johnathan Silver, "Report Finds Almost 7,000 In-Custody Deaths in Texas," Texas Tribune, July 27, 2016, https://www.texastribune.org/2016/07/27/over-6000-people-have-died-custody-2005-ut-project/.

[106] Office of the Attorney General of Texas. Custodial Death Reports 2005–2015. https://www.texasattorneygeneral.gov/criminal/custodial/report_deaths.php CSV Downloaded May 26, 2016.

[107] Reid Wilson, "Tough Texas gets results by going softer on crime," Washington Post, November 27, 2014, https://www.washingtonpost.com/blogs/govbeat/wp/2014/11/27/tough-texas-gets-results-by-going-softer-on-crime/; Olivia Nuzzi, "Prison Reform is Bigger in Texas," The Daily Beast, April 12, 2014, http://www.thedailybeast.com/articles/2014/04/12/prison-reform-is-bigger-in-texas.html.

[108] Legislative Budget Board, Statewide Criminal Justice Recidivism and Revocation Rates (January 2005), http://www.lbb.state.tx.us/Documents/Publications/Policy_Report/Statewide%20Criminal%20Justice%20Recidivism%20and%20Revocation%20Rates2005.pdf.

[109] Texas Sunset Advisory Commission. Texas Department of Criminal Justice Board of Pardons and Paroles Correctional Managed Health Care Committee, p. 10, 2006, https://www.sunset.texas.gov/public/uploads/files/reports/Criminal%20Justice%20Agencies%20Staff%20Report%202006%2080th%20Leg.pdf.

[110] Marc Levin, "Adult Corrections Reform: Lower Crime, Lower Costs," Texas Public Policy Foundation (September 2011), http://rightoncrime.com/wp-content/uploads/2011/09/Texas-Model-Adult.pdf.

[111] Jolie McCullough, "Dip in Texas Prison Population Continues Trend," Texas Tribune, Sept. 25, 2015, https://www.texastribune.org/2015/09/25/slight-dip-in-texas-prisoner-population-trend/.

[112] Ibid., 386.

[113] Council of State Governments Justice Center, States Report Reductions in Recidivism (September 2012), https://csgjusticecenter.org/documents/0000/1569/9.24.12_Recidivism_Reductions_9-24_lo_res.pdf.

[114] Legislative Budget Board, Statewide Criminal and Juvenile Justice Recidivism and Revocation Rates (February 2015), http://www.lbb.state.tx.us/Documents/Publications/Policy_Report/1450_CJ_Statewide_Recidivism.pdf.

[115] Texas Department of Public Safety, Crime in Texas, http://dps.texas.gov/administration/crime_records/pages/crimestatistics.htm; Texas Crime Analysis, http://dps.texas.gov/crimereports/14/citCh2.pdf.

[116] Texas Department of Criminal Justice, Rehabilitation Programs Division, Substance Abuse Treatment Program, https://www.tdcj.texas.gov/divisions/rpd/rpd_substance_abuse.html.

[117] Martinez, Alma and Michael Eisenberg, "Educational Achievement of Inmates in the Windham School District," Criminal Justice Policy Council, 2000, http://www.windhamschooldistrict.org/images/PDF/other/WindRev21.pdf.

[118] Windham School District. Annual Performance Report 2014–15 School Year, http://www.windhamschooldistrict.org/images/PDF/APR/2015/WSD-APR_2015-HR.pdf.

[119] Gaylene Armstrong and Cassandra Atkin-Plunk, Evaluation of the Windham School District Correctional Education Programs, 2014, http://www.windhamschooldistrict.org/images/PDF/other/Evaluation_Windham_School_District_Correctional_Education_Programs-SY2010.pdf.

[120] Cornell University Law School Legal Information Institute, *Furman v. Georgia,* https://www.law.cornell.edu/supremecourt/text/408/238#writing-USSC_CR_0408_0238_ZS; Michael H. Reggio, "History of the Death Penalty," *Frontline: The Execution* (PBS), http://www.pbs.org/wgbh/pages/frontline/shows/execution/readings/history.html.

[121] Death Penalty Information Center, Number of Executions by State and Region Since 1976, http://www.deathpenaltyinfo.org/number-executions-state-and-region-1976.

[122] Death Penalty Information Center, Death Sentences in the United States From 1977 By State and By Year, http://www.deathpenaltyinfo.org/death-sentences-united-states-1977-2008; Number of Executions by State and Region Since 1976, http://www.deathpenaltyinfo.org/number-executions-state-and-region-1976. In 1995, Texas executed 19 of the 51 people executed nationwide. In 2000, Texas executed 40 of the 84 people executed nationwide. In 2015, Texas executed 13 of the 28 people executed nationwide.

[123] Death Penalty Information Center, Execution List 2016, http://www.deathpenaltyinfo.org/execution-list-2016.

[124] Texas Legislature Online, Bill Analysis S.B. 60, http://www.legis.state.tx.us/tlodocs/79R/analysis/pdf/SB00060F.pdf#navpanes=0.

[125] ProCon.org, Top 10 Pros and Cons: Should the death penalty be allowed? http://deathpenalty.procon.org/view.resource.php?resourceID=002000.

[126] Innocence Project. Cameron Todd Willingham: Wrongfully Convicted and Executed in Texas, http://www.innocenceproject.org/cameron-todd-willingham-wrongfully-convicted-and-executed-in-texas/.

[127] Death Penalty Information Center, Innocence: List of Those Freed From Death Row, http://www.deathpenaltyinfo.org/innocence-list-those-freed-death-row.

[128] Adam Liptak and Ralph Blumenthal, "Death Sentences in Texas Cases Try Supreme Court's Patience," *New York Times,* December 5, 2004, http://www.nytimes.com/2004/12/05/us/death-sentences-in-texas-cases-try-supreme-courts-patience.html.

[129] State of Texas Judicial Branch, Annual Statistical Report for the Texas Judiciary, Fiscal Year 2014, http://www.txcourts.gov/media/885306/Annual-Statistical-Report-FY-2014.pdf.

[130] *Houston Chronicle,* 9 February 2001, 6.

[131] Michael Hall, "The Judgment of Sharon Keller," *Texas Monthly,* August 2009, http://www.texasmonthly.com/articles/the-judgment-of-sharon-keller/.

[132] Texas Board of Pardons and Paroles, Annual Statistical Report, Fiscal Year 2015, http://www.tdcj.state.tx.us/bpp/publications/FY%202015%20AnnualStatisticalReport.pdf.

[133] Brandi Grissom, "Under Perry, Executions Raise Questions," *Texas Tribune,* September 2, 2011, http://www.texastribune.org/texas-people/rick-perry/under-perry-executions-raise-questions/.

[134] Texas Department of Criminal Justice. "Death Row Information: Executed Offenders," http://www.tdcj.state.tx.us/death_row/dr_executed_offenders.html.

[135] Harris County Budget Management Department, Fiscal Year 2016–2017 Approved Budgets, Organizational Budgets, http://www.harriscountytx.gov/CmpDocuments/74/Budget/FY17%20Org%20Budgets.pdf; Office of District Attorney Devon Anderson, Harris County, Texas, https://app.dao.hctx.net/OurOffice/OurOffice.aspx.

[136] Dallas County Office of Budget and Evaluation, Fiscal Year 2016 Budget, FY2016 Approved Budget, http://www.dallascounty.org/department/budget/documents/FY2016_ApprovedBudget.pdf.

[137] Harris County Criminal Courts at Law, http://www.ccl.hctx.net/criminal/default.htm; Dallas County Court System, http://www.dallascounty.org/department/courts/county_criminal.php.

[138] Gallup, Death Penalty, October 2015, http://www.gallup.com/poll/1606/death-penalty.aspx; University of Texas/Texas Tribune, Texas Statewide Survey (May 2012),

https://texaspolitics.utexas.edu/sites/texaspolitics.utexas.
edu/files/201205-summary.pdf.

139 Kenneth C. Land, Raymond H.C. Teske Jr., Hui Zheng, "The
short-term effects of executions on homicides: Deterrence,
displacement, or both?" *Criminology 47*(4), November
2009, 1009–1043.

140 Death Penalty Information Center, Discussion of Recent
Deterrence Studies, http://www.deathpenaltyinfo.org/
discussion-recent-deterrence-studies.

141 Michael L. Radelet and Traci L. Lacock, "Do executions
lower homicide rates?: The views of leading
criminologists," *Journal of Criminal Law & Criminology
99*(2), 2009, 489–508. accessible at http://www.
deathpenaltyinfo.org/files/DeterrenceStudy2009.pdf.

142 Texas Department of Criminal Justice, "Death Row
Information," https://www.tdcj.state.tx.us/death_row/
dr_facts.html.

143 U.S. Census Bureau, Quick Facts, Texas, http://www.census.
gov/quickfacts/table/PST045215/48.

144 U.S. Census Bureau, "Poverty Thresholds for 2015 by Size of
Family and Number of Related Children Under 18 Years,"
xls file (https://www.census.gov/hhes/www/poverty/data/
threshld/)

145 Interest on Lawyers Trust Accounts, http://www.iolta.org/.

146 State Bar of Texas, Access to Justice, https://www.texasbar
.com/AM/Template.cfm?Section=Access_To_Justice_
Home.

147 For university legal clinics, see the University of Texas and
Saint Mary's University: see www.stmarytx.edu/law/index.
php?site=centerforlawandsocialjustice and https://www.
sll.texas.gov/self-help/where-to-go-for-help/legal-clinics/.
An example of a nonprofit organization is the Texas Civil
Rights Project. See http://www.texascivilrightsproject.org.

148 The Lawyer Referral and Information Service of the
State Bar, https://www.texasbar.com/AM/Template.
cfm?Section=Lawyer_Referral_Service_LRIS_.

149 Texas Access to Justice Commission, FAQ, http://www.
texasatj.org/faq.

150 Accetta, et al. *Indigent Defense Services in the United States,
FY 2008–2012–Updated.* U.S. Department of Justice,
Bureau of Justice Statistics: 2014, NCJ 246683, http://
www.bjs.gov/content/pub/pdf/idsus0812.pdf.

151 Texas Indigent Defense Commission, "Summary of Funding
for All Counties: FY 2015 Funds Disbursed," http://tidc.
tamu.edu/public.net/Reports/SummaryReport.aspx.

152 Bobby Cervantes, "Legal Aid to Low-Income Texans at
Risk, Groups Say," Texas Politics, *San Antonio Express
News* and *Houston Chronicle,* February 16, 2011.
http://blog.mysanantonio.com/texas-politics/2011/02/
legal-aid-to-low-income-texans-at-risk-groups-say/.

153 Editorial Board, "Texas Leads the Way in Needed
Criminal Justice Reforms," *Washington Post,* January 28,

2014, http://www.washingtonpost.com/opinions/
texas-leads-the-way-in-needed-criminal-justice-
reforms/2014/01/28/83919b72-879d-11e3-916e-
e01534b1e132_story.html; Office of the Governor
Rick Perry, "Drug Courts," https://web.archive.org/
web/20140518192648/http://governor.state.tx.us/priorities/
security/public_safety/drug_courts/; Olivia Nuzzi, "Prison
Reform Is Bigger in Texas," *The Daily Beast,* April 12,
2014, http://www.thedailybeast.com/articles/2014/04/12/
prison-reform-is-bigger-in-texas.html.

154 Mortimer B. Zuckerman, "Get a Little Less Tough on
Crime," *U.S. News & World Report,* May 9, 2014,
http://www.usnews.com/opinion/articles/2014/05/09/
its-time-for-prison-reform-and-an-end-to-mandatory-
minimum-sentences; Luna, Erik. "The Overcriminalization
Phenomenon." *American University Law Review 54,* no.3
(2005): 703–743. accessible at http://digitalcommons.wcl.
american.edu/aulr/vol54/iss3/5.

155 Right on Crime, Overcriminalization, http://rightoncrime.
com/category/priority-issues/overcriminalization/.

156 See Harvey Silverglate, *Three Felonies A Day: How the Feds
Target the Innocent* (New York: Encounter Books, 2009).

157 Derek M. Cohen, Texas' Mandatory Sentencing
Enhancements, Texas Public Policy Foundation (June
2016), http://www.texaspolicy.com/library/doclib/Texas-
Mandatory-Sentencing-Enhancements.pdf.

158 Byron Pitts, Jackie Jesko, and Lauren Effron, "Former
Federal Judge Regrets 55-Year Marijuana Sentence,"
ABC News, February 18, 2015, http://abcnews.go.com/
US/federal-judge-regrets-55-year-marijuana-sentence/
story?id=28869467; Matt McDonald, "Former federal
judge writes to White House requesting reduced sentence
for jailed Utah man," February 9, 2016, Fox 13, http://
fox13now.com/2016/02/09/former-federal-judge-writes-to-
white-house-requesting-reduced-sentence-for-jailed-utah-
man/.

159 United States Sentencing Commission, 2015 Report to the
Congress: Impact of the Fair Sentencing Act of 2010,
http://www.ussc.gov/research/congressional-reports/2015-
report-congress-impact-fair-sentencing-act-2010.

160 Texas Department of Public Safety, The Texas 1033 Military
Surplus Property Program, http://www.dps.texas.gov/
LawEnforcementSupport/texas1033.htm.

161 American Civil Liberties Union, Police Militarization, https://
www.aclu.org/issues/criminal-law-reform/reforming-police-
practices/police-militarization; Daniela Guzman, From
Warfighter to Crimefighter—The U.S. 1033 Program,
and the Risk of Corruption and Misuse of Public Funds,
Association of Certified Financial Crime Specialists, http://
www.acfcs.org/from-warfighter-to-crimefighter-the-us-
1033-program-and-the-risk-of-corruption-and-misuse-
of-public-funds/; also see ACLU, War Comes Home:

The Excessive Militarization of American Policing (June 2014), https://www.aclu.org/sites/default/files/assets/jus14-warcomeshome-report-web-rel1.pdf.

162 American Civil Liberties Union, Asset Forfeiture Abuse, accessed August 23, 2016, https://www.aclu.org/issues/criminal-law-reform/reforming-police-practices/asset-forfeiture-abuse.

163 Ibid; Right on Crime, Civil Asset Forfeiture, Texas Public Policy Foundation, http://rightoncrime.com/category/priority-issues/civil-asset-forfeiture/ .

164 "Deinstitutionalization: A Psychiatric 'Titanic,'" Frontline (PBS), excerpted from E. Fuller Torrey, *Out of the Shadows: Confronting America's Mental Illness Crisis,* (New York: John Wiley & Sons, 1997), accessible at http://www.pbs.org/wgbh/pages/frontline/shows/asylums/special/excerpt.html.

165 James, Doris J. and Lauren E. Glaze. Mental Health Problems of Prison and Jail Inmates Bureau of Justice Statistics. DOJ. December 14, 2006. http://www.bjs.gov/content/pub/pdf/mhppji.pdf.

166 Mary Beth Pfeiffer, "Cruel and Unusual Punishment," *New York Times,* May 7, 2006, http://crazyinamerica.com/html/articles.html#Anchor-62428.

167 Biennial Report of the Texas Correctional Office on Offenders With Medical and Mental Impairments (February 2007), https://www.tdcj.state.tx.us/documents/rid/TCOOMMI_Biennial_Report_2007.pdf.

168 Kate Murphy and Christi Bar, Overincarceration of People with Mental Illness: Pretrial Diversion Across the Country and the Next Steps for Texas to Improve its Efforts and Increase Utilization, Texas Public Policy Institute. (June 2015) p. 5, http://www.texaspolicy.com/library/doclib/Overincarceration-of-People-with-Mental-Illness.pdf.

169 Texas Specialty Courts, http://gov.texas.gov/files/cjd/Specialty_Courts_By_County_May_2016.pdf.

170 Sylvester Turner. Opinion: "Texas facing mental health crisis," January 22, 2014, http://www.chron.com/opinion/outlook/article/Texas-facing-mental-health-crisis-4214980.php.

171 *An Act relating to the creation of a mental health jail diversion pilot program.* S.B. 1885, Texas State Legislature (2013), http://www.capitol.state.tx.us/tlodocs/83R/billtext/pdf/SB01185F.pdf.

172 Mihir Zaveri, "Pilot program gives hope to inmates with mental health needs," *Houston Chronicle,* March 15, 2016, http://www.chron.com/news/houston-texas/houston/article/Pilot-program-gives-hope-to-inmates-with-mental-6892205.php.

173 The Center for Health Care Services. Blueprint for Success: The Bexar County Model, 2011. http://www.jtvf.org/wp-content/uploads/Feb-22-2011-Convening/fina-jail-text%20(2).pdf. See also Cowell, Alexander, Arnie Aldridge, Nahama Brone, and Jesse M. Hind. A

Cost Analysis of the Bexar County, Texas, Jail Diversion Program, 2008,http://www.naco.org/sites/default/files/documents/Cost%20Benefit%20Study.pdf.

174 National Association of State Mental Health Program Directors Research Institute, Inc. (NRI), Table 1: SMHA Mental Health Actual Dollar and Per Capita Expenditures by State (FY2013), http://www.nri-incdata.org/RevExp2013/T1.pdf.

175 Texas Code of Criminal Procedure, Art. 45.046.

176 Kendall Taggart and Alex Campbell, Their Crime: Being Poor. Their Sentence: Jail. Buzzfeed.com, October 7, 2015, https://www.buzzfeed.com/kendalltaggart/in-texas-its-a-crime-to-be-poor?utm_term=.ytODVAALNv#.yxVx855opN.

177 Texas Commission on Jail Standards, Abbreviated Population Report for 8/1/2016, http://www.tcjs.state.tx.us/docs/AbbreRptCurrent.pdf.

178 Conference of Chief Justices. "Resolution 3" 2013. http://ccj.ncsc.org/~/media/microsites/files/ccj/resolutions/01302013-pretrial-release-endorsing-cosca-paper-evidencebased-pretrial-release.ashx.

179 Travis Leete, Overview of Pretrial Services and Bail in Texas, Texas Criminal Justice Coalition, accessed August 28, 2016, http://www.texascjc.org/sites/default/files/publications/Overview%20of%20Pretrial%20Services%20Bail%20in%20TX%20(Mar%202012).pdf; Texas Criminal Justice Coalition, Solutions for Pretrial, Defense & Innocence, accessed August 28, 2016, http://www.texascjc.org/basic-facts-0.

180 Ross Ramsey, "Analysis: Legislators Seeking a More Efficient Approach to Jail Policies," *Texas Tribune,* January 25, 2016, https://www.texastribune.org/2016/01/25/analysis-criminal-justice-reformers-take-police-an/.

181 Noonan, Margaret, Harley Rohloff and Scott Ginder. Mortality in Local Jails and State Prisons, 2000–2013–Statistical Tables. August 2015. US Department of Justice. Bureau of Justice Statistics. http://www.bjs.gov/content/pub/pdf/mljsp0013st.pdf.

182 Johnathan Silver, "Report Finds Almost 7,000 In-Custody Deaths in Texas," *Texas Tribune,* July 27, 2016, https://www.texastribune.org/2016/07/27/over-6000-people-have-died-custody-2005-ut-project/.

183 Dahle, Klaus-Peter, Johannes C. Lohner, and Norbert Konrad. "Suicide prevention in penal institutions: Validation and optimization of a screening tool for early identification of high-risk inmates in pretrial detention." *International Journal of Forensic Mental Health* 4, no. 1 (2005): 53–62.

184 Texas Administrative Code, Title 37 Chapter 265.

185 Texas Commission on Jail Standards, Non-Compliant Jails, http://www.tcjs.state.tx.us/index.php?linkID=340.

186 Dane Schiller, "Findings of Sandra Bland jail death probe released," *Houston Chronicle,* April 14, 2016, http://www.

chron.com/news/houston-texas/article/Findings-of-Sandra-Bland-jail-death-probe-7243359.php; K.K. Rebecca Lai, Haeyoun Park, Larry Buchanan and Wilson Andrews, "Assessing the Legality of Sandra Bland's Arrest," *New York Times,* July 22, 2015, http://www.nytimes.com/interactive/2015/07/20/us/sandra-bland-arrest-death-videos-maps.html?_r=0; Christine Hauser, "Sandra Bland's Family Settles $1.9 Million Civil Suit, Lawyer Says," New York Times, September 15, 2016, http://www.nytimes.com/2016/09/16/us/sandra-bland-family-settlement-19-million-lawsuit.html.

[187] Texas Forensic Science Commission, About Us, accessed August 28, 2016, http://www.fsc.texas.gov/about.

[188] Texas Forensic Science Commission, Letter to Legal Community Stakeholders, August 21, 2015, http://www.fsc.texas.gov/sites/default/files/documents/Unintended%20Effects%20of%20FBI%20Database%20Corrections%20on%20Assessment%20of%20DNA%20Mixture%20Interpretation%20in%20Texas%20NOTICE.pdf.

[189] Texas Forensic Science Commission, Fourth Annual Report, November 2014 - November 2015, p. 17, http://www.fsc.texas.gov/sites/default/files/2015%20FSC%20Annual%20Report%20Posted.pdf.

[190] National Registry of Exonerations, Exonerations by State, http://www.law.umich.edu/special/exoneration/Pages/Exonerations-in-the-United-States-Map.aspx; Exonerations in 2015, http://www.law.umich.edu/special/exoneration/Documents/Exonerations_in_2015.pdf.

[191] National Registry of Exonerations, Timothy B. Cole, https://www.law.umich.edu/special/exoneration/Pages/casedetail.aspx?caseid=3114. Also, note that Texas Civil Practice and Remedies 103.001 (2016) may also require a pardon even after a dismissal or an acquittal in order to be eligible for compensation for wrongful incarceration.

[192] Texas Department of Criminal Justice, Statistical Report Fiscal Year 2014, https://www.tdcj.state.tx.us/documents/Statistical_Report_FY2014.pdf.

[193] Texas Department of Public Safety, Texas Arrest Data, Texas Crime Report for 2014, http://dps.texas.gov/crimereports/14/citCh9.pdf.

[194] Kimberly Kindy, Marc Fisher, Julie Tate, and Jennifer Jenkins, "A Year of Reckoning: Police Fatally Shoot Nearly 1,000," *Washington Post,* December 26, 2015, http://www.washingtonpost.com/sf/investigative/wp/2015/12/26/2015/12/26/a-year-of-reckoning-police-fatally-shoot-nearly-1000/.

[195] Texas Department of Criminal Justice, Statistical Report Fiscal Year 2014, https://www.tdcj.state.tx.us/documents/Statistical_Report_FY2014.pdf.

[196] Texas Juvenile Justice Department, New Commitment Profile Fiscal Years 2006–2013, http://www.tjjd.texas.gov/research/profile.aspx.

[197] Texas Department of Public Safety, Texas Crime Analysis, Texas Crime Report for 2014, http://dps.texas.gov/crimereports/14/citCh2.pdf.

[198] Alex R. Piquero and Robert W. Brame, "Assessing the Race–Crime and Ethnicity–Crime Relationship in a Sample of Serious Adolescent Delinquents," *Crime & Delinquency* vol. 54 no. 3 (July 2008) 390–422.

[199] Fair Punishment Project, Too Broken to Fix: Part I An In-depth Look at America's Outlier Death Penalty Counties (August 2016), http://fairpunishment.org/wp-content/uploads/2016/08/FPP-TooBroken.pdf.

[200] American Civil Liberties Union, Racial Arrests in Tulia, Texas, https://www.aclu.org/racist-arrests-tulia-texas; Janelle Stecklein, "Tulia Drug Busts: 10 years Later," *Amarillo Globe,* July 19, 2009, http://amarillo.com/stories/071909/new_news1.shtml#.V8M-4pgrKM8;

[201] Ibid., 397.

[202] Manny Fernandez, Richard Perez-Pena and Jonah Engel Bromwich, "Five Dallas Officers Were Killed as Payback, Police Chief Says," *New York Times,* July 8, 2016, http://www.nytimes.com/2016/07/09/us/dallas-police-shooting.html.

[203] Texas Code of Criminal Procedure, Art. 2.01.

[204] Pamela Coloff, Jail Time May Be the Least of Ken Anderson's Problems, November 14, 2013, *Texas Monthly.* http://www.texasmonthly.com/articles/jail-time-may-be-the-least-of-ken-andersons-problems/#sthash.nz5UEobF.dpuf, last accessed May 24, 2016; Innocence Project, Michael Morton, http://www.innocenceproject.org/cases/michael-morton/.

[205] *AN ACT relating to discovery in a criminal case.* S.B. 1611 (2013) Texas state legislature, http://www.legis.state.tx.us/tlodocs/83R/billtext/html/SB01611F.HTM.

[206] *Setting the Record Straight on Prosecutorial Misconduct.* Report. Austin, Texas: Texas District and County Attorneys Association (TDCAA), 2012.

[207] Michael R. Bromwich,"Final Report of the Independent Investigator for the Houston Police Department Crime Laboratory and Property Room," June 13, 2007, http://www.hpdlabinvestigation.org/reports/070613report.pdf.

[208] Emily DePrang, Fake Lab Results Endanger Thousands of Drug Convictions, *Texas Observer.* July 8, 2013, https://www.texasobserver.org/fake-lab-results-endanger-thousands-of-drug-convictions/. See also *Ex Parte Coty* http://texastechlawreview.org/wp-content/uploads/CCA-1.151.pdf.

CHAPTER 13

Financing State Government

Texas Learning Outcomes

- Analyze state financing issues and policies in Texas.

A fundamental question in the realm of political science is, "What should government do?" Individuals answer this question in many ways depending on their **political values**, a set of beliefs about political processes and the role that government should play in our society. Any action taken by government requires an expenditure of resources— whether it is measured as an expense or by the time it takes to reach a decision. Today much attention is focused on federal spending, but few citizens realize that state governments also spend large sums of money to supply services to their citizens. In 2013, state and local governments combined spent $3.2 trillion.[1] The federal government provides some funding to state and local governments in the form of grants, but state and local governments generate a large portion of their revenue from their own sources. Texas reported net revenues totaling $109.4 billion in fiscal year 2015, 33.5 percent was received from federal sources.[2] On average, Texas generates approximately two-thirds of its revenue.

political values
A set of beliefs about political processes and the role that government should play in our society

Because the Texas legislature meets in regular sessions every other year (biennially), it approves budgets for two-year periods (biennial budgets). In May 2015, the legislature approved a budget of $209.1 billion for the fiscal years 2015 and 2016. Approximately one-third of the biennial budget revenue comes from the federal government. Sixty-three percent of those funds are allocated to Health and Human Services, the system that provides for state Medicaid recipients.[3] In the 2016–2017 biennium, Medicaid funding accounts for 81 percent of the total Health and Human Services funding request.[4]

Chapter Learning Objectives

- Explain why governments provide services to citizens.
- Describe sources of state revenue in Texas.
- Discuss the issue of equity in taxes in the U.S. generally and in Texas specifically.

- Discuss local taxes in Texas.

- Discuss nontax revenue sources in Texas.

- Describe Texas government expenditures.

- Identify and explain continuing issues in Texas state finance.

Why Do Governments Provide Services to Citizens?

Learning Objective: Explain why governments provide services to citizens.

Government provision ensures availability of many goods and services to the public. For instance, there are more than 5,000 local government units in the state of Texas alone, all providing crucial services such as public education, water treatment, fire protection, policing, and health care. Why are these vital services often left to government to provide? Why can't we rely on private businesses to adequately provide roads, bridges, flood control, or clean air? As we discuss in more detail, markets fail to provide these goods and services because of some unique characteristics shared by these types of goods, called **public goods**.

Characteristics of Public Goods

The goods and services briefly mentioned in the introduction to this section are all types of public goods. Pure public goods share two characteristics that distinguish them from private goods: they are both nonexclusive and nonexhaustive (also referred to as **nonrivalrous**).[5] **Nonexcludability** means that it is not practical to exclude people from receiving or enjoying the good or service due to nonpayment. In other words, it is not easy to separate payers from nonpayers. For instance, imagine that a city tried charging a fee for fire protection and only responded to calls from those who paid the fee. Now, suppose you have paid the fire protection fee, but your neighbor hasn't. The city could not deny fire protection to your neighbor who had not paid, because protecting your house could require preventing or putting out a fire at your neighbor's, the nonpayer's, house. Likewise putting out a fire in your house is fire protection to your neighbor and the other houses adjacent to your home regardless of whether the fee is paid by your neighbors or not.[6]

The second characteristic of public goods is **nonexhaustion**, which means that use of a good or service by one individual does not diminish the availability of that good or service for others to use. Street lights offer a good example. Well-lit streets are a benefit shared by everyone in a community. Your benefiting from street lights on a walk home from a friend's house does not reduce the lighting available to the jogger who passes you on the sidewalk. Another example is

public goods
Goods or services characterized by the features of nonexcludability and nonrivalrous consumption; they are often provided by governments

nonrivalrous consumption
Situation in which the use or enjoyment of a good or service by a person or persons does not diminish the availability of that good or service for others to use or enjoy

nonexcludability
The inability to practically prevent people from receiving or enjoying a good or service due to nonpayment

nonexhaustion
The availability of a good or service for others to use and enjoy will not diminish; i.e., consumption is nonrivalrous

flood control. A flood control system that protects your community offers the same level of protection to you as it does your neighbors and local businesses. The benefit you derive from flood protection does not lessen the level of benefit derived by everyone else.

Nonexcludability and nonexhaustion result in the failure of the free market to adequately provide public goods. If a service is nonexclusive, then a business cannot prevent nonpayers, or "free-riders," from enjoying the benefit of the service. In such a case, there is very little incentive for people to pay for the service, and if a business cannot charge a price that people will pay, there is no incentive for the business providing the service. Additionally, if a service is nonexhaustive, the marginal cost (defined as the cost for the last unit produced) of delivering the service to additional people is zero. Consequently, any price a business would charge for the service would be too high (higher than zero), and too few people would pay.[7] Efficient pricing is impossible, and the end result is too few public goods provided and consumed if left to the private market.[8]

Although pure public goods share both the characteristics of nonexcludability and nonexhaustion, several subtypes share one feature but not the other (See Figure 13.1). In economics these goods are referred to as quasi-public goods.

Types of Public Goods

Many goods provisioned by government are not pure public goods in that they may share only certain features of pure public goods, or there is a broader societal purpose for ensuring availability. Three important subtypes are worth discussing: social goods, tolls goods, and common-pool goods.

Social Goods

Social goods are goods and services that can be, and often are, provided by the private sector, meaning they are exclusive and can be exhausted. However, these goods are also provided by government, because there is a value to

	Exhaustive	Nonexhaustive
Exclusive	**Social Goods** Education Libraries Subsidized housing Vaccinations	**Toll Goods** Broadcasting airwaves National parks Toll roads Toll bridges
Nonexclusive	**Common-Pool Goods** Aquifers Fisheries Forests Groundwater	**Pure Public Goods** Clean air National defense Pollution abatement Street lights

FIGURE 13.1   Characteristics of Public Goods

society in ensuring that everyone has access to such goods regardless of an individual's ability to pay. Governments ensure availability of these goods either by providing them for free or through subsidization. For example, in public education, it would be easy to separate payers and nonpayers, and we do—there are private schools for which parents often pay substantial amounts in tuition. However, we do not exclude any child from education for nonpayment, and thus ensure access to free public education for all children. In fact, most states, including Texas, require students to attend school until they reach a certain age, because it is believed that there is a broader public purpose or benefit to having an educated populace. Thus, some government services are provided without charge because there is a benefit to society as a whole—a collective benefit.

Toll Goods

Toll goods (sometimes called club goods) are goods that are exclusive but non-exhaustive. Toll roads and bridges are the classic example. Nonpayers can effectively be prevented from utilizing certain infrastructure by controlling access and exit points, but your use of the toll road does not reduce the benefit to other people. Now, it only takes a moment to recall sitting in bumper-to-bumper traffic on a congested highway to realize an important caveat. Toll goods are often only nonexhaustive to a certain point. All roads, even toll roads, have a maximum volume of traffic that can be sustained before causing delays or hazardous conditions. The same is true for parks and beaches that can become crowded to the point of diminishing the benefit to additional people. At the point of congestion and overcrowding, toll goods like toll bridges or parks are more accurately common-pool goods.

Common-Pool Goods

The last subtype of public goods are common-pool goods. Common-pool goods are public goods that are nonexclusive but are exhaustive. Natural resources are generally common-pool goods. Either by nature or design, exclusion is impractical or impossible, and because all natural resources are finite, common-pool goods can be exhausted. Groundwater is a particularly salient example in Texas considering that many parts of the state have been in some stage of drought since 2010. Groundwater is treated as private property, meaning one has a right to drill and pump whatever water exists beneath one's private property (the rule of capture). There are some restrictions that can be imposed on the extraction of groundwater by landowners, but these restrictions are arguably weak. If water is pumped at a rate faster than the water supply can be replenished, then access to groundwater will become difficult in certain parts, and in some cases wells and springs can run dry. Without effective regulation, it is unlikely that groundwater would be managed sustainably. (See Chapter 11 for more on Texas water policy.)

Although some think the government provides too many services to far too many citizens, attempts to reduce services often result in protests from those affected. As we all know, everyone favors cutting budgets (and taxes), but no one wants his or her favorite program cut. Despite what services one would think could be cut, all services must be paid for (eventually), either with tax money or from service charges and fees.

Thinking Critically. . .

What goods and services do you think state government should provide? Consider the consequences of your answer. What would the possible impact to society be, given your position?

Source: National Park Service

Sources of State Revenue

Learning Objective: Describe sources of state revenue in Texas.

To pay for the many services a state government provides, revenue must be raised from many sources. For state governments, the primary source of revenue is taxes paid by citizens, not money derived from service charges or fees. The amount of tax money available for any given state depends on the wealth of the citizens of that state. Some states, like some individuals, have a higher income capacity than others. The measure of a state's potential to tax is called its **tax capacity**. This measure is a ratio of the per capita taxable resources of each state indexed to the per capita taxable resources of the United States as a whole, which is set at 100. States above 100 have a higher tax capacity, and states below 100 have a lower tax capacity.[9] Texas had a tax capacity index of 106.7 in 2013, meaning that it was just above the national average.[10] Map 13.1 groups the 50 states by per capita tax capacity in 2013.

tax capacity
A measure of the wealth of a state or its ability to raise revenues relative to all other states

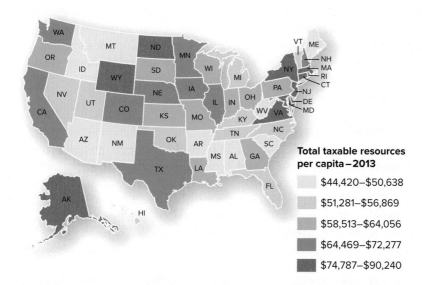

Total taxable resources per capita – 2013

- $44,420–$50,638
- $51,281–$56,869
- $58,513–$64,056
- $64,469–$72,277
- $74,787–$90,240

MAP 13.1   Total Taxable Resources per Capita, 2013

SOURCE: U.S. Department of the Treasury, Resource Center, "2015 Total Taxable Resources Estimates" (https://www.treasury.gov/resource-center/economic-policy/taxable-resources/Pages/Total-Taxable-Resources.aspx).

tax effort
A measure of the amount of revenue collected by a state relative to its tax capacity

Whereas a state's tax capacity measures its potential to tax, a state's **tax effort** measures its level of taxation. Ideally, a state's tax effort is a measure of the amount of revenue collected relative to its tax capacity. The tax effort in Texas using per capita revenue and per capita taxable resources data from 2013 is about 31, meaning that Texas is taxing below its capacity and that tax collection is low relative to other states. Thus, overall, Texas is a low-tax state; however, it is a high-tax state in terms of its dependency on sales and property tax when compared to other states.

Per Capita Taxes

per capita tax
The total taxes raised in a state divided by the number of residents

Another measure of state taxes is **per capita tax**. This is a simple measure obtained by taking the total taxes collected and dividing by the number of citizens in the state. Although this might be useful to know, it is not very informative about how much citizens actually pay in taxes. The primary point missed by the per capita tax measure is **tax exporting**. Sometimes taxes are exported to out-of-state residents.

tax exporting
The shifting of taxes to citizens in other states; a good example is Wyoming coal, which is exported to Texas to generate electricity

Alaska and Wyoming rank near the top on per capita tax burden. However, much of this tax is from oil in Alaska and coal in Wyoming and is exported to residents of other states—tax exporting.[11] Anyone who has ever observed a coal train hauling Wyoming coal to Austin, San Antonio, or Houston has seen tax burden being exported to Texas from Wyoming. This coal is used to generate electricity, and consumers pay the tax when they pay their utility bills. Thus, per capita tax is not a true measure of the tax burden on the citizens living in the state unless tax exporting is taken into account. For example, Texas receives about $1 billion in taxes on oil production and natural gas each year. However, much of the final product is exported to other states, and the tax paid is exported with the oil and gas and other petrochemical products.

Thus, if you rank all states on per capita revenues, the data does not tell us much about the actual taxes paid by a state's residents. A somewhat better measure is to compare the 15 most populous states on the amount of revenue raised per $1,000 of personal income. This still does not overcome the issues of tax exporting, but at least it compares the larger states' taxes as a percentage of income. By comparison, Texas is the fifth-lowest tax state, 46th out of 50 (see Table 13.1).

State Taxes in Texas

consumer taxes
Taxes that citizens pay when they buy goods and services—sales taxes

The most common, single sources of revenue for state governments are **consumer taxes**, such as sales and excise taxes on gasoline, tobacco, and liquor. Figure 13.2 shows the breakdown for Texas state tax revenue in 2014–2015, which totals $98.7 billion for the two-year period. As the figure shows, most revenue comes from consumer taxes paid by individuals when they make purchases. More than 80 percent of all tax revenue comes from consumer taxes (sales, motor vehicle sales, motor fuels, alcoholic beverages, tobacco taxes).

Because of high sales taxes, most of the taxes in Texas are paid by consumers and not by businesses. Business taxes are limited, taking the form of a corporate franchise tax. When compared to taxes on consumers, business taxes are minimal. This point is discussed later in this chapter.

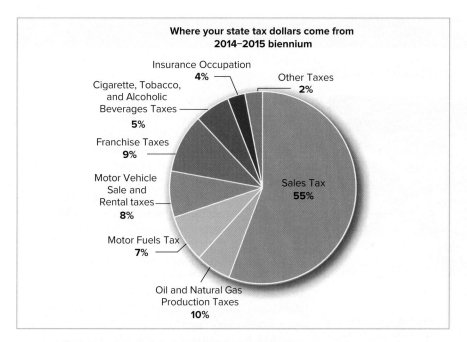

Where your state tax dollars come from
2014–2015 biennium

Insurance Occupation 4%

Other Taxes 2%

Cigarette, Tobacco, and Alcoholic Beverages Taxes 5%

Franchise Taxes 9%

Motor Vehicle Sale and Rental taxes 8%

Motor Fuels Tax 7%

Oil and Natural Gas Production Taxes 10%

Sales Tax 55%

FIGURE 13.2   **Total Tax Revenue in Texas, 2014–2015 Biennium: $98.7 billion.**

SOURCE: Texas Legislative Budget Board. *Fiscal Size-up 2014–15 Biennium,* February 2014, p. 27.

TABLE 13.1

State Tax Revenue per $1,000 for 15 Most Populous States, 2012

Rank Among 50 States	State	Per $1,000 of Personal Income	% of U.S Average
13	New York	$70.18	118
17	California	$65.67	111
20	Michigan	$64.68	109
22	Illinois	$63.15	107
23	North Carolina	$62.87	106
24	Massachusetts	$62.75	106
30	Pennsylvania	$59.19	100
32	New Jersey	$57.75	97
34	Ohio	$57.16	96
35	Washington	$56.27	95
37	Arizona	$55.02	93
43	Virginia	$47.06	79
45	Georgia	$45.32	76
46	**Texas**	**$44.97**	**76**
48	Florida	$42.34	71
	U.S Average	**$59.29**	

Source: U.S. Census Bureau; Texas Legislative Budget Board. *Fiscal Size-up 2014–15 Biennium,* February 2014, 52–53.

Focus On

Tax Contributions of Hispanic Households

© Siri Stafford/Getty Images

In 2013, the federal government collected approximately $1.6 trillion dollars in taxes. State and local governments collected $729.7 billion. What percentage do you think Hispanics contributed to those tax revenues? And, how might those numbers compare to their percentage of the overall population and household count? Let's take a look.

In the United States, according to 2014 estimates, Hispanics make up roughly 17 percent of the population (55 million out of 318 million) and also make up about 10.5 percent of the total households (12.2 million out of 116 million).[12] According to a report by the Partnership for a New American Economy (PNAE), "Hispanic households are estimated to contribute more than $123 billion in federal taxes," about 8 percent of the total 1.6 trillion dollars collected.[13] In addition, while U.S.-born Hispanics account for the majority of the total Hispanic population, just over 30 percent are foreign-born, i.e., immigrants.[14] Households headed by foreign-born Hispanics contributed about 44 percent ($54 billion) of the total Hispanic federal tax payment.

According to PNAE, of the total $729.7 billion tax dollars collected by state and local governments, Hispanic

households paid $66.7 billion, of which $31.9 billion came from immigrants. For Texas in particular, see Table 13.2.

It is also important to include the contributions of unauthorized Hispanic immigrants (noncitizens) when looking at tax data. The Pew Hispanic Center notes, in 2014, roughly 11.3 million individuals were classified as unauthorized immigrants and, of those, 49 percent were Mexican. Of the "5.6 million Mexican unauthorized immigrants living in the U.S.," many are concentrated in "California, Texas, Florida, New York, and Illinois."[15] This is notable because of how much that population contributes in tax dollars. In a report released in 2015 by the Institute on Taxation and Economic policy, unauthorized immigrants in general contribute "an estimated $11.84 billion" in state and local taxes.[16] In 2010, for example, Texas received more than 1.6 billion dollars in state and local taxes from families headed by unauthorized immigrants.[17]

Hispanics contribute significant tax dollars to federal, state, and local governments. "Federal taxes paid by Hispanic households go towards funding federal services—including the military, Social Security, and Medicare—that benefit all Americans."[18] At the state and local level, "Hispanic households help pay for critical local services like school districts, police and fire safety, local road and street maintenance, as well as emergency medical services."[19] Revenues at all levels of government increasingly depend on the relatively youthful Hispanic population, particularly as more move into the workforce.[20]

Critical Thinking Questions

1. Based on the data provided in Table 13.2, in Texas what percentage of all residents' federal and state/local tax revenues were contributed by all Hispanics?

2. As discussed in this chapter, all government services require an expenditure of resources. If all unauthorized immigrants left Texas, what would be the likely consequence for state revenue?

TABLE 13.2

Tax Contributions of Hispanic Households in Texas, 2013 (in billions)

	All Residents	All Hispanics	Foreign-Born Hispanics
Federal	$120.7	$23.6	$ 8.4
State/Local	$ 49.4	$ 11.4	$ 4.6
Combined Taxes	$170.1	$35.0	$13.0

Source: Partnership for a New American Economy, "The Power of the Purse: The Contributions of Hispanics to America's Spending Power and Tax Revenues in 2013," Table 3. December 11, 2014, http://www.renewoureconomy.org/wp-content/uploads/2014/12/ PNAE_hispanic_contributions.pdf.

Equity in Taxes

Learning Objective: Discuss the issue of equity in taxes in the U.S. generally and in Texas specifically.

The question of who should pay taxes raises many issues. Should those who benefit from public services pay taxes (**benefit-based taxes**), or should those who can most afford it pay the taxes? Some taxes are based more on the benefit a person receives, and others are based more on the **ability to pay**. For example, the excise tax on gasoline is an example of a tax based on benefit received rather than on ability to pay. A large portion of the gasoline tax is earmarked for highway construction. The more gasoline people buy, the more tax they pay, and the more benefit they receive from using the streets and highways.

For most taxes, other than the gasoline tax, showing direct benefit is problematic. Benefit received is more applicable to service charges and fees than to taxes. Sometimes the service charge covers the actual cost of providing the service, such as for garbage collection. In other cases, the service charge might cover only part of the cost of providing the service. College students receive most of the benefit from attending classes, and they pay tuition and fees to attend. In state-supported universities and colleges, however, not all of the cost of a college education is covered by tuition and fees paid by students. Some of the cost is still paid by taxpayers.

Generally, when individual benefit can be measured, at least part of the cost of the service is paid in the form of fees. People using a public golf course pay a greens fee, hunters pay for hunting licenses, and drivers pay a driver's license and tag fee. Often these funds go directly to the government unit providing the service. Taxpayers may pick up part of the cost through money paid in taxes. For example, greens fees paid by golfers often do not cover the total capital and operating costs of running a golf course. The difference is paid from revenue from other sources, typically from property tax revenues.

Other taxes, such as the federal income tax, are based more on ability to pay. The higher your net income, the higher your income tax bracket, and the higher the percentage of your net income you pay in federal income taxes. Most taxes, especially at the state level, are not based on ability to pay.

Regressive and Progressive Taxes

Using the criterion of ability to pay, taxes can be ranked as regressive or progressive. A **regressive tax** takes a higher percentage of income from low-income people, and a **progressive tax** takes a higher percentage from higher-income people. Economists also talk about **proportional taxes**, in which the tax paid is a fixed percentage of each person's income. Examples of proportional taxes are difficult to come by but, in theory, are possible. Perhaps the best example of a proportional tax is the tax on earned income for Medicare. One might argue that some state income taxes that tax each person the same percentage of income are proportional. No taxes in Texas can be described as proportional. The key to understanding this is not the total dollars paid but the percentage of income taken by the tax.

---

benefit-based taxes
Taxes for which there is a relationship between the amount paid in taxes and services received; motor fuel taxes are a good example.

---

ability to pay
Taxes that are not based on the benefit received but the wealth, or ability to pay, of an individual

---

regressive taxes
Taxes that take a higher percentage of income from low-income persons

---

progressive taxes
Taxes that take a higher percentage of income from high-income persons

---

proportional taxes
Taxes that take the same percentage of income from all citizens

Texas has one of the most regressive tax structures of all the states (see Table 13.3). The Institute for Taxation and Economic Policy, a Washington, D.C., advocacy group, issues a report that ranks every state by the progressivity or regressivity of their tax systems. Texas made the "Terrible Ten" list in the 2015 edition, ranking third among all states.[21] It is worth noting that the top four—Washington, Florida, Texas, and South Dakota—do not levy a personal income tax, and 6 of the top 10 states derive one-half to two-thirds of their tax revenue from sales and excise taxes.[22] Figure 13.3 shows tax revenue collected for major tax categories as a percentage of income by income group in 2015, and Figure 13.4 shows the U.S. average percentages of all states for each income group. As the figure shows, a Texas family in the lowest 20 percent of income will be paying about 12.5 percent of their income in taxes, whereas the national average for families in the lowest 20 percent of income is slightly less at 10.9 percent.

Figures 13.3 and 13.4 show that, although all state tax structures are regressive, the tax structure in Texas is more regressive than average. Table 13.3 shows that the top four states, including Texas, that have the most regressive tax systems have no personal income tax. These states also have the lowest taxes on the rich.[23]

The degree to which taxes are regressive or progressive depends upon many factors. Regressivity and progressivity are affected not only by the mix of taxes used in a state (income, sales, excise, property) but also by taxation rates and what is subject to tax. What is subject to taxation is called the **tax base**. For example, some states tax only unearned income (stock dividends and interest) instead of earned income (wages and salaries). Others do the opposite. Some states have a proportional rate for state income tax rather than a progressive tax rate.

With the sales tax, the tax base—what is subject to sales tax—is an important factor. If food and medicine are subject to a sales tax, the tax is more regressive because these are commonly consumed goods for which lower-income earners would pay a higher percentage of their income in order to pay the tax.

tax base

The items that are subject to tax; for example, the items subject to sales tax

TABLE 13.3

The 10 Most Regressive State Tax Systems (2015)

Taxes as Shares of Income for Non-elderly Residents

	Taxes as a Percent of Income		
Income Group	**Poorest 20%**	**Middle 60%**	**Top 1%**
Washington	16.80%	10.10%	2.40%
Florida	12.90%	8.30%	1.90%
Texas	**12.50%**	**8.80%**	**2.90%**
South Dakota	11.30%	7.90%	1.80%
Illinois	13.20%	10.90%	4.60%
Pennsylvania	12.00%	10.10%	4.20%
Tennessee	10.90%	8.40%	3.00%
Arizona	12.50%	9.50%	4.60%
Kansas	11.10%	9.20%	3.60%
Indiana	12.00%	10.60%	5.20%

Source: Institute on Taxation & Economic Policy, "*Who Pays? A Distributional Analysis of the Tax Systems in All 50 States,*" January 2015 (http://www.itep.org/pdf/whopaysreport.pdf),4.

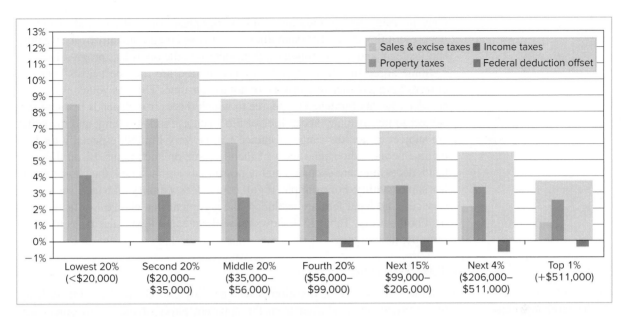

FIGURE 13.3   State and Local Taxes in Texas, 2015 State and local taxes imposed on non-elderly tax payers as share of income.

SOURCE: Institute on Taxation and Economic Policy, "Who Pays? A Distributional Analysis of Tax Systems in All 50 States," January 2015 (http://www.itep.org/pdf/whopaysreport.pdf), 115–116.

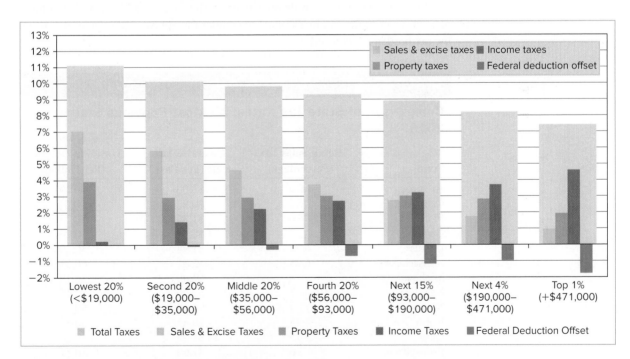

FIGURE 13.4   State and Local Taxes, All States, 2015 State and local taxes imposed on residents as share of income.

SOURCE: Institute on Taxation and Economic Policy, "Who Pays? A Distributional Analysis of Tax Systems in All 50 States," January 2015 (http://www.itep.org/pdf/whopaysreport.pdf), 131–132.

Only 17 states exempt food items, 44 exempt prescription drugs, and 11 exempt nonprescription drugs. By exempting services used predominantly by the wealthy, such as legal and accounting fees, from sales tax, the tax is less progressive.

Some argue that taxes based on consumption are the "best taxes" because citizens have a choice to consume or not to consume. The less you consume, the smaller your tax burden. The degree to which this is true depends upon what is subject to tax. If many necessities of life, such as food, clothing, and medicine, are subject to tax, the range of choice will be very limited, especially for low-income people who spend most of their income on such items. If, on the other hand, necessities are excluded and nonessentials are included, the choice theory has some validity. For example, if golf course fees, country club fees, accounting services, and legal fees are excluded, the argument that choice is a factor takes on a hollow ring. Table 13.4 shows rates of state and local sales taxes in the 15 most populous states.

Tax Shifting

tax shifting
Passing taxes on to other citizens

tax incidence
The person actually paying the tax

Another tax issue is the question of who actually pays the taxes, or **tax shifting**. Some taxes can be shifted from the apparent payer of the tax to others who become the true payers, or the **incidence**, of the tax. For example, a business may respond to a tax rate increase in three general ways: (1) by shifting the tax onto the consumer through increased prices; (2) by shifting the tax onto workers in the form of lower wages or fewer benefits; and (3) by absorbing the cost of the tax through lower profits to its owners or, in the case of publicly traded companies, in lower returns to investors.[24] No matter the approach, the goal of shifting the tax burden is achieved.

TABLE 13.4

Comparison of State Tax Rates: 15 Most Populous States, 2013

State	Retail Sales Tax (Percentage)	Cigarette Tax Rate (Per Pack)	Gasoline Tax Rate (Per Gallon)
Arizona	6.6	$2.00	$0.19
California	7.5	$0.87	$0.43
Florida	6	$1.34	$0.17
Georgia	4	$0.37	$0.20
Illinois	6.25	$1.98	$0.20
Massachusetts	6.25	$2.51	$0.21
Michigan	6	$2.00	$0.19
New Jersey	7	$2.70	$0.15
New York	4	$4.35	$0.27
North Carolina	4.75	$0.45	$0.38
Ohio	5.75	$1.25	$0.28
Pennsylvania	6	$1.60	$0.31
Texas	**6.25**	**$1.41**	**$0.20**
Virginia	5	$0.30	$0.18
Washington	6.5	$3.03	$0.38

Source: Federation of Tax Administrators in Legislative Budget Board, *Fiscal Size-Up 2014–15*, p. 56, Figure 69.

Students renting apartments near their campus and who never receive a property tax bill provide another example of tax shifting. The landlord pays the tax each year; however, the landlord will try to pass along the property tax as part of the rent. Market conditions will determine when 100 percent of the tax is passed along to the renter and when the landlord has to lower prices and absorb part of the tax in lower profits.

Except for personal income tax, all taxes can be shifted to others, and market conditions will decide when taxes are shifted. People sometimes argue against business tax increases by advancing the argument that such increases will "simply result in higher prices to the customer." If taxes on businesses could always be shifted forward to customers as higher prices, no business would object to tax increases. Except for the inconvenience of collecting the tax and forwarding it to the government, there would be no cost involved. Obviously, taxes cannot always be shifted to the customer as higher prices, and businesses resist tax increases.

CORE OBJECTIVE

Being Socially Responsible . . .

Texas taxes prepared food items, but does not tax unprepared food items (e.g., raw meats and fresh produce). If, as noted earlier in this chapter, individuals can be excluded from receiving services, such as electricity, because of the inability to pay, how does taxing prepared food impact our state's poorest citizens?

© Editorial Image, LLC/Alamy

Local Taxes

Learning Objective: Discuss local taxes in Texas.

In addition to taxes collected at the state level, local governments in Texas also collect taxes from two primary sources—property tax and local sales tax. Almost all units of local government collect property tax. For school districts, the property tax is the single largest source of revenue, exceeding state contributions. For so-called rich school districts, all of the cost of running local schools may come from the property tax. The property tax is also an important source of revenue for cities and counties. In addition, most cities, many counties, and all local transit authorities collect a local sales tax. In Texas, the local sales tax is fixed by state law at no more than 2 percent of the value of sales. Thus, in most urban areas in Texas, there is a 6.25 percent state sales tax plus a 2.0 percent local tax, for a total of 8.25 percent total sales tax.

There is effectively no state-level property tax in Texas. All but a small portion of property tax revenue collected goes to local governments. In calendar year 2014, the most recent year for which data is available, local governments in Texas levied approximately $49.1 billion in property taxes, an increase of 11 percent in real dollars since 2009. Table 13.5 shows the property tax collections by

TABLE 13.5

Property Tax Collections by Local Governments in Texas, 2009–2014 (numbers in millions)

Type of Government	2009	2010	2011	2012	2013	2014
School Districts	$21.8	$21.5	$22.0	$23.1	$24.9	$26.8
City Governments	$ 6.6	$ 6.8	$ 6.7	$ 7.0	$ 7.3	$ 7.8
County Governments	$ 6.5	$ 6.6	$ 6.7	$ 7.1	$ 7.6	$ 8.1
Special Districts	$ 5.1	$ 5.4	$ 5.0	$ 5.5	$ 5.5	$ 6.4
Total Property Tax	$40.0	$40.3	$40.4	$42.7	$45.3	$49.1

Source: Comptroller of Public Accounts in Legislative Budget Board, Fiscal Size-Up 2014–15, p. 42, Figure 50.

TABLE 13.6

Comparison of Property Tax Rates per $1000 of Personal Income: 15 Most Populous States, 2011

State	Revenue	Rank among 50 states
New Jersey	$55.17	1
New York	$45.64	6
Illinois	$42.96	11
Texas	**$38.42**	**12**
Michigan	$37.89	13
Massachusetts	$37.72	14
Florida	$34.33	21
California	$32.52	23
Arizona	$31.26	24
Pennsylvania	$30.82	25
Ohio	$30.12	27
Virginia	$29.74	29
Georgia	$29.31	30
Washington	$28.95	31
North Carolina	$24.83	39
U.S. AVERAGE	**$34.23**	
Texas as % of U.S.	$112.2	

Source: U.S. Census Bureau in Legislative Budget Board, Fiscal Size-Up 2014–15, p. 54, Figure 68.

local government type from 2009 to 2014. Texas local governments, especially school districts, are heavily dependent upon property tax revenue. Texas is not a low-property-tax state. Table 13.6 shows the comparison with the 15 most populous states. Nationally, Texas has the 12th-highest property tax rates per $1,000 of personal income, and the 4th highest among the top 15.

Comparison of State and Local Tax Revenues

Local taxes are often lost in the focus on state revenues and expenditures. Over the past several decades, the legislature has paid for less and less of the cost of local government services, especially school districts. Figure 13.5 shows the total state and local tax revenue picture for the State of Texas in 2014–15. As the

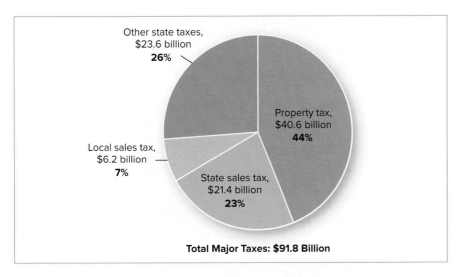

Total Major Taxes: $91.8 Billion

FIGURE 13.5 **Major Tax Revenue in Texas as a Percentage of Major Taxes in Texas in 2014–2015 Biennium (numbers in millions)**

SOURCE: Texas Comptroller Office in Legislative Budget Board, *Fiscal Size-Up 2014–15.*

figure shows, property taxes in Texas are almost half of all state and local revenues collected (44 percent). If the local sales tax is added to the local property tax, local tax revenues constitute 50.9 percent of total taxes collected in the state. Thus, local governments collect and pay just over half the total cost of government in Texas. If the current trend of the state spending less continues, local governments will be picking up a greater share of the cost of providing services to the citizens of the state.

The fact that local governments collect over half of state and local revenues combined in Texas is an indication of the declining role of the state government in funding services, especially schools. This has been a trend in school financing for several decades and the root cause of much of the objection to property tax increases.

Nontax Revenue Sources

Learning Objective: Discuss nontax revenue sources in Texas.

Service charges and fees are a source of **nontax revenue** for state governments. Governments often charge service charges and assess fees when a person can be excluded from receiving the service for nonpayment. When this exclusion is not possible, tax revenue usually finances the service. Figure 13.6 shows nontax revenue by source for the State of Texas in 2014–15. Nontax revenue sources make up about 34 percent of state revenue. Whereas state governments obtain only a small percentage of their revenue from service charges and fees, some local governments, especially cities, are heavily dependent upon service charges and fees to finance their services. Cities usually impose service charges or fees for water, sewer, and solid waste collection. Seventy-two cities

nontax revenue

Governmental revenue derived from service charges, fees (tuition), lottery, and other sources

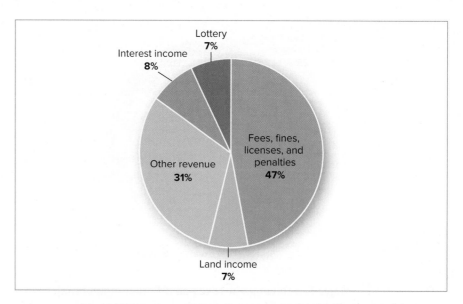

FIGURE 13.6   Total Nontax Revenue for Texas 2014–2015 Biennium: $35.5 Million

SOURCE: Texas Comptroller Office in Legislative Budget Board, *Fiscal Size-Up 2014–15*, p. 27, Figure 39.

in Texas also operate an electrical system and receive revenue for providing this service. The largest cities with electrical systems are San Antonio, Austin, Lubbock, Brownsville, Garland, Bryan, and College Station.

The trend in recent years has been to increase service charges and fees as a way to increase revenue and avoid raising taxes. All students attending state colleges and universities in Texas have experienced these increases as higher tuition and service charges (see Chapter 11). In terms of total dollars in the state budget, the various service charges and fees provide 15 percent of total state revenue.

The state lottery and interest income generates about 1.5 percent of all (total) state revenue. Even though the Texas Lottery has been the most successful lottery in history in terms of total dollars raised, it contributes only a small portion of the state's total budget and will never be a significant player in providing revenue. In recent years, revenue from the lottery has declined.

Federal aid makes up about 35.5 percent of the Texas 2014–2015 biennial budget. As shown in Figure 13.7, the largest part (61.8 percent) of these federal funds goes to health and human services for Medicare or Medicaid payments and welfare payments. About 15.5 percent of these funds goes to education, and about 16 percent goes to business and economic development. The remainder is divided among various other federal programs.

The Budget "Fix"

The legislature is limited in the amount of discretion it has in spending money. Much of the state's budget (82.7 percent) consists of restricted funds that can be spent only for specific purposes as stipulated by constitutional provisions, enabling legislation, fund formulas, or by external providers such as the federal government. Although the legislature could change legislation and funding formula rules, these are often politically difficult. Generally, special interests have a strong attachment to these appropriations and will fight to maintain them. Table 13.7 shows how much of the state's budget is restricted. These restrictions primarily are the results of funds being **earmarked** for specific programs (see Chapter 2).

On the revenue side, many of the taxes and fees collected are either dedicated or nondedicated. Like restricted funds, **dedicated revenue** is specified for a particular purpose either by constitutional provision or state law. For example, the proceeds from the state lottery go to education and the motor fuel tax goes

earmarked
Money dedicated to a specific expenditure; for example, the excise tax on gasoline funds highway infrastructure

dedicated revenue
Money dedicated to a specific expenditure by constitutional provision or law

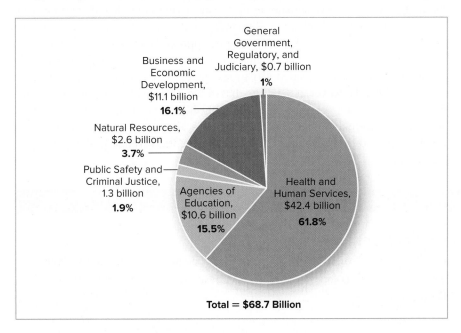

FIGURE 13.7   Total Federal Funds by State Function 2014–2015 Biennium (numbers in billions).

SOURCE: Legislative Budget Board, Fiscal Size up 2014–15, p. 6, Figure 9.

TABLE 13.7

General Fund Restricted Appropriations, 2014–15 Biennium

Function	In Millions Appropriation	Percentage of Total Appropriation
Appropriations or allocations of revenue dedicated by constitutional or statutory provisions	$ 45,753.4	44.7%
Appropriations influenced by federal law, regulation, or court decisions	$ 27,213.7	26.6%
Appropriations influenced by formulas	$ 11,602.8	11.3%
Total Restricted Appropriations	**$ 84,551.9**	**82.7%**
Nonrestricted appropriations	$ 17,555.4	17.2%

Source: Legislative Budget Board, *Fiscal Size-Up 2014–15*, p. 9, Figure 16.

nondedicated revenue
Money available for general spending

discretionary funding
Those funds in the state budget that are not earmarked for specific purposes

primarily to state and local road programs. **Nondedicated revenue** is revenue available for general spending. The earmarking of revenues obviously limits the ability of the legislature to change budget priorities or to react to emergency situations. If one fund is short, movement of money from another fund may not be possible. Last year's budget becomes the best predictor of next year's budget. Changes in the budget occur incrementally, in small amounts, over a long period of time.

Table 13.7 indicates that most funds in Texas are fixed. Only 17.2 percent of general revenue funds are nonrestricted and, therefore, considered **discretionary funding**. This does not give the legislature much leeway in making changes in the budget without new legislation or constitutional amendments approved by the voters in a statewide election. Remember, before constitutional amendments make it to voters on the ballot, they must be approved by two-thirds of members in both houses. That is not to say that amendments don't happen. After all, the constitution has been amended 491 times since 1876, and 59 times in the past ten years alone. However, it is telling that of the 64 amendments proposed since 2005, only two were amendments changing how dedicated revenue is apportioned. Both were adopted. The latest, in 2015, dedicated certain sales and use tax revenue and motor vehicle sales, use, and rental revenue to the state highway fund.

CORE OBJECTIVE

Source: National Park Service

Communicating Effectively . . .

Consider Table 13.7, which illustrates how specific appropriations are restricted. What percentage of funds is not restricted? How does restricting funds impact budget flexibility?

Expenditures: Where the Money Goes

Learning Objective: Describe Texas government expenditures.

The pattern of expenditures for Texas differs little from most states in terms of the items funded. In most states, three items consume most of the state budget—education, health and welfare, and transportation. In recent years, an increase in the prison population has greatly increased the amount spent for public safety, which includes prison operations. After these items, everything else pales in comparison. Figure 13.8 shows the major expenditure items in the State of Texas 2014–2015 biennial budget.

Although education takes the lion's share of the state budget (about 37 percent), local school districts contribute about 60 percent of the funds for local schools.

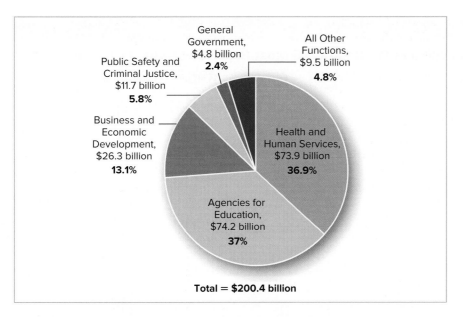

Total = $200.4 billion

FIGURE 13.8   Total Appropriations by Function, 2014–2015 Biennium (numbers in billions).

SOURCE: Legislative Budget Board, *Fiscal Size up 2014–15,* p. 6, Figure 2.

The state currently finances about 40 percent of the cost of elementary and secondary education. This is a decline in state contributions from a decade ago. The state's contribution has been steadily decreasing, and school districts have been forced to pick up a greater share of the cost of local education, which they are covering by assessing higher local property taxes.

Health and human services accounts for about 37 percent of the state budget and is funded primarily with federal grants to the state. The State of Texas contributes less than most states to the cost of providing these services. The Texas Constitution prohibits spending more than an amount equal to 1 percent of the state budget on welfare. These are the redistributive services discussed previously. Neither the tax structure nor the political culture supports such activities. Many students of budgeting have made the point that a budget is a statement of policy in monetary terms. What and how much money a state spends largely expresses its priorities. The budget becomes a statement of the dominant values in the state. A comparison of Texas with other large industrial states on the primary budget items will tell us something about what Texans value.

As shown by examining the 15 most populous states, Texas ranks near the lower-mid range in expenditures for health and human services (Table 13.8). Although Texas spends much money in total dollars, it tends to spend less than the average comparable state in per capita dollars for most items. In recent years, most of the growth in state expenditures has been driven by population increases alone. In terms of per capita expenditures, the state has remained at about the same level over the past decade.

TABLE 13.8

State Government Expenditures Per Capita, 15 Most Populous States, Fiscal Year 2011

State	Total	Education	Highways	Hospitals	Welfare	Corrections	All Others
Washington	178	80	11	15	14	13	44
New Jersey	166	38	7	20	10	10	81
North Carolina	160	68	11	21	1	22	37
Virginia	154	68	9	18	3	17	38
Michigan	147	77	3	19	10	15	23
Massachusetts	139	47	4	9	10	9	60
Pennsylvania	132	48	12	9	9	15	40
Georgia	126	56	5	7	9	18	31
New York	125	27	6	22	2	16	51
Texas	**124**	**52**	**5**	**10**	**9**	**17**	**32**
Ohio	120	60	6	14	2	13	25
California	108	42	5	12	1	16	32
Arizona	106	46	4	1	7	16	32
Illinois	102	48	5	9	7	9	24
Florida	97	29	4	2	5	16	40
U.S. AVERAGE	**140**	**55**	**7**	**13**	**7**	**15**	**43**
Texas as% of U.S.	88.80%	93.80%	72.40%	77.40%	120.70%	114.10%	74.20%

Source: U.S. Census Bureau in Legislative Budget Board, *Fiscal Size-Up 2014–15*, p. 62, Figure 76.

Continuing Issues in State Finance in Texas

Learning Objective: Identify and explain continuing issues in Texas state finance.

Over the past 20 years, Texas has experienced a number of fiscal shortfalls. The legislature has been forced to meet in special sessions to correct these problems. Many of the fixes have been short-term. An examination of several tax issues will help us understand the need for a long-term solution.

Tax Structure

In the past 20 years, Texas has experienced various financial problems. During the 1980s, there were 10 special sessions of the legislature to attempt to correct revenue shortfalls. These shortfalls were caused primarily by a decline in the state economy because of a drop in oil prices from a high of $40 per barrel to a low of less than $10. The fiscal crisis was worsened by the state's tax structure. Texas is very dependent on highly **income-elastic taxes** (85 to 90 percent) that rise or fall very quickly relative to changes in economic conditions. This means that when the economy is growing or contracting, tax revenue grows or contracts proportionately with the growth or contraction in the economy. For example, as retail sales grow, the sales tax grows. Texas is very dependent upon sales and excise taxes, which are highly income-elastic. The same is true for the tax on oil and gas extracted in Texas. As the price of oil increased on world markets, the economy of the state boomed, and tax revenue increased. When the oil bust came, the opposite happened, and Texas

income-elastic taxes

Taxes that rise and fall quickly relative to changes in economic conditions; the Texas tax system is very income-elastic

found itself extremely short of revenue. People quit buying goods and services subject to the sales and excise tax, and revenue fell accordingly. As the price of oil declined, oil revenue fell. Depressed oil prices also caused severe economic problems in Mexico and a devaluation of the peso. Fewer pesos flowed across the border, and some border communities experienced severe economic problems and declining local revenue along with the state revenue decline.

Figure 13.9 and Table 13.9 compare the tax dependency of the 15 most populous states. Texas is far more dependent on sales taxes than most other large states. Only Florida and Washington are about as dependent as Texas on consumer taxes. Washington, like Texas, lacks both a personal and a corporate income tax, and Florida lacks a personal income tax. Heavy dependency

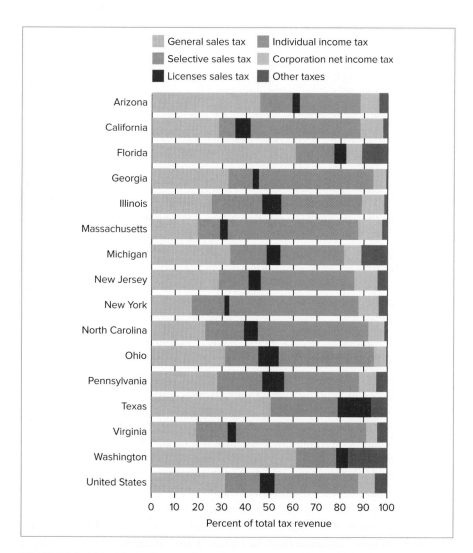

FIGURE 13.9   State Comparison, Percentage of Total Tax Revenue by Source

SOURCE: U.S. Census Bureau in Legislative Budget Board, *Fiscal Size-Up 2014–15*, p. 54, Figure 67.

TABLE 13.9

Sources of Revenue for 15 Most Populous States (in Percent), 2012

State	Total Sales Tax	General Sales Tax	Selective Sales Tax	License Tax	Individual Income Tax	Corporation Net Income	Other Taxes
Arizona	62.2	47.9	14.3	2.9	23.8	5.0	0.3
California	34.4	25.4	9.0	7.7	49.0	7.1	0.0
Florida	82.6	58.8	23.8	6.7	–	6.1	4.6
Georgia	43.8	32.0	11.8	3.1	49.1	3.6	0.1
Illinois	39.2	22.0	17.2	7.1	43.1	9.6	0.8
Massachusetts	32.1	22.3	9.8	3.9	52.3	8.8	2.8
Michigan	54.7	39.9	14.8	5.9	28.5	2.5	0.8
New Jersey	43.7	29.5	14.2	5.2	40.5	7.0	3.5
New York	32.0	16.6	15.3	2.7	54.2	6.4	4.8
North Carolina	42.0	24.5	17.5	6.5	45.7	5.4	0.4
Ohio	50.6	31.9	18.7	13.8	34.8	0.5	0.3
Pennsylvania	52.1	27.8	24.2	8.0	30.7	5.6	3.6
Texas	**77.0**	**50.4**	**26.6**	**15.5**	–	–	**7.5**
Virginia	32.3	19.2	13.0	4.3	56.3	4.6	2.3
Washington	80.4	60.2	20.2	5.6	–	–	3.2
U.S. AVERAGE	**47.2**	**30.5**	**16.6**	**6.8**	**35.3**	**5.3**	**3.9**

Source: U.S. Census Bureau in Legislative Budget Board, *Fiscal Size-Up 2014–15*, p. 54, Figure 67.

on consumer taxes makes for an income-elastic tax structure. In bad economic times, the state will face revenue shortfalls.

The Texas tax structure is very dependent upon highly income-elastic consumer taxes (such as sales and gasoline taxes), and when, not if, there is an economic downturn, the state will again experience revenue shortfalls. The potential for these problems to occur again is great.

Is There a Personal Income Tax in the Future for Texas?

Texas, Alaska, Florida, Nevada, South Dakota, Washington, and Wyoming are the only seven states without any form of personal income tax. In addition, New Hampshire and Tennessee have a limited income tax on unearned income (dividends, interest, and capital gains). Being in such a limited company of states without an income tax is not troublesome to most Texans. Politically there is great resistance to imposing such a tax. In 1992, the voters approved a constitutional amendment preventing the legislature from enacting an income tax without voter approval. Several legislative leaders felt that without voter approval, the tax would never be imposed by the legislature.

Texas will face another fiscal crisis as long as it is so dependent on consumer taxes. What recourse is available to the state? During past crises, the problem of revenue shortfall was often solved by raising sales and gasoline taxes and by increasing fees. Can these taxes be tapped again? Texas has one of the highest sales tax rates, currently sitting at 6.25 percent. Only California, Indiana, Mississippi, New Jersey, Rhode Island, and Tennessee have reached 7 percent. Raising the rate might not be possible.

Taking Personal Responsibility . . .

Although few individuals would express a preference for higher taxes, given the information in this chapter about the goods and services the state provides and the revenue data presented in Figure 13.9 and Table 13.8, should Texans advocate for a personal income tax? Why or why not?

Source: United States Department of Agriculture Agricultural Research Service

One suggestion, made by former Lieutenant Governor Bob Bullock and others, was to expand the base of the sales tax. Currently most services are not subject to a sales tax; most notably excluded are legal and financial services. Politically, given the large number of attorneys in the legislature (35 percent), pushing such a change through the legislature might be difficult. The proposal was killed in the past several sessions of the legislature, including a special session in 2004.

As of July 2016, the state tax on gasoline or motor fuel in Texas is at 20 cents per gallon, plus 18.4 cents in federal tax. The highest state gasoline tax is in Pennsylvania, at 51.4 cents per gallon.[25] There might be room to raise the gas tax a few cents per gallon, but if prices at the pump continue to rise, the prospect of this happening is unlikely.

Over the past few decades, the tax on oil and natural gas production, which is based on the dollar value of the oil and gas extracted from the ground, has generally increased. Since the cost of crude bottomed out in 1998 to the effect of $11 per barrel, production began falling off and prices began to steadily rise. The long-term outlook is for these taxes to rise, with the natural gas tax rising more than the oil tax.[26] In 2008, however, along with the global financial crisis, there was a huge surge up to $150 per barrel, then a huge plunge to back below $50 per barrel. When the economy began to recover, so did the price of crude, reaching back up to a stable $100 per barrel from 2010 to 2014. There was another price dive in 2014 as, even though global demand was slowing down due to various international crises, the United States has been increasing production and the Middle Eastern producers decided to maintain their own output to keep their market share. As of mid-June 2016, the price is roughly $50 per barrel.[27] As can be seen, the long-term price of a barrel of oil is very much tied to national and international factors. New oil from Russia and the U.S., continued war in the Middle East, and many other factors can affect the price of oil and the amount of revenue available.

Texas has a form of corporate "income tax" that is called a **franchise fee**. Originally it was assessed only on corporations doing business in the state. It did not apply to limited partnerships, corporations, limited liability companies, business trusts, professional associations, or business associations. Some businesses and corporations changed their structure to avoid the tax. The legislature was forced to eliminate many of these loopholes in 2007 and apply the franchise fee to most businesses in the state. The tax was first collected in 2008. As of 2014,

franchise fee
Major business tax in Texas that is assessed on income earned by corporations in the state

the franchise fee is the second-largest source of tax revenue ($9.3 billion, behind sales and use taxes, which total $48.9 billion).[28] The franchise fee seems to be a much improved source of business tax and may be filling the loopholes in the older franchise fee.

The franchise fee is rather complicated, but basically the tax is applied to the gross receipts of most businesses, with deductions allowed for some expenses such as wages, salaries, and employee benefits. Taxable entities with revenues of $300,000 or less owe no tax; however, all businesses must file a report. The tax rate is 0.5 percent for wholesalers and retailers and 1 percent for most other taxable entities. This tax is applied to most businesses in the state.

Conclusion

Although the budget for the State of Texas is large in total dollars, the state ranks toward the bottom (46th) in terms of per capita expenditures.

Some important conclusions should be drawn from analyzing government financing in Texas. First, although Texas is a resource-rich state, its tax effort is low compared to its tax capacity. Texas has one of the lowest tax burdens of any state, which is in keeping with the political culture of Texas and the emphasis on limited government. Yet, despite Texas's low tax status, Texas has one of the most regressive tax structures. The state government is heavily reliant on the regressive general sales tax, and the state does not have a personal income tax, which tends to be progressive in structure. It should be no surprise that the majority of states with the most regressive tax structures do not have a personal income tax.

Second, it is important to understand that it is difficult to achieve substantial changes in the state's budget.

Nearly 83 percent of the state's budget is fixed by constitutional, statutory, or federal mandates. Nearly 40 percent of the state's budget is provided through transfer payments from the federal government and, with that, less budget flexibility.

Finally, Texas will have to decide how best to manage growing fiscal challenges. While the Texas economy continues to be one of the strongest in the country with economic growth outpacing the national average, there is growing concern that state revenues will not keep pace with the demand for services like transportation and education in the coming years. Unlike the federal government, Texas, like all states (Vermont is the only notable exception), is required to balance its budget. It remains to be seen how the state will meet these challenges, although any changes to the tax structure are highly unlikely.

Summary

LO: Explain why governments provide services to citizens.

Markets fail to provide certain goods and services because of some unique characteristics shared by these types of goods, called public goods. Pure public goods are both nonexclusive and nonexhaustive (also referred to as non-rivalrous). Some goods, however, are quasi-public goods, which the government also provides. These are not pure public goods in that they may share only certain features of pure public goods, or there is a broader societal purpose for ensuring availability. There are three important subtypes: social goods, tolls goods, and common-pool goods.

LO: Describe sources of state revenue in Texas.

For state governments, the primary source of revenue is taxes paid by citizens, not money derived from service

charges or fees. The amount of tax money available for any given state depends on the wealth of the citizens of that state. The most common, single sources of revenue for state governments are consumer taxes, such as sales and excise taxes on gasoline, tobacco, and liquor. These account for roughly 80 percent of all state tax revenue.

LO: Discuss the issue of equity in taxes in the U.S. generally and in Texas specifically.

A major question regarding taxes is who should pay, and why. Should those who benefit from public services pay taxes (benefit-based taxes), or should those who can most afford it pay the taxes? It is difficult to determine who most benefits from public and quasi-public goods. Generally, when individual benefit can be measured, at least part of the cost of the service is paid in the form of fees. Other taxes, such as the federal income tax, are based more on ability to pay. The higher your net income, the higher your income tax bracket, and the higher the percentage of your net income you pay in federal income taxes. Most taxes, especially at the state level, are based on benefits.

LO: Discuss local taxes in Texas.

Local governments in Texas collect taxes from two primary sources—property tax and local sales tax. Almost all units of local government collect property tax. There is no state-level property tax, yet property tax accounts for a major percentage of total state revenue. The fact that local governments collect over half of state and local revenues combined in Texas is an indication of the declining role of the state government in funding services, especially schools. In addition, most cities, many counties, and all local transit authorities collect a local sales tax (set at no more than 2 percent).

LO: Discuss nontax revenue sources in Texas.

Nontax revenue is derived from service charges, fees (tuition), lottery, and other sources. Governments often charge service charges and assess fees when a person can be excluded from receiving the service for nonpayment. Nontax revenue sources make up about 34 percent of state revenue. Whereas state governments obtain only a small percentage of their revenue from service charges and fees, some local governments, especially

cities, are heavily dependent upon service charges and fees to finance their services. Cities usually impose service charges or fees for water, sewer, and solid waste collection. Governments use nontax sources as a way to prevent tax increases.

LO: Describe Texas government expenditures.

A state's budget is a monetary expression of its politics. What and how much money a state spends largely depends on its priorities. In Texas, Education and Health and Human Services are the main areas of expenditure, accounting for nearly 80 percent combined. The state currently finances about 40 percent of the cost of elementary and secondary education, though local governments are increasingly taking on that financial burden. Texas spends less on Health and Human Services than most other states due to its regressive tax structure and political culture.

LO: Identify and explain continuing issues in Texas state finance.

Texas is very dependent on highly income-elastic taxes that rise or fall very quickly relative to changes in economic conditions. These kinds of taxes include sales and excise taxes and the tax on oil and gas extracted in the state, which make up a huge percentage of Texas's total revenue. For example, as the price of oil and gas rises and falls, so too does state revenue. This means that when there is an economic downturn, the state will experience revenue shortfalls.

Key Terms

ability to pay	nonexcludability	regressive taxes
benefit-based taxes	nonexhaustion	tax base
consumer taxes	nonrivalrous consumption	tax capacity
dedicated revenue	nontax revenue	tax effort
discretionary funding	per capita tax	tax exporting
earmarked	political values	tax incidence
franchise fee	progressive taxes	tax shifting
income-elastic taxes	proportional taxes	
nondedicated revenue	public goods	

Notes

[1] U.S. Census Bureau, "State and Local Government Finances Summary: 2013," http://factfinder.census.gov/faces/tableservices/jsf/pages/productview.xhtml?src=bkmk.

[2] Texas Comptroller of Public Accounts, "Revenue by Source for Fiscal Year 2015 (All Funds, Excluding Trust)," http://www.texastransparency.org/State_Finance/Budget_Finance/Reports/Revenue_by_Source/.

[3] Legislative Budget Board, *Summary of Appropriations for the 2016–17 Biennium*, 6, Figure 9, http://www.lbb.state.tx.us/Documents/Budget/Session_Code_84/2580_84_BillSummary.pdf.

[4] Texas Health and Human Services System, Consolidated Budget: Fiscal Years 2016–2017, https://www.hhsc.state .tx.us/about_hhsc/finance/2016–2017.pdf.

[5] Tyler, Cowen, "Public Goods," *The Concise Encyclopedia of Economics,* 2nd Edition, ed. David R. Henderson, (Indianapolis: Liberty Fund, Inc., 2007). Also available at http://www.econlib.org/library/Enc/PubligGoods.html. This is a nice general introduction to the concept, and it generally informs the treatment here. The classic work on the subject of public goods is Paul A. Samuelson, "The Pure Theory of Public Expenditure," *Review of Economics and Statistics* 36:4 (November 1954): 387–389.

[6] There is some debate on the classification of public goods. For example, see Nobel Prize-winning economist Richard H. Coase's classic piece, "The Lighthouse in Economics," *The Journal of Law and Economics,* Vol. 17, No. 2. (October 1974): 357–376. For more on this debate, see David E. Van Zandt, "The Lessons of the Lighthouse: 'Government' or 'Private' Provision of Goods," *Journal of Legal Studies* 22:1 (January 1993): 47–72; and William Barnett and Walter Brock, "Coase and Van Zandt on Lighthouses," *Public Finance Review* 35 (November 2007): 710–733.

[7] John L. Mikesell, *Fiscal Administration: Analysis and Applications for the Public Sector,* 8th ed., (Boston: Wadsworth, 2011), 5–6.

[8] Cowan, "Public Goods."

[9] J. Richard Aronson and John L. Hilley, *Financing State and Local Governments,* 4th ed. (Washington, D.C.: Brookings Institution, 1986), 37–40.

[10] U.S. Department of the Treasury, Resource Center, "2015 Total Taxable Resources Estimates," https://www.treasury. gov/resource-center/economic-policy/taxable-resources /Pages/Total-Taxable-Resources.aspx.

[11] Texas Research League, "The Rating Game," *Analysis 11* (August 1990): 2.

[12] U.S. Census Bureau, QuickFacts, http://www.pewresearch. org/fact-tank/2015/11/19/5-facts-about-illegal-immigration-in-the-u-s/; U.S. Census Bureau, "FFF: Hispanic Heritage Month 2015," Release Number: CB15-FF.18. September 14, 2015, https://www.census.gov/ newsroom/facts-for-features/2015/cb15-ff18.html.

[13] Partnership for a New American Economy, "The Power of the Purse: The Contributions of Hispanics to America's Spending Power and Tax Revenues in 2013," December 11, 2014, p. 11, http://www.renewoureconomy.org/wp-content /uploads/2014/12/PNAE_hispanic_contributions.pdf.

[14] Pew Hispanic Center, "Characteristics of the U.S. Hispanic Population: 2013," in Statistical Portrait of Hispanics in the United States, 2013, http://www.pewhispanic.org/ files/2015/05/2015-05-12_statistical-portrait-of-hispanics-in-the-united-states-2013_final.pdf.

[15] Jens Manuel Krogstad and Jeffrey S. Passel, "5 facts about illegal immigration in the U.S.," Pew Research Center, November 19, 2015, http://www.pewresearch.org /fact-tank/2015/11/19/5-facts-about-illegal-immigration-in-the-u-s/.

[16] Matthew Gardner, Sebastian Johnson, Meg Wiehe, Undocumented Immigrants' State and Local Tax Contributions, The Institute on Taxation and Economic Policy, April 2015 (p. 1), http://www.itep.org/pdf /undocumentedtaxes2015.pdf.

[17] American Immigration Council, "Unauthorized Immigrants Pay Taxes, Too," April 18, 2011, http://www .immigrationpolicy.org/just-facts/unauthorized-immigrants-pay-taxes-too.

[18] Partnership for a New American Economy, "The Power of the Purse: The Contributions of Hispanics to America's Spending Power and Tax Revenues in 2013," December 11, 2014, p. 11, http://www.renewoureconomy. org/wp-content/uploads/2014/12/PNAE_hispanic_ contributions.pdf.

[19] Ibid.

[20] Charles P. Garcia, "Opinion: Want to save Social Security? Embrace Latinos," CNN, April 10, 2015, http://money.cnn. com/2015/04/10/news/economy/social-security-latinos /index.html.

[21] Institute on Taxation and Economic Policy, "Who Pays? A Distribution Analysis of the Tax Systems in All 50 States," 5th ed. (Washington, D.C.: 2015), http://www.itep.org/pdf /whopaysreport.pdf.

[22] Ibid.

[23] Ibid.

[24] Mikesell, John L., *Fiscal Administration Analysis and Application for the Public Sector,* 8th ed., (Boston: Wadsworth, 2011), 355.

[25] American Petroleum Institute, State Motor Fuel Taxes: Notes Summary, Rates Effective 7/1/2016, Revised 8/9/2016. http://www.api.org/~/media/Files/Statistics/ State-Motor-Fuel-Excise-Tax-Update-July-2016.pdf.

[26] Texas Comptroller of Public Accounts, www.cpa.state.tx.us.

[27] Nasdaq, "Crude Oil," http://www.nasdaq.com/markets/crude-oil.aspx?timeframe=10y.

[28] Legislative Budget Board, *Fiscal Size-Up* 2014–15, 29, Figure 40.

GLOSSARY

A

ability to pay Taxes that are not based on the benefit received but the wealth, or ability to pay, of an individual

absentee voting A process that allows a person to vote early, before the regular election; applies to all elections in Texas; also called early voting

acting governor When a governor leaves a state, the position is held by the lieutenant governor, who performs the functions of the office

Adelsverein Society An organization that promoted German immigration to Texas in the 1840s

agenda setting The power of the media to bring issues and problems to the public's attention

agents of socialization family, teachers, peer groups, religious institutions, geographic location, class, gender, race/ethnicity, mass media; those societal forces and institutions which surround individuals from early childhood onward

Anglo Here, refers to non-Hispanic white North Americans of European descent, typically (but not exclusively) English speaking

annual registration A system that requires citizens to reregister to vote every year

appellate courts Higher-level courts that decide on points of law and not questions of guilt or innocence

appointive-elective system In Texas, the system of many judges gaining the initial seat on the court by being appointed and later standing for election

astroturf A political term for an interest group that appears to have many grassroots members but in fact does not have individual citizens as members; rather, it is sponsored by an organization such as a corporation or business association

at-large election system System where all voters in the city elect the mayor and city council members

attorney general Chief counsel to the governor and state agencies; limited criminal jurisdiction

B

Baker v. Carr Court case that required state legislative districts to contain about the same number of citizens

ballot form The forms used by voters to cast their ballots; each county, with approval of the secretary of state, determines the form of the ballot

ballot wording Description of a proposed amendment as it appears on the ballot; can be intentionally noninstructive and misleading to voters in order to affect voter outcome

benefit-based taxes Taxes for which there is a relationship between the amount paid in taxes and services received; motor fuel taxes are a good example

bias The actual or perceived failure of the media to report news objectively

bicameral Legislative body that consists of two houses

biennial session Legislature meets every two years

bill of rights A list of individual rights and freedoms granted to citizens within a constitution

blanket primary system A nominating election in which voters could switch parties between elections

block grants Grants that may be used for broad purposes that allow local governments greater discretion in how funds are spent

boards and commissions Governing body for many state agencies; members appointed by the governor for fixed term

budget fix State laws and constitutional amendments that set aside money to be spent on specific items; the best example is the state gasoline tax being committed to state highways

budgetary powers The ability of a governor to formulate a budget, present it to the legislature, and execute or control the budget

burden of proof The obligation associated with providing evidence sufficient to support the assertion or claim made by the individual bringing suit in a court of law

C

calendars Procedures in the house used to consider different kinds of bills; major bills and minor bills are considered under different procedures

capture The situation in which a state agency or board falls under the heavy influence of or is controlled by its constituency interest groups

categorical grants Grants that may be used to fund specific purposes as defined by the federal government

caucus A meeting of members of a political party to nominate candidates (now used only by minor political parties in Texas)

ceremonial duties The expectation that a governor attends many functions and represents the state; some governors become so active at this role that they get caught in a ceremonial trap and neglect other duties

435

checks and balances   Power granted by the Constitution to each branch of government giving it authority to restrain other branches

chief legislator   The expectation that a governor has an active agenda of legislation to recommend to the legislature and works to pass that agenda

citizen journalism   The collection, dissemination, and analysis of news and information by the general public, especially by means of the Internet

citizen legislatures   Legislatures characterized by low pay, short sessions, and fewer staff resources

city manager   Person hired by the city council to manage the city; serves as the chief administrative officer of the city

civil law   Defines private relationships as well as financial matters or damages to property committed by businesses or other individuals to a person

closed primary system   A nominating election that is closed to all voters except those who have registered as a member of that political party

closed rider   Provisions attached to appropriations bills that are not made public until the conference committee meets

collective bargaining   Negotiations between an employer and a group of employees to determine employment conditions, such as those related to wages, working hours, and safety

collective benefit   Goods that are provided with no charge because there is a broader public benefit associated with the good

commission form   A form of local government where voters elect department heads who also serve as members of the city council

commissioner's court   Legislative body that governs a Texas county

Committee on Calendars   Standing committee of the house that decides which bills will be considered for floor debate by the full house and to which committee they will be assigned

Committee on Local and Consent Calendars   Committee handling minor and noncontroversial bills that normally apply to only a discrete area

commute   The reduction in punishment for an individual convicted of a crime

comptroller of public accounts   Chief tax collector and investor of state funds; does not perform financial audits

confederal system of government   A system of government that divides power between a weak national government and strong, independently sovereign regional governments

conference committees   Joint committees of the house and senate that work out differences in bills passed in each chamber

constitution   The basic document that provides a framework for government and limits what the government can do

constitutional convention   An assembly of citizens which may propose changes to state constitutions through voter approval

consumer taxes   Taxes that citizens pay when they buy goods and services—sales taxes

conviction   Following adoption of articles of impeachment by the lower legislative house, the senate tries the official under those articles; if convicted, the official is removed from office

council-manager form   Form of government where voters elect a mayor and city council; the mayor and city council appoint a professional administrator to manage the city

county chair   Party official elected in each county to organize and support the party

county executive committee   Committee made up of a county chair and all precinct chairs in the county; serves as the official organization for the party in each county

county government   Local unit of government that is primarily the administrative arm of a state government; in most states, it does not provide urban-type services

county sheriff   Elected head of law enforcement in a Texas county

creatures of the state   Local governments are created by state government, and all powers are derived from the state government; there are no inherent rights for local governments independent of what the state grants to them

criminal law   Statutory law that defines both the violation and the penalty the state will seek to have imposed upon the defendant

crisis manager   The expectation that the governor will provide strong leadership in times of a natural or man-made disaster

critical journalism   A style of soft news that focuses on political scandal, vice or mistakes of the government or politicians

crossover voting   Occurs when voters leave their party and vote in the other party's primary

cumulative voting   A system where voters can concentrate (accumulate) all their votes on one candidate rather than casting one vote for each office up for election

D

dedicated revenue   Money dedicated to a specific expenditure by constitutional provision or law

delegate   Representational role of member stating that he or she represents the wishes of the voters

"deregulated" tuition   A decision by the state legislature to allow state colleges and universities to set the rate of tuition charged to students

discretionary funding   Those funds in the state budget that are not earmarked for specific purposes

Due Process of Law Clause   Clause in the Fifth and Fourteenth Amendments of the U.S. Constitution that requires states to treat all citizens equally and that the state must follow certain rules and procedures

Duverger's Law   A scientific law indicating that the electoral system strongly conditions the type of party system that will result

E

earmarked   Money dedicated to a specific expenditure; for example, the excise tax on gasoline funds highway infrastructure

earmarked revenue   Tax revenue set aside for specific purposes; in Texas about 80 percent of revenue is earmarked

economic regions   Divisions of the state based on dominant economic activity

electioneering   Various activities in which interest groups engage to try to influence the outcome of elections

empresario   A person who contracted with the Spanish or Mexican government to recruit new settlers to Texas in exchange for the ability to claim land

enhanced punishment   The application of the next most serious penalty for repeat offenders

Equal Protection Clause   Clause in the Fourteenth Amendment of the U.S. Constitution that requires states to treat all citizens equally

equal time rule   Provided that a broadcaster permitting one political candidate access to the airwaves must afford equal opportunities to all other such candidates seeking the same office

exculpatory evidence   Material evidence that could assist the accused in proving that he or she was innocent of the offense charged

exoneration   The official absolution of a false criminal conviction and release from incarceration

extra legislative powers   Legislative leaders serve on boards outside of the legislature

extraordinary session   A specially called meeting of the legislature, outside the regular session, to discuss specified matters

extraterritorial jurisdiction   City powers that extend beyond the city limits to an area adjacent to the city limits

F

fair use   Law that permits the limited use of copyrighted material without acquiring permission from the rights holders

federal system of government   The division of powers between a national government and regional governments

felony   A serious criminal offense, punishable by death or incarceration

filing fee   A fee or payment required to get a candidate's name on the primary or general election ballot

focus group   Panel of "average citizens" who are used by political consultants to test ideas and words for later use in campaigns

fragmented government structure   A government structure where power is dispersed to many state agencies with little or no central control

framing   Framing describes the media's attempts to focus attention on certain events and places them within a context for meaning

franchise fee   Major business tax in Texas that is assessed on income earned by corporations in the state

Full Faith and Credit Clause   Clause in Article 4 of the U.S. Constitution that requires states to recognize the judgements, legislation, and public records of other states

G

general elections   Regular elections held every two years to elect state officeholders

general law city   Cities governed by city charters created by state statutes

geographic distribution   A characteristic of some interest groups in that they have members in all regions of the state

gerrymandering   Drawing district boundary lines for political advantage

government organizations   Interest groups that represent state and local governments; also called SLIGs, for state and local interest groups

graded penalties   Punishments that differ based upon the seriousness of the crime

grand juries   Juries of citizens that determine if a person will be charged with a crime

H

hard news   Factual, in-depth coverage of public affairs that contributes to citizen's understanding of political events and leaders in the public sphere

Higher Education Assistance Fund (HEAF)   The HEAF is money set aside for use by those universities not benefiting from the PUF

home rule city   Cities governed by city charters created by the actions of local citizens

Hopwood Decision   Decision by federal courts to end affirmative action in Texas schools; these programs had provided for special treatment for minority students in being accepted to colleges and professional schools

Hunt v. Cromartie   Court case that ruled while race can be a factor, it could not be the primary factor in determining the makeup of legislative districts

I

ideology   Basic belief system that guides political theory and policy; typically conceptualized as falling along a conservative/moderate/liberal continuum

impeachment   The process by which some elected officials, including governors, may be impeached (accused of an impeachable offense) by the lower house adopting articles of impeachment

in loco parentis   Latin for "in the place of a parent"

income-elastic taxes   Taxes that rise and fall quickly relative to changes in economic conditions; the Texas tax system is very income-elastic

incorporation   Process of creating a city government

independent candidate   A person whose name appears on the ballot without a political party designation

independent school district   School districts that are not attached to any other unit of government and that operate schools in Texas

individualistic subculture   Government that benefits the individual rather than society in general

informal qualifications   Additional qualifications beyond the formal qualifications required for men and women to be elected governor; holding statewide elected office is an example

informal rules   Set of norms or values that govern legislative bodies

information   Messages provided that concern social events occurring or services available in a community to its members

information or administrative hearing   A hearing before a judge who decides if a person must stand trial; used in place of a grand jury

initiative   A process that allows citizens to propose changes to the state constitution through the use of petitions signed by registered voters; Texas does not allow constitutional revision through initiative

intake   The procedures involved with the arrest and detention of an individual before a bail hearing

interest group   An organization of individuals sharing common goals that tries to influence governmental decisions

intergovernmental coordinator   The expectation that a governor coordinates activities with other state governments

interim committees   Temporary committees of the legislature that study issues between regular sessions and make recommendations on legislation

Interstate Commerce Clause   Article in U.S. Constitution that gives Congress the exclusive power to regulate commerce between the states; Congress and the courts determine what is interstate commerce

investigative journalism   Deeply researched stories that uncover serious crime, corruption or corporate wrongdoing

J

judicial powers   The ability of a governor to issue pardons, executive clemency, and parole of citizens convicted of a crime

L

land commissioner   Elected official responsible for administration and oversight of state-owned lands and coastal lands extending 10.3 miles into the Gulf of Mexico

land-based economy   An economic system in which most wealth is derived from the use of the land

League of United Latin American Citizens (LULAC)   The oldest organization representing Latinos in Texas, established in 1929

Legislative Budget Board   State agency that is controlled by the leadership in the state legislature and that writes the state budget

legislative power   The formal power, especially the veto authority, of the governor to force the legislature to enact his or her legislation

legislative professionalism   Legislatures with higher pay, longer sessions, and high levels of staff support are considered more professional

Legislative Redistricting Board (LRB)   State board composed of elected officials that can draw new legislative districts for the house and senate if the legislature fails to act

libel   A published false statement that is damaging to a private individual's reputation

lieutenant governor   Presiding officer of the Texas Senate; elected by the voters of the state

line-item veto   The ability of a governor to veto part of an appropriations bill without vetoing the whole bill

lobbying   The practice of trying to influence members of the legislature, originally by catching legislators in the lobby of the capitol

M

magistrate functions   Preliminary hearings for persons charged with a serious criminal offense

majority-minority   Minority groups make up a majority of the population of the state

mediatization   A theory that argues that the media shapes and frames the processes and discourse of political communication as well as the society in which that communication takes place

membership organizations   Interest groups that have individual citizens or businesses as members

merit system, or Missouri system   A system of electing judges that involves appointment by the governor and a periodic retention election

military powers   Powers giving the governor the right to use the National Guard in times of natural disaster or civil unrest

minor party   A party other than the Democratic or Republican Party; to be a minor party in Texas, the organization must have received between 5 and 19 percent of the vote in the past election

misdemeanors   Less serious criminal offenses, punishable by fine, incarceration, or both fine and incarceration

moralistic subculture   Government viewed as a positive force to achieve a common good for all citizens

multimember districts   Districts represented by more than one member elected to the legislature

N

name familiarity   Practice of voting for candidates with familiar or popular names; a significant issue in Texas judicial elections

Necessary and Proper Clause (Elastic Clause)   Statement in Article 1, Section 8, paragraph 18 of the U.S. Constitution that says Congress can pass any law necessary and proper to carry out other powers

network neutrality   The principle that Internet service providers should enable access to all content and applications regardless of the source, and without favoring or blocking particular products or websites

news   Stories that provide timely information about the important events or individuals in a community, state, nation, or world

noncompetitive districts   Districts in which a candidate from either party wins 55 percent or more of the vote

nondedicated revenue   Money available for general spending

nonexcludability   The inability to practically prevent people from receiving or enjoying a good or service due to nonpayment

nonexhaustion   The availability of a good or service for others to use and enjoy will not diminish; i.e., consumption is nonrivalrous

nonmembership organizations   Interest groups that represent corporations and businesses and do not have broad-based citizen support

nonpartisan election   Election in which party identification is not formally declared

nonrivalrous consumption   Situation in which the use or enjoyment of a good or service by a person or persons does not diminish the availability of that good or service for others to use or enjoy

nontax revenue   Governmental revenue derived from service charges, fees (tuition), lottery, and other sources

O

objectivity   The appearance that courts make objective decisions and not political ones

office block format   Ballot form where candidates are listed by office with party affiliation listed by their name; most often used with computer ballots

open primary system   A nominating election that is open to all registered voters regardless of party affiliation

ordinances   Laws passed by local governments

P

pardon   Grants forgiveness by the state for a conviction and requires that the convicted receive no punishment; does not erase the criminal record

parens patriae   Latin for "parent of the fatherland"

partial veto   The ability of some governors to veto part of a nonappropriations bill without vetoing the entire bill; a Texas governor does not have this power except on appropriations bills

partisan election   Method used to select all judges (except municipal court judges) in Texas by using a ballot in which party identification is shown

party chief   The expectation that the governor will be the head of his or her party

party column format   Paper ballot form where candidates are listed by party and by office

party dealignment   View that a growing number of voters and candidates do not identify with either major political party but are independents

party raiding   Occurs when members of one political party vote in another party's primary in an effort to nominate a weaker candidate or split the vote among the top candidates

per capita tax   The total taxes raised in a state divided by the number of residents

permanent party organization   Series of elected officials of a political party that keep the party organization active between elections

permanent registration   A system that keeps citizens on the voter registration list without their having to reregister every year

Permanent University Fund (PUF)   The PUF is money set aside in the state constitution to benefit the University of Texas at Austin and Texas A&M University

petit juries   Juries of citizens that determine the guilt or innocence of a person during a trial; pronounced petty juries

plural executive system   System in which executive power is divided among several statewide elected officials

podcast   A digital audio file made available on the Internet for downloading to a computer or portable media player, typically available as a series, new installments of which can be received by subscribers automatically

police power   The ability afforded states under the 10th Amendment of the U.S. Constitution, to regulate behavior and enforce order within its geographic territory

policy liberalism index   A measure of how liberal or conservative a state is on some state policies

political action committees (PACs)   Spin-offs of interest groups that collect money for campaign contributions and other activity

political communication   A field of study that focuses on how information is disseminated and shapes the public sphere

political culture   A system of beliefs and values that defines the role of government and the role of citizens in that government

political gerrymandering   Drawing legislative districts to the advantage of a political party

political participation   All forms of involvement citizens can have that are related to governance

political party   Organizations that act as an intermediary between the people and government with the goal of getting their members elected to public office

political socialization   The development of political attitudes and beliefs through agents of socialization, such as socioeconomic factors, family, religion, school, community, the media, etc.

political values   A set of beliefs about political processes and the role that government should play in our society

poll tax   In place from 1902 until 1966 in Texas, a tax citizens were required to pay each year between October and January to be eligible to vote in the next election cycle

popular sovereignty   The idea that power granted in state constitutions rests with the people

precinct chair   Party official elected in each voting precinct to organize and support the party

preferential voting   A system that allows voters to rank order candidates for the city council

presentation bias   the act of writing or presenting news stories that reflect a significantly distorted view of reality, favoring one party over another in the case of political parties

presidential primary election   Election held every four years by political parties to determine voters' preferences for presidential candidates

primary   An election used by major political parties in Texas to nominate candidates for the November general election

priming   The ability of the media to help shape public opinion respecting an event or a person in the public sphere

Privileges and Immunities Clause   Clause in Article 4 of the U.S. Constitution that prevents states from discriminating against citizens of other states and requires those citizens to be treated in like manner

professional associations   Organizations promoting the interests of individuals who generally must hold a state-issued license to engage in their profession

progressive taxes   Taxes that take a higher percentage of income from high-income persons

proportional taxes   Taxes that take the same percentage of income from all citizens

public goods   Goods or services characterized by the features of nonexcludability and nonrivalrous consumption; they are often provided by governments

public policy   "Whatever governments choose to do or not to do."—Thomas Dye

public sphere   A community's arena that allows individuals to freely discuss and identify societal problems, and influence political action

R

racial gerrymandering   Legislative districts that are drawn to the advantage of a minority group

Raza Unida (United Race)   Minor party that supported election of Hispanic Americans in Texas in the 1970s

realignment   "a lasting shift of party loyalty and attachment"(as defined by James L. Sundquist in *Dynamics of the Party System: Alignment and Realignment of Political Parties in the United States*, p. 4)

reapportionment   Refers to the process of allocating representatives to districts

recall   The removal of the governor or an elected official by a petition signed by the required number of registered voters and by an election in which a majority votes to remove the person from office

recidivism   The rate at which criminal offenders commit crime after they leave the state's custody

redistributive goods   Those goods where government takes money from one group of citizens and gives it to other citizens; welfare is a good example

redistricting   The drawing of district boundaries

referendum   A direct public vote on a single political issue

registered voters   Citizens who have formally gone through the process of getting their names on the voter registration list

regressive taxes   Taxes that take a higher percentage of income from low-income persons

regulations   Administrative rules implemented by governmental regulatory agencies to guide or prescribe specific conduct by industry or business

regulatory goods   Good, activity, or resource that the government regulates to prevent overuse; an example is pumping water from a commonly owned aquifer

rent seeking   The practice of trying to secure benefits for oneself or one's group through political means

reprieve   The temporary 30-day stay of execution the governor may grant

resonance   The reinforcement and magnification of existing beliefs about reality and commonality of events due to the presentation of reality by the media

retail trade associations   Organizations seeking to protect and promote the interests of member businesses involved in the sales of goods and services

Reynolds v. Sims   Court case that required state legislative districts for both houses to contain about the same number of citizens

rider   Provision attached to a bill that may not be of the same subject matter as the main bill

right-to-work laws   Legislation stipulating that a person cannot be denied employment because of membership or nonmembership in a labor union or other labor organization

Robin Hood Plan   System for funding the state's primary and secondary public school education whereby rich districts send money to the state, which then distributes those funds to poor school districts

Roe v. Wade   Texas court case that limits what states can legally do to prevent abortions

runoff primary   Election that is required if no person receives a majority in the primary election; primarily used in southern and border states

S

same-day registration   Voters are allowed to register on Election Day; no preregistration before the election is required

secretary of state   Chief election official and keeper of state records; appointed by the governor

selection bias   The systematic selection of particular news that presents a distorted view of reality

semi-closed primary system   A nominating election that is open to all registered voters, but voters are required to declare party affiliation when they vote in the primary election

semi-open primary system   Voter may choose to vote in the primary of either party on Election Day; voters are considered "declared" for the party in whose primary they vote

senatorial courtesy   The courtesy of the governor clearing his or her appointments with state senator from the appointee's home district

separation of powers   Power divided between the legislative, executive, and judicial branches of government

sine die   Legislature must adjourn at end of regular session and cannot continue to meet

single-member district   A system where the city is divided into election districts, and only the voters living in that district elect the council member from that district

single-member districts   Districts represented by one elected member to the legislature

social capital   The networks of relationships that become part of the public sphere, which are built and maintained by people who live in a community

social contract theory   The idea that all individuals possess inalienable rights and willingly submit to government to protect these rights

socioeconomic factors   Factors such as income, education, race, and ethnicity that affect voter turnout

soft news   Information, presented as news, that serves to entertain, titillate, or overdramatize events but lacks substance and value with respect to contributing to citizen's understanding of political events and leaders in the public sphere

"sore loser" law   Law in Texas that prevents a person who lost the primary vote from running as an independent or minor party candidate

speaker of the house   Member of the Texas house, elected by the house members, who serves as presiding officer and generally controls the passage of legislation

special purpose district   Form of local government that provides specific services to citizens, such as water, sewage, fire protection, or public transportation

special sessions   In Texas, sessions called by the governor to consider legislation proposed by the governor only

standing committees   Committees of the house and senate that consider legislation during sessions

stare decisis   Court decisions depending on previous rulings of other courts

state and local interest groups (SLIGs)   Interest groups that represent state and local governments, such as the Texas Association of Counties

state executive committee   Committee, made up of one man and one woman from each state senatorial district as well as a chair and vice-chair, that functions as the governing body of the party

state party chair   Heads the state executive committee and provides leadership for the party

statutes   Laws passed by state legislatures

straight ticket voting system   System that allows voters to vote for all candidates of a single political party by making a single mark and that has resulted in an increase in the number of Republican judges

straight-ticket voting   Casting all your votes for candidates of a single party

straw polls   Unofficial, ad-hoc personal interviews surrounding a formal vote

streaming services   The transferal of music or video data over the Internet, generally through a subscription service provider

strong mayor form   Form of local government where most power rests with the mayor

Sunset Advisory Commission   Agency responsible for making recommendations to the legislature for change in the structure and organization of most state agencies

supremacy clause   A clause that makes constitutional provisions superior to other laws

T

tax base   The items that are subject to tax; for example, the items subject to sales tax

tax capacity   A measure of the wealth of a state or its ability to raise revenues relative to all other states

tax effort   A measure of the amount of revenue collected by a state relative to its tax capacity

tax exporting   The shifting of taxes to citizens in other states; a good example is Wyoming coal, which is exported to Texas to generate electricity

tax incidence   The person actually paying the tax

tax shifting   Passing taxes on to other citizens

temporary party organization   Series of meetings or conventions that occur every two years at the precinct, county, and state levels

Tenth Amendment   Amendment of the U.S. Constitution that delegates or reserves some powers to the state governments or to the people

tenure of office   The ability of governors to be reelected to office

term limits   Limitations on the number of times a person can be elected to the same office in state legislatures

Texas Code of Criminal Procedure   The rules created by the Texas Supreme Court to govern the proceedings of trials in Texas

Texas Ethics Commission   State agency responsible for enforcing requirements for interest groups and candidates for public office to report information on money collected and activities

Texas Penal Code   The statutory law that defines criminal offenses and punishments in Texas

Texas Railroad Commission   State agency with regulation over some aspects of transportation and the oil and gas industry of the state

tort   "A civil wrong, recognized by law as grounds for a lawsuit, which can be redressed by awarding damages" *Source:* Cornell University Law School, Legal Information Institute, Wex Legal Dictionary

trade associations   Interest groups that represent more specific business interests

traditional media   The term associated with conventional forms of media such as television, print, radio, direct mail, and billboard signage

traditionalistic subculture   Government that maintains the existing political order for the benefit of a small elite

trial courts   Local courts that hear cases; juries determine the outcome of the cases heard in the court

trial de novo courts   Courts that do not keep a written record of their proceedings; cases on appeal begin as new cases in the appellate courts

trustee   Representational role of a member that states that the member will make decisions on his or her own judgment about what is best for voters

turnover   The number of new members of the legislature each session

unitary system of government   A system of government where all functions of government are controlled by the central/national government

voter registration   The act of qualifying to vote by formally enrolling on an official list of voters

voter turnout   The proportion of people who cast ballots in an election

Voting Rights Act   A federal law aimed at preventing racial discrimination in the operation of voter registration and elections at the state level

voting-age population   The number of people age 18 and over

voting-eligible population   The voting-age population, corrected to exclude groups ineligible to vote, such as noncitizens and convicted felons

W

weak mayor form   Form of government where the mayor shares power with the council and other elected officials

white primary   From 1923 to 1945, Democratic Party primary that excluded African Americans from participating

write-in candidate   A person whose name does not appear on the ballot; voters must write in that person's name, and the person must have led a formal notice that he or she was a write-in candidate before the election

evolution of, 260–263

governors expected to be leaders of, 142

strength in a state, 320

in Texas, 259–295

in the United States, 260–263

weakening of, 264–266

political reforms, parties weakened by, 264

"political slush-funds," for Republican politicians, 334

political spending, as a form of protected speech, 317

political values, 409

politics

from Democrat to Republican, 13–16

one-party in Texas, 9

Texans participating in, 232

Polk, President, 5

poll tax, 203, 216, 218, 223

polling, essential to campaigns, 263

polling places, 249, 289

pollsters, conducting survey research, 262

"Polo Road Gang" of Republican legislators, 98

Pomper, Gerald, 273

popular sovereignty, 36

population

in the 2010 census, 92

density, 18

as the distinguishing feature of county government, 201

growth of, 16–17

statistics, 16

populism, defining, 29

Populist movement, 223

postgubernatorial office, 124

post-Reconstruction Texas, 9–22, 30

Potter, Lloyd, 26

poverty

access to legal services and, 391–392

rates in Texas, 23–24, 336

as a strong indicator of educational attainment, 24

poverty hearings, Texas courts not conducting, 394

Powell, David Lee, 391

power

of an interest group, 318–319

orderly transfer of, 239

to tax and spend, 59

powers

formal of governors, 126–143

granted to both the national and the state governments, 58, 59–60

prayer, school-conducted, 29

precinct chair, election of, 289

precinct convention, 291

precincts, 288–289

"preclearance," of redistricting maps, 92

preexisting condition, causing denial of insurance coverage, 338

preferential voting, 195, 198

Premier Election System, 240

"preponderance of evidence," 371, 400

preregistration, 219

president of a state university, selection of, 134

President of the United States

line-item veto and, 141

Texas general election results for, 1992-2016, 284–285

using judicial appointive powers to select federal judges, 166

presidential candidates, winning the popular vote in Texas, 268

presidential elections, Texans supporting Republican candidates, 268

presidential primaries, 222–223, 293, 294

pretrial confinement, 395

pretrial diversion programs, 394

primary elections, 243, 293

administration and finance of, 247–248

becoming the "general election," 225

describing, 245–247

turnout low for, 229

voter turnout for, 223

primary system, determining to the national party conventions, 293

"prior appropriation," 354

prison construction program, 378

prison population

decline of, 386

growth of, 378

managing, 379–380

prisons

comparing private vs. public, 383

mental illness in, 393–394

overcrowding of, 378

private corporations, contracted to operate facilities, 380–381

private individuals, with a pet project or issue, 311

private life, governors retiring to, 124

private organizations, political parties as, 225

private prisons, 380–384

private property, legal definition of groundwater as, 355

private-to-private eminent domain transfers, Texas and, 335

Privileges and Immunities of Citizenship, 66

pro bono publico ("for the public good"), 391

pro se, low-income Texans representing themselves, 392

probate courts, 161

probation, minors on, 376

pro-business climate, fostering, 278

pro-business environment, in Texas, 333

product-liability claims, plaintiffs suing businesses for, 336

professional associations, 303, 304–305

professional campaign consultants, 253

professional licensing and examining boards, 137

professional lobbyists, hired to represent a client, 311

professionalism, of the state legislature, 320–321

Progressive causes, 272

Progressive Democrats, 14

Progressive Era (1890-1920), 13, 264

Progressive movement, taking up some Populist causes, 271–272

progressive taxes, 417

"progressive transinstitutionalism," 393–394

prohibitionism, striking a chord with certain segments of the Texas population, 272

property, crime involving, 370

property law, 370

property ownership, restricting the right to vote in Texas, 225

property tax

counties relying almost exclusively on, 206

as the primary source of local funding of education, 339

as a source of revenue, 421–422

property tax division, of the comptroller, 128

proportional representation systems, disincentive for smaller parties, 287

proportional taxes, 417

Proposition 8 in California, 65

prosecutors, failing to follow procedure, 398

prostitution courts, 380

Protestants, of the black church tradition, 22

provinces, in Canada, 57

provincial attitudes, of county officials, 207

YOUR VOTE MATTERS!

Get Informed and Get Registered:
campusvoteproject.org

Why Student Voting Matters

Young adults (ages 18-29) made up about **21%** of the voting eligible population in **2014**, but voter turnout for this demographic has reached record lows in recent years.[1]

Young people have the power to make a difference. An important way to achieve this is to make their voices heard at the polls on Election Day.

[1]Source: The United States Census Bureau Current Population Survey